Documents of European Economic History

Documents of European Economic History

VOLUME ONE

The Process of Industrialization 1750–1870

S. Pollard

Professor of Economic History, University of Sheffield

C. Holmes

Lecturer in Economic History, University of Sheffield

Edward Arnold

First Published 1968 by
Edward Arnold (Publishers) Ltd.
41 Maddox Street, London W1

SBN 7131 5378 4

Printed in Great Britain by
Robert Cunningham and Sons Ltd., Longbank Works, Alva

Table of Contents

Introduction

The interest now displayed among English-speaking modern economic historians in the economic development of the European Continent is of fairly recent origin. Historians of diplomacy, or of war, for example, have always had to take developments outside the British Isles into account, and, at the least, the history of the Great Powers has for long formed part of any respectable History course. But most of those who concentrate on economic development have for too long thought the study of the United Kingdom to be adequate for their needs, accompanied, perhaps, by the contrapuntal themes of the linked economies of the Colonies or the U.S.A., and many were not above declaring the history of the peoples across the Channel to be derivative, imitative or even, where it did not coincide with the British or American, simply an aberration.

This is not the place for an inquiry into the reasons for the change in outlook, though one suspects that the more subordinate role played by Britain today in the world's manufactured exports, capital supply and inventiveness may not be unconnected with it. Whatever the cause, the teaching and research in Great Britain and the U.S.A. increasingly shows an awareness of the intrinsic interest to be found in the paths of development of Continental economies, with their differences and similarities to the British or American patterns, and those who are concerned with 'economic development' as such, are particularly grateful for the multiplicity of case studies opened out to them.

Researchers, perhaps, can fend for themselves, but as far as undergraduates are concerned, there are two major barriers facing those who would understand the economic history of the Continent over the past two centuries. One is the barrier of language, and the other, more difficult to surmount, is the barrier of the differences in traditions, assumptions, social structure, political and legal power, against which the industrialization of the European economies was and is being carried through. When found implanted within such different societies, even familiar and apparently analogous institutions may take on fundamentally different roles, and others, for which there are no parallels here, may be incomprehensible, and may therefore too easily be ignored altogether.

The collection of documents offered here is intended to help towards bridging this gap in comprehension. In illustrating these economic developments on the Continent, the attempt has been made to concentrate on those countries and those trends which were of the greatest significance in the process of industrialization, though some, like the growth of overseas trade or the growth of population, are by their nature difficult to encompass in this way and have therefore not received their due in these pages. Particular attention has been paid to those features which showed fundamental differences from those in the English-speaking countries, and which therefore British and American students are likely to find the most difficult to interpret. At the same time, and in defiance of the title, this collection does not include documents on British economic history as such, partly because that background will already be familiar to English-speaking students, and partly because the existing literature is more easily accessible, and has recently been greatly enriched.*

The years covered in this volume, c. 1750–1870, the first of a planned two-volume collection, are those in which several of the major economies of Europe experienced their industrial revolution, and others had moved to the threshold of industrialization. These terms, however, have to be understood against a background of different European societies, which greatly varied their pace, their sequence, their emphasis and their significance. Moreover, the timing of economic changes was most uneven across the Continent. Some countries or major regions, such as Belgium, Saxony or Alsace, appeared at times to be very closely behind the British pioneer economy; others, like Russia or Spain, had hardly even reached a meaningful 'threshold' in 1870. And these economies, at different stages, reacted on each other as much as the British reacted on them all.

Nevertheless, some order has to be imposed on the mass of material available. It is presented here in three parts. The first is designed to describe the traditional economies before the 'take-off'. Agriculture, much the most important occupation of the people, is still, nearly everywhere, carried on in a feudal or semi-feudal framework, in which payments are unrelated to economic services, and initiative and incentives to improving the methods of production are absent or severely hampered. As a result, again with some significant local exceptions, techniques are traditional and immobile. Actual conditions of serfdom or restraint differ enormously among the regions and these differences, explained by historical background and geography, are giving rise to very different responses to the new stimuli provided by the market for agricultural produce. Industry and even trade are equally restricted, by gilds, monopolies, privileges and, in the East, even by the operation of serfdom itself, and mobility is little greater there than in the agrarian

* E.g. M. W. Flinn, *Readings in Economic and Social History* (Macmillan, 1964); W. H. B. Court, *British Economic History, 1870–1914* (Cambridge University Press, 1965); E. Royston Pike, *Human Documents of the Industrial Revolution* (Allen & Unwin, 1966); beside other more specialized collections.

base. Despite its potential importance for the future, manufacturing industry is, viewed in society as a whole, only a marginal occupation, and much of it is carried on within households and does not yet enter the market. But within industry, some sectors like mining, metallurgy and the domestic system organized by large merchant houses, carry within them the seeds of further capitalistic development. Commercial policy, in those conditions, is dominated by mercantilist or cameralist ideas, and the State not only frequently takes the initiative, but generally takes it in its own political-military interest, rather than in the interests of economic growth. Commerce is, no doubt, the most dynamic element in this society, but outside Holland and England it is also only marginal, and the primitive state of the financial and transport systems betokens its relative weakness. The social problems are those appropriate to this traditional setting, and the most effective section of the population clamouring for reform is the bourgeoisie which feels increasingly thwarted in its opportunities.

The second part illustrates the economic aspects of the French Revolution and the emancipation of the serfs in Central and Eastern Europe. The juxtaposition is deliberate, for in France, as well as in such countries as Prussia and Russia, the reforms give freedom of occupation and of mobility not only to the countryside, but also to the towns. In each country, the peasantry plays a major part in the change, but the peasantry appears essentially as a conservative element and is quickly satisfied, or else unable to impose further changes, though it is now better able to adopt new methods and increase output. By contrast, the bourgeoisie finds growing opportunities and growing powers, once the fetters are broken, and is in a position to use both to change the character of economy and society. Despite the continuation of many outward forms, the break with the past appears, in retrospect, almost complete. The difference in the time scale, however, is important: the Russian Statutes of Emancipation are promulgated almost three generations after the abolition of feudal dues in France.

In the third part, some of the multi-coloured aspects of 'industrial revolutions' are highlighted. Agriculture, despite its structural limitations, becomes much more responsive to the market, and is helped in this by costly improvements in means of transport. Industry, traversing its many stages of extended domestic or centralized 'manufacture', breaks out of its restrictions of gild and craft, and gradually attaches former independent or agricultural workers to itself in expanding factories, ironworks, shipyards and mines. Rapid technical innovations transform sources of power, instruments and machinery, and means of transport. Capital becomes a key factor, and spills over into new industries and new countries. A complex financial superstructure is built up, and Europe is linked up by railways, by stock exchanges, and by common commercial fluctuations. The needs of the new industrial capitalism affect ultimately also the policy of governments: protection and stimulation are used and manipulated apparently as before, but now they bear much more clearly the imprint of a desire for economic growth according to the British, and soon, also, the French, Belgian or German model. At the same time, the new rule of capital is scarcely in the saddle before it is being attacked by a new class, a new interest group fashioned in parallel with the new agglomeration of power and resources: the proletariat appears, and challenges by its trade unions and its Socialist ideas the new system before it has even had time to consolidate. By 1870, France, Germany and Belgium were becoming recognizably mature industrial economies; the transformation had well begun in Italy, Sweden and parts of Austria-Hungary; and even Russia was moving lumberingly in the same direction. The foundations of the modern industrialized world had been laid in Europe.

Any attempt to illustrate between the covers of a single volume these momentous developments, extending over 120 years and over a dozen countries, must inevitably leave large and grievous gaps. Every reader will have his own list of key documents that have been omitted. We are only too well aware of this particular shortcoming. We have attempted to remedy it as far as lies in our power by choosing, wherever possible, documents that will illustrate more than one point we wish to make; by limiting our own contribution to brief chapter introductions and the minimal indications of sources and explanations of unfamiliar terms in the text; and by thus letting, as far as we are able, the contemporary documents speak for themselves. It is clear that this volume can be used effectively only in combination with other, narrative works, and we are heartened by the growing, and increasingly competent, literature on European economic development now available in the English language.

This volume carries an unusually long list of acknowledgements, reflecting the extent of the help we have received in its making. Professor G. P. Jones and Dr W. O. Henderson have contributed unstintingly from their own collection of documents, many of them translated by them, and Mr M. E. Falkus has gone out of his way to help us with some Russian language sources, translated for us by Mr A. G. Waring. We are also greatly indebted to Mr. Th. Shanin for help with Russian sources. We have received unfailing kindness and helpfulness from the Librarians and staffs of the following Libraries: Sheffield University Library, the British Museum, the London Library of Political and Economic Science, the Goldsmith Library of the University of London, the London University Institute of Historical Research, and the Birmingham Public Libraries. Part of the research has been made possible by a grant from the Sheffield University Knoop Research Fund. Miss Helen Trippett triumphed over the intricacies of typing a difficult manuscript with her usual calm efficiency.

Editors.

Abbreviations

Ed. Tr.	= Document translated by the editors
G.P.J.	= Included with the assistance of Professor G. P. Jones
M.E.F., A.G.W. Tr.	= Included with the assistance of M. E. Falkus, translated by A. G. Waring
W.O.H.	= Document included with the assistance of Dr W. O. Henderson
W.O.H. Tr.	= Document included with the assistance of Dr W. O. Henderson and translated by Dr W. O. Henderson

Acknowledgements

The Editors and Publishers wish gratefully to acknowledge permission given by the following to reproduce documents in this volume: Musterschmidt-Verlag, Göttingen, for documents 7/2 and 7/9; Akadamie-Verlag, Berlin, for documents 2/16, 8/5, 8/6, 10/3, 15/15 and 15/17; Holzner-Verlag, Würzburg, for document 7/7; Veb Deutscher Verlag der Wissenschaften, Berlin, for documents 2/6, 2/10, 2/25, 5/3, 5/8a, 5/11, and 5/12; University of Michigan Press for document 12/8; D. Van Nostrand Co. Inc., Princeton, N.J., for document 8/4; Cornell University Press for document 15/10; University of Chicago Press for document 3/13; Harvard University Press for document 15/3; Swets & Zeitlinger N. V. for document 13/6; Basil Blackwell & Mott Ltd., Oxford, for documents 5/14 and 6/3; Longmans, Green & Co. Ltd., London, and David McKay Co. Inc., New York, for document 5/1a; Associated Book Publishers Ltd. for document 10/1; Cambridge University Press for document 4/26; Staples Press, London, for document 9/10; Macmillan & Co., New York, for documents 5/10, 6/2, 6/4, 6/5a, and 14/1; Librairie Armand Colin, Paris, for documents 3/11b, 14/15, 15/18 and 15/19; Editions du Temps, Paris, for documents 15/22 and 15/23; Librairie Honoré Champion, Paris, for document 2/26; Economic History Society for document 12/5b; Kress Library of Business and Economics, Boston, Mass., for document 14/2.

PART I

The Eve of Industrialization

Chapter 1 Agriculture

Introduction

Europe before its revolutions was predominantly agrarian. This was true not only in the sense that agriculture formed the largest single source of wealth and gave rise to more employment than any other sector of the economy, but also in the sense that land was the key factor in social and political structure and power. Outside a few cities, the European's place in society was determined by his relationship to the land, by the amount of it that he held, and by whether he owned it, administered it or worked it, and on what terms. The political and legal structure of each country, in turn, represented essentially a series of systems developed over the centuries, for diverting the agricultural surplus from those who worked the land to landlords, burghers and governments, and for sharing it out among them.

The systems based on serfdom proved remarkably stable. The landlords were among the most conservative groups in society, and as long as they were not disturbed by trade or the money economy from the towns, by wars and rising taxation or rent demands from outside, or by population pressure, there were strong conservative elements among the peasants also. The open-field system, for example, typically based on a two-field or three-field rotation, held sway over the northern half of Europe with remarkable tenacity since the Middle Ages (1/2). Other medieval relics, like the famous Spanish Mesta (1/1), were equally long-lived if they affected the means of livelihood of the majority of the population, and in areas untouched by modern trade routes, like large parts of Russia, techniques and implements also showed no signs of progress (1/3). In the West, however, wherever there was a class able and willing to profit by improvements, as among free peasants or progressive, market-orientated landlords, the 'new husbandry' developed in Holland and Great Britain made some headway in the eighteenth century. German landlords, particularly if within reach of the Baltic grain export routes, experimented with new rotations and new crops (1/4). In France, also, there were individual improving landlords (1/5, 1/7), although most of the country was still comparatively backward, and British travellers marvelled both at the fertility of the soil of the kingdom and at its neglect (1/6).

European agriculture cannot be understood without considering the system of land tenure and serfdom. By the eighteenth century this had almost everywhere ossified into a structure made firm and unified within each country by law, though there might be great variation between countries, and between different regions of one country. Serfdom was most complete in Russia, the last country to come under its sway in Europe, and there the peasants were divided into distinct groupings, like Crown serfs and private serfs. In the Tsar's empire, the differences in exactions also (determined by differences in soil and climate), such as labour dues, dues in kind or in money, were systematized over wide areas (**1/8, 1/9, 1/10**), and not only the stewards, bailiffs and domestic servants, but even factory workers, artisans, merchants and miners were serfs within the same system (**1/10, 2/24, 11/1**) right up to the emancipation.

Moving westward across Europe from Russia, into Poland, Austria-Hungary and the German States, we find serfdom only a little less oppressive and comprehensive. Various reforms had been set in train in the eighteenth century, in the Hapsburg lands, in Prussia, and elsewhere (**1/16, 7/1, 7/2**). Where there were little or no marketing opportunities, as in Poland and Hungary, the stagnation, the lack of incentive for improvement or even purposeful work, were among the most obvious characteristics of the surviving servile society (**1/11, 1/16, 1/17**). In Germany, where there were enormous differences between the various independent states, the more advanced state of industry, and the opportunities provided by trade and by developed urban markets had led to modifications everywhere. In the older parts of Brandenburg-Prussia, for example, the authority of the Junker over his serfs had been circumscribed by the needs of the powerful state for a tax base and an army recruiting base among the peasantry (**1/12**); in Silesia, incorporated into the kingdom only in 1740, the system was being modified because of the widespread existence of manufactures (**1/13**). There, as in Hanover (**1/14**), the disincentives of serfdom to exertion on the part of the peasant were increasingly criticized by contemporaries. In the West of Germany, where the peasantry had enjoyed greater freedom for longer than in the East, the system was radically different, being based, not on large-scale estate or demesne farming, but on dues from the smallholders; but there, progress was hampered by the poverty of the peasants, who rarely had sufficient land, and from whom all investible surpluses were extracted with great thoroughness by the landlords, as in Westphalia (**1/15**).

Further westward still, in France, most of the personal attributes of servitude had disappeared, though the exactions on the peasants were as harsh, and as inhibiting to progress, as in the East. The more advanced economy had, however, permitted large and progressive farmers to establish themselves in some parts of the kingdom, while elsewhere *métayage*, or share-cropping, had become important, a system sufficiently flexible to be considered as based on 'free' contract by the bourgeois governments of the

Revolution, and therefore left to survive unchanged into the nineteenth century (**1/18, 6/7**).

The modern historian may be struck by the inhibiting influence of the exactions of landlords, of the governmental tax systems (Chapter 4), and of the Church (**1/19**), which did not allow the peasant to rise above subsistence level, and therefore gave him no reason to exert himself, on the economic progress of Continental economies as a whole. Few contemporaries were moved by such secular considerations: it was the consensus of innumerable individuals, who saw their own opportunities to rise through the application of new techniques and the supply of new markets barred by the *ancien régime*, that drove them to provide the indispensable popular support for revolution and peasant emancipation in one country after another.

1/1 The Mesta, 1786

JOSEPH TOWNSEND, *A Journey through Spain in the Years 1786 and 1787* (3 vols., London, 1791), II, pp. 61-64, 284. (G.P.J.)

October 4, as we descended towards Leon, we overtook a Merino flock, belonging to the monastery of Guadalupe, in Estremadura. These monks have sufficient land near home to keep their flock during the winter months; but in the summer, when their own mountains are scorched, they send their sheep into the north, where, having no lands, they are obliged to pay for pasturage. They were on their return towards the south.

The great lords, and the religious houses, to whom belong these transhumantes, or travelling flocks, have peculiar privileges secured to them by a special code, called laws of the Mesta; privileges, by many considered as inconsistent with the general good.

This institution has been traced back to the year 1350, when the plague, which ravaged Europe for several years, had desolated Spain, leaving only one-third of its former inhabitants to cultivate the soil. But perhaps we ought to look for its origin in more remote and distant ages, when the whole country was occupied by shepherd nations. . . . Occupying the hills with their numerous flocks and herds, it was natural for them in winter to quit a country then covered deep with snow, and to seek the more temperate regions of the south; till these, burnt up by the returning sun, refused them pasture, and drove them back again to the mountains of the north, which, during the summer months are covered with perpetual verdure by the gradual melting of the snow.

The numbers of the Merino sheep are continually varying. Cajaleruela, who wrote A.D. 1627, complained that they were reduced from seven millions to two millions and an half. Ustariz reckoned in his time four millions; but now they are near five. The proprietors are numerous, some having only three or four thousand, while others have ten times that number. The Duke of Infantado has forty thousand. Each proprietor has a mayotal or chief shepherd, to whom he allows annually one hundred doblons, or £75, and a horse; and for every flock of two hundred sheep, a separate shepherd, who is paid according to his merit, from eight shillings a month to thirty, besides two pounds of bread a day for himself, and as much for his dog, with the privilege of keeping a few goats on his own account.

The produce of the wool is reckoned to be about five pounds from every ewe, and eight from the wethers; and to shear eight of the former, or five of the latter, is reckoned a good day's work. Some indeed allow twelve sheep to every shearer; but even this comes short of what we do in England, where a common hand will dispatch sixty in a day, and a good workman has been known to finish half as many more. . . .

When the sheep are travelling they may feed freely on all the wastes and commons; but, in passing through a cultivated country, they must be confined within their proper limits in a way which is ninety varas wide. Hence it comes to pass that, in such inhospitable districts, they are made to travel at the rate of six or seven leagues a day; but where pasture is to be had, they are suffered to move very slow. When they are to remove, either in the spring or autumn, if the lord has no lands, where his flocks are to be stationed, the chief shepherd goes before, and engages agistment, either of those proprietors who have more than sufficient for themselves, or of the corporations, who, in Spain, have usually extensive wastes and commons round their cities.

It is to these claims of the Merino stock that some political writers have attributed the want of cultivation in the interior provinces of Spain. . . .

Farms, if enclosed, let much higher than those which are open, because the latter are liable to be fed by the Merino sheep; whereas should they enter the former one-fifth of the number trespassing would be forfeited. This, however, proves a never-failing source of quarrels and contentions between the occupiers of land and those who may be called graziers, that is, the proprietors of the Merino stock who, under the sanction of a peculiar code, claim the privilege of feeding, not only in the common pasture, but even in the plantations of olives. The murders consequent on these quarrels have been more than two hundred in the space of a few years; and the litigations have cost the contending parties more than the value both of their sheep and their olives.

1/2 Field Systems in Russia, 1797

HEINRICH FRIEDRICH VON STORCH, *Historisch-statistisches Gemälde des Russischen Reichs* (9 vols., Riga, 1797–1803), II, pp. 281–291. (Ed. Tr.)

The field systems can be divided according to their nature into the following three main categories: the arable open fields, the steppe fields and the woodlands, which in some areas are also called brushlands. By arable open fields we mean, of course, the fields which are under permanent cultivation or are being worked every year. All over Russia, as elsewhere, the division into summer crops, winter crops and fallow is common (called in Russian, 'Yarovaya, Osimovaya, Yar'), to which some would add assarted fields ('Novina'), which we have made into a category of their own. Since these terms are unlikely to need explanation for most readers, we may merely remark here that the summer crop is sown and harvested in the same year, while the winter crop is sown in the previous autumn, to be harvested in the following summer. The former is sown in most parts of Russia with summer wheat, summer rye, barley, millet, buckwheat, flax, hemp, peas, poppies and oats; the latter is sown only with rye or wheat. After the field has been under a winter crop, it lies fallow, and remains uncultivated for the rest of the summer, the autumn and the whole of the winter; but at times the Russian peasants will sow even in the year following the field last under a winter crop, only with a crop which does not take much out of the soil, and allow it to rest under this form of rotation. The recent proposals of some agricultural economists to abolish the fallow completely, are considered even by enlightened husbandmen to be extremely difficult or wholly impossible to work because of the short summer in most Russian Provinces. Since the summer crop is gathered in only in August or even in September, in many areas, there is neither time nor the right climate to prepare the soil properly for the winter crop, and the late-sown rye is prevented by night frosts from reaching the strength to withstand the rough autumn and spring weather.

The steppe fields may be put in the same class as the out-fields known elsewhere; for although there are some differences, they agree in this, that they are cultivated for a short period without any manure, to be left again to a state of nature afterwards. In the great steppe lands which are found in the Russian empire, where everyone is free to occupy any area he likes, the only form of cultivation that is known is single ploughing, single harrowing, followed by the sowing. Even in areas having a poor soil this sort of cultivation is quite common, especially for sowing flax; but for growing corn on grass land, it is more usual to plough and harrow repeatedly for a year before the sowing, so that the soil is properly broken up and better able to suck in the fertilizing particles of air; the technical term for this is: acidulating the land. Such careful treatment is, however, uncommon in the steppe lands.

Woodlands or brushlands, finally, are fields which are made fertile by fire, achieved by two main methods. Either a forest is felled or brushwood is laid over the land, and the timber burnt down after being spread out and dried; or alternatively, the timber is cleared away, the land ploughed up, and the bundles of brushwood and split faggots are covered with soil before being ignited. The first process is called Clearing, and the second, 'Küttis', but several variations of both are found in different areas. In the inner provinces of Russia the peasants are content to cut down an area of forest land about St. Peter – St. Paul's day, or June 29, leaving the felled timbers on the ground until the following spring, when they are burnt. The first crop on such assarted land is generally flax, followed by barley or oats, and finally winter corn. If the soil is by nature fertile, it is turned into permanent arable; otherwise, the cultivated assarted fields are left again after a few years, and they gradually come to carry timber again, to be ready after fifteen or twenty years for renewed assarting by fire.

However difficult this form of cultivation, it nevertheless yields a large and certain return, so that it can be recommended with certain restrictions, in all regions possessing a true surplus of wooded land. In the Gouvernement* of St. Petersburg, the yield in the first four years after a clearing, even on average land, is ten to fifteenfold, and after a Küttis, ten to twentyfivefold. It is true that some agronomists have recently asserted that Küttis makes the soil totally infertile for many years; but this view is contradicted in Russia by experience going back over more than a hundred years. – More important than this objection is the damage which assarting or 'novinas' cause to the woodlands. Apart from the area staked out by the peasant for cultivation, there are frequently considerable stretches of other first class woodland which are burnt down in the process; in addition, the peasant cuts down all trees indiscriminately including trunks which could in due course, be used in shipbuilding. It would, therefore, be immeasurably more beneficial for the cultivation of this country, if instead of this assarting by fire, which helps to aggravate the increasing shortage of timber, they would dry out the marshlands, which exert a most adverse influence on the population, on the livestock, and even on the cultivation of corn, and the elimination of which would repay the labour expended on it by the richest dividends in the form of most fertile soil. In the Gouvernement of St. Petersburg, where the attempt has been made for some time now to gain cultivable land by this useful means, the first harvests return twenty, thirty, even thirty-five times the seedcorn, so that not only is the yield higher than the average of the Küttis

* See Glossary.

fields, but one of the by-products is the permanent creation of good arable land, especially in high-lying areas.

This description of agricultural implements and field systems will allow us to pass a general judgment on the course of husbandry. There is surely no other country in Europe in which agriculture as a whole is conducted so negligently, and yet yields such large and important returns; but there are also few countries to which nature is so kind as the bulk of the areas of central and southern Russia. – It is impossible to fix a generally valid date for sowing and harvesting in a country as large as Russia. The central provinces tend to sow their winter corn between the beginning of August and the middle of September and to harvest it in July or August of the year following, so that this type of grain stays on the average some eleven months in the soil. The summer crops are generally sown in May and harvested in August; they therefore stay only from three to four and a half months in the soil. While the peasants of the South rest after the summer sowing those of the North manure their future winter field, followed by haymaking and the harvest. In the autumn, both are occupied with the winter sowing; but while the former husbandman can be idle over the whole of the winter until the summer sowing and need concern himself only with his domestic duties, the latter has to manure his field in Lent, before Easter. The former will get away with a single ploughing and harrowing; the latter must do the work twice over. – In most regions the peasant sows his corn, especially in the spring, on the fallow of one or several years, without manuring; he walks behind the light plough, and turns the soil over; a second horse follows with the harrow, without a man to lead it, and this completes the work. Only in new first ploughings does he use the deeper coultered plough. The soil is manured only where the existence of livestock permits; hardly anywhere does the peasant think of manuring with marl, lime, pond mud or even with heaps of foliage. Only on a few noble farms are attempts being made to improve the soil by these means; apart from assarting by fire and natural manure, the peasant knows no other fertilizer, and even these are not universally in use, particularly not in Siberia. Since the harrows are very light, few fields are harrowed clean, particularly where the soils are heavy and clayey. Corn is cut partly by sickle, and partly by scythe. In some Provinces it is threshed by hand flail, in others the corn is trodden by horses or men; in some cases the corn is dried by the wind beforehand, but mostly it is dried by fire.

1/3 Russian Agricultural Techniques, 1861

American Consular Reports, 1861, pp. 190–191: F. S. CLAXTON, Consul in Moscow, 2 January 1861.

The great grain-growing district of Russia, whose annual yield is sufficient for the wants of the European continent, lies to the south of its centre, and between the 40th and 70th degrees of east longitude. It comprises the governments or provinces or Volhynia, Poltava, Kiev, Podolia, Kharkow, Voronezh, Saratov, and Samara. It may be considered as a tract of land over twelve hundred miles long by about four hundred broad. Not over one-tenth of this area is in wood, the other nine-tenths being arable land of such unprecedented richness that, notwithstanding the centuries it has been under cultivation, and that year after year it has been called upon to feed the many millions in this empire, as well as to supply the deficiency in the grain markets of Europe, it still continues to render a generous return for the seed sown, and bids fair, to all appearance, to be equally responsive for ages yet to come to the demands which may be made upon it. How much the percentage of yield may be increased can only be judged by those more familiar with agriculture than myself. But when I beheld the primitive plough with which the land is opened, and which scarce penetrates the surface, and certainly does not open a furrow much wider than one's hand; and when I witnessed the slow process of cutting the grain with the long since abandoned sickle, of about two and a half feet in length, I could not but conjecture that with improved implements, such as yearly compete for the prizes at our State fairs, the return from the land must be largely increased, whilst the labor of harvesting the crop will be reduced in still greater proportion. Again, the present process of threshing results in great loss; for, if the operation is performed on a large scale, the grain is scattered over an enclosure into which are turned the almost wild horses of the steppes – a drove of which is attached usually to each estate – and it is by their trampling hoofs, whilst urged here and there by the cries and long whips of the attendants, that the wheat and rye are separated from the straw. A large quantity, naturally, is hidden under foot, and an equal proportion is scattered by the wild movements of the frightened drove. But in a country where the standing crops have no protection, and where whole caravans of ox-carts turn their beasts amongst the ripe grain to feed and graze, no account is taken of the loss. The peasant who desires to prepare his limited crop for market sweeps clean a space in front of his cabin door, and there, with the ordinary flail, beats out the few bushels he may have to dispose of, or which he requires for the supply of the wants of his family. But over the many thousands of square miles embraced in the grain-growing district, and amidst the thousands of rich proprietors who claim the title to this remarkable soil, not one in a hundred possesses a deep-soil plough or improved drill, a patent reaper or a modern threshing machine.

1/4 German Agricultural Methods, 1794

Communications to the Board of Agriculture, I, Part IV (1794), pp. 379-384: Letter by DR. A. THAER* on Hanover.

The two systems of rural economy, best proved by experience, and acknowledged to be the most perfect, are, *the plan of stall-feeding, and the Mecklenburg Holstein Schlag, or Koppeln economy.*

The Koppeln or Schlag economy, consists in an equal partition of fields, into a certain number of portions, and in a fixed or regularly varied use of them, either for cultivation, meadow, or pasture. It differs according to the nature of the soil, and has from seven to thirteen portions, established upon certain determinate general principles. There is certainly no system of husbandry more regular, or more to be depended on, so far as it goes. The number of the oxen, of milch cows, the manure, the different kinds of ploughs, the sowing, the succession of crops, every thing is fixed in the most accurate manner. Every work has its proper time, and its regular succession, so as to be done with the smallest possible expence, either by the strength of men, or of cattle. The produce, unforeseen accidents, and unfruitful seasons excepted, is always certain. A possession of 20,000 acres is kept in order with the same ease as one of only 500. This system resembles a clock, which is wound up once a year by consulting the registers: the value of an estate, managed in this manner, and the rent it can afford, may be determined at once. The conditions on which the ground may be let, are, upon general principles, capable of being determined with such accuracy, that it is not in the power of the farmer to impoverish the land.

This system, therefore, is certainly the most eligible for the proprietors of extensive estates, whose principal aim is to draw a certain income from them, either by letting them out, or by farming them; without, however, being obliged to pay them any particular attention. Hence, it would probably meet with the most decided approbation of the proprietors of land in England, where, it is supposed that the real principles of the system are not yet universally known.

But whoever wishes to draw the highest possible produce from his lands,

* Albrecht Thaer (1752-1828), founder of the scientific study of agriculture in Germany.

though undoubtedly with a greater expence of money, labour, and attention; whoever chooses to employ a greater number of hands in the useful occupations of husbandry, and to keep a greater number of cattle to advantage, will, beyond a doubt, prefer the mode of stall-feeding.

That I may explain these principles more accurately, I must beg leave to present you with a short description of this system, as carried on at a farm called Essenrode, five miles distant from this place*, belonging to our director, Baron de Bülow.

Before I proceed, it is proper to mention, that the lands contained in his farm, formerly lay scattered in single pieces among those which belonged to the villagers; and that the stubble and the ley lands were used in common for the feeding of their cattle and flocks. The farm produced a rent of only 1000 dollars†; Mr. De Bülow persuaded the villagers to transfer to him, as his independent property, a common of about 700 acres, consisting of grass-land; in return for which, he made a cession to them of all his arable land, and gave up his right of feeding his cattle on the other commons with theirs.

This extent of grass-land, which, as was discernible by its furrows, had been tilled many centuries ago, consisted of a very good clay soil. It was broken up by Mr. De Bülow, and laid out in seven partitions (Koppeln), close to one another, each consisting of ninety acres, and an additional one of sixty acres, adjoining to the farm.

The farm has, besides, 24 acres of meadow, and 22 acres of garden ground.

The smaller portion is destined partly for lucerne, and partly for cabbage, for roots and vegetables for sale.

The seven main partitions (Koppeln) are managed in the following manner:

One year, manured for beans, peas, cabbages, potatoes, turnips, linseed, &c.; 2. Rye; 3. Barley, mixed with clover; 4. Clover, to be mowed either 2 or 3 times; 5. Clover, to be mowed once at St. John's, then to be broken up, ploughed 3 or 4 times, and manured; 6. Wheat; 7. Oats.

The stock of cattle amounts in all to 100 head; namely, 70 heavy Friesland milch cows, or oxen to be fattened, which are *continually* kept in the stable, and about 30 head of draught oxen and young cattle.

A management of this kind‡, affords a triennial manuring per acre of 10 *fuder* of good stable dung; and as to this is united a complete and regular tillage, and succession of crops, a double produce of corn may at least be expected, thus:

* Hanover (Ed.).
† See Glossary.
‡ *I.e.* stallfeeding (Ed.).

				rix dol.
90 acres wheat yield at	20*	1800	at 1	1800
90 acres rye	20	1800	24	1200
90 acres barley	24	2160	24	1260
90 acres oats	36	3240	12	1080
90 acres manured ley-crop, and 30 acres in the small portion (Koppeln) 120 acres at 15				1800
The heavy Friesland cows, fed with the same plenty both winter and summer, or the oxen that are yearly shut up twice in the stables, fattened, and sold at 40 rix dollars a head, produce				2800
Thus the farm produces				9940†

That we may be able to ascertain the relative proportion in point of produce, of our two most renowned systems of rural economy, we shall now consider the same farm, as managed after the Koppeln system of Mecklenburg.

According to the quality of its soil, which is very good, yet stands in need of manuring, it ought to be divided into nine portions, of 77 acres each; the reasons for which will soon appear.

These are, according to experience, most advantageously appropriated in the following manner.

1. Fallows ploughed during the whole summer, and left unsown; 2. wheat unmanured; 3. barley; 4. manured ley land, with ley-crop; 5. rye; 6. oats with clover; 7. clover once cut, then pastured; 8. pasture; 9. pasture.

By this mode of management, 77 acres are manured every ninth year, each acre with 10 *fuder*. As one head of grazing cattle yields eight *fuder*, 97 head ought to be kept. Each head, on this soil, requires 2 acres for its pasture; consequently 97 head require 194 acres, or two and a half Koppeln. Hence follows the division into nine portions mentioned above.

It may be admitted, that among these cattle there are about 80 milch cows, the rest draught oxen. This kind of economy seldom rears young cattle, but buys them. The cows are of the smaller breed, or else the pasture would not be sufficient for them. During the winter they live upon nothing else but straw; for what little there is of clover hay is destined for the draught oxen; hence it comes that they do not produce more than ten rix dollars a head.

* The translator could not make out what this weight or measure was. (Footnote in original.)

† In foreign computations the value of a rix dollar varies, but is, in general, about three shillings sterling; in Hanover it is three shillings and sixpence. *Fuder*, signifies a cart load. (Footnote in original.)

Though by this system the land is manured only once every nine years, which, according to the system of stall-feeding, is done every third year; yet this is made up in such a manner, by a three years' rest, and the ley left quite unsown, that the return of the corn may be admitted at the same rate, but not higher; consequently,

77 acres wheat yield at	20	1540	at 1	1540
77 acres rye	20	1540	24	$1026\frac{2}{3}$
77 acres barley	24	1848	21	1078
77 acres oats	36	2772	12	924
77 acres ley-crop	15			1155
			produce of the farm	$6533\frac{2}{3}$
From this ought to be deducted for the expence of housekeeping, &c. nearly				1500
			Remains clear produce	$5033\frac{2}{3}$

But as such complaints are made of the expences of housekeeping, &c. attending the system of stall-feeding, though in this case the young cattle are not bought, as in the other, which is a considerable saving; yet we will admit the highest possible sum, viz. the double, or 3000 rix dollars, to be deducted from the *general produce of* 9940 *rix dollars.*

Hence there remains of clear profit by the system of stall-feeding 6940 rix dollars. Consequently it produces, upon 700 acres, a greater profit than the Koppeln economy of Mecklenburg, amounting to $1906\frac{1}{3}$ rix dollars; and every acre of its land is employed at a greater advantage of $2\frac{2}{3}$ rix dollars.

1/5 The New Husbandry in French Agriculture

a 'Successful cultivation of the potato in the plain of Sablons and Grenelle'; extract from a communication from MR. PARMENTIER, in *Bibliothèque Physico-Economique*, Part I (1789), pp. 48-50. (Ed. Tr.)

b COUNT CHAPTAL, *De l'Industrie françoise* (2 vols., Paris, 1819), I, pp. 147-149. (Ed. Tr.)

a Two Arpent* were taken at random in this vast uncultivated plain, were worked and planted at the same time, without any kind of manure; and despite the most unfavourable circumstances, since the potatoes could not be planted until the 15 May, i.e. six weeks after the normal period of planting, and that for a whole month and five days they did not receive one drop of

* See Glossary.

water, their growth was nevertheless considerable, so much so as to make it seem that the dry soil in which the crop rested provided an excellent ground, that it had received a great deal of labour, aided by the best dung, and that the time of its development had the advantage of having been favoured by the weather. From this trial resulted 520 bushels of potatoes, without counting the quantities which avarice or curiosity had abstracted earlier. The whole harvest was given to the Philanthropic Society; since this whole first trial was only in the nature of a preliminary experiment, it was important to repeat it on a large scale on the same kind of soil; thus in place of two Arpent, 37 were taken: the potato was planted in the furrow behind the plough, at a depth of about 5″ and at 1 ft. distance: between the rows sufficient space was left to allow the small American plough to undertake the different works of tillage, and to show at the same time how one could save trouble, time and expense by this method, while the products, intended to be distributed among the poor of the countryside and of Paris, will develop among the people some taste for a food which is so fit for its constitution and its health.

But it was not enough to prove by an incontrovertible fact that the driest soil could grow potatoes, and that that plant could also be used, with great profit, after the March sowings, to supply food in the years threatened by an approaching famine; it was also necessary to multiply the best varieties, and even create new ones, to rejuvenate by new seedlings those which had degenerated and to provide sure means to prevent their degeneration everywhere: 17 Arpent in the plain of Grenelle are going to fulfil this useful object, and the harvest which the Intendant* has promised to his Province, will substitute very soon the better qualities for the poor potato which exists in our market; there is no longer even a corner in the Kingdom where the Society has not got correspondents to bring its immeasurable advantages to the districts which they inhabit.

Here, then, are 54 Arpent of soil of which the very name indicates sterility, and which, in the memory of man, have not carried any product, devoted today to give a lesson of practical agriculture, to provide numerous acts of benefit, to introduce to France new varieties of potatoes, and to fix in an irrevocable manner those which suit every territory, every position and every climate: what more imposing example for the inhabitants of the capital, than to have almost under their very eyes the sands of such an ungrateful soil, covered at present with green, in July with flowers, and containing in the autumn, within inches of their surface, several thousands of sacks of a precious root almost as nourishing as bread, which during six months of the year constitutes the main food of several districts, and which has already saved several of them from famine.

* See Glossary.

b The potato, despised for so long, has finally assumed its place as one of the most useful agricultural products; today it is cultivated everywhere, because everyone recognized its value in the years when cereals were extremely scarce in France. This important product, which the poor rejected, is admitted today on to the tables of the rich, and it is rightly regarded by everyone as the best substitute for wheat.

The potato is cultivated not only in fields and gardens, but it is even sown on the edges of landed property, on river banks, and in those places where the vine does not grow, and wherever the plough cannot be used: it can be cultivated on good earth, and it can grow even on the poorest land: unlike other foodstuffs its harvest very rarely shows any variation: the crop is not always guaranteed, but at the same time is always profitable for the proprietors of the land.

. . . The potato does not require any preparation, and nevertheless everyone finds it pleasant to eat, and it can be prepared in almost any way without losing its essential qualities.

The potato is one of the best and most economical winter foodstuffs for cattle.

In all respects the potato is one of the most important agricultural discoveries of the century. We can even hope that its cultivation and the habit which people have developed of having it for food, and mixing it with bread, will reduce the gravity of the cereal shortages, which we have hitherto experienced.

1/6 The State of Agriculture in France

a ARTHUR YOUNG, *Travels during the years 1787, 1788 and 1789, Undertaken more particularly with a view of ascertaining the Cultivation, Wealth, Resources and National Prosperity of the Kingdom of France* (2 vols., Bury St. Edmunds, 1792–1794), I, pp. 393, 351 and 346.

b *Ibid.*, I, pp. 503, 505–507, 510–511.

c EDWARD RIGBY, *Letters from France etc. in 1789*; edited by his daughter, Lady Eastlake (London, 1880), pp. 96, 9–10.

a The marvellous folly is that in nine-tenths of all the enclosures of France the system of management is precisely the same as in the open fields; that is to say, fallows as regularly prevail, and consequently the cattle and sheep of a farm are nothing in comparison of what they ought to be . . . . Sologne is enclosed, yet it is the most miserable province in France, of the same rank with Bretagne itself. The Bourbonnais and great part of the Nivernais are enclosed; yet the course pursued is 1. fallow, 2. rye, and 1. fallow, 2. rye, 3. left to weeds and broom – and all these on soils, as Bretagne, Sologne and the Bourbonnais, highly improveable and capable of the best Norfolk husbandry. With such miserable systems of what use are enclosures? – Hence we may draw this conclusion, that when we find half of France enclosed, we are not to suppose that kingdom in the state of improvement and cultivation which this circumstance implies among us. On the contrary, it indicates no such thing; for some of the poorest and most unimproved provinces are precisely those which are enclosed.

Throwing these several rich districts together . . . we cannot but admit that France is in possession of a soil, and even of a husbandry, that is to be ranked very high amongst the best in Europe. Flanders, part of Artois, the rich plain of Alsace, the banks of the Garonne, and a considerable part of Quercy are cultivated more like gardens than farms. . . . The rapid succession of crops, the harvest of one being but the signal of sowing immediately for a second, can scarcely be carried to greater perfection; and this in a point perhaps of all others the most essential to good husbandry, when such crops are so justly distributed as we generally find them in these provinces, cleaning and ameliorating ones being the preparation for such as foul and exhaust. These are provinces which even an English farmer might visit with advantage.

When we see some of the finest, deepest and most fertile loams that are to be met with in the world, such as those between Berney and Elbeuf, and part of the Pays de Caux, in Normandy, and the neighbourhood of Meaux, in the Isle of France, destined to the common barbarous course of 1. fallow, 2. wheat, 3. spring corn, and the product of this spring corn beneath contempt, the whole exertion and produce being seen in a crop of wheat, we must be convinced that agriculture in such a kingdom is on the same footing as in the tenth century. If those lands were then tilled at all, they were in all probability as well tilled as at present.

b It is a remarkable circumstance in the agriculture, or rather in the domestic œconomy of France, that the culture of hemp or flax for home uses pervades every part of the kingdom. It is a curious question how far this is beneficial or not to the general interests of the national prosperity.

Of the Influence of Manufactures on Agriculture

NORMANDY – *Rouen to Barentin.* – A noble soil and full of manufactures, but the most execrable husbandry I have yet seen; every field a bed of weeds and couch.

Yvetot. – A noble track of land; richer or deeper loams hardly to be seen, but all miserably cultivated; an exception to the common case in France, where fine soils are usually well cultivated: the crops in this country are a perfect contrast to the soil.

Havre. – This whole country, from Rouen, the Pays de Caux, is a region more of manufactures than agriculture. The fabric is what the great population of this district depends on, their farms being but a secondary object. The number of small properties, and consequently population is very great, which is the reason for the price and rental of land through this country being vastly out of proportion to the products. Landlords also divide their farms according to the demand, as the rise of rent tempts it; but he often finds himself depending for the rent of his land on the prosperity of a fabric. The whole country forms a curious spectacle; a vast fabric, and an immense employment, and population having been absolutely mischievous to agriculture. This has been the result throughout the Pays de Caux, the soil of which may be ranked among the finest in France. Had it been a miserably poor, rocky, or barren territory, the result would have been beneficial, for the fabric would have covered such a district with cultivation. But the farmers of the Pays de Caux are not only manufacturers, but have an inclination also for trade; the large ones engage in commercial speculations at Havre, particularly in the cotton trade, and some even in that of the West Indies. This is a most pernicious and mischievous circumstance; the improvement of their cultivation being never the object or result of their growing rich, but merely the engaging more largely in trade or manufacture. If they get a share in an American adventure, no matter whether thistles and docks cover their fields.

BRETAGNE – *St. Brieux*. – Meeting here with a linen merchant, and some other well-instructed persons, I demanded information concerning the state of husbandry in the central parts of the province, and particularly the districts in which the great linen manufacture (one of the most considerable in Europe) is carried on. All I had seen of the province was such a wretched and almost deserted waste, that I supposed the other parts much better. I was informed, that the whole province was alike, except the bishoprick of St. Pol. de Leon; that where the linen fabrick was chiefly established, there husbandry was most neglected, from the people depending on their linen alone; that this state of things could not be helped, as it was impossible to attend both to their fabric and their land; and the former being found of the most importance, the latter was left quite neglected; and that the *landes* in the linen parts of the province were enormous.

L'Orient. – Here, in conversation concerning the wastes of Bretagne, I was again assured, that the *landes* were of very great extent in the linen country of Pontivy, Loudeac, Moncontour, and St. Quintin; and that what is cultivated is as rough as any I have seen; for the weavers are amongst the very worst farmers in the province.

Auvergnac. – A person, intimately acquainted with every part of the province, informed me, that the linen fabric in Bretagne is almost always found amidst bad agriculture, which he attributed to their always sowing hemp or flax on their best lands, and neglecting corn; but where corn is found, as about this place, they depend on it, and are not equally solicitous for hemp and flax.

Elbœuf to Rouen. – A desert.

The geatest fabrics of France are the cottons and woollens of Normandy, the woollens of Picardy and Champagne, the linens of Bretagne, and the silks and hardware of the Lyonois. Now, if manufactures be the true encouragement of agriculture, the vicinity of those great fabrics ought to be the best cultivated districts in the kingdom. I have visited all those manufactures, and remarked the attendant culture, which is unexceptionably so execrable, that one would be much more inclined to think there was something pestiferous to agriculture in the neighbourhood of a manufacture, than to look up to it as a mean of encouragement. Considering the fertility of the soil, which is great, Picardy and Normandy are among the worst cultivated countries I have seen. The immense fabrics of Abbeville and Amiens have not caused the inclosure of a single field, or the banishment of fallows from a single acre. Go from Elbœuf to Rouen, if you would view a desert: and the Pays de Caux, possessing one of the richest soils in the world, with manufactures in every hut and cottage, presents one continued scene of weeds, filth, and beggary; a soil so villainously managed, that if it were not naturally of an inexhaustible fertility, it would long ago have been utterly ruined. The agriculture of Champagne is miserable, even to a proverb; I saw there great and flourishing manufactures, and cultivation in ruins around them. Let us pass into Bretagne, which affords but one spectacle, that of a dreary, desolate waste; dark as ling – *sombre* as broom can make it. – You find yourself in the midst of one of the greatest linen manufactures in Europe. . . .

Hence the following facts cannot be controverted:

I. That the agriculture of France, after a century of exclusive and successful attention to manufactures, was in a wretched state.

II. That the manufacturing districts in France and England are the worst cultivated.

III. That the best cultivation in England, and some of the best in France, must be looked for where no manufactures are to be found.

IV. That when the fabrics spread into all the cottages of a country, as in France and Ireland, such a circumstance is absolutely destructive of agriculture: spinning only excepted, which is almost universal in every country.

V. That agriculture alone, when thoroughly improved, is equal to the establishment and support of great national wealth, power, and felicity.

And from these facts, the following corollaries are clearly deducible:

I. That the best method of improving agriculture, is not by establishing manufactures and commerce, because they may be established in great extent and perfection, and yet agriculture may remain in a miserable state.

II. That the establishment of a flourishing agriculture, inevitably occasions the possession of such manufactures and commerce, as are equal to the support of numerous and flourishing towns; and to whatever is necessary to form a great and potent society. The lesson to governments is deducible in few words: first, secure prosperity to agriculture, by equal taxation, and by absolute liberty of cultivation and sale. Secondly; do no more to encourage manufactures and commerce, than by letting them alone, a policy exclusive of every idea of monopoly. We may safely affirm, and our assertions are founded on unquestionable facts, that any country will attain the utmost prosperity of which its government is capable, that steadily pursue this conduct.

c We left Paris early on Sunday morning, July 19, without any difficulty, as the tumult had entirely subsided and the Police of the City was restored to its usual regularity. Our journey from Paris to Dijon has been a most pleasant one; the weather has been favourable, the roads good, and no obstacles of any kind have interrupted us. I wonder who it was that told me that travelling was so inconvenient in France; that the roads were execrable, the horses so bad that they could not get on, etc. We have had sufficient experience of these things and they are not so, and that many other reports that prevail in England, unfavourable to this country and its inhabitants are equally untrue.

My astonishment at the magnitude of this empire, its wonderful population, the industry of the inhabitants, and the excellence of the climate only increases the further we penetrate into the country. We have now travelled between four and five hundred miles in France, and have hardly seen an acre uncultivated, except two forests and parks . . ., and these were covered with woods. In every other place almost every inch had been ploughed or dug, and at this time appears to be pressed with the weight of the incumbent crop. On the roads, to the very edge where the travellers' wheels pass, and on the hills, to the very summit, may be seen the effects of human industry. Since we left Paris we have come through a country where the vine is cultivated. This grows on the sides and even the tops of the highest hills.

It will also flourish where the soil is too poor to bear corn, and on the sides of precipices where no animal could draw the plough.

... ...

From near Calais the country is flat, and there is a good deal of pasture land, but full of small villages and cottages. Trees are everywhere planted on each side, willows, elms, Lombardy poplars, etc. The most striking character of the country through which we passed yesterday is its astonishing fertility. We went through an extent of seventy miles, and I will venture to say that there is not a single acre but what was in a state of the highest cultivation. The crops are great beyond any conception I could have had of them – thousands and ten thousands of acres of wheat superior to any that can be produced in England; oats extraordinarily large.

There is also an immense quantity of beans, a good deal of flax, some tobacco and wood . . . we were told at Calais of the scarcity of corn, but there is no appearance of it here. To behold the fact of this country one would suppose a scarcity could never take place; but when we come into the towns the crowds are so large that a prodigious quantity of corn must be consumed.

1/7 An English Farm in France

ARTHUR YOUNG, *Travels during the years 1787, 1788 and 1789, etc.* (see **1/6a** and **b** above), II, pp. 139–141.

Among the most interesting observations which the Duke of Liancourt had made, in the various visits he paid to England, was that of the superiority to which the industry of that kingdom was carried beyond the practice of France; and above all, to what a degree of perfection agriculture had attained, founded on experiment, and manifest in an infinitely greater production of corn and of live stock than is to be found in almost any other country, extent and quality of soil considered. Impressed with this fact, he had long cherished the hope of introducing into his own country this source of increasing wealth, flowing as well from the augmentation of produce, as from that of the people employed to raise it: but sensible, at the same time, that the most useful innovations could be introduced by example only he determined to attempt, as soon as it was in his power, an essay of English agriculture; but as he was desirous of having his example followed, it was necessary that these essays should be so conducted as to ensure success.

His friend, Mons. de Lazowski's residence during three years, in England, whither he consented to accompany the sons of the Duke, facilitated these means. Mons. de Lazowski, who I had the pleasure of knowing intimately, acquired that knowledge in agriculture, which much inquiry, assiduous application, and frequent conversations with the best farmers, could give to a mind very capable of, and much accustomed to observation: he was likewise no stranger to the projects of Mons. de Liancourt; and in this instance, as on every occasion, his unexampled friendship made him eager to second his views.

In 1789, Mons. de Liancourt, on becoming the proprietor of a large estate, situated at thirteen leagues* from Paris, resolved immediately to execute the plan he had so long projected: he accordingly engaged an English farmer to come over from Suffolk, with his family, and a common labourer; this English colony carried with it every kind of farming implement; they had with them likewise five oxen, a bull, and five cows, from Sussex, to perpetuate that breed, if the country into which they were transported would admit of it; to these were added a Suffolk polled bull and five cows.

The farmer was placed in a farm that had hitherto yielded about two hundred pounds a year; the land was in some parts good, in others bad; it was so divided in quality and in situation, as to render one part fit for the reception of sheep, and the other part for the feeding of cattle; these two objects were those which Mons. de Liancourt was most anxious to attain, in the agricultural system he was about to introduce; because they were most advantageous, in a country surrounded by great markets, and very near to that of Paris; he added a large extent of land to the farm, taken from his park, and from other farms, consisting of about eight hundred arpents*; two hundred and fifty of which were appropriated to sheep, and the rest to the feeding of cattle; he designed to have made such additions to each part, as would have enlarged the whole to fifteen hundred arpents; to which, in process of time, he would have nearly dedicated the whole of his park. Whilst the Englishmen were beginning their operations, and forming the labourers of the country to the use of the new sort of plough imported from England, instructing the common workmen as to the construction of the new implements, and teaching the women servants of the farm the management of the dairy, the making of cheese, &c. Mons. de Liancourt had sent two young labourers, out of the environs of Liancourt, to England, who, being placed by me with good farmers in my neighbourhood, qualified themselves to replace, at a future day, the English family, in case these should grow tired of living in France, or to assist them if, as Mons. de Liancourt hoped, they were disposed to remain. The artizans of Liancourt learnt to imitate the implements, the plough and the cart brought from England, and made them very well.

To the cows, from England, were added twenty-four more from Normandy and Switzerland; the whole herd, a very fine one, amounted, in 1792,

* See Glossary.

to a hundred and five head, and hopes were entertained of increasing the number to three hundred, and of supplying them completely with a sufficiency of food. The young beasts were not then of an age to allow of any decision being made, whether the produce of the Suffolk or of the Sussex breed would best succeed, but the whole afforded the most flattering hopes.

With regard to the flock of sheep – the Spanish ram crossed with the ewes of Berry and the Spanish ewes, and the Berry ram with the Flemish ewes, were the two breeds designed to be established and improved; an English ram from Romney Marsh was also crossed with the Berry ewes, all of which answered perfectly well: the lambs were fine, but as this branch of business had been began later than the other, the prospect of its success, although well founded, could not be entirely ascertained.

The lands had been put into excellent condition, in a country where inclosures were unknown; every field of the farm was inclosed by deep and broad ditches, with well planted hedges; gates were erected in all; the dry lands were irrigated, and the marshy meadows drained, by cuts underground; old lands, for ages past, judged incapable of yielding any produce, were burnt and rendered fruitful; the buildings on the farm were modelled to the new system, and to the management of the culture that was introduced. The two young French labourers were returned from England, and the English farmer (Mr. Reeve), an excellent one, and a very honest man, satisfied with his situation, with his success, and with the treatment he met in the country, thought only of continuing his employment, of increasing his success, and of seconding the intentions of his master. He was ordered to keep an exact and daily register of all the business transacted on the farm, to shew it to whoever chose to see it, and to answer all their questions with truth, mildness, and patience, but not to intice any person to undertake an imitation of the English method of farming; Mons. de Liancourt thinking, that in every innovation, nothing less than self-conviction ought to actuate those who attempt it; and that by raising their expections too highly they risk the success, which sooner or later would not fail to attend their efforts. The cows of the district were covered by the bulls of the farm whenever they were brought, and the produce from them was already found, by the people of the country, to be much finer; the culture of turnips and of cabbages, for the feed of cattle, absolutely unknown before in the district, began to be introduced; some proprietors inclosed their fields; several others had made, for their own use, farming implements after the English model, and found them answer best the purpose; many more hands were employed, of all ages and of both sexes, in the farms; the English were received with pleasure in the country, and treated in the most cordial manner; every thing succeeded to the utmost wish, and these successes were, in great measure, due to the indefatigable and enlightened vigilance of Mons. de Lazowski, whose heart is equal to his capacity.

1/8 Russian Serfdom, 1784

WILLIAM COXE, *Travels into Poland, Russia, Sweden and Denmark* (5 vols., London 1784; 4th ed., 1792), III, pp. 174-181.

The peasants of Russia, a few excepted, are all serfs, or slaves. They may be divided into, 1. Peasants of the crown. 2. Peasants belonging to individuals.

1. The former inhabit the imperial demesnes; and probably comprehend, including those belonging to the church lands, which are now annexed to the crown, about the sixth part of the Russian peasants. They are immediately under the jurisdiction of the imperial officers or bailiffs. Although liable to great exactions, by the tenure of their subjection, from these petty tyrants, yet they are much more secure of their property; and being under the protection of the sovereign, any flagrant instances of oppression are more easily made known and redressed. Many of these vassals, in particular districts, have been franchised, and permitted to enrol themselves among the merchants and burghers: the whole body will gradually receive more and more privileges, as the spirit of humanity and policy penetrates further into these regions; and as the empress can venture to realize the generous system of diffusing a more equal freedom among the subjects of her vast empire.

2. Peasants belonging to individuals are the private property of the landholders, as much as implements of agriculture, or herds of cattle; and the value of an estate is estimated, as in Poland, by the number of boors,* and not by the number of acres. No regulations have, perhaps, tended more to rivet the shackles of slavery in this empire, than the two laws of Peter the Great; one which renders the landholder accountable to the crown for the poll-tax of his vassals; and the other which obliges him to furnish a certain number of recruits: for by these means he becomes extremely interested, that none of his peasants migrate without permission from the place of their nativity. These circumstances occasion a striking difference in the fate of the Russian and Polish peasants, even in favour of the latter, who in other respects are more wretched. If the Polish boor is oppressed, and he escapes to another master, the latter is liable to no pecuniary penalty for harbouring him; but in Russia the person who receives another's vassal is subject to an heavy fine. With respect to his own demands upon his peasants, the lord is restrained by no law, either in the exaction of any sum, or in the mode of employing them. He is absolute master of their time and labour: some he employs in agri-

* See Glossary.

culture: a few he makes his menial servants, and perhaps without wages; and from others he exacts an annual payment.*

Each vassal, therefore, is rated according to the arbitrary will of his master. Some contribute four or five shillings a year; others, who are engaged in traffic or trade, are assessed in proportion to their supposed profits. Several instances of these exactions fell under my observation: a mason, who was rated £.6 per annum; a smith £.12; and others as high as £.20. With regard to any capital which they may have acquired by their industry, it may be seized, and there can be no redress; as, according to the old feudal law, which still exists, a slave cannot institute a process against his master. Hence it occasionally happens that several peasants, who have gained a large capital, cannot purchase their liberty for any sum; because they are subject, as long as they continue slaves, to be pillaged by their masters.

The mode adopted by many landholders with their peasants, reminds me of that formerly practised by the Romans in regard to their slaves. Atticus, we are told, caused a numerous body of slaves to be instructed in the art of copying manuscripts, which he sold at a very high price, and raised by that means a considerable fortune. Upon similar principles some of the Russian nobility send their vassals to Moscow or Petersburgh for the purpose of learning various handicraft trades: they either employ them on their own estates; let them out for hire; sell them at an advanced price; or receive from them an annual compensation for the permission of exercising trade for their own advantage.

In regard to the lord's authority over their persons, according to the ancient laws, he might try them in his own courts of justice, or punish them without any process; he could inflict every species of penalty excepting the knoot, order them to be whipped, or confined in dungeons; he might send them to houses of correction, or banish them into Siberia; or, in short, take cognizance of every misdemeanor which was not a public offence. He had, indeed, no power over their lives; for, if a slave was beat by order of his

* The empress thus expresses herself on this head: There is hardly a village which does not pay its dues in money. The landlords, who never or very rarely see their villages, impose dues of one, two and up to five roubles,† without troubling to find out how the peasant is to earn those sums.

It will be most necessary to lay down laws for the landlords which will force them to use more care in the manner in which they exact the payment of their dues, and to exact them in a way which will have the least ill-effect on the peasant's house and family. By these means we shall build up a strong agriculture, and the propulation of the Empire will grow. [Ed. Tr.]

This custom of obliging the peasants to pay an annual sum in money, without their having always sufficient resources to procure that sum, frequently drives the necessitous to the most desperate modes of acquiring it. (Footnote in original.)

† See Glossary.

master, and died within the space of three days, the latter was guilty of murder, unless other reasons could be assigned for his demise. . . . By the new regulations, this enormous power of the lords is reduced by restrictions more consonant to the humane principles which distinguish all the regulations of the present empress; and the right of inflicting punishment is lodged, where it ever ought to be, in the hands of the public magistrate. Abuses, however, still subsist; but must, in time, yield to the influence of such salutary institutions.

1/9 Russian Serfdom, 1799

WILLIAM TOOKE, *View of the Russian Empire during the Reign of Catherine the Second and to the Close of the Present Century* (3 vols., London, 1799), III, pp. 317-320.

. . . The value of an estate is estimated partly by the situation and quantity of the lands, and principally by the number of male boors* belonging to it. At the sale or mortgage of a piece of ground, the latter forms the basis whereupon the price of the estate is calculated, in proportion to which the other natural advantages are taken into the account, and even the magnitude of an estate is in common occurrences never otherwise determined than by the number of the *souls*, by which term only the boors of the male sex are understood. By these likewise the income arising from the estate is generally settled. Some proprietors distribute all the reserved land among their boors, taking from them only the obrok*; others retain, besides the obrok, a part of the lands to their own use, which the boors are obliged to till by feudal service; others again take no obrok, but deliver to the boors only so much land as is necessary for their support, and cause all the rest to be laboured for their own immediate benefit. Though the disposition of the estates is reducible to these three main kinds, yet in real practice a great difference obtains, as the fixing of the obrok, the feudal service, the proportion of the manor-grounds and peasantry lands, &c. depends occasionally on the will of the proprietor, who in this matter is limited by no law. A great part of the nobility never live on their estates, and consequently never addict themselves to farming. Where merely an obrok is to be collected, the personal presence of the owner is unnecessary, as every village pays its tribute yearly to its stahrost or alderman, who transmits it to the feudal lord; in the two other cases, the estates, in the absence of their proprietor are managed by what are called disponents, or even only by prikaschtschiki or clerks, with full powers, which latter are chosen from the vassal servants, in whom some confidence may be reposed.

* See Glossary.

1/10 Russian Serfdom, 1853

ROBERT HARRISON, *Notes of a Nine Years' Residence in Russia from 1844* to *1853* (London, 1855), pp. 104-109. (G.P.J.)

The owner of the soil, in return for the labour which is to make that soil productive, gives to each of his serfs a portion of land, which the latter cultivates for his own use and advantage, being furnished besides, from his lord's forests, with materials for the construction of a dwelling-house. The week is divided into two *troikas*, or sections of three days, one of which is devoted to the master's service, the other is the peasant's own. When this arrangement is equitably carried out, the condition of the *moojik*,* when happily situated with regard to soil, is by no means unfavourable, especially as he religiously avails himself of the saints' days and holidays (formerly so numerous, but now reduced by a recent Ukase, to fifteen in the year) which fall within the landlord's *troika*. Now, it has been for some years past a growing difficulty with landowners and their stewards, to find means to eradicate from the serf's mind the conviction that the house and land occupied for a number of years by himself and his forefathers is *bona fide* his own, and to meet this difficulty, the *Pameshtchiks* (Proprietors) resort to the cruel expedient of making 'a deserted village' by transporting its inhabitants to another part of the estate. Sometimes too these changes arise from the mere superfluity of land and scarcity of population. The fertility of the soil in one spot being worked out, that locality is left to lie fallow for years, and the peasantry are transferred bodily to a new, unexhausted region. That was certainly a great and wise step of the Emperor Alexander, which emancipated the serfs belonging to the apppanages of the Crown, for though the habit of dependence on a master may have made it seem hard to them at first to pay their own taxes in a direct manner, to battle with the official authorities, and to incur other responsibilities of comparative independence, yet I have ascertained by incidental conversations with the men themselves that the Crown peasants are happier and more generally prosperous than the bondsmen of the boyars*. . . .

There are serfs living in situations favourable to trade who have become millionaires, and some of the richest shopkeepers in St. Petersburg belong to Count Sheremetieff, who receives only about £1 a year each from them, as *obrok*,* or tribute, yet will neither give nor sell them their freedom. . . . Serfs of this description do give sometimes large sums of money for the purchase of their freedom. The gentleman whose property I have been

* See Glossary.

describing told me that one of his 'people' had bought his liberty with 33,000 roubles (£1500), the sum offered being fixed by the man himself. . . .

The *obrok* paid to their owners by traders and artisans is a commutation of the labour *troika*, which the master claims from every serf; and except in a few cases . . . the amount of it rises with the gains of the peasant. When a peasant boy displays an aptitude for some calling that can be pursued profitably in a town, he is sent to undergo a rough apprenticeship with a master of the art, and afterwards to work his way up in the world. If he should fail his owner is burdened with him again in his native village; if he succeed he will have to make a hard bargain with his master, who holds him fast by means of a passport renewable every year, or in some cases every six months. At each renewal the *obrok* must be paid; for by withholding the pass the landlord confines the serf to his own village, since not only the police authorities of a town are bound to see that every resident has documentary authority for living in that part of the world, but every employer is responsible for his workmen and servants, and must see that their passports are of the right date and in order.

1/11 Peasantry in Poland, 1825

WILLIAM JACOB, *Report on the Trade in Corn and on the Agriculture of the North of Europe* (London, 2nd ed., 1826), pp. 63-67.

In general, this Peasantry is in a condition of great distress, and involved in debt to their lord. They are no longer slaves, or *adstricti glebæ* [sic]. By the constitution promulgated in 1791, they were declared free, and that part of the Constitution suffered no alteration under the dominion of the Russians and Prussians; was confirmed when the king of Saxony became Sovereign; and was again assured in 1815, when the Emperor of Russia was enthroned as King of Poland.

The practical effects of the privileges thus granted have hitherto been very inconsiderable. The peasants can leave their land, but must first acquit the pecuniary demands of their lords. . . .

These people live in Wooden Huts, covered with thatch or shingles, consisting of one room with a stove, around which the inhabitants and their cattle crowd together, and where the most disgusting kinds of filthiness are to be seen. Their common Food is, cabbage, potatoes sometimes, but not generally, pease, black bread, and soup, or rather gruel, without the addition of butter or meat. Their chief Drink is water, or the cheap whiskey of the country, which is the only luxury of the peasants; and is drunk, whenever they can obtain it, in enormous quantities. They use much salt with their vegetable food, and in spite of the heavy tax on that commodity, can never dispense with the want of it at their meals. I was informed, and saw reason to credit the accounts, that when the peasants brought to the market towns their trifling quantities of produce, a part of the money was first used to purchase salt, and the rest spent in whiskey, in a state of intoxication that commonly endured till the exhaustion of the purse had restored them to sobriety. In their houses they have little that merits the name of furniture; and their clothing is coarse, ragged, and filthy, even to disgust.

Very little attention has been paid to their Education, and they are generally ignorant, superstitious, and fanatical. They observe about twenty Holidays in the year, besides the Sundays; and pass much of their time in pilgrimages to some favourite shrine, in counting beads, and similar superstitious occupations.

This Representation of the condition and character of the Peasantry, though general, cannot be considered so universal as to admit of no exceptions; some rare instances of perseverance in economy, industry, and temperance, are to be found; and unfavourable as their circumstances may be for the creation of such habits, they are here attended by the usual correspondent results. Some few peasants have been enabled to gain three or four allotments, and to employ their sons or hired servants to work for them; and there are instances of such persons making a still further progress, and being enabled to purchase estates for themselves. Such cases as these, however, occur so rarely, that though they produce individual comfort and wealth, they have no perceptible influence on the general mass of society, or on the surplus quantity of agricultural productions.

As may be naturally inferred, from the system under which labour is applied to the land, that labour is performed in the most negligent and slovenly manner possible. No manager of a large estate can have his eye constantly on every workman; and when no advantage is gained by care in the work, it will naturally be very imperfectly executed. All the Operations of Husbandry struck me to be very ill performed: the ploughing is very shallow and irregular; the harrows with wooden tines do not penetrate sufficient to pull up weeds in fallowing; the roller is almost unknown; and thus the land is filled with weeds of all descriptions. I observed the same want of attention in threshing; and it appeared to me that a much greater proportion of the grain was left among the straw, than in that which has passed under an English flail. In short, the natural effects of the system of duty work was visible in the whole of the administration of the large estates where it is followed, with the exception of those few proprietors who have intelligent and active managers, and are free from pecuniary embarrassments.

The common Course of Cropping is the old system of a whole year's fallow, followed by winter corn, and that by summer corn, and then a fallow again. Thus one third of the land bears nothing. The winter crop in the northern part of Poland consists of Wheat and Rye; the Proportion of the latter to the former, is nearly as nine to one, and the Wheat enjoys the benefit of what little manure is preserved. Thus the Wheat actually cultivated, does not occupy more than one thirtieth part of the arable land. In the southern part of the kingdom, the Wheat bears a larger proportion to the Rye, amounting, on the more tenacious soils, to a fifth, and even in some cases, to a fourth part of the Rye.

1/12 Peasantry in Pomerania, 1810

C. W. ZIMMERMANN, Report of November 22nd, 1810, on the Tenant Farmers in Pomerania; printed in G. F. KNAPP, *Die Bauernbefreiung und der Ursprung der Landarbeiter in den älteren Teilen Preussens* (2 vols., Leipzig, 1887), I, pp. 330–332. (W.O.H. Tr.)

The main facts concerning the relationship of leaseholding peasants to their lords of the manor in Pomerania and the New Mark are as follows:

1. The peasants who occupy holdings on [short] leases

(a) accept responsibility for all State and local taxes and obligations including the duty to provide horses [to the parish for carting];

(b) agree to perform services for the lords of the manor. The extent of the services depends on the nature of the manorial estate and of the leased holdings. In the most fertile districts and places the leaseholder renders daily manual labour and service with horses in the summer and also performs extra services with horses. In the winter however he performs manual labour and renders service with horses on only three days [in the week]. In addition he discharges his obligations by spinning – with flax or wild flax provided either by the lord of the manor or by himself – from 6 to 8 lengths of yarn. He also pays the 'meat tithe' (Fleischzehnt) and performs his [normal] village duties.

According to the nature of the district and the productivity of the manorial estate these services are proportionately reduced to two days manual labour and service with horses each week; the spinning of 6 lengths of yarn annually; the tithe and payments in cash and kind. If the rent is paid in cash it is usually fixed at between 20 and 150 Thalers.*

The lord of the manor, on the other hand, undertakes

(a) according to the custom of the district to provide winter seed if the

* See Glossary.

lease starts on Lady Day and also summer seed if the lease commences on Midsummer Day. It is a matter of mutual arrangement between the parties concerned as to whether the leased farm is provided with stock and implements or whether the leaseholder

(b) provides these things himself. It is also mutually arranged whether the lord of the manor – if he owns heathlands himself – provides the leaseholder with free domestic fuel or whether he pays for it. The former arrangement is the more usual.

(c) The lord of the manor must pay the premiums on the fire insurance. But a few years before the outbreak of the (Napoleonic) wars this obligation was imposed upon the leaseholders. If new buildings or repairs are required the lord of the manor provides the materials and pays the (skilled) craftsmen but the parish provides cartage and other (unskilled) labour not covered (by the peasant's services).

The lord of the manor is under no (legal) obligation to remit rent or services. The leaseholders must be satisfied with the remissions granted by the Local Authorities. Similarly the lord of the manor is not [legally] obliged to assist the leaseholder in the event of fire, losses of cattle or other misfortune. But it is obvious that the lord of the manor must at his own discretion pay some compensation to meet such misfortunes if he desires to preserve his own property from ruin. For the same reason the Lord of the manor must ease the terms of the lease, services and so forth in proportion to the burdens that have fallen upon leaseholders owing to the local exigencies of war. Allowance must be made [by the lord of the manor] for the changed circumstances [of his tenants].

2. The length of a lease is usually fixed at 6 years. Less frequently it is 3 years. Still less frequently it is 9 years.

3. In former times – until about 1780 – leaseholders were usually granted a renewal of their leases when the old ones expired. So grandfathers, fathers and children followed each other as occupiers of a holding and it was rare for rents to be raised when leases were renewed. But since 1780 rents have gradually been raised to a considerable extent and divisions of holdings have occurred. These changes have been accompanied by the granting of leases to new tenants and so many of the older tenants have left their holdings. . . .

4. In the more prosperous districts purchasers of hereditary copyholds will always be forthcoming if a farm that has been leased is disposed of in this way. It does not matter whether the former leaseholder rendered services; paid cash as well as rendering services; or simply paid a money rent. Normally a farm that has been rented (on short lease) is in a worse condition than one which is held by hereditary copyhold tenure. Experience shows that the peasant who occupies landed property on a hereditary tenure farms his hold-

ing far more efficiently because he knows that he alone benefits from his industry. Anyhow those anxious to take over on hereditary tenure farms formerly rented [on short lease] prefer to acquire holdings that were held for money rents to those for which services were rendered.

The advantage to the lord of the manor of an arrangement whereby a peasant continues to render to him the services and payments in kind formerly made by the leaseholder – the lord no longer being responsible for State and local taxes – is enhanced if it is accompanied by a stipulation fixing the sum that the peasant should receive as compensation for any misfortune in the event of the farm being held on a hereditary tenure. A system of fixed compensation protects the lord of the manor against having to pay out large sums for major disasters since the copyholder will take care of his formerly leased farm. The lord can publicly auction the lease of the holding of an incompetent farmer and can hope to get a better tenant. I am sure that both lords and hereditary copyholders will benefit from such changes and that the prosperity and the revenue of the State will increase. . . .

C. W. Zimmermann

Bockshagan
22 November 1810.

1/13 Peasantry in Sprottau, Silesia, 1821

J. G. ELSNER, *Landwirthschaftliche Reise durch Schlesien* (4 vols., in 2, Breslau, 1823) II/I, pp. 82–84. (Ed. Tr.)

I asked how it was that the peasants did not begin to plough up the fallow any sooner? – 'Well!' was the reply, 'they are not allowed to'. 'But this is curious', I replied; 'if the land is theirs, they are surely free to do with it what they please'. 'Oh no!' was the retort, 'the Lord has the right of grazing sheep, and as long as there is stubble grazing, we have to let the fallow lie'. – It is possible that they are exaggerating, and that this is not the literal truth. But there must be something in it, or else one or the other would surely have started his ploughing. – I asked them further, why they had not commuted their services. 'We would dearly like to', they replied, 'but the lord does not want to. We have made offers, but they have not been accepted'. – It is of course possible, that here also they were trying to make a case, since I could not apply the *audiatur et altera pars*.*

Now a very aged peasant came up to me and said confidentially, 'Believe me, the lord loses as much by this as we do. Cultivation is always inferior,

* The other side should also be heard. (Ed.)

and even if there is one or the other among us who wants to improve his tillage, he will get no thanks for it and will be laughed at by the rest. And why should we make special efforts, since we receive no recognition, and the steward and bailiff treat us as people whom one uses and does not care about afterwards?'

I believe that these words explain the whole of the situation described above. What could not mutual trust and a closer approach achieve here!...

If I have told you above, that the peasants have so much robot (service dues), and that everyone has, in addition to a great deal of ploughing and carting, also to send one person daily for labouring duties to the lords' home farm throughout the summer, you will probably wonder how a farm of one Hube,* in reasonably good condition, could fetch 2,000 Rthlr,* and this on a soil which could hardly be called more than medium rye soil. But the matter is easily explained by the fact that here the Hube has about 100 Morgen,* and contains therefore about double as much as elsewhere.

The services of the cottars and borders are less onerous than the service dues of the peasants; since in their case they are at least limited to a certain number of days. Their property to be sure, is of small value, and that of the cottar (Häusler) consists only of a small allotment, often less than half a Morgen. For them, commutation would be less desirable, since they are able to perform their services on the side; whereas by contrast they would find it hard to raise the commutation payment. Even if their service dues were commuted into annual rent payments, it would not be easy for them to pay them: since they would not always be able to find work and earn cash, and they would have to spend as much time spinning flax to raise it as they would have spent in labour services.

1/14 Peasantry in Hanover, 1820

THOMAS HODGSKIN, *Travels in the North of Germany* (2 vols., Edinburgh, 1820), II, pp. 77-92. (G.P.J.)

The land of Hannover is divided amongst persons who may be conveniently classed thus:- The sovereign, the nobles, town and religious corporations, persons not noble.... One-sixth at least belongs to the sovereign, and possibly more than three-sixths may belong to the nobles, one-sixth to the corporations, and less than one-sixth to persons not noble. That which belongs to the sovereign is again divided in general into large

* See Glossary.

portions . . . now let by the crown in their entire state. They may contain from 500 to 3000 acres. . . . These large portions are sometimes cultivated entirely by the first tenant, sometimes they are again divided into many small portions, which are held by the bauers according to some ancient tenures and some certain conditions, called either *Meyer* or *Leibeigen*. . . .

There are 644 noble properties in the kingdom, several of which are united in the hands of one person; but there is no one nobleman whose income amounts to more than 30,000 Thalers, or £5000 per year. . . . I have met with three instances . . . of nobles cultivating their own estates; but in general there are no houses on the properties of the nobles, other than the houses of the farmers; and few of the nobles ever live in the country. Those who retain their property in their own hands generally live in the towns. . . . Some of the nobles have full power over their properties and can let them all to one person and on what terms they please; in which case they make respectable farms and may contain from 100 to 500 acres. . . . But more generally the nobles have not full power over their property. It is divided into small portions of 5, 10, 20, 30 or 80 acres, which are held on certain conditions, either of doing service, or of paying rents which have been long ago established, and which the landlord has no power whatever to alter. . . . The use of these small portions of land on certain conditions is the property of the occupier, which he can sell; as the stipulated rent and services are the property of the landlord. The bauer has an hereditary right to the use, the landlord an hereditary right to be paid for that use. . . .

The occupiers of small portions of land, whether held under the crown, under the nobles, or corporations, may be conveniently divided into two classes. . . . The first class are called *Meyers*, half *Meyers*, or quarter *Meyers*, according to the size of their farm. It is, however, very rare for a whole meyer, in any of the fertile districts, to possess so much as one hundred *Morgen* of land, about eighty acres; from thirty to forty acres is the more usual size of their farms, while the half and quarter meyers have much less. The conditions by which the meyers have the use of their land consist in paying to the landlord a certain fixed yearly sum, or yearly quantity of corn, for rent. The landlord cannot alter these conditions, neither can he refuse, except when the heir is an idiot, or the rent has not been paid, to renew the lease on the death of the occupier. I never found the rent, in the fertile districts, to exceed twelve shillings per acre; generally it was between this sum and seven shillings. . . . The meyers have also to give the landlord a certain sum when, from death or from sale, the occupier is changed. . . .

The conditions by which the leibeigener holds his land are also fixed, they are not the arbitrary will of his lord, and it descends with these to his children; but they are conditions of service so onerous, that they reduce him almost to slavery. He is obliged to cultivate the land of his lord a certain number of days in the year, to neglect his own harvest while he is carrying in that of his lord, to employ his horses to bring home his lord's wood, to supply his lord with coach-horses when he demands them; in short, to do all sorts of feudal services. This relation of the two parties to one another is equally prejudicial to both. If the landlord had to hire labourers, he might have his work tolerably well performed, but it is now shamefully performed, because the people who have it to do have no interest whatever in doing it well and no other wish but to perform as little as possible within the prescribed time. The people acquire from this sort of labour habits of slothfulness and neglect, which they never lay aside, even when performing their own work. . . .

. . . the occupiers of small farms, whether leibeigeners or meyers . . . have this in common, that neither of them have, in general, much more capital than their necessary implements, two or four horses, and money to support themselves and families. When they have servants, they are generally the junior members of their own families; but they think of what is to be done, and they themselves are the persons who do it. This is by far the most numerous class of cultivators, and they are what we call peasants; in German they are bauers. Probably four-fifths of the country is cultivated by them.

A class of men, resembling strictly our agricultural labourers, that is, who work merely for hire, are in no part of Germany very numerous. They are found in the marsh lands; some are met with at all large farms, but at both these places they have, in general, also some little property of their own.

1/15 Peasantry in Minden, Westphalia, 1819

WILLIAM JACOB, *A History of Agriculture, Manufactures, Statistics and State of Society of Germany and Parts of Holland and France* (London, 1820), pp. 103-105.

. . . The far greater part of these provinces is divided into small farms, the occupiers of which reside together in considerable villages. The average of these farms does not exceed, if it reaches so much, as forty acres. The rent to the lord of the manor is paid, under various titles, sometimes in the produce of the soil, sometimes in a fixed number of days'-labour of the tenant, occasionally of his horses, and sometimes, though but rarely, in money. It however, very commonly, consists of a mixture of each of these different modes. The occupiers are generally a kind of copy-holders, under the proprietor, to whom they are bound as their feudal lord, and are called his subjects (*unterthaner*.) The lands descend from father to son, and the work is generally performed by members of the family.

In such a state of things the division of labour can scarcely take place, nor the labour be all productively applied. There are many seasons when such farms can afford no occupation to those who are established upon them; their neighbours being in the same state; as no employment can be obtained in any other way, much time, and consequently labour, must be thus lost. The number of horses kept on these small farms, is far greater in proportion to their extent than is required on larger ones; and hence arises a consumption which, in different circumstances, would be an actual surplus, and by the natural process of reproduction would create or augment the capital. The increase of population, is indeed promoted by this plan of small farms, and the employment which long and extended wars offered to the young men, prevented the evil of that increase from being felt; but the peace has returned numbers to their homes in this country, who cannot find occupation, and would be an unsupportable burden on their families, if the general introduction of potatoes for subsistence did not keep them from the extreme of want.

No improvements in agriculture, except that just alluded to of growing potatoes instead of corn, can be introduced into a district so oppressed by want, as those are where only such small farmers are employed in cultivation. They have no hope to rise above their present situation and no stimulus consequently to great exertions, either of intellect or of labour. They have the bare necessaries of life, as their ancestors had before them, and enjoying these are too indolent to better their condition; though besides living as poor and working as hard as the day-labourer, they are subject to cares and anxieties to which he is a stranger.

1/16 Serfdom in Hungary, 1831

RICHARD JONES, Peasant Rents (1831; reprinted 1895, New York and London), pp. 23-25. (G.P.J.)

In Hungary, the nobles alone are allowed to become the proprietors of land, either by inheritance or purchase. They constitute about one part in twenty-one of a population of eight millions. Of the other inhabitants, a great majority are peasants; for in 1777 there were only 30,921 artizans in Hungary, and their number is said to be not much more increased. These peasants occupy about half the cultivated surface of the country, and all pay labor rents.

Till the reign of Maria Theresa their situation was nearly similar to that of the Russian serf. . . . By an edict of hers, which the Hungarians call the Urbarium, personal slavery and attachment to the soil were abolished, and the peasants declared to be '*homines liberae transmigrationis*'. On the other hand, they were declared mere tenants at will, whom the lord at his pleasure might dismiss from the estate. But an interest in the soil, though denied to them as individuals, was attempted to be secured to them as a body. The lands on each estate, before allotted to the maintenance of serfs, were declared to be legally consecrated to that purpose for ever. They were divided into portions of from 35 to 40 English acres each, called Sessions. The quantity of labor due to the proprietor for each session was fixed at 104 days per annum. The proprietor might divide these sessions, and grant any minute portion of them as he pleased to a peasant; but he could stipulate for labor only in proportion to the size of the holding: for half a session 52 days, for a quarter 26 days, and so proportionably for smaller quantities.

The urbarium of Maria Theresa still continues the magna charta of the Hungarian serfs. But the authority of the owners of the soil over the persons and fortunes of their tenantry has been very imperfectly abrogated; the necessities of the peasants oblige them frequently to resort to their landlords for loans of food; they become laden with heavy debts to be discharged by labor.

1/17 Serfdom in Hungary, 1839

JOHN PAGET, *Hungary and Transylvania* (2 vols., London, 1839), I, pp. 305-307.

... I believe that many of these laws have an injurious effect on the peasantry. The system of rent by *robot* or forced labour – that is, so many days' labour without any specification of the quantity of work to be performed – is a direct premium on idleness. A landlord wishes a field of corn to be cut; his steward sends out, by means of his Haiduks,* information to the peasants to meet at such a field at such an hour with their sickles. Some time after the hour appointed a great part of them arrive, the rest finding some excuse by which they hope to escape a day's work; while others send their children or their wives, declaring some reason for their own absence. After much arranging they at last get to work; a Haiduk stands over them to see that they do not go to sleep, and between talking, laughing, and resting, they do get something done. Where horses are employed, they are still less inclined to hurry; lest they should tire them for the next day, when they use them for their own purposes.

Now how much does the reader suppose such workmen perform in one day? Count S—— says, just one-third of what the same men can do easily when working by the piece; and he has accordingly compounded his peasants' one hundred and four days' robot for a certain amount of labour, which they generally get through in about thirty-four days.

* See Glossary.

Another evil of the robot is the ill-will it begets between the masters and the workmen: their whole lives seem to be a constant effort, on the one hand, to see how much can be pressed out of the reluctant peasant; and, on the other, how little can be done to satisfy the terms of agreement, and escape punishment. Mutual injury becomes a mutual profit; suspicion and ill-will are the natural results.

1/18 System of Land Tenure in Pre-Revolutionary France

A. M. R. TURGOT, *Œuvres*, et documents le concernant, ed. G. SCHELLE (5 vols., Paris, 1914), II, pp. 448-450. (Ed. Tr.)

1. What really distinguishes the area of large-scale farming from the areas of small-scale production is that in the former areas the proprietors find farmers who provide them with a permanent revenue from the land and who buy from them the right to cultivate it for a certain number of years. These farmers undertake all the expenses of cultivation, the ploughing, the sowing and the stocking of the farm with cattle, animals and tools. They are really agricultural entrepreneurs, who possess, like the entrepreneurs in all other branches of commerce, considerable funds, which they employ in the cultivation of land. When their lease falls in, if the proprietor no longer wishes to continue it, they find another farm to which they can transfer their wealth and develop in the same way.

... They have not only the brawn but also the wealth to devote to agriculture. They have to work, but unlike workers they do not have to earn their living by the sweat of their brow, but by the lucrative employment of their capital, just as the shipowners of Nantes and Bordeaux employ theirs in maritime commerce.

2. *Métayer System* The areas of small-scale farming, that is to say at least 4/7ths of the kingdom, are those where there are no agricultural entrepreneurs, where a proprietor who wishes to develop his land cannot find anyone to cultivate it except wretched peasants who have no resources other than their labour, where he is obliged to make, at his own expense, all the advances necessary for tillage, beasts, tools, sowing, even to the extent of advancing to his *métayer* the wherewithal to feed himself until the first harvest, where consequently a proprietor who did not have any property other than his estate would be obliged to allow it to lie fallow.

After having deducted the costs of sowing and feudal dues with which the property is burdened, the proprietor shares with the *métayer* what remains of the profits, in accordance with the agreement they have concluded. The proprietor runs all the risks of harvest failure and any loss of cattle: he is the real entrepreneur. The *métayer* is nothing more than a mere workman, a farm hand to whom the proprietor surrenders a share of his profits instead of paying wages. But in his work the proprietor enjoys none of the advantages of the farmer who, working on his own behalf, works carefully and diligently; the proprietor is obliged to entrust all his advances to a man who may be negligent or a scoundrel and is answerable for nothing.

This *métayer*, accustomed to the most miserable existence and without the hope and even the desire to obtain a better living for himself, cultivates badly and neglects to employ the land for valuable and profitable production; by preference he occupies himself in cultivating those things whose growth is least troublesome and which provide him with more foodstuffs, such as buckwheat and chestnuts which do not require any attention. He does not worry very much about his own livelihood; he knows that if the harvest fails, his master will be obliged to feed him in order not to see his land neglected.

1/19 Church Exactions from Spanish Agriculture

WILLIAM JACOB, *Travels in the South of Spain in Letters written in A.D. 1809 and 1810* (London, 1811), pp. 99-101.

The most important branch, of the ecclesiastical revenues, is that accruing from tithes, which are collected with a strictness that far exceeds what is known in any other part of Europe. The tithes collected in Andalusia extend to every agricultural production, and are rigidly exacted, not, as with us, on the ground, but after it has gone through all the necessary processes to fit it for the use of man. Thus wheat and barley must not only be cut, but threshed and winnowed, before the tithes are taken. Olives, which form a most important article in this vicinity, when they are sold in the state in which they are grown, pay the tithe only on the quantity carried away; but if there be a mill, and oil-presses on the farm, one-tenth of the oil is taken by the collector. In the same manner the tithe upon grapes, when the grapes are sold, is paid in fruit, but when made into wine within the district, the church receives one-tenth of the liquor.

The principle upon which this is founded seems to be, that the church may receive one-tenth of the produce in the first stage in which it becomes fit for use; for if wine be made into brandy, or vinegar, the church receive its due from the wine, and not from those articles into which it is afterwards converted. The more valuable productions of the field, such as liquorice, and sumach, as well as the minuter articles of the garden, such as melons, pumpkins, onions, garlick, peas, and beans, all contribute an equal proportion to the support of the ecclesiastical establishment. The right to tithes has been lately extended to such wild fruits as can be sold, even for the smallest sums:

thus the tumas, or prickly pears, the figs growing on the opuntia, a wild fruit with which the hedges abound, and consequently of little value, have lately been subjected to the tithing system. One-tenth also of all the domesticated animals is delivered to the tithe-collector, as well as the wool annually shorn from the sheep.

Composition for tithes is a practice wholly unknown in Andalusia. The Cabildo* annually sells the tithes by a species of auction, and where no person bids sufficiently high, the articles are taken into its own hands, and collected in storehouses within the district. In either case, the collectors of the tithes have no common interest with the farmers, who, from submission to the church, frequently suffer the grossest impositions without an effort for redress, knowing that in any appeal they might make, priests would be their judges. Before the revenues are collected, the Cabildo issues its billets of repartimiento to the different claimants on their fund, which entitle the bearer to a certain sum of money, or a specific quantity of produce, and being easily transferred, are frequently sold by the necessitous clergy. Those who have billets for produce, receive it at the storehouses where it has been deposited by the collectors, but those who have billets for money, receive it from the treasurer of the Cabildo, as the purchasers of the tithes make their payments. There is an uniformity in this system which produces effects diametrically opposite to those which are felt in England. In Spain, it is the clergy who oppress, and the farmer who is defrauded; in England, it is the farmer who imposes, and the clergyman who is the sufferer.

The monastic bodies depend for their support on the lands they possess, and many of them have estates of considerable extent and of great value. The Carthusians are the richest as well as the most rigid order in Andalusia; they let large tracts of land to farmers, who pay them partly in produce and partly in money: at the same time they occupy very extensive farms themselves, and have for many years been the greatest breeders and proprietors of the best Andalusian horses, but their revenues are ill administered. The voluptuous lives of the priors, and the peculations of the procuradores, have involved the convents in embarrassments which have placed them under the necessity of anticipating their resources, and of lessening them by borrowing money on mortgages. The convent of St. Heronymo de Buena Vista possesses a tract of land highly productive of corn, wine, and oil. I was informed by the monks of St. Heronymo, that they could travel to the city of Carmona, which is about twenty-four miles from Seville without treading upon any soil which did not belong to their convent; yet with this valuable estate, from bad management, they are deeply in debt, and obliged to retrench.

* See Glossary.

Chapter 2 Industry and Industrial Policy under Mercantilism

Introduction

The quickening of economic life in the eighteenth century, largely stimulated by the development of trade, was marked by a powerful expansion and a series of fundamental organizational changes in the manufacturing industry of Europe. The mercantilist policies of the major states fastened on manufacture as one of their main points of interest and support. Nevertheless, a substantial share of industrial activity was, and remained, restricted by the gild system, inherited from the Middle Ages. Although the gilds, with their assumptions of local industrial interests, limited and defined markets, a static technology and the single master, working in his own workshop with perhaps one or two journeymen and apprentices as the typical productive unit, were plainly becoming an anachronism, yet the momentum of their own power and organization, and the complex legal framework they had built up, allowed them to fight for their survival with great tenacity.

Nowhere did the gilds survive more firmly than in Germany. Improved communications even seemed to strengthen them, and an Imperial Edict of 1734 tended in the same direction, by associating the territorial authorities more closely with the gild powers, and regularizing the recognition of members of one gild in the town of another. A spate of local enactments to enforce this edict left all the old restrictions intact, and merely proscribed personal abuses (**2/1**). Other legislation, some of it of mercantilist origin, made gild regulations so complex that special legal compendia (**2/2**) had to be printed for the information of members. While the gild system was at its strongest in the handicraft trades proper (**2/4**), it was also found in modified form elsewhere, including the iron industry (**2/3**).

The rise of capitalist manufacture was bound to undermine the gild system. In new or favoured or rapidly expanding industries, it was broken by economic logic (**2/6**); in France, attempts were made to end it by legislation (**2/5**); and the breakdown of the old order is also signalized by the rise of independent journeymen's organizations, which reached their most highly developed form in the French *Compagnonnages* (**5/11, 2/7**). In some rural industries it never developed at all (**11/1**). Yet, where it was not swept away by revolution, as in France, it lingered on well into the nineteenth century (**11/24**).

The new manufactures, whether centralized or scattered as domestic industry (or a mixture of both) were rarely allowed to grow up on the Continent without the intervention of governments. On the whole, government action was favourable, as mercantilist rulers believed that home manufactures would strengthen their countries in various ways, and would make them less dependent on imports. In certain industries, official support took the form of creating 'royal manufactures', directly under the control of the ruler or set up with his financial support (**2/8, 2/9, 2/10, 2/11, 2/12**). Much attention and care was lavished on them (though rarely with adequate economic returns), and they were always specially privileged by monopolies, tax concession and numerous other means. Other manufactures, financed privately, were also given special privileges of a similar kind (**2/13, 2/14, 2/15, 2/16**). Considerable efforts were made to attract skilled workmen and technologists from abroad by subsidies and other privileges, to foster or develop industries which the country did not possess, or possessed only to an inadequate extent and to introduce new methods (**2/11, 2/13, 2/14, 2/20, 2/21**). The attempts to introduce English methods were particularly significant, and became much more pronounced in the nineteenth century (**2/17, 2/18, 10/3, 10/4, 10/6**). More general protection and support was also given, for example by limiting official purchases to home manufactures (**2/19**) or by privileges to trading companies (**3/7, 3/9, 3/10, 3/11**).

In this final transitional stage between the handicraft (gild) type of industry and the factory system, several forms of organization developed according to needs and circumstances. The iron industry, still scattered in numerous small units, was in many countries organized on capitalistic lines (**2/22, 2/23**). In Russia, on the other hand, even large-scale mining was undertaken in servile conditions (**2/24** also **1/8, 1/9**). Most important, however, was the domestic or putting-out system particularly in the expanding textile industries of Germany and France (**2/25, 2/26**). Some of these manufactures in Germany grew up inside the gild organization; elsewhere, as in France, they may be linked to free overseas trade and thus appear to be on the threshold of factory industry.

The growing industries, stimulated by the influx of capital, by growing markets and the new science and technology, frequently felt themselves hampered by the restrictiveness of gilds, monopolies and privileges. Yet contemporaries were aware that economic development might be hampered not only by the regulation of industry as such, but by the attitudes and values of society as a whole. The role of entrepreneurship, or of the profit-maximizing motive as a positive driving force, could be inhibited by such general factors as the survival of serfdom, the pretensions and attitudes of the nobility, and the social and caste structure (**2/27, 2/28, 11/2**).

2/1 Gild Regulations in Germany

Regulations relating to the gild of locksmiths, lorimers, gun, watch and spring makers: Brandenburg-Prussia, 1734. Printed in C. O. MYLIUS, *Corpus Constitutionum Marchicarum* (5 vols., 1737-40), V, Part II, Appendix, pp. 61-63. (Ed. Tr.)

III. A journeyman asking to be admitted to mastership of his craft, who has applied in due manner to the general assembly of the trade, shall make the following as his masterpiece:

A locksmith:

(1) A proper French or English lock.

(2) A table lock besides a padlock, with two keys in two levers, with rotating pinions, inside and out properly and well finished.

A lorimer shall make as his masterpiece:

(1) Two pairs of coach poles, exactly alike, no matter how they are paired,

(2) Two pairs of riding poles, similarly.

(3) A pair of stirrups, the bottoms and crosspieces welded in.

(4) A pair of spurs with hollow pricks.

A gun maker shall make as his masterpiece:

(1) A drawn musket, the barrel of five spans' length worked up in the most delicate manner, together with the stock and all other parts.

(2) A pair of pistols after the present fashion, of iron, brass, yellow metal* or silver, so that each part is interchangeable with the other, no matter which of the two it is screwed into, with handle and accessories, all complete.

(3) A shotgun, the barrel of two ells length, with an ordinary lead, the lock to have a catch so that it cannot be fired without cocking and does not work loose, together with the stock and accessories, all complete.

The barrels and main components are to be forged by him according to the pattern shown to him in the gild, and within four weeks of the forging he must bring before the trade the barrels bored and filed as required, with screw threads and firing holes, when they will be tested by firing two bullets with full-strength powder.

A clockmaker shall make as his masterpiece:

A standing clock which chimes at the quarter hour, shows the state of the moon and the days of the month, and goes for eight days before re-winding, with a drum-cylinder, and a long pendulum, to be used in a

* This is the metal said to derive from Prince Rupert of the Palatinate (d. 1682), consisting of 3 parts copper and 1 part zinc. (Ed.)

drawing room or bedroom. If he has been trained as a locksmith also and wishes to pursue that trade at the same time, he must make the masterpieces like other locksmiths.

A watchmaker shall make as his masterpiece:

A spring pocket watch in the fashion of Augsburg, which chimes at the quarter hour, shows the position of the sun, the moon and the planets, and the phases of the moon.

A springmaker, if he wishes to set up on his own, shall make as his masterpiece, a tension spring, and a balance spring, but if he wants to pursue the trade of a locksmith at the same time, he shall make the pieces of a locksmith also, and it shall be open to every journeyman to keep, to sell, or do as he pleases with the articles made as his masterpiece; but no one shall be precluded, on any pretext, from making more than the pieces indicated here.

IV When the journeyman has been permitted to enter for the mastership by making his masterpiece, he shall forge it in the house of a master craftsman and in his presence, within 18 weeks. Clock and watch makers who wish to enter for both, should be given more time. But it is by no means necessary for more than one master to be present: and all the feasting usually associated with these occasions is here prohibited.

V When the masterpiece is finished, the candidate shall notify the master of the craft and the assessor, and ask them to inspect and judge his work, and this shall then take place as soon as possible in the presence of the assessor.

If the completed masterpiece shall be found to have such faults as to show that the maker is not yet full master of his craft, he shall be ordered to improve the knowledge of his craft for a further period, but he shall not be rejected for the sake merely of minor and petty faults . . . nor must the alleged minor faults, still less the masterpiece itself, be bought for money, but the masterpiece must be accepted or rejected as a whole, and if there should be any disagreement, the matter shall be put before the magistrate and, if necessary, other impartial masters: and if it shall be found that difficulties have been made for the candidate maliciously and without proper cause, those responsible for it shall bear the costs.

In addition, we are graciously pleased to command that in everything concerning the determination of the masterpiece and the years as tramping artisan,* no distinction shall be made between a stranger and a native, a master's son, or anyone marrying the daughter or widow of a master, but all

* See Glossary.

alike shall show the skill needed for the rights of mastership. If however anyone who has been a master elsewhere, whether at home or abroad, intends to settle as master and to join the gild, he shall be accepted as such without making a further piece, at a fine laid down in the following Art. VI; but he shall be obliged to show documentary evidence from the authorities of his former place of residence that he has been accepted by his former gild as master after performing his masterpiece, and has plied his craft as such.

VI The candidate performing his masterpiece successfully shall pay 8 Rthlr.* into the masters' chest; 2 Rthlr. for refreshments to the masters as a whole for meeting twice; 1 Rthlr. to the magistrate's assessor; 2 Rthlr. to the master in whose house he made his masterpiece, which however must not be paid by those who have already been masters elsewhere; 2 Rthlr. to the Town Treasury; and 1 Rthlr. to the church, instead of the usual wax; and he shall on no account, nor on any pretext, pay more than these total costs adding up to 16 Rthlr.; and as long as he has acquired rights of citizenship or at least applied to the Town Hall, he shall be accepted as fellow master of the craft and enjoy all the privileges of the gild.

2/2 Gild Regulations in the Woollen Industry, Prussia

Extracts from a Collection of Gild Rules applicable to the Woollen Trades. Printed in G. F. VON LAMPRECHT, *Kameralverfassung und Verwaltung der Handwerke, Fabriken und Manufacturen in den Preussischen Staaten* . . . (Berlin, 1797), pp. 531-562. (Ed. Tr.)

§ 760

Although it is laid down in the General Privilege (8 Nov. 1734) that it shall not be necessary to produce a masterpiece in order to gain the master's freedom; yet it was ruled afterwards: that anyone aspiring to the freedom of the gild, shall (22 November 1772) apart from being examined by the Inspector of Manufactures and the Gild Master whether he be properly experienced in sorting and fulling, wool shearing and preparing and threading the looms, also weave a piece of cloth of mixed colour from wool dyed by himself.

§ 765

The woollen weavers may sell by retail and cutting-up home produced cloths and baizes on condition that they and their fellow gild members may

* See Glossary.

not only sell in their own town the goods made locally, but may also offer them for sale at fairs and annual markets. The latter, however, is limited to this extent (1772 and 1791): that a gild member may not take part in any market or fair unless he has at least 12 pieces of cloth for sale, though it is permissible (18 December 1791) for two of them to enter a fair and to offer cloth for sale if they have at least 12 pieces of cloth between them; at the same time, this privilege is extended also to weavers (1772) who are no longer practising their trade themselves.

§ 766

The woollen weavers of Salzwedel, however, may not sell the cloths produced by themselves, by retail and cutting-up, even in their own town, because the local cloth cutters' and tailors' gild enjoys, according to its old privilege (1233, 1323 and last confirmed on 26 January 1715) the sole right of cutting up woollen and similar cloth for sale, so that neither the local merchants, nor the mercers, nor the woollen weavers of the town, whose rights were recently confirmed, have the right to cut up woollen cloth for sale.

§ 767

Woollen weavers may not trade in woollen cloths made outside their own town, unless they have been specially granted this right, because this would infringe the privileges granted to the merchants; in small towns, however, where no merchants are established or likely to become established, weavers have been given special trading concessions, but such concessions are not normally granted largely because the makers of cloths might otherwise take up this easy and profitable trade and neglect their main occupations: thus the woollen weavers of Eberswalde have recently (30 March 1786) been refused this concession.

§ 768

. . . Neither finishers nor croppers, dyers or other craftsmen (1772) are permitted to trade in woollen cloths or undertake putting-out agencies on pain of losing their craft privileges.

§ 769

In the countryside (28 August 1723, 14 November 1793) neither linen (?) weavers, nor vergers or schoolmasters, nor husbandmen themselves, are permitted to manufacture woollen or worsted cloth not even for their own use. Neither are town linen weavers permitted to make goods wholly of wool.

§ 770

Woollen weavers are permitted to dye their own cloths, but neither they nor the merchants are permitted to have the cloths made in the Electoral Mark finished or dyed in foreign towns, on pain of confiscation of the goods. While the export of unfinished and undyed cloths is permissible (1772), merchants and woollen weavers should be persuaded (26 October and 10 November 1791) to export only dyed and finished cloths.

§ 771

Woollen weavers may not (1772) keep their own tenting frame and stretch their own cloths, but must leave this finishing process to the cloth finishers. They have however the concession (28 October and 11 November 1773) that they may keep 10-12 frames, but on these they may only stretch 3/4 widths, and twill flannels. This originally applied to the Berlin Gild only, but has since been extended to all woollen weavers who make this sort of twill flannel. Afterwards, however, the Berlin woollen weavers were granted permission (27 November and 26 December 1782) to erect as many frames as they need to dry their flannels, as long as they were kept so narrow that no full cloths could be stretched on them and later still (18 November and 1 December 1783) the excess number of frames to be kept beyond the original maximum of twelve, was limited to seven. . . .

§ 798

On pain of requisition and, for repeated offences, on pain of loss of the freedom of the gild, better yarn may not be used for the ends of pieces of cloth than is used for the middle. No weaver is permitted to keep frames of his own, on pain of loss of his gild freedom, and he is obliged to take his cloths to the master shearmen; tanned wool and wool-fells may not be woven into pieces, but must be made only into rough goods and horse blankets. Finally it is laid down in detail how each type of woollen and worsted cloth shall be manufactured; and weavers have been advised several times to observe closely the detailed rules and regulations of the woollen and worsted order (20 September 1784, 9 September and 8 October 1787). . . .

§ 800

It is further laid down as a general rule, that all cloths shall be viewed by sworn aulnagers, of whom eight shall be elected in large companies, six in medium sized ones, and two to four among small ones, and they shall be viewed three times, and sealed accordingly after each time. The first viewing shall determine that the piece is woven with sufficient and satisfactory yarn, woven sufficiently closely and without flaws, and of the correct length and width. The second, held on the frame, shall determine whether the cloth is overstretched, and has wholly pure wool, is fulled cleanly and free of errors in fulling, and the third, held on the frame after dyeing, whether it has suffered by the dyeing. . . .

§ 805

[Here follows a complete table of all gilds, with their membership in 1776 and 1795, and the date of their privileges. This is a summary – Ed.].

37 Gilds, Membership:

	1776	1795
Masters	1,652	1,889
Journeymen	451	610
Apprentices	180	384

2/3 Gild System in the German Iron Industry

JOHANN PHILIPP BECHER, *Mineralogische Beschreibung der Oranien Nassauischen Lande* (Marburg, 1789), pp. 584–590. (Ed. Tr.)

The persons employed in the furnaces and forges of Siegen belong to Three Gilds.

The first includes the iron furnacemen and forgesmiths, the second the steel furnacemen and the third the steelsmiths. Of the first there exist since 1689 separate Gilds for Catholics and those belonging to the reformed religion – religion has divided the brothers since a part of the country went over to the Catholic religion – but the Gilds do not differ from each other in their organization. The steelsmiths in the district of Hilchenbach and Krombach, as well as those living in Freudenberg, have two separate Gilds but the same organization and the same Charter. The members of these Gilds are of two types.

Those who have learned their trade by the work of their hands form one class, and include all masters and journeymen. They have always been bound by an oath to ply their trade only within the country, and to train only natives of the country in it.

The other class includes the Raitmeisters, who though they do not occupy themselves in handicrafts, yet are entitled to trade in iron and steel. A Raitmeister has to own either two forge days or six furnace days and must be free of the Gild, since without the latter, the owners of the furnace or forge days may not work these themselves on their own account, but have to lease them out to others.

To the definition of the Raitmeister given already, the following should be added; he who transfers any of his 'forge days' to a hammersmith in such a way, that he delivers the pig-iron to the hammersmith, who then provides his own coal necessary for forging and returns the bar iron on payment of the forge wages; or he who sub-contracts the 'forging time' of someone else delivering him the pig-iron on condition that the bar iron is returned to him on payment of the forgers' wage, fulfils the conditions of a Raitmeister. The hammersmith who forges the iron for the Raitmeister is called the wage-smith.

The wage-smith has to forge the iron for the Raitmeister according to a certain formula. If there is a shortage, he has to replace it, but if there is a surplus, or if he saves coal, he receives special payment or compensation.

The wage of the wage-smith is regulated by the price of coal: since he has to buy out of it not only, as already mentioned, the coal, but also has to pay his assistants and to repair and maintain the hammer and equipment . . . as well as the building.

Perhaps something over 100 years ago the larger part of the forges together with the iron trade was in the hands of the Raitmeister who lived in the city of Siegen.

At present they are largely in the hands of the hammersmiths, living in the country, who have acquired them since the rise of the drawn bar trade and with it the rapid turnover of goods.

The days on which the Gilds meet annually, are known as the duty days. On those days the Charters are publicly read out, in order to renew them and keep them in memory, the transgressors of them are reported and punished, apprentices are indentured, two new masters of the Gild are elected, the accounts audited and completed, buildings, weights, etc. are inspected, and those who have been remiss in looking after them, punished.

The formerly common fining days have been abolished for the last ten years, they existed in order to punish those who had broken the terms of the Charter.

The duty day of the iron furnace and forge gild is the 1st May, the beginning of the furnace year. On that day the accounts of the furnaces and forges are closed, and new ones are started.

The period which the furnaces and forges are allowed to work are called the 'journeys'. These are divided into 'days' and the 'days' into 'hours'.

Each furnace is as a rule entitled to one journey only, which begins at the end of summer or in autumn. But a few furnaces are privileged to have one and a half, two and even three journeys, in which case one takes place in the spring and one in the autumn.

Formerly . . . the journey contained 48 days. Today, however, it has been fixed at 60 days. These consist of the starting day, the concluding day, one poor's day, the furnace clerk's day, eight general days and 48 ordinary days. It is the ordinary days which are divided among the members. Everyone sub-contracts or supplies himself for those days with the necessary material of coal and ironstone, and to that end everyone has his own coal and ironstone shed. The other days belong to the whole of the Gild, apart from the poor's day, which is leased out for the benefit of the poor.

Generally, every member contributes some coal and ironstone for the starting day, so that the blast furnace can be brought into operation by mixing the several grades and types of ironstone. It is up to the furnace clerk to collect sufficient material to keep the furnace going for the whole day. He is also responsible for the repairs to the furnace, the bellows, etc. It is a further part of his duty, to have the furnace ready for the journey, to clean the area around it, etc. He is also responsible for the common expenses which he has to meet out of the sales of the general iron, produced in the general days. In general, he is the plenipotentiary of the Gild. In recompense he gets the benefit of the furnace clerk's day, but for that he has to provide all his own material at his own cost.

The organization at the furnace itself is as follows. I shall begin with the steel furnaces.

As mentioned, each day has a natural division into 24 hours, and usually begins with the beginning of the day.

But since in 24 hours only three steel castings can take place, and the last is not always finished with the end of the day, but sometimes occurs before and sometimes after, it is obvious that the furnace day cannot have such a fixed beginning and ending as the natural day. The variations are entered into the book every day, and the hour is noted at which the third and last steel ingot has been run in. It is from that moment that the next day begins. As soon as the bellows are started, the first hour of the starting day begins, and the journey ends with the last hour of the concluding day.

For a further explanation of general days, I remark that this is the period in which the furnace is worked by the gild as a whole, dividing the benefits and losses among themselves. The reason for this arrangement is as follows. It is well known that the furnace never works as well in the first week as later when it is thoroughly heated and there is a good draught. So that no member should suffer from this circumstance, these days are worked together by the whole gild as general days.

2/4 A Potters' Gild in Alsace

E. GERSPRACH, *Documents sur les anciennes faïenceries françaises et la manufacture de Sèvres* (Paris, 1891), pp. 8-20. (Ed. Tr.)

STATUTES OF THE MASTER EARTH POTTERS of the Province of Alsace between Basle and Strasbourg, of 17 January 1740

The King in his Council has approved and confirmed the said Statutes and thereby orders the following:

Article 1 Every year on Whit Monday the Gild Statutes shall be read and then the names of the masters, to whom it is forbidden to have apprentices.

Article 3 Whoever wishes to be received as master in this Brotherhood must present himself at the Special Assembly which meets every year in Colmar. He shall be obliged to take an oath, to observe the present Statutes, and he shall then be admitted and received to the said Mastership.

Article 4 Anyone guilty of uttering a lie during the General or Special Assembly shall be fined 1 sol 4 deniers.*

Article 6 A General Assembly shall meet every three years and every year a Special Assembly, at which the attendance of the three chiefs of the métier,* together with the jurés* and the law officers of the métier shall be required, in order to settle internal disputes in the presence of some officials of the magistrature.

Article 8 No-one can be received as master if he has not wrought the usual customary masterpiece, and whoever assumes this rôle, without being received Master, shall be fined 8 livres 6 sols 8 deniers.*

Article 12 If a master is guilty of bad conduct and leads an unruly life and keeps an unruly house, he shall be prevented from exercising his trade and having compagnons until he has mended his ways, and convinced the other masters that he has reformed his habits.

Article 14 The Assembly of the Brotherhood of Master Potters living in Alsace between Strasbourg and Basle, shall keep the day of St. Louis in the town of Colmar, which feast shall be observed and kept by all the masters in all their houses on penalty of half a livre* of wax in fine, which shall be paid by each guilty party to the Brotherhood.

Article 20 If the chiefs of the Brotherhood give an order to a master, he shall be obliged to obey them, provided that it is not contrary to the public good, otherwise he shall be fined 6 sols 8 deniers.

Article 21 The compagnon who binds himself to two masters shall lose his customary two weeks wages in fines.

Article 22 If a master were to allow a boy or compagnon to work illegally

* See Glossary.

with another master . . . it shall likewise be illegal for all compagnons to work with the master in question under a penalty of a fine of 3 sols 4 deniers.

Article 23 Those who wish to be received Master Potters in the Brotherhood shall be required to work for a masterpiece three pots, each of three-quarters of an aune* in height, a Colmar measure round, and of a proportionate width, and each of these three pots shall be seen and examined by six master examiners, three of whom shall be nominated from Higher and three from Lower Alsace, who shall carry out this task under oath. The young master who wishes to make his masterpiece shall be obliged to make and complete it in the town of Colmar on the day of the Assembly . . . and shall pay 8 écus, each écu counting as 7 livres, which sum shall be used to pay for the examiners' fees and the meal which the young master is obliged to provide for them.

Article 24 No-one may sell earthen pots or other similar merchandise in Alsace between the said towns of Basle and Strasbourg where the Brotherhood is established if he has not made the pots himself, if he has not been incorporated and received into the Brotherhood, and if he does not conform to the Statutes and Rules of the latter; with the exception of Cologne stoneware pottery, or other similar goods which are not made between Basle and Strasbourg.

Article 25 In the case where a master makes a financial endowment to the Brotherhood and allows a year to pass without payment, such a person shall be forbidden to have servants and compagnons until he has discharged his obligation to the Brotherhood.

Article 27 The three chiefs of the Brotherhood shall give account of their administration and of their receipts and expenses every year in the presence of twelve jurés and the law officers of the Brotherhood.

Article 31 To overcome the abuses and misunderstandings which have hitherto prevailed between the Masters and the Compagnons . . . it has been agreed that henceforth before being received into the mastership, an apprentice shall be obliged to attend for two consecutive years the Assembly of Master Potters, held annually in the town of Colmar, to show his certified letters of apprenticeship, and each boy apprentice shall be obliged to pay to the said Assembly, for each of the said two years, 40 sols tournois,* to subsidize the expenses of the Brotherhood.

Article 34 Each year the names, surnames and geographical origins of each compagnon potter shall be inscribed in a register on the day of the Assembly of the Brotherhood, so that it can be ascertained how many years each one has held that position.

Article 36 It shall be forbidden to anyone to become an apprentice, who is the

* See Glossary.

son of a hangman, or anyone like that, who mingles with, or helps to execute criminals.

Article 37 When a boy is received as an apprentice, two masters and two compagnons must be present and the boy shall be obliged to indicate which family he is from, and to enrol in the register in which the masters are inscribed.

Article 38 Anyone who wishes in the future to learn the trade shall be obliged, following accepted procedure, to make his agreement with the Masters for three years, and to pay for his apprenticeship 66 livres 16 sols 4 deniers, half of it fifteen days after the agreement, and the remainder twenty-eight months later. And the same apprentice shall be obliged to continue the said three years without abandoning either the master or the trade.

Article 39 In the case of some stranger or foreign worker wishing to learn the said trade who cannot pay 40 florins, he shall be obliged to make his agreement for four years, and it shall be impossible for him to obtain a discharge from his apprenticeship before the expiry of the four years.

Article 41 If either a master or an apprentice, acts contrary to the terms of the present Statutes, he shall pay 40 florins making 6 livres 13 sols 4 deniers fine to the Brotherhood.

Article 43 And finally, it shall not be permitted to the Master Potters of foreign territories, who are not members of the Brotherhood, to set up furnaces, nor to work their craft in the area where there are Masters in Alsace between Basle and Strasbourg on the penalty of five florins fine, unless these foreign masters make a piece of pottery which the Masters of the Brotherhood are unable to manufacture.

2/5 Suppression of Gilds in France, 1776

Edict of 1776. Printed in ROBERT JACQUES TURGOT, *Œuvres* . . . avec les notes de Dupont de Nemours (2nd ed., 2 vols., Paris, 1844), II, pp. 302-307.(Ed. Tr.)

In nearly all the towns of our Kingdom the practice of different arts and crafts is concentrated in the hands of a small number of masters, united in a corporation, who alone have the exclusive right to manufacture and sell particular articles; so that those of our subjects who, through wish or necessity intend to practise in these fields, must have attained the mastership, to which they are admitted only after very long tests which are as difficult as they are useless, and after having satisfied rules or manifold exactions, which absorb part of the funds they need to set up in business or even to exist.

Those whose circumstances do not allow them to satisfy this expense, are reduced to having a precarious existence, under the domination of the masters, to languishing in poverty or taking out of the country skills which might have been used to the State's advantage.

Citizens of all classes are deprived of their right of using workers whom they would like to employ and the advantages which competition confers in relation to the price and perfection of finished articles. One cannot execute the simplest tasks without having recourse to several workers from different corporations, without enduring their slowness, their dishonesty and extortions, which are necessitated or encouraged by the claims of these various corporations and the vagaries of their arbitrary and selfish rules.

As far as the State is concerned, these bodies ensure an incalculable reduction of commercial and industrial activity; the majority of our subjects suffer from a loss of wages and the means of subsistence; the inhabitants of the towns in general are affected by subjection to exclusive privileges similar in their effects to a real monopoly, which works against those who exercise it, when they in their turn, need the goods or services of another corporation.

The basis of these statutes is firstly to exclude by law whoever is not a member of the corporation from practising the trade; their general spirit is to limit, as far as possible, the number of masters, and to make the acquisition of the mastership an almost insurmountable difficulty for anyone except the children of the present masters. It is to this end that the multiplicity of expenses and formalities of admission are directed, and the same applies to the difficulties surrounding the masterpieces which are always arbitrarily judged, and, above all, to the dearness and duration of apprenticeships and the prolonged servitude of compagnonnage. . . .

Among the countless number of unreasonable regulations, which are always dictated by the interests of the masters of the corporation, is that which excludes altogether all those who are not sons of masters or those who marry widows of masters.

Others reject all those who are called strangers, i.e. those born in another town.

In a large number of corporations it is sufficient to be married to be excluded from apprenticeship, and consequently from the mastership.

The spirit of monopoly which has prevailed in the drawing up of these Statutes has been pushed so far as to exclude women from the tasks which are most suitable to their sex, such as embroidery, which they cannot practise on their own account.

Finally, the custom prevailed of regarding these obstacles to employment as a matter of common law. The government gradually made a financial expedient of the taxes imposed on the corporations and their innumerable privileges.

Doubtless it is this financial attraction which has continued to disguise the immense harm which the existence of the corporations inflicts on industry and the extent to which it is an infringement of natural law.

With some people this illusion has been carried to the point of advancing that the law to work was a royal law, that the Prince was able to sell and his subject had to buy. We hasten to reject such a maxim.

God, in giving man needs, by making work necessary, has made the right to work a universal prerogative, and this is the first, the most sacred and the most indefeasible of all rights.

We regard it as one of the first duties of our law, and one of the acts most worthy of our charity, to free our subjects from all attacks against the inalienable right of mankind. Consequently, we wish to abolish these arbitrary institutions, which do not allow the poor man to earn his living; which reject a sex whose weakness has given it more needs and fewer resources, and which seem, in condemning it to an inevitable misery, to support seduction and debauchery; which destroy emulation and industry and nullify the talents of those whose circumstances have excluded them from membership of a corporation; which deprive the State and the arts of all the knowledge brought to them by foreigners; which retard the progress of these arts through the innumerable difficulties encountered by inventors with whom different corporations dispute the right to exploit their discoveries . . . which, by the huge expenses artisans are obliged to sustain to obtain the right to work, by their various exactions and frequent fines for alleged illegalities, by all kinds of expenditure, waste and interminable law suits, resulting from the respective claims of all these corporations on the extent of their exclusive privileges, burden industry with an oppressive tax, which bears heavily on the people, and is without benefit to the State; which finally, by the facility they provide for members of corporations to combine to force the poorest members to submit to the laws of the rich, become an instrument of privilege and encourage developments, the effect of which is to raise above their natural level the price of those goods which are most essential for the people.

2/6 Breakdown of Gilds in Germany

Explanation by von Philippi and von Eisenhart to the General Directory on working 'free'; Berlin, 22 September 1788. Printed in HORST KRÜGER, *Zur Geschichte der Manufakturen und der Manufakturarbeiter in Preussen* (Berlin, 1958), pp. 474–475. (Ed. Tr.)

Following the repeated complaint of the woollen and worsted weaver named Ast, calling himself a manufacturer of woollen materials, about the runaway apprentice Leder, Your Majesty demanded on 10th and 21st inst. to be informed what the term 'to work free' means. It is well known that the woollen and worsted weavers in Germany and abroad are without a gild, that is to say, do not belong to a company which is governed by certain rules or privileges, but follow their trade as woollen and worsted weavers without regulation. For in an organized trade with its own Charter within which it has to operate and which has as an assessor appointed whose task it is to see that it is observed, no apprentice may be taken on, unless he first proves by his birth certificate or patent of legitimacy that he was born in wedlock, or legitimized by royal patent. Further, according to the rules of apprenticeship, no apprentice may be given his freedom until his years of apprenticeship are ended according to the registry, and his master declares before the assembled trade when his indenture as journeyman is made out that he has an adequate knowledge of his craft. Similarly, no one can achieve the rights of mastership without having completed two years as journeyman as laid down, and produced the appropriate masterpiece.

All these regulations are omitted in the case of the free weavers. For there are really no masters, journeymen and apprentices among them; but if a weaver is able and has the resources to set up looms, he sets on workers, usually lads or those who have some knowledge of the trade, who may call themselves apprentices or journeymen, but are not recognized and esteemed as such by those within the gild, since the employer has not produced a masterpiece, the journeymen and apprentices have no indentures or birth certificates, they have no privileges, no assessor, and thus live without a regulation. Such a woollen or worsted weaver will then be called a 'free worker'. . . .

If such woollen weavers, who have mostly been attracted into the country by the large manufacturers, want to set up here on their own, although they have not been properly brought up within their company, and cannot be accepted as masters, they can receive permission, for themselves only, 'to work free'. Many of the weavers working 'free' have felt the disadvantages of exclusion from their gild, so that some years ago, after some long-drawn-out disputes between the organized and unorganized weavers, they were granted the concession, on certain prescribed conditions, to be accepted as members of their gilds, whereby the number of unorganized ones has been much reduced, except for the large manufacturers and their workers, who are largely still unorganized.

Such outsiders as have risen to the level of manufacturers, by which it is meant that they man several, perhaps many, looms with unorganized workers, have never been granted this concession, but have, as the term goes, 'worked free'; and since they cannot become masters and therefore are not allowed to use the term of master, have termed themselves woollen manufacturers, in order to distinguish themselves from the other excluded, but minor, weavers.

2/7 Compagnonnage in France

a Police Ordinance, Orléans, 18 July 1767. Printed in G. MARTIN, *Les associations ouvrières du XVIIIe siècle (1700- 1792)* (Paris, 1900), pp. 270-272. (Ed. Tr.)

b Complaint from Toulouse, 1783. Printed in E. MARTIN SAINT-LÉON, *Le compagnonnage* (Paris, 1901), p. 63. (Ed. Tr.)

a On the basis of what has been indicated by the Procureur du Roi* in the signed petition which he has presented to us, that the Compagnons* of the different arts and crafts corporations have for some time formed associations, which have several times warranted the attention of the law; that these associations which, at first, were designed simply to help needy compagnons, and to give financial help from common funds to compagnons who were unemployed, have resulted in abuses which have far outweighed their advantages; that a spirit of animosity has developed among the compagnons of the different associations, which results in reciprocal violence and acts of terrorism, and that they usually combine to use force against compagnons who are reluctant to accept the principle of association; that, moreover, by means of these associations the compagnons impose laws on the masters in each corporation, 'blacking' the shops of those against whom they believe they have a grievance; that these abuses have been caused partly by the ease with which the compagnons can assemble in bars, in numbers which are forbidden by law, and partly because the corporations have not established an office to which the compagnons may address themselves on arrival, in order to find employment, which has led the compagnons of various associations, to elect individuals whose task it is to indicate sources of employment and . . . who point out those establishments which are 'black'; that, to remedy this situation he (the Procureur du Roi) thinks it is necessary to renew the laws forbidding the compagnons to assemble more than three in number, under any pretext, under penalty of prison and 50 livres fine for the compagnons, and 100 livres fine on all bar owners who receive them; to urge the police chiefs to make visits to the bars and to summon before us and to have arrested the compagnons who break the law; similarly to urge policeman on duty and the cinquanteniers* to arrest, after a proper warning, the compagnons who are breaking the law and to make them prisoners . . .: also to

* See Glossary.

urge all the compagnons who arrive in Orléans to appear before the most senior member of each corporation on the day of their arrival, to sign the register, which shall be kept by him for this purpose, after which he shall give them a card bearing a certificate of the registration . . . for which the compagnon shall pay 5 sols . . .; to forbid the compagnons to enter into the service of another master without the said certificate, and to forbid the master to accept the compagnons without their being carriers of the latter, under the penalty of prison for the compagnons and 100 livres fine on the masters; to allow the jurés*, after obtaining our permission, to have the guilty compagnons arrested and imprisoned; similarly to make it illegal for any individual to undertake to find work for any compagnon without this certificate under penalty of 100 livres* fine, and for the masters of each corporation under the same penalties to receive any compagnon without a certificate from his former employer; moreover, to direct that the most senior juré of the corporation shall be obliged to note in a special register the names of the masters who need workers, and to indicate such vacancies to compagnons as they arrive in Orléans; and to inform us of any refusal on the part of the compagnons to enter into such employment; and for this registration they shall be authorized to take 3 sols from each master, and that the ordinance shall be pronounced, published and posted in the streets, places and carrefours, which shall serve as legal notice for the most senior juré of the corporation, who shall be obliged within the month, on penalty of 100 livres fine, to produce the registers to the Procureur du Roi.

After having considered the matter, assenting to the remonstrance of the Procureur, we order that the following regulations be carried out in the manner in which they are intended. [After this follows a number of restrictions related to the activity of the compagnons, based on the Procureur's recommendations].

b To you gentlemen, the magistrates of Toulouse.

The jurés* . . . of the body of master joiners of the towns . . . have the honour of informing you that for a considerable time, in Toulouse and other towns in the kingdom, associations have been formed among the compagnons who have divided themselves in several groups; one composed of young men from all areas and known amongst themselves as Dévorants . . . members of the other group are called Gavots; that these two groups, which are engaged in constant conflict, meet at the houses of individuals whom they call 'mothers' whenever they are hatching some plot; that apart from these illegal assemblies they also gather together in inns and bars, which meetings are nearly always followed by disputes and quarrels which threaten

* See Glossary.

public order: that most compagnons wander from town to town and obtain a situation with various masters, without a certificate or any form indicating their birthplace. The petitioners have attempted several times to stop these disorders or to forestall them, but always to no avail, since the majority of the compagnons have carried wickedness to such an extent as to gather in groups, about one hundred strong, armed with cudgels and sticks, and to march into the centre of the town, to seek out those whom they regard as their enemies.

2/8 The Royal Meissen Porcelain Factory

Patent of 23 January 1710. Printed in CARL AUGUST ENGELHARDT, *J. F. Böttger, Erfinder des sächsischens Porzellans* (Leipzig, 1837), pp. 301–305. (Ed. Tr.)

We, Frederick Augustus, by the grace of God King of Poland and Elector of Saxony, etc. etc. Whereas we wish to help our Electoral Saxony and our other countries in their miserable condition, caused by the Swedish invasion four years ago, etc. . . . We have decided among other means that the restitution of the blessings of food and work can be achieved mainly by manufacture and commerce, and we have applied our care particularly to search for the treasures in the ground in our country, which have formerly lain dead but now might be made useful; and having ordered accordingly certain scientific and knowledgeable men to use their experience and their industry to the purpose, and our intention having so far been blessed that materials in our country formerly not used have now been employed in making red vessels, exceeding the Indian, from so-called *Terra Sigillata*, as well as various specially coloured and painted ware which, despite their delicacy are so hard, that they may be ground, cut and polished like jasper or porphyry, and having other qualities which have been known only among the Indian vessels; moreover, they having put before us numerous experimental pieces of white porcelain, glazed and unglazed, which show sufficiently that it is possible to make from material found in our land a porcelain which matches both in transparency and in other qualities the china from the East, and it may be assumed that in future with proper organization such white porcelain, as in the case of the red ware, may be made to exceed the Indian in beauty and quality, and may produce large pieces, like statues, columns or table services very much better than the Indian; wherefore these men have petitioned, that a Commission be established in order to enquire further into the manufacture of this invention, using solely materials from within our land, so therefore we decided to grant this fair request, and now the Commission has reported that these manufacturers will be of great benefit to us and our subjects. Therefore . . . to this end we have nominated a special manufacture directory, with the task of setting up the above kind of manufactures, and have given it the particular instructions that both the manufacture and the trade arising from it shall be ordered in proper mercantile fashion, that proper books and journals shall be kept, true credit maintained, and with God's blessing any surplus shall be used for the growth and multiplication of new manufactures. From which our subjects may learn sufficiently that our intention is merely to help the well-being of our whole country, and we are therefore entitled to ask them to provide a fair share of the very large sums which will be required to set up such a large and important manufacture, particularly since our subjects will ultimately gain much benefit from them. But to the end that the artists and artisans shall not be frightened off by the Gilds or the jurisdiction of our local councils, nor fear in other ways to be subject to high taxes and obligations; we intend to promise them the immunities and liberties, which we have in former edicts granted to immigrant artists and artisans and have indeed granted these to them, and they shall be under no other jurisdiction than that of our directory of manufacture, unless they buy property elsewhere or engage in any other occupations, in which case they shall in respect of such property or occupations be subject to the jurisdiction of the local authorities, but as far as the work within the manufacture is concerned, they shall be subject to the directory only; and we shall issue the necessary instructions.

And we shall be particularly delighted if we are able by the setting up of the said manufactures and useful inventions, to provide not only useful work and nourishment for our subjects, but to attract to our land, particularly our capital city of Dresden, skilled artists and handicraftsmen, and provide more occupations for those resident already, letting the arts and the sciences flourish in future, and with God, happier times. . . .

2/9 The Royal Porcelain Factory, Berlin

FRIEDRICH NICOLAI, *Beschreibung der königlichen Residenzstädte Berlin und Potsdam* (3rd ed., 3 vols., Berlin, 1786 [1st ed. 1769]), II, pp. 537–539. (Ed. Tr.)

It was the merchant Wilhelm Kaspar Wegely who first started in 1751 to make porcelain. He erected a large building for the purpose in the new Friedrichstrasse next to the King's Bridge, and had a great deal of porcelain made in it, mostly of fairly good quality. But he could not have made a profit at it, for he gave up his concern again and sold off his considerable stock of goods by public auction. In 1760 the local merchant Johann Ernst Gotzkowsky took his place, after the secret of making true porcelain had been imparted to him by Ernst Heinrich Reichardt for a certain sum of money. He fitted up the house in the Leipzigerstrasse bought from the Dorville heirs, but discontinued it in 1763. The work thus started was taken over by the King, and Gotzkowsky was paid the sum of 225,000 Rthlr* for it. The King had not only the buildings of the manufactory enlarged and considerably increased, but also put everything in train for making it more perfect. He appointed a separate manager for it (at present Councillor Grieninger); an inspector; and he confirmed the scientists, whose task it is to improve constantly the clay, the colours, etc.; besides the supervisors of all workers, who number 500.

The manager is directly responsible to the King, and at the end of each month he has to hand in personally his report on the progress and activity of the works, together with a summary of the accounts, and is always asked to report back the next day. The board of the porcelain factory consists of the manager and the inspector (at present Councillor Klüpfel). The porcelain factory has its own power of jurisdiction, which is carried out by the manager and a special judicial officer.

The King hardly ever comes to Berlin without viewing the porcelain factory and its products. He places occasional orders himself after his own ideas, and when they are carried out well, he shows his special satisfaction. Encouraged thereby, all those who are engaged in the works are therefore eager to make them more perfect all the time. And it is already the case that experts prefer Berlin porcelain to all others because of its material, colour and painting.

The main warehouse is in the front building, where all china in stock may be viewed, where all kinds of china may be bought or orders placed. Apart from this main warehouse there are depots in Warsaw, Dantzig, Hamburg, Königsberg, Breslau, Stettin and Magdeburg, to facilitate purchases by foreign collectors. Yet it has to be noted: that although these depots and factor's holdings each have been made, by contract, sole sales agents for certain Provinces and areas, and no one else is allowed to sell porcelain within them, yet it is open to each individual to apply to the main warehouse in Berlin itself, and to order there for his own use whatever he likes.

2/10 Royal Woollen Manufactory, Berlin

Complaint by German and French manufacturers to the Chamber of the Electoral Mark about the monopoly of the Berlin storehouse†; Berlin 4 March 1739. Printed in KRÜGER, *Geschichte der Manufakturen* [*see* Document **2/6**], pp. 476-477. (Ed. Tr.)

Although H.M. our Gracious Lord and Sovereign, when he set up the

* See Glossary.

† Lagerhaus, = the central premises of the royal woollen manufactory. (Ed.)

storehouse, had no other end in view, but simply and solely to have the cloths and kerseys required by the army manufactured there, without damaging the interests of the merchants and manufacturers; yet nevertheless experience has shown that while formerly the regiments of cavalry (and) infantry, had their own sources of supply from the towns and regions where they were quartered, now that the regiments are obliged to draw their uniforms from the storehouse, many hundreds of the manufacturers in H.M. dominions, especially in the New Mark, have been forced, since their income has been totally taken from them, to retire partly to Poland and partly to Saxony, as the local officials duly reported at the time, and as is still in recent memory. If the loss which H.M. has suffered by the emigration of so many hundreds of families were to be set against the alleged profit to be expected from the storehouse, careful calculation would show that the latter would bear no comparison to the former, and H.M. would be shown to be greatly the loser, since the merchant community in H.M. dominions has since fallen into such decay that it is not possible to conceive their restoration; further, if a detailed enquiry were to be held in all towns of the realm how many merchants and manufacturers of different trades have since emigrated abroad, it would be made clear how impossible it is that both the merchants and manufacturers and the storehouse should co-exist at the same time, since the establishment of the storehouse will lead as surely to the total ruin of the merchants and manufacturers, as the shadow follows the body. If now the storehouse is not satisfied with supplying the army with the necessary uniform cloth, but has started, for some time, to send out travellers with all kinds of saleable goods and cloths, which it mostly does not manufacture itself but buys from us, to all home and foreign fairs, and sells to other merchants, trading like ordinary merchants and traders, and mixing with them, at the same time lowering the price of the woollen goods at home to our detriment to such an extent that if this evil is not ended quickly, we shall all of us be under the necessity of leaving our trade and looking elsewhere for our living: and it should not go unmentioned that the storehouse does not need

(1) to reflect the costs of dyeing and finishing its own goods, also
(2) gets the profits on the goods acquired from us,
(3) has no need to add, as we have to, costs of the journey and storage rent.

(4) Since the storehouse has free capital sums for making and buying in its stocks of goods, allowing it to give credit for 12 or 18 months despite the low price, which no manufacturer can compete with, unless he owns the necessary capital himself (which few of us do) when he has to live on it, but

if he is forced, as are most of them, to borrow this at interest, then it is obvious that the manufacturer cannot stand up to the storehouse and must go under, and

(5) as is well known, the storehouse has nothing to risk in granting such long credit to its debtors, for in case of bankruptcy it has right to primacy, so that others, if they do not want to lose their possessions, must refrain from giving credit.

Since however H.M. would never allow that we should not only be prevented from visiting the fairs, by the storehouse, but should be totally ruined, we petition . . . that the storehouse shall in future refrain from making all kinds of saleable goods and cloths, and leave them solely to us, so that we may not be placed under the necessity to appeal direct to H.M. for redress.

2/11 The Royal Small Arms Factory in Berlin

GOTHSCHE, *Die königlichen Gewehrfabriken* (Berlin, 1904), pp. 1–5. (Ed. Tr.)

When King Frederick William I ascended the throne of the young Prussian Kingdom in 1713, it was his intention . . . to become independent of foreign countries in the supplies for his Army; and in 1721 he ordered Colonel von Linger of the Artillery, to get in touch with suitable people from Liège, where the small arms manufacture was particularly flourishing, for the purpose of establishing a 'small arms manufactory' in Potsdam.

This officer succeeded with the help of the merchant house of Splittgerber & Daun, in attracting the arms manufacturer Henoul (or Henouville), who provided the necessary plans, after he had found sufficient water power for the driving of drilling and grinding machines in Spandau.

The management and administration of the planned factory were to be handed over to the merchants Splittgerber & Daun, who appeared particularly suitable by their experience and connections abroad. . . .

The King provided 15,900 Thlr.* for the building of the necessary structures and works in the first instance, and ordered the provision of the necessary timber and building materials. The building ground in Spandau was particularly difficult and the prisoners in the house of correction had to ram in 1,800 piles for laying the foundations.

At the same time, the first barrel-smiths were brought in from Liège and first of all put on a waiting wage; and by royal order of 26 February 1722 the employment of one rifle maker and one stock maker for each infantry regiment was ordered, at a monthly wage of 9 Thlr.

The negotiations with Splittgerber & Daun regarding the administration of the small arms factory in Potsdam and Spandau were completed in 1722.

* See Glossary.

The agreement concluded with them, by which the foundations of the royal small arms manufactory in Prussia were laid, received royal approval on 31 March 1722.

From this agreement the following important provisions may be noted:
1. The merchants Splittgerber & Daun shall take over from the state as entrepreneurs the buildings necessary for a small arms factory, the mills and large tools as well as bellows, etc. in Potsdam and in Spandau; on the other hand it is their duty to maintain the works in good condition and to provide the small tools.
2. The arms workers entering from abroad shall receive free transport for themselves, their families and goods; they shall be permitted to maintain their own religious services, if they are Roman Catholics; they are protected from impressment into the Army and receive free rights of citizenship and of mastership; finally they are permitted to drink gin, but 'since H.M. has prohibited all sale of gin in the town of Potsdam having regard to the garrison there; the workers of the factory shall be free to drink gin and to have a supplier; but he shall not dare, on punishment of running the gauntlet, to supply any of it to the soldiers'.
3. The entrepreneurs shall be paid 6 Thlr. 12 Sgr.* for each musket, and receive free powder for the trial of the barrels.
4. The musket shall be taken in charge by an officer, who shall make the trial firings and, if they are passed, shall mark them with an eagle; similarly he will test every lock.

The entrepreneurs succeeded even in 1722 in attracting 116 workers from Liège to Spandau and Potsdam. . . .

The completion of the buildings and works in Potsdam and Spandau had proceeded far enough by the end of 1722 to allow the manufacture of arms by the beginning of 1723, but the original sum proved insufficient. Though the King granted additional sums, he ordered that an officer of the artillery should help to supervise the building, and keep a tight rein on the cash. . . .

One Sergeant was employed to supervise the cleaning of the dwellings and to train the Fire Brigade. When the whole works were completed by the end of 1724 the set-up was as follows:

In Spandau the barrels, bayonets and ramrods were manufactured, they were then brought by water to Potsdam, where the stocks, locks and other fittings were made, and the muskets were assembled.

Large water-driven machinery was limited to Spandau and consisted of boring, grinding, polishing and hammer works. The most difficult job was the production of the barrels. Work began by drawing out the iron plates under a drawing hammer into the necessary length and width. The plate-

* See Glossary.

forger welded these drawn plates into barrels, which were then bored with the appropriate borers to the right calibre.

A large proportion of the welded barrels were likely to burst, if the plate-forger made the slightest mistake in the welding. The outer shape of the barrels, ramrods and bayonet was ground by water-driven grindstones, and the components of locks and shafts were finished by hand. Since all these works were completed by one workman for each musket, it required an enormous amount of skill to meet all these requirements. The workmen were free to work when and where they wished, they could use the large water-driven drills free, but had to pay for the iron, wood and coal required for each musket to the entrepreneur and received an appropriate price for the muskets finished and ready for use.

Apart from the privileges granted by the King, the workers were also given by the state, free dwellings, free fuel, free medical attention for themselves and their families, as well as an old age pension for themselves and a pension for widows. . . .

2/12 Industrial Training for French Royal Manufactures

E. GERSPRACH, *La manufacture nationale des Gobelins* (Paris, 1892), pp. 263-267. (Ed. Tr.)

Arrêt of the Council of State of the King

The King, being informed that the rules established by the Edict of November 1667, for the instruction of the pupils in the manufacture of Gobelins, have been neglected for a long time, and that it is important for the continuation of this manufacture to make a new regulation to ensure the education of these pupils; His Majesty, being in his Council, has ordered that:

Article 1 One of the rooms in the Royal Manufacture of Gobelins shall always be open as an academic school for the study and practice of the art of design.

Article 2 All the children supported by the King in the said manufacture, and others being apprenticed there . . . shall be required to assemble each day of the week in the school, except Sunday and feast days, to draw for two consecutive hours, and to profit from lessons which shall be given by the Professor appointed for this purpose, and in his absence by one of his assistants.

Article 3 The said two hours devoted to the exercise shall be fixed between 6 and 8.00 in the evening during the summer and 5 and 7.00 in winter, spring and autumn, subject to their being brought forward during the two latter seasons, if it is necessary.

Article 4 None of the said children and apprentices may, under any pretext, absent themselves from the said school at the prescribed hours and from remaining there for the space of time indicated in the two preceding articles, unless they suffer illness or have some other legitimate complaint; under penalty of 10 sols* for each offence, and double fines in case of repetition of the action in the course of the same week; the fine to take the form of a retention by the King from his maintenance funds, to be supplemented by the worker who has deterred his apprentice from going to the said school, or who has not paid sufficient attention to oblige him to go there. . . .

Article 6 The studies and exercises of the said school shall be conducted and directed by the Professor and divided into three classes, in accordance with the capacity of the students.

Article 7 The first class shall contain the young beginners and those who have not yet any idea of the art of design. . . .

Article 8 The second class shall be made up of those children and apprentices who are already acquainted with some of the principles of the art of design, or who have acquired such knowledge in the first class.

Article 9 The said apprentices who show ability and have acquired more sophisticated knowledge of the art of design and who appear suitable to become chief officers shall form the third class. . . .

Article 10 The drawings of all the children and apprentices of the said three classes shall be marked with the name of the pupil who has executed them and handed to the Professor, to enable the latter to assess their progress. This judgment shall precede the distribution of prizes, which shall be made, every six months to those who have passed the school's examinations.

Article 11 These prizes shall consist in each case of the distribution of three silver medals, one for each class; the first – for the third class – shall be worth 40 livres*; the second – for the second class – 20 livres, and the third – for the first class – 10 livres.

Article 12 The pupil who gains the prize in the first class shall move into the second class, and the one who obtains it in the latter, to the third class, mention of which shall be made in the [class] register referred to in Article 5.

Article 13 It shall be permissible for the workers at the manufactory who are out of the apprenticeship stage to compete for these prizes . . . provided, however, that they have followed the said exercises without interruption for the term in which the prizes are declared.

Article 14 His Majesty shall choose as Professor in the said school Le Clerc, former Professor of the Royal Academy of Painting and Sculpture, and Professor in Perspective at the said Academy.

Article 15 The Inspector of the said Manufacture as well as the entrepreneurs

* See Glossary.

of the school engaged in high and low warp work shall concern themselves with everything relating to the discipline and work of the school and shall assume appointments as assistants to the Professor, as is the case at the Royal Academy of Painting and Sculpture.

Article 16 They (the staff) shall divide among themselves in turn each month the administration of the said school, in order to be present and to preside in case of the absence of the Professor and to ensure that the school is never without the Professor or one of his colleagues to undertake its supervision and direction: when the assistant is on duty he shall make the necessary comments in the [Academy] journal as is prescribed in Article 5.

Article 17 And as far as discipline, decency and good order are concerned, the teachers and assistants shall take care to have observed Articles 2 and 3 of the Statutes and Rules of the said Royal Academy of Painting and Sculpture of 24 December 1663. Given at the Council of State of the King. His Majesty being there, held at Versailles, 16 April 1737.

(*Signed*) Philippeaux.

2/13 Royal Privilege for English Potters in France, 1775

Arrêt of 15 May 1775. Printed in E. GERSPRACH, *Documents sur les anciennes faïenceries.* [See Document **2/4**], pp. 120-123. (Ed. Tr.)

Regarding the petition presented to the King in his Council by Messrs. Clark, Shaw & Co., natives of England, which indicated that they have begun to set up an establishment for the manufacture of English pottery at Montereau, that the tests they have made of the clay found in the surroundings of the town have indicated its suitability for the production of English pottery called Queen's ware; that the earth is such that they can produce pottery of this kind which is superior to that made in England, since it is possible to produce the pottery with the highest degree of whiteness; that consequently the petitioners propose to extend their manufacture and for this purpose to recruit workers and apprentices whom they shall train for this work, in order to supply the public with this type of pottery which, as regards perfection and durability is unsurpassed by any in the Kingdom, and which shall be cheaper than any pottery hitherto produced there: that the petitioners who have wives and children and who, together with two other workers whom they have brought from England . . . have been involved in the expense of changing their residence, that moreover an enterprise of this kind shall require considerable capital, involving them in unlimited expenditure, without counting the cost of training French workers and apprentices to proficiency in a new activity, as well as the losses they have already experienced and which they shall still have to sustain before they are proficient in the use of wood fires, since in England exclusive use is made of coal; [and that] they do not think they should enter into this project without previously having recourse to the bounty of the King, for him to authorize the scheme and to grant them the privileges they need.

The King . . . wishing to aid the said manufacture

Article 1 Has permitted and permits Messrs. Clark, Shaw & Co. to establish in the town of Montereau or in its neighbourhood, the manufacture of pottery, similar to that made in England, and to sell and retail the said pottery throughout all the Kingdom and abroad.

Article 2 His Majesty wishes that the said Messrs. Clark & Shaw, their widows, their children or legitimate heirs, including also their foreign workers and their widows, shall be exempted from all escheat duty, (droit d'aubaine)* and consequently that they shall share all the rights and privileges enjoyed by the other subjects of His Majesty.

Article 3 Messrs. Clark & Shaw and their children shall be exempt from guêt, garde*, corvées* and other public burdens, and their houses and buildings used in the said manufacture shall be exempt from the quartering of troops.

Article 4 His Majesty grants Messrs. Clark and Shaw and their children and four of their principal workers exemption from militia duties.

Article 5 His Majesty authorizes the said Messrs. Clark, Shaw & Co. to enter into any necessary contracts with the workers, who shall be obliged to honour the same; His Majesty forbidding all entrepreneurs in such manufacture from attracting or taking the said apprentices or workers unless they are bearers of a valid ticket of leave, indicating that they have carried out their period of apprenticeship.

If they have legitimate reasons, the said workers or apprentices, can ask for leave, and if Messrs. Clark, Shaw & Co. refuse to grant this, they may apply before the Intendant of the Généralité* of Paris.

Article 6 His Majesty orders that all disagreements which may arise between Messrs. Clark, Shaw & Co. and their workers or apprentices, shall be brought before the Intendant and Commission resident in the Généralité of Paris, to be judged by the Intendant, subject to appeal to the Conseil. His Majesty undertakes to enforce the present decree.

* See Glossary.

2/14 Royal Privilege for French Glassworkers, 1786

ELPHÈGE FRÉMY, *Histoire de la manufacture royale des glaces de France au XVIIe siècle et au XVIIIe siècle* (Paris, 1909), pp. 422-427. (Ed. Tr.)

Archives of the Company of St. Gobain.

Louis, by the grace of God King of France and Navarre, etc.... Our friends involved in the royal manufacture of glass, associated under the name of Louis Renard and Company have had it brought to our notice that the advantages this manufacture has provided since it began in France are well known, that the first privilege, granted in 1665, limited itself to imitating blown Venetian glass, but that soon the inventive genius of the nation, gave rise to another privilege, for moulded glass; that the foundation of these establishments was difficult and costly, in spite of the various exemptions and privileges which were granted to them and which they have enjoyed; that it is only since the union of these two privileges in 1695 and the order established in the Company by the Arrêt of the Council and the Letters Patent of 22 August and 23 October 1702 that the enterprise has prospered and acquired the degree of stability indicated by its numerous achievements, which were rewarded by a new privilege granted to the same company by the Letters Patent of 20 February 1727; that since this time they have given considerable attention to the improvement of their manufacture; that they have undertaken considerable investment to improve the quality of their production, which allowed them not only to supply internal demand for glass, which had previously been obtained from abroad, but even to contribute to exports; that this activity has warranted a new exclusive privilege, granted to the same company under the name of Renard on 22 October 1757, granting exemption from all export duties . . . ; that although the privilege granted by the Letters Patent of 22 October 1757 has not expired, the same motives which determined the granting to them of the said Letters Patent more than five years before the expiry of the 1727 privilege militate again in favour of their obtaining new Letters Patent for 30 consecutive years from 23 October 1792.... We have ordered, and order, that the said interests in the royal glass manufacture associated under the name of Renard and Company shall enjoy for 30 consecutive years, beginning on 23 October 1792, the exclusive privilege of manufacturing and having manufactured throughout the Realm by such workers as they regard as satisfactory, whether noble or common, glass of all sizes, forms and colours, which are blown or moulded or made by any other method, as well as the privilege of grinding and polishing them in conformity with the Letters Patent of 1 May and 15 October 1695 and 23 October 1759, on the undertaking by those involved in the said manufacture to make the price of glass conform to the 1757 assessment and to the increase of 10% in consequence of new duties imposed by the edict of August 1781; we order similarly that the said Renard and Company may make and manufacture jointly with those who have the privilege, crystal, white glasses and all sorts of large and small pieces of glass ware. We forbid anybody to introduce into our realm to have manufactured and to sell under any pretext whatever any glass other than those made by Renard, on penalty of confiscation of the articles, and the materials and tools used in their manufacture, the demolition of their furnaces and 3,000 livres fine* for each relevant contravention, one-third of the fine going to the denunciator, one-third to the General Hospital and the remaining one-third to the profit of Renard and Company. . . . We order also that the same fine shall be incurred, for each contravention, by the workers of such glass, which shall be confiscated to the profit of the Company; together with the boats, carts and other vehicles and carriages which are used to transport the goods; the clerks and superintendents of the said Renard and Company may make any necessary visits to assist the nearest Police Judge; and they may carry defensive arms like those used in our Farms; we order that the said Renard and Company shall continue to enjoy exemption from the duties of the Five Large Farms* and in general from other duties and impositions of any sort, levied or about to be levied on land, toll bars, etc. . .; we order, moreover, that the said entrepreneurs shall remain exempt from the obligation to provide barracks for soldiers . . . and that the other principal workers and clerks shall be exempt from the corvée* and the militia; we order, moreover, that the said Renard and Company shall remain authorized to gather any materials necessary in glass manufacture from any part of the Kingdom, payment being made either by mutual agreement or on the advice of experts knowledgeable in the trade; also the said Renard shall be able to bring into his enterprises such persons as he wishes, nobles or commoners, artisans, foreigners, without the nobles in question being supposed or reputed to have disparaged their nobility as a result of their action, and that these foreign workers, after three consecutive years in the same manufacture, shall enjoy the rights of citizens, without having to take any Letter to this effect. . . .

Given at Versailles in the month of February in the year of grace 1786, in the eleventh year of our reign. Signed, Louis.

* See Glossary.

2/15 Privileged Ironworks in Prussia, 1768

PRIVILEGIUM für die Hütten-Bediente und Arbeiter bey den Königlichen Chur-Märkschen, Pommerschen und Neumärckschen Eisen Hütten und Blech Werken (Berlin, 1 November 1768), pp. 3-4. (Ed. Tr.)

Whereas H.M. the King of Prussia is graciously animated by loving care for his subjects, and in order that the newly discovered iron stone in Pomerania, the Electoral Mark and the New Mark shall not be without benefit but be used for the good of his lands and loyal subjects in Pomerania, the Electoral Mark and the New Mark, by setting up iron furnaces and rolling mills; now therefore H.M. is graciously pleased, for the greater advance and progress of these works so useful to the country, to grant the following liberties to their servants and workmen, or those to be employed by them in the future.

(1) It is H.M. highest wish and command that each and every man and servant accepted by the said works or volunteering for them, shall be exempt together with all his family from all quartering of troops, whether during their marches or otherwise, also from all taxes and services, such as Contributions, Cavalry Tax, Land and Roof Tax, War contribution, Income Taxes, and all other burdens, of whatever title, which have been enacted or may be enacted in the future, for now and for evermore as long as they remain employees of the furnaces, but if they buy or otherwise acquire estates bearing service or tax dues they shall remain responsible for meeting the obligations belonging to these.

Further, the said servants and workmen employed about the furnaces shall remain subject to the laws of the land regarding prohibited goods and in other respects, and shall refrain from smuggling, on pain of incurring the usual penalties, provided that the searches which may become necessary in this regard about the furnaces shall be in the presence of the appropriate factor, so that disorders may be avoided and the factor be made responsible for the prevention of smuggling.

(2) The furnace servants and workmen are hereby given the right and the liberty to purchase all that they need for themselves and their families in the way of necessities, food, drink and otherwise, from anywhere in the King's dominions, either in the country or in the towns, wherever they can best be got.

(3) All the servants and workmen employed in the said iron furnaces and rolling mills, such as factors, managers, blast furnacemen or smelters, casters, loaders, hammermen and other iron and plate forgemen, iron miners,

charcoal burners, and all others of whatever degree, as well as their families, shall be wholly exempt from impressment and recruitment.

(4) They shall be paid their wages promptly and in cash, and they shall in no manner be forced to accept against their will food or other truck in place of ready cash, as happens quite often at other furnaces, and whereby the poor workmen may be cheated of their hard-earned wage.

(5) All furnace servants and workmen receive free lodging and firing, but the latter is to consist of windfall twigs and branches only, gathered by members of their families.

(6) If one or other of the furnace servants or workmen should wish, after the expiry of the term of his binding, to remove to his home or elsewhere with his property, brought with him, acquired later or earned in the Royal dominions at work at the furnace, he shall be allowed to do so freely and without hindrance, and no deduction shall be demanded from his goods or money.

(7) H.M. wishes to protect the above furnace servants and workmen in the enjoyment of their liberties and grants, against everyone of high or low degree, and take them under his particular care in case of any infringement. In return for which they are reminded to prove themselves to be loyal, honest, obedient and tireless furnace servants and workmen, and to obey the furnace order and rules which are to be published for them.

As witness his Royal hand
Frederick

2/16 Privileged Calico-Printing Works in Saxony, 1787

Patent, printed in RUDOLF FORBERGER, *Die Manufaktur in Sachsen vom Ende des 16. bis zum Anfang des 19. Jahrhunderts* (Berlin, 1958), pp. 237-8. (Ed. Tr.)

We, Friedrich August, by the grace of God Duke of Saxony (etc), declare by these our Letters Patent for ourselves, our heirs and successors: whereas we have been informed by Christian Samuel Lorent, Johann Liebegott Stöszel and Carl Heinrich Caspari, that they intend to start up a calico printing works in Zwickau, and have for this purpose acquired by purchase the so-called bleach yard and the nearby dyeworks of Schmidt, now disused, and have prayed that we may graciously award them a patent of privilege, *cum jure prohibendi*, together with other liberties and grants; we have examined this prayer, and grant the said Lorent and associates:

(1) the privilege asked for, *cum jure prohibendi*, for ten years from this

date, in such manner, that within this period no one shall be permitted to start up a calico printing works in a radius of four miles from Zwickau to print calico or to have it printed; from which prohibition, however, not only the existing print works, but also Chemnitz with its suburbs and Messrs. Steiner Brothers of Zwickau are expressly excluded;

(2) permission for the grantees for themselves, their heirs and successors, to adopt the style for their print works, of Electoral Saxon Privileged Lace and Cotton Factory, Zwickau; and

(3) mark the goods manufactured in their factory with the swords of our coat of arms and the words Zwickau Privileged Lace and Cotton Factory;

(4) exemption for ten years from property taxes applying to the Zeidler bleach yard and the Schmidt dyeworks purchased by the said Lorent and associates, and exemption from personal taxes for the same period, provided that this shall apply only to the entrepreneurs themselves and their fulltime indoor workers, as listed regularly in the due reports to be made to the town council of Zwickau, and shall not apply to those working outside the factory for a wage, and provided further that the manufactory is maintained in proper production, and we have already transmitted our appropriate order to the Tax Office;

(5) exemption from the land and general excise duty on all materials used in the manufacture, as well as on timber for firing, for ten consecutive years, *per modum restitutionis*, as well as a promise of reduced land and general excise rates at the end of that period;

(6) exemption of the factory buildings from the obligation of quartering troops, such as lies upon other citizens, but continued liability for a moderate service contribution;

(7) exemption, for their regular workmen, from impressment, conscription and choosing by lot.

We therefore order . . . all our officials, and particularly the Town Council of Zwickau, to protect these our patentees, so that they may enjoy the benefit of this instrument, though we expressly reserve the right, for ourselves, our heirs and successors, to increase, reduce or withdraw these privileges, according to changed times and circumstances. . . .

2/17 Foreign Entrepreneurs in France

Memorandum, *c.* 1754, attributed to John Holker. Printed by P. BOISSONADE in *Revue d'Histoire Économique et Sociale*, VI (1913), pp. 68–77. (W.O.H. Tr.)

Mr. Holker, Captain in Ogilvy's Scots Regiment, has satisfactorily fulfilled the engagements which he has undertaken both with regard to the establishment of a factory for the making of velveteens and cotton cloths resembling those made in Manchester and to the construction of cylinders or calenders of the English type designed to finish and give a gloss to thread-fabrics and cotton cloths which are made in Normandy.

Cotton velveteen, ribbed cloths, heavy and fine cotton cloths and many other new types of cloth – the manufacture of which Holker has introduced into Rouen during the past eighteen months – leave nothing to be desired when they are compared with English samples. Their quality has been proved by the use to which they have already been put and there has been a considerable demand for them not only in Paris but also in Rouen and the provinces.

A similar success has been achieved by four calenders (i.e. cylinders) that Mr. Holker has constructed and set to work in Rouen. [These machines] finish plain or figured cloths, handkerchiefs and, in general, all kinds of thread-fabrics and cotton cloth by passing them alternately through hot and cold rollers of wood and copper. The dressing given by the calenders is in no way inferior to that given by English machines and this has enabled us to open up a new branch of commerce on the Guinea coast by the manufacture of . . . cloths which the English and Dutch export to the negroes and which we could not copy without using the cylinders set up by Mr. Holker. Several manufacturers in Rouen have, during the past year, devoted their attention to the imitation of these various cloths and they have succeeded.

All that has to be done now is to multiply the factories set up by Mr. Holker and so extend our trade in these new products, which so far have been brought to perfection only in the Royal Factory at Rouen – although several establishments of the same kind have already been set up, such as those of Ricquier at Vernon, Moëlien at Rouen, Veillot at Yvetot, François at Saint-Clair, and Fromenteau at Tours. The managers of the Royal Factory at Rouen have had thirty-seven looms running continuously for four months and the demand for these fabrics has increased so much that one hundred looms could be installed and even then it would be impossible to meet demands even of customers from Rouen alone. In order to expand this industry we need new buildings capable of holding a larger number of looms and apprentices. This will depend not only upon Mr. Holker's exertions but upon the activities of his colleagues and of those capitalists who may wish to contribute to the enterprise.

2/18 Foreign Workers in France

From a Report of John Holker to Trudaine, 1766, on the Commerce of Orleans. Printed in J. HAYEM (ed.), *Mémoires et documents pour servir à l'histoire du commerce et de l'industrie en France* (12 vols. 1913), III, pp. 18-20. (Ed. Tr.)

M. de Mainville's business has become very considerable. He employs daily between 140 and 150 men, boys and women, all from the town, without taking into consideration the spinners and weavers for the production of linen cloth, which may amount to 2,500-3,000 aunes.* These cloths are not made up in the Généralité.* He obtains them from Beaujolais, Rouen, Troyes, Sens and Montignac.

In addition, M. de Mainville has several Dutchmen who are employed as colourers, engravers and printers, who are a very heavy charge to him, since he pays the colourers 2,400 livres,* board and lodging, and the engravers and printers 24 livres each week, irrespective of whether it includes feast days. These workers absorb a large proportion of his profit and as they are all jealous of French workers, it is difficult for M. de Mainville to finish his goods and I envisage that if some misfortune were to happen, his enterprise would crack, for the apprentices whom he trains and has brought up himself are a charge rather than a profit. Thus I proposed to M. de Mainville to make arrangements with the Dutch printers to train apprentices, otherwise they would never reach the necessary degree of perfection, since they have neither the theory nor the practice necessary for their task, which situation will always make him dependent on foreign workers, and yet it is to be presumed, because the Dutch would only diminish their wages in passing on their techniques, they will not lend themselves to the idea unless they derive some concrete advantage from it. I have proposed to M. de Mainville that he should engage one of the Dutchmen for life at one Louis per week* more than he would earn in working for him, [and] that he should give him two Louis for each apprentice printer he trains . . . assuming a maximum of fifty apprentices. He is fully aware of the need for such action and would like nothing better than to undertake it, but he would like to be sure that the Conseil would give him some financial assistance, because he fears that as soon as the workers are trained they would leave him to work elsewhere, which could happen, since they are used in all branches of manufacture. . . .

There is an absence of skilled engravers in France. Our manufacturers of calicoes have to resort to the Dutch and the Swiss for this purpose, which is costly, and they are always uncertain about their control over such workers. It would be a great help if one of the Dutchmen could train some French pupils in the skill of engraving. . . . I have had several conversations

* See Glossary.

with the most skilful engraver and he would undertake this if he were paid 2,000 livres for each pupil. I think this is exorbitant and we could obtain his services for half that sum. If this can be achieved, M. de Mainville would like four apprentice engravers and will contribute to the expenses, by providing engraving blocks and paying the apprentices during their period of apprenticeship, etc.

2/19 Royal Support for the Prussian Linen Industry

Frederick the Great to the Chamber of the Electoral Mark; Berlin, 16 March 1748. Printed in GUSTAV MENDELSSOHN-BARTHOLDY, *Der König* (16th ed., Bielefeld, 1954), pp. 220–221. (Ed. Tr.)

Although for many years, in reign after reign, various beneficial edicts and regulations have been issued, and orders have been given in them to advance the growing of flax and its spinning, besides the settlement of linen weavers in the villages belonging to us as well as in those belonging to the nobility, yet experience has shown that little has been done so far, and neither you nor the royal officials have taken any special interest in this useful work.

If we now graciously and earnestly demand that our regiments and all the remainder of the population of the country shall not buy and use any linen other than that produced at home, it will be necessary to devote more attention to the growing of flax and the spinning and weaving of linen than hitherto, and it will require untiring efforts; therefore we hereby order you expressly to promulgate regulations in all places and villages for our subjects to devote themselves more earnestly to the cultivation of flax, and attend rigorously to their spinning. To this end, they shall be required to deliver up, instead of the spinning tax in coin, certain lengths of yarn, which the farmers-general shall take from them in place of ready money, and shall then turn into cash, for which the increase in linen weavers will give them plenty of opportunity.

In general, you and every member of your commission must use all your effort, and likewise instruct your officials, not to let our subjects and their children spend the long evenings of the autumn and winter in idleness, but employ them in spinning and weaving as is the case in the other Provinces, and raise themselves by it, as well as getting used to habits of industry, inasmuch as the laziness of our subjects in the Electoral Mark is the only reason why they find themselves in straitened circumstances, fall into arrears with their dues both nationally and on their estates and are always coming to our magazines for advances, and, further, since they have no by-employment, they look merely to their husbandry, expect to feed themselves and their families merely out of the barns and the sacks of flour, neglecting their gardens from which they might supplement their maintenance during the winter, and therefore find it necessary to ask our estate offices or the magazines for advances of corn.

We do not lack beneficial regulations whereby to improve the food supply of our subjects. What is lacking is that you and your subordinate officers and local officials, who are not industrious enough, should give adequate instruction, which you will have to attend to more efficiently than has hitherto been the case. . . .

The official who shall show the greatest diligence in this respect, may expect promotion and reward to come to him before all others.

2/20 Encouragement for an Ironworks in Prussia

THOMAS PHILIPP VON DER HAGEN, *Beschreibung der Kalkbrüche bey Rüdersdorf, der Stadt Neustadt-Eberswalde. . . .* (Berlin, 1785), pp. 121-125. (Ed. Tr.)

As soon as the peace of 1742 with Austria was concluded, the King had ordered the building of an iron and steel manufactory [at Eberswalde] as well as the recruitment of the necessary workmen, such as knifesmiths and scissor-makers from the territories of Gotha and Eisenach.

This was put into operation, and in 1743 the first two scissor-makers arrived in Eberswalde from Eisenach. They were quartered with some townsmen, and two grinding wheels were built for them, one behind the town mill, later moved to the Wolfswinkel, and one on the Rogösen-Fliesz. They were soon followed by 17 knifesmiths from Schmalkalden and areas thereabouts, who with their families made in all 70 people, and many more continued to arrive in Eberswalde in the following years, so that by 1750 there were 60 families of colonists settled there, consisting of 300 persons.* They were known as the Ruhla colony, since most of them had come from the village of Ruhla.

Originally a special suburb was to have been built for them in front of the Lower Gate, along the dyke towards the George Hospital, but the plans were changed later, and houses were bought in the town for some of the manufacturers, while the others were quartered as tenants among the townspeople. Eight public furnace hearths were built for them along the town

* These colonists received, out of the royal exchequer, not only their daily expenses from the day of their departure to Eberswalde, at the rate of 4 gr. per man, 3 gr. per woman and 2 gr. per child, but continued to receive them after their arrival, until they were in full work and had been allocated their apartments and hearths. (Footnote in original source.)

wall at royal expense. However, as their numbers grew, the colonists began to suffer from lack of space. It was decided, therefore, to move some of them to the River Drage in the Neumark Province, Marienthal district, where a bar mill and power hammer were already in existence. However, the colonists complained that not enough grinding wheels could be built along the Drage, for it was shallow and froze over easily; and they protested against the removal for various other reasons. Finally, in 1749, after the town walls had been breached and a new gate made, a new suburb was built for the colonists on the Kiehn-Werder, together with a few houses near the Rogöse grinding wheel, and all the manufacturers were given apartments there. A new grinding wheel was built in front of the new gate outside the town wall, together with another . . . for which the water had to be collected from mountain streams, so that there are now four grinding wheels in all.

All the buildings and works were put up at the King's expense, and although the manufactory was at first limited to knives and scissors, it was soon making several types of iron and steel goods such as files, drills, candle-snuffers, locks, etc., and the concern was deservedly known as an iron and steel goods manufactory.

Therefore in 1750 all foreigners were prohibited from importing foreign-made knives, scissors, locks, etc., since the knife dealers of the County of Lingen had offered to carry stocks of iron and steel goods from Eberswalde, besides foreign ones.

This prohibition was re-affirmed in 1751, and at the same time the official price of all goods made in Eberswalde was published in a printed list.

On the 5 August of that year, all foreign made iron and steel goods were prohibited throughout the country, and this was re-enacted in 1756. From the beginning until 1752 the manufactory was administered directly. The local authority was put in charge, and Town Clerk Schleich was employed as factor, with a separate inspector appointed in 1751. The manufacturers bought their own raw materials for their products, which were at first bought from them in bulk by the factor, and later by the knife dealers of Lingen. But in 1753 the manufactory was handed over to the bankers Splittgerber and Daun for 20 years free of rent, and on 9 May last, *i.e.* before the 20 years were over, it was transferred to them free of charge, on condition that they maintained all its buildings at their own cost. Since then the manufactory has been enlarged and improved, and its market has been expanded.

The houses in the suburb on the Kienwerder are specifically designed to take two families each, each of whom has its own hearth or furnace. Apart from the houses built for the manufacturers there are also two large buildings, for the storing of raw materials and finished goods, and for the counting house, the apartments of the manager and the other officials.

The raw materials, such as iron, steel, tinplate, wire, brass, tin, lead, all kinds of horn and bone materials, ivory, coal, etc., are bought in by the proprietors of the manufactory in bulk, and are given out to the workmen at fixed prices; the finished goods, which they deliver once a fortnight to the warehouse, are paid for in cash also at fixed rates. This delivery and payment does not take place by the piece, but by the dozen, gross, pack etc.

Three inspectors are paid by the masters to check and judge the quality and workmanlike manufacture of the finished goods, and it is their special duty to inspect the goods carefully before delivery and to report on them, and those which do not come up to standard are rejected. If the workmen are dissatisfied with the verdict of the inspectorate, three or four other disinterested masters are called in, and the workmen have to accept their arbitration decision.

2/21 Encouragement of Foreign Workers and of Manufacture in Russia

HEINRICH VON STORCH, *Historisch-Statistisches Gemälde* [*see* Document **1/2**]I, pp. 464-473, III, pp. 38-42. (Ed. Tr.)

As early as December 1762 Catherine II issued a Proclamation inviting foreigners to settle in her realms under favourable conditions. In July 1763 the Empress set up an Office of Tutelage or Protection of Foreigners which was given the same rights as the other National Colleges. The main intention at its foundation was that the Office should take the newly arrived foreigners under its protection and lead them to their destination according to the Proclamation. It was given an annual budget of 200,000 roubles* which, apart from the purchase of an office building, was to be wholly used for the provision of seed-corn, livestock, implements etc. for the settlers, and for the setting up of manufactories. The Tutelage Office was charged with the further duty of collecting information about all wastes and unoccupied lands, directing the setting up of the new establishments, watching over their preservation and progress, and maintaining contact with Russian representatives abroad. Finally, it was given the privilege of reporting direct to the Empress.

At the same time a second Proclamation was issued, laying down in greater detail the advantages and privileges by which foreigners were invited to settle in the Russian Empire. Since this document has become the basis for all later attempts to attract settlers from abroad, and the regulations it con-

* See Glossary.

tains have become, as it were, the legal constitution of a numerous and not unimportant section of the population; it may not be out of place to summarize here its main provisions.

All foreigners may settle anywhere in the Empire, and need in this respect to report merely to the Tutelage Office or, in the case of the frontier districts, to the Governors and Commandants. If they do not possess sufficient property of their own to finance their journey, they will be supplied with funds from the Russian Ministers and Residents at foreign Courts and brought to Russia at the expense of the Empress. Immediately on arrival, they are to state what kind of husbandry or what industry they intend to pursue, and after swearing the oath of allegiance, they will be assisted to their destination without delay. The favours and privileges which the Government extends to them consist in the main of the following: the right to free religious observance; the right to build churches (but not monasteries), and to maintain clergy; without, however, attempting to make conversions, with the exception of the Muslim frontier tribes, whom anyone is permitted to convert to Christianity in a proper manner, and who may be subjected to serfdom by anyone; freedom from taxation for a certain period, which is fixed, according to the value of the colony to the State, at five, ten or thirty years; six months' free settlement, calculated from the day of arrival. Those who intend to engage in agriculture, industry or manufacture will be granted sufficient cultivable land and all aid possible for their settlement. The Imperial Exchequer will advance the sums necessary for buildings, livestock, tools, implements and materials, without interest and repayable after ten years in three instalments. Internal administration is wholly left to the discretion of the settlers who settle in complete villages; but they are subject to the general civil jurisdiction of the Empire. Duty-free import of their property, including even a quantity of commodities, which may, however, not exceed 300 roubles per family. – Exemption from civil and military service. – Board and free transit from the frontier to their destination. – Duty-free sale and duty-free export for ten years of any commodities produced by the settlers which have not hitherto been mined or produced in the country. – Foreign capitalists establishing factories, manufactories or workshops may buy as many peasants or serfs as they require for their enterprises. – The settlers may set up markets or fairs without paying any dues whatsoever. – All these privileges are extended to the children of settlers, including those born in Russia. Their years of privilege will be calculated from the date of arrival of their parents or ancestors; at their conclusion, they will be liable to the usual taxes and services. All those who wish to leave again, are free to do so on payment to the Imperial Exchequer of a fifth of their property acquired in Russia in the case of settlement of one to five years, and a tenth in the case of settlement of five to ten years. If the settlers require further privileges, they may apply to the Tutelage Office.

These invitations and privileges have attracted a large number of foreigners, particularly Germans, to Russia. The regions in which most of them settled were the Gouvernements* of St. Petersburg, Voronezh, Chernigov, Yekaterinoslav and Saratov; the last-named, in particular, attracted the most numerous and most important settlements on both banks of the Volga and the Medveditsa, and as a result it became necessary to set up an office of the Tutelage Commission in Saratov. . . .

The settlers in the Gouvernement of Saratov are mostly engaged in arable and animal husbandry; but there are many skilful artisans among them who have settled in the towns of the Province, especially in Saratov, where their work is in great demand and provides them with a good income. . . .

In the Gouvernement of St. Petersburg the settlers are mainly engaged in arable husbandry and market gardening; since the products of their industry can easily be sold in the capital, they are all doing well. – In the Gouvernement of Chernigov, where they number about 3,000, they live in five villages which possess two churches, one Lutheran and a Roman Catholic minister. – But nowhere is the mixture more diverse or more curious than in the Gouvernement of Yekaterinoslav, in which settlers form more than half the population. Here may be found Germans, Swedes, Italians, German Mennonites, Greeks, Bulgars, Serbs, Arnauts, Albanians and Armenians. The last-named are not only among the most numerous, but also among the most useful, of the settlers in this Gouvernement. . . .

. . . The numerous establishments which arose gradually as a result of this invitation, though they were given considerable advances by the Crown, yet were not set up wholly at its cost; it was thus easier for Catherine to venture this attempt also of encouraging industry, though no great hopes could be entertained for it after the many examples of failures abroad. The results here prove once again that concerns of this kind flourish only under free enterprise; most of the manufactories set up at the cost of the Imperial Exchequer and administered on the Crown's behalf either failed after a short period, or could be maintained only at great sacrifice.

Among all the examples of unsuccessful projects of this type to be found in Russia, perhaps none can provide a better object lesson than the history of the manufacturing settlement of Yamburg. The formerly insignificant and neglected hamlet of Yamburg, lying on the high road between Riga and St. Petersburg, was to have become the location of industrial manufacturing establishments of the most elaborate kind. The management of the whole undertaking was put into the hands of Yelagin, a well-known Imperial

* See Glossary.

contractor now deceased, who had been one of its leading projectors, and who proposed such grand schemes for commercial and industrial enterprises that even the survival of the neighbouring town of Narva might have been in danger, had not this proximity, as well as the proximity of the Court itself, been a major handicap for the realization of his projects. The plan for the building of the new town of Yamburg was extensive and splendid. Its location might be unpropitious for the proposed scheme, but it was well enough placed for the erection of large, stone-built houses which Yelagin ran up, since the most important building materials were found in great quantity in the immediate vicinity. A market hall, built of stone, was constructed, large enough for a major trading city. While these and numerous other buildings were being erected, Yalagin attempted, at great expense, to attract industrialists to Yamburg, particularly those engaged in the final stages of manufacture. A number of enterprises had, in fact, been started, when the Empress herself visited this new industrial settlement. She was shown the first fruits of the products of local craftsmanship, and her attention was drawn to the rapid transformation of the miserable huts which had once stood there, into palatial buildings. Although the Empress showed her satisfaction, her keen eye did not miss the true considerations which should guide the development of these costly properties. Yelagin was ordered to suspend any further town development, since hardly any purchasers had yet been found for the large buildings, no matter how cheaply they had been offered, and how convenient the terms of payment. The manufactories already started either began to stagnate or were formally discontinued soon after. The manufacture of cambric, begun on three looms by a French weaver who worked them in a damp cellar, was viewed with displeasure by the Empress and was, therefore, quickly given up. A manufacture of silk stockings and gloves, which had imported its complicated frames from abroad, as well as manufactures of mock-velvet, baize, and leather gloves, shared the same fate a little later. Only the famous woollen manufacture of Yamburg, supplying the finest cloth and worked exclusively for the Crown, managed to survive for a time, though not without a large subsidy.

The most important and most fruitful measure which Catherine II took for the encouragement of industry, was undoubtedly the foundation of the bourgeois estate in the famous Constitution of Towns, in which the existence, the duties and rights of this separate class were not only acknowledged and secured, but the separate classes of bourgeois were distinguished from each other, and each put in charge of a separate branch of industry. Up to then there had been no order among the bourgeois industries in Russia; urban industries were often managed by peasants; the bourgeois in the towns might engage in commerce, in handicrafts, in gardening, in carting, and at times even in agriculture, in rapid succession. In such conditions, it was hardly likely that any branch of industry would develop to any degree of perfection. The Constitution of Towns limited the practice of manufacturing industry exclusively to the bourgeois, and divided the latter into Gilds and Companies.

2/22 The French Iron Industry

Mr. William Wilkson's account of the iron made in France, 5 February 1787. (Boulton & Watt Collection, Birmingham Public Libraries.)

Mr. Degros of Chalons sur Saône in Burgundy has for several years past – had the Care of receiving the Iron from the Interior part of France and forwarding it down to Lyons, and the South of France. He has frequently told me that there has for many years previous to 1782 passed through his Hands 30,000,000 pounds or 15,000 tons Short Weight of Barrs. This Iron comes chiefly from the Provinces of Franche Compté, the Northern Part of Burgundy, and the Southern parts of Alsace and Champagne, and serves to supply Lyons, Languedoc, Dauphiné, Provence and Marseilles as there are no Iron Forges south of the Latitude of Chalons on the East Part of France. The Iron sent is nearly half Coldshort and is chiefly consumed in Forez in the Nail and Iron Manufactories of St. Etienne and St. Chaumont, and I have always been informed from the Director of the Farmes at St. Etienne who receives the Duties on it, that they consumed in those Fabrications 6,000 tons yearly. The Prices were at Chalons untill 82 about 260 to 280 Livres the Ton s.w. or from 10. 16. 0. to 11. 12. 0. English. Common Merchant Iron from 13. 10. 0. to 14. 10. 0. and fine drawn ½ inch squares etc. – 15. 10. 0. to 16. 10. 0. Since that time I am informed the Prices have rose considerably and the quantity lessened from 15 to 2,000 tons owing to the Quantity of Wood which has been destroyed. All this iron has paid the Mark de fer* of 17/- English per ton.

I have been informed from the Officers who receive the Mark de fer that about 30,000 tons are consumed of home made iron, but as the Provinces of Alsace, Lorrain or Rousillon does not pay for what they consume at home and as they smuggle their Manufactories into France it is difficult to say what they may furnish; Luxembourg, in which there are several Forges, chiefly supplys the manufactory of Charleville and neighbourhood; that iron is supposed to pay the duty on coming into France, but I am told by some capital Men in that Trade that they do not pay the half. Charleville consumes in every line about 6,000 tons – not 1/6 of which is made in France, but comes

* See Glossary.

from the Pais Messin and Luxembourg. Champagne supplys Paris iron tender and Coldshort; a few forges in the [?] about Joigny and Montbard in the North of Burgundy do the same, Iron Coldshort entirely. The castings of all parts used in Paris come from Champagne, Normandy, Perche, Berry supplys along the Loire as well as Nivernais; this last is chiefly coldshort – the former is of a good nature but improperly treated as such does not keep up its ancient credit. Périgord Angoumois supply Bordeaux and Rochelle with Bars and Castings of which last great numbers of Sugar Pans are yearly sent to the West Indies – Iron chiefly tough.

Rousillons Works all by Bloomerys. I have seen 8 of them – they make about 2 tons a Week each. This Iron is very good and tough what is more than sufficient to supply the Province and which Perpignan and Port Vendres takes much is smuggled into Spain in small Articles – manufactured in the Province as nails and Articles of Husbandry, etc.

I have a particular Detail of the Nivernais and Berry Works in Wales. At present I do not recollect it. Very few works in Britany and those coldshort. The duty on importing into that Province from France and its situation and trade to the North renders Swedish & Russia Iron much in use there and cheaper than the French as the duties are only 5/- per ton. Anjou and Touraine have not one Ironwork that I have ever heard of – Maine and Perche a few – Picardy none – nor Artois; Provence none, or Languedoc or low Gusine the same. In Dauphiné they have about 28 finerys for making the steel from pig iron which they get from Alvart,* and other Furnaces from the Savoy which works from a white spathic ore. This steel is reported good for small articles, but not for heavy strong tools.

2/23 Swedish Iron Manufacture

H. WRAXALL, Jun., *A Tour through some of the Northern Parts of Europe*, etc. (2nd ed., London, 1775), pp. 168-171. (G.P.J.)

I have almost made the complete tour of the Province of Upland. The country is chiefly a horrid desert. . . . Nature has, however, made them in some degree amends for this parsimony, by enriching these barren wastes with inexhaustible mines of copper, iron and silver. The peasants are chiefly employed in the manufacture of these metals, and I have visited six or seven forges on my journey, each of which constantly employs from four to fourteen hundred workmen only in iron. Wherever there is a country seat, you may be certain to see one of these fabrics and no Cyclops were ever more dexterous in working their materials. I have seen them stand close to, and

* Allevard (Ed.).

hammer, in their coarse frocks of linen, a bar of ore, the heat and refulgence of which were almost insupportable to me at ten feet distance. . . . I had the pleasure of viewing the whole process used to reduce the ore into iron, and must own it is very curious and instructive. They first roast it in the open air for a considerable time, after which it is thrown into a furnace, and when reduced to fusion, is poured into a mould of sand, about three yards in length. These pigs, as they are then denominated, are next put into a forge heated to a prodigious degree; they break off a large piece with pinchers when red hot, and this is beat to a lesser size with hammers. It is put again into the fire, and from thence entirely finished by being laid under an immense engine resembling a hammer, which is turned by water, and flattens the rude piece into a bar. Nothing can exceed the dexterity of the men who conduct the concluding part of the operation, as the eye is their sole guide, and it requires an exquisite nicety and precision. . . .

2/24 Mining Industry in Russia

STORCH, *Historisch-Statistisches Gemälde* . . . [*see* Document **1/2**], II, pp. 520-532 (Ed. Tr.)

As mentioned above, most private owners of mines are nobles, but a few are bourgeois and merchants. Now that the family Pokhadyashin has sold its copper mine to a bank, the richest of such mines belong to the families Turchaninov, Luginin, Stroganov *et. al.*; the most important ironworks, to the Demidov, Yakoblev, Stroganov, Tverdichev, Lazarev, Luginin and Batachev families. The Stroganov family owns some 540,000 verst* square in the Gouvernement* of Perm alone, on which it possesses, according to the last but one revision, 83,453 male serfs. Among the private ironworks and villages there are many which exceed in the size and splendour of their buildings and the number of their inhabitants, most of the towns of this Gouvernement.

According to the Law of 28 June 1782, no Court or Magistrate may interfere in the administration of these private mines, and the establishment and management of mining is left to the sole discretion of the owners. These usually leave the management in the hands of a 'prikachik' or steward, a job for which they pick a clever fellow among their serfs who is master of the great arts of reading, writing and reckoning; many select deliberately a member of the Old Believers' sect, because they are not (quite as much) the victims of drink, and watch for the errors of their orthodox neighbours with eagle eyes. Such a man is often in charge of most extensive mines and smelt

* See Glossary.

works, offices with difficult accounts, and some thousands of servile and free workmen; he supervises the mining and the smelting, arranges for court cases about boundaries and pits, pays the taxes, buys in the cheapest market and makes his master rich, for a pay of a mere forty to one hundred roubles,* besides some other perquisites. Although some private works employ free men, such as merchants or retired army officers, yet in most cases it is a serf prikachik who controls, with his assistants, vast mining enterprises, the products of which, as in the case of those of Demidov or Yakoblev, run into millions, and for the management of which other countries would have to have whole mining councils, with their councillors, assessors and clerks.

The labour on the royal as well as the private mining enterprises is performed partly by Crown artisans, partly by ascribed peasants, partly by serfs and in part also by free labourers. The class of master artisans has developed out of the Crown serfs and of the men destined for army recruitment who were ordered into the mines. Together with their descendants they belong forever to the Crown or private mines to which they have been ascribed, and are wholly kept by the Crown or the private works owner. In order to describe the activities and the fate of this class in greater detail, we shall quote parts of the description of those of Kolüman, by Renovanz.

Although the miners and smelt-workers are all called master artisans as a group, they are divided into masters, deputy masters, apprentices, hewers, miners, carters, washers and sorters. Their wages depend on their skill, and range from 15 to 30 roubles a year. Their board, supplied by the warehouse, is deducted from this wage.

The number of master artisans on the books of Kolüwan runs to 4,186, but from this a considerable portion must be deducted as consisting of old paupers, the sick and the hospital nurses, supervisors in the mine and iron offices, 'denshchiki'* for the officers etc., and there is a further annual diminution by desertion. From the remaining number, all the auxiliary workers have to be deducted, so that only a relatively minor part is left for mining proper, which in the case of the Schlangenberg itself does not amount to more than about 600 men. – The children of the workers and soldiers, numbering 1,029, are partly educated in the schools, and partly, as they grow up, they work on the sorting banks. The increase in the workforce depends on recruitment; but since mining and smelting are unhealthy and shorten the life expectancy, the losses can hardly be replaced by such means. The true increase comes from the children of the miners, of whom a boy of fourteen can do more useful work than a fully grown peasant yokel. – The administration, the treatment and the punishments of the miners are almost wholly of a military nature. They receive promotion like the non-

* See Glossary.

commissioned officers in the army; their crimes are tried by courts martial, at which, if necessary, mining officers may be present.

Since there are neither markets for victuals nor handicraftsmen in the Altai Mountains, the miner must look to his own supplies; for this purpose, the numerous state and church festivals are most useful, as they free him of all official work. His first care is to possess his own cottage, round which he cultivates his garden and keeps some animals to supply his food. If new pits are sunk elsewhere, he has to make do temporarily with a hut built of stakes and covered with turf, or he digs a dwelling and an oven in the ground. But as soon as the mine appears to have a settled future, he at once builds himself a proper cottage, and brings along his possessions and his livestock. Thus it happens not infrequently, that in the thickest and most inaccessible forests, or in the endless wastes of the steppes, whole streets and villages of miners spring up within a few years. If he has to leave, the miner does not stand to lose, for he can easily sell his hut to a peasant, who may erect it at some other spot twenty or thirty verst distant.

In general, the miners and smelters of the Altai Mountains, especially those who spring from miners' families, are men who will fit in anywhere and can turn their hands to anything. Many develop their talent for artistic craftsmanship quickly and happily with some little assistance. There are some boys among them who can copy the prettiest hand drawing; common blacksmiths construct huge metal striking clocks, and wherever there is a chance of making money, their spirit of industry is roused, which seems to be developed, rather than suppressed, by their wearisome and hard work. Almost every miner in the Altai is, besides, an excellent hunter, a clever horseman and, in case of necessity, is certain to be a first-class soldier.

The ascribed peasants, mentioned before, came into being as follows. Most of the early mines were initially set up on Crown land, and, apart from the Crown itself, were mostly begun by persons not of noble quality and therefore without serfs of their own. In order to deal with the shortage of labour, which was all the more troublesome then, as no free workmen could be found to work for a money wage in the beginning, and in order to further the mining industry, the Sovereign commanded that the Crown peasants who happened to be in the vicinity of the works should work off their poll tax which the works owner was then obliged to pay on their behalf. Most of the private mines which had such peasants in their neighbourhood thus received a sufficient number of workmen who could, until 1779, be used for any work and in all seasons.

The uncertainty of this regulation led to a double abuse. Not only was the ascribing of the peasants done very freely, at the expense of the Crown, but these poor people were so burdened with arbitrary long hours and arduous work, that in their desperation they were more than once driven to revolt. As soon as Catherine II ascended the throne, she sought to end these abuses. In 1766, accordingly, a Commission including some of the most respected civil servants was set up to inquire into the situation and make recommendations for its improvement; but since the completion of this important matter was held up by all kinds of obstacles, the Empress dealt with the worst abuses by interim measures, until the praiseworthy Edict of 23 May 1779 which determined the fate of these ascribed peasants fairly and humanely. Not only was their wage raised, but their hours of work, and the kind of work, were laid down in detail, and breaches of the regulations were made punishable. As a result, these peasants are now required to perform only five kinds of task, which each male soul has to work off, according to the fixed daily rate, to the extent of 170 copecks, and these should take him normally no more than four weeks in the year and should leave him plenty of time for his own husbandry and domestic duties.

Where persons of noble birth own mining enterprises on their own soil, they have to provide all labour, from among their own serfs; but if they commence mining on other land, they may also use ascribed peasants. – Free labour is almost everywhere the smallest part, and if mining had to depend on them, most works would soon have to close down. But many copper and ironworks in the Ural Mountains have most of their ore carted to them by hired carters, since the ascribed peasants will have usually worked off their poll tax in cutting timber and leading charcoal. – Since nowadays all Crown peasants in the neighbourhood of these mines already belong to the mines in one way or another, it has become virtually impossible for anyone who does not possess his own serfs to enter the mining industry to advantage, since in most districts it is most difficult to attract good volunteer workmen even at the highest wages, and since, further, a large capital sum is needed, generally much beyond a single fortune. These are probably the reasons why, since the Proclamation of 1782, which firmly secured and increased the liberties of mining, not a single new mining enterprise has been started up.

2/25 Putting-out System in German Textiles

Report by Wintgens to v. Buggenhagen on the woollen industry in Aachen; Duisburg, 8 February 1781. Printed in KRÜGER, *Geschichte der Manufakturen* ... [*see* Document **2/6**], pp. 508–510. (Ed. Tr.)

Yours, which reached me only on the 5th inst., concerns the large-scale woollen manufacture at Aachen and Verviers, and especially its costs, for materials as well as labour costs for all necessary processes, from the scribbling to the finishing, about which I am to report. In fulfilling this assignment, may I note first of all that in the local manufactories (which are not entirely unknown to me as a former inhabitant of Aachen) there are five main types of persons involved, viz. the entrepreneur, or manufacturer, the weaver or draper, the fuller, the dyer and the finisher or shearer. Each of these plays a leading part or has his own independent business, which in the case of the dyer, weaver and finisher is protected by a gild which ensures that they are not subordinate to the entrepreneur, otherwise than in completing, like other independent handicraftsmen, the work ordered from them for cash, so that the manufacturer need only supply the Spanish or Portuguese wool, which is exclusively used there.

The weavers form a gild, containing numerous good and bad master workers, who can count on more or less work according to the degree of their skill and the rates of payment charged: for the entrepreneur picks the weaver according to his convenience and need, and supplies him with the necessary wool, weighed out in proportion to the number of pieces required. These weavers then have to get the wool washed, cleaned or scribbled, carded, spun, woven and the nap raised, in other words, manufactured according to the fineness, the length and breadth ordered, and delivered to the house of the manufacturer, so that the weavers (drapers) of Aachen, taking into account the work performed within their stage, may be held to be entrepreneurs themselves, since the scribbling, washing and spinning is not done by their own workmen, but by others engaged for the purpose, some of whom live scattered in the villages and the countryside.

When the pieces have been inspected, and passed, they are sent to the fuller who sends them back to the entrepreneur's house after fulling. Now the finishers have their turn, also forming a gild like the weavers, and equally numerous.

Here also the entrepreneur picks the men who suit his interests best. These finishers, after the cloths received by them have been cleaned, drawn, teased and cropped twice, three or four times according to the quality (except black cloths, which are cropped only after dyeing) and once more and thus prepared for dyeing, hand them over direct to the dyers nominated by the entrepreneurs, the former also belonging to a gild of their own.

After dyeing, the cloths are returned to the finishers who have put them out, and they then provide the finishing touches, and when they have been stretched on the frame to the required length and dressed, they are delivered back to the entrepreneur for dispatch. Thus in Aachen the citizen or his friends, if he has enough resources to buy wool, and knows how to sell the cloths favourably, can become an entrepreneur or manufacturer, even if he has no other knowledge or skill of the cloth manufacture; at the same time such manufacturers may not start up weaving, dyeing or finishing works on their own account in their own houses, but have to get these tasks performed by the existing specialists. Only the Roman Catholics may enter the dyeing or finishing trade, but even they only on condition that they are properly apprenticed and members of the gild, without which no one receives permission to do so, no matter how high his status.

But the sons of rich entrepreneurs rarely condescend to become apprentices, and it is the Protestants who maintain the largest manufactories; and besides, the wages paid to finishers and dyers are so low, that they could not undercut their costs unless they worked on a large scale themselves. There are also but few dyers. A few manufacturers are known to me who began by serving in the lowly state, and on becoming wealthy, maintain their own finishing and dye works.

This constitution and organization of the manufacture leads among others, to the following advantages:

(1) The weavers, finishers and dyers are enabled by their certain income, which cannot be withdrawn from them, to work on a large scale and therefore to produce cheaply. One drives the other, and young men, who have their way to make, have to try to gain customers by working skilfully and cheaply, so that wages are everywhere the lowest possible, especially if there are fewer orders from outside.

Aachen is not entirely without well-to-do weavers, dyers and finishers, who undertake to weave, finish or dye 100 or more pieces of cloth and return them completed by a certain date, and even grant credits to the poorer entrepreneurs from one fair to the next, so that these represent really the main entrepreneurs within their special branch, employing often as many as 200 workers at one time.

(2) The entrepreneurs can wholly rely on getting even the largest orders for cloth completed in the promised time, when the job is distributed among the several master-workers, once their completion has been promised by them, since they may not, on any excuse, fail to complete them and have to compensate the entrepreneur for any damage arising out of any delay.

(3) Beginners may enter the market on the same terms as the largest entrepreneurs, and need not fear to be swallowed up by them, since they both enjoy the same advantages regarding the rates at which weaving, finishing and dyeing are available for them, and any advantage of one over the other must arise either out of cheaper wool purchases or faster turnover of finished goods. I know a theology student and other individuals who, having acquired a superficial knowledge of the woollen manufacture, had cloths made on their own account and gradually rose to be among the largest entrepreneurs and capitalists.

From this rough sketch of the organization of the Aachen manufacture Your Excellency will be able to judge the large difference from, and the advantages over, the organization here, where the manufacturer, if he wants to set up, has to found willy-nilly his own finishing and dyeing shops, for which he needs capital, and has to look after his own spinners and weavers, and has to get them to work by raising their wages, so that the smaller manufacturers who lack the means, have to have their work done in the establishments of the larger ones, and therefore cannot compete with them; and even the large manufacturers cannot compete with those of Aachen, since each dye works and finishing shop is of small size appropriate to each separate manufactory, and built out of its capital, and cannot be expected to work as favourably as the large-scale concerns, not to mention that not every kind of cloth can be dyed here, and if anything special is demanded, it has to be sent for dyeing to Aachen at great cost in freight; and the local manufacturers are embarrassed by special orders which they cannot complete here for lack of skilled labour, and have reluctantly to leave them to outsiders. . . .

2/26 Putting-out System in French Textiles

FRANÇOIS DE LA ROCHEFOUCAULD – LIANCOURT, *Voyages en France (1781-1783)* (ed. J. Marchand, 2 vols., Paris, 1933-8), I, pp. 4-5. (Ed. Tr.)

I then saw the material called cotton check (*cotonnades*). There are all sorts of cotton manufacture made up at Rouen and in the area 15 leagues* around it. The peasant who returns to the plough to work his fields, sits at his cotton frame and makes either *siamoises*† or ticking or even white, very fine, cotton cloth. One must admire the activity of the Normans. This activity does not interfere at all with their daily work. Land is very dear and consequently very well cultivated. The farmer works on the land during the day and it is in the evening by the light of the lamp that he starts his other task. His workers and his family have to help. When they have worked all week they come into the town with horses or carts piled up with material. Goods are sold in the Hall, which is all that remains of the palace of the former Dukes of Normandy, on Thursdays. It is a truly wonderful sight. It takes place at a surprising speed. Almost 800,000 francs* worth of business is transacted between 6.00 and 9.00 in the morning. Among those who do the buying there are many agents who buy for merchants and then the goods pass to America, Italy and Spain. The majority goes to America. I have seen many pieces destined to become shirts for negroes; but their skin will be seen through the material, since the cloth is thin and almost

* See Glossary. † Common cotton goods. (Ed.)

sufficiently coarse to make ticking. It costs 17, 20 and even 25 francs* per aune* in the Hall.

2/27 Class and Entrepreneurship in Poland

a WILLIAM JACOB, *Report on the Trade in Foreign Corn* [see Document **1/11**], pp. 78-79. (G.P.J.)

b Report on Poland by Frhr. v. Stein, 9 November 1781. Printed in ERICH BOTZENHART (ed.), *Freiherr vom Stein: Briefwechsel, Denkschriften und Aufzeichnungen* (Berlin, 1931, 7 vols.), I, pp. 56-58. (Ed. Tr.)

a Among the real Poles, there are no regular gradations of ranks between the noble proprietor and the wretched peasantry. There may be, and visibly are, differences in the condition of the peasantry, depending on the personal character of their lords, and upon the more or less embarrassed state of the property on which they may be settled. There is also a difference between the landed proprietors, owing to the different degrees of activity, economy, and attention that they exercise; but there is not a middle class of Poles. The Polish gentry are too proud to follow any course but the military career; and the Government, by its large standing army, encourages the feeling, though the pay is scarcely sufficient to supply the officers with their expensive uniforms. The Church has too few prizes, among many thousand blanks, to induce any but the lower classes to enter on that profession. The offices of Government can employ but few, and those are ill paid, and said to depend on small peculations, rather than on their salaries. Whatever difficulties may present themselves to the placing out of young men of good family, none have had recourse to commerce; and if they had, such would be treated by others as having lost their caste, and descended to a lower rank of society. The manufacturers and the artisans in Poland are almost all of the German nation. If a joiner, painter, mason, tailor, shoemaker, or a person of other similar occupations, including too the medical profession, is wanted, he will commonly be found only among the Germans. The merchants, bankers, and traders, are nearly as exclusively of the Jewish race; and that too of all classes, from the importer of wines and colonial produce to the dealer in rags and old clothes; from the monied man, who traffics in foreign loans and foreign exchanges, down to the lender of small sums, which the poor can obtain by pledging their miserable furniture or implements.

* See Glossary.

b INDUSTRY.

It is not possible to design a tableau of national industry. Since it is widely known, from the many unfinished attempts made by authors and civil servants hitherto, how difficult it is to design any proper tableau of national industry, it must be obvious that a nation which has always looked upon its own welfare and its own conditions with indifference and has never attempted to get to know them, would find it impossible to develop such a tableau. We will therefore have to content ourselves with the following general considerations, in order to judge the state of industry in Poland.

The Pole produces raw materials only. The Pole is concerned merely with the use of raw materials, namely grain, cattle, skins, also some furs, timber, potash, ochreous ash, honey, hemp, saltpetre, and plain cloth for the use of home consumption only in the district of Fraustadt, Lissa, as well as some iron in the areas of Sandomier, Cracow and Sieradz. Formerly, the product of his country included salt and plain linen, but these came from the Carpathian Mountains which now are part of Austria.

His Manufactures and Factories are Insignificant. The attempts made hitherto by Count Tyzenhausen on the Royal Estates in Lithuania have partly failed, and partly they are too insignificant to be taken into consideration here. From what has been said so far, it can easily be seen that in general the state of industry in Poland is most insignificant, and the value of its products cannot be expressed in figures. It may appear curious that goods of refined luxury, such as English furniture and commodities, are produced in large quantities in Warsaw, but the mystery is solved when we consider that these commodities are largely produced for the foreigners who live in Warsaw, and for grandees for whom price is no consideration.

Industry is Insignificant because of Serfdom. The reasons why this nation is so backward compared with its neighbours merit some consideration. The property and wealth and the personal rights of the largest part of the nation are entirely subordinate to the whim of a tiny minority, which enjoys the fruits of the work of the former, so that the drive to activity which is a consequence of the desire to happiness is lacking. In Poland the whole middle or bourgeois class, which normally can be expected to provide enlightened human beings for the state, is missing.

Because of the Gross Sensuousness and Carelessness in the National Character. To this we have to add the character of the nation, the carelessness regarding the consequences of its actions, and the laziness and contentment with the mere satisfaction of the physical needs, so that all the attractions of work and industry are missing, which vanity, imitation, habits and refined taste and economic wisdom contain in themselves. The ordinary Pole is a careless being, who continues to enjoy as long as the supply lasts, who dresses and feeds himself and lives miserably and who knows no joy but debauchery and revelry. By contrast, the nobility uses its wealth in an excessive luxury which can be satisfied only by imported goods from abroad. On the one hand, therefore, one finds a lack of cleanliness to a degree unknown in the rest of Europe, a miserable style of building and block houses, a lack of linen and a shortage of even the first necessities of life, for example bread, and on the other hand, with the nobility, one finds the most debauched and excessive waste of all kinds. Putting these causes of serfdom and general laziness together, we have as a consequence that there is no other trade known than agriculture, no other incentive to work than the satisfaction of the minimum needs and brute force, and that all industry of such a nation is imperfect and little varied, and its population weakened in proportion with its rates of subsistence. From what has been said so far, it is possible to answer the question whether Poland will soon grow to a higher state of refinement and to a more varied industry.

In the near future, Polish industry will not grow because the government is poor and weak, the nobility is extravagant, and wages are high. It is the weakness and policy of the Government which prohibits them from using strong means to direct and support commerce, with which other countries are able to effect rapid revolutions. All attempts hitherto to erect factories have failed because of lack of money; and the limitation of harmful luxury by sumptuary laws was never obeyed. The wealth of the nation is in the hands of the aristocracy, which wastes it in an unreasonable manner, and uses it for frivolities, and not on goods which could increase national wealth. Moreover, in a nation in which all are either noble or slave, the number of manufacturing workers available to refine the national product is small, and the wages are consequently high. Workers from abroad who enter the country either rapidly become victims of drink and the inglorious manner of living of the Poles, or they leave the country in which earnings are moderate and necessities are sold to them by the natives of the country only at a high price, while the customs are very different from their own. To this has to be added the lack of money and the high rate of interest of 10%, . . . Manufactures which require the concurrence or permission of natives, whose own products are not sold to consumers and who when fixing their prices know no other law but their own will, cannot develop in the near future, into the kind of manufactures which could be sold to merchants or consumers who can determine price by calculation and comparison, even if neighbours did not increase the cost of transit by bad practices still further.

2/28 Class and Entrepreneurship in France

J. NECKER, *De l'Administration des finances* (3 vols., Paris, 1784), III, pp. 116–117.

The multitude of privileges which is conferred by noble status and which can be acquired for money, is a prop to vanity, which encourages people to leave commercial or manufacturing establishments at the very time when, as a result of an increase in wealth, they could make their greatest contribution. . . . It is then, indeed, that merchants can be content with smaller returns on their capital; it is then that they can facilitate exports, by the granting of loans; it is then that they can take greater risks and open up new lines of business. . . . I have no hesitation in saying that these attitudes prevent France from realizing her full commercial potential, and that they are among the principal factors which allow nations where social distinctions are less marked, and the resultant pretensions are not a cultural obsession, to maintain their commercial and industrial superiority.

Chapter 3 Commerce, Transport, and Commercial Policy

Introduction

The late eighteenth and the very early nineteenth century belong essentially to the pre-railway age. In this earlier stage of transport development, the emphasis falls upon rivers (**3/1**), roads and canals (**3/4**). It was by these means that Europe transported and exchanged its goods. It is clear that the European transport system exhibited grave deficiencies and it is equally clear that in many areas these drawbacks continued to characterize the system until well into the nineteenth century (**13/3**, **13/4**, **13/5**). Not only did the system mean a certain slowness in the movement of goods, but, inevitably, entrepreneurs incurred heavy costs. As late as 1828 Jacob could write of 'the expenses of conveyance' in Mecklenburg, amounting to 'somewhat more than 13%' on the sum farmers received for their produce (**3/2**). When it is recalled that Europe's problems were exacerbated by the incidence of heavy tolls and customs duties (**3/3**, **4/7**), which continued into the nineteenth century (**3/13**), it can be appreciated that consumers and producers were both inevitably affected. This situation was aggravated by the restrictions placed on the internal grain trade which existed for a considerable period in the eighteenth century. In years of harvest failure this helped to raise prices, accentuate suffering and create social tension (**5/1**). It is hardly surprising that Governments devoted considerable attention to remedying such problems (**3/11** see also **5/2**).

The great fairs were an important feature in pre-railway economies. It was at these meetings that the large-scale exchange of goods occurred. Most travellers to Eastern Europe felt obliged to devote some attention to the fairs at Pesth (**3/5**), Kharkov and Nijni Novgorod (**3/6**). The fairs extended over a considerable period. Nijni Novgorod, for example, opened annually on 27 July and closed on 22 September N.S. (**3/6**), and was an unrivalled exchange market. There is a direct correlation between the persistence of such fairs, general economic backwardness (**3/5**) and the retardation of rail transport. Once the railway permitted quick, cheap and frequent contact between the leading commercial and industrial centres, the necessity for the large-scale fair was reduced and retail specialization and the department store assumed their place in the European economy.

External trade was characterized and influenced by the mercantilist tradition. Large-scale trading organizations were still being sponsored by the State (**3/7**, **3/8**, **3/9**). Such intervention went far beyond the granting of trading privilege and monopoly and included material aid and help to the privileged companies throughout the period of their existence (**3/9**): trade policy was closely related to industrial policy, since an industrial base was regarded as 'the mother of useful trade' (**3/7**).

French trade in this period was still heavily under Colbertian influence, in the sense that traders depended heavily on state-sponsored schemes and in the sense that protectionism remained a salient feature in French commercial policy until the Eden-Reyneval Treaty in 1786 (**3/12**). Then, for a brief period, France departed from her traditional commercial policy, until the old system was restored during the Revolutionary and Napoleonic period, when France once more surrounded herself with a tariff wall, and at the latter point, attempted to involve all Europe in her schemes (**10/11**). Reyneval's dream of bringing together France and England and of destroying 'the system of envy and hatred' proved an illusion, and it was 70 years before France once more ventured towards free trade (**12/5**, **12/6**, **12/7**, **12/8**, **12/9**, **12/10**).

On the whole the eighteenth century was a period of French commercial expansion (**3/10**). Arnould indicates quite clearly that France was heavily involved in trading with the new world of America and Africa, and that the importance of this type of commercial contact increased throughout the century. In its turn this helped to lay the basis for some of the wealthy trading families, whose affluence impressed Arthur Young, and who gathered in expanding ports like Bordeaux. But there were other consequences. The excursion into free trade policy had deleterious effects upon certain sectors of the French economy, and this affords a sharp contrast with the picture presented by Arnould. It would be unwise to regard the 1786 Treaty and the consequent competition from British industry as the sole factor behind the distress of the immediate pre-revolutionary period, but there is little doubt that in certain areas it had a damaging effect on French industry and aided the development of discontent, which attained its climax in the revolution (**3/13**, see also **4/5**, **4/6**, **4/7**, **4/8**, **5/1a**, **b**, **c**, **5/14a** and **b**).

3/1 River Transport in Russia

H. F. VON STORCH, *The Picture of St. Petersburg* (London, 1801), pp. 262-263.

The buying up of the foregoing articles, and their conveyance from the midland, and partly from the remotest regions of the empire, form an important branch of the internal commerce. The majority of these products are raised on the fertile shores of the Volga; this invaluable river, which, in its course, connects the most distant provinces, is at the same time the channel of business and industry. Wherever its water laves the rich and fruitful coasts, industry and diligence have fixed their abode: its course marks the progress of internal culture. But even from a distance of between five and six thousand versts,* from the heart of Siberia, rich in metals, St. Petersburg receives the stores of its enormous magazines. The greater part of them, at least the hardwares, are brought hither from the easternmost districts of Siberia, almost entirely by water. The Selenga receives and transfers them to the Baikal, from which they proceed by the Angara to the Yenisey, and pass from that along the Oby into the Tobol; from it they are transported over a tract of about four hundred versts by land to the Tchussovaiya, out of this into the Kamma, and then into the Volga; from which they go, through the sluices at Vishney-Volotshok, into the Volkhof, and out of that into the Ladoga lake; from which they lastly, after having completed a journey through two quarters of the globe, arrive in the Neva at the place of their destination. This astonishing transport becomes still more interesting by the reflection that these products conveyed hither from the neighbourhood of the north-eastern ocean, tarry here but a few weeks, in order then to set out on a second, perhaps greater voyage: or after being unshipped in distant countries, return hither under an altered form; and, by a tedious and difficult navigation, come back to their native land. How many scythes of the siberian boors* may have gone this circuit.

3/2 Roads in Germany

WILLIAM JACOB, *Report . . . to the Board of Trade respecting the Agriculture and the Trade in Corn* (London, 1828), pp. 363-364.

The state of roads in countries which export corn deserves attention when, calculating the cost of production, less on account of the slow pace of travelling on them, than on account of the small quantity of corn which each team of horses can draw. Thus, for instance, in England, the usual load of a waggon with four horses is ten quarters of wheat, weighing about 4,800 lb, whereas in the districts, the roads of which are noticed in this report,† the usual load is not more than half that weight. . . .

It may not be amiss here to introduce the calculation furnished by a very enlightened and accurate gentleman.

This proprietor and excellent cultivator of a good estate in Mecklenburg,

* See Glossary.

† *i.e.* the south shores of the Baltic. (Ed.)

gives the following calculation, grounded on the real cost of his expenses of conveyance, on an average of 5 years.

The estate in question is distant 5 German, or 24 English miles, from the market-place to which its surplus corn must be carried.

The regular load on this estate for a waggon with 4 horses is 2,400lb. weight, or 40 Rostock sheffels of rye, being nearly equal to 45 imperial bushels, of 53lb. weight; but for the subsistence of the cattle backwards and forwards, 180lb., or about 3 bushels and a half, of the corn must be carried, and deducted from the quantity to be sold, which will then be 41½ bushels.

The expenses in money, on each journey, on an average of the last five years, for the keep and wages of the men, and various small incidents, is found to amount to 4*s.* 8*d.*; and the value of the corn carried for the horses, at the price of the place where, if not consumed, it would have been delivered for sale, taken at 3*s.* the bushel, amounts to 10*s.* 6*d.*, thus making a deduction of 15*s.* 2*d.* on 41½ bushels.

	s.	*d.*
The amount, then, of the 41½ bushels, at 3*s.*, is	124	6
Cost of conveyance, in money and corn	15	2
Net produce	109	4

The expenses of conveyance thus amount to somewhat more than 13 per cent. on the sum which the cultivator receives for his rye.

No additional charge is made in the statement for the wear and tear of carriages, harness, or cattle, nor any for the loss of the manure made by the horses, for the interest on the capital which is invested in cattle and implements, and gradually diminished in value; nor is any notice taken of the expense of maintaining the horses and men for those portions of their time, when by inclement weather, or other circumstances, they are doomed to remain in a state of inactivity.

3/3 Tolls in Germany

T. HODGSKIN, *Travels in the North of Germany: describing the present State of the Social and Political Institutions in that country; particularly in the Kingdom of Hanover* (2 vols., Edinburgh, 1820), II, pp. 193-201. (G.P.J.)

There are no less than twenty-two tolls on the Weser betwixt Münden and Bremen, seven of which belong to the sovereign of Hannover. . . . At every toll every vessel is stopped and her whole cargo examined. On an average, more than one hour is employed at each toll to examine each vessel; so that every one loses one whole day in passing between these two towns. This is mere waste, a loss of times to all the parties, more injurious probably than the duties which the merchants have also to pay. I have been informed that not one of these sovereigns who levy these tolls, except the King of Prussia, has ever employed one farthing of the money thus collected in clearing the river. . . . It is said the expence of collecting the tolls equals the receipts. . . .

On the Leine, about twenty-four vessels capable of carrying eighty tons each, though they are seldom more than half loaded, pass and repass in a year between the towns of Bremen and Hannover. They are about sixty miles apart, and there are no less than five tolls in this distance. . . . On the average each vessel has to pay in descending the river about 200 Thalers, or more than £30 Sterling. In ascending the charge is double. . . .

Similar tolls and impediments are known to exist on every river of Germany. . . . The cargo of the raft on which I passed from Munich to Vienna was nothing but trees, deals and three bales of goods; yet we were frequently detained both in Bavaria and Austria for hours to have it examined. Boats whose cargoes were more complicated than ours were sometimes detained half a day. . . .

Tolls on roads are perhaps not less numerous, though less pernicious, than tolls on rivers. The loading of a waggon is much sooner examined than the cargo of a ship . . . they are in general domanial tolls, the produce of which goes into the pocket of the sovereign, and he repairs the road or not as he pleases. I do not know what number of these may anywhere exist, but I can state that in Hannover they are numerous and rigidly levied. . . . Such domanial tolls are common on all the roads of Germany, and in some parts they belong to nobles. . . . Tolls are generally heavier for foreigners, under which term is included the subjects of other German powers, than for natives; and sometimes it appears that the sovereigns cannot agree on the conditions under which their respective subjects may be allowed to traverse the dominions of each other. Thus, the post which ought to go from Bremen direct through Oldenburg to Embden, a distance of seventy miles, goes all round by Osnabrück, which is at least twice as far; and it requires three days, without employing a messenger expressly for the purpose, to convey a letter from one of these two towns to the other. . . .

Let any person conceive what would be the effect on the commerce of the Thames if there were twenty tolls between London Bridge and the Nore, and that every vessel . . . had to stop and be examined at every one of those tolls, and he may know accurately the extent of the impediments which the water tolls of the sovereigns of Germany throw in the way of the commerce of the country. . . . Let any person further conceive custom-houses placed at the border of every county in England, custom-house officers examining every loaded waggon . . . and he may then also know accurately the impediments which the land-tolls of the sovereigns throw in the way of commerce.

3/4 Trade on the Canal du Midi

F. ANDREOSSY, *Histoire du canal du Midi* (Paris, 1800), pp. 281-284. (Ed. Tr.)

The main seasons for transport on the canal du Midi are the periods leading up to the Fair of Beaucaire, which begins on the 4th thermidor [22 July] and lasts eight days; and towards the times of the two Fairs of Bordeaux which last 15 days each, the first of which begins on the 25 vindémiaire [15 October] and the second, on the 11th ventôse [1 March].

The merchandize brought from Bordeaux by the Garonne river consists of dye-woods and medicine-woods, salt, fish, tobacco leaf from Holland and coffee and sugar from America, of the last of which at present there is none because of the war. But in peace-time this last branch of trade was greatly increased after it was no longer diverted by the customs of Valence, which forced the merchandize to by-pass the canal, which was its natural route, and to proceed instead to Lyons and neighbouring areas via the mountains of Auvergne.

Grain loaded between Toulouse and Carcassonne, forms the main commodity transported on the canal du Midi; it provides two-thirds of its revenue.

From Cette a large quantity of wines and spirits are exported, which the Swedes, the Danes, the Hamburgers and the Ligurians carry to their own countries and to Russia, Prussia and the Hanse cities.

The main imports consist of olive oil of all qualities from Liguria, of herbs, cork, wood for making barrels and for dyes, brought by the Spaniards to France, and soap from Marseilles and other merchandise like drugs, spices, etc. from the Levant. Since salt has become a free merchandize, the consumption of it has doubled, and the revenue from its transport by the canal increased in proportion. It is above all through the port of Agde that the departments of the Bouches-du-Rhône, Alpes-Maritimes and Mont Blanc are supplied with sugar, coffee, dye-woods and other objects from America, sent via Bordeaux and the canal. From the same point grain, wine and spirits are also sent, either to the merchants of these departments or to Liguria, as well as military and naval munitions required by the army of the Republic and her allies.

The only article of grain which was sent from Agde during the seven months beginning with Brumaire, year VIII* amounted to 400,000 quintals.†

* October-November 1799. (Ed.) † See Glossary.

The major part of the commodities entering by the port of Agde consists of oil and soap from Genoa and the surrounding countryside, of products of the Levant, of French wines and fruit, and of raw materials such as wool, cotton, etc. for the factories of the southern Departments.* The port of Nouvelle handles the same types of merchandize as the ports of Agde and Cette.

3/5 The Market of Pesth

J. G. ELSNER, *Ungarn durchreiset, beurtheilet und beschrieben* (2 vols., Leipzig, 1840), I, pp. 44-51. (Ed. Tr.)

Let us now return to the banks of the river and continue our walk. Below the bridge, downriver, we see the steamer 'Kaiser Franz', arrived from Semlin. There are always fewer passengers from there than from Vienna, which is not surprising, but there are more goods on board. The speed of transport, as well as the freight charges which are on the whole not much higher, ensure that steamers are preferred to other vessels. For with the rapid flow of the Danube the latter have to be pulled upstream by horses. A great number of these are needed, and even if they are cheap, as the cost of their fodder is low, the increase in costs is considerable. In addition, much time is lost, while for many commodities speed is important. . . .

If we now proceed from the bridge along the right-hand bank of the river, we come upon a milling mass of people through which we can advance only with difficulty. We choose a morning for our walk. I can paint the picture which meets our eyes here only with a few strokes of the brush, and would need much more space than I have available to do full justice to it. The space between the water's edge of the Danube and the first row of houses is about 10 fathoms wide. Along the middle of it a solid line of waggons is formed, quite impenetrable, but with occasional passages. Here are the peasants who have brought their produce to market, unhitching their horses, tethering them to the waggons and throwing them some fodder, often bivouacking day and night, living quite off their own. Everything that can be found in the markets for fruit, vegetables, poultry or other produce is found here together. Between August and October an important commodity is the melon (the water and sweet varieties). They are stacked up in large pyramid-shaped heaps, of which I have counted up to 80, not including the smaller quantities offered for sale here and there from the waggons. If we ask where all these quantities which are always being renewed, disappear to, we are answered: they are consumed by the people. The incredibly low price at which they are sold (melons weighing 4 to 5 lb at 11-15 kr. W.W., *i.e.*

* See Glossary

5-6 kr. Conv. M.)* ensures that the Jew boy can buy them as easily as the most respectable gentleman, and that peasant lads can be met with everywhere in their tattered clothes, eating sweet melons. The soldiers also eat not a few. Habit and a glass of wine consumed afterwards may obviate the ill consequences, which such consumption would otherwise be likely to entail.

Let us fight our way through the crowds around the parked waggons. Here the purchases of food are made. Vegetables, fruit, cheese, bacon, poultry and a mass of similar goods are set out, and all around are housewives and maidservants, quarrelling and bargaining over the products on offer. We can hear them arguing in three languages: here in German, there in Hungarian, and there again in the Slavonic tongue. The calm and patience of the horses and oxen tethered to the waggons are to be admired, they are quite oblivious of the pushing and shoving going on around them, and consuming their hay with philosophic calm. Of course, they are not among the best-fed specimens, and consist largely of skin and bones. For despite the rich soil of Hungary, it does not yield anything like the produce it could easily bring forth, if it were worked with intelligence and application. On one side, close to the houses, a few pedlars have set up their stalls and offer their wares with loud cries to the passers-by. . . .

Beside all this the Danube has to be imagined flowing past, alive with craft, some of which arrive to increase the market, others leaving with large numbers of people who have finished their business and are hurrying home.

Following the river further down, the crowds gradually thin out, and we meet merely the arriving and departing waggons, as well as individuals wandering along the river bank. Here we have the leisure to turn left into the town and to inspect the fish market. . . . The Danube yields a harvest as varied as the Seine, so that the fish market here is as richly supplied as the one there.

The last object in our picture is the salt depot. . . . A train of waggons is about to arrive from Szolnok on the Theiss river, loaded with rock salt. All the vehicles appear to have been cast in the same mould. They are small, short, of about six-foot length, with low laddered sides scarcely one ell high and low wheels, pulled by two or three horses each; they all crowd around to be dealt with quickly. At Szolnok their salt has been weighed out to them, certified in a note which they have to deliver here. A balance erected in the open checks the weight. If the load is short, a deduction is made from the carter's wage, but this happens only rarely. It is bad for these carters if they are caught in the rain. In that case, though some allowance may be made on delivery of the salt, yet it may happen that the shortage is noted and a deduction made. As soon as the salt is delivered and signed for, they receive

* I.e. *c.* ½d a pound (Ed.). See Glossary.

their payment, for which they also crowd eagerly, so that there is a constant jostling and shouting going on.

It is well known that Pesth is the centre of the commercial traffic of the whole of Hungary with all its attached provinces. The peculiarities of the conditions of this country would alone give a special shape to this commerce, even if the variety of its inhabitants and the wealth of its produce had not done so already. In more developed countries, as for example Germany, France, or England, there is an internal exchange in trade and industry, as in a living body, and only what is lacking is imported, and the surplus exported. In Hungary it is quite different. This country sends most of its raw products abroad, has them worked up there and, as far as it needs them, imports them again. As a result, its commercial relations develop quite differently from the other countries named. They become more broken down into simpler components. Vast depots of raw materials are required, for they are nearly all produced on a large scale. Let us take wool as an example. The mass available, and the consequent easy oversupply of the market depresses the price frequently, to the great gain of the buyers. Thus it is easily explained how it comes about that enterprising foreigners, particularly the Germans, have in the past made and are still now making quick fortunes, and it is evident how the Jews, partly as jobbers and intermediaries, partly as jumped-up merchants, are enabled to amass riches rapidly, especially since their natural talents are speculative and quickly grasp the advantages of the situation. Just as the raw products of the country are collected in huge depots, so are the products of handicraft and industry. It is here that nearly all the merchants and shopkeepers of all the smaller towns of Hungary obtain their supplies, and their demand is substantial since, as is well known, the towns are considerable distances apart and set in the midst of well-populated villages. Even if the latter are a good few miles from the nearest market towns, yet their inhabitants have to visit them to buy all their necessaries. This happens particularly at the annual fairs, when the towns are always overcrowded. From all this it must follow that the import and export trade of Pesth is most extensive and is bound to be very profitable.

Apart from the large wool depots there are others for other natural products of the country. Wax, honey, bacon, wine, potash, etc., are all being brought here in large quantities and collected for export. Hungary's wines are well enough known and are sometimes esteemed too highly, but usually too little. For the latter, the carelessness with which they are treated, and the frequent dishonesty towards the customers, are responsible. . . .

There is much elegance and good taste in the display of goods of skilled craft and luxury. This is in most laudable imitation of Vienna, and it has succeeded so well that it is possible to find as much entertainment and pleasure here as there, even after hours of gazing at shop windows, containing so much of the beautiful, the artistic and the splendid, displayed with so much artistry and good taste. How many cities of Northern and Eastern Germany are still far behind in this respect!

Considering that the largest part of these commodities have been imported from abroad, mainly from Vienna, so that costs of transport and customs duties have had to be met, it is astonishing that they are being sold at a price which only slightly exceeds their price at their place of manufacture. This can be understood only by considering how large and rapid is the demand, and how many foreign trading firms have their agents here, so that they merely add on the two items of costs mentioned, and apart from these, which do not weigh heavily on individual goods, they sell at the same prices as at home.

In the commodities imported from abroad also, several large merchants have made good bargains and have enriched themselves.

3/6 The Fair of Nijni-Novgorod

American Consular Reports, 1870, pp. 340–344: GEO. T. ALLEN, Consul in Moscow, 31 March 1870.

Nijni-Novgorod, or Lower Nijni, as distinguished from Novgorod the Great, is at the confluence of the Volga and Oka Rivers, in latitude 56° 30′ north, 273 miles by rail nearly due east from Moscow. It has ordinarily a population of 40,000, which is increased to 150,000 or 200,000 during the fair, and is the chief city of the province. . . .

From the top of the tower of Minin a very grand panorama is presented. The fair is spread before you, like a city of shops, on a triangular tongue of land, between the Volga and Oka Rivers, which can be seen for many miles, with their many steamers. The forest of masts on the Oka looks like a vast floating town. The numerous barges, arriving from the most distant parts of the empire, will be seen below discharging and receiving their cargoes by aid of an army of Tartars. In another direction will be seen the arched gateways, whitewashed towers, and crenellated walls of the kremlin; while the green, blue, yellow, and brown roofs of the houses below, pressing through the green foliage of many gardens, during the summer fair, afford charming diversity to the view. . . .

The great fair opens annually on the 27th of July and closes on the 22nd of September, N. S., and may be most advantageously seen during the last week of August. The realities of this fair, including clouds of dust, unpaved, and often muddy, streets, the temperature sometimes tropical, and a population unattrative in appearance, form a repulsive contrast to the panorama previously enjoyed. An American would be disappointed in not meeting here crowds of gorgeously dressed Asiatics, after reading what has been written on the subject by many travelers; for he will see neither Chinese, Kamschatkans, nor Asiatic Esquimaux; Persians, Armenians and Tartars, in small numbers, being usually the only Asiatics in attendance. It is not, however, so much the types of the people met here as the extent and nature of the trade that would attract the attention of the stranger, for here we see a rude and ancient form of buying and selling that the introduction and extension of railroads, and the establishment of banks and credit, will soon tend to render obsolete. Here iron that was brought from Siberia at an immense expense, over bad roads, in awkward carts, or floated down narrow tributaries to the Ural, the Kama, or the Volga, in clumsy barges, and, perhaps, to be sold to dealers who live within a few miles of the place where it was produced, is stored in shops that extend a mile, and in which no other article is sold. Custom compels the manufacturer to offer his goods to the public at established markets and at certain seasons of the year, involving a great loss of time in slow travelling, and greatly adding to the cost of the goods. Sales being periodical and at long intervals, purchasers are forced to buy very large stocks at these times, and they, therefore, demand one or two years' credit, and this also augments the price to the consumer. Trade is very tenacious of old customs, and railroads have not yet either interrupted, injured, or modified the business of this fair, simply because they have only been extended east as far as Nijni. . . .

The house of the local governor is in the center of the fair, and the lower story of his residence is converted into a bazaar for the sale of manufactured goods and fancy articles of European production; yet the stalls of hardware from Tula, of silks from Persia, of precious stones and curiosities from Bohkara and other parts of Central Asia, and of geological specimens and cut stones from Siberia, make it really the cosmopolitan center of the mart.

A boulevard extends from the rear of the official residence to the cathedral, the Tartar mosque and the Armenian church, all of which stand in tolerant, and, therefore, in laudable juxtaposition. The shops of silversmiths, jewelers, drapers, furriers, and drysalters, line the boulevard, and the plate and silver ornaments are curious and beautiful, and travelers usually purchase small articles as souvenirs. Behind the shops of the boulevard is the 'Chinese Row,' characterized by its Chinese architecture. The tea trade is less flourishing than it was before the prohibition to import sea-borne tea, which now stocks the market, was removed. This trade is now in a transition state, the land-carriage and the sea borne tea traffic opposing each other and alternately triumphing. Much depends upon the relative quantities offered for sale, the prices being forced down one year by excessive importation of the previous one, and they are apt to rise the next because of short supply. In the progress of time, Canton and water-carriage will triumph, notwithstanding the groundless prejudices against the pernicious effects of salt air on this delicate article, until railroads will have been extended from Nijni to the tea regions of the Orient. The Russians are great tea-drinkers and are accustomed to the better qualities of tea from northern China; but these are as easily obtained from Canton as from Kiakhta. The Kiakhta tea, after crossing Asia to Perm on the Kama River, is forwarded thence by water down the Kama and up the Volga. There are several teas that seldom, if ever, enter the American or English trade, viz: the yellow and the brick teas. The former has a delicious fragrance and is very pale; it is passed around after dinner in the place of coffee, but is injurious to the nerves if frequently and freely enjoyed. The brick tea is thus named because it is pressed into the shape of a brick in its curing. This forms the drink of the Kalmucks and Kirghizes of the Steppe.* The best yellow tea sells for about 35 English shillings a pound, and is put up in very pretty Chinese boxes.

The wharves are more than ten miles long, and will amply reward the labor of a thorough inspection. Every stranger will feel interested in observing the gangs of sturdy Tartars as they unload the almost mediaeval boats, laden with grain, hides, wooden boxes, water-melons, wine-skins from the Caucasus, madder, and cotton from Bokhara, and with nearly every description of goods that the earth yields and the industry and ingenuity of man produce.

The huge and clumsy steamers that have long been in use here for towing vessels are being rapidly replaced by steam-tugs, and the many fine steamers now employed on the Volga remind one of American rivers. There are now more than four hundred steamers engaged in the trade of this stream, and most of these were built in England and Belgium. Some were brought here in pieces and put up at Nijni; others were carefully piloted to the Volga through the seas, lakes, rivers, and canals, which so unite as to furnish an uninterrupted fluvial intercourse throughout European Russia. The first war vessel built in this empire was launched at Nijni, in the seventeenth century, by a company of Dutch merchants, who had obtained permission to open trade with Persia and India, through the Caspian Sea.

The outskirts of the fair are quite as interesting a study as the interior. The continued succession of drojkies† carts, and queer wagons, in long lines; the busy throngs of strange-looking laborers; the knots and concourses of earnest, long-bearded traders; the itinerant venders of liquid refreshments – principally tea – and white rabbit-skins; the filthy, lazy monks, collecting

* The brick is a black tea. (Footnote in original source.)
† See Glossary.

kopecks of the faithful; the legion of squalid beggars, living upon what they beg or steal, usually from foreigners, all attest the importance of Nijni during the fair.

The sales of a single exposition represent more than £16,000,000 sterling in value, transacted by 150,000 to 200,000 traders, engaged in thus exchanging the produce and manufactures of Europe for those of Asia. The bakers are compelled to report daily the amount of bread they sell, and a rough estimate is thus made of the attendance.

Cured fish are sold at Nijni in immense quantities. The annual sales of sturgeons caught in the Volga exceed 2,500,000 rubles, and as many as 30,000 barrels of caviare, or fish eggs, have been shipped from Astrakhan per annum. The sterlet, one of the finest fishes in the world, is very abundant in the Volga.

Two other fairs than the one I have attempted to describe are held at Nijni-Novgorod, one in January, on the ice, and the other in July. The former is devoted to the sale of wooden-wares, and the latter to that of horses. Great numbers of people attend at such times from the neighboring villages. . . .

. . . The completion of the railroad from St. Petersburg, in the north, and of the one from Odessa, in the south, to Moscow; the certainty of the completion of that from Dünaburg, on the line from Berlin to St. Petersburg, through Smolensk to Moscow, during the summer of 1870, and the extension of a road from Moscow to Nijni, completed in 1864, have benefited the Nijni fair, by rendering it possible for traders and manufacturers throughout Europe to forward to it goods and machinery that would not have reached it in any other way, and by enabling thousands of merchants and travelers to attend it who would otherwise have been deterred from undertaking so long, tedious, difficult, and dangerous a journey.

The Russian government has now surveyed two lines for railroads eastward from Nijni through Siberia, and it is supposed that one if not both of these will be speedily built; but those who must decide this question are declared to be deterred from prosecuting these enterprises through fear of annihilating the ancient and time-honored institution of Nijni. . . .

No one doubts that the completion of a railroad eastward from Nijni through Siberia would remove the necessity for continuing such a fair and cause it to die of inanition, and the question now agitated is, will the government of Russia be more benefited by perpetuating the fair at Nijni than by opening to commerce and travel the *terra incognita* of interior and eastern Siberia, in spreading throughout Asiatic Russia such a net-work of railroads as is now demanded by the interests of civilization everywhere.

3/7 Austrian Trading Companies and Commercial Policy

FRIEDRICH NICOLAI, *Beschreibung einer Reise durch Deutschland und die Schweiz im Jahre 1781* (8 vols., Berlin and Stettin, 1783–1796), IV, pp. 402–409. (Ed. Tr.)

In order to facilitate the Imperial Board of Commerce's task of increasing trade, it was thought necessary to create large artificial powers, in proportion to the weight of the trade. As a result, trading companies were set up at once, no fewer than six in number:

(1) The Fiume Company, which was to exchange sugar for goods from the hereditary Hapsburg lands.
(2) The Temesvar Company, which was to trade to Italy, Spain and France with Hungarian corn, potash and wool. The capital was 1 million Gulden.*
(3) The Janoschaz Company, which was to sell the same goods to Turkey. Capital, 800,000 Gulden.
(4) The Bohemian Linen Company of Vienna, which was to export Bohemian linen via Trieste and Cadiz to America. Capital 1 million Gulden.
(5) The Egypt Company of Vienna, which was to increase industry in particular, by promising to export Austrian manufactures to Asia and as far as Egypt, and import in exchange only raw materials which could be worked up at home.
(6) The Kilianova Company at the mouth of the Danube, on the Black Sea.

Efforts were made, in view of these far-reaching opportunities for trade, to found also a large number of factories and manufactories. Of course, large scale trade which is to be of benefit to the State cannot develop until industry has been created first. Industry must be the mother of useful trade, as well as the mother of the circulation of money. But they did not think as far ahead in those days. They held the generally accepted, but so little examined, view: 'that in order to keep the money at home, it was necessary to grow and produce everything yourself'. Thus, whoever wanted to undertake anything of that kind, was welcome and received an advance. The Emperor Francis I, it is well known, was himself very keen on trading ventures on his own account. The great nobles followed his example. Titled gentlemen thronged to the largest factories and manufactories wanting to get rich quick; and they accepted merchants either as partners or as managers of the manufactories; a type of administration of manufactures which I think on the whole (there are occasional single exceptional cases) is equally harmful to the State as is the practice of nourishing the desire among the merchant class to enter the nobility, which is also all too common in Austria. The

* See Glossary.

businesses of the merchant and the manufacturer have to be carried on with freedom, consideration, frugality and above all industry. That is how, Nuremberg and Augsburg flourished and flourish still. But every trading or industrial town in which work is begun without those mercantile qualities, or in which one of them is lost later, will go under like Florence and Antwerp. If a merchant of good sense is to run a manufactory with the capital of a noble partner, and the latter demands measures which his whim or the counsel of his boon companions dictates; how can the former act freely following his own opinions? If a merchant enters the ranks of the nobility, then the luxury and the circumstances of his higher status will, in four cases out of five, prevent the frugality if not the industry in the second generation, so necessary for carrying on business. On the other hand the nobility has, according to the present Constitution of the State, its special relationship to the sovereign, to whose service it is particularly devoted, and to the State, as landowners. Without landed estates which remain in the family the nobility may be brilliant, but never lasting. The merchant can only perform his supreme duty, the advancement of industry, with perfect application, he will be happiest himself and most useful to the State, if he is satisfied in his own mind with his status, and is willing to work within it to extend his field as far as he can. Since, according to the present Constitution, the distinctions among the estates are indispensable, it is not the same thing to be the first in ones own estate, or the last in another.

But I return to the factories started in Austria. Not all of them had the hoped-for success, as is not uncommon in over-hasty enterprises. In order to favour them, foreign goods were prohibited in 1764; and since they still refused to blossom forth, the prohibitions were finally enlarged in 1769 and 1770 to the point where nearly everything from abroad was banned, including commodities which, as was soon evident, they could not or would not do without. However much they believed to have proved to themselves that the prohibition of all imports would allow home industry to reach the highest peak, they soon had to take off some of the import prohibitions again. Now all imports were permitted, since they could not be provided in sufficient quantities at home, but they were burdened by heavy duties. . . . in the Edict of 14 October 1774. In this edict it is further ordered, that if any exported goods are re-imported, they shall be regarded as of foreign origin and accordingly pay the high duty or be prohibited, as the case may be. Such regulations, which one finds in other countries also, must necessarily be very troublesome to the calculations of the merchant, who is supposed to advance native industry by his exports. But, it may be said, otherwise smuggling cannot be prevented. Very well. But can it be prevented at all? And is not the remedy worse than the evil, if the high duties call smuggling into being?

(for the more a man without property may gain by smuggling, the more he is likely to be drawn into it) – and if, in order to prevent smuggling, one prevents trade also?

In 1775 a new tariff and new customs laws were published. As well as a high imports duty, all commodities also carry a high export duty which must surely often interfere with trade. Transit duties are still fairly moderate. There is also a special frontier duty at Engelhartszell; and in Vienna all consumption goods carry a special duty according to a separate tariff, as well as city tax and manorial tax. Ships pay duties, whenever they tie up in Vienna. Among large ships, this is calculated according to their length, thus a skiff from Hockenau or Kolb pays 20 Xr.* per shoe up to 10 shoe, then 30 Xr. One of Kellheim pays 10 Xr. per shoe up to 10, over 10, 15Xr. Imported building timber is charged, e.g. double posts 3 Fl. 12 Xr. per pound, hardwood double posts 5 Fl. per pound, roof slats 20 Xr. a pound, square slats 26 Xr. per pound. Presumably these are ships' pounds or something similar. . .

But what then was the success of the great measures taken for the benefit of trade and industry? – If a foreigner judges about measures, as they deserve, no matter how useless they are, or even if he omits to praise them; then in all parts of Germany this will be put down to envy, ill-will, or I don't know what. So little are we Germans, who so often boast about our truthfulness, yet used to hear the truth. – I shall therefore talk about the success in the words of the sensible and impartial Austrian patriot, Mr. v.W: 'Finally, all credit was lost by the merchant class. – The manufacturers' stocks piled up, in many packs, unwanted and unused, in vaults and depots. The shareholders of the trading companies received no dividends. – In a word, all these great enterprises failed; the fortunes hoped for disappeared into the mist; and more than half of those fortunes which were ventured were swallowed up by the sea'.†

3/8 French Privileges for Traders to the Baltic

Arrêt du Conseil d'État du Roi, qui accorde différentes faveurs au commerce du Nord; 25 September 1784 (Paris 1784). (Ed. Tr.)

The King wishing to aid the Northern commerce of his subjects: having heard the report of Calonne, Councillor to the Royal Council, Controller

* See Glossary.

† It is said that the various experiments cost the Imperial-Royal Exchequer some 500,000 Gulden, a sum which may be looked upon as large or moderate. Acc. to Mr Büsching, the Treasury of the Imperial-Royal Board of Commerce had in 1770 an income of 1,194,940 Fl. and an expenditure of 1,080,390 Fl. (Footnote in original source.)

General of the Finances; His Majesty, being in his Council, has ordered and orders the following:

Article 1 The victuals necessary for the provisioning of vessels destined for Northern commerce shall be exempt from all export duties on the taking of an excise bond, which shall be issued by the Consuls or Vice-Consuls of France, in the Northern ports where the King maintains Consuls, or by municipal officers in those parts where Consuls are not maintained, on the understanding that the said exemption on wines and spirits shall be limited to 1 pint of wine or 2 pints of beer or cider and a $\frac{1}{4}$ pint of brandy, Paris measure, for each crew member, for each day that the Chamber of Commerce in the province of the port of departure estimates for the duration of the voyage; any surplus of the said wines and spirits shall pay export duties.

Article 2 Northern merchandize carried by French vessels into French ports where the entrepôt police is established, on justification of their origin, shall enjoy the said entrepôt for a period of six months and in the said term of six months such goods may be re-exported without payment of any duty.

Article 3 For four years, bounties shall be paid to the Captains or owners of the French boats which ply the Northern commerce. For the first year the bounties shall be calculated from the day of publication of the present Arrêt, at the rate of 10 livres* for each port tonnage of the boat, when the said boats have been registered with a French house established in the Baltic; and similarly 5 livres per ton when they have been registered with a French house in a German sea-port or a North Sea port.

The second year, the said duties . . . shall be 6 livres per ton for the Baltic Sea and 3 livres per ton for the German or North Sea.

In the third year they shall be 4 livres per ton for the Baltic Sea and 2 livres per ton for the German or North Sea.

In the fourth year they shall be 3 livres per ton for the Baltic and 1 livre 10 sous for the German or North Sea.

When the merchandize carried by a French boat has been sent to a French house, the said bounties shall be paid on the return of the said ships, on the certificate of the appropriate Consul, by the Receiver General of Farms.

Article 4 When the boats carrying out the trade have not dealt with a French house the said duties shall be reduced by a half.

Ordered in the Council of State of the King, His Majesty being there, held at Versailles, 25 September 1784; signed Le Mal de Castries.

* See Glossary.

3/9 New French Company of the Indies

Arrest du Conseil d'État du Roi, portant Établissement d'une nouvelle Compagnie des Indies; 14 April 1785 (Paris, 1785). (Ed. Tr.)

(Extract from the Registers of the Council of State).

The King . . . as a result of the accounts given to him of the behaviour of exports from his kingdom and imports from Asia since the suspension of the privilege of the Company of the Indies has recognized that competition, which is beneficial in other branches of commerce, could only result in injuring this particular trade; indeed experience indicated that European cargoes which were neither co-ordinated nor related to the needs of the places to which they were sent sold at low prices, whilst competition of His Majesty's subjects in the markets of the Indies raised the price of local goods; on the other hand imports, which were characterized by an abundance of some goods and a complete absence of others, served the interests neither of the merchants nor the Kingdom. On consideration that to these inconveniences, which arise through lack of co-ordination, is added the absence of sufficiently large resources among individuals to sustain the hazards of distant commerce and the long-term loans it necessitates, His Majesty has been convinced that it was only a privileged company with resources, credit and special protection, which could profitably conduct trade with the Indies and China; consequently His Majesty has accepted the proposition, put forward by a group of merchant capitalists, whose ability, zeal and intelligence are known to him, enabling it to exploit for a limited period of time, the commerce of Asia. . . . Since the principal causes of the losses suffered by the former company resulted from political problems, expenses of government and an over-complicated administration, it seemed proper that the new company should be freed entirely from such burdens, that nothing should divert its resources from commercial ends, and that it should be ruled completely by its own interested parties; at the same time, His Majesty has concerned himself with the means of preserving for the kingdom all the advantages compatible with the exercise of the privilege; His Majesty has granted them the trade to and from India, the slave trade, the free exchange of their produce with European goods and everything which seemed necessary to guarantee the provision and support of this deserving colony. Having heard the report of Calonne, Councillor Ordinary to the Royal Council, Controller General of the Finances, the King, being in his Council, has ordered and orders the following:

Article 1 The privilege of the Company of the Indies and China, which had been suspended by the Arrêt of the Council of State of 17 August 1769, shall not affect the said Company since His Majesty wishes that the new company, founded with his consent for trade with Asia, shall be substituted for seven peace-time years in the exercise of the said privilege and that it shall enjoy it under the same name. . . .

Article 14 His Majesty forbids all his subjects, within the period of the exclusive privilege of the said Company, to trade with the centres included in the said privilege under penalty of confiscation, for his profit, of the warehouses engaged in such trade and of their merchandize, arms, munitions and other effects. . . . His Majesty also wishes that all goods from places included in the exclusive privilege of the Company, which come to France in boats other than those owned by the Company or those chartered by the Company, be confiscated for his profit.

Article 15 All the operations of the said Company shall be directed and administered by twelve administrators, approved by His Majesty, who shall be obliged to conform to the decisions reached by discussion in the General or Special Assemblies and to establish the soundest and most economical management of the Company.

Article 16 The funds which are needed to carry out this exclusive privilege, granted by the present decree, amount to 20 million, 6 million of which shall be provided by the twelve administrators, in the form of 500,000* livres each or 500 shares of 1,000 livres each; the remaining 14 millions shall be divided into 14 thousand shares of 1 thousand livres denomination, for which certificates shall be granted to those who wish to take a financial interest in the Company.

Article 24 The administrators shall publish every year, starting in 1787, the general balance sheet of the Company's business, after which they shall remit it to the General Controller of Finances. . . .

Article 26 The general administration of the Company's business shall be established in Paris, in a building specially designated for this purpose, which His Majesty shall grant free of charge to the Company for its meetings and offices during the term of the privileges.

Article 31 His Majesty shall protect and defend the Company if necessary to the extent of using force to maintain its commercial privileges . . . he shall provide it at all times with the officers and sailors it requires.

Article 35 His Majesty grants and allows the said Company, for the duration of its privilege, the free use in the Eastern ports, of buildings,† warehouses, cellars, shipyards, ropeyards, workshops, lighters, implements and port facilities and other buildings and loading berths necessary for the construction, repair, fitting out and arming of its own boats, or those which it charters, as well as for the receipt and disposition of its merchandise and imports and exports. His Majesty wishes that all the said buildings, bridges and workshops,

* See Glossary. † i.e. office buildings (Ed.).

etc. following the demands made upon them by the Company be immediately returned to him, after being repaired at the expense of His Majesty, who shall remain obliged to bear the cost of all major repairs, throughout the duration of the privilege of the said Company. . . .

Article 43 His Majesty guarantees the Company against all kinds of demands and claims made against it, either in Europe or in the Indies, which arise out of the privileges of the former Company of the Indies. . . .

Article 50 The said Company shall be empowered to export annually from the Kingdom the gold and silver needed for its commerce, notwithstanding the prohibitions made in the ordinances against all transport of gold and silver to foreign countries . . . but its administrators shall be obliged to inform the Controller General of Finances of the value of their annual exportation, and His Majesty, wishing to treat it favourably, also frees it from the agreement with the Fermier Général des Messageries* . . . concerning the transport of gold and silver specie . . . and allows it to conclude with the said Fermier Général such agreements as they regard as mutually convenient. . . .

Article 55 His Majesty forbids anyone, irrespective of rank or status, to load goods or merchandise or to have them loaded onto any of the Company's ships or those they have hired, which are coming from, or going to the countries with which it has concessions, without previously having them included in the loading invoices, by written permission of the administrators or customs officers . . . any infringement of which shall result in the confiscation of the goods and the dismissal of the captains and officers.

Article 57 His Majesty orders that the present decree shall be printed, published and posted in all the necessary places. . . .

Transacted at the Council of State of the King, His Majesty being present, held at Versailles, 14 April 1785; signed Le Bon de Breteuil.

3/10 Expansion of French Overseas Trade

A. ARNOULD, *De la balance du commerce et les relations commerciales extérieures de la France* (2 vols., Paris, 1791), I, pp. 299–302, 326–328. (Ed. Tr.)

At the end of Louis XIV's reign or during the first years of Louis XV's, French trade with the West Coast of Africa, in rubber, elephants' tusks and leather, increased to around 500,000 livres,* and the number of slaves bought there was perhaps 2,000, who, sold in the American Colonies, for 1,000 livres each, brought in a total sum of 2 million livres. Goods exported from France to the coast of Africa, amounted altogether to 650,000 livres.

* See Glossary.

At the time of the Revolution, French exports to the West Coast of Africa alone rose to 18 millions, more than 10 millions of which were in goods of foreign origin, particularly cotton goods, whilst 8 millions were the products of French agriculture and industry.

Today, rubber, elephants' tusks and leather brought back to France from this part of Africa have increased during 1785, 1786 and 1787 to a yearly average of approximately 14 million livres. At the time of the Revolution, *i.e.* taking the average for the years 1786, 1787 and 1788, about 30,000 black slaves were introduced into the American Colonies by French privateers; each one was sold there for 1,300 livres, French money, giving a total of 39 million, which was paid over in the form of colonial goods, the value of which was realized in Europe, according to the prevailing price of those goods in the European market.

Since the end of Louis XIV's reign, French trade with Africa has progressed beyond all expectations . . . if we concern ourselves simply with the number of black slaves seized by French privateers, before the last war, the increase is more than half.

This increase can be related partly to the interest taken by the Government since the peace of 1783 to extend and protect French establishments on the West Coast of Africa, and partly to the nature and extent of the financial encouragement provided by the Government for French privateers.

Importations into France from all our possessions, either in the Archipelago or the North American Territories, at the end of the reign of Louis XIV, increased to 16,700,000 livres. That is:

1. 11,000,000 livres of sugar and cocoa;
2. 4,081,000 livres of indigo and rocou;
3. 775,000 livres of cotton, leather, furs and approximately 200,000 livres of tobacco.

Our exports to our American possessions increased at the same time to 9 million livres; that is to say:

1. 4,160,000 livres in manufactures and finished goods;
2. 1,900,000 livres in foodstuffs;
3. 1,564,000 livres in wines and brandy;
4. 1,548,000 livres in wood, hoop iron, metals and other articles of smaller importance.

At the time of the revolution, France received from its American colonies 185,000,000 of merchandize. That is to say:

1. 134,000,000 in sugar and coffee;
2. 26,000,000 in cotton;
3. 7,600,000 livres in indigo and rocou and dyes; and
4. 10,000,000 in cocoa and ginger, etc.

3/10 *Expansion of French Overseas Trade*

Exports from France today amount to 77,900,000 livres in five principal categories:

1. 42,447,000 livres of manufactured goods;
2. 19,611,000 livres of foodstuffs, flour, vegetables, salted meat, cheeses, etc.;
3. 7,285,000 livres of wine and brandy;
4. 6,513,000 livres of wood, cask wood, hoop iron, metals, etc.

Finally, 2,057,000 livres of goods of a different kind and of less importance.

Before concentrating upon any connection between the trade of the two periods, we must recall that at the time of the Revolution France no longer possessed Canada, Louisiana nor the Isle of Granada, which belonged to the English after 1763, nor St. Bartholomew, ceded to the King of Sweden by virtue of the agreement of July 1784.

3/11 Free Trade in Grain and Internal Free Trade in France

a Edict of the King, July 1764. Printed in CHARLES SMITH, *Three Tracts on the Corn Trade and Corn Laws* (2nd ed., London, 1764), pp. 165–171.

b Arrêt of 29 August–21 September 1789, authorizing internal free trade in grain and forbidding its exportation. Printed in J. JEANNENEY and M. PERROT, *Textes de droit économique et social français, 1789–1957* (Paris, 1957), pp. 6–8. (Ed. Tr.)

c J. NECKER, *Comte rendu au Roi* (Hamburg, 1781), pp. 97–99. (Ed. Tr.)

a Translation of the *French* King's EDICT relative to the Exportation of Corn, *&c.*

EDICT of the KING.

Concerning the LIBERTY *of the* EXPORTATION *from, and* IMPORTATION *of Grain into the Kingdom.*

Given at Compeigne,* *in the month of* July, 1764.

REGISTRED IN PARLIAMENT.

LOUIS, by the grace of GOD, King of *France*, and *Navarre*, to all present and to come, Greeting;

The attention which we owe to every thing that may contribute to the welfare of our Subjects, hath induced us to give a favourable hearing to the petitions which have been addressed to us from all parts, to establish an entire Liberty in the Corn-trade, and to revoke such Laws and Regulations as have been heretofore made to restrain it within too strict bounds. After having taken the opinion of persons the best acquainted in the affair, and

* Sic in Smith. (Ed.)

having carefully deliberated in our Council. We thought it necessary to comply with the solicitations which have been made to us for the free Exportation and Importation of Corn and Meal, as proper to encourage and increase the cultivation of the most real and certain riches of a state, to maintain plenty by Magazines and the Importation of foreign Corn, to prevent Corn from being at a price which discourages the Grower, to banish Monopoly by an irrevocable exclusion of all particular permissions, and in the end, by a free and entire concurrence *or competition* in the Trade, to keep up between different Nations, that communication of exchanging superfluities for necessaries, so conformable to the order established by divine providence, and to the views of humanity which ought to animate all Sovereigns. We are convinced, that it is worthy of our continual care, for the happiness of our people, and of our justice towards the proprietors of Lands and the Farmers, to grant them a liberty which they so earnestly desire; and we have, moreover, thought it necessary to secure, by a solemn and perpetual Law, the Merchants and Traders from all fear of the return of prohibitive Laws; but to remove the fears of those who are not as yet fully convinced of the advantage which the liberty of such a commerce must produce. It seemed to us necessary to fix a price of Corn, above which, all Exportation out of the Kingdom should be prohibited, when Wheat shall have risen to that price. And as we ought not to neglect any occasion to excite industry, we have resolved to encourage at the same time the *French* navigation, by securing to *French* vessels and seamen, exclusively of all others, the carriage of Corn to be exported. For THESE CAUSES, and others moving us hereto, with the advice of our Council, and of our certain knowledge, full power and royal authority, we have by this present, perpetual, and irrevocable Edict, ordered, decreed, and ordained, ordering, decreeing, and ordaining, willing, and it is our pleasure, as follows:

I.

Our Declaration of the 25 *May*, 1763, concerning the free transportation of Corn within our Kingdom with permission to establish Magazines, together with the Letters patents, explaining the same of the 5 *March* last, shall be executed according to their form and tenor; consequently, it is our pleasure, that the said interior circulation, *shall not be in any wise obstructed.*

II.

Also, we permit all our Subjects of whatever quality and condition they may be, even the Nobility and priviledged persons, to trade in every species of Corn, Seeds, Grain, Pulse, and Meal, whether it be with natives or foreigners, and to form, for that end, such Magazines as they shall think proper, without being liable to be searched, disturbed or bound by any formalities other than those mentioned by this present Edict, nor shall the said Nobility and privileged persons be subject to any impositions by reason of such Trade *only*.

III.

It is our pleasure, to that end, that the Exportation, to foreigners, of all Corn, Seeds, Grain, Pulse, and Meal, shall be entirely free, both by land and by sea, with the exceptions and limitations only laid down by the following articles. We strictly prohibit and forbid all our officers and those of *Lords* to oppose or hinder such Importation in any wise, in any case, or under any pretence whatsoever.

IV.

The Export of Wheat, Rye, Maslin, and Meal shall not be permitted, when by sea, as to the present, untill it shall be, by us, otherwise ordered, except from the ports of *Calais*, *St. Valory*, *Dunkirk*, *Fécamp*, *Dieppe*, *le Havre*, *Rouen*, *Honfleur*, *Cherbourg*, *Caen*, *Granville*, *Morlaise*, *St. Malo*, *Brest*, *Port Louis*, *Nantes*, *Vannes*, *la Rochelle*, *Bourdeaux*, *Blaye*, *Libourne*, *Bayonne*, *Cette*, *Vendres*, *Marseilles*, and *Toulon*, and the Exportation may not be carried on but on *French* vessels, of which, the Captain and *two thirds* of the mariners at least shall be *French*, under pain of confiscation.

V.

Being desirous to provide, by the introduction of foreign Corn into our Kingdom, so that Corn may not rise to a price burthensome to our people, we permit all our subjects and all foreigners to bring freely into our Kingdom, on all kinds of Vessels without distinction, all Corn, Seeds, Grain, Meal, and Pulse, coming from abroad, paying the duties imposed by this present Edict.

VI.

In case, nevertheless, when, contrary to our expectation, and notwithstanding the reasonable hopes which the free Importation of such foreign Grain gives; the price of Wheat shall be risen to twelve livres ten sous the quintal* and upwards, in any one of the ports or places situated on the frontier of our Kingdom, and that the said price shall be kept up in the same place, for three following market days: It is our pleasure that the liberty granted by the foregoing Articles shall remain suspended in such place, absolutely, and without there being need of any new regulation. We therefore prohibit, and most expressly forbid, in the said case, all our subjects to

* About 48s. the quarter, *London* measure. (Footnote in Smith.)

*export,** or cause any Grain to be exported, from the said place, until that, upon the representations of the officers of the said place, which are to be addressed to the Controller General of our Finances, the opening of the said place hath been ordered in our Council, to the end, to re-establish there, a general and indefinite liberty for the Import and Export of Grain, without which, no particular permissions in this respect shall or may be given in any case by our Governors, Commandants, Commissaries in their departments, or other our officers.

IX.

We repeal all Edicts, Declarations, and Regulations contrary hereto, nevertheless, without making any innovation, as to the present, in the rules of the police, hitherto observed, for victualling our good City of *Paris*, which shall continue to be observed, as heretofore, untill it hath by us been otherwise ordered.

Registered, &c. in due form *at Paris, in Parliament, all the Chambers assembled*, 19 *July*, 1764. Signed *Dufranc*.

b The King, being informed of grain prices in various parts of his Kingdom, of the laws made successively for the trade in grain, and the measures which have been taken to assure the peoples' subsistence and to prevent high prices, has recognized that these measures have not met with the success which had been expected.

He has seen with the greatest satisfaction that the plans necessary to make his peoples' subsistence less dependent on the vicissitudes of the seasons are consistent with true justice, the maintainance of property rights and the just liberty of his subjects. Consequently, he has resolved to grant freedom to the internal grain trade, which he regards as the only possible means of preventing excessive irregularities in prices and the increase of the just and natural price which should characterize foodstuffs and which is determined by seasonal variations and the strength of demand.

The diversity of the seasons and differences in land create very great inequalities in production: in areas and years affected by harvest failure people are absolutely dependent either on grain brought from areas with a surplus or on that stored from previous years: thus, after production, the transport and storage of grain are the only means of preventing scarcity, because they are the only means of exchange which permit the distribution of surplus production to the needy.

This exchange, effected by the transport and storage of grain, can be

* *Export or* is not in the original. (Footnote in Smith.)

established in only two ways, either by private enterprise or by Government intervention.

Reflection and experience alike prove that free trade is the surest, promptest method of satisfying the needs of the people, and it is the least expensive and the least subject to inconvenience.

Thus the more commerce is free and brisk, the more the nation is effectively and abundantly provided for; prices are proportionately more uniform, they deviate proportionately less from the average and customary price by which wages are necessarily regulated.

Government agents, not having any interest in economy, buy more dearly, transport at greater cost, conserve with less precaution, and much grain is lost or spoilt.

Whatever methods the Government employs, whatever sums it dispenses, experience has shown that it is never able to prevent wheat from being dear when harvests are deficient. If, by coercive measures it succeeded in delaying this inevitable result, it can do it only in certain places for a very short time, and whilst it believes it is helping the country, in effect, such action only aggravates the situation.

By assuming control over the transport and storage of grain the Government can only compromise the sustenance and tranquillity of the people.

It is by trade alone, and by free trade, that harvest irregularities may be corrected.

c By His decree on tolls, Your Majesty has already indicated Your Majesty's desire to facilitate internal commerce: consequently the necessary information has been gathered to put Your Majesty in a position to carry out his wishes, as soon as the financial situation permits it; and I see in advance that success in this sphere will not require great sacrifices. There are a large number of tolls which are almost as expensive to collect as the contribution they make to income; and either as a result of this, or through a concern for public welfare, several proprietors have offered Your Majesty the gratuitous abandonment of their rights. But the entire suppression of these tolls will have only imperfect results, as long as the Kingdom, independently of its divisions into the areas of the Gabelle tax,* contains other absolutely distinct divisions, known as the Provinces of the Five Great Farms, the Provinces Reputed Foreign, and the Foreign Provinces*; divisions which require Bureaux de Visite to demand the duties levied on all goods which pass between the Provinces. It must be agreed that this situation is quite unsatisfactory; but it results from the gradual growth of the Kingdom, as well as projects which have remained unfinished either as a result of diffi-

* See Glossary.

culties which we have not known how to overcome or have not wanted to solve.

A simple and splendid plan would be to abolish all internal duties; but as the duties which are paid from Province to Province, or from one transit place to another, must be considered as duties on consumption, it will be necessary, in suppressing them, to make up the deficiency by increasing the duties on goods entering or leaving the Kingdom; to do this would be to risk real harm to our foreign trade. Thus, in concerning myself with this important subject, I felt it was necessary to begin by examining what would be the most suitable import and export tariff which reconciles political ideals with fiscal necessities: if the revenue from this tariff, once it has been perfected, did not balance with the loss of internal duties, . . . it would be necessary to make up the deficiency in some way. I am preparing various plans in this respect, in order to be ready to implement them when peace returns. But in the middle of a war, when the return on frontier duties is much less than in peace time, it would be insane to carry out such a plan.

3/12 French Views on Freedom of Trade

Declaration of principles on which France ought to conduct commercial negotiations with England, by GERARD DE REYNEVAL, to the Conseil d'État; 21 May 1786. Printed in COMTE HIS DE BUTENVAL, *Établissement en France du premier tarif général de douanes, 1787–1791* (Paris, 1876), pp. 149–151. (Ed. Tr.)

It is neither through magnanimity nor a liking for France that Mr. Pitt is disposed to brave the prejudices of his country to establish regular commercial relations with France. The fact is, that he is convinced the system of prohibition followed hitherto by England, is without real advantage for industry and commerce and prejudicial to the revenue of the Treasury.

In reflecting on the interests of France, the French Government reaches the same conclusions as Mr. Pitt.

To ensure wise negotiation, it is necessary to take certain principles as a base; we are now going to enumerate these principles.

1. The greater the amount of excess production in a country, the more it must try to increase its exports.
2. The most useful and well-established commerce is in the natural products of a country; it encourages agriculture, which consequently makes industry flourish.
3. Agriculture must assume first importance in the negotiations; if there are sacrifices to be made, they must be made in its favour.
4. It is a dangerous error to want to manufacture everything in France which

can be manufactured elsewhere; because commerce is maintained only by exchange, and these exchanges are impossible when a nation wants to give everything and to receive nothing.

5. In general, lack of competition is prejudicial because it introduces monopoly, increases the prices of goods and reduces the care taken by the manufacturer, who is too certain of his gain. It is a wise policy to admit foreign competition.

6. Any manufacture, the products of which are 10 and even 5% dearer than similar goods which enter as contraband, does not deserve to be supported, because it would require support which would be burdensome for the State, and result in a double charge on consumers.

7. The freedom of the consumer is an essential part of his happiness: he must have preference over the manufacturer and the merchant. The latter are only a very small group vis-a-vis the rest of the nation. This rule does not admit of any exception, except when the State has a major interest.

8. Protection encourages smuggling. It is, therefore, essentially vicious, since it kills legitimate commercial enterprise, and diminishes the source of public revenue instead of increasing it.

It follows that it is in our interests to make a commercial treaty with England and to export to her our agricultural surplus.

England will pay us in part with industrial goods, but as far as we are concerned, protection has destroyed neither the market nor the sale of such goods, nor our liking for them.

Apart from our wines, brandy, vinegars, and oil, etc., we can sell to England, linen cloth, cambrics, silks and our fashions; let us try to establish a fair balance of exchange between Great Britain and ourselves.

She will never compete successfully with our agricultural products, and perhaps we shall capture from her the superiority she enjoys in industrial production. Competition ensures the perfection and success of our manufactures.

Suppose this result is not attained, is it preferable to make several iron and steel manufacturers wealthy or to further the prosperity of the realm? to increase the number of manufacturers or the number of farmers? and suppose we are inundated with English iron goods, is it impossible for us to re-sell them to Spain or some other country?

Since the prohibitive system is essentially vicious and vexatious, it would be useful to adopt the opposite system. We should move closer to England, as hereafter there would no longer be any goods in which trade is prohibited between the two nations.

Your Majesty will have manifested, in a manner consistent with your greatness, your wish to bring together the two nations, and indicated a path along which it is to be presumed that one day the court of London will believe it is possible to venture, in order to destroy for ever the system of envy and hatred which has hitherto dominated all commercial arrangements between France and Great Britain.

3/13 Effects in France of the 1786 Anglo-French Commercial Treaty

Reply from the Inspector of Manufactures in Champagne to the Bureau du Commerce. Printed in *Journal of Modern History*, Vol. XI (March-December 1939), pp. 42-48. (Ed. Tr.)

Châlons sur Marne, 9 October 1788

To M. Bruyard.

Monseigneur,

Troyes, with its manufacture of cotton cloth, dimity and other linen and cotton goods, presents the most disquieting situation in this Généralité.* The demand for these goods having slackened without interruption since the month of May 1787 to the extent that exports since then have never been more than half of their customary level, merchants in the trade have suspended their purchases and have been prepared to buy only at prices which are ruinous to manufacturers, all of whom have been obliged to cut back production and several of them, lacking resources, have been reduced to becoming workmen. As a result, of the 2,600 frames engaged in this branch of production in the town and suburbs of Troyes, at the end of 1786, 1,100 remained in business, which, on the assumption that there are six workers to each frame, has resulted in 9,000 workers losing their jobs.

The cotton hosiery trade, which still forms an important branch of manufacture in Troyes, has also experienced the dreadful effects of the commercial treaty with England and shares in the distress. 200 of the 500 frames in the town and suburbs of Troyes have been dismantled in the last eighteen months, with the result that 1,200 workers are still unemployed.

People are well aware that this stagnation . . . cannot last, and that as the English goods which are sold in competition are recognized as being of inferior quality, as in effect they are, the former (goods manufactured at Troyes) will regain favour; but in the meantime it is extremely important to provide subsistence this winter for the unfortunate, unemployed workers, to prevent their leaving the area, and also to forestall the disorders which despair would induce them to commit if they were without food.

The number of workers deprived of their customary jobs through the disruption of manufacturing production at Troyes amounts to almost

* See Glossary.

10,200; but as the majority of foreign labour has returned home it is estimated that approximately 4,200 workers are in need of help.

The sale of the goods manufactured at Rheims has also been very difficult and sluggish for eighteen months, as a result of the Treaty of Commerce and the falling off in business experienced in the principal commercial towns of Spain. Production has not diminished as much as these circumstances lead us to fear it would, the manufacturers of this town generally having pooled all their resources to support the greatest proportion of their workers in the hope of better prospects in the future. The most unfortunate aspect of the problem is that manufacturers and merchants are today burdened with manufactured goods, which will result in a considerable number of businesses suspending work, if trade does not revive. At present . . . it is impossible to count more than 600 workers, for the subsistence of whom it is necessary to provide this winter.

Production at Rethel has been hit by those factors which have affected production at Rheims, but as it works up principally dauphines* and twilled material, which constituted a large profitable sale at the last Guibrai fair, a sum of 3,400 francs† that the provincial assembly has granted for the setting up of an Atelier de Charité† for the unemployed workers, appears sufficient to see them through the difficult period which lies ahead.

The manufacture of prints at Courcelles sur Blaise has been almost entirely stopped owing to the lack of suitable linen cloth because of the prohibition of the Order of Council of 10 July 1785, as a result of which approximately 150 workers are affected, whose situation will improve if the entrepreneurs are granted the request they have made to draw sufficient cloth from abroad to keep in business. . . .

The decline of business activity in the manufacturing centres of Chaumont, Wassy and Joinville, occasioned by the fall in consumption of small cotton goods which are manufactured there . . . deprives a number of workers of their livelihoods, i.e. 400 approximately at Chaumont, 200 at Wassy and 100 at Joinville, if we include the Arrondissements† of the Bureaux‡ established in these towns; but the custom which prevails among workers of returning at such times to the cultivation of their smallholdings and other work in the countryside helps them out of their difficulties.

From these details it can be estimated that there are approximately 4,800 workers in the manufactures of the Généralité of Champagne, who are utterly dependent upon public charity and Government assistance. 4,200 of these are in Troyes and 600 at Rheims.

* Small coloured, woollen articles. (Ed.) † See Glossary.

‡ The precise nature of the bureaux referred to here is not clear. . . . It is possible that bureau in this reference means simply the Central Office of an Atelier de Charité [footnote in the Journal of Modern History].

The Provincial Assembly has already earmarked 11,100 livres* for this purpose, 7,400 livres for Troyes, and 3,700 livres for Rheims, but this sum is far from sufficient.

The best way of administering this help and any supplement the Government regards as necessary would seem to lie in the opening in these two towns of Ateliers de Charité in the form of public works, to which the manufacturing workers alone would be admitted, on presenting a certificate indicating their trade. . . . This kind of help cannot be abused by the poor, who, unable to pursue their customary employment, cannot then say that they have neither work nor bread, and, moreover, it does not have the disadvantage of duplicating the work of the manufacturers and merchants, as happened . . . last year at Troyes.

Such, Monseigneur, is the result of the information which I have gathered carefully to satisfy the wishes of your letter of the 9th of last month. . . .

I am, with profound respect, Monseigneur, your very humble and very obedient servant,

Taillarda de Ste. Gemme.

* See Glossary.

Chapter 4 Banking and Finance

Introduction

By the end of the Middle Ages, many of the rising centres of commerce had developed a system of credit and of paper money in addition to coins made of precious metals and a token coinage. Institutions specializing in these monetary and credit transactions came to be known as banks, though the term included a wide variety of agencies from pawn-('lombard') and money-changing shops to important centres of international finance. All, however, were based on the needs of commerce or of public (including papal) finance, and only to a very minor extent on the needs of industry and agriculture, and all bore the marks of this origin.

Of the main types of banks which had evolved by the eighteenth century, the Bank of Amsterdam represented the most advanced. Benefiting from the sack of Antwerp and the economic decline of the Austrian Netherlands, it was based on the economic and commercial power of the Dutch, and rose with that power to become the centre of international trade and investment. The security and expediency of the method of banking evolved were of a very high order, and greatly strengthened the Dutch economy, just as later it was to decline with the decline of Dutch power (**4/1**). A similar system, on a narrower scale, had been adopted in Hamburg, another free centre of international trade and investment (**4/2**). Another kind of bank was the *Caisse d'Escompte*, dealing mainly in bills of exchange and having, like the Bank of England, as one of its main functions the raising of a loan for the King, although unlike the latter, it had no monopoly (**4/3**). The least successful banks were those based on land mortgages, though it was natural that they should be devised in countries in which land was the main source of wealth. The Russian example, typically for a country in which there were few centres of wealth, was set up with the help of the Crown (**4/4**).

In such special cases, as also in the support of certain selected industries (Chapter 2), the State might appear as an economic benefactor; but in general, the growing appetite of absolutist rulers for ever higher taxation, for mounting war expenditures, rising conspicuous consumption, and for defraying the staggering costs of collection, and servicing and paying off arrears, became increasingly harmful to economic prosperity and development. Whether levied on income and wealth, or on the movement and consumption of commodities, taxes came to be regarded as among the most irksome fetters imposed by the *ancien régime* on the productive and progressive classes, leading frequently to their utter poverty and ruin.

In France, as in some other countries, matters were made worse by the inefficiency and corruption of the method of collection, and by the glaring unfairness of incidence, including the exemption of the Church and the Nobility, and the great variety of burdens, based on long-standing traditional privileges, among the regions. A vast literature of protest arose (**4/5**, **4/6**, **4/7**, **4/8**), forming an important part of the general attack on the social and political system ruling in France. In the process, principles of fair taxation, in contemporary terms, were evolved in theory (**4/9**), and repeated attempts were made to end some of the worst abuses (**4/10**, **4/11**). In the event, however, it proved impossible to make the taxes more progressive than the system they were levied to uphold, and the opposition to the tax system merged with the other interests which finally could see no way forward but by the destruction of the whole of the *ancien régime*.

Taxes that were not only unfair, but positively harmful to economic well-being, were not found in France alone, but were found all over the Continent. An important example of such a tax was the *Alcavala* levied in Spain (**4/12**).

4/1 Bank Money: The Bank of Amsterdam

ADAM SMITH, *The Wealth of Nations* (M'Culloch ed., Edinburgh, 1863), Book IV, Chapter III, pp. 211-215.

Before 1609 the great quantity of clipt and worn foreign coin, which the extensive trade of Amsterdam brought from all parts of Europe, reduced the value of its currency about nine per cent. below that of good money fresh from the mint. Such money no sooner appeared than it was melted down or carried away, as it always is in such circumstances. The merchants, with plenty of currency, could not always find a sufficient quantity of good money to pay their bills of exchange; and the value of those bills, in spite of several regulations which were made to prevent it, became in a great measure uncertain.

In order to remedy these inconveniencies, a bank was established in 1609 under the guarantee of the city. This bank received both foreign coin, and the light and worn coin of the country at its real intrinsic value in the good standard money of the country, deducting only so much as was necessary for defraying the expense of coinage, and the other necessary expense of management. For the value which remained, after this small deduction was made, it gave a credit in its books. This credit was called bank money, which, as it represented money exactly according to the standard of the mint, was always of the same real value, and intrinsically worth more than current money. It was at the same time enacted, that all bills drawn upon or negotiated at Amsterdam of the value of six hundred guilders and upwards should be paid in bank money, which at once took away all uncertainty in the value of those bills. Every merchant, in consequence of this regulation, was obliged to keep an account with the bank in order to pay his foreign bills of exchange, which necessarily occasioned a certain demand for bank money.

Bank money, over and above both its intrinsic superiority to currency, and the additional value which this demand necessarily gives it, has likewise some other advantages. It is secure from fire, robbery, and other accidents; the city of Amsterdam is bound for it; it can be paid away by a simple transfer, without the trouble of counting, or the risk of transporting it from one place to another. In consequence of those different advantages, it seems from the beginning to have borne an agio, and it is generally believed that all the money originally deposited in the bank was allowed to remain there, nobody caring to demand payment of a debt which he could sell for a premium in the market. By demanding payment of the bank, the owner of a bank credit would lose this premium. As a shilling fresh from the mint will buy no more goods in the market than one of our common worn shillings, so the good and true money which might be brought from the coffers of the bank into those of a private person, being mixed and confounded with the common currency of the country, would be of no more value than that currency, from which it could no longer be readily distinguished. While it remained in the coffers of the bank, its superiority was known and ascertained. When it had come into those of a private person, its superiority could not well be ascertained without more trouble than perhaps the difference was worth. By being brought from the coffers of the bank, besides, it lost all the other advantages of bank money; its security, its easy and safe transferability, its use in paying foreign bills of exchange. Over and above all this, it could not be brought from those coffers, as it will appear by and by, without previously paying for the keeping.

Those deposits of coin, or those deposits which the bank was bound to restore in coin, constituted the original capital of the bank, or the whole value of what was represented by what is called bank money. At present they are supposed to constitute but a very small part of it. In order to facilitate the trade in bullion, the bank has been for these many years in the practice of giving credit in its books upon deposits of gold and silver bullion. This credit is generally about five per cent. below the mint price of such bullion. The bank grants at the same time what is called a recipice or receipt, entitling the person who makes the deposit, or the bearer, to take out the bullion again at any time within six months, upon re-transferring to the bank a quantity of bank money equal to that for which credit had been given in its books when the deposit was made, and upon paying one-fourth per cent. for the keeping, if the deposit was in silver, and one-half per cent. if it was in gold; but at the same time declaring, that in default of such payment, and upon the expiration of this term, the deposit should belong to the bank at the price at which it had been received, or for which credit had been given in the transfer books. What is thus paid for the keeping of the deposit may be considered as a sort of warehouse rent. . . . No demand can be made upon the bank but by means of a recipice or receipt. The smaller mass of bank money, for which the receipts are expired, is mixed and confounded with the much greater mass for which they are still in force; so that, though there may be a considerable sum of bank money, for which there are no receipts, there is no specific sum or portion of it which may not at any time be demanded by one. The bank cannot be debtor to two persons for the same thing; and the owner of bank money who has no receipt, cannot demand payment of the bank till he buys one. In ordinary and quiet times, he can find no difficulty in getting one to buy at the market price, which generally corresponds with the price at which he can sell the coin or bullion it entitles him to take out of the bank.

It might be otherwise during a public calamity; an invasion, for example, such as that of the French in 1672. . . . In such emergencies, the bank, it is supposed, would break through its ordinary rule of making payment only to the holders of receipts. . . .

The bank of Amsterdam professes to lend out no part of what is deposited with it, but, for every guilder for which it gives credit in its books, to keep in its repositories the value of a guilder either in money or bullion. That it keeps in its repositories all the money or bullion for which there are receipts in force, for which it is at all times liable to be called upon, and which, in reality, is continually going from it and returning to it again, cannot well be doubted. But whether it does so likewise with regard to that part of its capital, for which the receipts are long ago expired, for which in ordinary and quiet times it cannot be called upon, and which in reality is very likely to remain with it for ever, or as long as the States of the United Provinces subsist, may perhaps appear more uncertain. At Amsterdam, however, no point of faith is better established than that for every guilder circulated as bank money there is a correspondent guilder in gold or silver to be found in the treasure of the bank. The city is guarantee that it should be so. . . .

The city of Amsterdam derives a considerable revenue from the bank. Besides what may be called the warehouse-rent above mentioned, each person, upon first opening an account with the bank, pays a fee of ten guilders; and for every new account three guilders three stivers; for every transfer two stivers; and if the transfer is for less than three hundred guilders, six stivers, in order to discourage the multiplicity of small transactions. . . . What is paid for the keeping of bullion upon receipts is alone supposed to amount to a neat annual revenue of between one hundred and fifty thousand and two hundred thousand guilders. Public utility, however, and not revenue, was the original object of this institution. Its object was to relieve the merchants from the inconvenience of a disadvantageous exchange. The revenue which has arisen from it was unforeseen, and may be considered as accidental.*

4/2 Bank Money: The Bank of Hamburg

a AN ENGLISH RESIDENT (WILLIAM REMNANT), *A Sketch of Hambourg* (Hamburg, 1801), pp. 101–103.

b PATRICIA JAMES (ed.), *The Travel Diaries of T. R. Malthus* (Cambridge, 1966), p. 38.

a In Hambourg there is no paper-money, except the bills of exchange, that pass between individuals; in *Altona* there are bank-paper-bills or notes from eight species or two pounds – up to an hundred pounds.

The principal treasure of Hambourg, lies in the Bank: the silver, not wanted for daily use, is deposited in cellars, secured with iron bars. The plan of this bank is the most simple, and on that account perhaps the best in Europe. Each burgher has a right by inheritance to his folio on its books, in which the sum is put down, that is at the same time deposited in bars of pure silver – The amount of the sum deposited is set down in the folio; if there are 10,000 marks in the name of one person, upon one folio and as much upon another, and one pays 3,000 marks to the other, the folio of the person paying is alter'd to that of 7,000 marks, and that of the person paid to that of 13,000; this is called writing off, and the same sum remains in the bank, altho standing in consequence of transfers, in different names.

All marks here are called marks banco, and average the value of 20d. English.

Nothing is paid in; but bullion or pure silver and gold, and it never discounts.

In consequence of this arrangement, there can be no forgeries – no trans-

* (J.R.M.C. footnote). The events that have transpired since the publication of the *Wealth of Nations* have shown that the directors of the Bank of Amsterdam had abused the confidence placed in them . . . . In 1795 the French invaded Holland, and the provincial government established in the city of Amsterdam was obliged to issue a declaration . . . informing the public that, during the last fifty years, the directors had successively advanced 10,624,793 florins to the East India Company, the Provinces of Holland and West Friesland, and the City of Amsterdam! . . . in consequence, bank money, which had previously borne a premium of 5 per cent over the current metallic money of Holland, immediately fell to 16 per cent. below it.

fer can be made by bill; the party *paying* must attend in person; if ill and confined, he is attended by a clerk from the bank, if abroad, he must send a power of attorney, and the person receiving such power, must be previously identified, before he can touch a shilling – let the Hamburgians alone for taking care of their money!

There is another part of the bank, where money may be paid in, and received back again, on drafts as in the case of common bankers.

The Hamburg bank is looked upon as one of the safest in Europe.

b [30 May 1799]

The bank of Hamburgh is merely a bank of deposit, and transfer, and issues no paper whatever. A merchant places a certain quantity of pure silver in the bank and has credit for a certain number of marks banco. The transfer of this capital forms the grand medium of circulation in the purchase of merchandize. A high penalty is attached to overdrawing, so that there are no merchants' bills in circulation that are not actually represented by bullion in the bank. It follows that if this bullion be drawn out of the bank and sent away, (as is said to be the case lately), capital must be scarce, and the interest of money rise.

A mark banco is the weight of a mark in pure silver, and therefore banco money is always above currency. Spanish dollars or bars of silver are the most common form of the bullion in the bank. Currency is sent very rarely as it must be melted and assayed before it be admitted. The banks gain no kind of profit whatever. The expences of the clerks &c. are paid by a small per centage when the money is drawn out. At present 3 marks banco are worth 3 marks 12 sou's currency. Banco is 25 per cent higher than currency.

4/3 Regulations concerning the Caisse d'Escompte, 1776

A. M. R. TURGOT, *Œuvres, et documents* etc. [*see* Document **1/18**], V, pp. 354–358. (Ed. Tr.)

Regarding the petition presented to the King, being in Council, by Jean Baptiste-Gabriel Besnard, that he wished to establish a discount bank in the capital, all the operations of which would tend to lower the rate of interest and which would afford the public a source of security and saving, by undertaking to receive and to hold without charge . . . funds belonging to individuals . . .; that to this end he would beseech Your Majesty to authorize him to form a company of shareholders, according to the proposals, clauses and conditions laid down below;

4/3 *The Caisse d'Escompte, 1776*

Article 1 The shareholders of the said Company shall be associated *en commandite** under the name of Caisse d'Escompte.

Article 2 The operations of the said company shall consist:

Firstly, in discounting bills of exchange and other negotiable instruments, at the pleasure of the administrators, at a rate of interest which shall never exceed 4% a year; secondly, in dealing in gold and silver; thirdly in accepting ... payments from individuals ... without being able to demand any sort of commission, return or deduction for these services.

Article 3 The Company undertakes never to borrow at interest, nor to enter into any liability which is not payable on sight. It is prohibited from engaging in any transport of merchandize, maritime trade, insurance and commerce of whatever kind, beyond that clearly designated in the preceding article.

Article 4 The shareholders shall establish a fund of 15 million livres,* for which they shall receive 5,000 shares of 3,000 livres each, in return for a single payment in ready cash; of the 15 million, 5 million shall be used to begin operations and the other 10 million shall be deposited in the Royal Treasury, on 1 June 1776, as a surety for the liabilities of the said bank, in such a manner as indicated in Article 6; Your Majesty shall be asked to accept the 10 million livres as a loan and to grant receipts from the Royal Treasury to the value of 13 million francs, payable in thirteen years, in order to effect the repayment of the capital and interest of the said sum of 10 million, which receipts shall be divided and paid in twenty-six equal payments of 500,000 livres each, the first of which shall become payable on 1 December 1776, and so on, every six months on 1 June and 1 December of each year, up to and including the 1 June 1789.

Article 5 As surety for payments which have been stipulated in the previous article, Your Majesty shall be asked to assume the revenue of the postal farm and to order the keeper of Your Royal Treasury, as part of his duty, each year to deliver to the Treasurer of the Company, as payment for the 500,000 livres due on each occasion, an assignment drawn on the controller of the said postal farm.

Article 6 The 13 million livres constituting the total amount of the above mentioned financial receipts, or what shall be outstanding, having regard to the payments already made, shall be used exclusively to provide the element of security and guarantee in the bank's operations: and the administrators cannot, under any circumstances, sell, alienate, transfer or mortgage the amount of the loan which remains unredeemed.

Article 7 The said discount bank shall be opened on 1 June next, in such a place in Paris as the shareholders shall judge appropriate.

* See Glossary.

Article 9 *and* 10 (Nomination of De Mory as General Treasurer and requiring the possession of twenty-five shares to have deliberative votes).
Article 11 The said company shall be ruled by seven administrators, who shall be elected, by plural votes, in the said first General Assembly; in their administration they shall be required to conform to the wishes of the General Assembly; they shall appoint employees, fix their salaries and dismiss them, if they deem it necessary for the good of the Company.
Article 12 Each administrator shall be the holder of fifty registered shares.
Article 13 None of the administrators may be dismissed except by the votes of two-thirds of the shareholders present at the General Meeting, or by the unanimous vote of six other administrators or by ceasing to possess fifty shares in the Company, in conformity with the preceding article.
Article 14 The administrators shall not draw salaries whilst profits remain below 150,000 livres per half year. At this point and above it, one tenth of the profits shall be allocated to them.
Article 15 Every year two General Meetings of shareholders shall be held, in January and July, to discuss the company's affairs; to receive and examine the account of the half year which precedes the Meeting, which account shall be certified as accurate, and signed by the administrators, and also to decide the half yearly dividend payment.
Article 17 A deposit for shares shall be opened at the bank, for those which the holders wish to deposit there as a precaution against accidents, theft, or fire, and which may be withdrawn at any time; for those put there as a result of a notarial decision; and finally for those of which the deposit is ordered by law.
Article 18 The said discount bank shall be deemed and accounted to be the personal and domestic bank of each individual who has his cash there; and it shall be accountable towards these said individuals, in the same way as their personal financial advisers.
Article 19 Seeing the said request, the proposals made and the conditions proposed, the King authorized the said Jean Baptiste-Gabriel Besnard, to establish the said discount bank under the conditions outlined above, without the said authorization affecting the liberty which bankers and merchants have enjoyed in the past, and shall continue to enjoy in the future, to discount, to trade in gold and silver and to receive the cash of individuals who desire to place it with them.

4/4 Government Interest in Early Banking in Russia

H. F. VON STORCH, *The Picture of St. Petersburg* [see Document **3/1**], pp. 210-212.

On a more extensive plan and of greater importance is the LOAN BANK for the nobility and the corporations. This extremely remarkable institution owes its origin to a no less remarkable ukase. . . .

. . . Catharine the second, in the year 1786, made a deposit of two and twenty millions of rubles* for the nobility, eleven millions for the corporate towns, and three millions for the province of Taurida, to be lent out for the improvement of rural œconomy, of social industry and the benefit of civilization in general. The conditions under which all this was to be executed were essentially as follows.†

The bank lends only on real estates. The value of a landed estate in Russia being estimated according to the number of boors† upon it, the bank adopts the last revision as the rule of its proceedings in this respect, taking the boors at forty rubles per head; so that the proprietor of an estate, requiring the loan of a thousand rubles, must give five and twenty boors as his pledge. The loan is made for twenty years; the mortgager paying annually five per cent interest and three per cent on the capital, so that after twenty years he has paid back the whole of his loan.

The loans are subject to no other limitations than what arise from the value and the security of the pledge; every one being allowed to apply for and to receive as much money as he is capable of laying down a lawful pledge for. The bank, however, lends no sum under a thousand rubles, and only by thousands, for the sake of avoiding the perplexities of extensive and intricate accounts. Consequently only twenty-five, or seventy-five, or a hundred, &c. boors can be pledged.

The mortgaged property is subject to no suit, to no confiscation, or to any demands from the crown or private individuals. – Every four years, one part of the pawn is discharged, equal in value to the part of the capital already paid. – The bank can redeem estates elsewhere mortgaged or appropriated to the payment of debts: and mortgaged estates may be sold; but in that case, the purchaser takes upon him all the obligations which the seller was under to the bank.

The municipal magistracy of the government vouches for the worth of the pledge, and must be responsible for it. The interest is paid annually. The bank gives ten days grace; whoever exceeds one month pays a stated penalty per cent, and this likewise holds good of the second and third month. If payment be delayed beyond three months, the mortgaged estate is taken

† See Glossary.
* Ukase of the 2d of July, 1786. (Footnote in original source.)

into charge by the noble court of wards. The interest and fines are paid from the incomings of the estate and the remainder is paid to the proprietor.

The inhabitants of towns obtain loans on their real estates, paying yearly four per cent interest and three per cent capital; and are consequently freed from their debt in two and twenty years.

With the bank is connected a DEPOSITO-FUND, which accepts money at four and a half per cent. The sums deposited may at any time be withdrawn. In regard to sums of very large amount a previous notification is necessary.

4/5 Irregularity of taxation in various areas of France under the Ancien Régime

J. NECKER, *De l'Administration des finances* etc., [*see* Document **2/28**], I, pp. 186–187. (Ed. Tr.)

1. *Irregularity of taxation between areas*

The Généralité* of Chalons contains 600,000 people fewer than the Généralité of Bordeaux; it has more manufactures but much less commerce; and yet the revenue of the Généralités is almost equal. The fact is that La Guyenne, freed from the Salt Tax, is also exempted from aides,* whilst Champagne is subjected to, and pays one of the largest gabelle taxes*. These two taxes place on Champagne an additional burden of about 7 millions; and this particular tribute balances any additional burden the Généralité of Bordeaux pays in taille*, vingtièmes*, capitations*, tabac*, droits de traites*, de contrôle* and other taxes, of the sort which are assessed according to the wealth of the population.

2. Champagne has only one fifth more people than the Franche Comté and yet it pays at least six times more taxes. The fact is that the Franche Comté is exempt from aides and the exclusive privilege of tabac and the Treasury sells salt there at a quarter of the price fixed for Champagne. Thus these two taxes alone produce almost 6½ millions more in Champagne than the Franche Comté. The 3 vingtièmes in Champagne amount to 2.900,000 livres*; as a result of long standing agreements, those of the Franche Comté do not amount to 1,600,000 livres. Finally, the taille, capitation, and all the general impositions, are still greater in Champagne than the Franche Comté.

* See Glossary.

4/6 Inequalities in the payment of the Taille

A. M. R. TURGOT, *Œuvres, et documents* etc. [*see* Document **1/18**], V, pp. 170–173. (Ed. Tr.)

1. Ecclesiastical proprietors, noblemen, or those enjoying the privileges of nobility, can run a four-carucate farm, [*une ferme de quatre charrues*], which in the Paris area usually carries 2,000 francs* tax, without being liable to the taille*. This is the first advantage enjoyed by the privileged proprietors.
2. The same privileged people pay absolutely nothing on the woods, meadows, vineyards, ponds and enclosed lands belonging to their chateaux, irrespective of their extent, without this affecting the *privilège des quatre charrues**. There are some very large cantons* where most of the land is used either as meadow or for viticulture; thus the noble who farms his estates is exempt from the taille. . . . This is a second immense advantage.

I cannot resist observing that this privilege encourages people to use a great deal of land as meadow or for viticulture which could be devoted to wheat. The contrast which this legislation provides with the prevailing fears that freedom of commerce in grain deprives the realm of subsistence, merits the attention of the King.

3. The nobles pay only the vingtième* on seigneurial rents, and dîmes infeodées* and all the profits of the fief. Although these burdens are not very important around Paris, in the provinces they account for a large percentage of the net revenue arising from land.
4. In the provinces where there has been a desire to establish the taille on a proportionate basis, an attempt has been made to share the imposition between the proprietors liable to the tax and his farmers. In certain provinces the farmers have been made to pay half the imposition levied on the land, i.e. the 'taille of exploitation'; the other half has been paid by the proprietors, the so called 'taille of property'; in other areas, the 'taille of exploitation' has been regarded as two-thirds of the total imposition and the 'taille of property' as one-third. It follows from this that in the provinces, apart from the exemption which the nobles enjoy on what they themselves produce, they also enjoy exemption from one half or one third of the impositions on the land they rent out. This constitutes a fourth advantage.
5. The capitation tax* is levied on the nobles as on those who are liable for the taille, but not in the same proportion. By its nature the capitation is an arbitrary tax. It has proved impossible to levy it on all citizens, except in the most capricious fashion. It has been found more convenient to take the already compiled taille rolls as a basis for the capitation tax. Thus to those liable to the taille, the capitation tax has become an additional burden. A

* See Glossary.

special tax roll was compiled for the nobles; but since the nobility can safeguard their interests, and those who pay the taille have no-one to speak for them, the capitation of the nobles has been reduced in the provinces to an extremely modest level, whilst the capitation burden of those subject to the taille, is almost equal to the principal of the taille itself. Consequently, all the privileges with which the lands of the noble are endowed, result in a proportionate privilege as regards capitation tax, although at its inception it was intended that, this latter tax was to be levied on all the King's subjects according to their ability to pay. A fifth advantage of the nobles.

6. I have had the opportunity to express to the King the difference between the provinces where land is exploited by the rich farmers who profit from cultivation, and pledge, by a lease agreement, to pay a fixed sum each year to the owners; and other provinces where, because of the absence of wealthy farmers, the proprietors are obliged to grant the land to poor peasants, who are unable to make a profit, to whom the proprietor furnishes beasts, ploughs, seed and the wherewithal to maintain themselves until the first harvest; then all the fruits are divided, half to the proprietor and half to the farmer, which is called the métayer system of agriculture.* This custom, which is almost a law . . . was introduced at a time when the taille and the other taxes were not established; it is true that then it was advantageous to all parties; the proprietor drew an adequate profit from the land and the farmer could earn a living and maintain his family quite easily. It is evident that when the taille and all the taxes were placed on the unfortunate métayer, the equality in this system was shattered and the métayer was reduced inevitably, to a state of misery. His ruin was more or less absolute, depending upon the fecundity of the soil, the outlay necessitated by the land, and the price of foodstuffs. This is the sixth advantage enjoyed by the proprietors over those cultivators who are liable to the taille. It must be admitted that the disadvantage for the latter is greater than the advantage to the former.

7. Only the farmer and the tenant are on the tax roll, it is against them that proceedings can be directed; it is they, therefore, who bear all the expenses, all the consequences which result from delays in tax payment, the distraints, the activities of bailiffs and collectors, in short, all the vexation and trouble which results from the collection of a burdensome, badly distributed tax, levied on a part of the population which, because of its poverty and ignorance, cannot defend itself against any sort of problem. A seventh advantage of the privileged classes over the people; but as in the preceding instance, it is much more of a disadvantage to the people.

8. The impossible situation in which the farmer liable to the taille is placed, of calculating exactly his tax liability before he settles the conditions of his

* See Document 1/18.

lease . . . can also be regarded as another great disadvantage to those liable to the taille but really without any advantage to the proprietors. It is well known that the impositions resulting from the taille often undergo variations, which usually increase rather than reduce the amount of taxation.

4/7 Complaint Relating to French Taxes and Tax Farmers

DARIGRAND, *L'Anti-Financier, ou Relevé de quelques-unes de malversations* (Amsterdam, 1763), pp. 41-45. (Ed. Tr.)

To indicate all the inconveniences of the present administration I should need several volumes and a knowledge I do not possess; for you know that those who practise something do not allow the outsider to acquire their secrets; but I will cite several inconveniences, chosen at random, . . . relating to aides and controles.*

At the entry to Paris, a consignment of wine pays 32 or 33 different duties; the receipts delivered with it prove this.

Who would believe that this same consignment of wine has paid almost as much before arriving in Paris? This is certainly true of wine grown in the Pays d'Aides.*

If any wine has been re-sold, most of these duties are doubled.

If the wine arrives by water a duty is levied at every bridge passed on the journey.

The duties on the retail sale of wine are equally numerous, and everybody knows that they are levied on each pint.

. . . To collect these innumerable duties levied on the harvest, the making, the transport of the wine, on its entry into the towns, and on its wholesale and retail transactions, together with the duties collected on the road and on each stage of the road, an army of officials is required, some of whom surround the towns, and others, carrying out their searches, disturb the domestic peace of our citizens; . . . the roads are infested, the thoroughfares are watched by the militia, which is hated by those whom they oppress.

. . . Will posterity find it possible to believe that in the century of Louis le Bien Aimé, a Frenchman did not possess a single room to which he could forbid entry to the tax officials, that he did not even have a chest or a cupboard which he could refuse to open to them? It should not be believed that only the innkeepers are victims of this constraint (I do not speak of the gabelle,* the tabac,* the duty on leather and other impositions which carry the right of search, I speak only of the duties on wine). It is known that at harvest time the tax officials possess entreé to all houses, so that they can com-

* See Glossary.

pile their inventories. It is well known that in all the places subject to the duty called 'Inspecteurs aux Boissons',* all the inhabitants are subject at all times to visits of tax officials. It is known that in all the municipal towns, the common people as consumers are treated as if they were innkeepers and pay retail duties for exceeding their allocated consumption of wine, just as if they had sold this amount retail.

It was not sufficient to have the most odious inquisition established in the houses of the citizens, it was not sufficient to have their consumption limited to a certain amount of wine, a kind of subjection which had escaped the imagination of every Asian tyrant and the invention of which is due to the financiers; to have the consumption of wine, which has been encouraged, regarded as a crime; finally, to have men punished without their being convicted; all that remained was for the financiers to leave their employees absolute masters of the fate of these citizens whom they judged guilty of any sort of fraud which seemed appropriate.

According to the laws of the civilized world, legal conviction operates by the unequivocal evidence of at least two irreproachable witnesses. These laws do not bind the financiers; they obtain a conviction without witnesses; their officials are the accusers, or rather the informers; on these accusations and denunciations citizens are condemned, and the ruin of the latter is the price of this spy system, of this system of denunciation and false testimony. I must develop my ideas.

All France knows that all the tax officials in every branch of taxation, irrespective of their rank, have a share in the fines and confiscations, which is assured to them by tax farmers and which forms the biggest part of their salaries. As a result, their ability, zeal and work are judged by the number of law suits they bring, which is the only way they can obtain promotion; their present needs and their hopes of a fortune in the future . . . are the factors exploited by the financiers to corrupt 2,500 tax officials, whom they let loose over all the kingdom, where, armed with procès verbaux they carry out their principals' wishes, to earn their living and so obtain promotion into the ranks of the élite.

4/8 Total Burden of Taxation in France, 1788

G. F. LE TRÔNE, *De l'administration provinciale et de la reforme de l'impôt* (2 vols., Basle and Paris, 1788), I, pp. 46–51. (Ed. Tr.)

We have no other direct tax today except the dixième [the tenth], and it yields only 40 million: but it yields so little because the revenue of the terri-

* See Glossary.

tory is absorbed, removed and wiped out by a mass of other taxes which are destructive of our national produce, either because of their arbitrariness, as in the case of the taille, or because of their enormous costs of collection, which reduce their value and total consumption. But since these taxes have multiplied to excess, above all in the past century, one could at least have assumed that the State would have had an income, which, though derived, it is true, by means which place a heavy burden on the nation, was at any rate very substantial. Nevertheless, it remains true, though it seems like a paradox, that the public revenue is now less than it was under Louis XI and Louis XII* not only relatively to the increased needs, but even absolutely.

Under Louis XI, the taille brought in 4·7 million livres,† but the value of the mark weight of silver was then 10 livres, *i.e.* nearly as eleven to two compared with today's. Thus the 4·7 million livres represented 470,000 marks of silver. This weight in silver, expressed in today's money, would be worth 26 million.

But we have to go further, and compare the exchange value of silver against commodities. The mark of silver was worth 200 sous tournois†: the septier† of corn, Paris measure, was worth 13 sous tournois, or one-fifteenth of the mark of silver; 470,000 marks of silver thus represented 7,050,000 septiers . . . this, in today's money, is 141 million livres. . . .

But today the territorial dixième [tenth] brings in only 40 million. Thus the taille of those days at 140 million, which was only levied at one-tenth was worth, in today's terms, 3½ tenths. . . . But we have to note that under Louis XI there were only two-thirds of the Provinces which today are directly under the Crown, so that, to collect today the same value in a territory larger by one-third, the tenth over the whole Kingdom should provide 210 million. . . . In fact, the taille, added to the tenths, representing a one-third levy and not one-tenth, yields today only 130 million. . . .

. . . The state of the country is thus much changed. And what else could have caused this but the nature and multiplicity of the taxes, their enormous costs of collection, and their destructive effects, which have progressively undermined the advances of production and dried up the sources of further taxation?

Let us look now at the state of the public revenue under Louis XII, the father of his people; who raised no new taxes, and lowered all the existing ones, both overall and in their costs of collection; under Louis XII who reigned over a France smaller by one-third than today's.

Louis XII received, net, 7.75 million l. as appears from Sully's '*Économies Royales*'. To reduce this sum to real values, we have to compare it with the

* i.e. 1461–1483 and 1498–1515. [Ed.].
† See Glossary.

price of the principal commodity. In his time, the septier of corn was worth 18–20 sous. Let us say 20 sous. Thus the revenue amounted to 7,750,000 septiers. Besides this, there were levied in the Provinces large sums which did not pass through the State Exchequer and were used for provincial expenditures, roads, fortifications, provisions and equipment for the gendarmerie. These sums seem to have totalled an equivalent of 7½ million septiers. Thus the total levied in the country was 15 million septiers. Estimating today's value of the septier at 20 l., this would represent at today's prices, 300 million l. But since it is perhaps uncertain how much was actually collected in the provinces that did not enter the Exchequer, let us reduce this sum to 4·25 million l. only; with the 7·75 million l. which did pass through the Exchequer, this would total 12 million, worth 12 million septiers, or 240 million l. at today's values.

In 1776 the King enjoyed a revenue of 377 million, while the Kingdom had grown by a third. Let us see whether this is as large as that enjoyed by Louis XII. 377 millions, divided by 20, give 18,850,000 septiers. We must, to start with, deduct one third, since the Kingdom has grown by a third since then. One third would be 6,280,000 septiers; deducted from 18,850,000, it leaves for a true comparison, 12,577,000 [*sic*] septiers.

The King has thus 12,577,000 septiers compared with Louis XII, who had 15 million, or at least 12 million; but Louis XII had 12 million septiers to spend freely, on nothing but public expenditure. The present King, by contrast, owes 130 millions in arrears, or 140 million including mortgages. This sum of 140 million l. divided by 20 l., the present price of the septier, is 7 million septiers, with which the public revenue is burdened. The King then has only 5,577,000 septiers available for current public expenditure, compared with Louis XII, who on a similar extent of territory, i.e. on two thirds of the present territory, enjoyed 12 million. What an enormous difference!

The burden of 140 million l. of arrears and mortgages has arisen out of the loans and creation of offices by which it had been attempted, from reign to reign, to make up the shortfall in taxes by all possible means. It is thus clear that, the more direct taxes are increased, the more the national income and the public revenue are damaged; the more is borrowed, the more the public revenue becomes inadequate; so that the debt service charges reduce the tax income, and the disorganized taxation system, by damaging the national wealth more and more, forces new borrowings and additional taxation, a double progress of misfortune which nothing can halt except a return to order.

It is worth noting that under Louis XII the people were happy and well off, and paid their value of 12 million septiers without additions; an incontestable proof of the healthy state of the economy. Today, while the Kingdom is larger by one-third, it is notorious that the population is sucked dry, while the King only receives 18,850,000 septiers. The reason is (1) that while the King only receives 18,850,000 septiers, the population pays 34 million, because a part of the tax is levied by means which cost double what they bring in; (2) that the taxes are of a kind which destroy values and productive powers; (3) that the arbitrariness which rules the distribution of the other parts of the tax burdens form yet another obstacle to the prosperity of the economy.

4/9 18th-Century Views of Fair Taxation

a Frederick the Great in an interview with Boden on 11 May 1772. Printed in C. A. ZAKRZEWSKI, *Die wichtigeren preussischen Reformen der direkten Ländlichen Steuern im achtzehnten Jahrhundert* (Leipzig, 1887), pp. 82–83. (Ed. Tr.)
b (Marquis) C. L. DUCREST, *Sécond mémoire sur l'administration des finances* (Paris 1787), pp. 18–20. (Ed. Tr.)

a 'The general welfare of the country and that of every individual rests mainly on the basis, that the burdens of the State shall be borne equally and at the same rate. All authorities, subjects and inhabitants without exception shall contribute in such measure as corresponds to their fortune, condition and income. . . . But in Pomerania there were many poor people, and poor land, especially near Friedland, Hammerstein, Tuchel and on to Konitz. A *pro rata* would have to be worked out; *e.g.* a rich man with an income of 5,000 Thaler* could be made to pay 2,500, and would still have enough left to live on; but a poor man, with an income of 80 Thaler, could not pay one half, for then he could not live; for him it would be sufficient to pay one out of 80 Thaler.'

b Let us begin by discussing taxes in relation to their influence on the fortune, the freedom, and the peace of mind of every citizen, considered as an individual, and let us try to establish the sequence of principles in the natural order from which they derive.

I. In every Government, the best system of taxation is that by which the distribution is the most equal, and the incidence the least arbitrary. Every inequality is unjust, every arbitrariness is vexatious; and in the matter of taxation the contributors can complain of two things only, injustice and vexation.

II. In order to make the distribution equal, one need not take into account all the means of every citizen, but only the excess beyond what he strictly needs to sustain

* See Glossary.

life. This principle is self-evident. To make taxation just in regard to the taxpayer, he should be able to look upon it as a proportional contribution towards public and general expenditure *from which he receives support and protection*. Could he then regard it in this way, if it takes away from him what he needs to live, and condemns him to languish for a time before dying of hunger and poverty?

III. If there is in a Society a class of citizens who have not the necessary minimum means of life: not only should it not pay anything but it should receive something out of the total taxes collected, and the richest should pay more accordingly. This principle is also obvious; for, since the *first object* of taxation is to provide support and protection to all members of Society, the rich, who enjoy that support and protection, should at least ensure the subsistence of the poor.

IV. Every citizen should contribute to the public expenditure out of his surplus beyond what he requires strictly to sustain life, in a proportion which should become higher, the richer he is. The more comfort grows, the nearer it approaches surfeit, and surfeit should obviously pay more than comfort, for the same reason that comfort should pay a little more so that necessity should be entirely exempt.

4/10 French Tax Reform: Uniform Assessment, 1768

Declaration on the Assessment of the Taille; Versailles, 7 February 1768: Preamble. Printed in MARCEL MARION (ed.), *Les impôts directs sous l'ancien régime* (Paris, 1910), p. 159. (Ed. Tr.)

Whereas by our declaration of 13 April 1761 . . . we have made rules on the assessment of the taille,* and made known our intention to end, as soon as possible, the arbitrariness in the drawing up of the tax lists; and we have therefore announced by our declaration of 21 November 1763 the establishment of a tax register to carry out our wishes in this respect; yet, nevertheless on the basis of information we have received on how the laws, made in this respect by ourselves and our predecessors, are being applied in the different provinces and parts of our Kingdom, we now recognize that one of the greatest obstacles to that execution lies in the differences in the manner in which the assessment and the formation of the register are carried out, and in the abuses inherent in the right granted to taxpayers by the declaration of 17 February 1728 to have themselves assessed in the parish of their domicile for all their incomes arising in other parishes; all of which creates obscurity and uncertainty in an operation which, by its nature and object, ought to be

* See Glossary.

simple, clear and uniform. In order to achieve a more equitable distribution of their tax burden at once, to be followed by a certain and always uniform assessment, we have provisionally ordered the intendants and the inspectors (*commissaires*) distributed over the districts of the *pays d'élection** to act uniformly and in accordance with the models which we had sent to them† in the assessment of the taille for the current year 1768, advising them to observe the rules and to enjoin the inspectors appointed by them to conform to them. We have already had the satisfaction of seeing the success of this method in the small number of parishes in each district in which the attempt has been made; and, since we cannot let the rest of our taxpaying subjects enjoy the same advantage too early, we are eager to give the method all the publicity and authority necessary for its earliest implementation. We do not doubt that our tax courts and inferior courts concerned with the matter will join with zeal in the execution of this present declaration, of which the sole object is the ending of arbitrariness in the assessment of the taille. Therefore...

4/11 French Tax Reform: Abolition of Contrainte Solidaire, 1775

Declaration; Versailles, 3 January 1775. Printed in MARCEL MARION (ed.), *Les impôts directs* ... [*see* Document **4/10**], pp. 165-166. (Ed. Tr.)

In the misfortunes which afflicted our country during the civil wars, the resultant irregularity in the collection of taxes made it necessary for our predecessors to authorize the tax receivers to make the principal inhabitants of parishes collectively responsible (by *contrainte solidaire*) for the taxes due from the parish, either in the case of rebellion, or in the case of non-assessment, or non-appointment of collectors, or, finally, when the collectors, after a summary count of their movable property, were found to be insolvent ... (now) it seems to us that rebellion alone should be the exceptional case in which we should give our tax receivers this power, with the proviso that we hope that they will never be reduced to that extremity: our affection for the population moves us to abolish, in the other two, less extreme contingencies ... these rigorous measures which threaten the loss of liberty or property for our principal tax-payers, spread fear in the countryside, discourage agriculture, the most worthy object of our care and protection, and oblige the tax (taille) receivers, against their will, to involve in considerable expenses those inhabitants whom it is their duty and their interest to foster. We take the appropriate measures, at the same time, to ensure the payment of our dues in these circumstances, and to indemnify the

* See Glossary.

† Refers to the Circular to the Intendants of 4 August 1767. (Ed.)

tax receivers, charged with making their payments within the limited terms, against the arrears that will arise. Therefore. . . .

Article 1 *Contrainte solidaire* shall be imposed on the principal taxpayers of each parish only in case of proved rebellion against the State. . . .

Article 2 We order . . . our Intendants, to choose among those of the Estates who shall pay the highest taille each year, those who shall undertake the office of tax collector, where no other nomination has been made, or where an insufficient number have been nominated.

Article 3 In case the collectors appointed by the parishes or by the ntendants according to the previous Article refuse or neglect to assess the taxes or to pay them over according to the regulations, they shall be forced to pay them by the usual means and following the terms of the said regulations.

Article 4 In case the collectors shall become insolvent, after a summary account of their movable property and report of a search of their persons, made on the request of the tax receivers, the said tax receivers shall use the good offices of the said Intendants to reimpose the taxes due from the parishes, and these re-impositions, after they have been communicated to the inhabitants and have been agreed, shall be paid over to the next Department,* including the interest and the legitimate expenses of the said receivers, by all the tax payers of the said parishes. . . .

4/12 Effects of Alcavala Tax on Spanish Industry

a J. KIPPAX (trans.), *The Theory and Practice of Commerce and Maritime Affairs*, written originally in Spanish by D. G. DE UZTARIZ (2 vols., London, 1751), 2, pp. 236–238.

b WILLIAM JACOB, *Travels in the South of Spain. . . .* [See Document **1/19**], pp. 169–170.

a After the strictest inquiry, and a most mature consideration of the duties, imposed upon commodities and goods in Spain, and other kingdoms and states, I have not been able to discover in France, England, or Holland, nations that best know the value of commerce, that they have ever laid any duty upon the sale or barter of their own woven and other manufactures, either upon the first, or any future sale. As then I find Spain alone groaning under this burden, and it is so very oppressive, as to lay ten per cent. for the primitive Alcavala, and the four one per cents annexed to it, a duty not only chargeable on the first sale, but on every future sale of goods, I am jealous, it is one of the principal engines, that contributed to the ruin of most of our manufactures and trade. For though these duties are not charged to the full in some places, a heavy tax is paid. And as the subsidies of the Millones,*

* See Glossary.

which are also very high, and an additional load, as also the city excises and Arbitrios,* all of them laid, as it were, upon provisions, which the labourer consumes, it is easy to apprehend, as I have intimated already, that all these imposts will excessively raise the price of our goods; and as on this very account there can be little demand for them, either at home or abroad, our manufactories must be at a stand, and those of foreigners flourish, who will introduce their own goods, and easily dispose of great quantities, as they can afford them cheaper; and this proceeds from their not being so heavy loaded with taxes in their respective countries, and favoured with great indulgences in the Spanish custom houses, as I have already declared in several other chapters.

It is a confirmation of what I have advanced, that most of our fabricks of middling cloths and stuffs, that now succeed in Spain, are confined to certain seignories, where there is great allowance made by the lord upon the first sale, and sometimes an entire exemption from it, with other encouragements. This instance and the favourable consequences of it suggest, that we ought to pursue the same plan in other places belonging to the crown. I am obliged also to observe, that though great abatements be made in charging the Alcavala and Cientos* in many places, yet our evil genius still haunts in this interesting transaction of trade, so that at Sevil, Granada, and other considerable cities, where our silk manufactories were most numerous and in greatest perfection, and therefore stood most in need of powerful encouragements, these mechanicks have been most persecuted, and saddled with the heavy burden of paying the 14 per cent. entire,

'and other severities, that have been the ruin of them. For a proof of it I cannot forbear particularising Sevil, as an instance. The silk weavers, pleaded their cause, in the year 1722, before the superintendant of that kingdom, in the runious situation they found themselves, their manufactories being already reduced to less than a hundred looms, and owing to this; that besides 14 per cent. paid at entry in that custom house, there was charged to his majesty another 14 per cent. on their being sold again. For while this duty from the calamitous circumstances of the times and a general decay in commerce ought to have been proportionably eased, the contrary prevailed; for the under farmers every year created new vexations and oppressions in collecting it, especially in the years 1720, 1721, and 1722, when there was a rigorous administration, that occasioned them to make repeated scrutinies and researches, to plant guards over them, and sometimes lock up the goods in a chest, and carry away the key, leaving a centinel over it; and all this, with a view to oblige them to terms and submit to pay even above the 14 per cent. After all, though they charged this duty entire, it yielded only 31,764 reals, and deducting out of it 7340 reals, the salaries and charges of administration, the farmer had but 24,424 reals net money. In the year 1722, it amounted to no more than 23,244 reals, and after deducting the charges of administration was reduced to 15,904 reals, and there is still found every year a farther reduction of this branch of the revenue.'

b There is an impediment to all commerce, to all exchange of necessaries in

* See Glossary.

Spain, so impolitic and oppressive that it is scarcely credible; and the only wonder is, that under such circumstances any commerce should exist at all; I mean the tax called Alcavala, a duty of six per cent on the sale of property every time it changes owners. The obvious effect of such a tax needs no comment; but the consequences of it are felt far beyond the mere payment of the money. At each gate of this and other cities, bands of the lowest class of revenue officers are stationed with power to search the baggage and examine the person of everyone who passes: a power often rigorously exercised, towards those who do not grant them a gratuity, and therefore particularly oppressive to the lower orders of the community. To enforce this tax, the custom house, or perhaps, according to our English usage, the excise office, requires every person coming to the city, with anything for sale, to make an entry, and pay this as well as other municipal duties; and, in a similar manner, any person making purchases within the city must take out a clearance from the proper office. Thus a peasant's melons, onions or garlick must wait for the dispacho, as it is called; and when he purchases the necessaries which are required for his village consumption, he must again apply for a clearance before he can return. Thus their time is lost, and the officers of the Government multiplied without producing a revenue at all correspondent to the expence.

By some late regulations this practice does not extend to corn, which is now allowed to come in without any formal entry; but meat is rigidly subjected to it, as well as other vexatious interpositions of authority. An ox brought to the city for the butcher must be first carried to the public slaughter house, without the Puerto del Carne, where it is killed by an authorized matador, and the hide, horns and hoofs are his fee. The duty of Alcavala, another called Millones and some municipal taxes must be paid; and then a permit is issued, allowing the meat to be sold within the wards. These duties in meat amount to rather more than the original price and therefore, though oxen are cheap, meat is as dear in Seville as in London.

Chapter 5 Social Policy and Conditions

Introduction

Four main themes are concentrated into this discussion of social policy and conditions in the eighteenth century. The importance of agricultural fluctuations in creating social discontent, contemporary attempts to obtain a disciplined labour force, social policy itself, with special reference to poverty and disease, and finally, social discontent, with reference to action and protest arising from the 'lower orders'.

Contemporaries were well aware of the importance of agricultural stability for the maintenance of social harmony. Europe was a predominantly agrarian economy, and the majority of the population still found employment in agriculture. Any dislocation in agricultural production resulted in increases in the price of basic necessities, and if prolonged, a serious contraction in rural demand which affected the entire economy. General prosperity, therefore, was tied closely to agricultural prosperity (**5/1a**). One of the features of French society in the years before the revolution was the severity of agricultural depression. With an increasing population, the crises tended to become acute. The comments of Turgot and Young make it quite clear how the fate of many individuals was tied to the harvest situation and illustrate the all-pervading concern and distress which could be caused by agricultural failure (**5/1b, c**). Knowledge of such consequences lay behind the attempts made in the course of the eighteenth century to establish freedom of trade in grain in France. By such means it was hoped to iron out inequalities in production (**3/10**), whilst in Prussia attempts were made to solve the problem by Royal grain provisioning (**5/2**), which achieved some measure of success. The Law of the Maximum of 29 September 1793 may be regarded as a later attempt to achieve some degree of harmony between prices and wages, to ensure the minimum amount of social discontent. The decree achieved very little; there were positive advantages for some in violating it, and there were few agencies to enforce it (**5/9**).

With the development of industrialization in the eighteenth century some concern was expressed at the reluctance of workers to accept the standards associated with capitalist society (**5/3**); and it is possible to see attempts being made to create a disciplined labour force. Order, regularity and discipline were prerequisites for advance, and any pre-industrial attitudes had to be quickly relegated to oblivion. The consequence was the appearance of rules and regulations, governing almost all aspects of an individual's working life (**5/4**, see also **15/17**), virtually identical in their underlying psychology with those which appeared in Britain.

Poverty and disease were the chief problems which pressed on eighteenth- and early nineteenth-century charities. Contemporaries were able to draw neat lines between 'deserving' and 'undeserving' poor, and were prepared to prescribe different treatment according to classification (**5/8**). Analysis of causation was characterized by a moral tone, and there was a strong emphasis on personal responsibility (**5/8**, **5/9**). Disease and sickness were treated mainly by charitable and particularly religious organizations (**5/5**), although in Venice the authorities intervened to combat such problems (**5/6**). One of the most impressive charitable institutions for the relief of the needy and sick in the eighteenth century was found in Gratz, which was well endowed with charitable institutions. One of the outstanding features of this particular institution, was its comprehensive range of relief activities (**5/7**).

Finally, mention must be made of social discontent. It is possible to examine this in town and countryside at a local and national level. The 1783 petition of the Berlin Calico Printers, who were faced with unemployment as a result of an over-supply of labour brought about through the training of large numbers of apprentices (**5/11a**) and who were simultaneously being imprisoned on the instigation of their employers is an interesting example of urban discontent (**5/11b** and **c**). The violence characterizing these relationships is reminiscent of that between the gild masters and the compagnons in France at the same period (**2/7a** and **b**). It is also possible to trace disturbances in the countryside, of which perhaps the most important example is the Pugachev rebellion of 1775 (**5/13**). Agrarian unrest was not simply a Russian phenomenon. Unrest occurred in Saxony in 1790 (**5/12**) when the peasants drew up their broadside denouncing rapacious landlords, their hireling lawyers, and tax collectors, all of whom were characterized and castigated as oppressors of the people (**5/12**). The chief centre of unrest in the eighteenth century, however, was France. Pre-revolutionary distress is seen quite clearly in the cahiers, which not only listed the grievances felt by the population against the *ancien régime*, but also provided the authorities with suggestions for reform (**5/14**. See also **4/5**, **4/6**, **4/7**, **4/8**). Overall, the cahiers formed an impressive indictment of a system of political, economic and social organization which had dominated the eighteenth century, and the dissatisfaction with this régime, when it was sharpened by the distress resulting from the effects of the 1786 Eden-Rayneval Treaty (**3/13**), and the harvest failures of 1778-89, led to the Revolution in 1789.

5/1 Effects of Harvest Failure in France

a Reports from Government officials at Aumale and Rouen, 1755, 1756 and 1768. Printed in J. LOUGH, *An Introduction to Eighteenth-Century France* (London, 1960), pp. 66–67. (Ed. Tr.)

b Report on the 1769 harvest by Turgot. Printed in W. W. STEPHENS (ed.), *The Life and Writings of Turgot* (London, 1895), p. 50.

c A. YOUNG, *Travels in France during the years 1787, 1788 and 1789*, etc. [*see* Documents **1/6a** and **b**], 1, pp. 18, 83, 134, 104, 123–124, 128–129, 130.

a

1

. . . Cheap food has always been regarded as the dynamic behind the internal commerce of the Kingdom; thus since this year's abundant harvest manufacturers have been filled with optimism and taken on all the wool they could possibly work up.

2

. . . Experience always shows that nothing has more influence on commerce at Aumale than the price of foodstuffs. In fact, this single factor regulates all other forces. For as soon as there is an increase in wheat prices trade starts to fall off and prices fall and the supply of goods diminishes. The increase in industry in Aumale seems to prove this reasoning, since for a year now wheat has remained at a reasonable price and the supply and price of goods have increased. The reason for these changes is easy to understand but an example will serve the purpose better. Suppose the father of a family earns 6 livres per week*; he must still work every day to earn this amount and he needs 2 bushels of wheat per week. If wheat costs only 25s., he still has sufficient left to clothe himself and his family and to provide for other requirements. But if it costs 50s., as it has done for about 5 years, with the exception of this year, what can he do? Wages remain constant, yet his obligations are the same, he earns just enough to keep himself, he cannot buy anything else. How many people are in this state, and consequently, what is the effect on consumption, and, as a result, on commerce at Aumale?

3

. . . Bread has become so dear that the day labourers, artisans and workers and factory hands have great difficulty in earning sufficient to buy necessary foodstuffs for their families. The price of bread is the key to production, since production falls off when bread is dear . . . The manufacturers are burdened with unsold goods, and to avoid more stockpiling, they have been obliged

* See Glossary.

to shut down a large number of their workshops. This necessary action has resulted in the unemployment of a considerable number of workers.

b Everyone has heard of the terrible dearth that has just afflicted this generality.* The harvest of 1769 in every respect proved to be one of the worst in the memory of man. The dearths of 1709 and 1739 were incomparably less cruel. To the loss of the greatest part of the rye was added the total loss of the chestnuts, of the buckwheat, and of the Spanish wheat – cheap food stuffs with which the peasant sustained himself habitually a great part of the year, reserving as much as he could of his corn, in order to sell it to the inhabitants of the towns. . . . The people could exist only by exhausting their resources, by selling at a miserable price their articles of furniture and even their clothes. Many of the inhabitants have been obliged to disperse themselves through other provinces to seek work or to beg, leaving their wives and children to the charity of the parishes. It has been necessary for the public authority to require the proprietors and inhabitants in better circumstances in each parish to assess themselves for the relief of the poor people; nearly a fourth of the population is dependent upon charitable contributions. After these melancholy sufferings which the province has already undergone, and with the reduced condition in which it was left by the dearth of last year, even had the harvest of the present year been a good one, the poverty of the inhabitants would have necessitated the greatest efforts to be made for their relief. But we have now to add the dismal fact of our harvest being again deficient. . . . We can scarcely think without shuddering of the fate that menaces this part of the province, already so cruelly exhausted by the misfortunes of the past year.

c Pass Payrac, and meet many beggars, which we had not done before. All the country girls and women are without shoes or stockings; and the ploughmen at their work have neither sabots nor stockings to their feet. This is a poverty that strikes at the root of national prosperity; a large consumption among the poor being of more consequence than among the rich. . . . It reminded me of the misery of Ireland.

. . . Pass by several cottages, exceedingly well built, of stone and slate or tiles, yet without any glass to the windows; can a country be likely to thrive where the great object is to spare manufactures? Women picking weeds into their aprons for their cows, another sign of poverty I observed during the whole way from Calais.

To Combourg, the country has a savage aspect; husbandry not much further advanced, at least in skill, than among the Hurons, which appears incredible amidst enclosures; the people almost as wild as their country, and

* See Glossary.

their town of Combourg one of the most brutal filthy places that can be seen; mud houses, no windows, and a pavement so broken, as to impede all passengers, but ease none; yet here is a chateau, and inhabited. Who is the Mons. de Chateaubriand, the owner, that has nerves strung for a residence amidst such filth and poverty?

To Montauban. The poor people seem poor indeed; the children terribly ragged, if possible worse clad than if with no clothes at all; as to shoes and stockings they are luxuries. A beautiful girl of six or seven years playing with a stick, and smiling under such a bundle of rags as made my heart ache to see her. They did not beg, and when I gave them anything seemed more surprised than obliged. One third of what I have seen of this province seems uncultivated, and nearly all of it in misery. . . .

Walking up a long hill, to ease my mare, I was joined by a poor woman, who complained of the times, and that it was a sad country. On my demanding her reasons, she said her husband had but a morsel of land, one cow and a poor little horse, yet he had a franchar (42 lb.) of wheat and three chickens to pay as a quit-rent to one Seigneur; and four franchar of oats, one chicken and 1s. to pay to another, beside very heavy tailles and other taxes. She had seven children, and the cow's milk helped to make the soup. . . . It was said, at present, that something was to be done by some great folks for such poor ones, but she did not know who or how, but God send us better, *car les tailles et les droits nous ecrasent.* This woman, at no great distance, might have been taken for sixty or seventy, her figure was so bent, and her face so furrowed and hardened by labour; but she said she was only twenty-eight.

Everything conspires to render the present period in France critical; the want of bread is terrible; accounts arrive every moment from the provinces of riots and disturbances, and calling in the military, to preserve the peace of the markets. The prices reported are the same as I found at Abbeville and Amiens; 5s. [2½d.] a pound for white bread, and 3½s. to 4s. for the common sort, eaten by the poor; these rates are beyond their faculties, and occasion great misery. . . .

It was represented to him [the King] that the want of bread was so great in every part of the Kingdom that there was no extremity to which the people might not be driven; that they were nearly starving, and consequently ready to listen to any suggestions, and on the qui vive for all sorts of mischief; that Paris and Versailles would inevitably be burnt. . . .

He [Young's barber] gave me a frightful account of the misery of the people; whole families in the utmost distress; those that work have a pay insufficient to feed them – and many that find it difficult to get work at all, I inquired of Mons. de Guerchy concerning this, and found it true. By order of the magistrates no person is allowed to buy more than two bushels of wheat at a market, to prevent monopolizing. . . . Being here on a market-day, I attended, and saw the wheat sold out under this regulation, with a party of dragoons drawn up before the market-cross to prevent violence. The people quarrel with the bakers, asserting the prices they demand for bread are beyond the proportion of wheat, and proceeding from words to scuffling, raise a riot, and then run away with bread and wheat for nothing. This has happened at Nangis, and many other markets; the consequence was that neither farmers nor bakers would supply them till they were in danger of starving, and prices under such circumstances must necessarily rise enormously, which aggravated the mischief, till troops became really necessary to give security to those who supplied the markets.

Conversation here, as in every other town of the country, seems more occupied on the dearness of wheat than on any other circumstance; yesterday was market-day, and a riot ensued of the populace, in spite of the troops that were drawn up as usual to protect the corn. It rises to 46 livres (£2. 0. 3d.) the septier, or half-quarter, and some is sold yet higher.

5/2 Royal Grain Provisioning in Prussia

a Royal rescript to the Chamber of Pomerania; Berlin, 19 May 1741;

b Rescript of the General Directory to the Chamber of Königsberg; Berlin, 19 May 1741;

c Rescript of the General Directory to the Chamber of Pomerania; Berlin, 31 August 1756. Printed in ACTA BORUSSICA *Getreidehandelspolitik* (3 vols., Vol. 3, ed. G. Schmoller, W. Naudé and A. Skalweit, Berlin, 1910), pp. 359–360; 569–570. (Ed. Tr.)

a You will see, from the written enclosure, what the Magistrates of the districts of Stolpe, Schlawe, Rumalsburg and Greiffenberg have reported in regard to the poor condition of our subjects and the existing shortage of bread grains and summer seed.

We therefore order you to institute exact, thorough and reliable enquiries, and report to us as soon as possible whether it be true, that some of our subjects are constrained to grind chaff and husks up to nearly half the quantity into their bread grains and eat such bread, while others, lacking nutritious bread, find themselves subject to fatal diseases. At the same time, you will admonish the Members of the Nobility that it is their duty to take the necessary care to maintain their subjects, and wherever the subjects are unable to provide their own seed and bread corn, to provide these for them, and you should take steps against those of the noble estate, who do not undertake this task with sufficient care and thoroughness. At the same time, you will bear the consequences, if you do not carry out this instruction with sufficient force and if serious results should arise from this neglect.

b We have received your report of 12th of this month regarding the shortage of bread corn, summer seed and fodder. It seems hardly credible, in view of the particularly rich harvest of last year, that there should be a shortage of seed grain this year, if you had taken the proper precautions. Meanwhile you are ordered to see to it that all fields are properly sown and that there should nowhere be a shortage of seed.

c We have received your report delivered to us on the 20th of this month, on this year's poor harvest in the province, and the shortage of grain feared as a result. Since you omitted to follow our Rescript of 16th May of this year, ordering you to enquire into the alleged poor harvest, as well as to follow the General Order to investigate the damage to the standing corn, we shall leave it to your own sense of duty and power to decide how you are going to deal with the expected shortage of grain, particularly since your own investigations are not likely to be completed before the end of October, after we have already ourselves, following the report of our subjects, permitted the free import of foreign grain, so that little more should be expected of us at present; in particular, your own proposal to buy 7,419 wispel in order to fill the corn stores and magazines, the wispel at 24 Rthlr,* whereas the same could not even be got in Danzig, free of costs of transport, at this price, and nothing can be expected from Prussia, would require 178,056 Rthlr, which cannot possibly be entertained by the magazine account, the more so since it already suffered large losses in the past year; therefore, since nothing can be issued from our own magazines, each particular land government must use the permission to import freely and look after the imports for its own subjects.

5/3 Alleged Luxury and Lack of Economy among German Workers

Report by Peltre, clerk of the Neustadt-Eberswalde Knife and Steel Goods manufactory, to Mining Councillor Gerhardt, Chairman of the Commission of Enquiry into the Conditions of Manufacture; Neustadt-Eberswalde, 16 October 1784. Printed in KRUEGER, *Geschichte der Manufakturen* [*see* Document **2/6**], p. 591. (Ed. Tr.)

. . . I have . . . to draw attention here to the fact that it would be possible to reduce the price of the goods much more† if these good people were able

* See Glossary.

† The selling price in Eberswalde steel goods was too high; there was therefore a

to economize a little, or at least could be made to be more economical by domestic supervision by their overseers, since the present leniency seems to do no good. As it is, they are the opposite; the men make fools of themselves over their wives, and the women over their children; here is the origin of the excessive luxury, and the rottenness is carried on from one generation to the next. Since these things have to be said, Your Excellency will permit me to state, for your information, that they take their wives, not from among the honest well-brought up daughters of the local town or countryside, but like the Jews, they choose them for reasons of infatuated love and passion, from the spoilt people of Ruhle. As soon as they clap eyes on each other, they get betrothed, and all they then think about is getting the banns called and living together. Thus the wife knows nothing of cooking, washing, sewing, spinning or other domestic duties, the man who has to work gets hungry, eats the meat raw from the pot before dinner, but often because of poor preparation the whole dinner has to be thrown out into the yard and still the husband does not see that he has bought a pig in a poke. So his money runs through his fingers, the husband wastes money on his wife and the wife on the child, on a whole lot of useless finery and tinsel. The townspeople and the Jews know how to profit by this, lend them money until they are deep in debt, cheat them over putting it on the slate, and when it comes to paying up, there is constant litigation to the benefit of the town's arbitration tribunal, the bias is always in favour of the townspeople, and these manufacturing workers, who really need someone to look after them, lose all they have, and a lot more could be said about it, but has already been put on record.

5/4 Government Control over German Miners

Regulations for the miners in the Duchy of Cleve, Principality of Meurs and County of Marck, 6 May 1768. Printed in GERHARD ADELMANN (ed.), *Quellensammlung zur Geschichte der Sozialen Betriebsverfassung* (*Ruhrindustrie*), Vol. I (Bonn, 1960), pp. 14-16. (Ed. Tr.)

Whereas H.M. the King of Prussia, our gracious Sovereign, etc., has awarded a general privilege to the miners of the Duchy of Cleve, the Principality of Meurs and the County of Marck, dated Berlin, 16 May 1767, and has been graciously pleased to grant them a gild charter; it is therefore necessary for everyone to know in future how to conduct himself after swearing the oath of loyalty and obedience, and therefore the Royal Mining Office is issuing the following regulations:

slump in demand. The attempt was made to make prices competitive by cutting wages. (Krüger's comment.)

(1) All miners below and above ground shall register in the Royal register of miners and swear an oath by Almighty God to remain loyal to our gracious King of Prussia . . . and to show obedience to the Cleve-Meurs-Marck Mining Office set above them.
(2) They shall live honourably and respectably, and appear on all working days at the mine at the proper time for the morning service: on penalty for those who are absent of half a shift's wage for the first offence, and a whole shift's wage for the second time, but for the third time, if offending deliberately, they shall be discharged without a discharge note and never be re-employed in any of this country's mines.
(3) After morning service they have to make ready for the work to which they are ordered by managers, overmen or deputies, and perform it loyally and diligently, and not leave it until the end of the shift.
(4) They must not change shifts without permission, on any pretext whatever.
(5) They must stay at their work and keep their binding and not leave it, but if they have good reason to leave their work and their contract, they must give previous notice, when their wage and leaving certificate will be handed to them: anyone leaving his job without sufficient notice shall not only not receive his discharge note, but shall also be punished, and his wages due to him shall be forfeit to the miners' benefit fund.
(6) Anyone leaving his shift or bond without previous knowledge of overman or deputy, or leaving the pit before his time, shall be fined 5 Stbr.* for each offence.
(7) Coal hewers shall
(a) hew the coal as far as possible in large lumps;
(b) complete the task work set them every shift and not leave their stall until it is put in such condition that work can start next day at once; but if
(c) it should befall that for accidental causes the set quantity of coal cannot be produced, they shall nevertheless stay on for the whole of the 8 hours of the shift.

Whoever is found deliberately offending against this, shall be fined one shift's wage for the first offence, 2 shifts' for the second, and shall be discharged without discharge note at the third time.
(8) All workers shall obey willingly any order by their overmen or deputies to work a by-shift in special cases, and to move to a different pit on similar penalty.
(9) They shall be satisfied with their fixed wage and, on penalty of 10 Rthlr.,* shall not accept any tips, on any pretext.
(10) All miners, in all mines, and pits . . . shall behave decently, quietly and

* See Glossary.

peacefully, without invective, swearing, blasphemy, fighting or brawling, avoiding all riot and tumult, still less being guilty of raising one or helping to raise one, and in general conduct themselves as befits an honest miner. Whoever offends against this, shall be punished, according to the royal mining regulations . . . in proportion to the gravity of the offence.

(11) In case of fire or other accident in the mines or in the buildings nearby, they shall at the first sign or notification hurry without fail to the aid of those affected, and assist them as much as lies in their power to prevent further damage.

(12) They shall also wear, without exception, miners' habit, otherwise they shall not be employed or kept in employment. Finally

(13) On entering their name in the miners' register they shall pay once and for all the sum of 10 Stbr. to the miners' benefit fund, and out of each Rthlr. wage they shall pay over another Stbr: from which each of them shall enjoy all possible assistance in case of accident or illness in the mines, for medical expenses as well as maintenance, and in case he shall prove incurable or be unable to work further because of age, shall receive a pension as long as he lives.

(*Signed*) Hagen, 6 May 1768.

Form of oath:
I . . . promise and swear a solemn oath by Almighty God that I will keep the above regulations, which I have read or at least well understood, in all respects; so help me God and his Holy Word, through Jesus Christ.

5/5 Hospitals in France

J. HOWARD, *The State of the Prisons in England and Wales . . . with an account of some foreign prisons and hospitals* (2nd ed., Warrington, 1784), pp. 149–151.

PARIS: HOSPITALS

L'Hôpital de St. Louis for the sick, and *L'Hôtel Dieu*, are indeed the two worst hospitals that I ever visited. They were so crowded, that I have frequently seen five or six in one bed, some of them dying. In one of my visits at *L'Hôtel Dieu*, I observed the number of patients written up to be three thousand six hundred and fifty-five.*

But though these two hospitals are abominable, and a disgrace to Paris, it has many other charitable foundations which do honour to it; and from

* Over one of the gates of this hospital is the following inscription, which, from its application to *such a place*, has an air of ridicule and even of profaneness. '*C'est icy la Maison de Dieu, et la Porte du Ciel.*' [This is the house of God, and the gate of heaven.] (Note by Howard.)

which this country may derive useful information. – This is a subject foreign to my chief purpose, and I have perhaps already enlarged too much upon it. I cannot help, however, just mentioning a few of these foundations.

In the *Hôpital de lá Pitié* there were about one thousand four hundred and twenty boys, who are clothed, and taught to read, spin &c. These boys are admitted at about four years of age, and put out apprentices at thirteen or fourteen.

L'Hôpital des Incurables is designed for the aged, infirm, and distorted, who are here clothed in a neat uniform, the *men* in gray, and the *women* in black. The *nuns* attend upon them.

Le Quinze Vingt Hôpital is appropriated to blind persons.

L'Hôpital des petites Maisons et des Insensez is situated in a spacious garden or court, containing a number of small houses for the aged and infirm of both sexes, and an hospital for the *insane*. Here are also infirmaries for the sick, which the *nuns* kindly superintend. The neatness and cleanliness I observed in them gave me such pleasure as engaged me to repeat my visit. Each person of the insane has a separate room; and they also are taken care of by the good sisters. . . .

The *Hôtel Dieu* at Lyons is by the river side (the Rhone.) The principal building is in the form of a cross, near three hundred feet from end to end both ways. The wards thirty-two feet wide, and twenty-five feet high; with apertures between the joists of the floor above, and two tier of windows; in many of them two casements. Three rows of iron bedsteads in each ward. Under a dome in the centre is an octagon altar, in view from every part of the cross. Prayers, which are read there twice a day, can be heard through the wards. This part of the house is for those that have *fevers*. There are other wards for the *wounded*; for *lying-in-women*; for *foundlings*; for the *insane*: all separate: and a room for chirurgical operations. The cross-wards are so airy, as not to be in the least offensive: and yet there are, in another part of the house, two upper rooms still more airy and pleasant, (*chambres de convalescence:*) to these they remove patients that are recovering: and those whom I saw there said they were very refreshing. They come down from them at meals to a refectory. These rooms soon complete the patients recovery; and seem an excellent precaution against the slow hectic fever, of which our hospital-physicians so frequently complain; and it is chiefly on account of these that I mention the house.* The whole was clean and quiet. There are eight chaplains; nine physicians and surgeons; and twelve sisters. These are ladies of a

* I was induced to take such particular notice of this hospital, from the recollection of something similar to these *chambers of convalescence* proposed by my ingenious friend Mr. Aikin of Warrington, in his *Thoughts on Hospitals*. I had not the pamphlet then with me, but have since turned to the passage, and find he advises that 'all patients capable of sitting up, should remain through the day in large airy halls.' (Note by Howard.)

religious order, dressed in a neat uniform, who make up, as well as administer all the medicines prescribed; for which purpose there is an elaboratory and apothecary's shop, consisting of five or six apartments, the neatest and most elegantly fitted up that can be conceived.

5/6 Public Health in Venice

J. HOWARD, *An Account of the Principal Lazarettos in Europe....* (Warrington, 1789), pp. 12–17.

The *health-office* at Venice was instituted by decree of the senate in the year 1448, in the midst of a very destructive pestilence, and afterwards confirmed and regulated by various subsequent decrees, till reduced to the excellent order in which it stands at present. This important office is governed by three commissioners, annually chosen by the senate, whose duty it is to attend every day to the business of the office; and to them are added two assistant commissioners, and two extraordinary, who have formerly served as junior commissioners, or are gentlemen of wisdom and experience: these last take their seats at the board when they think it requisite, or when cases of difficulty and danger require their counsel. The power or authority of this court is very extensive; for, when all the seven magistrates sit together, their judgments are decisive and without appeal, as well in civil as criminal affairs that relate to public health, all which fall under their cognizance; by which means this court is one of the most respectable in the government, and accordingly is always filled by persons of approved integrity and reputation, and in easy circumstances, in order to be less exposed to corruption, as their emoluments are very small, although it is a step towards more lucrative employments. . . .

. . . The court is always attended by a secretary, who is a notary public, advocate fiscal, and several clerks, who are for life or during good behaviour, and have their respective salaries. The priors of the lazarettos are subjected to this board, as are the guardians of health, and messengers, whose particular duties I shall afterwards describe. It maintains overseers in different parts of the city to inspect the provisions sold in the public markets, shops or otherwise, who make their report of whatever they find that might have a tendency to affect the public health; their business is also to superintend beggars, to prevent loathsome and noxious distempers being derived from want and misery, or other obvious causes; they keep an exact register of deaths, and the bodies of those who die without any previous malady, are accurately examined by the physician and surgeon immediately belonging to the office; both these have a fixed salary, and are consulted by the board in cases relating to their respective professions; they are also obliged in contagious emergencies to shut themselves up in the lazaretto to take care of the sick.*

The city of Venice has two lazarettos appropriated to the expurgation of merchandise susceptible of infection, coming from suspected parts, and for the accommodation of passengers in performing quarantine; as also for the reception of persons and effects infected in the unhappy times of pestilence. . . .

The internal government and direction of these lazarettos is committed in each to an officer called a *Prior*, who is chosen by the board of health, and accountable to it alone for his management; he has an assistant chosen by himself, and confirmed by the magistrates; both these have a competent salary, and are obliged to reside in the lazaretto, where a convenient habitation is assigned them. . . .

RULES.

He must see all the gates and doors of the different apartments locked every evening by sun-set, as well the outward gates as those of the apartments occupied by passengers, merchandise, and porters; he takes the keys into his possession, and suffers them not to be opened before sun-rise. And where there is any suspicion of infection, the gates must be kept constantly locked, and opened only for necessary occurrences, in the presence of the prior.

PRIOR'S DUTY.

He must not suffer dogs, cats or other domestic animals to go loose in the lazaretto.

He must neither buy nor sell, nor make bargains or contracts with passengers or others within the lazaretto, nor permit others to do so; neither are contracts of any kind, purchases or sales, nor even powers of attorney or other notarial acts allowed there, without express leave from the board; otherwise they are null and void.

He suffers no fishing boats, nor other small craft to come within a certain distance of the lazaretto, nor any communication between those in quarantine, and such boats.

He keeps a book wherein are regularly noted all persons who perform quarantine, together with a general inventory of their effects, and a particular distinct one of all goods and merchandise, copies of which he transmits to the health-office, at least once a month.

* Besides the health-office at Venice, every city, or town of any note or commerce has one of its own, upon the same plan as that of the metropolis, directed by gentlemen of the place not concerned in trade, who serve *gratis*, and think it an honour to watch over the health of their fellow-citizens; the necessary ministers and clerks are paid by the respective communities; and all these courts of health are dependent on that of Venice, and accountable to it in every respect. (Note by Howard.)

He cannot receive persons nor effects to perform quarantine without a mandate from the office, which mandate must be always accompanied by a messenger, and in the same form at their discharge. Neither can he admit visitors to those in quarantine without such a mandate, which (for visits) is given *gratis* from the office.* But public brokers are excluded from these visits, even if they had obtained a mandate for that purpose.

He is to take care that quiet and good order be maintained among the passengers and porters, and must not permit gaming, drinking, nor even such exercises and diversions as might produce a mixture of persons in different quarantines, or offend the circumspection of the place.

When a passenger or porter falls sick, the prior by means of the respective guardian takes care that he is separated from others in the same apartment as much as possible, and immediately gives notice to the board, who send their physician to examine diligently the nature of the disease, and any other physician may be called jointly with him; but they are not to transgress the cautions prescribed, or they would be detained in the same apartment, till the quarantine ended. The prior is authorized to execute the office of notary public in cases of necessity, for no notary is admitted without express order from the board; he therefore may draw up wills and testaments of those within his territory, but it must be done in the presence of five witnesses. When any person dies there, unless the physician of the office, together with the surgeon declare that his death proceeded not from any contagious cause, and that they are quite clear and explicit in their report, all those in his quarantine must begin it anew, and that as often as any suspected death happens in it. There is a burial place within the lazaretto, and the dead are all buried naked, by those of their respective apartments, and if there is any suspicion of infection, a quantity of quick-lime is thrown upon the corpse in the grave, which is digged five or six feet deep.

It is the *prior's duty* to see that the guardians of the respective quarantines cause the passengers to expose their apparel, and other effects to the open air every day, and that they give all proper assistance to those under their guard.

He ought to visit every apartment under quarantine at least twice a day, once in the morning, and once after noon, to see that the passengers are properly served and supplied with necessaries, and that every thing goes on according to the rules and cautions of health. He is to take into his possession all sorts of arms belonging to passengers, which are to be restored when the quarantine is finished. . . .

When letters are written from the lazaretto they must be fumigated in the

* Adjoining to the prior's house, there are *parloirs*, where these visits are made generally in the presence of the prior, sub-prior or guardian, and sometimes of all of them. (Note by Howard.)

usual way by the guardian who superintends the apartment, then reached to the prior by means of a cane, or other stick split in the end for that purpose, and by him sometimes perfumed and sent away. He causes the porters employed in expurgation of goods, to sweep and keep clean their respective sheds, and all around them, suffering no bits of wool, cotton, or such like to fly about, or to lie on the ground when there is any passage; and attends with the most vigilant exactness to the porters in the discharge of their daily duty. . . .

The *prior* and his substitute must carefully avoid touching either goods or passengers in quarantine, and for that end, in their walks and visits always carry a cane to keep passengers at a proper distance; but if by an unfortunate accident they should be contaminated by touch, they must perform the quarantine from whence the suspicion of infection was derived, and others would be appointed in their room, *pro tempore*. If they were touched by malicious design, the person offending is liable to such punishment as the nature of the offence requires, and the magistrates of health judge adequate.

Neither the prior nor his substitute must leave the lazaretto, except when called by the magistrates, or upon business with them relative to his office; and not without express permission, on his private affairs.*

GUARDIANS.

There are sixty *guardians* belonging to the health-office of Venice, of whom part are appointed to inspect the quarantines of passengers, merchandise, and the porters attending it in the lazaretto, and part superintend the quarantines of ships and their companies, on board which they are sent immediately on their arrival, and continue till their discharge; all these have a fixed daily allowance, from the passengers, masters of ships or merchants in whose service they immediately are. Their duty in the lazaretto is to attend on passengers, to assist them in their accommodation and otherwise, and strictly to observe that no mixture of different quarantines happens; as every apartment of passengers by the same ship, or if goods and porters have their respective guardian, none of them are permitted to go without the limits of their allotted apartment, unless accompanied by the guardian, who has his cane to keep others at a due distance. . . .

The duty of *guardians* on board ships is still more strict, and requires greater attention; for, not having the prior to direct them in any emergency, as in the lazaretto, they must correspond directly with the office, and give an account of every thing that happens immediately. On their going abroad,

* On desiring the prior to shew me the rules for the officers of the lazaretto, he presented me with a printed copy, entitled *Commissioni in via d'istruzione, ad nuovamente eletto Priore del lazaretto*. In Venezia 1726, quarto, 48 *pages*. (Note by Howard.)

they must take an exact roll of all the ship's crew, which they transmit to the office, and they must see them all mustered every day, that no sickness be concealed, nor elopement made. They must also take a distinct and minute note of all goods and effects on board without exception, a copy of which they also transmit to the office, in order to prevent contraband goods being clandestinely retained. After this they must on no consideration allow any thing to go out of the ship, nor must they suffer any bark or other vessel to come near without a mandate; and when visits are permitted to the captain or crew, the guardian must always be in sight of the interview, that the due cautions of health be carefully observed. They are to take care that the sutlers appointed to serve ships in quarantine, perform their duty faithfully, and with due regard to the rules of health, in like manner as in the lazaretto.

5/7 Charitable Institutions in Gratz (Styria)

RICHARD BRIGHT, *Travels from Vienna through Lower Hungary* (Edinburgh, 1818), pp. 631–633.

Gratz is rich in charitable institutions, and in establishments for education; of the former, the principal is a comprehensive institution for the *care of the poor*. This is divided into seven separate departments. *1st*, The hospital in which the patients are received, according to their circumstances, either gratis, or on paying at the rate of 10 kreutzers, 30 kreutzers, or a florin per day.* *2d*, The lying-in charity, of which, as it differs much from any thing in this country, I shall give some particulars, extracted from the rules of the house. The object is to afford to unfortunate women an asylum, and not only to shield the mother from public shame and from want, but to give protection to the guiltless infant. The patients consist of four classes, like those of the general hospital, the first class having separate chambers and nurses. Those who pay are received from every part of the country, without any regard to their condition in life. Those who are received without pay, and for whom ten beds are appropriated monthly, must bring proof of their real poverty, and of their having become pregnant within the limits of the city, or of having lived there during ten years at some former period of their lives. If, however, in very urgent cases this rule is dispensed with, the mother is obliged to take charge of her own child, or to pay herself the appointed sum to the parish on which the burden falls. Married women can have no claim to be received into this house, and exceptions are made in very few instances.

The women who pay are only required to speak to the surgeon in chief,

* See Glossary.

who is also the accoucheur, respecting their admission, and may at any time be received on paying for a month in advance; but if they are sufficiently recovered to leave the house before the expiration of that time, the balance is restored to them, and the surgeon gives all the requisite information to the board of directors regarding the circumstance of the admission.

Those who wish to be received gratis, must apply to the governor and committee of the institution, and shew their proper certificates; and when these are satisfactory, the patient is referred to the surgeon, who takes the patient under his care, and communicates the circumstance to the board.

It is not requisite that any woman who is received, whether gratuitously or for pay, should declare herself to any other than those above mentioned; and as secrecy is the great rule of the establishment, all inquiries respecting the father, or other circumstances not immediately connected with the prescribed rules of admission, are strictly prohibited.

When the patient has been declared a proper object, she may come to the house at any hour either of the day or night, and the porter will shew her to the room prepared for her reception, or if she does not chuse to apply to him, the surgeon will do it. Women who pay a florin, or 30 kreutzers, are not even required to declare their true names. It is, however, necessary that they should write their real Christian and surnames upon a ticket, sealed up, and in that way shewn to the surgeon; this the woman keeps in her own possession, having the number of her chamber and bed marked upon it, so that, in case of death, the offices may give the proper information to the relatives. Those who pay are likewise at liberty to disguise themselves with masks or veils, or in dresses of any kind they please, may enter at the very hour of labour, and may leave the house as soon as they please, or, if the surgeon think it proper, may remain longer than the usual period. They may either take the child with them, or put it to board at their own expence, or deliver it, on payment of 18 florins, to the provincial foundling institution, just as suits their views.

The *third* department of this institution comprises the orphan and foundling house. The former provides for children who are bereft of their parents by death, the latter for illegitimate offspring and children who have been exposed. Where poverty is proved, the children are taken free of all expence; in other cases, a certain small sum is paid at the time the child is received; and in the case of exposed children, the parish pays the sum required.

The *fourth* department is an asylum for lunatics; the *fifth* an alms-house for old people; the *sixth* consists of a fund for pensioners connected with the hospitals; and the *seventh* of a similar fund in connection with the alms-house. I was conducted over the greater part of the buildings appropriated to the different objects of this national charity, and, in general, the whole appeared to be conducted with much care and judgment.

5/8 The Berlin Poor-House

a Order to end begging in streets and houses; Berlin, 20 December 1774. Printed in KRUEGER, *Geschichte der Manufakturen* ... [*see* Document **2/6**], pp. 615-617. (Ed. Tr.)

b J. D. F. RUMPF, *Beschreibung von Berlin und Potsdam* (Berlin, 1804): *Part I, Berlin*, pp. 422-423. (Ed. Tr.)

a Whereas His Majesty, on the 16th inst., has renewed the prohibition of begging in the streets and in houses and has made all giving of alms punishable; it has been decided to inform the public of the present measures for the relief of the poor, and to acquaint it with the main outlines of the above order:

1. In the new workhouse, now under the jurisdiction of the Royal Poors' Directory, the genuinely needy and the poor deserving sympathy shall be cared for better than hitherto, but the deliberate beggars shall more resolutely be made to work.

2. The past organization of this house has therefore been totally altered, so that all persons to be received in it shall be divided into two entirely separate main classes, differentiated both in the status of their work and its location, in their dormitory and in their board.

3. The first class is meant for the old and for other persons deserving help and sympathy, who cannot entirely live by their work and do not wish to beg. Those report to the Poor's Chest in the Town Hall of Berlin, with a certificate from the Minister of their Church, showing their hitherto unblemished character, and after their references have been checked, they shall be accepted. They spin in the house as much wool as their age and health permits, and if they spin more than the cost of their keep, the surplus shall be paid out to them.

4. Other respectable poor (*pauvres honteux*) who report for reception in this house shall also be received after due examination, in special rooms set aside for the purpose, shall be provided with food and decent work, and their payment shall be made as in the last case.

5. The second main class is destined for those who do not wish to make use of this benefaction, but would rather live by begging. These deliberate beggars will be arrested by the Poor Law Constables, if necessary with the assistance of the Police, irrespective of age or status, whether they be vaga-

bonds, journeymen, citizens, discharged soldiers, their wives or children, and will be sent to the workhouse.

6. Those who are caught begging for the first time shall be put into this class for three months at least, for the second time, for a year, and for the third and later times for several years, and according to circumstances, for life.

7. Similarly, this class is destined for those who after due process of law have been sent for punishment as runaway servants and apprentices, for a period of time determined by the Court.

8. All the persons under numbers 5, 6 and 7 shall be forced to spin and prepare wool, and shall be kept on a minimum standard, clearly differentiated from the first class, both in the status and quantity of their work, in their board and their lodging.

9. The children shall be cared for separately, after they have either been found begging themselves, or merely belong to beggars arrested, and shall receive education for several hours a day by the specially appointed schoolmaster, but in their work they shall be under the charge of a person of the first class.

10. Before a beggar is discharged, he must, in order that he shall not again become a public nuisance, prove an occupation in prospect or the existence of relations or of other persons, who will look after him and will put him up at once. . . .

16. No-one is allowed, on pain of 10 Rthlr.* to give shelter to a beggar without previous knowledge and permission of the Poor Directory.

b The Poor-House in the Royal Suburb has joined to it a hospital for the respectable poor (*pauvres honteux*). They are occupied spinning wool; but anything they earn above their keep is paid to them in cash. The other class consists of those entered as a punishment, the beggars, their wives and daughters arrested by the constables, the apprentices and servants who have run away, women who ply their clandestine trade of whores, and those cured of venereal disease; all those are kept in until they can prove that they can earn their living outside; they have to spin daily a certain quantity of wool on threat of punishment. In 1802 there were 297 hospital inmates, and 945 undergoing punishment. There is a church and a school in the building.

* See Glossary.

5/9 Comments on Poverty in Eighteenth-Century Spain

BERNARDO WARD, *Proyecto Economico en que se proponen varias providencias dirigidas a promover los intereses de España, con los medios y fondos necesarios para su plantificacion: escrito en el año de 1762* (Madrid, 1779), pp. 196–199. (Ed. Tr.)

Because the profitable employment of men is the most fundamental object of any economic system, in this chapter we shall deal with those who are usually wasted, *i.e.* the poor.

The poor are made up of three groups: 1. the old people and the sick who cannot work; 2. the idlers and vagabonds who do not want to work; and those who are in the majority; 3. the poor citizens who work hard, but because they have heavier burdens than they can support, suffer much misery.

The proposal in this work is directed mainly to the benefit of the last group. . . .

To aid the helpless poor, it is unnecessary to herd them into poor-houses, as is the case in other countries, but rather to grant to them a portion of the alms given to the prelates, convents and others, which today, as a result of deficient distribution, is largely responsible for sustaining idleness and feeding this vice amongst people who deserve punishment rather than pity, so that even before God Himself the former would be more acceptable than the latter.

To ensure that alms benefit only those who deserve them, it is necessary to prohibit completely all vagrant begging; this will be attained by the vigorous and stringent enforcement of the laws of the Kingdom on this matter, as is the case in England since the introduction of the law that no poor person may beg beyond his parish. . . .

Lately I have come to believe that begging has deeper roots in our Catholic countries than in the Protestant areas, because of the abuses which prevail in the great religious houses and as a consequence of the false interpretation which the vicious man wilfully imparts to the sacred activity of alms giving, so that he can call his own inclination a virtue.

The humility of a friar who, being able to satisfy his needs by such means, subjects himself to living off alms, is without doubt a powerful and estimable example; but when the child sees its mother kiss the hand of the friar when she gives alms to him; to see veneration joined to mendacity in such a manner creates in the child from an early age an impression which, among uneducated people, who cannot differentiate between religious poverty and culpable mendacity, inclines them unconsciously towards a life of begging. In those countries where there are neither mendicant religious nor pilgrims and where poverty is not seen in such a favourable light, the horror with which it is viewed by most people is a powerful factor working in favour of diligence and industry.

For this reason Spain needs some vigorous provision to uproot this inclination towards vagrancy; and it would be desirable to establish by law throughout the Kingdom that no one should be admitted into any royal or municipal employment nor into any brotherhood (*Hermandad o Confradia*) unless he could show that he had been continuously employed in his own village or elsewhere in some honest occupation; and that whoever absented himself from home for one year after the age of 18, and could not provide evidence that he had been honourably employed should be regarded as a vagabond; if this is rigorously observed, in time mere exclusion from the Hermandad and Confradia would impress a stigma of infamy on vagabondage.

To this provision it is appropriate to add punishment for those who do not want to be reformed; and the best form of state action would be to condemn them to public works, on roads and canals, etc.

As a result of rooting out mendacity, the real poor will be few, and known to the authorities, and charity and social policy will contrive a thousand ways of relieving their misery.

5/10 The Law of the Maximum

Law of the Maximum, 29 September 1793. Printed in J. HALL STEWART, *A Documentary survey of the French Revolution* (New York, 1951), pp. 499-500.

1. The articles which the National Convention has deemed essential, and the *maximum* or highest price of which it has believed it should establish, are: fresh meat, salt meat and bacon, butter, sweet oil, cattle, salt fish, wine, brandy, vinegar, cider, beer, firewood, charcoal, coal, candles, lamp oil, salt, soda, sugar, honey, white paper, hides, iron, cast iron, lead, steel, copper, hemp, linens, woolens, stuffs, canvases, the raw materials which are used for fabrics, wooden shoes, shoes, colza and rape, soap, potash, and tobacco.

2. Among the articles specified in the above list, the *maximum* price for firewood of the first quality, that of charcoal, and of coal, are the same as in 1790, plus one-twentieth. The decree of 19 August on the fixing of the prices of firewood, coal, and peat by the departments is revoked.

The *maximum* or highest price of tobacco in rolls is twenty *sous** per *livre*,* eight ounces; that of smoking tobacco is ten *sous*; that of a *livre* of salt is two *sous*, that of soap is twenty-five *sous*.

3. The *maximum* price of all other commodities and merchandise specified

* See Glossary.

in article 1 shall be, throughout the entire extent of the Republic and until the month of September next, the price of 1790, as stated by the market prices or the current prices of each and every department,* plus one-third; deduction being made for fiscal and other fees to which they were then subject, under whatever denomination they may have existed.

4. The tables of the *maximum* or highest price of each of the commodities specified in article 1 shall be drafted by each district administration, posted within a week of receipt of the present decree, and dispatched to the departments.

5. The *procureur-général-syndic** shall dispatch copies thereof, within the ensuing fortnight, to the provisional Executive Council and to the National Convention. . . .

7. All persons who sell or purchase the merchandise specified in article 1 for more than the *maximum* price stated and posted in each department shall pay, jointly and severally, through the municipal police, a fine of double the value of the article sold, and payable to the informer; they shall be inscribed upon the list of suspected persons, and treated as such. The purchaser shall not be subject to the penalty provided above if he denounces the contravention of the seller; and every merchant shall be required to have a list bearing the *maximum* or highest price of his merchandise visible in his shop.

8. The *maximum* or highest figure for salaries, wages, manual labor, and days of labor in every place shall be established, dating from the publication of the present law until the month of September next, by the general councils of the communes, at the same rate as in 1790, plus one-half.

9. The municipalities may put in requisition and punish, according to circumstances, with three days' imprisonment, workmen, manufacturers, and divers laborers who refuse, without legitimate grounds, to do their usual work. . . .

17. During the war, all exportation of essential merchandise or commodities is prohibited on all frontiers, under any name or commission whatsoever, with the exception of salt.

18. The items above specified which are destined for export and are intercepted in contravention at a distance of two leagues on this side of the frontier, and without a permit from the municipality of the place of the driver, shall be confiscated, with the vehicles, beasts of burden, or vessels transporting them, for the benefit of those who detain them; and a penalty of ten years' imprisonment shall be imposed upon the contraveners, owners, or drivers.

19. In order that the crews of neutral or Frenchified vessels may not abuse the courtesy of hospitality by carrying off the surplus comestibles and

* See Glossary.

provisions of maritime cities and places, they shall present themselves to the municipality, which shall cause whatever they need to be purchased.

20. The present decree shall be dispatched by special messengers.

5/11 Dispute of Berlin Calico Printers over Apprenticeship, 1783

a Petition by the men to the King, to stop the further training of apprentices; Berlin 11 April 1783;

b Protest to Minister von Heinitz against the arrest of eleven calico printers; Berlin, 18 June 1783;

c Sentence on the accused calico printers; Berlin, 21 July 1783. All printed in KRUEGER, *Geschichte der Manufakturen* . . . [*see* Document **2/6**], pp. 560–562, 640–642. (Ed. Tr.)

a Our poor living and the real fear that the larger part of us, the calico printers, must necessarily soon be totally impoverished, drive us to ask Your Majesty humbly

> to be graciously pleased to order the calico manufacturers to refrain for the time being from taking on any more apprentice lads.

The shortage of work has induced many of us to turn their backs on this country, leaving their needy families behind, to which sorry fate we are all liable in the future. That this is a fact is based on our sad experience, that in the calico works here journeymen calico printers have to leave for reasons of poverty and inability to find work because there are so many apprentices employed, yet nevertheless there are 15 still out of work at present, who are in the sad position of not being able to provide a living for themselves and their families. It is no wonder, for in the last 10 years 130 new men have been trained up.

There are among us older men, who work as well as their powers allow, and can make a reasonable living, yet because, in view of their age, they cannot work as fast as lads just out of their time, they have to expect daily to be discharged by the manufacturer, which is the greatest injustice, and they may then go begging for all they care, for even if they have worked for a firm here for 20 or 30 years, they still have nothing to hope from the owner. It is true that apprentices are more profitable to the employers than journeymen, for they work for 5 years at only half-wages, from which it must follow, that older calico printers, no matter how many years they have behind them, are sacked because of the many new apprentices and have to leave the country, and we can prove to your Majesty that the shortage of work has forced even registered ones to emigrate.

The manufacturers allege falsely that an apprentice or a man just out of his time works better than an old printer, but it stands to reason that a man who has been in the works for many years understands more than an apprentice or a man just out of his time, and it is just that the latter is more profitable to the employer.

It has even come to pass in the works here that one apprentice has to instruct another, which is totally unheard of. The manufacturer himself is either a merchant or a Jew, and therefore cannot teach anyone the trade, because he does not know it himself, and since we journeymen, because so many are now idle, neither can nor will teach any more, we are immediately threatened with the sack, and, as stated above, one apprentice is set to teach another.

We are prepared to offer that if the further training of apprentices is suspended for the time being, then those who emigrated in secret shall be brought back, and if they and the unemployed are put back in work, and there is a shortage of printers in the works, then we promise to start taking apprentices again, yet since at present the works, far from being enlarged, are being reduced in size, the teaching of more apprentices is totally unnecessary if we older printers are to earn our bread.

But if the training of new apprentices is found necessary, we journeymen are prepared and willing to teach them, but on condition that the apprentices, until the training is complete, shall belong to the printer and not to the merchant, since the latter is not a printer and consequently cannot teach any lads, nor ought he to draw any profits from it. For just as the merchants would not allow that any of us should go into their business, so the teaching is our business.

Further, our earnings are not so high as to allow one, in one's old age, to settle down at leisure and live without working, but on the contrary we have to work until the end, as long as we are able. Our work only runs for three-quarters of a year, since we cannot work by artificial light, and for a quarter of the year we have to live miserably from our savings.

In every other trade, the masters can live in their old age on their journeymen and apprentices, but we must always remain journeymen and can therefore not look forward to this for our old age. Although we have a sick and funeral fund, this cannot keep the old and unemployed printers; we pay them a small sum out of our wages, but it is not enough, and the manufacturers don't give them a penny. In order to alleviate this sorry situation and in order to remain able to support those who are already impoverished and out of work, and the widows, we would humbly beg Your Majesty to be graciously pleased,

after proper enquiry of the above facts, to order the local calico manufacturers not to take any more apprentices for the time being, and to consider the trade of calico printer as closed until a shortage shall be felt. . . .

b Your Excellency,

The whole of the body of calico printers make so bold as to present this petition in humblest submission.

The employer, Ermler, has had the audacity to have eleven of the printers in his employ arrested by the guard on the 15th inst., at his arbitrary decision, without the Courts, without cause, therefore out of caprice, and to have them led in public through the town to the new market place and from there to Calands Hoff, where they are still being held.

This action of Ermler is severely punishable, since it may be the practice to treat in this way common rogues or those guilty of attempting violent or murderous assault, but not good citizens who have wives and children, and who, if they were in fact punishable, which does not apply in this case, could be found at any time, for it would in truth be intolerable if a manufacturer had the power to arrest arbitrarily any printer employed by him.

We would like to represent to Your Excellency what may have induced Ermler, though unlawfully, to have the eleven printers arrested. They will have been picked out,

> since we are in dispute with the manufacturers before the General Directory about the taking on of too many apprentices, where one lad has to teach the others, for which there has not been a decision as yet.

Despite this, this Ermler has nevertheless taken on another seven apprentices, although the dispute has not yet been settled, from which it may be concluded that he intends

> to discharge six or seven of his printers out of the fourteen that he employs, in his works. We questioned him about it with the greatest moderation, and told him that if he did not get rid of the boys and sacked seven printers instead, the rest of his printers would give notice, and this is the real reason why eleven printers have been arrested by him. We therefore ask Your Excellency most humbly and submissively, to order the immediate liberation of the printers arrested by Ermler, since the whole of the body of calico printers engage themselves to stand surety that the said printers shall present themselves before the authorities whenever they are desired to do so.

We hope for a gracious consideration,

All the calico printers. . . .

[Marginal comment, Proepken; Berlin, 19 July 1783:
Decision of the Chamber following the Rescript of 16th. If the calico printers arrested by Ermler have stirred up their comrades about the dispute (which

has since been decided against them) over the apprentices to be set on by the entrepreneurs, or inveigled them into laying down their tools, or into committing other illegalities of equal damage to the general interest of the country's factories, they shall be punished according to the Law. But if they have been guilty of only minor offences, or have been sent to Calandshof by Ermler in revenge, they shall be freed from arrest at once, and Ermler in addition shall face the consequences. They shall, under the resolution of the 16th, be warned again to behave quietly and in obedience to the Law, if they do not want to suffer the penalties enacted for those who stir up journeymen.]

c Since no calico printer can order his employer which journeymen he is to keep, what work he is to give to any of them and how many apprentices he shall train, but all this depends entirely on the arbitrary decision of the entrepreneur.

(1) It is in consequence an obvious obstruction and punishable riot, if those who were not discharged attempted to force Ermler to keep on the others;
(2) Accost him in his house, moreover,
(3) in large number, meddle in other people's affairs, and start a common riot against Ermler, conducting themselves in a coarse and uncivil manner.

so therefore all the eleven arrested calico printers are to be punished for obstruction and riotous assembly, in addition to the arrest already suffered, by four days' prison, half on bread and water, and warned that in future, riots will be punished much more severely, as an example and warning to others, according to the sentence, by imprisonment in the fortress or public pillory, and if the ringleaders cannot be found, those shall be considered guilty who show an interest for others or who declare that they are giving notice or dictating to their employer for the sake of others, and they shall remain under arrest until such time as they name those who have uttered the threats. Since Blumenberg Jr. and Crone, who escaped arrest, were equally guilty of riotous assembly, they shall be punished by eight days' prison, of which the first and last two days shall be on bread and water. After their punishment, Ermler has to give a proper discharge to those with whom he cannot agree on further terms of employment, with the comment that they have been discharged because there is no further need for them in his factory.

But if in future any calico printer shall be discharged because of rioting, he will have to face the fact that this will be entered in his discharge note, as an example and warning to others.

Philippi. Troschel.

5/12 Peasant Unrest in Saxony, 1790

Broadside of rebellious peasants; Dresden, 1790. Printed in PERCY STULZ and ALFRED OPITZ, *Volksbewegungen in Kursachsen zur Zeit der französischen Revolution* (Berlin, 1956), Appx., pp. 1–5. (Ed. Tr.)

We, united by solemn oath and covenant, numbering 20,000, wish all our readers grace, wisdom, understanding and blessing, particularly our dear Elector Frederick August, his friends and relations.

Oh Lord from the beginning and in all eternity, great King and Lord of all Lords, of the heavens and the earth, put our Elector into a state of prosperity, crown him with wisdom and understanding, bless him from your great height and give him grace from your throne, allow the streams of your benediction to flow on to him and our land, so that we may all together live in peace. Therefore we beseech you, let wisdom flourish and grow in our Electoral Saxony, wherefor we will give you thanks. We also ask you that in your goodness right and justice should find room here and that our land should be cleansed of all injustice. That it should enjoy prosperity and that our house of Saxony should again reach a fair state of comfort, and ask God to bless with heavenly wisdom our Elector Frederick August so that he should see the injustice which now covers our land and whereby the poor people are being tortured, and among the stewards and chamberlains at Court, the nobles and others of their fellows, and even the ordinary people from swineherds up to royal councillors, there is nothing but corruption.

In the name of God the All Highest of the Holy Trinity, the wise Regent and King of Kings, and Lord of Lords,

We hereby give notice to all and sundry, that because of the great suffering in our land of Saxony a rebellion has broken out and we hereby make known to our people and ask them to take note. . . .

FIRST

Risk your life, your property and your blood to save us from misery and want, and do not get cast down by fear, for we can die once only, and then all our misery and want will be ended; therefore hold fast, do not turn aside to the right or to the left, and remain steadfast. Herewith we put ourselves into the hands of God. Amen.

1. We bid the nobles . . . those fiends calling themselves Lordships in our country and attempting to be Gods on earth, but who should be in truth called devils, unless these nobles should free all their subjects from their services, rents, labour dues, grain dues, protective moneys, hereditary rents, St. Michael's rents, and in total for all services, they shall suffer great depreda-

tions; their estates shall be sacked, destroyed and burnt, and all nobility that shall rise on our land shall be beaten to the ground and hunted from the land; the tongues of these hounds of hell shall be torn from their mouths and shall be put to public exhibition in all streets, wherever there shall be no help for the poor and the miserable, and where they do not cease to torment and to oppress and to torture, such wages will await you, nobles of this land. In the name of God.

2. There shall be the same wages to the lawyers, who are the devils and companions of these nobles, suck the poor man's blood and don't cease from it, before they have made them into beggars. In the name of God.

3. The inspectors, collectors, scriveners, excise officers, are equally devils and hounds of hell, sucking the blood of the poor people, and their wages shall be equal those of the nobles, you dogs of hell. In the name of God.

4. Equally, the collectors of the meat tax, hounds of hell who will suck the blood of the poor people, shall expect the same wages as the noblemen. In the name of God.

5. The collectors of the beer tax shall have the same wages, and the devils and hounds of hell should have wages like noblemen. In the name of God.

6. No nobleman shall alone form any government, but should always select wise men from the country who shall try to help the poor people, and help to raise the prosperity of the Prince, who shall love right and justice and improve the Commonwealth. In the name of God.

7. The poll tax, squeezed and tormented out of the small people, and many a labouring man has to give the money which he had to work for by the sweat of his brow to some rich lordling and being thereby so tormented that he had to beg for his bread, and nevertheless the rich lordling makes money, torments the small people and cheats the Prince. For how much of it does the Elector himself get? Hardly more than one penny in a hundred: from a thousand thaler he gets hardly ten thaler, such is the extent of the corruption in Saxony. No one shall have pity on these hounds of hell, but they shall all pay with their head; for it is possible to protect yourself against thieves and rogues, but not against such people who have the power to torment the poor. You hounds of hell. In the name of God.

8. You also, you citizens of Liebstadt . . . you have brought misfortune on your heads, as you have failed to free our brother Geisler, and if you do not make the effort to free this man again and to hand over this notice personally into the hands of the Elector, no house, no village, neither shall Liebstadt itself be spared, but all the houses shall be burnt down; no man from your Lordship shall remain alive, from the smallest to the greatest, so see to

it that this notice is handed over to the Elector; and if you don't, you have been warned, and it will happen to you as I have written.

To be smuggled to Liebstadt.

Twenty Thousand Conspirators of the land of Saxony.

LAST

No man shall dare to do service to the lords and nobles, whether in rents, boon-work, grain dues and other services, . . . no one should dare to offer any services to the nobles; but he who shall dare to work further for the Lords, shall be hunted from the country, and he who shall in future dare to hand over his grain dues or any other, whatever its name, shall lose his property and his life, further if anyone should be traitor or informer to the nobles, he shall have his tongue cut out or torn out. You have been warned. In the name of God.

And if the lords shall not freely give up their services, there shall be a hard time for them such as has never been from the beginning to the end of time. There shall be no further nobility in our country; if they do not release their subjects from their services and burdens, there shall be no house of any noble or any squire left in our towns and countryside, but they shall all be destroyed, sacked and rased to the ground whenever they fail to free their subjects; and their plague shall last as long as they shall continue to oppress, torture and torment their subjects.

In Jerusalem, one man cried during the destruction 'woe, woe, woe'. And now to you nobles, over your Estate, we also shout 'woe, woe, woe'. This shall be our decision, from all of us, 'Woe, woe, you nobles, woe to your nobility, woe to your life, woe to your estates and castles'.

We, united by league and oath, twenty thousand men of the land of Saxony, put our name to this, all of us.

5/13 The Pugachev Rebellion

a A Pugachev Manifesto. Printed in *Materiali po istorii chuvashskoi A.S.S.R.* (4 vols., Cheboksary, Chuvashgosizdat. 1957–60), I, p. 332. (M.E.F., A.G.W. Tr.)

b Deposition of two cossacks, among others interviewed about the part they played in the Pugachev uprising and the battles on the Rivers Proleyka and Mechetraya; 18 August 1774. Printed in A. P. PRONSHTEIN (ed.), *Don i Nizhnee Povolzhe v period Krestyanskoi voiny, 1773–75 godov: Sbornik Documentov* (Rostov, Izdatel'stvo, Universiteta, 1961), pp. 81–83. (M.E.F., A.G.W. Tr.)

a We grant by this decree in our name in our regal and paternal mercy that all who were formally peasants and serfs of the landowners be loyal servants of our crown and we reward them with the right to practise their ancient faith, with leaders and elders, and freedom and liberty as cossacks, for ever, exemption from military service, poll or other money taxes, and the right to possess land, forest, hayfields, fishing rights and salt lakes without purchase of obrok,* and we abolish all taxes and oppressions imposed upon the peasantry and the whole people by the evil nobility and the corrupt judges, resident in the towns. And we wish you salvation and a quiet life in this world . . . for the sake of which we suffered persecution from the said nobility, and as our name flourishes now by the will of the Almighty, we order by this, our ukase, that these noblemen, enemies of our rule, and suppressors of the peasantry, be caught, punished and hanged and suffer similar treatment to that which they, not having Christian feelings, inflicted on you, the peasants. And after the destruction of these enemies, everyone will be able to experience the quiet life, which will go on for ever.

b On 18 August 1774, two Cossacks of the Don army were brought in with a report from the Starshiny† Vasily Grekov, Peter Kulbakov and Osip Lashchilin and were questioned in the cossack army office. . . .

They made the following depositions:

1. (Vasily Ivanovitch) Malakhov – 54 years of age, not very literate, was born in the Bukhanovskaya village, son of a Cossack (had sworn to serve the Tsar faithfully. . . .)
2. (Ivan Grigorevitch) Melekhov – 36 years of age, a Cossack, can read and write, was born on the Medveditsa river in the Skurishinskaya village, and after moving from it in 1770 now lives in the Berezovskaya village (had sworn to serve the Tsar faithfully. . . .)

Upon secondment to serve with Essaul† Petr Fomin in 1774 in Saratov in the supervision office, as members of the squadron of 200 men for watching the colonists and hunting brigands, Malakhov was a Sotnik† and Melekhov a Quartermaster under the command of Brigadier Ladyzhenskii.

On the third of this August, when the news reached there that the criminal and traitor Pugachev with his following was on his way to the town of Petrovsk, the aforesaid Essaul Fomin, together with them and also with two khorunzhii† and sixty Cossacks, were sent by Brigadier Ladyzhenskii to that town, under orders (as the aforesaid Essaul Fomin told them on the way) to gather intelligence about the rebel and to defend that town, and in case this should be impossible, to throw the cannons and gunpowder into the water and remove the treasury to Saratov; they were to be accompanied by Guards officer Derzhavin, who was then in Saratov and for whom fresh

* See Glossary.

† See note on Ranks below. (Ed.)

horses were prepared, but he did not join them. On their approach towards evening of the next day, the 4th, to within a kilometre of Petrovsk, Officer Gogilev on behalf of the said officer of the Guards caught up with them. At the same time they caught sight of the host of followers of the criminal and barbarian Pugachev, of whom the leading horsemen were already entering the town of Petrovsk from the hill, while the horsemen in the rear were bringing in quite a large number of waggons, without any resistance from the town, as the local inhabitants, it should be noted, and the clergy therein met him with icons, with the ringing of church bells, and with bread and salt; then Essaul Fomin and the officer assigned to him, who had come to join him on his (Fomin's) horse, and another officer who had met them on the road, a praporshchik* by the name of Shkuratov, taking some ten Cossacks with them, rode nearer to this crowd in order to investigate and find out how many there were of them, and what kind of people they were. Shortly, one after another two Cossacks were sent to them from Fomin, the first to say that those with poor horses should go off ahead, and the other to say that they should wait. Then the officer who had come to them, and after him Essaul Fomin and the other officer, galloped past, and the essaul (in Malakhov's hearing, since Melekhov was about 30 sazhens† away from the Cossacks at the time because he was suffering from the fever), began to shout: 'What are you waiting for? The enemy is here in Petrovsk. Get away!' and he held his own horse by the reins, facing along the road. At this point Malakhov told him why he would not join in the withdrawal: 'Some Cossacks have poor horses. It will be better for us to die here in the service of Her Imperial Majesty.' Fomin then declared that he would ride after Officer Gogilev and, having got his own horse back from him, would return to them, leaving the other officer, he said to get away, using the horses he came on in relays. And after that they did not see Fomin again.

At that very moment that they disappeared from view, they saw riders on horses galloping towards them carrying nine banners with various images of saints on them (however, without borders or gold and silver stars, only certain ones had embroidered small stars and also some had gold braid round the edges and others were without any border), and a horde of some 150 men surrounded them all, although they all had loaded muskets and were on horseback; and halting about 150 sazhens away, they sent a Yaik Cossack up to them. Malakhov heard this man, whose name he does not know, address them from a distance of about 20 sazhens, as follows: 'Do not resist with force of arms. His Majesty Petr Fedorovitch is here himself', and everyone got off their horses, whereupon the brigand rode back to his chief. Then another Yaik Cossack coming to them from the rebel said they should halt

* See note on Ranks below. (Ed.) † See Glossary.

their horses: 'The All-highest himself is coming up behind, and as soon as he rides up, put down your weapons and bow down on your knees.' And this Cossack did not ride away from them, and the rebel himself arrived with banners, and by such extremes they were forced, falling on their knees, to bow down and call him 'Your Imperial Majesty', as the Yaik Cossack ordered them to do. And he, sitting on his horse, asked them 'Who are you?', and hearing that they were Don Cossacks and had been in Saratov and calling them children, said: 'God and your Sovereign forgive all your sins, come and join me in the camp.' He then asked them who had run away from them, and finding out that it was the essaul and two officers, the chief rebel himself, changing his horse, set off after them on a brown horse with a javelin taken from a Cossack, with four of his men, and the remaining villains took all of them together with their image of the Mother of God and the horse-tail standard (which they had captured in the spring of that year, riding beyond the Volga to Yaik on the River Bol'shiye Uzenya, from a troop of ten rebel Yaik Cossacks commanded by Ivan Besshtan whom they had defeated) to their camp which was near the town of Petrovsk itself between the rose willows in the meadow, where there were two tents of this same rebel between which the Yaik Cossacks were located, and the third of a Yaik Cossack, Alexei Ivanov, calling himself the rebel's secretary; and putting them amongst the rank and file, they enrolled them in the regiment of the Yaik Cossack Afanasy Petrov. Towards evening the rebel himself arrived at the camp where they heard from the Yaik Cossacks that they had not managed to track down the essaul and one of the officers, but the other officer, Shkuratov, had been speared to death by one Yaik Cossack.

Then the rebel called both of them, Melekhov and Malakhov, and khorunzhii* of different villages, Vasily Popov from Ust'-Khoperskaya and Stepan Kalavrodov from Ust'-Medveditskaya to his tent in which supper was ready for them, and ordering them to sit, ordered them each to be served with two vessels of wine, saying: 'Drink, children, in my presence', and reminding them that they must serve faithfully, asked them: 'What pay do you get from the Empress?', and they said to him: 'We are satisfied with the salary received from our most merciful Sovereign', and he said: 'No, although you are satisfied, that is not enough to buy a saddle, never mind a horse. If you serve with me you won't have to be satisfied like that, but you will go about in gold, while as you are now the masters eat up your pay.' And at the same time he said: 'Listen my friends, I was three years in Egypt, three years in Tsaregrad, and in a third place (he, the witness, does not

* The Army ranks may be translated as follows:
Czarist Army: poruchik – lieutenant; podporuchik – second lieutenant; praporshchik – ensign. *Cossack Army*: essaul – captain; sotnik – lieutenant; khorunzhii – cornets. (Ed.)

remember where) three years.' And he has learnt all the foreign examples, not just ours: 'I know how to deal with the masters.' He confirmed that they should come to him morning and evening. And after these conversations ordered them to go and rest for the night.

5/14 Cahiers of the French Revolution

a Extract from the cahier of the Tiers État of Paris. Printed in J. M. THOMPSON (ed.), *French Revolution Documents* (Oxford, 1948), pp. 8–11. (Ed. Tr.)

b Preliminary cahier of the parish of Longnes. Printed in J. M. ROBERTS and R. C. COBB (eds.), *French Revolution Documents* (Oxford, 1966), p. 75. (Ed. Tr.)

a FINANCES

Article 1 All the taxes collected at present shall be declared null and illegal; and yet by the same act they shall be provisionally re-established, until the Estates General fix a time for their abolition and the commencement of collection of the freely-imposed subsidies.

Article 2 The debt of the King shall be verified, and, after examination, consolidated and declared a national debt, and in order to facilitate its discharge and to diminish its burden, it shall be decreed that the domaines engagés, and land sold or enfeoffed since 1556 shall be restored to the nation. Regarding these, the Estates General shall order the review of those claims which have not been legally established and afterwards take such action as they regard as in the best interests of the nation. . . .

Article 4 All discriminatory impositions of whatever kind . . . shall be suppressed and replaced if necessary by general taxes borne equally by all citizens and classes.

Article 5 Tolls shall be taken only at the entry to the Kingdom and customs posts shall be pushed back to the frontier.

Article 6 The Estates General shall concentrate particularly on the suppression of the unfortunate aides* and the gabelle tax* and the means of replacing them. They shall also concern themselves with the suppression of the tobacco farm, and its replacement by another tax.

Article 7 In replacing these taxes, the Estates General shall concentrate principally upon direct taxes, which bear equally on all citizens, and the collection of which is both easy and inexpensive.

AGRICULTURE

Article 1 The Estates General are specially and instantly invited by the Assembly to take into consideration at the earliest possible moment the

* See Glossary.

present dearness of grain and to seek out the cause and the perpetrators and to occupy themselves with measures for providing an effective and permanent remedy of the situation.

Article 5 Every property owner shall have the right to enclose his own ground and to cultivate all suitable crops and to work all the mines and quarries which are found there.

Article 6 The capitaineries* extend over 400,000 sq. leagues* and perhaps more; they constitute a perpetual scourge on agriculture. The deputies shall be especially charged to ask for the abolition of the capitaineries; they are . . . so opposed to every principle or morality that they cannot be tolerated. . . .

COMMERCE

Article 1 The various commercial treaties concluded between France and foreign powers shall be examined by the Estates General to ascertain and assess the effects of these treaties on France; and in future no treaty may be concluded unless the project has been communicated to all the Chambers of Commerce and the Estates General.

Article 2 A Chamber of Commerce composed of twenty merchants, traders, manufacturers, skilled workers and the most respectable artisans shall be established in all the principal towns. . . .

Article 3 National goods exported abroad shall be exempt from all export duties and foreign goods shall be subjected to an entry duty in accordance with their nature and value.

Article 4 The exportation from France of raw materials, vital for French manufacture, shall be forbidden, and all raw materials necessary for manufacture, and which are imported, shall be exempt from all duties.

Article 5 A request shall be made for bounties to be paid on French goods which are exported abroad.

Article 7 The Estates General shall be asked to determine, whether it is consonant with our commercial interests to conform rigorously to the rules regulating manufacturers, or whether it is necessary to modify them, or to grant to our manufacturers unrestricted freedom of activity.

Article 8 And in those instances where freedom cannot be granted, the inspectors and sub-inspectors of manufacture shall be chosen by a majority vote by the Chambers of Commerce, and shall be obliged to make reports on their visits, whenever required.

Article 9 All tolls, bridge tolls and other impositions of this kind shall henceforth be provisionally suppressed, subject to the reimbursement of those proprietors who exercise such rights by law.

* See Glossary.

Article 12 No re-coining of money, and no change in fineness or value may be undertaken without the consent of the Estates General.
Article 13 Uniformity of weights and measures shall be established throughout the Kingdom.

b We, the syndics* of the Parish of Longnes, as a result of the command addressed to us by the King, have convoked the general assembly of all the inhabitants of the parish, on this 8 March, to draw up their doléance, in conformity with the King's Command.

1. We beseech Your Majesty to abolish the gabelle and to throw open the trade in salt.
2. If it pleases You, we want Your Majesty to abolish all illegal taxes (*maltoute*) or taxes which are levied on foodstuffs and other kinds of basic necessities.
3. We want the contrôle* limited to a fixed amount, which is lower than its present level and also a reduction in the influence of notaries.
4. We want Your Majesty to grant that the taille* and the capitation* taxes together with additional impositions and duties which we pay to support the State, should be levied on real estate, such as chateaux, houses, farmland, meadow, wood, coppice, forest, vineyards, moors, ponds and streams and all other such things.
5. We want to have publicised such abuses as the opening of some road which ennables the seigneur to reach his chateau, but which does not have any general purpose.
6. We want taxation proceeds to be taken to the bureau in the provincial town and passed immediately into the King's coffers.
7. We want Your Majesty to grant to us the right to kill game, particularly rabbits and pigeons, which cause considerable damage in the countryside.
8. In view of the resulting abuses, we want the abolition of privileges relating to mills.
9. We want the execution of the stealers of horses and other beasts, in accordance with the rule of law.

Drawn up and decreed . . . this 8 March 1789.

* See Glossary.

PART II

The French Revolution and Peasant Emancipation in Europe

Chapter 6 The Revolutionary Legislation and Agrarian Settlement in France

Introduction

The effects of the revolution in France extended far beyond the borders of the Kingdom. This was so, not only because of the size and power of France, and the might of her armies which carried the revolutionary message across the length and breadth of the European Continent, but also because the intolerable conditions the revolution was trying to relieve, and the solutions it offered, were relevant and appropriate in greater or lesser degree in the rest of Europe also.

The forces radiating from Paris which changed the course of world history were too momentous to be easily described under a single head. Some were unleashed by men seeking to gain political influence or end legal disabilities. Others were stirred by new philosophies, by rationalism and the wider horizons opened out by the progress of science. But there can be no doubt that somewhere near the heart of these stirrings there lay the economic grievances and demands, just as there can be no doubt that the consequences of the Revolution in the economic field were among the most important and the most enduring.

There was scarcely a member of French economic life which did not suffer under the *ancien régime*, and there was scarcely an interest group that did not become convinced that piecemeal reform was no longer possible, and that only the total destruction of the oppressive rule of nobles and clerics, and ultimately of the King, could open the road to progress. The peasantry, the largest sector of the population, was sucked dry by feudal exactions, and searched in vain for a system of incentives that would allow it to increase its output and break through the vicious circle of growing pressure of population upon the land, leading with increasing frequency to famines and food shortages (**1/6**, **1/8**, **5/1**). Together with merchants, industrialists and the professions, they suffered from a taxation system that laid on them unfairly heavy burdens and gave them an unfairly low share of the benefits (**4/5**, **4/6**, **4/8**). Manufacturers and merchants suffered not only under the oppressive internal toll system (**4/7**), but also from the economic privileges of the gilds, and from those granted to favoured manufacturing and trading companies (**2/5**, **2/14**, **3/8**, **3/9**, **3/10**), and the social privileges withheld from them as a class (**2/18**). As a succession of Ministers proved unable to solve the internal problems and contradictions of the French economy, and the system proved unable to reform itself fundamentally, dissatisfaction came to a head when a series of calamities such as harvest failures (**5/1**, **5/10**, **5/14**), the competition of newly admitted English manufactures (**3/13**) and further tax demands were superimposed on an already overstrained situation in the last years and months before the events of 1789. Local rebellion turned into national revolution.

The significance of the social and economic forces which plunged France and Europe into turmoil may perhaps be judged best by what they achieved. The bourgeois classes emerged not only with a large share in political power, and the end of their legal disabilities, but had used these to gain a number of other important aims. Privileges and restrictions on their enterprise were swept away; internal tolls were abolished, but protective tariffs were raised against foreign imports (**6/2**); coinage, weights and measures were rationalized (**6/5**, **14/3**, **14/4**, **14/5**); the tax system was remodelled in their interest (**6/4**, also **14/1**, **14/2**); and, in apparent defiance of the 'principle' of liberty, but very much in the interests of employers, workmen's combinations were prohibited, and their general freedom of contract restricted (**6/3**). Hardly any demand common to the class as a whole was left unsatisfied.

The gains of the peasantry appear, at first sight, to have been equally satisfactory. One of the earliest actions of the National Assembly in 1789 was the abolition of feudal obligations and the manorial system in France, in the famous 'August 4th Decrees' (**6/1**), which also laid down the principles of equality before the law and the abolition of tax and other privileges. The result of the changes imposed on the basis of these principles during the revolutionary years, when the power of the nobility was at its lowest ebb, was the creation of a strong peasantry, firmly anchored to its land, but condemned, by its very success, to till the land in units that were too small for efficiency, and were worked with inadequate capital. The practical adoption of gavelkind reinforced the tendency towards small holding in the nineteenth century (**6/6**, **6/9**, **6/10**).

Thus, while the general economic developments of the century following the revolution allowed the bourgeoisie to register great advances from the base fortified in the earlier years, the peasantry, equally successful at first, found that in the long run most of its gain turned out to have been hollow. Those working under some form of métayage went on as before, and under much the same hardships (**6/7**, **6/10**, also **1/18**). Those who now held their own land, but in minute holdings, generally found themselves condemned to exceptionally hard work for low returns, and were at the mercy of harvests and market conditions which would force them deeper into debt, and ultimately drive them off the land, if they turned adverse (**6/8**, **6/9**, **6/10**). The tenacity with which the French peasant held on to his land also made recruitment into the factories more difficult, and thus may have helped to hold back their expansion. Those who saw merit in the system of *petite culture* did so more for the incentive it produced for hard work, than for the returns it yielded to the cultivators (**9/1**). In Flanders, the system of dwarf holdings led to greater poverty still (**6/11**).

6/1 Abolition of Serfdom in France

Decrees of 4 August 1789. Printed in STEWART, *A Documentary Survey* [*see* Document **5/10**], pp. 107-110.

* * *

1. The National Assembly abolishes the feudal regime entirely, and decrees that both feudal and *censuel* rights and dues deriving from real or personal *mainmorte* and personal servitude, and those representative thereof, are abolished without indemnity, and all others declared redeemable*; and that the price and manner of redemption shall be established by the National Assembly. Those of the said dues which are not suppressed by the present decree, however, shall continue to be collected until reimbursement has been made.

2. The exclusive rights to *fuies* and *colombiers* is abolished; pigeons shall be confined at times determined by the communities; and during such periods they shall be regarded as game, and everyone shall have the right to kill them on his own land.

3. The exclusive right of hunting and open warrens is likewise abolished†; and every proprietor has the right to destroy and to have destroyed, on his own property only, every kind of game, conditional upon conformity with police regulations relative to public security.

All *capitaineries*,‡ even royal ones, and all hunting preserves, under whatever denomination, are likewise abolished; and provision shall be made, by

* The distinction implied here is one between servile or personal dues and contractual or real dues, the latter being deemed worthy of compensation. Unfortunately, the Assembly was unsuccessful in maintaining this distinction throughout its work on the feudal regime. (Stewart's note.)

† The right of hunting was vested in the King, who shared it with the nobles by issuing licenses; rabbit warrens, for example, could not be established without a license. The emphasis placed on hunting rights in the *cahiers* indicates that they had become a grievous burden to the peasantry. (Stewart's note.)

‡ See Glossary.

means compatible with the respect due property and liberty, for the preservation of the personal diversions of the King.

The President shall be charged with requesting the King for the recall of persons exiled and consigned to the galleys simply for hunting, the release of prisoners now detained, and the cancellation of existing proceedings in that connection.

4. All seigneurial courts of justice are suppressed without any indemnity; nevertheless, the officials of such courts shall continue in office until the National Assembly has provided for the establishment of a new judicial organization.

5. Tithes of every kind and dues which take the place thereof, under whatever denomination they are known and collected, even by subscription, *possessed by secular and regular bodies* by beneficed clergymen, *fabriques* and all persons in *mainmorte*,* even by the Order of Malta and other religious and military orders, even those abandoned to laity in substitution for and option of *portion congrue*,† are abolished, subject to the devising of means for providing in some other manner for the expenses of divine worship, the maintenance of ministers of religion, relief of the poor, repairs and rebuilding of churches and parsonages, and for all establishments, seminaries, schools, colleges, hospitals, communities and others, to the maintenance of which they are now assigned. Meanwhile, until such provision is made and the former possessors are furnished with their equivalent, the National Assembly orders that collection of the said tithes shall continue according to law and in the usual manner. Other tithes, of whatever nature, shall be redeemable according to the regulations of the Assembly; and until such regulations are made, the National Assembly orders that the collection thereof also be continued.

6. All perpetual ground rents, either in kind or in money, of whatever species, whatever their origin, to whatever persons they are due . . . shall be redeemable; *champarts*† of every kind and denomination likewise shall be redeemable at a rate established by the Assembly. No nonredeemable due may be created henceforth. . . .

18. The National Assembly shall repair *en masse* to the King to present to His Majesty the decree just pronounced, to bear him the homage of its most respectful gratitude, and to supplicate him to permit the *Te Deum* to be sung in his chapel, and to be present there himself.

19. Immediately after the Constitution, the National Assembly shall undertake the drafting of laws necessary for the development of the principles

* *i.e.* by institutions possessing the property in accordance with the principles of mortmain. (Ed.)

† See Glossary.

established by the present decree, which, with the decree of the tenth of this month, shall be dispatched immediately by the deputies into all the provinces, there to be printed; proclaimed also at the parish sermons, and posted wherever necessary.

6/2 Abolition of Internal Tariff: Uniform Tariff Abroad

Decree of 31 October 1790. Printed in STEWART, *A Documentary Survey* [*see* Document **5/10**], pp. 163-164.

The National Assembly, considering that commerce is the source of all agricultural and industrial development and strength, and that it may function effectively only in so far as it enjoys adequate liberty; considering that it is now handicapped by innumerable obstacles, that the present customs duties established under divers denominations at the boundaries separating the former provinces of the kingdom, regardless of their capacity and needs, disturb, by the method of their collection as well as by their rigor, not only commercial speculations but even individual liberty; that they render different parts of the State foreign to one another; that they restrict consumption, thereby harming the production and increase of national wealth, decrees as follows:

1. Dating from 1 December next, all customs duties and all bureaux established in the interior of the kingdom for the collection thereof . . . are abolished.

2. The suppression pronounced by the preceding article shall include likewise the special fees of *abord* and *consommation** . . . as well as the fees . . . collected on wines and other beverages from abroad, without any changes being made for the present in those of the said fees due on beverages exported or passing from areas of *aides** into those exempt therefrom, and *vice versa*, which shall continue to be collected until the time of replacement or modification of rights of *aides*.

3. Dating likewise from 1 December next, the special tariffs of 1664, 1667, and 1671 . . . ,† and all other tariffs serving for the collection of fees on the [commercial] relations of the divers parts of the kingdom with one another and with foreign lands, shall cease to be enforced and shall remain annulled . . .

Said tariffs and fees shall be replaced by a single, uniform tariff, which shall be decreed immediately, and the fees of which shall be subject to collection dating from 1 December next on all imports and exports of the kingdom

* See Glossary.

† *i.e.* the essentials of Colbert's system. (Stewart's note.)

save the exceptions, bonded warehouses, and transit duties recognized as necessary and determined immediately according to reports to be made thereon to the National Assembly.

4. To assure the execution of the above articles, officials shall be provided immediately under the title of Superintendents of the Police of External Commerce and of the Bureaux, . . .

7. Until the promulgation of the new tariff and the new code of customs duties, the present tariffs and the laws thereon shall continue to be enforced.

8. The departmental* assemblies, the chambers of commerce, and all merchants of the kingdom may direct, both to the National Assembly and to the administration, memoirs and observations stating the interests of agriculture, commerce, and industry with respect to the effects of the new tariff and possible changes therein, without prejudice, however, to the execution of the law.

9. The King shall be requested to sanction the present decree, and, in order to assure its prompt execution, to entrust it to seven special administrators, among whom His Majesty shall be requested to include the members of the general *ferme* who have co-operated with the Committee on Agriculture and Commerce in the work on customs duties.

6/3 Le Chapelier's Anti-Combination Law, 1791

Passed 14 June 1791. Printed in J. M. THOMPSON, *French Revolution Documents* [*see* Document **5/14**], pp. 84-86. (W.O.H. Tr.)

1. Since the abolition of all types of associations of citizens belonging to the same class and occupation was one of the fundamental bases of the French Constitution their re-establishment in any shape whatever is hereby forbidden.

2. When persons belonging to the same occupation or profession – employers, shopkeepers, workers and journeymen (*compagnons*) of all kinds – meet they may not appoint a chairman, or secretaries or trustees, they may not keep records and they may not deliberate or pass resolutions or make rules to advance their supposed common interests.

3. Municipalities or public bodies may not receive any address or petition from any occupation or profession and no reply may be made to such representations. They must declare null and void all deliberations so made, and must take great care to ensure that nothing comes of them.

4. If – contrary to the principles of liberty and of the Constitution – people belonging to the same occupation or profession do deliberate to-

* See Glossary

gether or make agreements among themselves which would lead to their refusing, in concert, to use their skill or labour, or to their using these only for wages which they demand, then all such deliberations and agreements – whether made on oath or not – are declared to be unconstitutional, to be subversive of liberty and the Declaration of the Rights of Man, and to be null and void; and it is incumbent on public bodies and municipalities to declare them to be such. The instigators and leaders who have called such meetings or have presided over such deliberations shall be cited by the Prosecutor of the Commune* to appear before a magistrate and will be liable to a fine of 500 livres,* the loss for one year of all their rights as citizens, and the right to be elected to the primary assemblies.

5. No public authority or municipality, on pain of its members' being held individually responsible, may employ or admit or allow to exercise their skill on any public works those employers, workers and journeymen who have instigated or subscribed to the aforementioned deliberations or agreements, unless such offending persons shall, of their own accord, have presented themselves before the magistrates in order to retract and disavow their acts.

6. If these associations put up posters or distribute circulars containing any threats to employers, artisans, workers or foreign workers who are working in the district or to those who are prepared to work for lower wages, then each of the authors, instigators and signatories of these acts or writings shall be punished by a fine or 1000 livres and 3 months imprisonment.

7. Those who utter threats or offer violence against workers who exercise the liberty granted by the laws of the Constitution to those who work or are engaged in industry shall be dealt with according to the Criminal Law and will be punished as disturbers of the public peace with all the rigour of the law.

8. All assemblies composed of artisans, workers, journeymen and day labourers, in which there is incitement against the free exercise of the right that belongs to every citizen to work or to engage in industry under all sorts of conditions materially agreed upon, or against police action and the execution of Court judgments in such matters, as well as against sales by auction of, and public adjudications upon, various enterprises – all these are held to be seditious assemblies. As such they shall be dispersed by the public authorities empowered to do so, acting on the legal requisitions made to them, and the authors, instigators and leaders of these assemblies, and all of those who have committed acts of violence, shall be punished with all the rigour of the law.

* See Glossary.

6/4 Personal and Sumptuary Tax

Decree of 25 July 1795. Printed in STEWART, *A Documentary Survey* [*see* Document **5/10**], pp. 560-561.

1. All French citizens enjoying their rights or incomes, and all foreigners, shall pay a personal tax of five *livres* per year* as hereinafter stated.

2. Laborers who subsist only by their work and whose daily wages do not exceed thirty *sous*,* are exempt from said tax; nevertheless, they shall be permitted to pay it voluntarily.

3. Taxpayers include those who enjoy an income in excess of 365 days of labor, evaluated as in the preceding article.

4. Men and women over thirty years of age, and unmarried, shall be required to pay one-fourth over and above all their personal and sumptuary taxes. Widowers and widows who have children, or who are widowed only after the age of forty-five, are exempted from such payment.

5. Apart from said personal tax, sumptuary taxes shall be paid as follows: chimneys, other than those of the kitchen and the bakehouse, shall be taxed, 1st, in cities of 50,000 or more inhabitants, five *livres* for the first, ten *livres* for the second, and fifteen *livres* for each additional one; 2nd, in cities of fewer than 50,000 but more than 15,000 inhabitants, the tax shall be one-half the above; 3rd, in communes* of fewer than 15,000, one-fourth. Computation of chimneys for taxation shall be made by each household.

6. No chimney may be exempt, even though not ordinarily used, unless it is closed on the inside and sealed with masonry.

7. Stoves shall be taxed at one-half the above rates, in the same proportion relative to population.

8. Said taxes shall be paid by the tenants or by owners occupying the houses themselves. The owners or principal tenants shall be responsible for said tax.

9. Likewise a tax shall be paid in proportion to the number of male domestic servants attached solely to personal and household service, other than those ordinarily and principally occupied with the work of agriculture and attendance upon and care of stock: to wit, ten *livres* for the first, thirty *livres* for the second, ninety *livres* for the third, and so on in triple proportion.

Domestic servants over sixty years of age, or those incapable of working because of their infirmities, shall not occasion the above taxation.

10. For superfluous horses and mules not ordinarily used for commerce, manufacturing, mills, plowing, carting, posts, stagecoaches, transport, or haulage, without distinction of saddle or draught horses, twenty *livres* shall be

* See Glossary.

paid for the first, forty *livres* for the second, eighty *livres* for the third, and so on in double proportion.

Stallions, brood mares, colts under three years of age, and the horses of licensed horse dealers are exempt from the above tax.

11. For carriages on springs, state coaches, and cabriolets, by pair of wheels, twenty *livres* shall be paid for the first carriage, forty *livres* per pair of wheels for the second, one hundred and twenty *livres* also per pair of wheels for the third, increasing in the same proportion, according to the number of carriages, whether or not the owner has horses, or whether he has them for only one carriage. Litters drawn by horses or mules shall pay as two-wheeled carriages; two-wheeled carriages shall be counted first for taxation.

12. Renters of horses, four-wheeled carriages, and cabs, contractors for stagecoaches or private carriages, other than those who have dealt with the government, shall pay only five *livres* for each horse, and ten *livres* per carriage wheel, without progression for a number thereof.

Saddler-coachmakers are not included in the tax on carriages and equipages....

6/5 Metric System of Weights and Measures

a Decree of 1 August 1793. Printed in STEWART, *A Documentary Survey* [*see* Document **5/10**], pp. 504-505.

b *Le manuel républicain* (Paris, an VII), pp. 79, 88-89. (Ed. Tr.)

a The National Convention, convinced that uniformity of weights and measures is one of the greatest benefits that it can offer to all French citizens:

After hearing the report of its Committee on Public Instruction concerning the work which has been done by the Academy of Sciences in accordance with the decree of 8 May 1790;

Declares that it is satisfied with the work, which has already been accomplished by the Academy on the system of weights and measures; that it adopts the results thereof in order to establish said system throughout the entire Republic, under the nomenclature of the table annexed to the present decree, and in order to offer it to all nations.

Accordingly, the National Convention decrees as follows:

1. The new system of weights and measures, based on the measure of the meridian of the earth and the decimal division, shall be used uniformly throughout the entire Republic.

2. Nevertheless, in order to allow all citizens time to become acquainted with the new measures, the provisions of the preceding article will not be

obligatory until 1 July 1794; citizens are merely invited to make use thereof before that time.

3. Craftsmen chosen by the Academy of Sciences shall make standard models of the new weights and measures, which shall be sent to all departmental* and district administrations.

4. The Academy of Sciences shall name four commissioners taken from its midst, and the Committee on Public Instruction shall name two, to supervise the construction of said standard models; they shall verify the exactness thereof, and shall sign the instructions that are to accompany the shipments, which shall be made by the Minister of the Interior.

5. The Academy of Sciences shall send the Committee on Public Instruction a specific estimate of the costs necessitated by the construction of the standard models, in order that the Convention may decree the necessary funds therefor.

6. Said standard models shall be kept with the greatest care in a place intended for such purpose, the key to which shall remain in the hands of one of the commissioners of each administrative body.

7. In order to prevent the debasement of standards, the administrative bodies shall name, in each departmental or district seat, a well-informed person who is to be present when the craftsmen have access to said standards for the purpose of constructing instruments for measurement and weight for the use of the citizens.

8. As soon as the new standards have reached the district administrations, all the municipalities of each and every district shall be required to have instruments constructed for measurement and weight which [instruments] shall remain in the communal hall.

9. The collection of the several memoranda, drafted by the commissioners of the Academy up to the present, including the details of the methods whereby the new system of weights and measures was achieved, shall be printed, and shall accompany the dispatch of the standards.

10. The Convention orders the Academy to compose, for the use of all citizens, a book containing simple instructions on the manner of using the new weights and measures, and on the application of the arithmetical calculations pertaining to the decimal system.

11. Instructions on the new measures, and their relation to former measures most generally used, shall be introduced into the elementary arithmetic books written for the national schools.

[Appended to this decree was an elementary table of the new weights and measures, with their equivalents under the old system. The point of departure was one-quarter of the meridian, or the distance from the pole to the equator. This distance was, in terms of old units of measurement, 5,132,430 *toises*. And the basic unit of linear measurement adopted

* See Glossary

was the ten-millionth part of this quarter meridian, or 0·5132430 *toise*. This unit was called the metre, and, since the *toise* = 6·39459 feet, the metre equalled 3·281979 feet or 39·383748 inches. The present U.S. standard of the metre is 39·37 inches.] (Stewart's note.)

b The usefulness of a uniform system of measures cannot be doubted; it is one of the unfortunately all too few points on which there has been agreement in the past at all times, in all places, irrespective of political differences.

If the reader of this article has placed in his mind the terms of measurement, mètre, are*, stère,* litre, gram and the seven prefixes, déca-, hecto-, kilo-, myria- for the multiples, and deci-, centi-, milli- for the submultiples, he possesses the entire vocabulary of the new measures, and at the same time he knows their connections and relationships. By contrast, it would require several volumes to assemble all the various denominations of measure used in the Republic; to explain the meaning of those denominations and to indicate their value and interrelationships.

In Paris alone there are forty-five different names for weights and measures, all of which are distinct and arbitrary choices. They do not allow a person to feel the relationship of the measures; what is called 'voie', 'gros', 'minot', could equally be called 'corde', 'once', or 'mine'. . . . In general, the denominations which are used are misleading even when they seem straightforward. Take for example 'setier' or 'septier'. When this is used as a measure of liquids it designates eight pints; who wouldn't assume that the demi-setier must be the equivalent of four pints? Would a foreigner suspect that the name is given to a quarter of a pint? But isn't the very word 'setier' or 'septier', which seems to indicate one-sixth or one-seventh of some other measure, in itself misleading? Moreover, when it is used it is necessary to state whether reference is made to solids or liquids. The same applies to 'muid', and everybody is aware of the confusion created by the word 'livre' which is used to indicate both weight and money. Finally, the same meaning is not always attached to the same word. For example, without going out of the Department* of the Seine, . . . the word 'arpent'* has five different meanings. . . .

6/6 French Law of Succession

JAMES PAUL COBBETT, *A Ride of Eight Hundred Miles in France* (London, 1824), pp. 167-171. (G.P.J.)

Before the Revolution the law of *primogeniture* and of *entail* appears to have existed in a very extensive degree in Normandy, while it did not so exist in the other provinces of the kingdom, except with regard to a com-

* See Glossary.

paratively small part of the community . . . as far as the positive law can go, the Revolution has destroyed this custom. All is now laid level. The law does, in fact, *make a man's will for him*: and it divides and sub-divides his property, till, in some cases, a farm of 100 acres is, at the death of the owner, cut up into allotments of *six* or *seven* acres; it has been said that 'the law of primogeniture *has but one child*' and that it devotes all the rest to *beggary*. On the other hand it is said that, even if this be admitted, the law of primogeniture has an advantage over the *law of scattering*, as it may be called; for that the law of primogeniture has *one* child, while the other has *no child at all*; that the law of primogeniture devotes to beggary *all but one*, while the law of scattering saves *not one*, but disperses the *whole*, and makes them *all beggars*. . . .

I hear on all sides, here in Normandy, great lamentations on account of the effects of this revolutionary law. They tell me that it has dispersed thousands of families, who had been on the same spots for centuries; that it is daily operating in the same way; that it has, in a great degree, changed the state of the farm buildings; that it has caused the land to be worse cultivated. . .

It is not natural to expect that an owner of a farm, for instance, will have the same regard for, or consider himself bound to take the same care of, the farm which he has purchased of a stranger as he would of the farm upon which he himself had been born and bred up . . . which his father had tilled, and which he had inherited in his father's name. Nor can it be any more expected that the father while he lives should pay the same attention to the farm which is to be *sold away*, or cut up *into lots* sorely against his will, as he would to that which must remain in the hands of his son after he is gone. . . . The farms here are not, I am assured, in anything like the same fine condition that they used to be. . . .

I have been assured that in many families . . . the several members have come to an agreement with each other to act according to the ancient custom, and thus prevent the parcelling out of their estates and the extinction of their families. This *may* now-and-then take place, but generally it cannot; and it is clear that, if the present law remain, the land must *all* be cut up into *little bits*; that a farm house must become a rare sight; and that a *tree* worthy of the name of *timber* will scarcely be seen in a whole day's ride.

6/7 Métayer Tenure in France

RICHARD JONES, *Peasant Rents* (New York, 1831, repr. 1895), pp. 79–85. (G.P.J.)

In spite of the cultivation by vassals and serfs . . . the metayers [sic] had in their possession before the revolution four-sevenths of the surface of France.

Another one-sixth or one-seventh was in the possession of capitalists finding their own stock and paying money-rents. The remainder was held by the proprietors, or by serf or feudal tenantry.

The terms on which the French metayers held their farms differed much from age to age: these variations do not immediately strike the eye of an observer because the nominal rent, and nominal share of the tenant, have changed but little and the metayer still very generally takes that portion of the produce, viz. the half, from which his original name of mediatarius was derived. But while the metayers tenant pays nominally the same rent, his own share of the produce may be diminished in two modes: by his being subjected to a greater quantity of the public burthens: or by the size of his metairie being reduced. By this second mode of reduction, I am not aware that the French metayer suffered much: fifty acres was not an unusual size for a metairie; in poor districts they comprised a much larger quantity of land.

By the first mode of reducing his share of the produce, that is, by an increase of the public burthens which he had to bear, the metayer suffered to an extent fatal both to his own comforts and to the prosperity of agriculture; a circumstance which had a great share in converting the peasantry into those reckless instruments of mischief which they proved in many instances to be during the revolution. . . .

. . . In spite of the multiplication of small proprietors since the revolution, metayers are supposed still to cultivate one-half of France. Their actual condition is little improved, it appears, by the change which has taken place in the system of taxation, and their sufferings are aggravated by the spread of a class of middle-men (always existing to some extent) who without changing the terms on which the actual cultivator holds the soil, pays a money rent to the proprietor, and grinds and oppresses the tenant to make his bargain profitable.

6/8 Critique of the French System of Tenure

a A. B. REACH, *Claret and Olives* (London, 1852), pp. 257-264.

b M. L. MOUNIER, *De l'agriculture en France, d'après les documents officiels* (Paris, 1846), pp. 174-176. (Ed. Tr.)

a The French are undoubtedly at least a century behind us in agricultural science and skill. This remark applies alike to breeding cattle and to raising crops. Agriculture in France is rather a handicraft than what it ought to be – a science. As a general rule, the farmers of France are about on a level with the ploughmen of England. When I say this, I mean that the immense majority of the cultivators are unlettered peasants – hinds – who till the land in the unvarying, mechanical routine handed down to them from their forefathers. Of agriculture, in any other sense than the rule-of-thumb practice of ploughing, sowing, reaping, and threshing, they know literally nothing. Of the *rationale* of the management of land – of the reasons why so and so should be done – they think no more than honest La Balafrè, whose only notion of a final cause was the command of his superior officer. Thus they are bound down in the most abject submission to every custom, for no other reason than that it is a custom: their fathers did so and so, and therefore, and for no other reason, the sons do the same. I could see no struggling upwards, no longing for a better condition, no discontent, even with the vegetable food upon which they lived. All over the land there brooded one almost unvaried mist of dull, unenlightened, passive content – I do not mean social – but industrial content.

There are two causes principally chargeable with this. In the first place, strange as it may seem in a country in which two-thirds of the population are agriculturists, agriculture is a very unhonoured occupation. Develop, in the slightest degree, a Frenchman's mental faculties, and he flies to a town as surely as steel filings fly to a loadstone. . . . Again, this national tendency is directly encouraged by the centralizing system of government – by the multitude of officials, and by the payment of all functionaries. From all parts of France, men of great energy and resource struggle up and fling themselves on the world of Paris. . . . Nine-tenths of those who have, or think they have, heads on their shoulders, struggle into towns to fight for office. Nine-tenths of those who are, or are deemed by themselves or others, too stupid for anything else, are left at home to till the fields, and breed the cattle, and prune the vines, as their ancestors did for generations before them. Thus there is singularly little intelligence left in the country. The whole energy, and knowledge, and resource of the land are barrelled up in the towns. You leave one city, and, in many cases, you will not meet an educated or cultivated individual until you arrive at another – all between is utter intellectual barrenness. . . . I do not mean to say that here and there, all over France, there may not be found active and intelligent resident landlords, nor that, in the north of France, there may not be discovered intelligent and clear-headed tenant-farmers; but the rule is as I have stated. Utterly ignorant boors* are allowed to plod on from generation to generation, wrapped in the most dismal mists of agricultural superstition. . . .

A word as to the subdivision of property. . . .

The tendency of landed properties, under the system in question, is to continual diminuition of size.

This tendency does *not* stop with the interests of the parties concerned – it goes on in spite of them.

* See Glossary.

And the only practical check is nothing but a new evil. When a man finds that his patch of land is insufficient to support his family, he borrows money and buys more land. In nine cases out of ten, the interest to be paid to the lender is greater than the profit which the borrower can extract from the land – and bankruptcy, and reduction to the condition of a day-labourer, is sooner or later the inevitable result.

The infinitesimal patches of land are cultivated in the most rude and uneconomical fashion. Not a franc of capital, further than that sunk in the purchase of spades, picks, and hoes, is expended on them. They are undrained, ill-manured, expensively worked, and they would often produce no profit whatever, were it not that the proprietor is the labourer, and that he looks for little or nothing save a recompense for his toil in a bare subsistence. It is easy to see how the consumer must fare if the producer possess little or no surplus after his own necessities are satisfied.

It is not to be supposed from the above remarks, that I conceive that in no circumstances, and under no conditions, can the soil be advantageously divided into minute properties. The rule which strikes me as applying to the matter is this: – where spade-husbandry can be legitimately adopted, then the extreme subdivision of land loses much, if not all, of its evils. The reason is plain: spade-husbandry, while it pays the proprietor fair wages, also, in certain cases, develops in an economical manner the resources of the soil. The instance of market-gardens near a populous town is a case in point. . . .

Are small properties, then, in cases in which spade-husbandry cannot be economically applied, injurious to the social and industrial interests of the community in which they exist?

The following propositions appear to me to sum up what may be said on either side of the question:

Small landed holdings undoubtedly tend to produce an industrious population. A man always works hardest for himself.

Small landed holdings tend to breed a spirit of independence, and wholesome moral self-appreciation and reliance.

On the other hand –

Small landed holdings, by breeding a poor and ignorant race of proprietors, keep back agriculture, and injure the whole community of consumers; and –

Small landed holdings tend to grow smaller than it is the interest of their owners that they should become. Capital, borrowed at usurious rates of interest, is then had recourse to for the purpose of enlarging individual properties – and the result is the production of a race involved, mortgaged, and frequently bankrupt proprietors.

At this present moment, I believe the proprietorship of France to be as bankrupt as that of the south-west of Ireland. The number of 'Encumbered Estates' across the Channel would stagger the stoutest calculator. The capitalists, notaries, land-agents, and others in the towns, and not the peasantry, are the real owners of the mortgaged soil. The nominal proprietors are sinking deeper and deeper at every struggle, and they see no hope before them – save one – Socialism. French Socialism is simply the result of French poverty.

Whether a Poor-law, and a change in the law of heritage might not check the evil, I am not, of course, going to inquire; but the present state of rural France – all political considerations left aside – appears to me to point to the possibility, if not the probability, of the world seeing a greater and bloodier *Jacquerie* yet than it ever saw before.

b This state of things [the division of landed property] creates enormous difficulties, which have been emphasized by many writers.

There is not a single agronomist who has not deplored the inevitable and often disastrous consequences of this state of affairs, which is consecrated by our present social order; a situation which is so much more difficult to reform, since it relates to the most holy and inviolable of all social principles, property. . . .

This division of land, this parcelling out into small pieces, . . . is, and nobody will deny it, one of the most difficult obstacles to overcome, as regards the introduction of improved techniques and the production of those things which large-scale agriculture should provide for us.

The following observations apply almost exclusively to large-scale agriculture. . . .

First of all, there is the loss of time sustained by the farmer (*laboureur*), in visiting in turn all his properties, which are often considerable distances apart, whenever he is involved in ploughing, sowing, weeding, clearing thistles, carrying and spreading manure, gathering in the harvest and transporting it to his farm.

This loss of time is compounded by an increase in the costs of cultivation; the innumerable sunken tracks; the difficulty of watching and protecting the crops. . . .

Add the expenses which arise inevitably from the sowing of seed on each of these small, contiguous pieces, sown by different cultivators, through the encroachments necessarily made on the previously sown adjacent plot by the horses or beasts pulling the plough . . . to obtain some idea of the consequences.

But, most of all, it is impossible for an individual to cultivate his land as he wishes; to establish the succession of harvests required or permitted by the quality of the soil; to plant the grasses and the trees, which today are so vital; to make artificial meadows; and to undertake enclosure for pasturage; to get away from the old disastrous fallow system; since the owner who is better informed about nature, who wanted to cultivate all his lands every year, following an appropriate method, suited to the laws of vegetation, and local circumstances, and who had the resources to do this, would be frustrated in his aim if his land were surrounded by that of neighbours who make their land fallow and continue in the use of the harmful common pasture system.

The man who would do otherwise would see his cultivation subjected to the continual ravages of the village cattle, and if to preserve himself from this, he undertook the expense of enclosing his land, he would undoubtedly see his enclosures violated every day by the other village inhabitants.

Moreover, even if his enclosures were successful, it would be a very expensive business and would take land out of cultivation, since the surface occupied by walls, hedges and ditches would be more significant than usual, because of the small size of the enclosures.

The excessive division of land has been the reason why artificial meadows and pasture ground have not been introduced.

The use of fallow and common pasture, either in the same or a different commune,* have arisen to compensate for the absence of pastureland and artificial meadows.

These practices, have, in their turn, made it impossible to create artificial meadows and pasturage, which, it was falsely believed, they could replace; and apart from their uselessness, they have become detrimental to agriculture; they have assumed a tyrannical character to which some are obliged to submit their intelligence and desire for better cultivation, and together with other factors they perpetuate ignorance and misery. . . .

6/9 Small Farms in France

T. E. CLIFFE LESLIE, 'The Land System of France', in J. W. PROBYN (ed.), *Systems of Land Tenure in Various Countries* (London, 1881), pp. 292–296.

. . . We may accept as a close approximation to the actual situation the following estimate by M. de Lavergne:

> Of our five millions of small rural proprietors, three millions possess on the average but a hectare† a-piece. Two millions possess on the average six hectares. . . . Two million independent rural proprietors, a million tenant-farmers, as well as the million farmers, for the most part proprietors of land; such is approximately the composition of our rural population.‡

* See Glossary.
† Not quite two acres and a half. (Leslie's note.)
‡ 'Economie Rurale de la France,' last Edition. (Leslie's note.)

Four millions of landowners cultivating the soil of a territory only one-third larger than Great Britain, may probably appear to minds familiar only with the idea of great estates and large farms almost a *reductio ad absurdum* of the land system of the French. Those, on the other hand, who have studied the condition of the French cultivators not merely in books, but in their own country, and who have witnessed the improvements which have taken place in it and in their cultivation year after year, will probably regard the number with a feeling of satisfaction. One thing, at least, is established by it, that property in land is in France a national possession; that the territory of the nation belongs to the nation, and that no national revolution can take place for the destruction of private property.

But the inquiry proper to the present pages leads us to examine, in the first place, the causes of so wide a distribution of landed property in France, and, secondly, its economic effects.

The French law of succession, which limits the parental power of testamentary disposition over property to a part equal to one child's share, and divides the remainder among the children equally, is the cause commonly assigned in England for the continuous subdivision of land in France. The real effects of the French law of succession cannot be understood without taking into account a process of subdivision taking place in France from a different cause, one really indeed traceable in part to the structure of French law, but not the law of succession – namely, continual purchases on the part of the peasantry of small estates or parcels of land. On this subject notaries in many different parts of France have given the writer surprising information in recent years; and it has indeed for many years been a subject of such common remark in the country, that even mere railway passengers through it can hardly have failed to have come upon evidence of it. M. Monny de Mornay states with respect to it, in the chapter of his report on the division of land: 'The fact which manifests itself most forcibly is the profound and continuous alteration in the distribution of the soil among the different classes of the population. In the greater number of departments the estates of 100 hectares might now be easily counted; and taken altogether they form but an insignificant part of the national territory. The proportion cannot be stated in figures, because it varies from one Department* to another; one must confine oneself to saying that the west and south have preserved more large estates than the north and east.' The north and east, he might have added, are the wealthiest and best-cultivated zones, though the south is now rapidly improving in cultivation and wealth, and, as will presently be shown, the process of subdivision, keeps step with this improvement. After referring to the disappearance of estates of even moderate size, M. de Mornay proceeds:

* See Glossary.

'All that has been lost to the domain of large estates, all that is lost day by day to that of estates of middle size, small property swallows up. Not only does the small proprietor round his little property year by year, but at his side the class of agricultural labourers has been enriched by the rise of wages, and accedes to landed property in its turn. In the greater number of departments 75 per cent. at least of them are now become owners of land. Peasant property thus embraces a great part of the soil, and that part increases incessantly. The price of parcels of land, accordingly, which are within reach of the industry and thrift of the peasant, increases at a remarkable rate. The competition of buyers is active, and sales in small lots take place on excellent terms for the seller, when the interval has been sufficient to allow fresh savings to re-accumulate.' This is in some degree an official statement, and official statements in France are sometimes suspected of exaggerating the prosperity of the nation at large; but it is confirmed by a superabundance of unofficial and unquestionable authority not on the side of Imperial Government. In one of several passages to the same effect, in his 'Economie Rurale de la France,' and other works, M. Léonce de Lavergne, for instance, says: 'The small proprietors of land, who, according to M. Rubichon, were about three millions and a half in 1815, are at this day much more numerous; they have gained ground, and one cannot but rejoice at it, for they have won it by their industry.' And in a communication* to the present writer, M. de Lavergne observes:

> The best cultivation in France on the whole is that of the peasant proprietors, and the subdivision of the soil makes perpetual progress. . . . All round the town in which I write to you (Toulouse) it is again a profitable operation to buy land in order to re-sell it in small lots. . . .

Along with the subdivision of landed property thus taking place, there is also a movement in the land market towards the enlargement of peasant properties, the consolidation of small parcels, and even in some places towards the acquisition of what in France are considered as large estates; as, in like manner, contemporaneously with the subdivision of farms, and the more minute cultivation of the soil, there is also a counter-process of enlargement of little farms, and in some places even a development of *la grande culture* on a splendid scale.

* November 6, 1869.

6/10 Land Tenure in France, 1860–1

NASSAU WILLIAM SENIOR (ed. M. C. M. Simpson), *Conversations with distinguished Persons during the Second Empire from 1860 to 1863* (2 vols., London, 1880), I, pp. 19, 77–78, 197–198. (W.O.H.)

(M. de Kergorlay 1860)

. . . The co-heirs, in their mutual jealousy, often require each field to be divided. If partitions were managed as they are with you, and the whole property were divided into only as many lots as there are heirs, there would not be much '*morcellement*'. But according to the practice of our peasants an estate of twenty fields may be divided by two co-heirs into forty fields, and in the next generation into eighty, without an increase of population. . . . The expenses of a sale, including the tax to the State, are above ten per cent of the value, or more than three years' income, to which must be added the expenses of a suit to decide whether a sale shall take place or not, which is at the discretion of the tribunal. . . .

(Marquis de Vogué, 1860)

I defend it (*métage*) [sic] in such a country as this (the Berri-region) – a country in which there is little capital, little population and much land. Of course I prefer *fermage* (i.e. tenant farmers paying cash rent) where good *fermage* is practicable. If I could get . . . a man with large capital, intelligence and knowledge, I should prefer it, but such men are rare. . . . Here we have . . . to choose between *fermage* by a tenant with little capital, *exploitation* by the proprietor himself and *métage*. In the first case the land is unproductive, yet exhausted; in the second you must employ a bailiff, on whom you seldom can depend, or you must personally superintend these details – a business for which a gentleman is seldom fit, and which in our large estates is, in fact, impracticable. Under the *métayer* system you have a tenant whose interest is yours, who, having studied nothing but agriculture, knows it well, who, what is equally important, knows the specialities of every field, and who is not above seeing that the day labourer works, or above higgling with purchasers and sellers in the market. . . .

(Gustave de Beaumont, 1861)

. . . Real property is so desired in France, that the construction of estates goes on as rapidly as their dissolution, Our conveyancing system, though very expensive, is simple. To be a land-jobber . . . is a considerable profession. It is so easy to buy and sell, that the land of the country is supposed to change hands on an average once in twenty years. This is one of the reasons which make it difficult to get tenants and farm servants. If a man has capital, he had rather spend two thirds of it in buying a farm and the other third in stocking it, then employ the whole on another's land. I have not a servant who has not his field. To have none is a degradation. My labourers are constantly telling me: 'I cannot come tomorrow, as I have to sow my barley. I cannot come another day because I have to dig my potatoes.'

6/11 Land Tenure in Belgium, 1869

Letter from WILLIAM MURE in *The Times*, December 1869. Printed in *Journal of the Statistical Society* (vol. 33, 1870), pp. 148–151. (G.P.J.)

. . . The Cadastre survey, published in 1856, states that in West Flanders the arable land, amounting to 677,005 acres, is divided among 86,225 occupiers, showing the proportion of 7½ acres to each. In East Flanders, the division of 545,245 acres among 88,225 occupiers reduces the mean size of holding to 5½ acres. In West Flanders the number of persons engaged in husbandry is in the proportion of 20 to 100 acres. On the same extent in East Flanders forty-one are employed, whereas in England the proportion is only twelve. The average pay of the day labourer in East Flanders is 7s. a week, for (? from) which he has to find food and lodging. In West Flanders it is 6s 10d. Women, in the two provinces respectively, can earn 5s 6d. and 4s. 6d. These figures are taken from the Government statistics published in 1856, subject to modification in consideration of the ten years which have elapsed. . . .

The *Pays de Waes*, which lies between Ghent and Antwerp, is, perhaps, the best type of Flanders, as it embraces both the alluvial and sandy land. Here extreme subdivision prevails and spade husbandry is chiefly practised. In this region, too flat for subsoil drainage, superfluous waters are carried off by a system of open ditches. The fields, which vary in size from 1½ to 6 acres have all, by careful manipulation, been worked into convex platforms, the watershed being in the centre. . . . In this system of drainage, which necessitates the parcelling out of the land into very small fields, and in the light friable nature of the soil, we find in some measure the origin of excessive subdivision and spade husbandry. Along the ditches and roads Canada poplars are planted. They belong to the proprietors and are valued at 1 fr. a year. They do immense injury to the growing crops. . . .

Much has been said about the *spade husbandry* of Flanders. The Pays de Waes is *par excellence* its dominion . . . in the light soils it is used universally as an auxiliary, and in the following admirable manner. Every seven years the farmer trenches his soil to the depth of 2 feet in order that the juices of the manure, which during that period have percolated beyond the reach of the plough, may be brought again to the surface and utilised. This practice is enforced in leases and agreements. 'The spade is the peasant's gold mine' is an old proverb. Leases from three, six, to nine years are the rule throughout Belgium; tenancy-at-will is the exception. Notwithstanding the natural poverty of the greater part of the soil, the produce, owing to the industry of the peasant is enormous.

Here I must digress in order to remove a most erroneous impression which prevails in this country regarding the much vaunted *petite culture* – an impression which seems to have derived additional force from the error into which Mr. Stuart Mill and other writers have fallen, by quoting the Flemish peasant as an example of the small proprietor who tills his own soil. . . . The following is the truth. Upwards of 80 per cent. of the fertile land in Flanders, though the property in fee of small proprietors, many of whom are peasants, is let in minute farms to a rack-rented but industrious tenantry. . . .

With regard to the tenant, there is really no country in Europe, far less Ireland, where his tenure is less secure. In the Pays de Waes, commonly called the 'Paradise of Belgium' he holds at will, without even a written agreement, and is subject to summary eviction. . . . In this district. . . . The little homesteads are generally the property of the tenant, who hires land to cultivate as near home as he can get it. The landlords are chiefly the wealthier peasants, attorneys, and people of their class. It is not uncommon to find a tenant holding from more than one landlord, who in his turn is also a tenant. Thus, though owing to precarious tenure, and the custom of summary eviction, together with the leverage which the fixed residence of the tenant gives the landlord, oppression and tyranny are common, they find no compact forces to oppose them. The tenant who is harshly treated to-day has a certain sympathy with the facilities which the law affords to rapacity, as to-morrow he may wish to avail himself of them in the management of his own little property hard by. . . . The peasant tenant of Flanders is the descendant of a race of peasant proprietors who, by their skill and industry, have snatched hundreds of thousands of acres from the dominion of the sea, forged wealth out of pure silica, and converted a howling wilderness into a fruitful garden. The fruitful garden remains, but it has now, under the pressure of competition, to fulfil the threefold mission of land which has arrived at commercial value, viz. to provide rent for the landlord, profit for the tenant and wages for the labourer. The peasant proprietor, cultivating his own land, has disappeared, and with him likewise security of tenure. The tendency of the law of testamentary division is not only to break up extensive estates, and root out the land monopolist, but also to keep continually forcing a large area into the market in small parcels, within the means of that very numerous class whose love of land amounts to a passion. As generations succeed each other, and population increases, and with it competition, the proprietor, finding it impossible without excessive labour to extract from his land a fair return for his capital, and unable to resist the temptation of high offers, soon learns to prefer the ease and petty power of the landlord to the toil of the husbandman. The tenant enters rack-rented, and, with the dreaded rent day ever hanging over him, is obliged to sacrifice every other consideration to the cultivation of his land. His children from their earliest years having to take their share in the daily routine of labour and anxiety, grow up in complete ignorance, and the land, under the high pressure of intense industry, is clothed, fed, and adorned by a lavish use, or rather abuse, of the energies of the overwrought slaves who 'water it with their sweat'.

Speacking of Flanders, Mr de Lavelaye . . . says:–

But* there also we are struck by the sad contrast between these splendid harvests and the miserable life of those who grew them. . . . Unfortunately, the condition of the cultivators who have brought agriculture to such a high degree of perfection bears no relation to the quantity of produce which they bring in. The agricultural labourer of Flanders is perhaps the worst fed among all the workers of Europe, the small farmer hardly lives any better, and if one takes a close look, one comes to the conclusion that far from drawing the 10% from his capital considered necessary in England, he does not reach 3% over and above the wage he would deserve for his own labour.

* Ed. Tr.

Chapter 7 Peasant Emancipation in Germany and the Austrian Empire

Introduction

Economic development proceeded more slowly in Germany and the Hapsburg lands than in the Kingdom of France, and some of the more acute problems of the French peasantry, such as the growing land hunger and the contrast between reality and market opportunities, were slower in making their appearance, except in certain advanced economies, as in Saxony (**5/12**). Moreover, the differences in the economic problem, the legal framework, and the stages of development reached were even greater among the provinces of Germany and Austria than they had been within the domain of the French Bourbons. At the same time the doctrines of the 'Enlightenment', to which the rulers of France had at best been indifferent, made a strong appeal to sovereigns like Frederick the Great of Prussia and Joseph II of Austria (as well as Catherine the Great of Russia), as a means of catching up with and thus equalling the power of the West.

Unlike the abolition of Feudalism in France, therefore, peasant emancipation in the major states of Central and Eastern Europe was imposed from above (helped, it is true, by the largely urban revolutions of 1848), rather than conquered from below. From the middle of the eighteenth century onwards, the rulers of Brandenburg-Prussia had attempted to modify the conditions of serfdom, and the commutation had begun in earnest on the royal estates in 1773 (**7/1**). At much the same time, Joseph II attempted to end personal subjection in some of his dominions, without, however, abolishing the burden of feudal dues (**7/2**).

These early measures illustrated the problems of emancipation from above, that is to say, emancipation carried out in conditions of undiminished powers of rulers and landlords. For while it had to preserve the livelihood of the peasantry, and its ability to act as a tax base and a reserve of army recruits, the legislation also had to avoid harming the feudal nobility which remained strong enough to prevent the implementation of any decree threatening its own incomes. The need to balance these three divergent interests of State, nobility and peasantry explains most of the difficulties, setbacks and delays in the course of peasant emancipation.

The most significant step forward in this part of Europe was the emancipation of the serfs in Prussia as part of a general movement of nationalist enthusiasm that arose in response to humiliation by Napoleon's armies. The Edict of 1807 abolished personal servitude (**7/3**, **7/4**), but this was only a first, negative step. New definitions and regulations of legally free relationships on the land were required in addition, and they were laid down in the Edict of 1811. This enactment, basing itself on the experience in the royal domains in 1807–10, contained the terms of the transfer of part of the land to the peasantry, while leaving sufficient in the hands of the nobility (**7/5**). Though it was relatively generous to the latter, it was evident that many landlords were not satisfied with their compensation (**7/6**, **7/7**); and they retained sufficient legal, political and social power to delay its execution, in many cases by over thirty years. It was only legislation following the Revolution of 1848 which finally completed the legal framework of a free peasantry and agricultural proletariat in Prussia (**7/8**). Similarly, Austrian emancipation was completed only in 1848 (**7/9**).

In Saxony and in many of the western and southern States, serfdom had been less complete even before the French Revolution (**1/14**, **1/15**). The progress to legal freedom and the terms of compensation, differed widely among them, but the outcome was a peasantry closer to the smallholding agrarian system of the French than to the larger Junker estates of the eastern provinces of Prussia, a peasantry which was suffering from many of the same problems as in France (**7/10**, **7/11**, **7/12**).

7/1 Security of Tenure and Early Attempts of Emancipation in Prussia

LEOPOLD KRUG, *Geschichte der staatswissenschaftlichen Gesetzgebung im preussischen Staate* (Berlin, 1808), pp. 130–137. (Ed. Tr.)

(*a*) SILESIA

By a Regulation of the Silesian Chambers of 15 May 1763 local officials were reminded to work as far as possible for the extinction of servitude and of indeterminate service dues, wherever they still survived, and to report on the matter itself and on the results of their efforts. . . .

According to an Order of the Silesian Chambers of 26 July 1764, it has been noted with satisfaction that a good start has been made in various districts with converting certain holdings into heritable tenancies, and the officials are reminded to make renewed efforts in this matter and to remove any obstacles which might be found to impede its progress; they are to travel personally about their districts, and attempt to draw up fair contracts between the landlords and their subjects, or to report on the difficulties that stand in the way. Henceforth no estate which has not made all its holdings heritable shall be entitled to the smallest subsidy or rebate, whether for the demesne farm or for the rest of the land, and the estate shall be ordered to 'hand over all the subsidies which would have been made over to it from the Royal Exchequer, to the subjects thus evicted'.

On 28 January 1765 yet another Order was issued by the Breslau Chamber to its District officials, with the instruction: to contribute as much as possible to the conversion to heritable holdings of holdings cleared by the landlords, and to be on the spot to negotiate with the landlords and their tenants about the commutation payments and the other dues; and on 10 September 1766, again, another order went out to the officials of the Departments regarding the 'making heritable of the remaining tenancies-at-will', demanding the 'completion without fail' of this business in the course of the year. . . .

A circular of 11 July 1798 reads explicitly: 'that in several estate offices, particularly in Upper Silesia, a large part of the holdings are not yet heritable;' it is therefore ordered that the process of making them heritable should begin in earnest, and that every estate office shall produce a list of all heritable and non-heritable holdings. Exactly the same duty is laid upon the officials in relation to the Upper Silesian nobility. The officials of the two areas recently added to Silesia are also commanded to look into this matter, and they are asked to recommend: how best to speed there the conversion into heritable tenancies.

(*b*) REST OF PRUSSIA:

The conditions of the peasants in Pomerania are described by the Peasant Order of 30 December 1764 as follows:

> While the peasants cannot be called slaves, to be given away, sold or treated as a commodity, and they are therefore able to own property, accumulated by diligence and industry, beyond the holding given them by the lord, and may dispose of it freely and bequeath it to their children; yet nevertheless it is beyond dispute that their fields, meadows, gardens and dwellings, unless explicitly determined otherwise in certain villages by contract of sale or by other means, belong to the landlord as *res soli*, and besides they have received their Seedcorn and other supplies from him; they themselves are not hereditary tenants, but servile subjects of the manor or *glebae adscripti*, and pay for the farmsteads, fields and meadows assigned to them but a small annual rent; at the same time they have to perform all sorts of services, and their children are not permitted to leave the estate without previous knowledge and consent of the lord, etc. . . .

By an order of 8 November 1773 the obligations of the subject peasants in East and West Prussia were defined more closely. Personal subjection and slavery are abolished by this law, particularly in the royal domains and on the noble estates, but hereditary subjection and *glebae adscriptio* remain. Neither the release from the obligations of this subjection, nor the amount of the commutation payment is left to the discretion of the manorial lord, but the conditions in which a subject may ask for release are laid down specifically, as:

(1) If he has the opportunity to acquire elsewhere some land in freehold, or to set up as an artisan in a town; provided he has learnt his trade with the lord's consent.
(2) If he wants to study, and is capable of benefiting by higher education.
(3) If a female has the opportunity of marrying elsewhere.
(4) If a subject is granted a royal office sufficient to maintain himself.
(5) If the lord treats a subject so cruelly as to endanger his life or health.
(6) If the lord is incapable of providing bread or the minimum of subsistence for his subject.
(7) If a lord intends to sell or give away a subject without the estate to which he belongs.

The commutation payment for a male subject, irrespective of the extent of his property, is fixed at 20 Rthlr.*; for a female, at 10 Rthlr.; for a son under the age of 14, at 6 Rthlr.; and for a daughter under 12, at 3 Rthlr. – Incidentally, the estate offices of the royal domains are *ordered* to facilitate commutation, and of the noble estate offices it is *hoped* that they will do likewise.

7/2 Abolition of Personal Servitude in Bohemia, 1781

Patent of Joseph II, 1 November 1781. Printed in WERNER CONZE, *Quellen zur Geschichte der deutschen Bauernbefreiung* (Göttingen, 1957), pp. 55–56. (Ed. Tr.)

We, Joseph II . . . to our subjects in Bohemia, Moravia and Silesia, Greetings: Whereas we have considered that the abolition of personal servitude and the introduction of a moderated subject status in the manner of our Austrian hereditary lands would have a beneficial influence on agriculture and industry, and that reason and humanity support this change;

We have taken the step of abolishing personal servitude completely, and putting in its place a moderated subject status, and we hereby command the landlords, their officials and the subjects as follows:

1. Every subject has the right to marry merely by putting up the banns and filling in a form without payment.
2. Every subject has the right (without prejudice to the army recruiting regulations) to leave his lord and settle or take employment anywhere in the country. But those who wish to leave their lordship in order to settle elsewhere have to demand a free leaving certificate, showing the new lordship that they have been discharged from their former duties to the landlord.
3. All subjects may learn any art or craft and seek their livelihood without leave of a guild.

* See Glossary.

4. The subjects are no longer obliged to perform work on the seigneurial farm, except that
5. orphans who have lost both their parents have to render the common orphan years' service to the manorial lord on his demesne, but the service shall not exceed three years and shall be performed in their place of settlement only
6. All other robots,* natural and money dues appertaining to the land to which the subjects will be liable after the abolition of personal servitude are laid down in the *Urbarium* patents, and beyond this no further burdens may be placed on them, and least of all, since they shall no longer be considered as serfs, are any dues to be demanded of them on the grounds of their former servitude.

It goes without saying that the subjects, even after the abolition of personal servitude, owe their manorial authorities due obedience in accordance with the law. . . .

7/3 Peasant emancipation in Prussia: Law of 1807

Edict of 9 October 1807. Printed in J. R. SEELEY, *Life and Times of Stein* (3 vols., Cambridge, 1878), I, pp. 442–445. (G.P.J.) For another translation see R. B. D. MORIER, 'The agrarian legislation of Prussia during the present century', in J. W. PROBYN (ed.), *Systems of Land Tenure* . . . [see Document **6/9**], pp. 369–372.

. . . it accords equally with the imperative demands of justice and with the principles of a proper national economy, to remove all hindrances which hitherto prevented the individual from attaining the prosperity which, according to the measure of his powers, he was capable of reaching. . . . We . . . accordingly ordain as follows:

I. Freedom of Exchange in Land.

Every inhabitant of our States is competent, without any limitation on the part of the State, to possess either as property or pledge, landed estates of every kind: the nobleman therefore to possess not only noble but also non-noble, citizen and peasant lands of every kind, and the citizen and peasant to possess not only citizen, peasant, and other non-noble but also noble, pieces of land, without either the one or the other needing any special permission for any acquisition of land whatever, although, henceforward as before, each change of possession must be announced to the authorities.

II. Free Choice of Occupation.

Every noble is henceforth permitted without any derogation from his position, to exercise citizen occupations; and every citizen or peasant is

* See Glossary.

allowed to pass from the peasant into the citizen class, or from the citizen into the peasant class. . . .

VI. Extinction and Consolidation of Peasant Holdings.

When a landed Proprietor believes himself unable to restore or keep up the several peasant holdings existing on an estate which are not held by a hereditary tenure, whether of a long lease or of copyhold, he is required to give information to the government of the province, with the sanction of which the consolidation, either of several holdings into a single peasant estate or with demesne land, may be allowed as soon as hereditary serfdom shall have ceased to exist on the estate. The provincial Authorities will be provided with a special instruction to meet these cases.

VII. If on the other hand the peasant tenures are hereditary, whether of long lease or of copyhold, the consolidation or other alteration of the condition of the lands in question is not admissible until the right of the actual possessor is extinguished, whether by the purchase of it by the lord or in some other legal way. In this case the regulations of VI also apply. . . .

X. Abolition of Villainage.

From the date of this Ordinance no new relation of villainage, whether by birth, or marriage, or acquisition of a villain holding, or by contract, can come into existence.

XI. With the publication of the present Ordinance the existing condition of villainage of those villains with their wives and children who possess their peasant-holdings by hereditary tenures of whatever kind ceases entirely both with its rights and duties.

XII. From Martinmas, 1810, ceases all villainage in Our entire States. From Martinmas, 1810, there shall be only free persons, as this is already the case upon the Domains in all Our provinces; free persons, however, still subject, as a matter of course, to all the obligations which bind them as free persons by virtue of the possession of an estate or by virtue of a special contract. . . .

Given at Memel, 9 October 1807.

FRIEDRICH WILHELM

7/4 Emancipation in Prussia: Definition

Publicandum of 8 April 1809* defining the rights of the Lord of the Manor abolished by the Edict on the Emancipation of the Serfs. Printed in G. F. KNAPP, *Die Bauernbefreiung* . . . [*see* Document **1/12**], II, pp. 174-175. (W.O.H. Tr.)

(7) . . . It should be observed that the following are abolished:

* This statement referred only to Silesia. Its provisions were extended to the other provinces of Prussia by an Edict of 24 October 1810. (Eds.)

(*a*) the right of the lord of the manor to demand compensation in cash or in kind in return for emancipating hereditary serfs;

(*b*) the right of the lord of the manor to demand three years' service on his estate – in return for a nominal payment – from all children of his serfs;

(*c*) the right of the lord of the manor to demand from such children of serfs financial compensation in lieu of the service mentioned in section (*b*);

(*d*) the right of the lord of the manor to demand from the children of those who have hitherto been in a servile or other subservient position to him – even after they have completed their (full-time) service on the estate – that they should render (part-time) service on the estate or should be allocated by the lord for service with the manorial gardeners or threshers in return for a payment called *Fremdenlohn*;

(*e*) the right to demand financial compensation if a serf seeks employment elsewhere than in the village on the lord's estate;

(*g*) the right to require every serf to undertake paid employment in the village on the lord's estate on the completion of his twenty fourth year;

(*h*) the right to decide, on the death of a serf, who is survived by more than one child, which of the children shall succeed to the serf's holding. . . .

(9) As soon as he ceases to be a hereditary serf a villager is free to marry and to learn a townsman's craft without the permission of his lord.

7/5 Peasant Emancipation in Prussia: Edict of 1811

R. B. D. Morier, in J. W. PROBYN (ed.), *Systems of Land Tenure* . . . [*see* Document **6/9**], pp. 375–379.

The legislation of 1811 mainly consists of two great edicts, both bearing the same date, that of the 14th of September. The one entitled, 'Edict for the Regulation of the Relations between the Lords of the Manor and their Peasants.'

The other, 'Edict for the better Cultivation of the Land.'

The first is concerned with the creation of new title-deeds for the peasant holders, and with the commutation of the services rendered in virtue of the old title-deeds.

The second surveys the whole field of agrarian reform, and introduces general measures of amelioration. . . .

The first edict branches off into two main parts.

The first dealing with peasant holdings in which the tenant has hereditary rights; the second with holdings in which the tenant has no hereditary rights.

PART I.

All tenants of hereditary holdings – *i.e.*, holdings which are inherited according to the common law, or in which the lord of the manor is bound to select as tenant one or other of the heirs of the last tenant – *whatever the size of the holdings*, shall by the present edict become the proprietors of their holdings, after paying to the landlord the indemnity fixed by this edict.

On the other hand, all claims of the peasant on the manor, for the keeping in repair of his farm-buildings, etc., shall cease.

'We desire that landlords and tenants should of themselves come to terms of agreement, and give them two years from the date of this edict to do so. If within that time the work is not done, the State will undertake it.

'The rights to be commuted may be thus generally classed:–

'I. Rights of the landlord.

1. Right of ownership ('dominium directum').
2. Claim to services.
3. Dues in money and kind.
4. Dead stock of the farms.
5. Easements, or servitudes on the land held.

'II. Rights of the tenant.

1. Claim to assistance in case of misfortune.
2. Right to gather wood, and other forest rights, in the forest of the manor.
3. Claim upon the landlord for repairs of buildings.
4. Claim upon the landlord, in case tenant is unable to pay public taxes.
5. Pasturage rights on demesne lands or forests.

'Of these different rights only a few, viz., the dues paid in kind or money, the dead stock, and the servitudes, are capable of exact valuation.

'The others can only be approximately estimated.

'To obtain therefore a solid foundation for the work of commutation, and not to render it nugatory by difficulties impossible to be overcome, we deem it necessary to lay down certain rules for arriving at this estimate, and to deduce those rules from the general principles laid down by the laws of the State.

'These principles are:

'1. That in the case of hereditary holdings, neither the services nor the dues can, under any circumstances, be raised.

'2. That they must, on the contrary, be lowered if the holder cannot subsist at their actual rate.

'3. That the holding must be maintained in a condition which will enable it to pay its dues to the State.

'From these three principles, as well as from the general principles of public law, it follows that the right of the State, both to ordinary and extraordinary taxes, takes precedence of every other right, and that the services to the manor are limited by the obligation which the latter is under to leave the tenant sufficient means to subsist and to pay taxes.

'We consider that both these conditions are fulfilled when the sum-total of the dues and services rendered to the manor do not exceed one-third of the total revenue derived by an hereditary tenant from his holding. Therefore, with the exceptions to be hereafter described, the rule shall obtain:

'That in the case of hereditary holdings the lords of the manor shall be indemnified for their rights of ownership in the holding, and for the ordinary services and dues attached to the holding, when the tenants shall have surrendered one-third portion of all the lands held by them, and shall have renounced their claims to all extraordinary assistance, as well as to the dead stock, to repairs, and to the payment on their behalf of the dues to the State when incapable of doing so.'...

PART II.

The class of holdings treated of in the second part are those held at will, or for a term of years, or for life. In these cases the landlord gets an indemnity of one-half of the holding under much the same conditions as in the case of the hereditary holdings. When the conditions differ, they do so in favour of the lord of the manor....

7/6 Resistance of the Landlords, 1811

G. F. KNAPP, *Die Bauernbefreiung* ... [*see* Document **1/12**], II, pp. 270–274. (Ed. Tr.)

The general attitude among landlords is made clear by the following correspondence.

Under date Berlin, 17 July 1811, Count Schlieben sent a memorandum to the Chancellor, Frh. v. Hardenberg, referring as follows to the 'Law on the Transfer of Property':

In Prussia, where the landlord enjoys real rights over the peasant holdings, [this law] is of the utmost importance: for the estates which are structurally based on peasant services must cease functioning at once, for these reasons:

(*a*) Most estates with peasants are so organized that the home farm as such has virtually no stocks necessary for arable cultivation.

(*b*) The peasant's stock, as a rule, is advanced by the landlord, e.g., 4 horses, 2 oxen, 2 cows, sheep, pigs, chickens, ducks, geese, seed-corn for both fields and 20–40 Scheffel* bread corn, besides field and domestic implements.

In many areas, the peasant has double the livestock, for which he requires as a rule

* See Glossary.

about 2 Huben* Kulm land (equals 4½ Magdeburg Huben), rented at absurdly low rent, . . . so-called chicken rent. But in return he is obliged to

(*c*) undertake the whole of the arable cultivation, so that the lord has no daily or domestic servants' wages to meet, no bed or board for servants, 'truly not a trivial matter'. Finally, no tied cottages are required on the home farm, except for herdsmen and craftsmen.

Now, when the transfer of property to the peasants is about to be enforced, all these expenses will suddenly have to be met, and where is the money to come from? and how shall the necessary tied cottages on the home farm and the missing stables and sheds be built, without compulsory services to draw upon?

By far the larger part of the Prussian peasantry has been so impoverished by the unfortunate war, that it hardly knows how to survive from day to day without the help of the landlord. How then can the peasant find the capital sum to pay off his lord for the stock, the services and the dues?

Land alone will not do, since the landlord cannot raise the cash to equip and stock his own estate farms. But even if money could be found, so that the peasant could compensate his lord, where are the hands to come from, for haymaking and the harvest, with all their difficulties in the Prussian climate? Even before the war Prussia was short of people; it is more so now.

Schlieben himself had been unable to provide stock for his peasants after the war, and had instead stocked up the home farm himself and worked it with direct labour in compulsory service: therefore, he says, he ought to be awarded part of the peasant's land in compensation. In general, he demands that the transfer of property shall be suspended, and the landlord be granted part of the land allocated to the peasantry.

The landlords of the Stolp District write to the King on 2 November 1811 for permission to make their own arrangements with their peasants and other holders of land in accordance with their own rights and with local conditions, and that these arrangements should not be rendered over-hasty by setting excessively short terms for them.

In justification, they call attention to the fact that even Frederick the Great sanctified the peasant constitution of Eastern Pomerania by his 'peasant order.' According to its terms, they allege, the landlord of Eastern Pomerania was always the proprietor of the peasants' holdings and was only under the single obligation not to allow the peasant households on his estate to lapse.

In these conditions, it would be contrary to the principles of justice to force us to make over larger sections of peasant holdings, which are our property at this moment, to our peasant farmers into their hereditary ownership. We should then, on our own estates, come upon the property of others at every step, and there will be no salvation therefrom otherwise than by re-purchasing what was formerly our property, and re-uniting it with the rest of the estate (according to §32 of the Edict of 14 September 1811).

When the peasant has become a proprietor, where shall the landlord find the labour to work his own home farm? The abolition of serfdom has already caused a considerable disturbance but we made this sacrifice at the time without complaint; but if the peasant is to become a proprietor himself, he will not only withhold the labour of his own family from the estate farms, but will employ the labourers' families of the rest of the village, and take them in to live under the roof of his own farmstead; and as far as our

* See Glossary.

own living-in servants are concerned, he will take great care not to let his own children go into our service, quite apart from the fact that our poor soil will hardly bear the cost of living-in or day labour.

Our estates will become hell on earth to us, if independent peasant proprietors are to become our neighbours.

7/7 Resistance to Emancipation, 1822

Report of East Prussian General Provincial Directory to the Prussian Ministry of Agriculture, 16 November 1822. Printed in HANS WOLFRAM GRAF FINCK VON FINCKENSTEIN, *Die Entwicklung der Landwirtschaft in Preuszen und Deutschland 1800–1930* (Würzburg, 1960), pp. 128–129. (Ed. Tr.)

The peasant regulations, which might have become so beneficial as a result of the proposed regulations for the agriculture of the Province in general and for the conditions of each landed proprietor in particular, but only after a series of years had elapsed and the transition had been fairly and practicably made, are terrible in their effect at the present unhappy time, when they are being enforced by the authorities against the wishes of the landlords and by setting aside so many lawful and historic institutions. This Province in particular must find it most difficult to make the transition from an agriculture based on payments in kind to one based on money, precisely because this Province has been so terribly impoverished in the past fifteen years, and because its monetary circulation will remain among all Provinces the weakest as long as its maritime trade continues in a state of depression, since half the agricultural rents and other interest payments and surpluses are being paid over to Berlin, without attracting back a comparable proportion by any existing means.

At this moment of great and progressive impoverishment, the husbandry on several hundred former demesne farms is suddenly expected to be entirely transformed by the regulations, about 224,000 Morgen* to be newly brought under cultivation, and 524 day-labourers' cottages and 76 home farms to be newly built.

The monetary compensation, not infrequently made in other Provinces and very favourable to the landed proprietor, is very rare in this Province. Because the peasants are unable as a rule to meet regular rent payments, the landlords are obliged to accept their compensation in the form of land.

Many, even among the best-placed landed proprietors, who could otherwise have profited greatly by the regulations, have been put to the greatest embarrassment and danger by the present transition, and many will be ruined during the period of transition, unless rapid and powerful help can be found for them. . . .

* See Glossary.

7/8 Commutation of Dues, Prussia, 1849–50

Report of the Prussian Ministry to the King on the Draft Laws concerning (i) the relations between Lords of the Manor and Peasants, and (ii) the establishment of a Land Mortgage Bank, 10 April 1849. Royal approval granted on 2 March 1850. Printed in G. F. KNAPP, *Die Bauernbefreiung* . . . [*see* Document **1/12**], II, pp. 430–431. (W.O.H. Tr.)

The main principles of the new Laws are as follows:

(1) In addition to those obligations due to the lord of the manor – arising from submission to the manorial court, manorial police and so forth – which were abolished by Article 40 of the Constitution (of 5 December 1848) those obligations which merely impose burdensome restrictions on the occupation of land and are of little or no real advantage to the lord of the manor shall also be abolished without compensation. These obligations became due under entirely accidental circumstances and are therefore not capable of valuation or compensation in monetary terms. They consist of various personal obligations due to the superior authority of the lord of the manor and include payments on renewal of hereditary leases, the right of pre-emption, and the right of escheat. They include also certain types of payments due to the lord of the manor when property on his estate changes hands which have either been found to be particularly oppressive owing to the changed circumstances of the present day – for example, more frequent changes of occupation of the holdings subject to or benefiting from feudal obligations or an increase in the value of holdings – or which are of dubious legal validity owing to conflicting decisions of courts of law.

(2) All holdings occupied on a permanent tenure shall be held in full ownership.

(3) It is proposed to abolish all payments in kind – with the sole exception of taxes and similar public dues and services – associated with holdings always held in full ownership, with holdings held in full ownership as the result of former legislation, and with holdings to be held in future in full ownership as a result of this proposed Law.

(4) To secure this abolition all such payments in kind shall be changed into fixed annual payments.

(5) The principle must be observed that holdings under obligation to make such payments remain legally liable for the payments.

(6) A person who is liable to make such payments may pay a single lump sum equivalent to 18 of the proposed fixed annual payments.

(7) A person who is liable to make such payments and is unable or unwilling to take advantage of this offer [*i.e.* to pay a lump sum] shall owe nine tenths of the sum that has been fixed to the Land Mortgage Bank that is to be

established. The Bank shall pay the whole lump sum to the creditor in the form of stock worth 20 full annual payments and 4% interest shall be paid on the stock.

(8) The $7\frac{1}{2}$% profit which shall thus be made by the Land Mortgage Bank shall be used every six months to secure the gradual redemption of the stock so that after 56 years the extinction [of the debt] shall be completed and the liability to make annual payments will cease.

(9) But during this period of 56 years the person making such annual payments has the right to deposit his savings – even the smallest amount – in the Land Bank for the partial or total redemption of the debt. The savings will help to pay off the interest and the principal so that the total debt shall lessen from year to year.

(10) The State will assume responsibility for the cost of running the Land Bank and will also guarantee the financial obligations that the Bank shall, by law, be required to assume.

(11) In future when a holding is transferred under the provision of a will the holding must be transferred in full ownership and the only debt to be handed on will be the liability to continue fixed payments. Moreover

(12) The burdening of a holding with a loan is not redeemable and shall not be allowed and [the proposed Law] makes possible the redemption of [formerly] irredeemable loans.

If these principles are carried out an end shall be made to every surviving restriction on the free and most profitable use of landed property and to every kind of peasant servitude to the lord of the manor in respect of a holding. At the same time the financial relationship between the peasant who occupies a holding and the lord of the manor, that follows from the payment of dues and rendering of services, shall come to an end in a simple and prompt manner. This will be accompanied by the abolition of the legal distinctions of status associated with such a relationship – an abolition which is required by the revised national Constitution – and which should be desired as much by the lords of the manor as by the peasants who hold land.

7/9 Abolition of Serfdom in Austria, 1848

Edict of Ferdinand I, 7 September 1848. Printed in WERNER CONZE, *Quellen zur Geschichte der deutschen Bauernbefreiung* (Göttingen, 1957), pp. 205-206. (Ed. Tr.)

We, Ferdinand I of Austria, Constitutional Emperor, have resolved, by and with the advice and consent of our ministers and the Constituent Reichstag, and order as follows:

1. The status of servitude and all laws relating to it are repealed.

2. The soil is to be freed; all differences between dominical (lords') and 'rustical' (peasant) land is abolished.
3. All burdens, services and dues derived from the status of servitude, as well as all natural, service and money dues deriving from manorial status, from the tithe, protective,* fruit, wine and manorial rights, including fines and heriots, are now abolished.
4. There shall be compensation for some of these dues, and not for others.
5. All rights deriving from the servile and protective* status, and from manorial rights and privileges, are abolished without compensation, and burdens derived from them are to cease.
6. For the service, dues in kind and money dues, payable to the landowner as such, or to the tithe owners or their tenants, fair compensation shall be fixed as soon as possible.
7. Right of forests and meadows, as well as of service, shall be compensated, but not the manorial right over flowers and meadows, and the manorial right of fallow and stubble-grazing.
8. Details of these orders are to be worked out by a Commission representing all Provinces, and shall include decisions on:
   (a) Money compensation of mutual obligations derived from agreements on the partition of property.
   (b) The abolition on burdens on the land not enumerated under 3 above.
   (c) The manner of the abolition and regulation of the rights enumerated under 7 above.
   (d) The scale of compensation payable and the Fund, set up separately by each Province to meet the compensation payment laid down by the State.
   (e) Whether the dues to be abolished under 2, 3 and 8b above, but not to be compensated under 5 and 6 above, shall have some compensation, and if so, how much.
9. The manorial authorities are to continue provisionally their administrative and political functions at the State's expense, until the State is in a position to take them over.
10. The Commission under 8 shall have the right to modify the provisions of compensation, under 6.
11. The manorial rights over brewing and distilling are abolished. . . .

* The reference is to the legal fiction, according to which the feudal lord, in return for the dues and services received by him, has to protect his subjects from external attack.

7/10 Peasant Tenure in Germany, 1842

WILLIAM HOWITT, *The Rural and Domestic Life of Germany* (London, 1842), pp. 40–41.

In Germany the peasants are the great and ever-present objects of country life. They are the great population of the country, because they themselves are the possessors. This country is, in fact, for the most part, in the hands of the people. It is parcelled out amongst the multitude; and wherever you go, instead of the great halls, the vast parks, and the broad lands of the nobility and gentry, as in England, you see the perpetual evidences of an agrarian system. The exceptions to this, which I shall afterwards point out, are the exceptions, they are not the rule. The peasants are not, as with us, for the most part totally cut off from property in the soil they cultivate, totally dependent on the labour afforded by others, – they are themselves the proprietors. It is perhaps from this cause that they are probably the most industrious peasantry in the world. They labour busily, early and late, because they feel that they are labouring for themselves. The women and children all work as well as the men, for it is family work; nay, the women often work the hardest. They reap, thrash, mow, work on the fallows, do anything. In summer, without shoes and stockings, clad in a dark blue petticoat and body of the same, or in other colours, according to the costume of the neighbourhood, and with their white chemise sleeves in contrast with their dress, and with their hair burnt of a singed brown, or into different hues, with the sun, they are all out in the hot fields. Nay, you may even see women driving a wagon, in which two or three men are sitting at ease smoking. They take the dinners to the fields, frequently giving to the lesser children a piece of bread, and locking them up in the cottage till they come home again, the older ones being at school till they join them in the afternoon.

This would be thought a hard life in England; but hard as it is, is not to be compared with the condition of labourers in some agricultural parts of a dear country like England, where eight or nine shillings a week, and no cow, no pig, no fruit for the market, no work in the winter, but dependence for everything on a master, a constant feeling of anxiety, and the desperate prospect of ending his days in a Union workhouse, is too commonly the labourer's lot. The German peasants work hard, but they have no actual want. Every man has his house, his orchard, his road-side trees, as we have seen, commonly so hung with fruit that he is obliged to prop and secure them all ways, or they would be torn to pieces. He has his corn-plot, his plot for mangel-wurzel, for hemp, and so on. He is his own master; and he, and every member of his family, have the strongest motives to labour. You see the effect of this in that unremitting diligence which is beyond that of the whole world besides, and his economy, which is still greater.

7/11 Peasant Tenure in Germany (Ruhr, Rhineland), 1846

T. C. BANFIELD, *Industry of the Rhine: Series I, Agriculture* (London, 1846), pp. 51–53, 88–90.

As the traveller approaches Elberfeld, the seat of the silk and cotton manufactures, the face of the country presents a totally different aspect from the adjacent districts of the county of Mark that we have just traversed. Neat peasants' houses with small plots of land fill the rather narrow valley, the hills enclosing which are covered with wood for the use of the numerous steel-manufacturers. Here is the place to study the allotment system, although not in its best form. The factories are nearly all worked by waterpower, and are consequently scattered along the course of the Wüpper, according as the fall in its bed allows. Between them the peasants' houses stand, often at a distance of a mile or two from the factory, a portion of whose inmates are the labourers employed. These houses have a garden, fields that produce grain and fodder, and usually a piece of meadow on the river's bank that helps to feed a cow. . . . The small holdings are tilled with care, but produce on an average rather less grain than the large farms. Cabbages, carrots, small patches of flax and rape-seed, point to the wants or prevailing market crops of German peasants. It must be owned that a labouring population, so scattered and rurally disposed, forms a pleasing contrast to the dingy rows of cottages that are met with at the entrance to our manufacturing towns. . . .

The pride of the German peasant is to be a small landowner. The sacrifices made to gratify this longing are incredible, as is the tenacity with which he clings to his land in all changes of fortune. The price paid for small lots of land in the valley of the Wüpper and the adjoining districts would frighten an English farmer. From 500 to 700 dollars* per morgen, or 117*l.* to 150*l.* per acre, is no unusual price for arable and meadow land. What interest he gets for his investment seems never to cross a peasant's mind. The rent of small patches adjoining these houses is not proportionately high, although dear enough; 10 or 12 dollars per morgen (2*l.* 10*s.* or 3*l.* 0*s.* per acre) is constantly paid in situations remote from the influence of towns. Building sites, especially those favourable for trade or manufactures, sell also as high as in England. The sum of 3000 dollars was paid a few years back for about an acre and a half of ground on which some zinc-works now stand at Duisburg. This was equal to 500*l.* per acre. . . .

* Thaler. (Ed.)

The village or common property comprises woodland as well as grazing-land, and, as has been said, frequently includes watercourses, public places and buildings, as well as money invested in the public funds. The revenue derived from all these sources is applied, as far as it goes, in alleviation of parochial and county taxation. From this fund the few poor persons that become chargeable are supported. We have been told of parishes where the members of the village corporation receive a dividend out of the common property. To obtain admittance to the rights of a villager a stranger must pay a certain sum, which is large or small according to the wealth of the corporation. He then enjoys the grazing and fuel rights, and the modification in taxation which the annual revenue procures. In the Rhenish districts the fee on admittance is high when compared with Central Germany. It is, we believe, highest in Rhenish Bavaria, where, in some villages, it amounts to 1500 florins, or 120*l.*

The various official personages of the village, such as the field-police, the cow, swine, and goose herd, the schoolmaster, the headborough and his officer or bailiff, receive their salaries from this fund, out of which, too, all public expenses, where it suffices, are defrayed. The church has generally its own foundation. . . .

To the mill of the lord of the manor, to which the peasants, while serfs, were bound to bring their grain to be ground, a village mill has succeeded, occasionally forming part of the corporation property, sometimes owned by shareholders who have purchased the mill of some once privileged owner. As it is still usual all over Germany for peasants to grind their own corn, there may be seen a table in all these mills in which the miller's fee, usually a portion of the meal, is expressed for all the quantities commonly brought. The feeling of security conveyed by the power of doing without extraneous help, a relic perhaps of the times when communications were liable to constant interruption, and bad roads made carriage difficult or impossible, still gives value to these mills. We have known instances of large sums being refused for mills that were sought for manufacturing purposes; the ground assigned being that the village could not do without its mill.

A public baking-oven is another appendage to a German village, although every rich peasant has his own. The oven is heated in succession by those who use it, each person bringing his own wood. In autumn the flax, after steeping or dew-rotting, is dried in this oven. The tendency of modern times is to dispense with these efforts to attain, by association, what was difficult or expensive for individuals to establish. We cannot help thinking that more may be said in defence of these common institutions than in praise of much that has superseded them. The great article of consumption, bread, is, for instance, enjoyed at least in purity by the aid of the village mill. Cheapness of course is at present not attained by the peasant, who never calculates the value of the time he spends in procuring food, and who certainly does not rank the exemption of the females of his family from drudgery amongst his luxuries. They are allotted their full share of outdoor work, as well as all the care of the household.

7/12 Land Tenure in Germany (Saxony)

HENRY MAYHEW, *German Life and Manners as seen in Saxony at the Present Day* (2 vols., London, 1864), I, pp. 6-11. (G.P.J.)

Möhra . . . lies on the borders of Saxe-Meinigen, close to Saxe-Weimar. . . . It contains about as many distinct families as there are houses and numbers altogether just upon six times as many inhabitants as families, or not quite 500 men, women and children. . . . The people here are mostly *Ackerbauern** and day labourers (Tage-löhner), and possess altogether, among them, some 4000 acres of land . . . an average of about half a hundred acres to each of the four-score families located in the village. Some, however, have as many as 150 and even 200 acres and many, on the other hand, only one; while owing to the law of 'Gavelkind' which prevails here, and gives to each member of the family an equal share of the land, on the decease of the former proprietor, the soil has come to be so divided and subdivided that even they who are lucky enough to hold more than a hundred acres are the owners of as many different strips of land, situate in as many different places. Hence the large farms in Möhra are merely an aggregation of petty ones, made up of an infinite variety of small patches . . . all the appliances of 'high farming' are entirely unknown in Möhra . . . the utter absence of all such implements as reaping machines or threshing machines, even in the largest 'economies' (as the farms are called). . . . There is only one carpenter among the Möhra population, and even he, from dearth of work, has been forced to take to the more lucrative occupation of swineherd. . . . Nor are there any builders, for the houses are all of . . . 'wattle and daub' . . . so that neither masons nor bricklayers are required. . . . On the other hand, just a tithe of the four-score householders . . . are woodcutters . . . even the few craftsmen . . . can hardly be said to be handicraftsmen proper, being . . . half-boor† half-artisan; for the smiths and the tailors are, many of them, small farmers; while the weavers, like the woodcutters, ply their trade only in the winter, and in the summer, abandon the shuttle, as the others lay aside the axe, for the sickle and the scythe, the spade and the hoe. . . the Herr Pastor has his flock, not only in a figurative but in a literal sense of the term. . . . The schoolmaster . . .

* Arable farmers. (Ed.) † See Glossary.

is renowned for breeding the biggest calves in the parish, and cultivates early peas and young potatoes. . . .

But if there are few pure mechanics and artizans there are still fewer tradesmen in Möhra . . . you might as well look for a shop in Belgrave Square as in the *Ober-* and *Unter-gasse* of the Thuringian village. . . . The *Gasthaus*, or hostelry, is the only Magazin in the place . . . for there, and there only, are coffee, sugar, candles, tobacco and salt retailed, together with the most watery beer and the most fiery '*Schnapps*', to the villagers. . . . So that one went along wondering what on earth the boors did with their money . . . for, as they generally pay their wages in kind, and grow not only their own food but also the shirts and chemises, coats and petticoats of the entire family, it was not at all improbable that even the richest bauers, though they might be worth some thousands in pigs, cows, sheep and land, had hardly a paper thaler or a plated groschen to bless themselves with.

Chapter 8 Peasant Emancipation in Russia

Introduction

In Russia, as in Prussia, emancipation was preceded by reforms on the domains of the Sovereign which served as experiments and as pacemakers for the more difficult steps of freeing the peasantry in the possession of the nobles (**8/1**). The Russian 'State' serfs formed about one-half of the total, and in addition the serfs in several of the western provinces had been freed earlier (**8/2**), so that there was no lack of experience to guide the Commission set up to complete the process of emancipation. Nevertheless, in the conditions in which it was undertaken, in an absolutist Empire in which the nobility retained all its political influence and its local domination in the provinces, the task of 'freeing' some 22 million serfs and arranging for satisfactory 'compensation' to their landlords which would leave them no worse off than before, yet allow the new peasantry sufficient land to survive and pay taxes, proved a formidable one. In addition to the difficulty, similar to the Prussian one (Introduction to Chapter 7), of reconciling three conflicting sets of interests, the Russian law-makers had to face the problems of applying terms to a vast and varied area, including fertile regions in which the landlords clamoured for the maximum amount of land to be given them (and a minimum to the peasants, who would thus be forced to labour on their estates), and infertile zones, in which the landlords had little interest in land, but all the more in the maximum share of the peasant's earnings, whether received for work in the villages or in the towns, factories or mines elsewhere (**11/1**, **11/14**). Partly for this purpose of being able to 'attach' a tribute from the peasant's outside earnings, partly because of the backwardness of the Russian administrative apparatus, and partly in response to tradition, the peasants' new property, though calculated in terms of individuals, was transferred to them, not individually, but as local communities or '*mirs*', which were also made the tax units.

The resulting Statutes of 1861 formed a code of exceptional length and complexity, of which only the barest hint can be given here (**8/3**). That the terms were even more favourable to the landlords than in Prussia is indicated by the relative mildness of their complaints. Against this, the peasantry was bitterly disappointed, believing (not without some historical justification) that the land had always been theirs, though they themselves belonged to their lords, and that any compensation in land to the landlord was therefore unjust. Numerous local rebellions, when the terms were announced, were witness to their views, and the brutality of their repression could have done little to convince them otherwise (**8/4, 8/5**). The reactions in the servile mines and factories were no less hostile, and as might be expected, it was there that pressure from below had been strongest before the reforms of 1861 (**2/24, 8/6**).

8/1 Peasant Emancipation: The Tsar's Estates, 1831

RICHARD JONES, *Peasant Rents* [*see* Document **1/16**], pp. 20-22. (G.P.J.)

The domains of the Russian sovereign are immense, and perhaps more than equal the estates of all his subjects. This fact is indicated by the number of royal serfs: of these, in 1782, ten millions and a half belonged to the crown. To extract labour rents from such a body of people, that is to employ them as they are employed by subjects, in raising produce for the benefit, and under the superintendence, of their owner, was a work clearly beyond the administrative capacity of any government. Induced therefore partly by the necessity of the case, partly, we may believe, by a wise policy, the Russian government has attempted to establish on the crown domains a different system of cultivation, including an almost total abolition of labour rents, and a voluntary and very considerable modification of the sovereign's power, as owner of the serfs. The villages inhabited by the peasants of the crown have been formed into a sort of corporation; the surrounding lands are cultivated by them at a very moderate fixed rent or abroc*: the serfs may securely acquire for themselves and transmit to others personal property, and what is a more important privilege, and one not always conceded to their class in neighbouring countries of more liberal institutions (in Hungary for instance) they may purchase or inherit land.† In the tribunals instituted especially for the management of their corporations, two peasants, chosen by the body, have a seat and voice with the officers of the emperor. But the right to their personal services has not been wholly abandoned. The serf is so far attached to the soil as to be forbidden to leave his village unless with a special licence, which is only granted, when granted at all, for a limited period. The Russian monarchs have manufactures and mines conducted on their own account. The serfs on the crown lands are still liable to be taken from their homes and employed on these. They are hired out occasionally to the owners of such

* See Glossary.

† This privilege was given in 1801, and in 1810 the peasants of the crown had purchased lands to the value of two millions of roubles in Bank assignations. . . . (Jones' note.)

similar establishments as it is thought politic to encourage; and in some of the foreign provinces *united* to Russia, though not lately, it should seem, in Russia proper, they are liable to be sold, or to be given away, or granted with the soil for a term, to individuals whom the court wishes to enrich. . . . The tenants on the royal domains already appear to be, on the whole, in a condition superior to that of the serfs of individuals, but the progress of their improvement is retarded by causes not likely soon to lose their influence. However earnestly the Emperors of Russia may shake off the character of owners of slaves, they will evidently be obliged for some generations to retain that of despots, and there is some danger that the ordinary defects of their form of government will mar their really humane efforts as landed proprietors. The officers of the Russian government are proverbially ill paid; oppression and extortion still afflict the peasantry, and the condition of the serfs of the crown is sometimes even worse than that of the slaves of the neighbouring nobility. . . .

8/2 Russian Serfdom – Statistics, 1858

ARTHUR DE BUSCHEN, "On the Origin and Numerical Development of Serfdom in the Russian Empire', *Journal of the Statistical Society* (Vol. 24, 1861), pp. 320–323. (G.P.J.)

The numbers are derived from the tenth census, taken at the end of the year 1858. The total population of Russia, exclusive of Poland, the Grand Duchy of Finland, and the Caucasus, consisted of 62,000,000. In the following provinces, containing 3,251,000 souls, the serf system had ceased to exist, viz. Estland, Livonia, Kurland, and the country of the Cossacks of the Black Sea, Semipalatinsk, and of the Kirghis, Siberia. The provinces in which serfdom existed contained a population of 59,000,000, of whom 48,000,000, or nearly four-fifths of the whole, were cultivating land and presenting three distinct classes.

1. The freemen possessing land of their own, amounting to only 1,500,000.

2. The free peasants on land belonging to the State, numbering 23,300,000. This class consists of a great number of different denominations, with different rights; they pay *obrok** for cultivated land.

3. The serfs belonging to private proprietors, amounting to 22,563,086. They include 36 per cent, or about one-third of the whole population, and two-fifths of the rural population. In 1858 they were subdivided as follows:

* See Glossary.

(*a*) Serfs attached to the land:

Males, of all ages	9,798,938
Females of all ages	10,359,293
Both sexes	20,158,231

(*b*) Serfs not attached to the land, but held as the servants of the proprietors:

Males	723,725
Females	743,653
Both sexes	1,467,378

(*c*) Temporary serfs, held for stated periods:

Males	173,476
Females	180,848
Both sexes	354,324

(*d*) Serfs, the property of institutions, as corporations, churches, schools, hospitals, etc., generally legacies from private individuals:

Males	19,350
Females	21,204
Both sexes	40,554

(*e*) Serfs attached to manufactories and mines (mostly belonging to merchants):

Males	259,455
Females	283,144
Both sexes	542,599

These five classes comprise a total of:

Males	10,974,944
Females	11,588,142
Total of both sexes	22,563,086

... In sixteen governments* 50 per cent and upwards of the population were in a state of serfdom. Among these are the following belonging to the earlier Polish provinces, viz., Smolensk 70 per cent, Mohileff 64 per cent., Witebsk 57 per cent., Minsk 60 per cent., Podolia 60 per cent., Volhynia 56 per cent., Kieff 58 per cent. Seven governments of Great Russia, forming the centre of the Muscovite Empire, give the following proportions: Tula 68 per cent., Kaluga 61 per cent., Riasan 56 per cent., Nijni-Novgorod 58 per cent., Vladimir 57 per cent., Kostroma 57 per cent., and Yaroslav 57 per cent.... The proportion of serfs was lowest in the following governments, viz., Tauria (Crimea) 5 per cent., Olonetz 4 per cent., Viatka, Astrakhan, Stawropol 2 per cent., and Bessarabia 1 per cent....

Unquestionably the richest districts were Perm (with 9 700 serfs as an average to each owner), Viatka (530), and the three lesser Russian governments of Podolia (670), Kieff (721) and Volhynia (370). The average of the whole country was 211 serfs to each proprietor. Of the 107 000 proprietors, 1,396 were owners of no less than 6,500,000 serfs, or on an average about 4,600 each ... 3,462 proprietors with more than 3,000,000 serfs, had between 1,000 and 2,000 serfs, or about 1,200 on an average to each ... about 8,000,000 serfs were owned by 20,162 proprietors possessing from 200 to 1,000 each.... Over 3,300,000 serfs belonged to 36,179 proprietors, who possessed between 40 and 200 each.... The class of proprietors, each with less than 40 serfs, comprised 42,959 with 700,000 dependents (averaging sixteen to each owner).... Lastly, we find 3,633 proprietors with about 25,000 serfs but *without land* (averaging six to each). This class is nowhere considerable.... It is worthy of notice that in the governments where the land is held by the intermediate and small proprietors the disposition towards emancipation was the least favourable. Much more sympathy was found among the large proprietors, with a few exceptions.

8/3 The Statutes of Emancipation, 1861

a Part I. The General Statute, Obshchee Polozhenie o Krest'yanakh Vyshedshikh iz Krepostnoi Zavistimosti, St. Petersburg, 19 February 1861.†

b Part II. The Redemption Statute, Polozhenie o Vykupe.

c Part VI. The Local Statute for Great Russia, New Russia and White Russia, Myestnoye Polozhenie.... (M.E.F., A.G.W. Tr.)

(a) (1) The servitude of the peasants belonging to the landed proprietors ...

* See Glossary.

† A French version of important sections of the Act will be found in R. Portal, *Le statut des paysans libérés du servage, 1861–1961* (Paris, 1963), pp. 194–204.

is abolished for ever, in accordance with the rules laid down in the present Statute, and the Regulations published at the same time.

(2) Peasants and domestic serfs freed from servitude shall have the civil rights accorded to the persons and the goods of free rural subjects.

(3) While keeping the right of property over all their lands, the landed proprietors shall grant to their peasants in perpetuity, against the payment of rent, the enjoyment of the following:

the cottages and their appurtenances,

and, in addition, in order to ensure their livelihood and to permit them to fulfil their duties towards the State and the landed proprietors, an extent of cultivable land and other productive landed property that shall be determined by local Regulations.

(4) In return for the allotment which they shall receive under the preceding article, the peasants shall be obliged to render to the landed proprietors those dues in money and services laid down by the local Regulations. . . .

(7) There shall be regulatory deeds defining the new relationships of dependence between the landed proprietors and the peasants allotted to their land. The drawing up of these deeds is left to the care of the proprietors themselves. A term of two years from the promulgation of this Statute is laid down for their completion, confirmation and execution.

(8) Once the quantity of land has been conceded to the peasants in perpetual enjoyment, according to the local Regulations, the proprietors shall not henceforth be obliged, in any circumstances, to make further grants of land.

(11) The peasants have the right to purchase the full proprietorship over their houses and their appurtenances on the conditions prescribed by the local Regulations.

(12) With the consent of the landed proprietors, the peasants may acquire in full proprietorship, in addition to their houses with their appurtenances, any of the cultivable land and other properties which have been granted to them in perpetual enjoyment; following their acquisition in full proprietorship of their allotments . . . all the bonds of dependence between the proprietors and their peasants are at an end.

(14) In order to facilitate the acquisition by the peasants in full proprietorship of the land which has been granted to them in perpetuity, so that this acquisition may take place by amicable agreement between the landed proprietor and the peasants, or on the request of the proprietor alone, the government shall provide its assistance, to the extent and according to the procedure laid down by the special Regulation on redemption. . . .

(17) The freed peasants are grouped in village communes in all that relates to economic matters, and in districts for administration and local

justice. In each commune and in each district business shall be regulated by the assembly and its elected authorities. . . .

(18) The landed proprietor reserves for himself the right of seigneurial police and supervision of the rural communities, as long as the bonds of dependence regarding proprietorship remain in being.

(56) In localities covered by these Regulations, the share of the land acquired by the whole village commune (where communal utilization exists) must not be less than one-third of the upper limit of land per head, fixed by the aforesaid Regulation . . . and in the case of the Steppe land belt, one-third of the amount laid down by decree.

Where land is acquired in ownership, not by the whole commune, but only by one or a few householders (in those settlements where communal working of the land has been replaced by working by individual households), the strip of land acquired must be no less in extent than two single allotments of the upper limit (in the case of the Steppe land belt, of the decreed amount) as determined by the aforesaid Regulation. . . .

NOTE: This Article applies also to the land of the Don Army and to the Stavropol province on the basis of the supplementary rules specially drawn up for them.

(67) If the dues taken from the peasants before this Regulation was enacted and which remain unchanged in the Charter, are lower than the dues fixed for each locality according to the allotment on the basis of the present local Regulations, then the redemption payment is determined by 6% capitalization of the dues from the peasants and is made over to the landowner in the full amount without the deduction indicated in Article 66 of one-fifth (paragraph 1) or one-quarter (paragraph 2), as long as this capital sum does not exceed the size of the redemption alone, calculated by capitalization of the dues reckoned according to the size of the allotment with deduction of the aforesaid one-fifth or one-quarter.

If the capital sum exceeds the aforesaid size, then the redemption alone shall be taken as valid.

This rule applies only to those estates where, by mutual voluntary agreement between landowner and peasants, the entire allotment is acquired in ownership.

(b) (27) The sum which is paid over to the landed proprietor in the form of a guaranteed payment by the State, for the land and other property made over to the peasant is called 'redemption loan'.

(29) The payments made over by the State to the landed proprietors, consist in part of bills of the State Bank bearing 5% interest, and in part of

redemption certificates, with a guaranteed return, which will be progressively replaced by bills of the State Bank.

(31) It shall be open to the peasants to acquire in full proprietorship either the entire allotment granted to them in perpetual enjoyment, the houses, their appurtenances and the cultivable land, or only a part thereof.

(32) The redemption of the communal allotment arises from an amicable agreement between the landed proprietor and his peasants. This agreement determines the amount of compensation payable to the proprietor for the land granted, independently of the redemption loan by the State. The exceptions to this general regulation are indicated below.

(56) The land required by a rural commune (on which it cultivates its communal land) must not be less than a third of the total extent of the locality covered by the commune.

(65) In determining the amount of the redemption loan, the base shall be the amount of money repayments by the peasants to the landed proprietor as laid down in the regulatory deed as compensation for the communal allotment, the houses and the appurtenances and the cultivable land . . . if the peasants do not require their total allotment, but only a part thereof, the amount of the repayment is less according to the regulations laid down by the local acts for the calculations of money repayments.

(66) Annual repayment, due for the land in process of acquisition . . . is capitalised at 6%, i.e. it is multiplied by $16\frac{2}{3}$. The redemption loan granted to the peasants to be paid over to the landed proprietor is a fraction of the capital calculated as follows:

four-fifths if the peasants require the whole of the allotment indicated in the regulatory deed

three-quarters if they require less than the whole. . . .

(68) As regards additional payments made by the peasants over and above the redemption loan, the following rules shall be observed:

1. If the repayment is the result of an amicable agreement between the landed proprietor and his peasants, with the agreement of the State, only the loan of the State is fixed (cf. Article 65 and 66). The indemnity paid to the proprietor by the peasants in addition to the redemption loan is left to the agreement of the contracting parties.

2. If the repurchase is imposed by the proprietor alone (Article 35) and the peasants require the whole of their allotment, the landed proprietor does not have the right to demand additional payment . . . but if the peasants express the desire to acquire less than the whole of the allotment, and only a part thereof . . . they must at a time when they make a declaration of intent, transmit to the Treasury of the district the amount of the additional payment,

equal to one-fifteenth of the redemption loan, calculated on the extent of the land which they are about to acquire.

(113) The peasants who have acquired their allotment in full proprietorship by purchase, are required to pay each year to the Treasury in place of the repayments due to landed proprietors for that land, a sum equal to 6% of the redemption loan fixed by the State, and this should be paid until the amortisation of the latter. This is called the 'redemption payments'.

(114) The redemption loan is amortized by redemption payments over 49 years beginning from the grant of the loan.

(118) When the land is acquired by a whole commune, the method of dividing the redemption payments among its members is left entirely to the commune.

(c) (5) Each commune receives in perpetual enjoyment . . . the quantity of land necessary, according to local conditions, to ensure the livelihood of the peasants, and to permit them to fulfil their obligations towards the State and their landed proprietor. For this land the peasants shall either pay rent to the proprietor or perform labour services.

(6) The village commune to which the allotment is granted . . . consists of all the persons enumerated in the village according to the tenth census. . . *

(9) The extent of the allotment granted to the peasants in perpetual enjoyment is determined by amicable agreement between the proprietor and the peasant. . . . If such agreement cannot be reached, the granting of the allotment shall take place according to the Regulations indicated hereafter.

(10) The provinces to which the present Statute applies are divided into 3 zones.

(14) Each of the 3 zones . . . is divided into regions;

1. The 'non-Chernoziom' (non-Black Earth) zone – into 9 regions;
2. The 'Chernoziom' (Black Earth) zone – into 8 regions;
3. The 'Steppeland' zone – into 12 regions;

(16) To determine the quantity of land granted in perpetual enjoyment to the village commune, there shall be laid down for each region of the first and second zones two limits establishing respectively the maximum and minimum allotment per 'zone'. The annexe to article 15 indicates the number of dessiatines† of land which shall form in each region the maximum allotment per 'soul'. The minimum allotment shall be equal to one-third of the maximum.

* '. . . the statute of 1861 when dealing with the allocation of land to freed serfs, points out that "the subject of the right to land and house is not the peasant head of household (*domokhozyain*) himself, but all the family, all the household (*dvor*)." (Ed.)'

† See Glossary.

(17) The peasants of the first and second zones shall keep in perpetual enjoyment the landed property – houses with their appurtenances, arable fields, pasture, meadow ... – of which they had the use before the promulgation of the present Statute, as long as the amount of dessiatines which represent these landed holdings is no greater than the maximum communal allotment, except as shall be laid down in Article 20.

N.B. To obtain the extent of the maximum of the communal land, the number of 'souls' making up the commune is multiplied by the maximum allotment per 'soul', indicated in the annexe of Article 15, for the locality in question. . . .

(18) If the present allotment exceeds the maximum communal allotment, the landed proprietor has the right to re-possess the excess.

(19) If the present allotment is less than the minimum communal allotment, the landed proprietor has the choice of two solutions:

1. to supplement the allotment by adding to it the deficient quantity of land; or else

2. to reduce the rent in proportion to the deficiency. . . .

(20) If, in the first and second zones, the granting to the peasants of their present allotment should leave the landed proprietor with less than one-third of the extent of the property he previously possessed, he has the right to keep back sufficient to make up one-third ... provided, however, that the communal allotment is not reduced below the minimum. . . .

(26) The peasant allotments comprise only such land as is fit for cultivation.

8/4 Peasant Dissatisfaction with Statutes of Emancipation, 1861

S. I. NOSOVICH, *Krest'yanskaya reforma v Novgorodskoy Gubernii; zapiski S. I. Nosovicha, 1861–1863 gg.* (*Peasant Reform in Novgorod Province; Notes of S. I. Nosovich, 1861–1863*) (St. Petersburg, 1899), pp. 16–24, translated in STANLEY W. PAGE, *Russia in Revolution; Selected Readings in Russian Domestic History since 1855* (Princeton, N.J., 1965), pp. 15–18.

May, 1861

. . . The Governor of Novgorod had appointed me to the post of government representative at the district congresses of communes. . . . I arrived in Isakovo two months after the proclamation of the emancipation manifesto and was much amazed to find the landlords rather apathetic with respect to a matter so important to them as the emancipation of the serfs. . . . The peasants were ... in a tense frame of mind, mainly because they had no idea at all what awaited them either in the immediate or in the somewhat distant future. The published peasant statutes had been read to them – they had perhaps even read them themselves; but they could make no sense out of them.

8/4 *Peasant Dissatisfaction, 1861*

Earlier, passing through Demyansk District . . . I had heard of many misunderstandings that had risen between the landlords and their former serfs. I do not know whether the statements of my informants were fair . . . but I was told that all of the disagreements grew out of the stubbornness of the landlords, solidly opposed to the reforms, and that the flogging rods usually decided the issues to the disadvantage of the peasants who were forced to listen in silence not really knowing what was true and what was not.

Prior to my arrival at Isakovo the *obrok** peasants had been refusing to perform their field labor because of what they had understood the statutes to say. After much futile discussion the district leader of the nobility was called in, as was the police inspector, whose arrival frightened the peasants. However, the officials employed no harsh measures. They briefly explained to the peasants what their error was; that although the amount of their labor had been reduced, some labor was still required of them. It must be said that even before the arrival of the authorities . . . the peasants had invariably remained respectful and although protesting vigorously, always added such phrases as: – 'not wishing to blame your grace,' or 'we, little mother, were always devoted to you, but the people tell us that we no longer are obliged to do the work.'

There were other disagreements. *Tyaglo** exempt peasants did not want to fulfil their *barshchina** requirements. Others did not want to weave . . . and sometimes refused to do any kind of work. The woman's *barshchina* . . . had been set at two days a week . . . but many women did not care to do the work in the middle days of the week, regarding those days as inconvenient. Whatever the explanation for all the confusion in our village . . . , the main thing that can be deduced is that nobody on our estate, besides mother and sister, could understand the new arrangement.

Upon my arrival I asked all of the heads of [peasant] households to convene in the church on the first Sunday so that a thanksgiving service might be held to celebrate the emancipation. . . . Upon completion of the service I went out to the church square. There, surrounded by a crowd of peasants and women, I expounded upon [the great change] wrought by the grace of the tsar. I mention in passing that the tsar's prestige was unusually high in the eyes of the common folk of our parts. When the manifesto was read to the peasants, many of them said with feeling: 'See, the little father looks after all of us.' I tried to build upon this prestige in the hope that the peasants, seeing how the tsar . . . cared for them, would in their turn . . . respect the provisions of the statutes. At the same time I constantly suggested that they trust the persons whose task it was to carry out the regulations of the statutes with fairness and conscience.

* See Glossary.

I spoke to them of the major judicial, administrative and economic changes that were to come. The last interested them the most, being more comprehensible to them, and when I was on the subject of the land or of their obligations, their attention doubled and they pressed closer about me. I explained to them what their present obligations to the landlords were. . . . I assigned the *barshchina* peasants equal shares of work and read them the list drawn up to indicate to each by name his day of labor. Then I gave this list to our steward, whom I instructed daily to mark off the workers. I asked him to be most careful and not cause me or himself unpleasantness. I did not think the fulfilment of *obrok* payments a matter altogether fair to the peasants, but I could not touch upon that . . . in order not to undermine the influence and importance of the district marshal of the nobility who had categorically expressed himself to the peasants on that score. . . . In conclusion I explained to the peasants that they would be free hired workers commencing with the coming year; that I intended to deal fairly with them and give them land as specified by the statutes. I said I would place them all on an *obrok* basis in order to figure their payment and would equate six *desyatins** of land to nine silver rubles per peasant. Several times the peasants asked me how large a *desyatin* was and how the cost of inferior land would be reckoned. . . . [Many] peasants told me that they had little faith in what the masters told them, that the priests too were [interpreting the laws] in favor of the masters and that in many parts of our region the laws were being interpreted in a manner different from that explained to them by their masters.

I asked them about their personal views . . . and realized how greatly their hopes had been disappointed. All of them expressed the most communistic conceptions . . . and had expected that all the land '. . . would be divided among the peasants.' . . .

I have had talks with many manorial serfs. . . . They regard themselves as wronged in comparison with the peasants. All of them expected that the landlords would have to settle them on land; many still persist in their delusion. Some of the manorials want to have land not for themselves but for their children. They want to partake in the communal sharing of the commune fields so that they can lease out the land for added income. . . . They expect to continue working in their customary capacities but want the land to serve as a real estate fund to secure the future of their children. They think more about this now than formerly, since they want their children to become literate and they worry about their education and the like. The manorials should be settled on state lands and be given some aid in paying the cost. Many manorials have lately become smarter about marriage. Some feel they made mistakes in that respect, seeing that the whole brood of children will be

* See Glossary.

their full responsibility after exactly two years. . . . Previously the landlord, one way or another, provided for each growing child. The marriage of manorials required no foresight and nowhere were there as many children as in the manor. The old manorials are worried about their future and are constantly – by word as by deed – trying to win over their former masters . . . , fearfully envisioning themselves thrown out on the street in two years.

8/5 Reaction to Emancipation, 1861

Imperial Aide-de-Camp Count A. V. OLSUVIEV to Alexander II: Reports dated 28 March and 5 April 1861. Printed in WALTER MARKOV, *Die Bauernbewegung des Jahres 1861 in Russland nach Aufhebung der Leibeigenschaft* (Berlin, 1958), pp. 2–5. (Ed. Tr.)

The peasants of the estates of Turla, Mikhalishka, Chekha and Labudza in the Vilna Region, stated to their owner, Mr. Kotvich, after they had received a copy of the new edict, that they were no longer willing to perform any servile duties whatever. . . . The obstinate peasants would not listen to reason. They even succeeded in persuading the peasants of the neighbouring estates of Messrs. Mineyka and Abramovich to follow their bad example and refuse their labour services.

Thereupon Chief of Police Gregoriev and Staff Officer of Gendarmes Adamovich were ordered to proceed to the above-named estates to apprehend the guilty parties and bring them to deserved punishment. Further, the Governor-General ordered a company of the Libau Infantry Regiment 'Prince Charles of Prussia' from Vilna to the estates, which are about 60 km distant, in order to make the peasants submit to authority and, if necessary, to mete out punishment. A report arrived also of insubordination of peasants on the estate of Mr. Skirmunt in the Sventsiany Region which, though it is in a different Region, adjoins the above-mentioned estates.

I have the impression that the peasants are rebellious merely because of ignorance of their obligations, and I feel sure that, to restore order, nothing more is required than a sensible explanation of the new regulations, which have probably been deliberately misrepresented to the peasants by subversive elements. . . .

On the rest of the estates in the Vilna Region everything is quiet so far, thank God. The peasants remain respectful towards their estate-owners and fulfil all their obligations. . . .

(5 April 1861)

After a I had despatched my last report . . . 28 March, a report came in from Major Mikhnev, who is attached for special duties to the Governor-

General and who had been sent out to restore peace and order among the peasants on the estate of Mr. Skirmunt in Sventsiany Region, to the effect that the peasants remained obstinate and rebellious despite his efforts at peaceful persuasion.

As a result, the Governor-General considered my presence on the above-named estate advisable. On my arrival at Sventsiany, the Deputy Lieutenant, Mr. Svietecky, reported to me that the peasants of the landowner Count Mostovsky, some 700 souls, were also refusing to perform their labour services, and a rebellious mob had informed him that they did not believe the explanations given to them by the estate-owner and the local authorities regarding the new regulations, and refused to perform any service of any kind. . . . I ordered a company from the town of Sventsiany to the estate of Count Mostovsky, some 2 verst* distant. As soon as I arrived on the estate, it became clear to me that kindness and peaceful persuasion were by no means appropriate methods to end the unrest. I decided therefore to make an example of them, had two of the ringleaders arrested and taken under guard to the provincial capital, where they are now facing sentence as rebels. Further, I gave orders to whip six men. These strict measures had a beneficial effect on the riotous mob. The peasants saw common sense, and gave me the rueful promise to meet their obligations as laid down in the regulations.

On the following day I drove with the Deputy Lieutenant of the Region to the estate of Mr. Skirmunt, where we arrived at the same time as the company ordered there. Major Mikhnev, who had been attempting to exert persuasion on the 1,300 souls on the estate during the past fortnight and who was therefore well acquainted with all the troublemakers, designated five of the ringleaders, whom I arrested as being rioters and detrimental influences on the village community, and transported them to the provincial capital for sentence. Thirty-one men were whipped.

From the estate of Skirmunt we proceeded to the estate of Mrs. Bochkovskaya, where we also assembled the peasants of the nearby estates of the Deputy Lieutenant Svientecky and of Mr. Mosheyka. These peasants also followed the bad example of the Skirmunt estate in refusing to accept any orders, and refusing to recognize any authority. They remained deaf to all persuasion. I had again to use severity, and to have the worst agitators and rebels taken to the provincial capital for sentence, as well as one man from the Svietecky estate. In addition twenty-nine men from the three estates were whipped.

Your Imperial Majesty, I have reluctantly come to the conclusion that none of these rebellious peasants was willing to see reason without severe punishment. Only after the harshest measures had been used against their

* See Glossary

obstinacy, did they show any readiness to discuss the new regulations promulgated by Y.I.M. . . .

There is hope now that these unfortunate, but inevitable punitive actions may serve as a warning for the Gouvernement* as a whole and persuade the peasants to judge the new regulation, not by what is said by some disreputable agitators, but by what is said by the local authorities or the estate-owners.

8/6 Reaction of Factory and Mine Serfs to Emancipation, 1861

Imperial Aide-de-Camp G. A. KRIEGER to Alexander II: Reports dated 4 April and 2 May 1861. Printed in WALTER MARKOV, *Die Bauernbewegung* . . . [*see* Document **8/5**], pp. 158-160. (Ed. Tr.)

The local Zemstvo authorities have succeeded in ending the unrest in the works of Preobrazhensky, Voskresensky, Verkhotorsky and Arkhangelsky. The troublemakers from the Kargalinsky mines who had returned without permission to their works of origin, have learnt their lesson and have gone back without delay to their places of work. In the concerns themselves a state of perfect order continues. The workers are meeting their obligations, wherever they are set to work, and a peaceful progress of production seems as good as certain for the future. Among the workmen who had run away without permission from their work in the mines there were fifty men from the Voskresensky mine of the Pashkovs, who alone persisted in their disbelief and disobedience. But when it was proved to them that they had been misled by the peasant Lutukhin from the village of Beregovaya, on the Pashkov estate, they were induced to repent. They now saw the error of their ways, promised submission and returned to their work in the mines. The peasant Lutukhin, as chief troublemaker, was punished directly by the police with the Governor's permission. To go through the due processes of law would have led to a delay intolerable in the present circumstances. The highest degree of ignorance and stupidity was shown by the workers belonging to the Preobrazhensky concern of Lt.-General Pashkov who had also left their mine and were examined on their return to their works of origin. They would not even recognize the genuineness of the manifesto and of the new laws. Their attitude was determined by the rumours which they had heard earlier about an imminent liberation, so that they were expecting a manifesto which would give them immediate and unconditional freedom and the end of any dependence on the factory owner. Finally, however, they understood that such expectation was totally unrealistic, since all preconditions for it are

* See Glossary.

missing. On that occasion they were also informed what consequences they had to expect if they persisted in further acts of disobedience, and so they willingly returned to the mines. . . .

In order to see the position in the individual firms at first hand, I intend to make a tour of the region, with the Governor's permission. I would like to begin with the Shilvinsky works of the merchant Polyachev in the Menselin Region. This concern is peculiar in that the workers possess, apart from their huts, no field, no grassland and no woodland, so that they do not come under the additional regulations for peasants in factories and therefore demand special notice. . . .

On my journey to the Shilvinsky works in the Menselin Region, and the Sycheshlinsky mines, 86 verst* distant, belonging to it, I was joyfully greeted as representative of the Sovereign by the peasants who came to meet me. They fell on their knees before me and expressed their gratitude for the personal rights granted to them. A few among them, who had been to school, expressed their disquiet to me over future developments, since they understood quite well that the new regulations and additional clauses relating to peasants in factories are only applicable where the workers possess, unlike themselves, fields, grassland and woodlands, besides their huts. I had anticipated this question; the object of my journey was to clarify it. I began by explaining to the workmen that their conditions which were radically different from those of other concerns, would shortly be dealt with by a special regulation. But I pointed out in addition, that the present order obtaining in their works must be maintained until the introduction of the land transfer documents. About three years ago the Governor had sent troops into the works because of alleged mutiny, and had visited them in person. When enquiries were made into the reason for the dissatisfaction of the workmen, however, it was found that the demands of the workers against the owner, the merchant Polyachev, were fully justified. Since then the works have been handed over, by Imperial command, to trustees, and the conditions of the workers have been somewhat improved.

To me personally they complained about holding back their additional wage which had been promised them in September of last year by the trustee Belonovsky and the Chief of Police of the concern. They also asked for permission to use timber from the Imperial forests near the works. I have transmitted both these requests to the Governor for his decision.

Before setting out on my journey to the works, I studied the files relating to the former unrest, in order to gain an insight into the attitude of the factory workers. The main reasons for the rebellion and insubordination of the workers in the various private factories seemed to me to have been the

* See Glossary.

following: shortage of food, large difference in wages compared with the State factories, occasional rascality of the managers, unscrupulousness of the office staff, frequent indifference of the works chief of police and the constant absence of the factory-owner. Even in the present transitional period, so decisive for factory-owners and workers alike, the Governor was forced to turn to the Minister of the Interior and the Governor-General of Moscow, because the workers of the Voskresensky and Preobrazhensky concerns (proprietor, Lt.-General Pashkov) had not received the wages due to them, and the Beloretsky works (proprietor, Capt. Pashkov, ret.) would not advance them any money for the purchase of bread grains.

PART III

The Rise of Modern Industry in Europe

Chapter 9 Agriculture

Introduction

The belief in human rights and in personal freedom had played a large part in the emancipation of the serfs and the other great changes in land tenure and in status all over Europe, but behind them lay the demand for efficiency. The three great interest groups involved, namely the State, the nobility and the peasants, could be ultimately satisfied only if the new terms permitted an increase in agricultural output, and the examples of Holland, Great Britain and, later, France, had spread the conviction that an independent peasantry, or capitalist landlords and farmers employing free wage labourers, would have stronger incentives, and would be better able to develop and introduce improved techniques than the traditional and restrictive system they replaced.

On the whole, these expectations were justified. In the peasant agriculture of France (**6/6, 6/7, 6/8, 6/9, 6/10**) increased yields were obtained, though often in conditions of great hardship and overwork, both in the grain staples, particularly wheat, and, even more significantly, in such products as the great cash and industrial crops of wine, silk and sugar (**9/1, 9/2, 9/3**). Further, the major drawback of peasant agriculture, namely the tendency of people to cling to the land and the consequent over-supply (or disguised unemployment) of labour, could be partly alleviated in this period by the ease with which the peasant households could turn to part-time industrial employment, in France (**11/3**) as well as in other similar areas, like Saxony or Russia (**11/1, 11/7, 11/26**). The price paid for this concentration on cash and industrial crops was the dependence on the vagaries of a world market, and the vulnerability to crop failure, as in silk (**9/4**) or, later, in the vine.

Similar technical progress occurred in other peasant regions, like Flanders (**9/5**, but compare **6/11**), Western Germany (**9/6**) and Lombardy (**9/8**). Where large estates had evolved, as in the eastern provinces of Prussia, the incentives to technical progress were also present (**9/7**).

Before the demands for greater output could be met, two aids to progress were required by both peasant and estate agriculture: capital and technical advice. To furnish the first, a variety of institutions grew up, from the Crédit Foncier in France (**9/9, 14/7**) to the German agricultural co-operative credit societies (**9/10**). As regards the second, Continental farmers enjoyed a great deal of State support. Schools and colleges in France, Germany, Denmark and Switzerland, for example, taught practical farming to the peasants, and at the same time developed a trained scientific advisory service at a higher level, and the results could be seen in the better farming methods adopted (**9/6**, **9/11**, **9/12**). There was also growing government support, as well as local initiative, for exhibitions, agricultural societies, and the fostering of breeding stocks and new varieties of plants (**9/13**). It might, perhaps, be doubted whether the rigidly surviving partition into the relatively small holdings typical of Western Europe was the form of tenure best adapted to the new, increasingly scientific and increasingly mechanised techniques of the mid-nineteenth century; but, given the structure which it was politically impossible to change, the combination of private peasant initiative and government support ensured rapid progress within the limits set, as soon as market conditions permitted.

9/1 Agricultural Progress in France

T. E. CLIFFE LESLIE, 'The Land System of France', in J. W. PROBYN (ed.), *Systems of the Land Tenure* . . . [*see* Document **6/9**], pp. 298–299, 306–307.

'Almost everywhere the soil of France may be made to respond to the labour of man, and almost everywhere it is for the advantage of the community that manual labour should be actively bestowed upon it. Let us suppose ourselves in the rich plains of Flanders, or on the banks of the Rhine, the Garonne, the Charente, or the Rhone; we there meet with *la petite culture*, but it is rich and productive. Every method for increasing the fruitfulness of the soil, and making the most of labour, is there known and practised, even among the smallest farmers. Notwithstanding the active properties of the soil, the people are constantly renewing and adding to its fertility by means of quantities of manure, collected at great cost; the breed of animals is superior, and the harvests magnificent. In one district we find maize, and wheat; in another, tobacco, flax, rape, and madder; then again, the vine, olive, plum, and mulberry, which, to yield their abundant treasures, require a people of laborious habits. Is it not also to small farming that we owe most of the market-garden produce raised at such great expenditure around Paris?'* This passage was written sixteen years ago; and a communication to the writer cited above shows how the predictions it contains respecting the south of France, and the great future before *la petite culture*, are now being realised under the eyes of its author. But it is not in the southern half alone of France that the peasant cultivator finds a perpetually growing demand for all the most remunerative kinds of his produce. The 'Enquête Agricole,' for

* Lavergne.

instance, shows a great increase in the cultivation of the vine in the east, the west, and the centre, as well as the south; while in the north – where the vine is, on the contrary, giving way before the competition of the plant of more favoured skies – the demand for the produce of the market-gardens, the dairy, and the orchard, afford more than a compensation. It deserves, moreover, passing remark that the little gardens and orchards round the cottages of the peasantry form, by reason of their careful and generous cultivation, the greater portion of the class of land which in French agricultural statistics obtains the denomination of *Terrains de qualité supérieure*.

The raising and fattening of cattle for the market is another great department of husbandry which *la petite culture* has almost to itself in France; yet it must be confessed that it is – though a marked improvement is visible – not as yet generally carried on with the same skill as in Flanders; and the art of house feeding, which is the basis of the Flemish system of small farming, is still in its infancy in many French districts: a fact, however, which only opens a brighter future for *la petite culture* within them. While *la petite culture* is gaining ground and growing more prosperous as well as more perfect and more minute, large farming too has made great progress in France. Not only is there a great domain, within which *la petite culture* has exclusive or special advantages, but there is a common domain, for example, in the production of cattle, cereals, and roots, where both may co-exist and prosper; and there is, again, a domain within which *la grande culture* has its own superior advantages. There were no less than 154,167 farms in France of 100 acres – a number not far short of the total number of farms in England – at the date to which the latest agricultural statistics go back. There were, again, 2,489 steam threshing-machines in 1862, as against 1,537 in 1852; and it is natural to infer that the chief employment of these was on the larger farms. In the production of sheep, again, *la petite culture* has not shown itself successful in France; though it is proper to remark that the decline of sheep between 1852 and 1862 is attributed by the highest authorities, in the main, not to the subdivision of the soil (the decline in their number being a new phenomenon and subdivision an old one), but to a number of wet seasons followed by disease, to a contraction of the area of sheep-walks by the reclamation of waste land and the division of commons; to an extension of the surface under wheat; and to an improvement in quality as distinguished from quantity. Nevertheless, it appears certain that minute farming under French methods does not give sheep an adequate range, and tends to other productions. Again, both in Belgium and in France the cultivation of the sugar beet, in combination with sugar factories, is found to tend to *la grande culture*, and no finer, larger farms are to be seen in Scotland than many in France, of which beet is the principal produce.

In the Departments* immediately surrounding Paris large farming is to be seen in the highest perfection, of which the reader who has not visited them will find a description in M. de Lavergne's 'Economie Rurale de la France.' Yet, after noticing several magnificent examples, he adds: 'While *la grande culture* marches here in the steps of English cultivation, *la petite* develops itself by its side, and surpasses it in results.' The truth is, as we have said, that the large and the small farming compete on fair terms in France, which they are not allowed to do in England; and the latter has, to begin with, a large and ever-increasing domain within which it can defy the competition of the former. The large farmer's steam-engine cannot enter the vineyard, the orchard, or the garden. The steep mountain is inaccessible to him, when the small farmer can clothe it with vineyards; and the deep glen is too circumscribed for him. In the fertile alluvial valley like that of the Loire, *the garden of France*, his cultivation is not sufficiently minute to make the most of such precious ground, and the little cultivator outbids him, and drives him from the garden; while, on the other hand, he is ruined by attempts to reclaim intractable wastes which his small rival converts into *terrains de qualité supérieure*. Even when mechanical art seems to summon the most potent forces of nature to the large farmer's assistance, the peasant contrives in the end to procure the same allies by association, or individual enterprise finds it profitable to come to his aid. It is a striking instance of the tendency of *la petite culture* to avail itself of mechanical power, that agricultural statistics show a larger number of reaping and mowing machines in the Bas Rhin, where *la petite culture* is carried to the utmost, than in any other department. Explorers of the rural districts of France cannot fail to have remarked that *la petite culture* has created in recent years two new subsidiary industries, in the machine-maker on the one hand, and the *entrepreneur* on the other, who hires out the machine; and one is now constantly met even in small towns and villages, old fashioned and stagnant-looking in other respects, with the apparition and noise of machines, of which the large farmer himself has not long been possessed.

9/2 Successful Wheat Production in France

H. COLMAN, *The Agricultural and Rural Economy of France, Belgium, Holland and Switzerland: from Personal Observation* (London, 1848), pp. 123–128.

The crops cultivated in France are the usual cereal grains, wheat, rye, barley, and oats; but what may be called the peculiar crops, yielding an immense pecuniary value, are wine, silk, and sugar.

* See Glossary.

9/2 *Successful Wheat Production in France*

1. WHEAT. – In gross amount, the wheat grown in France constitutes an immense crop. With the exception of Russia, from which no accurate statistical returns have been obtained, and in European Russia comparatively little wheat is grown, the bread used being chiefly of rye, it is stated, that more than half of the wheat grown in Europe is produced in France. From the best statistical accounts that can be obtained, the wheat annually produced in the United Kingdom,

England, Scotland, Ireland, is 111,081,320 bushels.
In France it is 198,660,000 „

The amount of seed ordinarily sown to the acre is from two to three bushels. The return of crop for the seed sown is represented as, in the best districts, averaging 6·25 for one; in the least productive 5·40 for one; but the mean average return for the seed in the principal wheat-growing departments is reckoned at 6·07 for one. These accounts must be considered as uncertain. Any person having experience in the case, knows how difficult is even an approach to accuracy. My readers may be curious to know the calculations which have been made in regard to some other countries in this matter.

NORTH EUROPE

Countries	Year	Increase for seed sown.
Sweden and Norway	1838	4·50 for one
Denmark	1827	6 „
Russia, a good harvest	1819	5 „
———, Province of Tambof	1821	4·50 „
———, Provinces north of 50° latitude	1821	3 „
Poland	1826	8 „
England	1830	9 „
Scotland	1830	8 „
Ireland	1825	10 „
Holland	1828	7·50 „
Belgium	1828	11 „
Bavaria	1827	7 to 8 „
Prussia	1817	6 „
Austria	1812	7·05 „
Hungary	1812	4 „

Switzerland, 1825, lands of an inferior quality, 3; of a good quality, 8; of the best quality, 12.

France, inferior lands, 3; best lands, 6.

CENTRAL EUROPE

Countries	Year	Increase for seed sown
Spain	1828	6 for one
Portugal	1786	10 ,,
Tuscany	—	10 ,,
Plains of Lucca	—	15 ,,
Piedmont. Plains of Marengo	—	4 to 5 ,,
Bologna	—	15 ,,

Roman States. Pontine Marshes, 20; ordinary lands, 8.
Kingdom of Naples – best districts, 20; ordinary lands, 8.
Malta – the best lands, 38 to 64; ordinary lands, 22, 25, 30*. . . .

By the official returns in France, where much pains have been taken to render them accurate, it appears that within eighty years, while the population has increased in the proportion of twenty-one to thirty-three millions, the production of wheat has more than doubled; which shows an improvement in the comforts of the people. It is further stated, upon good authority, that the product of an acre of land is ordinarily double what it was three-fourths of a century ago; which shows a most gratifying improvement in the agriculture of the kingdom. It is an instructive fact, that the product of wheat in France has increased sixty-three per cent. since the close of Napoleon's wars – a fact which shows, in a most striking manner, the interruption which war brings into the useful arts of life, and the privations and wretchedness which are sure to follow in its train.

9/3 Successful Beet Production in France

a COLMAN, *The Agriculture . . . of France . . .* [*see* Document **9/2**], pp. 168–174.
b COUNT CHAPTAL, De l'industrie . . . [*see* Document **1/5b**], I, pp. 156–161. (Ed. Tr.)

a BEETS FOR SUGAR.—The history of the introduction of the culture of beets into France for the manufacture of sugar, is well known. The presence of sugar in the beet-root, in an available quantity, was the discovery of a distinguished chemist; . . . The Emperor Napoleon being cut off by the nations at war with him from those supplies of this article, which the people had been accustomed to receive from their colonies, conceived the plan of their supplying this great necessity from within themselves. His object, to a considerable degree, was accomplished. Since his time, the culture and manu-

* *Statistique des Céréales de la France*, par M. A. Moreau de Jonnès. Paris, 1843. Colman's note.)

facture have been immensely extended, and it bids fair to prove one of the greatest boons that was ever bestowed on agriculture.

The beet employed for sugar is called the Silesian beet, with a whitish skin and white flesh, but the most valuable kinds have a green neck and yellowish tint on the top. This is full as valuable for the feeding of animals as any of the others, and is decidedly the beet selected for its sugar properties. It will bear to be well manured, but it is not an extraordinary exhauster of the soil. It returns indeed a large amount of enriching matter to the soil in its abundant leaves.

That, exclusive of their sugar properties, they constitute a valuable green fodder for cows in milk, and fatting cattle, strongly recommends them to cultivation. They have this great advantage over turnips, that they give no disagreeable taste to the milk; and that when in the spring, turnips have become corky, and potatoes sprout abundantly, and seem to lose in a great degree their nutritious properties, the beet preserves its freshness, even into June.

It is not within my province to go into the subject of the manufacture of sugar, farther than as it is connected with agriculture. The greatest profits are realized where an individual unites in himself the character of cultivator and manufacturer. The pulp that remains, after the sugar is expressed, is employed in the fatting of cattle and sheep. An eminent farmer, whose cultivation was of the finest description, and who manufactured a large amount of sugar, informed me, that he estimated his pulp, for the feeding of cattle and sheep, as constituting seven-twentieths of the whole value of the crop. . . .

In 1842, the production of beet-sugar in France reached the enormous amount of 67,717,685 lbs. It had in some years, as it must evidently vary with the seasons, been even more than this; and there is no reason to suppose that it has decreased. In some parts of the country I have seen several factories of recent erection. . . .

A highly distinguished agriculturist in France, perhaps as competent as any man to speak on this subject, has recently given to the public a statement in regard to it, which must attract particular attention. I shall give his statement nearly in his own words. A hectare (about two and a half acres) produces in the Isle of Bourdon about 76,000 kilograms (a kilogram is about two pounds and a fifth of a pound) of cane, which will give 9,200 kilograms of sugar, and which costs in labour 2,500 francs.* A hectare of beet-root produces 40,000 kilograms of roots, which will produce 2,400 kilograms of sugar, and the expense of the culture of which costs 354 francs. The cost of the cane sugar in this case is 27 centimes, and of the beet-sugar 14 centimes only, per kilogram.

* See Glossary.

The production of beet-sugar is not by any means confined to France. Large amounts are produced in Belgium, where I found most extensive manufactories, and in several parts of Germany; but in none of these countries is industry in any form unrestricted; and a man hardly dares to be successful in any enterprise, at least to proclaim his success, lest the government by some impost or taxation should endeavour to avail itself of his success for its own advantages. It is thus that every where industry is checked and hampered, and enterprise scarcely rises from the ground, but is seen fluttering along upon one wing.

b In this recent period when France, cut off from the seas, and at war with all Europe, was reduced to its own resources, its industry showed itself superior to all these problems, and it is to these difficult circumstances that the prodigious industrial developments over the last thirty years may be related.

The cost of sugar had limited its consumption; only the rich could afford it: chemistry never despaired of being able to supply it; first of all, it perfected syrups by eliminating the taste and flavour which made some of them quite disagreeable; it succeeded in extracting from the grape a variety of sugar which . . . could replace sugar cane. There is no doubt that this was a great step forward, but it did not satisfy science, which aimed at providing Europe with sugar which was exactly the same as that shipped from the Indies.

It had been known for a century that the beet-root contained a sugar similar to that found in sugar cane; but we did not know that in Germany they had already attempted to extract it on a large scale and to market it as a commercial proposition; once we knew this all research was directed towards sugar beet; the cultivation of the root improved and became widespread; the methods of extracting and refining its sugar were varied and perfected; numerous factories were set up in all parts; but, the developments were badly directed, and carried out too quickly, and the result was inevitable. In some areas there were abundant supplies of beet but no establishments, in other areas establishments could not obtain supplies of beet; almost everywhere the machines were defective and the workers were unskilled in new techniques; nowhere did the promised results materialise; and this very important branch of industry would have been lost for ever if it had not been for the perseverance of men who knew how difficult it was to overcome prejudice and to develop new production methods . . . ; they knew that time and knowledge alone could improve the processes and overcome all difficulties; and it is to their enlightened perseverance that France owes this branch of agricultural prosperity. Their efforts are all the more praiseworthy since they had to overcome, simultaneously, manufacturing problems and French public opinion, which had become wary of sugar beet following several unsatisfactory results which characterised the initial stages of production.

Today, we have arrived at the point when we can establish two incontestable truths; in the first place there is no difference between sugar from beet and that from cane; secondly, the manufacture of sugar beet can compete with sugar cane even in peace-time Europe.

1. The growing of beet allows the farmer to intercalate a harvest between the clearing of the artificial meadow which occurs in winter and the sowing of wheat in the autumn. This activity improves the land and is valuable in preparing it for cereal plants.

2. The beet marc or residue . . . is excellent cattle food, especially for horned cattle; experience has shown that there is nothing better for fattening cattle or obtaining best-quality milk; beet is always dry, and, unlike winter fodder, does not cause stoppages, and is preferable to the wet grass of the spring and autumn, which is nearly always rotten.

3. The extraction of sugar beet is carried on during the winter months and provides work during this season. . . .

4. The growing of beet, far from harming the wheat harvest, increases it; beet is sown in springtime and gathered in October, the leaves can be cut and left in the fields, the seeds can be sown and planted without much trouble. The weeding of beet crops in the summer removes all the weeds and, in general, the wheat harvest yield is one-eighth higher in the lands where beet is sown.

5. . . . 50,000 hectares* of beet cultivation will produce 30 million kilograms of raw sugar, and 189 million kilograms of marc; thus 50,000 hectares can provide sufficient sugar to satisfy total French consumption and sufficient marc to feed 60,000 cattle, or to feed about a million sheep during the winter and to provide work for about twenty or thirty thousand people. Sugar sales would produce about four or five million francs* for the country areas, and the fattening of cattle would add another 6 million to this. . . . This result is deduced from an extremely rigorous examination of the situation over six consecutive years.

It seems to me that the situation warrants the Government's closest attention; it must be especially careful not to stifle the industry, in its early days, through its fiscal programme; the least fear, in this respect, would retard its progress; but in so far as the Government inspires confidence among the beet cultivators, the industry will establish itself and develop, and in a few years France will have inexhaustible supplies.

* See Glossary.

9/4 Effects of Disease on French Silk Production

F. MARSHALL, *Industry and Trade in France in 1861–1862* (London, 1862), pp. 258–264.

Up to 1854, the greater part of the French-grown silk was produced by the peasants themselves in little lots, but it seems probable that, if the trade should recover from its present critical state, large magnaneries will be successively established, and that the production will become more concentrated. Before 1854 the total cost of raising an ounce of seed (which is the quantity always calculated on in France) came out at 3*l.* 14s., not including labour. The 77 lbs. of cocoons were worth (previously to 1854) about 1s. 6d. per lb., which gives 5*l.* 15s. 6d. So that on this rough calculation the peasant growers got 2*l.* 1s. 6d. per ounce of seed for their trouble, irrespective of their gain on the leaves, which they generally cultivated themselves.

This was the state of the case down to 1853; in that year the total yield of cocoons was 26,000 tons, worth about 4,680,000*l.*, the great mass of which went into the pockets of the small farmers of Provence. The trade had assumed serious importance, for such a home production of high-priced raw material constituted a valuable addition to the national wealth. But just at the moment when French sériciculture seemed to have such brilliant prospects before it, the disease of the worm, which had lurked about the magnaneries of the alluvial plain of the Durance for some twenty years, broke out with violence, and in every direction, at the end of 1853. Under its influence the production of cocoons fell successively from 26,000 tons in that year to 7,500 tons in 1856, while their price, which had already got up since 1852 from 1s. 4d. to 1s. 6d. per lb., rose to 1s. 9d. in 1854, to 2s. in 1855, and to 3s. in 1856. Notwithstanding this rise of price, which the public had to pay, the damage to the worm-growers was very considerable, for they at once lost at least half of the large and easily earned income which the cultivation had hitherto brought them.

The disease, which still continues to ravage the magnaneries of almost all Europe, was at first supposed to consist solely in the decline or exhaustion of the worm, but it has since been proved that there are several distinct maladies, each producing special and different results. Its first effect was to reduce the quantity of silk; the second was to oblige the growers to give up the use of French seed, and to import it from countries still unattacked. But from 1855 the best foreign seed began to fail also, and up to the present date, notwithstanding the remarkable efforts which have been made, it has been impossible to obtain eggs which resist the contagion. Whether brought from Italy, Spain, Turkey, or China, they are all affected in various degrees.

The question for the magnaniers was where to get seed which would withstand the contagion. They have tried all sorts of experiments, but with no real result. M. Levert, prefect of the Ardèche, which is, or rather was, a great silk-growing department, reported in 1858, that the average crop of cocoons in his district was only 19 lbs. per ounce of hatched eggs, instead of the previous average of 77 lbs. The seed brought from Andrinople had succeeded the best, as it failed only 3 times out of 108 trials, while the French seed failed 97 times out of 109. But a few months afterwards the Andrinople seed caught the malady in its turn, and no longer produced a crop.

The disease continues to this day with almost the same virulence, and it is still impossible to express an opinion as to the final issue of the struggle between it and the worm-growers. It would, indeed, be deplorable if so thriving a trade were to be beaten by such a cause. Efforts are being made to turn the difficulty, and the scientific societies and the government are trying to introduce other species of worms, so as to prevent the trade from dying out. . . .

According to M. Dumas, France produced about a tenth of the value of all the silk of the world,* and it is certain that that proportion would have increased. It can only be hoped that the disease may yet be conquered, and that this eminently national industry may be preserved to France. It has thus far been essentially a poor man's trade, notwithstanding the great value it represents. . . .

9/5 Agricultural Improvements in Belgium

ÉMILE DE LAVELEYE, 'The Land System of Belgium', in J. W. PROBYN (ed.), *Systems of Land Tenure* . . . [*see* Document **6/9**], pp. 454-456.

We are often told that agriculture stands in need of capital, that institutions in aid of agricultural credit are wanting: I reply, good husbandry itself creates the capital needed.

In agriculture, the capital most needed is live stock, to furnish the manure by which rich harvests are secured.

The Flemish small farmer picks up grass and manure along the roads. He raises rabbits, and with the money they fetch he buys first a goat, then a pig, next a calf, by which he gets a cow producing calves in her turn. But of course he must find food for them, and this he does by staking all on fodder and roots; and in this way the farmer grows rich, and so does the land. The institution in Flanders in aid of agricultural credit is the manure-merchant, who has founded it in the best of forms; for money lent may be spent in a public-house, but a loan of manure must be laid out on the land.

* In 1853. (Ed.)

The poor labourer goes with his wheelbarrow to the dealer in the village to buy a sack or two of guano, undertaking to pay for it after the harvest. The dealer trusts him, and gives him credit, having a lien on the crop produced by the aid of his manure. In November he gets his money: the produce has been doubled, and the land improved. The small farmer does as the labourer does; each opens an account with the manure-dealer, who is the best of all bankers.

The large farmers of Hainaut and Namur do not buy manure, fancying they would ruin themselves by doing so. The Flemish small farmers invest from fifteen to twenty millions of francs in guano every year, and quite as much in other kinds of manure. Where does large farming make such advances?

§ 8. The chief objection made to *la petite culture* is, however, that it does not admit of the use of machinery, being reduced, as it is alleged, to the employment of the most primitive implements of husbandry, and never raising itself above the first stage of cultivation in that respect. This has been put forward as an incontestable axiom, baffling refutation, and I believe is so regarded in England.

To disprove this, I need point out that to Flanders are due the best forms of the spade, the harrow, the cart, and the plough – Brabant ploughs having for a long time been imported from Flanders into England. It may be said that these are primitive and not very costly implements. I need only reply, Look at what is going on in Flanders at the present day.

The most costly agricultural machine in general use in England is the locomotive steam threshing-machine. Well, this machine is to be found everywhere in Flanders. Some farmers will club together to purchase one, and use it in turn; or else a villager, often the miller, buys one, and goes round threshing for the small farmers, on their own ground, at so much per day, and per hundred kilos of corn. The same thing takes place with the steam-plough as soon as the use of it becomes *remunerative*.

To keep hops in good condition, very expensive machines are required to press it. At Poperinghe, in the centre of the hop country, the *commune* has purchased the machines, and the farmers pay a fixed rate for having their hops pressed – which is at once an advantage to them and a source of revenue to the town.

9/6 Progressive Agriculture along the Rhine

T. C. BANFIELD, *Industry of the Rhine* [*see* Document **7/11**], I, pp. 215-216.

Between Carlsruhe and Baden-Baden the traveller passes one of the richest agricultural tracts of country in Europe. The valley, or rather plain, that lies stretched at the foot of the Black Forest chain, is well watered by the streams that fall from this chain of hills, and its soil is an alluvial deposit of a very fertile nature. Farms are something larger in this part of the Rhine than lower down the river, and the marks of ease and even of wealth are easily distinguished in the houses of the greater landed proprietors, although their peasant-like appearance and manner rather belong to a poorer class. Respecting the management of the peasants' estates, . . . the crops grown here are the same with those of the Palatinate; poppies for oil, rape, Swedish turnips, tobacco, cabbages, and carrots, divide the fallow with the potato. The nature of the soil is here also minutely studied. The village system, however, is in full force in the whole of Baden, and it is rare for a peasant proprietor to live upon his land. On the other hand, there are many large estates in this neighbourhood, belonging to the members of the reigning family, and to some noble families, which are excellently managed by men who have been brought up in some of the agricultural colleges that we have mentioned. One of these colleges is at Darmstadt. A useful polytechnic school has recently been founded at Carlsruhe. The fruit of these excellent establishments has been chiefly to lay a foundation in the minds of a large class of the people that disposes them to industrious activity, and has prepared highly useful agents both for the management of farms and of manufacturing establishments. Few young men would now think of offering themselves for the place of bailiff or farming agent, without possessing testimonials of their fitness from some of these colleges. The scientific explanations which any inquiring traveller can receive at the hands of almost any young men so occupied on large estates, respecting the soil, climate, manners, &c. of the locality, will often perhaps excite surprise, and no less so the calculations by which they judge whether improved processes ought to be adopted, and where additional outlay or increased economy is the more judicious plan to follow.

9/7 Improving Landlords in Silesia

J. G. ELSNER, *Landwirthschaftliche Reise* . . . [*see* Document **1/13**], I/II, pp. 70–74. (Ed. Tr.)

In order to give you an idea of the larger estates in this region, I will take you into one of them, distinguished by the great industry and attention with which it is conducted; it is the Skarsine estate with its attached home farms. Herr von Keltsch may rightly be considered an agriculturalist who has, in the course of many years experience in his own practice, developed a method which ensures that he almost always gets good results. As a thoughtful agriculturalist, managing his widespread estates himself, he has made so many observations and abstracted from them so many rules, that their communication is of the greatest value to anyone seeking enlightenment, and I recognise this with the greatest gratitude.

First, we inspect his livestock. The cattle kept by him here are a genuine Swiss cross but are not as good as those he rears at Dobrischau; for the latter leave nothing to be desired as far as the shape and the posture of the animals is concerned. The strain is distinguished by strength, well-fed appearance and cleanliness. Comparing them with the miserable, starving and misshapen specimens one finds here and there, it hardly seems as though they were the same kind of animal.

Herr v. K's flocks of sheep have reached a fair degree of fineness in their wool, since he has done a great deal towards this in recent years, and they improve every year. The grasses and herbs of the fertile soil of this region have the power of improving not only the quality of the wool, but also its quantity. You may call this a paradox, but it is nevertheless true; for the beneficial effect of the grazing and fodder available here on the quality is confirmed by the high repute in which the fleeces of this region have been held for a long time among the wool buyers; and I do not know why it should be impossible, since grazing and fodder have a substantial influence on the character and the physical condition of animals. The quantity of wool is in the first instance dependent on the quantity of the fodder supplied; but I ask whether there is any other kind of soil, e.g. a humus-rich black soil, on which one could raise sheep with such a weight of wool that the annual clip from 100 sheep reaches 20, or even 21 stone; as is the case at Mr. von Lübbers at Michelwitz. I have had this confirmed not by him, but by several of his neighbours and by other trustworthy persons. It is true that his animals are of exceptional size, but they are no larger than I have seen among other flocks, where nevertheless the clip never exceeded 16–18 stone at the most. I have also heard it generally confirmed that sheep brought from elsewhere and from a different soil into this region immediately increase the quantity of their annual wool clip. . . .

I now turn to the arable system of cultivation of this region. The three-field system is still in the main observed here, though in view of the variety of the crops raised, this should more properly be called a variable system. If taken as a part of a three-field system, the so-called fallow has one part clover and one part peas and beans. Potatoes are frequently introduced into the summer field as a fourth crop; but where this is not done, they are planted in the fallow and followed by the winter, and sometimes even the summer crop. After the pure fallow comes wheat, but also in many parts some clover, which is then ploughed in time and broken up before sowing; the rest is sown with rye. After the wheat follows flax, where there has been clover, and barley with clover where there was pure fallow. It is always so arranged that flax and Clover are alternatives, i.e. where there was flax the last time, clover is sown, and vice versa; where there have been peas and beans, there follow oats, to become fallow the next year; it is made fallow about St. John's Day. Thus the sequence goes on, and in this way flax and clover return to the same field every twelve years. But if we look upon this as a variable system, we can distinguish a series of twelve years, and the following crop sequence would emerge: (1) fallow, (2) wheat (3) flax, (4) peas or beans, (5) rye, (6) barley or oats, (7) fallow or clover, (8) wheat, (9) barley, (10) clover, (11) rye, (12) oats.

Where potatoes are not grown in one of the two fallow periods, they are introduced in No. 6; at No. 7 the field is manured again.

9/8 Contrasts in Italian Agriculture at mid-century

M. SANTORO, *L'Italia nei suoi progressi economici dal 1860 al 1910* (Rome, 1911), pp. 117–118, 210–211. (Ed. Tr.)

Roman Agriculture

Before concerning ourselves in particular with the various treatises on agriculture in the Roman province before 1860, we feel it is desirable to relate these general considerations, drawn from a Memoria* published several years ago. . . .

'The immoral concentration of all wealth into the hands of a small number of parasites, the violence done to natural law in favour of the privileged classes, leaves agriculture with neither freedom nor protection, and as a result it has been reduced, especially in the vicinity of the capital, to the most deplorable condition. In the immense stretch of country, in the middle of which Rome rises like an oasis in a desert, the desolation is quite striking. The owners of the land, the leading Romans or religious orders, who do not possess any agricultural knowledge, who are disinclined to undertake economic activity, and have little financial motive to increase their returns, which are sufficient to support them in a semi-barbaric existence, lease the land to the bourgeoisie; and the latter convert the land to pasture which provides them with an assured profit, unaffected by agricultural fluctuations.

If this land were divided as in France, it would provide the inhabitants of Rome with all their necessities at low prices and endow society with a class

* Charles de la Verenne, *L'Italie centrale.* (Neuilly, 1859). (Ed.)

of robust and independent citizens and provide commerce and finance with immeasurable resources.

But none of this is seen by the theocratic Government which offers no encouragement, no hope of success, no help to attempts at improvement and the introduction of new crops, no laws to improve the condition of the agricultural workers, no protection to worker associations, which . . . would ensure the prosperity of the region and increase the population.

The Romans, who are mostly involved in agriculture as a result of their geographical position, do not possess an Agricultural Society. . . . What is the use of a clear sky, the fertility of the soil and our aptitudes if we cannot act? It seems that the Government does everything possible to prevent any increase in production from the land by creating so many obstacles to production, distribution and exchange.'

Lombard Agriculture

The soil of these areas, which is almost everywhere extremely fertile (since natural fecundity is enhanced by careful and judicious cultivation), has always been considered among the richest and most productive areas of all Italy, if not the very richest.

There is no better way to begin to deal with Lombard agriculture than by relating the vivid and accurate description of the area compiled by Carlo Catteono in this *Introduzione alle notizie naturali e civili su la Lombardia*

We can shew the foreigner our plain which is completely tilled and renewed by our own hands; thus the botanist complains about this agriculture which transforms each vestige of primitive vegetation. We have taken water from the deep river-beds and from the marshy valleys and distributed it over the arid land. Half of our plain – more than 4,000 square kilometres – is provided with irrigation; and a volume of water which is estimated at more than 30,000,000 cubic metres each day is directed by artificial channels. As a result of our own skill, a part of the plain becomes green in winter when everything around is touched by snow and cold. The damper earth has been converted to rice fields; on the same latitude as the Vendée, Switzerland and the Tauern mountains, we have established a type of Indian cultivation.

9/9 The Land Bank in France

A. COURTOIS, *Histoire de la Banque de France* (Paris, 1875), pp. 202-207. (Ed. Tr.)

HISTORY OF THE BANK OF FRANCE – THE LAND BANK

Let us sum up now the state and year by year activities of the Crédit Foncier de France from its origin up to 1873.

* Compiled in 1844. (Ed.)

The communal loans contracted between 1860 and 1873 amount to 1,416 and in capital to 755,886,500 francs.* . . .

Thirty-one short-term loans are now completely settled and repaid.

Of the long-term loans, amounting to 1,154,257,086 francs, 1,404 between 1852 and 1858 amounting to 75,961,130 francs were effected in specie loans and repayments; the others are repayable at the wish of the borrower in specie or bonds.

By adding to the long-term mortgage loans those for drainage works (1,431,322 francs) and those specially for Algeria (6,891,700 francs) the overall total amounts to 1,162,580,108 francs which we shall consider under the following different headings:

THE AMOUNT OF EACH LOAN

	Number	*Sum*
Loans below 10,000 fr.	7,483	39,669,278
from 10,000 to 50,000	8,161	215,708,245
from 50,000 to 100,000	2,672	204,337,634
from 100,000 to 500,000	2,418	492,654,951
from 500,000 to 1,000,000	121	85,530,000
more than 1,000,000	27	124,680,000
TOTALS	20,882	1,162,580,108

THE DURATION OF EACH LOAN

	Number	*Sum*
Loans of 10–19 years	601	13,972,189
,, ,, 20 years	664	19,401,258
,, ,, 21–30 years	1,258	37,537,081
,, ,, 31–40 years	258	10,421,493
,, ,, 41–49 years	1,746	148,413,949
,, ,, 50 years	14,473	846,862,138
,, ,, 60 years	1,882	85,972,000
TOTALS	20,882	1,162,580,108

* See Glossary.

THE RATE OF INTEREST

	Number	Sum
At the rate of 3·70%	290	22,445,300
" " " " 4·25%	212	11,070,300
" " " " 4·51% } " " " " 5·00% }	20,380	1,129,064,508
TOTALS	20,882	1,162,580,108

THE KIND OF PROPERTY

	Number	Sum
Urban Properties	15,875	930,862,792
Rural Properties	4,666	211,610,116
Mixed Properties	341	20,107,200
TOTALS	20,882	1,162,580,108

THE SITUATION OF THE PROPERTY

1. Seine, 12,153 loans amounting to	844,677,115
2. Seine-et-Oise (25 millions) Bouches-du-Rhône (23) Seine-Inférieure (15), Seine-et-Marne (14), Gironde (12), Alpes-Maritimes (10), Nièvre (9), seven Departments* in all, 3,210 loans amounting to	107,125,000
3. Cher (8 millions), Rhône and Dordogne (7-8 millions each); Calvados, Algérie, Allier (6-7 millions each); Indre, Oise, Aisne, Hérault and Eure (from 5 to 6 millions each); finally, Marne, Gard, Loiret, Saône-et-Loire, Orne, Haute-Vienne, Var, Nord and Loir-et-Cher (from 4-5 millions each); 19 departments in all and Algeria, altogether a total of 2,910 amounting to	112,449,835
4. Finally the rest of France (60 Departments plus Alsace-Lorraine) altogether a total of 2,609 amounting to	98,328,158
TOTAL: 20,882 loans amounting to	1,162,580,108

* See Glossary.

If we concern ourselves with the average loan, we arrive at the following results; for the Seine, 69,503 francs, for the seven successive Departments* it is 33,372 francs (maximum, Gironde 63,243 francs; minimum, Seine-et-Oise 12,161). For the twenty provincial divisions of the third paragraph we find an average of 38,462 francs per loan (maximum, Orne 88,755 francs; minimum, Algeria, 10,836 francs); and finally for the remaining sixty Departments, including Alsace-Lorraine the average loan is 57,726 francs (maximum, Aube, 130,827 francs; minimum, Haute Savoie, 6,734 francs).

It can be seen that the loans of the Crédit Foncier are unevenly distributed; to ascertain whether the blame attaches to the institution or to defaulting borrowers, one would need to know the Departmental distribution of the mortgage debt of France. It is thought that it must be approximately 10–12 milliard francs; its division by Department has never been published and hardly can be, since by their very nature many of the mortgage contracts escape from the control of administrative authority.

In spite of the absence of this piece of useful information, we can make a general judgment on the institution. The information we possess, and which is presented in abundance in the reports of the Crédit Foncier, allow us to state, regretfully, that the towns, and in the towns, buildings projects have been given marked preference; thus the Seine accounts for more than two-thirds of the total debt, and has more than thirty times as much debt as the next most favoured area. The division into urban and rural property, mentioned above, is even more eloquent; the former accounts for more than four-fifths of the general total, and the latter for less than one-fifth.

It can be seen that the Crédit Foncier banks, originally created to help in the liquidation of mortgage debt, have, as a result of their amalgamation, quickly become an important instrument for the general municipal building projects of the Second Empire.

We feel it is necessary to remind the reader of the judgment made about ten years ago by a publicist. . . .

> The system of landed credit has been modelled upon the already existing system of commercial credit, which is under the deplorable monopoly of the Bank of France. . . . The institutions of Nevers and Marseilles which had developed under the Empire . . . and which were more in touch with the proprietors who sought their help, better informed on the property they accepted as guarantee, and more personally involved with their clients and which, correspondingly, had previously given better service than the Paris Bank, have had to disappear. Consequently it was easy to foresee the small effect the new legislation would have on our agriculture, the trifling amount of help which small proprietors may expect to obtain from it, however much they need assistance, and however much land they possess.

* See Glossary.

9/10 Agricultural Co-operative Banks in Germany

C. R. FAY, *Co-operation at Home and Abroad: A Description and Analysis* (5th ed., 2 vols., London, 1948), I, pp. 49-50.

The Raiffeisen banks are thickest in the South-west of Germany, the home of the small peasant proprietors. Indeed, the change wrought in many of these villages is nothing short of a revolution. The experience of the parent village bank may serve in illustration:

> About an hour's walk from Neuwied on the Rhine is situated on a plateau bordering the Westerwald the little village of Anhausen. The district is not very fertile and the inhabitants are mostly small peasant proprietors, some with only sufficient land to graze a single ox or cow. An owner of ten acres is a rich man. Before the year 1862 the village presented a sorry aspect; rickety buildings, untidy yards, in rainy weather running with filth, never a sight of a decently piled manure heap; the inhabitants themselves ragged and immoral; drunkenness and quarrelling universal. Houses and oxen belonged with a few exceptions to Jewish dealers. Agricultural implements were scanty and dilapidated; and badly worked fields brought in poor returns. The villagers had lost confidence and hope, they were the serfs of dealers and usurers. Today, Anhausen is a clean and friendly-looking village, the buildings well kept, the farmyards clean even on work days; there are orderly manure heaps on every farm. The inhabitants are well if simply clothed, and their manners are reputable. They own the cattle in their stalls. They are out of debt to dealers and usurers. Modern implements are used by nearly every farmer, the value of the farms has risen and the fields carefully and thoroughly cultivated, yield large crops.* And this change, which is something more than statistics can express, is the work of a simple Raiffeisen bank.

9/11 Agricultural Education on the Continent

J. KAY, *The Social Condition and Education of the People in England and Europe; showing the Results of the Primary Schools and the Division of Landed Property in Foreign Countries* (2 vols., London, 1850), I, pp. 147-151.

The governments of Western Europe are doing a great deal, to enable the peasant proprietors to acquire a knowledge of the best systems of agriculture and management of cattle.

The cantonal governments of Switzerland have been earnestly engaged for several years in establishing, in various parts of the country, great schools, where the children of the farmers may be educated, at a very trifling expense, in the science of agriculture. I went over several, in company with M. de Fellenberg and M. Vehrli. I have described them more fully in the chapter on Swiss education.

To each of these institutions are attached, a large farm, barns, cowsheds, farm-yards, orchards, a plentiful supply of the best farm implements, a

* Quoted in, and translated from A. Wuttig, *F. W. Raiffeisen* (Neuwied, 1907[?]), p. 71. (Ed.)

laboratory, and class-rooms. The greatest portion of the expense of maintaining them is defrayed by the cantonal governments. Many of the sons of the peasant farmers enter these institutions after leaving the primary schools. They remain in them from one to three years. They learn there agricultural chemistry and practical farming. They are taught how to analyse earths; how to mix and manure them, so as to make them as fertile as possible; how to prepare and collect manures; how to drain land; how to tend, and fatten cattle; how to manage the dairy; how to breed cattle, so as best to improve the stock; how to vary the succession of crops, so as to make the most of particular soils; how to prune fruit-trees; and, in fact, the whole science of farming. Is it surprising that farmers educated in such a manner should be much more skilful, and should make much more out of their lands, than the farmers of our country? Similar colleges are being established throughout Germany and France.

But this is not all, that is being done in foreign countries, in order to secure a scientific system of farming among the peasant proprietors.

All the teachers of the village schools, as I shall hereafter show, are prepared for their duties in the villages, by a long and very careful preparation in the Normal colleges.

Among other things which they learn, in many of these colleges, are, botany, the art of pruning, and the art of gardening; and, in some of them, as in the Bernese Normal College, they are taught and practised in farming.

This is done for two purposes; first, in order to strengthen their sympathies for the peasants, among whom they have in after-life to labour, by accustoming them to all the habits of the peasants; and, secondly, in order to enable them to give the children in the village schools a rudimentary knowledge of pruning, gardening, and farming, so as to insure their being taught, at least, the first principles of these arts, and so as to stimulate their interest in them, and to teach them that there is a right and a wrong way of conducting them. Boys who have received these ideas in early life will not afterwards scoff at instruction, but will always be ready, not only to receive, but to seek out, advice and assistance.

Science is welcomed among the small farmers of foreign countries. Each is so anxious to emulate and surpass his neighbours, that any new invention, which benefits one, is eagerly sought out and adopted by the others.

The system of agriculture, therefore, good as it is among these intelligent peasant proprietors, is not at a stand still, but is making rapid progress. The governments, poor as they are, have ample funds to devote to the best possible education of all classes.

No one who has travelled through the Rhine Provinces of Germany, through Prussia, Saxony, Holland, the Protestant cantons of Switzerland,

and some of the Catholic cantons, as Soleure, Zug, and the upper part of the valley of the Rhone, can possibly deny the excellence, or the progressive improvement of the cultivation of the soil.

In all these countries the same evidences of progress and improvement may be seen among the peasants; viz., a laboriously careful tillage of the fields, and cultivation of the gardens; large, good, and substantial houses for the peasantry; orderly and clean villages; and great industry. I was assured, in the Rhine Provinces and in Saxony, that the face of the country had quite changed, since the laws tending to prevent the sale and division of the landed property had been altered; and that the system of farming, the character of the houses, and the condition of the peasants, had progressively improved and were still improving. Certainly, the appearance of the villages, houses, farms, and peasantry was singularly satisfactory. The cultivation of the land was as beautiful and perfect as I have ever seen. The careful manner in which the sods were broken up upon the ploughed fields, and the way, in which all the weeds, stones, and rubbish were removed from the ground, in which every disposable bit of ground was brought under cultivation, and in which the land was drained of all superabundant moisture and manured, filled me with surprise, at what Professor Rau most truly calls, the 'superhuman industry,' 'das ubermenschliche fleis', of the peasants.

9/12 Agricultural Education in Switzerland

COLMAN, *The Agriculture . . . of France . . .* [*see* Document **9/2**], pp. 86–87, 90–91, 100–105.

The institution at Grignon is designed to supply instruction both in the science and practice of agriculture, and the constitution and arrangement of the school seem admirably adapted to this end. . . . In England and in France a class exists of which at present, in the free portion of the United States, we know nothing; and it may be some time before they are required. These are the persons who manage the estates of large proprietors; who in England are called bailiffs or stewards; in France, agricultural engineers. Grignon may be said to be particularly designed to educate this useful class. At the same time, there are among the pupils several who seek this education for the management of their own estates; and these agricultural engineers are themselves, without doubt, hoping presently to become proprietors. In the south of France, land is held generally under what is called the *mettayer* system, or what is known in the United States as taking land upon shares. After certain deductions, the half of the produce is returned to the proprietor as the rent of the land. In either case such education must be highly valuable. In the case of a tenant, that he may be able to obtain the best return from the land, and, in the case of the proprietor, that he may know what to require, and how properly to direct the management of his estate.

The term of residence at Grignon is fixed at two years; but the pupil remains three months after his studies are completed, in order to digest and draw up the entire management of an estate, and describe its details in every department.

There are several distinct professorships. The Professor of Practical Agriculture gives two courses; the one written, the other oral; and, like the lecture of a clinical professor at the bed-side, it is given in the fields. This professor understands not only how a thing should be done, but how to do it; and he can put his hand to every form of agricultural labour, such as ploughing, harrowing, sowing, managing the teams, feeding the animals, handling every instrument of agriculture, buying, selling, &c. In the words of his commission, his object is at the same time to form the eye and the hand; to teach his pupil how to learn; to command, to direct, and to execute. To this end it was necessary to form a complete agricultural organization for practice, independent of the exercises attached to the departments of the other professors.

The farm is composed of

Arable land, about	670	acres
Land in wood and plantations	365	,,
Irrigated meadows	35	,,
Gardens, including vegetable, botanical, fruit garden, orchards, mulberry plantations, osiers, and nurseries	28	,,
Ponds and water-courses	15	,,
Road and lands in pasture	50	,,
Occupied by buildings	6	,,

The animals on the farm include

Animals of draught or labour of different kinds	18
Oxen for fatting	20
Cows of different ages and races, and different crosses	100
Sheep, embracing the different kinds	1100
Swine establishment	100

There are likewise on the establishment workshops or manufactories. . . .
For the making of agricultural instruments;
A threshing-house and machine for grain;

A dairy room for the manufacture of different kinds of cheese and of butter;

A magnanerie, or establishment for silk-worms;

A stercorary for the manufacture of compost manures.

To all these various departments the attention of the students is closely called, and they are required to take some part in the labours connected with them.

Besides the farm belonging to the establishment, there is a field of one hundred acres devoted exclusively to the pupils, and principally to the culture of plants not grown on the farm.

The study of the different kinds of soil, and of manures, with all their applications, and the improvements aimed at, take in a wide field. Under the head of soils there are the argillaceous, the calcareous, the siliceous, turf-lands, heath-lands, volcanic soils, the various subsoils, loam, and humus. . . .

All these studies are pursued in the first year of the course; and the time is so arranged as to afford the diligent pupil an opportunity of meeting his duties, though the period is obviously too limited for the course prescribed.

The second year enjoins the continuance and enlargement of these important studies; the higher branches of mathematics and natural philosophy; an extended knowledge of chemistry; and a thorough acquaintance with mechanics, when the scholars with their professor visit some of the principal machine-shops and factories in Paris, or its environs, in order to become practically acquainted with them.

The students are further instructed in the construction of farm-buildings of every description; in irrigation, in all its forms; in the drainage of lands; in the construction of roads; in every thing relating to farm implements; and in the construction of mills and presses.

As I have said, organic chemistry is largely pursued with the various manufactures to which it is applicable; and animal physiology and comparative anatomy are very fully taught.

These studies are followed by a course of what is called agricultural technology. This embraces the manufacture, if so it may be called, of lime, of cement, of bricks; the preparations of plaster; the making of coal by various processes; the making of starch; the making and purification of vegetable oils; the making of wines, of vinegar, of beer, of alcohol, of sugar from the beet-root, including all the improvements which have been introduced into this branch of manufacture; and the pupils, under the direction of the professor, are taken to see the various manufactories of these articles, so far as they are accessible in the vicinity. . . .

Next to this comes the culture of vines, and the establishment and care of a vineyard – a subject of great importance in France.

I have already spoken of the veterinary course of instruction. This embraces the whole subject of the breeding and rearing of animals; their training, shoeing, and harnessing, and entire management.

Under the head of farm-accounts, the establishment itself at Grignon is made an example; the accounts of which are kept most accurately by some of the students, and open to the inspection of all.

A journal of every thing which is done upon the farm is made up every night; and these accounts are fairly transferred into a large-book.

To this is added, a particular account of the labours performed, and the occupation of each workman on the farm.

Next, a cash-book, embracing payment and sales, which are adjusted every fortnight.

Next, an account with the house; charging every article supplied or consumed.

Next, a specific account of each principal department of the farm; such as the dairy, with all its expenses and returns; the pork-establishment; the granary, &c.; which are all balanced every month, so that the exact condition of the department may be known.

As the students are advanced, more general and enlarged views of the various subjects of inquiry are given; such as,

The taking of a farm, and the cultivation or management to be adopted.

The influence of climate and soil.

The crops to be grown; and the rotation of crops.

Agricultural improvements generally.

The devoting of land to pasturage; to dairy husbandry; to the raising of animals; to the fatting of cattle; to the growth of wool; to the production of grain; to the raising of plants for different manufacturing purposes; or to such a mixed husbandry as may be suggested by the particular locality.

The use of capital in agriculture; the mode of letting farms; cash rents; rents in kind; rents in service; laws regulating the rights and obligations of real estate; the conveyance of real estate; with the various forms of culture in large or in small possessions, or on farms of a medium size.

I have extended, perhaps beyond the patience of my reader, the account of the Agricultural School at Grignon, and yet have given an imperfect and abridged statement of the subject matters of instruction and study at this institution. The institution at Grignon may be considered as a model establishment; and a thorough education in the various branches referred to, must be, to any young man, an important and invaluable acquisition.

9/13 Government Measures for Agricultural Improvement in France

COLMAN, *The Agriculture . . . of France . . .* [*see* Document **9/2**], pp. 41–45.

The measures of the government for the advancement of agriculture have much to recommend them, if they are carried out in an intelligent and faithful manner.

1. DEPARTMENT OF AGRICULTURE.—In the first place, there is a department of agriculture, the secretary or minister of which, being one of the first men in the kingdom, is expected to look after this great interest; to obtain statistical returns of agricultural produce from all parts of the kingdom; to learn what is the condition of the art; what improvements have been made; what improvements are most required; and what is the condition of the agricultural population. . . .

4. IMPORTATION OF IMPROVED STOCK.—The government have imported from other countries some of the most valuable animals, such as bulls and stud-horses; and stationed them in different parts of the country, that the farmers may avail themselves of the advantages which they offer for the improvement of their stock. On account of the large demands made by government for horses for the cavalry, this becomes a matter of great importance. Whether the keeping of bulls would not be better left to private enterprise, is a question much debated. That which belongs to the public is seldom cared for like that which belongs to an individual; but the government have met this objection by disposing of their improved animals occasionally at public sales.

5. AGRICULTURAL AND VETERINARY SCHOOLS.—France has likewise several agricultural schools, established in different parts of the kingdom, of which I shall presently give an account, designed to furnish a complete scientific and practical education in agriculture. In addition to this they have veterinary schools, where comparative anatomy is thoroughly studied, and the diseases of all the domestic animals most carefully treated. These likewise may be supposed to grow in a great measure out of their army, where the medical treatment of their horses is obviously of great importance.

6. AGRICULTURAL SOCIETIES AND SHOW.—In various parts of the country agricultural societies are established, and assisted by the government, for the purpose of diffusing information; and these will, in all probability, extend themselves. A society in Paris, composed of some of the first men in the kingdom, meets regularly twice a month for the discussion of agricultural subjects, for the report of improvements, and, at the end of the season, for the bestowal of premiums. An agricultural show was undertaken the last year at Poissy, the Smithfield of France, where some excellent native, and some very good improved stock, though not to a large amount, was ex-

hibited; and here I saw sheep of the very best, and most profitable kind, especially for such a country as the United States, where good mutton, and particularly fine wool, are in demand. These were pure Merinos of a very large size, well-proportioned and fat, and with fleeces of an excellent quality. I have never seen animals of the kind combining more valuable properties. It is intended that these shows, of which this was a first attempt, should be continued annually.

7. An Agricultural Congress.—Previous to this show, an Agricultural Congress, composed of more than 300 gentlemen interested in agriculture, and sent as deputies from different parts of the country, had been sitting in Paris for a fortnight to discuss practical questions in agriculture, and likewise political questions bearing upon it; which was done with great ability. At Poissy, the Minister of Agriculture distributed premiums of large amount; and every circumstance indicated an active, an increased, and increasing attention to this great subject.

8. Conservatory of Arts and Trades.—Paris is, in the next place, distinguished by its direct means of scientific instruction. It has what is called a Conservatory of Arts and Trades. This is, properly speaking, a school for the industrial and mechanical classes. Here is a complete collection of models or of examples of agricultural buildings and implements—to say nothing of other arts – not only of those in use in France, but specimens of the best of every description which are used in foreign countries. Here, under accomplished professors, courses of agricultural lectures, or rather of chemistry and mechanics as applied to agriculture, are regularly given, to which access is entirely gratuitous, the professors being supported by the government; so that here is presented to inquisitive minds the best means of learning the application of science to agriculture.

9. Society for the Improvement of Wool.—Besides the Society of Agriculture, which meets in Paris twice every month, and is the centre of the correspondence of all the agricultural societies of the country, there is likewise a Society for the Improvement of Wool, who twice a year bestow valuable premiums upon persons who have made the greatest advances in the improvement of the fleeces of their flocks. This society has its public exhibitions of wool, and has undoubtedly accomplished much good.

Chapter 10 The Continental System and British Competition

Introduction

Much of European and world economic history, until 1870, can be written in terms of British impact and influence. This influence weakened with the growth of the European and American economies, but in the period under review, it was discernible at many points.

The free-trade policy inaugurated at the end of the *ancien régime* by the Eden-Reyneval Treaty of 1786 (**3/12, 3/13**) was reversed during the revolutionary period by the decree of 10 Brumaire, Year V. A protectionist policy was continued under Napoleon who, through the Berlin and Milan decrees of 1806/7 (**10/1**), attempted to prevent Britain drawing wheat and certain raw materials from the Continent, and simultaneously to deprive her of an important export market. The effects of the decree varied enormously. As far as Britain was concerned, markets were sought elsewhere, and some goods were still smuggled into Europe. The long-term effects were negligible since the French found it impossible to administer the system and to achieve the full co-operation of other Europeaan powers. In Europe itself, the consequences were mixed. From Chaptal it is clear that sugar beet production was stimulated by the scarcity resulting from the English counter-blockade (**9/3**) but in Eisenach the results were quite different. Here, during the blockade, entrepreneurs in the textile trade had been induced to concentrate on cotton rather than on woollen goods; and with the collapse of the system, and the renewal of British competition, the area was plunged into distress (**10/2**).

Once the war was over, rivalry continued, but this time through the forces of competition. It would seem that when the 1824 Select Committee on Artisans and Machinery was taking its evidence British cotton machines were 40% cheaper than their French equivalents whilst steam engines enjoyed a 30% advantage (**10/5**). Confirmation of this assertion was received by the same Committee from an English cotton operative who had worked in France, where he had been employed at Guebwiller (**10/6**). According to the same workman, the French were at least ten, and in some instances twenty years behind Britain in the manufacture of machinery (**10/6**).

By the mid-thirties Baines could still assert that the French cotton industry lagged behind that of Britain. He attributed this retardation to innumerable factors including shortage of capital, the small-scale French business unit, protection, political considerations and national character, without attempting to place these in any order of importance. Whatever the reasons for French backwardness, Baines found plenty of evidence to indicate that French manufacturers were afraid of, and unable to withstand, British competition (**10/7**, see also **12/4**).

This was not the position which had been assumed two years previously by Kirkman Finlay in his evidence before the Select Committee on Manufactures. He was impressed by the growing technological development on the Continent since the Vienna Treaty in 1815, and the labour advantages enjoyed in this respect by France, Switzerland and Flanders (**10/8**). The general body of available evidence (**11/11 a** and **b**, **11/12**, **11/13**, **11/14**, **12/3**) would tend to confirm Finlay's assertion. It was the development of this competition which led to the suggestion before the Select Committee on the Exportation of Tools and Machinery that the exportation of machines from Britain should be permitted to compete with this nascent engineering industry whilst it was still in its infancy. Such action, it was felt, would nip European progress in the bud (**10/9**).

The eighteenth century movement of labour from England to Europe (**2/13**, **2/17**, **2/18**) continued into the nineteenth century (**13/13a** and **b**, **10/6**), such movement holding out special attractions for those individuals such as Evans Evans who had the technical competence which the Europeans required and who could be tempted by financial inducements (**10/3**), and for Englishmen whose technical skill allowed them to enter into partnerships, based on their expertise and capital provided by local businessmen (**10/4**). By such means Britain helped to spread the process of industrialization, and was to see the fruit of her action later in the century.

10/1 The Decree of Berlin, 1806

Printed in H. BUTTERFIELD, *Select Documents of European History; III, 1715–1920* (London, 1930), pp. 87–89.

CONSIDERING

1. That England makes no recognition of the law of nations which is universally followed by all civilized peoples;

2. That she counts every individual belonging to an enemy state as himself an enemy, and consequently makes prisoners of war not only the crews of vessels armed for war, but also the crews of trading-ships and merchant-vessels, and even the commercial agents and traders who travel for business purposes;

3. That she extends to the ships and merchandise of traders and to the

property of individuals the right of conquest which can only apply to the property of the enemy state;

4. That she extends to unfortified towns and ports of trade, to harbours and the mouths of rivers, the right of blockade which, according to season and the usage of all civilized peoples, is only applicable to fortified places;

That she declares those places to be in a state of blockade before which she has not even a single warship, although a place is not in a state of blockade unless it is so invested that no attempt may be made to approach it without the incurring of imminent danger;

That she even declares to be in a state of blockade places which all her combined forces would be incapable of blockading, entire coasts and a whole empire;

5. That this monstrous abuse of the right of blockade has no other object but to impede communications between peoples and raise the commerce and industry of England upon the ruins of the industry and commerce of the continent;

6. That such being the evident aim of England, whoever trades in English merchandise upon the continent is by this fact furthering her designs and making himself her accomplice;

7. That this conduct of England – conduct in all ways worthy of the earliest ages of barbarism – has procured the advantage of this power to the detriment of all the others;

8. That it is a natural right to oppose an enemy with the arms which he himself makes use of, and to combat in the manner in which he combats when he repudiates all those ideas of justice and those liberal sentiments which are the effect of civilization upon human society:

We have resolved to apply to England the methods which she has sanctioned in her maritime code.

The dispositions of the present decree shall always be considered as a fundamental principle of the empire, until England has recognized that the laws of war are one and the same on land and sea; that hostilities cannot be extended either to private property of any kind whatever, or to the persons of individuals who are unconnected with the profession of arms; and that the right of blockade must be restricted to fortified places genuinely invested by forces of adequate strength;

We have in consequence decreed and do decree the following:

Art. 1. The British Isles are declared to be in a state of blockade.

2. All commerce or correspondence with the British Isles is forbidden. In consequence, letters or packets addressed either to England or to an Englishman, or written in the English language, will not be allowed to pass through the post and will be seized.

3. All individuals, subjects of England, of whatever state or condition they may be, who are in the countries occupied by our troops or by those of our allies, shall be made prisoners of war.

4. Any commercial establishment, any merchandise, any property of any kind whatever belonging to an English subject, shall be declared lawful prize.

5. Trading in English merchandise is forbidden; and all merchandise belonging to England or coming from its factories or its colonies is declared to be lawful prize. . . .

7. No ship coming directly from England or the English colonies, or having been there since the publication of the present decree, will be received in any port. . . .

10/2 Effects of the Continental System and of post-war British Competition on the German Textile Industry

J. RUSSELL, *A Tour in Germany and some of the Southern Provinces of the Austrian Empire in the years 1820, 1821, 1822* (2 vols., Edinburgh, 1825), I, pp. 323-324; II, pp. 155-160. (G.P.J.)

Eisenach is the most wealthy and populous town in the duchy of Weimar . . . With a population of not exceeding ten thousand inhabitants, it was reckoned, till within these few years, among the most flourishing of the manufacturing towns so frequent between Leipzig and Frankfort. Seduced by the protection which the Continental System seemed to promise, its capitalists forsook the manufacture of wool for that of cotton. They had just advanced far enough to entertain sanguine hopes of ultimately succeeding, when the unexpected changes in political relations again opened the German markets to England, and their cotton manufactures were blighted. One of the most ingenious and persevering among their capitalists told me that, during the former period, he had employed nearly four hundred persons in spinning cotton, – a large scale for an establishment in a small Saxon town. He attempted in vain to struggle on after the peace, found it necessary to follow the example of others, dismiss the greater part of his workmen, return with the rest to wool, adhere to the commercial congress of Darmstadt, and cry loudly for prohibitory duties against England. . . .

Hirschberg, the principal town of this part of Silesia . . . does not contain more than 7,000 inhabitants, and by no means promises to become more flourishing. It owed its eminence to the gauze and linen manufactures, of which it was the centre; but both these manufactures, which have been the source of all the prosperity of Lower Silesia, and on which the greater part of its population still depends, have miserably decayed during the last thirty years. . . . The Silesian linen found its way into all parts of Europe and South America, from Archangel to Peru. The quantities sent into Hungary and Poland were considerable; Russia was a still more profitable outlet; but by far the most important branch of the trade was the exportation to Spain, for the purpose of supplying the South American markets. Prussia, humbled at the feet of the conqueror, was compelled to receive his laws, and the prohibition against the importation of British wares, put an end to her own lucrative commerce with the new world. On the return of peace, Silesia endeavoured, but in vain, to regain the ground which it had lost; it found Britain firmly established as a successful rival in the markets of the new world; in Russia and Poland it was opposed by Bohemia; and the export, I was assured, is not one-third of what it amounted to before this calamitous period. . . . The linen exported from the department of Reichenbach in 1817 had fallen half a million of dollars below that of the preceding year. A great number of manufacturing houses have abandoned the trade; and in the neighbouring county of Glatz, it had sunk so low, that, in 1818, it was found necessary to provide other employment for a great proportion of the spinners and weavers. . . .

The Silesian weaver labours under the disadvantage of being, in some measure, a speculator. Our cotton-weavers receive from the manufacturer the materials of their labour; the price to be paid for any given portion of their work is fixed; however small the pittance may be, it is a certainty, and a gain; and, if the workman strain his weekly toil to the uttermost, he knows that he is adding to his weekly emoluments. But the Silesian manufacturers have always proceeded on a different footing; the artisan himself purchases the yarn, weaves the web, and brings it to market as a merchant. Thus he is never certain of gaining a farthing, for he is exposed to all the vicissitudes of the market. After he has spent days and nights at his loom, scarcely allowing himself time to snatch his miserable meal, he knows not but he may be forced to sell his cloth at a price which will not even cover the expence of the materials wrought up in it. Yet he must sell; the poor man has no capital but his hands; he cannot reserve his work for a more favourable opportunity; he must submit to starvation to procure the means of purchasing new materials. Thirty years ago, when the decay of the Silesian manufactures was only in its commencement, you might see weavers returning from the town to their distant villages, with tears in their eyes, and not a sixpence for the expectant family at home. The evil is now much more general.

10/3 A Welsh Engineer in Germany, 1808

Letter by the Welsh engineer, EVAN EVANS, to Councillor Sahr; Chemnitz, 5 May 1808. Printed in ALFRED SCHRÖTER and WALTER BECKER, *Die deutsche Maschinenbauindustrie in der industriellen Revolution* (Berlin, 1962), pp. 120–123.*

... When Mess. Bernhards applyed to Government for a Support or an Advance of Money, likewise a Priviledge, to build fine English Spinning Machines, called Mules, gave themselves also as Men capable of directing the Building of the Same. Every thing (as far as I have heard) was granted, they begun and set to work, for two or three years, or at least, so long untill they were convinced they could never bring any thing to bear.

At last they were forced to enquire about some Englishmen, or else they were entirely lost, as they themselves often acknowledged. They found One in Hamburg, and that was Watson, but this still was not enough, Watson knew that he himself had only a Knowledge in some Parts of the Bussiness, but not half enough, so he gave Bernhards a Direction to write to me; and after I received two or three very flattering Letters, I set off from Manchester the 12 of Feby 1802 and arrived in Harthau the 20th of the following March. In a very short time afterwards as every One (who was anywise interested in the Bussiness) knows, I brought several Machines into a go, and the Product (or Yarn) was very commendable.

Now, Messr. Bernhards made me such Promises as would really shame them at present if I had it only in Writing from them. By this time Charles Frederick was grown into a very Great Mechanic, he could build or direct the Building of the Mules himself, because forsooth, I had furnished him with all kinds of Models, and likewise learnt him Workmen in every Branche of the Bussiness: when they got the Great Engagement in Berlin, they begun to reward me, as they had for the course of three years and an half often promised.

However their Reward was binding me as I dane [dare] not give Direction to any body else of their Construction (as they called it for I had no Contract with them for so long a time in the Beginning) this I was so soft as to do, I only requested the Liberty of Building other Machines for myself what I have not given them, though they granted this, but as soon as I begun a little, they begun a begrudging it and demanding, I must build every thing as I had Knowledge of for them, by the Influence of the Contract, though the Contract did not specify any kind of Machine, but what he already had. ...

They did not neither when I first came to Harthau begin to command I

* The German editors claim to have preserved the orthography of the original manuscript. Two or three apparent misreadings on their part have been corrected between square brackets. (Ed.)

must do so and so, for they first waited untill they could learn Something from me, than they thought they could command me. Inhumane!!! Unmenschlich!!! muzzeling the Mouth of the Ox that thrashed the Corn.

As I was setting the Machines together in Harthau and making the Necessary Alternations on them, Watson to be sure, benefited not a Triffle by it, and it is entirely seems, he gave the most Directions to Whitefield to build Mules, but this still was not sufficient for Whitefield, for he endavoured to catch as many People as he could, who worked in Harthau, and was successful too; on [or] else perhaps he could not make a Beginning to spin upon Mules to this Day; this is universally known, and if this was not the Case, I should imagine it would be a Discredit to Whitefield to strive so much for People who I had learnt; to prove this, he (Whitefield) before he could make the least Beginning, has advertised in the News Papers for Mule Spinners and there was (at that Time) none existing in Saxony but them who I had learnt.

In short I know no Undertakings of Mule Spinning in Saxony this moment, but what is either Direct, or Indirect from me, that is, all through People who have benefited by me. Thomas in Lengefeld, Irmscher in Chemnitz, and Hanibal, a Fellow who I have had a deal of trouble with, for some yers in Harthau, I could mention some others, but it is not worth while; some of these had Supports, and I do not enevy it, but still, it cuts me rather when I think I can not bring it so for [far], or rather farther as the very first in the Bussiness, and one who has left his native Country to establish it in another.

1st Some few more Considerations or Observations I will make so free as to lay before Your Excellency Suppose I did not at that Time leave England and come to Saxony, it might possibly you had no Mule Spinning to this very Day; though, I will not say that you could yet [get] no other, but I will say that men of thoroughly Knowledge in the Bussiness are very seldom, even in England, for One man has one Branch and Another another. . . .

8thly If Your Excellency would only consider, that several have been supported with Money to through entirely away, and I could Employ 5 Thousands better than some Gentlemen 20. 30. 40 or 50 Thousands, such as Mr. Woehler, Messrs. Bernhards, or Mr. Thomas in Lengefeld; You yourself would think it almost a Cruelty as I can not obtain it.

The Counselor Dürisch asked me a few Days since how I would or could be supported by some other means, is very difficult at present to be obtained. I can only propose to you the three following Methods, as you could support me without ever having any Occasion to repent.

1st Gratification well considered, and not above my Merit would help me very much.

2ndly If you was to stipulate a small Premium for every Spindle as I could bring into a go every year, for Ten Years, or so many as you please (let them be for whom they will in the Land, for that is indifferent to the Nation). By this I wish to convince you, as I do not desire any, Reward for Idleness, Contrary, in every Respect according to Merit.

3rdly If a Pension is easier to be obtained than any other kind of a Support, According to Your Honour I hope you will fix such as would really help me, if it was only for a few Years. Your Excellency I know, will consider that I have been now a long time in Saxony.

If neither of theese Prepositions will succeed, then I am for ever done, To be sure, I have the greatest Occasion for a Building for myself, where I could have my Tools, Implements or Utensils, and Workmen together, in this respect, I labour under the Greatest Disadvantages and Inconveniences. . . .

By several means you might help me to this without hazarding a Heller. Such as buying me a Place and lend it me untill I could pay for it. Or if I was to buy it and You lend Money upon it, which is all one. In short, I believe every Thousand you would (at present) help me, would help the Saxon Manufactory in a short Time, Fifty Thousands. . . .

10/4 English Steelmakers in France

Articles of association between Robin, Peyret & Co. and James & William Jackson; 2 August 1817. Printed in, W. F. JACKSON, *James Jackson et ses fils: Notice sur leur vie et sur les établissements qu'ils ont fondés en France* (Paris, 1893), pp. 163-166. (Ed. Tr.)

Contract of Association between Robin, Peyret and Company, merchants of St. Etienne, and James & William Jackson father and son, manufacturers of cast steel; 2 August 1817.

The undersigned Robin, Peyret and Company, and James and William Jackson, father and son, agree to the following:

Article 1 The contracting parties enter into partnership for the manufacture and the sale of cast steel, case-hardened steel, wrought steel and steeled iron (?) and all other sorts of steel, all kinds of files, and other articles which they regard it as appropriate to manufacture.

Article 2 The principal site of the company shall be at Trablaine, in the commune* of Feugerolles, where furnaces and workshops have been established with funds provided by Robin, Peyret and Company.

Article 3 Business shall be carried on under the title of Robin, Jackson and Company. M. Robin shall control the Company and his obligations shall be the only ones which the Company has to honour.

* See Glossary.

Article 4 Robin, Peyret and Company shall have the sole responsibility of determining the kind and quantity of steel and other goods which the Company agrees to make, and of the day to day running of the Company.
Article 5 Each of the contracting parties shall be free to put into the Company any funds they can raise; interest shall be paid by the Company to each partner who does this, at the rate of 6% per year. At the moment, the Company is only liable for the sum for which Robin, Peyret and Company are the creditors, for advances or commissions which arise out of previous agreements with Jackson and Son; the Company is also accountable for the funds supplied by them and agreed upon today.
Article 6 The assets of the Company are made up of all the establishments at Trablaine, and all the liquid assets, equipment and stock which belong either to Robin, Peyret and Company or to Jackson and Son, of which an inventory shall be made. . . . The Company is committed to the agreements made by Jackson and Son both with the workers whom they employ and with M. Heurtieur.
Article 7 Jackson and Son shall take 3% of the net profit of the goods manufactured in payment for their contribution to production. 1% of the profit on sales shall also be allocated to them, which shall be divided between John and James Jackson.

Robin Peyret and Company shall deduct 1% from the total of raw materials bought by them on behalf of the Company and 6% from the sales of the manufactured goods, i.e., 3% for their investments in the company and 3% as commission.

The wages of the workers, the expense of correspondence and all other costs relating to the establishment, shall be borne by the Company: the same is true for any travelling which has to be undertaken for the sale of the Company's manufactured goods.
Article 8 After deduction for the costs of production, sales and purchases, commission and interest, the remaining profit shall be divided equally between Robin, Peyret and Company and Jackson, Father and Son. The losses shall be shared in the same proportion.
Article 9 If Robin, Peyret and Company wish to withdraw part of the investments they have put into the Company, they shall enjoy the right to retain half the profits which usually accrue to Jackson, Father and Son, until their investment is reduced to the amount contributed by Jackson and Son.
Article 10 Records shall be kept of the Company's operations and at the end of each year an inventory shall be compiled to draw up assets and liabilities.
Article 11 The company is valid for nine years from the present day. Nevertheless, Robin, Peyret and Company reserve the exclusive right of discontinuing the present arrangements by forewarning Jackson and Son one

month in advance, and by granting them six, nine and twelve months for the repayment, in equal portions, of the sums for which they are creditors and which relate to the enterprise, and in that case they alone shall be responsible for selling goods manufactured by the Jacksons until their repayments are complete, . . .

Article 12 Jackson and Son pledge themselves fully to work for the future progress of the Company, by devoting their work and all their time to its activities; they pledge themselves also on behalf of John and James Jackson, who shall work solely for the company, at their expense, and in case of John and James absenting themselves, they shall be obliged to provide a worker to carry out smelting operations instead of the former [John], and a clerk or a worker to replace the latter [James].

Made in triplicate at St. Etienne on 2 August 1817.

(*Signed*) Robin Peyret and Company
James Jackson
William Jackson

10/5 Machine Building in France, and English Exports, 1824

Evidence by Mr. Alexander. Third Report of SELECT COMMITTEE ON ARTIZANS AND MACHINERY (Parl. Papers, 1824 51. v), pp. 102–103.

Are you able to speak to the difference in value between the machinery made in France, and that made here? – A machine made in England is certainly superior in certain metals; as cast-iron, steel, and brass, and generally better finished; but if a Frenchman has a good model of a machine, he will certainly make it as well as any English mechanic, so that you cannot distinguish the one from the other; but the great difference is, that the same number of English workmen will turn out 16 machines in this country, when an equal number of French workmen will not turn out in France 4 of the same description. If I were to give an order in England, for 50 or 60 cotton-spinning machines, and give an order in France for the same number of machines, I should not be able to get 10 machines made in France in the time the whole 60 would be made in England. This dispatch is partly to be attributed to the superior knowledge of the workmen, but more to the great variety of tools used in the English manufactories.

You can get any quantity you please from Manchester? – Yes; any number; the only difficulty is in their exportation.

What is the difference of value, in the estimation of your manufacturers, between a machine made in Manchester, and one made in France? – About 40 per cent in favour of English machines.

Do you speak of any particular machines, or cotton machines generally? – I will state first as to cotton machinery, about 40 per cent. . . .

What is the difference in value between a steam engine of the same power, made in England and made in France? – The difference is about 30 to 35 per cent. A steam engine of ten horses power made in England, generally costs about 700*l.* and one in France, about 1,000*l.*

Are they of equal quality? – Yes; many persons like French engines as well, that are made by Mr. Edwards; he is an Englishman, and is the manager of Mr. Perrier's manufactory at Chaillot.

Where does he come from? – From London, I believe. Mr. Edwards is in competition with many steam-engine manufacturers in England. . . .

Have you any means of knowing what number of steam engines have gone to France, within the last two years? – One English engineer has stated, that he had sent 100 to France, within the last three years.

Have you any idea how many Mr. Edwards has made in that time? – Mr. Edwards has put up in France about 100, that he made in England; and since the increase of duty, he has put up 200, which he has made at Chaillot.

Are you able to state, whether any parts of the steam engines are made in England, and sent over to France, and then completed there? – Yes, several parts; particularly boilers.

Is that generally the case? – It is very often the case; the last steam-boat made for the French government, for the post-office at Calais, has been made by Messrs. Steel and Atkins, steam-engine makers at Paris; the boiler and a certain part of the engine have been made in London, and the remainder of the pieces of the engine have been made in Paris.

Are you aware whether the screws, which form a part of the steam engine, are made in France, or made in England? – They are made in England.

How can they send them from England? – They send them along with the engine concealed; no man would take an engine, if they did not send the screws with it. The complete machine must be imported into France, if one is ordered complete.

Do you know any manufacture of other machinery in other parts of France? – Yes, I know the manufacture of rollers for calico and cotton printing machines.

Where are they? – In Paris.

For any other articles? – They make every sort of machine in Paris, which is made in England.

Can you state within how many years any of these manufactories have been established? – They have improved and increased, particularly within these three or four years; a great number of these machine makers have been established many years ago, but the increasing demand for machinery began four or five years since.

Do you know whether any stocking machines are carried from England to France? – Not stocking machines, but lace manufacturing machines; I know a great number of them have been brought from England.

Where are they established? – Most of them are established at Calais, Douay, St. Quentin, Rouen and Paris; there is an immense number of Englishmen, in the neighbourhood of Calais, employed in that trade. . . .

Do they make any of those lace machines in France? – Yes, they make them now in considerable numbers.

Are the English lace machines much more prized than the French? – I am told that they work as well as the English machines, and I could not of myself make any distinction whether the English machines are better than the French; they both appear to work well.

10/6 An English Cotton Operative in France, 1824

Evidence by Adam Young. Fifth Report of SELECT COMMITTEE ON ARTIZANS AND MACHINERY (Parl. Papers, 1824 51. v), pp. 579–580.

WHAT are you? – I am a carder.

Where were you originally employed? – I worked five years at Mr. Burley's, at Manchester.

After having quitted Mr. Burley's service, where did you go? . . .

I went to Alsace, through Mr. Slombergher sending a letter for me.

What was the name of the town? – Guebeville.

In what capacity were you engaged? – As a carder.

How long did you remain with him? – About two years.

What wages did you receive? – Three guineas a week.

What were you receiving in England at that time? – Fifty shillings.

How many Englishmen were at work in the factory where you were? – Six; one carder, one spindle maker, one spinner, and one stretcher, &c.

How many natives were employed altogether? – I dare say about 600 or 700; he has three very large extensive mills there, all spinning mills.

What is the state of his machinery? – The very best in France, but nothing to be compared to ours in England.

How high numbers of twist does Mr. Slombergher spin? – We have spun 150 in French numbers, that is equal to 200 English, but not to make the yarn as in England.

Is he spinning that now? – No.

What prevents their making the yarn as good there as here? – There is sloth, that is one thing; they do not keep the machinery so clean, and it is not in such correct order, though it is made by English mechanics; and they have not the regular heat in their factories as we have here.

You mean to say that the machinery is kept in very bad order? – Yes.

The different things that are attended to in a Manchester manufactory, are neglected in France? – Yes.

Was the machinery you conceived to be the best in France, inferior to ours? – It is above twenty years behind us.

Do you allude to the machinery for the coarse or fine spinning? – Ten years for the coarse, and twenty for the fine.

Where was the machinery made? – Part in England, and part in France, and part borrowed from Mr. Lees, in Salford.

How do you mean borrowed? – They get the pattern in England, and get the work made here, and they fill it up with a little French work, and say it is French work. I have known my master buy yarn in England, and sell it for his own spinning.

Whilst you were there, did any machinery arrive from England? – Yes.

What part? – Spindles, and part of the rollers, and part of the box organ wheels.

Did you see any manufactories for those articles in France? – Yes, I have seen Job Dixon there; he worked at Manchester, where I did, as a machine maker.

Where was he working when you saw him? – At a place called Sernág; the gentleman has made him a large concern, and fitted him up a large house, and he is to make machinery for the French.

Were you at that place where this manufactory now is? – Yes.

Can you state what machinery he did make; and was it equal to the machinery in England? – No; inferior; he was forced to send to England to borrow instructions; and when he had made the machinery, he was obliged to send to England for somebody to *gait* it, that is, to set it a-going.

Did you find the spinners there as active and industrious as the spinners in England are? – No; a spinner in England would do twice as much as a Frenchman will do; they get up at four in the morning, and work till ten at night, but our spinners will do as much in six hours as they will in twelve.

Are all the workmen of that kind? – Yes; they are all of a lazy turn.

Had you any Frenchmen employed at the same work with you? – Yes, I had eight under me.

How much did they get? – Two francs a-day.

What did you get? – Twelve francs a-day; I was obliged to gait the machinery, and make the article to spin.

You were employed as a superintendent? – Yes.

Supposing you had eight English carders under you, how much more work could you have done than you did with the eight Frenchmen? – With one Englishman I could have done more than I did with those eight Frenchmen.

You do not mean to say that is the case generally in France? – Yes, it is, and worse in many places than it is there.

Is the machinery moved as quick as it is here? – No, it would frighten them; they would go into fits if they looked at it here.

They are not accustomed to that kind of expedition? – No, and never will be.

Can they make nearly as good a description of yarn? – No.

Do they make it at a greater expense? – Yes; although they have their hands for much less wages than in England.

Do they use a superior species of cotton wool than we do, to produce the same article? – Yes; by 2*d.* and 3*d.* a pound, for coarse yarn.

Judging from the habits of the artizans you have seen working in France, do you think they will be able to make as good machinery as we have in England? – Not unless you send our machinery there for them to make it by.

If they had it, could they work it so well? – Not so well; but it would improve their manufactures; and after they had got some machinery of ours, they would make others like it, and would then buy no more.

From what you have seen of the French machine makers, do you think they could ever make them so well as in England? – Yes, as well to look at; but not equal in speed; they have not the method of fluting rollers, as we have in England.

10/7 The European Cotton Industry and English Competition, 1835

EDWARD BAINES, JR., *History of the Cotton Manufacture in Great Britain* (London, 1835), pp. 512–515, 520–521, 526.

The French consume a somewhat larger quantity of cotton-wool than the Americans, and are indeed second only to England, though their production is only about one-fourth that of the English. In the silk manufacture the French are unequalled, though our own country is pressing hard upon them in this respect: they are pre-eminent in taste and fancy, possess much ingenuity, and rank very high in chemical knowledge. But they labour under such serious disadvantages for conducting manufactures on the large scale, that there is not the least prospect of their ever successfully competing with this country in the manufacture of cotton.

1st. The national character and habits of the French are unfavourable. Though they have an abundance of energy, they lack that close attention and persevering application, which are indispensable to the attainment of the highest skill, and to regularity of operations in an extensive manufactory. The weavers, and even many of the spinners, cannot be induced to work the year round at their looms or mules, but in the months of summer and vintage turn to agricultural pursuits for relaxation; – a practice which, however agreeable and healthful, is incompatible with high proficiency in any manual art, and most seriously interrupts the operations of the manufactory. It is the combination of perseverance with activity and intelligence, that makes the English artisan unrivalled.

2d. The political state of France is unfavourable. Wars, invasions, and revolutions, and the liability to their recurrence, have shaken credit, and prevented the manufacturing establishments from gaining that duration and firmness which are needful to the perfection of their arrangements, and to the full development of mercantile enterprise.

3d. France has natural disadvantages, especially in the comparative scarcity of fuel and iron. Coal is not largely found in that country, nor is it raised without considerable expense, and the supply of wood is inadequate to the wants of the manufacturer: the manufacturers of Paris use the coal brought from Mons, but it costs them ten times the price given for that article at Manchester. Iron is also far from abundant, and is therefore dear.

4th. The artificial state into which French manufacturing industry has been brought, from being propped up on every side with protections, and therefore incapable of free movement, greatly aggravates the natural disadvantages of the country. Coal and iron might be imported far more cheaply than they can be raised in France, but duties nearly prohibitory are levied upon those articles when imported, to protect the domestic iron and coal proprietors. Of course, these duties fall directly upon machinery, which is in consequence double the price in France that it is in England. The *protection* of the proprietors of iron and coal mines renders it necessary to *protect* the makers of machinery; and the protection of the latter renders it indispensable to protect the cotton manufacturer. The system is a grand series of blunders, and all its parts must stand or fall together. So long as they stand, the body of the French nation will pay for it dearly, in the high price of their cotton and other goods; and if it should fall, their manufacturers will atone for an unfair monopoly by extensive ruin. The manufacturers have been seduced by absurd legislation into a false and dangerous position, where they enjoy no real advantage, and from whence they have no retreat. They have the monopoly of the home market and of the French colonies, except in so far as the smuggler disturbs them; but they hold it under perpetual alarm, and on conditions which prevent them from ever enjoying an export trade of any moment.

5th. As an effect of the political and natural causes already mentioned, the manufacturing establishments in France are small: they are scattered in many parts of the country, in order to supply the wants of the inhabitants; and each spinner and manufacturer is obliged to make a variety of articles, to suit his customers. It is a necessary consequence of this state of things, that the attention both of the manufacturer and of his workmen is divided among several kinds of work, and they are prevented from acquiring excellence in any; whereas the concentration of the manufacturers in England, and the extent of their market, enables each to confine himself to one or to a few articles, which he brings to the highest perfection, as well as makes with the greatest economy of time and money.

6th. The defective roads and inland navigation of France render the carriage of raw materials and goods expensive.

7th. The duty on the importation of the raw material is 2 per cent, more in France than in England.

8th. Capital is much less plentiful in France, and fetches a higher interest.

These, with other minor causes, place the French cotton spinner and manufacturer in so disadvantageous a position, when compared with the English, as to forbid all prospect of successful competition. In the investigation now pending, before a Commission of Inquiry appointed by the French minister, every witness in the cotton trade hitherto examined has declared that their trade would be ruined in all its departments, if English cottons were admitted, even under a high duty. The delegates from the Chambers of Commerce of Rouen, St. Quentin, Lille, Alsace, Troyes, Amiens, Calais, and many other seats of the cotton manufacture, represent their constituents as feeling the utmost alarm at the proposition to remove the prohibition on foreign manufactures established by the law of February, 1816, which they declare to be their 'charter of industry,' and their 'tutelary ægis.'...

M. H. Barbet, manufacturer of indiennes at Rouen, gave in an estimate to the Commission, shewing that an establishment, calculated to produce 50,000 pieces of that article in a year, would cost for its outfit 450,000 francs in France, and 270,000 francs in England, and that the annual expenses of the former would be 182,000 francs, and of the latter 74,750 francs. According to M. Sanson Davillier, the delegate of the Chamber of Commerce of Paris, a manufactory of 300 power-looms would cost 610,000 francs to be established at Paris, and only 221,250 francs at Manchester.

The manufacture of bobbin-net in imitation of the Nottingham manufacture, has been carried on for about ten years at Calais and Douai, chiefly with thread smuggled from England; the number of lace-frames is about

1850; but the manufacturers have been conducting a losing trade. According to M. Abiet, lace manufacturer at Douai, English net is 58½ per cent. cheaper than French net; and, as has been seen, very large quantities of the former are introduced by the contraband trade. . . .

It is the opinion of Dr. Bowring, whose judgment, from the minute attention he has given to the subject, and from the opportunities he has enjoyed, is entitled to great respect, that the additional cost of French cotton goods above those of England is on the average from 39 to 40 per cent.; that the inferiority of French machinery is about 25 per cent.; and the inferiority of French labour, that is, the result of the labour of a given number of hands for a given number of hours, is about 20 per cent. . . .

It would be superfluous to enter into detail concerning the cotton manufacture in the other countries of Europe, seeing that none of them is in the least likely to compete successfully with that of Great Britain. The Swiss manufacture well, and print beautifully: their yarns are 20 per cent. below the French prices, but still they cannot compete with the English, except in the low numbers. The consumption of cotton in 1831 was 56,000 bales, or 18,816,000 lbs. The want of coal, – the limited water-power, already fully occupied, – and the expense of bringing the raw material from Genoa or Trieste, – must always keep down the manufacture in that country.

The Belgian cotton manufacture at Ghent, established during the war, sunk before English competition. The enactment of a protecting system by the government of the United Netherlands, and the monopoly which the Belgian manufacturers enjoyed of the supply of the Dutch colonies, forced up the manufacture to a very flourishing state. But the separation of Holland and Belgium, which has been followed by the loss to the latter of the trade with Dutch colonies, has crushed the manufacture again, and the weavers and spinners are at this moment in a state of the deepest distress.

In Prussia, Austria, Saxony, and Lombardy, this manufacture exists, and is spreading; but in each of these countries it is as yet insignificant. They are all very disadvantageously situated as regards the supply of the raw material; they are also more liable to be disturbed by wars and political commotions than England; and none of them can pretend to compete with England in this branch of industry.

10/8 The Competitive Power of the Continental Cotton Industry 1833

Evidence by Kirkman Finlay. Minutes of Evidence before the Select Committee ... (on) MANUFACTURES, COMMERCE AND SHIPPING IN THE UNITED KINGDOM (Parl. Papers, 1833, VI), pp. 37-38, 70-71.

652. At what period did you begin to feel the competition of foreign manufacturers in the foreign markets in the cotton manufacture? – When I first knew the cotton manufacture of this country, which was in the year 1787, and when I first entered into business extensively, which was in 1792, there was no manufacture of cotton of any importance in any part out of Great Britain. There were, perhaps, some domestic cotton manufactures carried on abroad, but there were no finer fabrics of any kind. I believe my house was amongst the first that ever exported cotton manufactures of fine fabrics generally to the continent of Europe, to Germany, to Italy, to France, and to Switzerland. In those times there was no cotton manufacture in France at all; none in Switzerland worth speaking of; none in any part of Germany. Then the practice came to export cotton twist; and I think it was about the year 1794 or 1795 when we first began to export a good deal of cotton twist. At that time there was no cotton twist spun in any part of Germany. Now there is not a single country in which there is not a great manufacture of cotton carried on. There is a very extensive spinning carried on in Switzerland; there is a very extensive spinning carried on in Austria, and a large cotton manufacture carried on there. By the recent accounts it appears that the Government has relaxed a little the prohibition against cotton twist, and that it may be introduced in future on the payment of a moderate duty. Their manufacture has, in my recollection, entirely grown up. The French manufacture, which did not exist at all at the period I first spoke of, in 1792, and which was very inconsiderable at the conclusion of the peace in 1814, when I was in France, and saw it, has become of late very formidable; and by the means that are taken, as I understand, by the regulation of the drawback, by which the manufacturer receives more amount of drawback than he pays of duty, there is a very formidable advantage given to the French manufacturer by that fiscal regulation.

653. You have stated that the French competition has grown up since 1814; what was the state of the other countries after the period of 1814? – In the United States there was no manufacture in 1814 worth speaking of.

654. Was there any in Austria and Switzerland? – It was beginning.

655. Then the principal foreign competition has grown up since the peace of 1815? – Yes, I think so.

656. Do you think that that competition is on the increase? – I think it is, decidedly.

657. And has been steadily on the increase since 1815, growing every three or four years greater and greater? – Yes, I think every year.

658. Can you state what advantages are particularly possessed by an foreign country in the cotton manufacture? – In the first place, in some countries, particularly in France, and Switzerland and Flanders, they have a body of workmen well trained to the other manufactures; to linen, for instance, which was the great manufacture in Flanders; and by that means they were prepared for engaging in the cotton manufacture.

659. Are there any other natural advantages that they possess? – The low price of labour.

660. Do the improvements in machinery, which are made originally in this country, pass very readily and promptly into those other countries? – They can easily get the improvement; but it is not very easy for them to work it with equal advantage. . . .

1158. What country do you consider the most formidable competitor with this country in the manufacture of cotton? – Most of the competitors in the cotton manufacture are merely competitors in their own market supplying themselves. If I were asked what country I would prefer to supply I would say France; France would take a greater amount of the cotton manufacture of this country than any other country in the world for their own consumption; but with reference to the supply of a third country, I do not apprehend that France is a very formidable competitor, although I know there are a considerable quantity of French cotton goods sold in the Brazils and in other parts of South America, and also in other countries. There are dyed cottons and printed cottons manufactured in France, and sold in considerable quantities. I apprehend that America is as formidable as any, but that it is only one particular article; I do not think at this moment exceedingly formidable for the supply of any third country.

1159. Do you apprehend anything from Switzerland? – Switzerland manufactures a great deal; every country that manufactures either for its own consumption or for the consumption of another, of course is a competitor.

1160. Do not you expect that they will become more formidable as they acquire more experience? – Yes; but we are always improving also, and if we take care and do not make any mistakes in our own legislation with respect to manufactures, I think we shall always enjoy a large share of the cotton business.

10/9 The Competitive Power of the Continental Engineering Industry, 1841

Evidence by G. Withers. Minutes of Evidence before the SELECT COMMITTEE . . . (on) THE EXPORTATION OF TOOLS AND MACHINERY (Parl. Papers, 1841, VII), pp. 71–74.

985. Do you consider the silk machinery of France to be of a superior character? – With respect to the machinery upon the continent, I think the Belgian machinery the best, and next to it, the French and Swiss.

986. Is there much silk machinery in Belgium? – Very little; they are now beginning to apply the Jacquard loom near Antwerp; there is an old silk trade in Antwerp which has existed for centuries, in what they call the black silk cravat; it has fallen off of late years; they are now wanting to renew it, and making some exertions for that purpose.

987. Lyons is the principal seat for silk manufactures in France, is it not? – It is.

988. Do you consider the machinery there to be of a superior class? – I think the silk machinery upon the continent is of a very inferior class; the Jacquard loom is a modern invention; that is good, but I understand it has been improved upon in England.

989. It is a French invention? – Yes; it is the invention of a man named Jacquard, a weaver of Lyons.

990. Do you know the date of that invention? – I do not; it is not many years since it was invented.

991. You are not so well acquainted with the silk machinery as the cotton and cloth machinery? – I have seen it; my impression is that it is very inferior, and the general impression is that it is very inferior.

992. Do you discover, in the present state of machine-making abroad, any reasons for the abandonment of our present policy, or any ground for apprehension as to the future, if it be persisted in? – Machine-making abroad is rapidly progressing towards perfection, and they are so very little behind us, that I am afraid they will go by us, if we do not push the thing a little ourselves; they have our best tools, and their workmen are rapidly improving, and I see no reason on earth why they should not pass us by. We have much practical superiority over the French, but they are a very ingenious people, and if we want to keep ahead, I think we must do all we can to arrest the progress of machine-making abroad.

993. Do you think that the opening of the trade would produce a great foreign demand for machinery? – I think it would not, for the moment; we should have a great demand in time, but not at first; we should begin by having a demand for Spain and for Italy and for Russia, and some parts of

Germany; and I hope afterwards that we should succeed in stopping the machine-making, to a great extent, in Belgium and in France, and become ourselves the furnishers of that machinery.

994. Then you think the arrest of the machine-making abroad will depend upon our allowing the exportation of machinery here? – Most decidedly.

995. You stated that unless we take great care, they will surpass us abroad in machinery; do you mean by surpassing us as to invention or execution or cheapness, or all three combined? – I mean surpass us in all respects; we do not pretend to possess all the inventive genius in the world; other nations may be able to invent as well as we can; it is a well-established proverb, 'that experience makes fools wise,' and we may apply that to the continental system of machine-making; if we hold out a premium to their manufacturers, they will become machine-makers, and by experience they will improve, and become as clever as ourselves; and if we can suppose that a nation may become as clever as ourselves, we may continue the idea, and suppose that they may become cleverer than ourselves, because they may gradually have more experience than ourselves, and consequently have more reason for becoming superior machine-makers; at all events it is a risk, and why should we run that risk when we have the opportunity of removing it? Do we, I would ask, get any thing by keeping back our machines? I imagine not any thing, but we do ouselves a great injury; if by keeping back our machines we could keep back foreign manufactures, I am the first man to say, keep back our machinery; but they possess all our machines and all our inventions; you have permitted them to have all our best tools; they have no longer any difficulty in making any machine, and we see every day that they are taking out patent inventions of their own; under those circumstances, therefore, I consider it would be good policy, on our part, to put a stop to that, by allowing our own machinery to go; they will then have less encouragement, and we shall draw the trade to England; and there is another advantage we shall gain, which is in favour of the manufacturers themselves. The French are a very inventive people, and invent a great many things which they cannot bring to bear, because of the state of manufactures in that country; if we encourage foreign inventors, they will come here with their inventions, and employ our capital and our workmen in perfecting those inventions, and by that means we shall reap the first fruits of them.

1003. Will you have the goodness to state to the Committee whether in your opinion the free exportation of machinery would lead to the imposition of additional duties by foreigners, and should you consider that advantageous or otherwise to this country? – I stated yesterday that I thought it probable that other countries might be induced, in order to protect their iron-masters, to lay on a duty upon English machinery, and I should consider that a bonus given to our manufacturers. If you lay a tax upon any thing, that tax falls upon the consumers; the consumer of machinery is the manufacturer; if he gets heavy protecting taxes, he always throws them to the account of his own profit and loss; the higher the price the manufacturer pays for his machinery, so much the better for our manufacturers; if a Frenchman pays 150,000*l.* for a factory which costs an Englishman 100,000*l.* he has 50,000*l.* extra laid out upon machinery, upon which you cannot reckon less than 15 per cent. for interest, less value, wear and tear, and other expenses; the other part of the question is therefore resolved at once, that a man so situated is placed in a disadvantageous position; the more foreign governments lay on as duties, so much the better for English manufacturers.

1004. You say that the unrestricted exportation of machinery would be beneficial to this country, and you gave your reasons for that opinion; would not the unrestricted exportation of machinery from this country be the means of giving to foreign countries our very best machines and machinery? – If you allow the exportation of machinery from one country, and the importation of it into another country, certainly you give the manufacturers of the country so importing the means of having the machinery you produce; but you do not thereby necessarily give them the means of competing with you in foreign markets.

1005. But assuming that it would, as you say, put them in possession of all our best machines and machinery, would it not give them facilities of supplying themselves at no considerable distance of time from their own means? – The question would be more relevant, to take the French for example, if you supposed that the French did not possess machinery equal to our own; if you suppose that the French are a century behind us, the question may have some relevancy; but that is not the case, for the French make as good machines as we do, and you merely give them the choice of two machines; will you purchase my machine, or will you purchase your own; my machine is perhaps lighter and more handsome in its general contour, but no better than your own, and mine is perhaps five per cent. cheaper than your own? I say, the French possessing all our machinery in the highest state of manufacture (for nothing can be more beautiful than many of the French fabrics, their mousseline de laines, for instance, which are produced from machines made by themselves), we give them nothing but the choice of two machines; I assume that our machine is cheaper than their own by five per cent; we give them no advantage whatever in giving them our machinery, except the saving of five per cent. if it exist.

Chapter 11 Large and Small-Scale Industry

Introduction

European industry between 1800-1870 presented a mixture of the old and the new. In many centres light industry was still characterized by the domestic system, which had prevailed in the eighteenth century (**2/25**, **2/26**). In Russia the domestic system provided support for the Obrok serfs, who were obliged to discharge their obligations in money terms. Agriculture was unable to provide them with an adequate livelihood, and manufacturing activity was a means of obtaining the wherewithal to satisfy their obligatory payments (**1/11**). Such a system did not lead to sophisticated techniques. The relationship between light industry and agriculture was a feature not only of Russia, but also prevailed in France and Germany (**11/4**) until well into the nineteenth century. In the 1830s the outdoor system was strong at Lyons, the second city in France, and the chief centre of silk manufacture, and a similar situation existed at St. Étienne (**11/8**, **11/9**, **15/8**; but see **11/6**). The domestic system was in evidence further eastwards in Saxony, where there was a concentration on stocking manufacture (**11/7**). In 1848 in the canton of Sobre-le-Château workers tended to move into the town during the winter months when agricultural activity was slowing down and return to the countryside during the summer (**11/3**; see also **3/13**). Paris was subjected to the regular influx of such labour, whose chief aim was to work for fixed periods in the city in order to accumulate sufficient funds to buy rural properties (**15/4**). Such attitudes were closely associated with the nature of property holding on the Continent (**6/6**, **6/8**, **6/9**, **6/10**). At a higher level, this division of interest between agriculture and industry was also characteristic of certain elements in the French business community. Chaptal noted the antipathy which prevailed in France towards business (**11/2**; see also **2/27**, **2/28**, for similar comments), a factor which has been much discussed in recent debates on French development.

The nineteenth century saw significant developments in European heavy industry. Progress was uneven; France and Germany assuming a greater importance than Russia (**11/25**), Austria (**11/24a** and **12/11**) or Spain (**11/26**). In Belgium the Cockerill plant at Seraing was of particular importance and represented an outstanding example of English initiative on the Continent. This was an establishment which was very soon equal to the production of almost all kinds of machinery which had hitherto been made in England, and the plant was soon exporting its products to the rest of Europe (**11/11**). Other significant developments in machine production occurred in Belgium, France (**11/12**) and Russia (**11/13**). In most of these establishments English influences, could be seen either in the form of entrepreneurs, workers or materials (**11/13**, **11/14**; see also **10/4**, **10/5**, **10/6**, and also **2/13**, **2/17**, **2/18**) and there were other indications of economic activity extending beyond national borders (**11/25**). Coal and iron formed the solid base of this general advance (**11/16**, **11/19**, **11/21b**, **11/27**).

Once again it should be emphasized that just as institutional attitudes suited to a pre-industrial society lingered on into the industrial age (**11/2**, **11/24a**), large-scale production and new techniques in heavy industry did not emerge overnight, and old forms of production continued to exist. Baudé's account of the French iron industry shows quite clearly that in 1829 charcoal processes were still important in this industry and co-existed with the new manufacturing techniques (**11/21a**). But the shape and organization of industry was changing rapidly. The Anzin Mines have been cited as a good example of a French concern 'wishing to live and let live', which was relatively unimpressed by the idea of absorbing its rivals. But this can be overdrawn. Anzin had an eye for its own prospects and its shareholders' interests, and was not averse to increasing the scale of its production by taking over its smaller rivals (**11/17**). In Germany, where merchants had urged a customs union as a means of stimulating national manufacture (**12/1**), Banfield noted the increasing scale of industrial operations at the workshops of Haniel, Huyssen and Jacobi, and how an entire community was being built around the works, with an existence inextricably tied to that of the firm (**11/15**). These developments increased the power of the employers. It is also clear that the repeal of the Prussian Mining Law in 1860, which left all contracts to be settled purely by the contracting parties, allowed for the increasing exploitation of the miners (**11/20**). A larger scale of operations and increasing power of the owners (**15/17**) were not the only factors indicating that Europe was forging ahead on the heavy industrial front. It was also clear to contemporaries that, whereas agricultural recessions and depressions had been the signal for general social economic disequilibrium in the eighteenth century (**5/1a**), in this period it was fluctuations in the coal industry which determined the general level of economic development (**11/18**; see also **14/7**, **14/8**).

In all these developments, a special place was held by Paris, which maintained and strengthened its position as the leading centre of creative craft work (**11/23**), and with the influence of the capital spreading into other regions, elegance and beauty of design were the general features of the French exhibits at the Great Exhibition in London in 1851 (**11/22**).

The period between 1815 and 1870 is, therefore, a period of contrast and change in technique, scale and organization with the overall industrial emphasis shifting from the textile sector to heavy industry. What emerges clearly from this is that by 1870 the leading areas of Western Europe had laid the groundwork of industrialization, particularly from the mid-century onwards, and were well prepared for further growth.

11/1 Peasant Industry in Russia

a BARON VON HAXTHAUSEN, *The Russian Empire: its People, Institutions and Resources.* Translated by Robert Farie (2 vols., London, 1856), I, pp. 151-155.

b D. M. WALLACE. *Russia* (London, 1877), pp. 102-105.

a In some parts of Europe, and also of Russia, a peasant cannot hesitate to bestow his labour upon the land, because there is no other way in which he can employ it: in such a case he cannot speak of loss, however much labour he may expend; the smallest advantage is better than none, and the case mentioned by Arthur Young then occurs. But in the Government* of Yaroslaf the labour of the peasant has a high pecuniary value, in consequence of the flourishing state of the manufactures.

Agricultural operations can only be carried on in the four summer months: during this period all the labour is employed, but in the remaining eight months, as far as regards agriculture, it is completely at rest. The consequence has been, from the earliest times, a remarkable development of manufacturing industry, as well in the country as the towns. The situation has always been favourable: By the comprehensive plan of Peter I. St. Petersburg was brought into connection with the Volga and all its tributary streams by means of three admirable systems of canals. These canals enter the Volga at Ribinsk; and, as it is necessary to reship all the goods into the canal boats, this formerly insignificant place has become the largest *entrepôt* in the Empire, and the centre of industry for the Government of Yaroslaf.

This industry was originally applied only to the raw produce of the district, which was converted into manufactures and carried to market by the inhabitants and producers in the eight winter months, during which agriculture left them at leisure. [It] was greatly strengthened by the institution of serfage. The majority of the serfs in this Government have always been *obrok* and not *corvée** peasants; the interest of the masters themselves led to this arrangement even in early times, as it was extremely convenient for the indolent nobles living in the towns. This circumstance gave an extraordinary stimulus to manufacturing industry. Agriculture yielded only a bare sub-

* See Glossary.

sistence, but no profit, and money had to be procured for the payment of the *obrok*. The raw products fetched low prices, but all manufactured articles high ones (a fact which still holds good throughout Russia, and must always be kept in view). Thus these raw products were converted into commodities; and carpenters, wheelwrights, makers of wooden shoes, bast-weavers, tar-boilers, boat-builders, spinners and weavers of linen and sailcloth, rope-makers, saddlers, curriers, and shoemakers, brought to market their various articles in wood, hemp, flax, and leather. These artisans however did not live scattered amongst the population, working only for the supply of the immediate wants of a neighbourhood: they worked together as in a factory, and produced articles for the markets; and in this way the remarkable spirit of association, which I have so often alluded to, was developed, grounded upon the organization of the Russian Communes.

In other countries those persons devote themselves to a particular occupation who have a taste or an aptitude for it: in Russia it is understood that everybody has a taste and a talent for every calling. There is indeed much truth in this, for the aptitude Russians display, almost without exception, for all kinds of handicraft, is nearly incredible. In general the wandering Russian tries his hand at various occupations, feeling himself disposed and fitted for them all, and then adopts the one which seems to promise the greatest amount of profit.

The various trades have in this manner mostly formed themselves into separate Communes: for instance, all the inhabitants of one village are shoemakers, those of another are smiths, of a third, curriers, etc. This arrangement possesses great advantages. As the Russians are accustomed to live together in large families, often two generations at a time, the division of labour takes place naturally which is so essential to manufacturing industry. The members of the artisan Communes also constantly assist each other with their capital and labour; purchases and sales are transacted in common, and they send their commodities together to the markets and towns, where they have shops for the sale of them: they do not form exclusive corporations, like those of the German artisans; but their associations are open to all, and the members are united only by the bonds of communal life. Every one is at liberty to assume a profession, or to give it up, commence another, and enter a Commune where his new occupation is carried on. This however is seldom the case, as a change would not often be advantageous; but no restraint is imposed by any of the communal regulations. They are voluntary associations of manufacturers, and again remind us of the St. Simonian theories.

The manufactures, carried on in this manner, yield great advantages to the population, and this Government, to which Nature has shown so little favour, enjoys great prosperity. But if it be asked, whether the arrangements above described have led to any improvement, either in the cultivation of the soil or in the various trades and employments, it must be confessed that there is little cause to boast. The manufactured articles are for the most part indifferent in quality, being slightly or carelessly made, and they remain always at the same stage of imperfection. However advantageous the result may be for the artisans, it can give little satisfaction to the public who purchase their articles. Economically however these artisan Communes are of immense importance, for, without material injury to agriculture, the labour which the latter cannot employ is turned to a useful purpose.

b Very often the peasants find industrial occupations without leaving home, for various industries which do not require complicated machinery are practised in the villages by the peasants and their families. Textile fabrics, wooden vessels, wrought iron, pottery, leather, rush-matting, and numerous other articles are thus produced in enormous quantities. Occasionally we find not only a whole village, but even a whole district occupied almost exclusively with some one kind of manual industry. In the province of Vladimir, for example, a large group of villages live by Icon-painting; in one locality near Nizhni, nineteen villages are occupied with the manufacture of axes; round about Pavlovo, in the same province, eighty villages produce almost nothing but cutlery; and in a locality called Ouloma, on the borders of Novgorod and Tver, no less than two hundred villages live by nailmaking.

These domestic industries have long existed, and have hitherto been an abundant source of revenue – providing a certain compensation for the poverty of the soil. But at present they are in a very critical position. They belong to the primitive period of economic development, and that period in Russia is now rapidly drawing to a close. Formerly the Head of a Household bought the raw material, and sold with a reasonable profit the manufactured articles at the 'Bazaars,' as the local fairs are called, or perhaps at the great annual *Yarmarka** of Nizhni-Novgorod. This primitive system is now rapidly becoming obsolete. Great factories on the West-European model are quickly multiplying, and it is difficult for manual labour, unassisted by machinery, to compete with them. Besides this, the periodical Bazaars and Yarmarki, at which producers and consumers transacted their affairs without mediation, are being gradually replaced by permanent stores and various classes of middle-men, who facilitate the relations between consumers and producers. In a word, capital and wholesale enterprise have come into the field, and are revolutionizing the old methods of production and trade. Many of those who formerly worked at home on their own account are now

* This term is a corruption of the German word Jahrmarkt. (Wallace's note.)

forced to enter the great factories and work for fixed weekly or monthly wages; and nearly all who still work at home now receive the raw material on credit, and deliver the manufactured articles to wholesale merchants at a stipulated price. . . .

However, the great factories have not hitherto contributed to the material or moral welfare of the population among which they have been established. Nowhere is there so much disease, drunkenness, demoralization, and misery, as in the manufacturing districts. . . .

In general there is no proper accommodation for the workmen in the neighbourhood of the factories, and in the smaller works no attention is paid to sanitary considerations. Thus, for instance, in the province of Novgorod there was in 1870 a lucifer-match manufactory, in which all the hands employed worked habitually in an atmosphere impregnated with the fumes of phosphorus; and the natural consequence of this was that a large number of the workers were suffering from disease of the jaw-bone and other complaints. Similar imperfections are seen in the commercial world. As very many branches of industry and commerce are still in their infancy, it often happens that some enterprising trader acquires practically a monopoly, and uses his influence in reckless fashion. Not a few industrial villages have thus fallen under the power of the *Kulaki* – literally Fists – as these monopolists are called. By advancing money the Kulák may succeed in acquiring over a group of villages a power almost as unlimited as that of the proprietor in the time of serfage.

Attempts are frequently made to break the power of the *Kulaki* by means of association. The favourite form of association is that recommended by Schulze-Delitsch, which has had so much success in Germany. What the ultimate result of this movement will be it would be hazardous to predict, but I may say that already some of these associations work remarkably well.

11/2 French Attitude to Entrepreneurship

COUNT CHAPTAL, *De l'industrie françoise* . . . [*see* Document **1/5b**], II, pp. 220-224. (Ed. Tr.)

Respect is the first requirement of the manufacturer and the trader; doubtless they can acquire it by irreproachable conduct, strict honesty and constant fidelity; but this distinction is insufficient for them; they still want respect for their profession, as such. The stupid prejudice which forbids the French nobility to engage in commerce and relegates the individual who is involved in any kind of industry into a lower class, has contributed not a little to arrest the progress of public fortune. The son of a merchant or a manufacturer scorned the status of his father; he tried to hide the source of his wealth; he aspired to live like a noble; in this way family fortunes were dissipated, establishments, hardly begun, disappeared; traditions were lost; development was stifled. Those who know how difficult it is to obtain a reputation for a commercial house, the importance which attaches to a revered name, an assured clientèle, and an esteem obtained only through time and unswerving honesty would readily agree that with such a system France has not been able to increase significantly her national wealth.

This fundamental institutional vice estranged the merchants and manufacturers from the Government; they all felt how useful they were to their country, but they realised their country did not care about them; from that moment they isolated themselves and separated themselves from the national interest, in order to concentrate entirely upon their own activities.

People are surprised at the absence of public spirit in France; but is it possible to have this when there is an absence of general common unity? Can public spirit exist in a country where the most useful men are rejected by the authorities from the first rank of citizenship? Can public spirit be formed in a nation where names, title and favour classify men, and establish so many divisions which have distinct rights and privileges? Could public spirit have been established in a country where the law was unequal, where taxes fell only on a section of the inhabitants, where government favours were the perquisites of a small number? Today, as our institutions place all Frenchmen under the same law, public spirit will doubtless develop in France, because there is a common interest; and the agriculturalists, merchants and manufacturers will praise for ever the Sovereign who has consecrated this right in a solemn act.

To ascertain the social respect which it is possible for commerce to attain, one need only look to England; there, the son of a peer does not blush to sit down in the commercial establishment of his ancestors; and when, in his turn, he is called to take his place in Parliament, he hands over to his children the proud commercial heritage which has been handed down to him. There, many English manufacturers and traders rise to the peerage; everything is measured, everything is calculated according to the degree of public utility; it alone creates classes or ranks, it alone dispenses favours and distributes respect; there, public interest is the interest of everybody. . . .

11/3 Rural Industry in France, 1848

Report of the findings of the Commission of Enquiry in the Canton of SOBRE-LE-CHATEAU, 8 August 1848. Printed in *Bulletin de la Société de Géographie de Lille* (No. 7, September-October, 1938), pp. 256-265. (W.O.H. Tr.)

In the Canton* of Sobre-le-Chateau the only industries – other than purely individual occupations – are: the manufacture of nails and chains; tanneries; wool-combing; cloth weaving; iron works; the quarrying and working of marble; pottery; glass making; forestry and agriculture. . . . There are . . . 3,372 workers of whom 142 marble-workers and 15 ironworkers come from outside the canton and are only temporary residents. The rest of the male working population consists of builders – masons, roof-makers and carpenters – while the women workers include seamstresses, linenworkers, washerwomen and charwomen. In addition to the agricultural workers already listed there are also day-labourers performing temporary duties on the land in the busy season as well as industrial workers who go harvesting in the summer. . . .

Manufacturing is not highly developed, yet since the population is small in relation to the area of the canton there is in normal times sufficient agricultural activity and enough work in the few factories and workshops to give employment and the means of existence to all the inhabitants. The factories are usually less busy in the summer and the surplus labour finds employment on the land. At haytime and at harvest-time there is no need – as is done elsewhere – to employ strangers. In the winter the artisans go back to their factories and resume their wool-combing or weaving until the next busy season on the land.

In our factories . . . labour is paid for by the day or by the piece without any obligation either on the part of the master to give employment or on the part of the workers to stay in a job for a definite period. Farm labourers in some communes do harvest work by the hectare.* They are paid in wheat – either 42 litres of wheat mixed with rye per hectare (harvested) or 84 litres of spelt.† A woman's rate of pay is one half that of a man. Threshing is paid by the 'fourteenth' – every fifteenth hectolitre of wheat threshed belonging to the worker. . . .

The only industrial establishments which cease work from time to time are the forges, the blast furnace and the glass works. The forges at Liessies and Consolver close down for five or six months in the year owing to lack of water. The blast furnace of Sors-Porteries usually closes down for six or eight weeks each year for essential repairs. It is not working at present and

* See Glossary.

† Spelt is a variety of wheat, also called 'German wheat'. (W.O.H.)

the date of a resumption of work is not known. The cause of this abnormal stoppage is the trade depression. Since the construction of railways and other public works is suspended there is no demand for castings and no orders are being received. Production in the glass works is suspended for about three weeks every year. The wool-combing and nail factories experience a slack season in the summer which amounts to a stoppage. This is solely due to the fact that the nailworkers are also masons or slaters while the wool-combers like to work in the fields [in the summer] and return to the workshops in the autumn....

The worker usually has good living accommodation, as rents are low; the population is scattered; and there are more houses than are needed. Almost always in the countryside, and often in the towns, the workers' cottages have gardens in which they grow vegetables in their spare time.

It is fortunate that local circumstances – brought about by the position and nature of the district – assist the worker by providing him with the means of growing winter vegetables. The local farmers have not got enough manure and therefore have to allow some of their land to lie fallow at intervals. There is not enough top-soil over the rock to permit the land to be cultivated year after year. The district is rather similar to the Ardennes, which are not far away. Plots of various sizes – according to the size and needs of the family – are temporarily left unused by the owner and are handed over free of rent to the worker on condition that he manures it adequately and plants it with potatoes. The worker can find withered leaves and moss; he brings ashes from his earth and dung from the roads for manure; and the spade does the rest. So at no expense and by using only manual labour the worker can produce a considerable amount of food cheaply and at the same time he is improving the land entrusted to him and is doing a good turn to the landowner who does not complain even if he has to furnish the worker with seed.

In the last two years the working population has been hard hit by the potato blight which has adversely affected their earnings in two ways. The artisan has had nothing to show for his work on the land and he has had to depend upon his wages from the factory for all his needs. Consequently the workers have not had enough to eat during the winters of 1846 and 1847 and their health has suffered considerably. Illnesses due to inadequate nourishment have been widespread.

11/4 Labour Supply in Germany, 1848

T. C. BANFIELD, *Industry of the Rhine: Series II, Manufactures* (London, 1848), pp. 235–236.

In dealing with the workmen the continental manufacturer occupies a different position from the English millowner. There is no floating mass of candidates for labour, who, if work is not to be had in one place, move off to a distant locality, and are never again heard of where they have been refused. The police and military arrangements prevent accumulations of strangers, unless there is some guarantee for their finding employment. The poverty that grows up with an increasing population, for which growing employment is not provided, is in Germany distributed amongst the peasants' homesteads, of course to the great relief of the parishes, but to the inconvenience of the manufacturer. It is from the peasantry of the immediate neighbourhood that he must take his hands. On the one hand he finds a responsible set of aids, but their number is limited, and if he wish to enforce strict discipline, they are fully aware of the annoyance to which they can expose him. Large and successful undertakings often contrive to establish a population of strangers round their establishments, in the manner that we have seen at Oberhausen, Hammerstein, and Nisterdale; but it can only be done at present by forming a community which is willing to submit to the organization prescribed.

11/5 Silk Industry in Germany, 1858

M. JODLBAUER, *Wirthschaftliche Wandernotizen* (2nd ed., Augsburg, 1858), pp. 16–17. (Ed. Tr.)

In silk, Crefeld and Elberfeld hold first position in the Customs Union; the great skill of the silk workers, their opportunities of becoming well-to-do in a short space of time and their relative independence combine to make the silk weavers into one of the most favoured classes. While the population in the Geldern District is engaged in producing plain silks, Crefeld supplies mostly fancy or flowered silks. Careful observers of the rapid expansion of that ambitious town give it as their opinion that it is overtaking its older sister and rival town for two reasons, first, because the merchants of the newer town of Crefeld are satisfied with much lower percentage margins than the houses of Elberfeld which are used to the high profits of silk manufacture and Turkey-red dyeing, and secondly, because the cost of living is kept down in Crefeld by the opportunities of leasing small allotments for growing potatoes and green vegetables, the labour on which could be looked upon as a kind of recreation in spare hours, whilst land in Elberfeld is tightly controlled, and all victuals have to be bought in from the Rhine. The royal Government in Düsseldorf is constantly attempting to persuade the local council to buy up some land in close proximity to the town and let it off in allotments.

The silk merchant is responsible for purchasing the silk, for providing the looms, for the sale of the finished goods, and for the provision of patterns which are transferred onto cardboard by means of stencils. The silk weavers are given one loom each to begin with, and as soon as their work is considered satisfactory, they are given more, employ journeymen and thus rise to become master weavers. It is said that it is by no means rare to find merchants whose fathers have been weavers. It is the opportunity of improving his status which forms the greatest attraction of the weaver's job. As in all fabrics, the yarn used in the weft is different from that used in the warp; the former is twisted less, and two or three untwisted strands are twisted together, while in the case of the latter, each strand is twisted separately, then several together, and then two or three, wound onto new bobbins, are twisted once again ('doubled'), before the silk yarns are used.

The Prussian silk industry is of some importance if we bear in mind that in Prussia in 1842, 15,700 looms were in operation, against a mere 300 in Bavaria; the District of Düsseldorf had 6,700 looms in 1831, 9,000 in 1834; Berlin is said to have increased its numbers of looms from 1,200 to 1,700 in the same period. Besides, silk weaving is the kind of trade which cannot bear a change of location easily because of the difficulty of acquiring the necessary skill, unless mass migration takes place.

11/6 Textile Industry in Alsace, 1851-1861

C. THIERRY-MIEG'S report to the Mulhouse Industrial Society, October, 1862. Printed in LOUIS REYBAUD, *Le Coton, son régime, ses problèmes, son influence en Europe* (Paris, 1863), Appendix, pp. 412-438. (W.O.H. Tr.)

. . . The textile industries take the first place in our industrial region. They are without question of the greatest significance from the point of view of both the importance of their products and the numbers of workers employed in them.

The printing of cotton cloth, which was introduced into Mulhouse in the middle of the eighteenth century, has gradually been followed by the introduction of weaving and spinning. This was followed by the establishment of the machine-building industry. Although the cotton industry is still the leading branch of the manufactures of the Eastern Departments* [of France]

* See Glossary.

woollen manufactures have also become of considerable significance and there are also some silk and linen establishments. . . .

Spinning of Combed (carded) Wool. Another industry which was introduced into Alsace not many years ago [1839] has developed rapidly, particularly in the first part of the period with which we are dealing.

In 1851 only five mills with 38,500 spindles were engaged in spinning combed wool but now there are six firms with 71,500 spindles and 300 looms to weave the merino wool. A new era of prosperity seems today to be opening out for this industry, after some slack years.

The chief improvements introduced since 1851 in this industry are: (i) the adoption of the Heilmann carding-machine which has led to a veritable revolution by producing much cleaner combed wool of better quality with fewer blemishes; (ii) the purification of the water for washing by a simple and practical process which uses less soap while cleaning the wool more thoroughly; (iii) the adoption of compressed winders with two rows of bobbins. . . .

The spinning of carded wool in Alsace has a turnover of 12 million francs and employs 2,200 workers – 32 per 1,000 spindles. It is one of the finest achievements of the manufacturers of Alsace. . . .

Weaving

The weaving industry in Alsace has made considerable progress in the last ten years. This is due partly to the great increase in the production of ordinary calicoes, which has necessitated the erection of many weaving sheds with mechanical looms. Most of these factories are in the Vosges where cheap labour is available and where waterfalls are used for power. But soon an inadequate flow of water or a dry summer obliged these factories to use steam power in addition.

When that happened the high price of transporting coal counterbalanced the advantage of water power and placed the Vosges weaving sheds in a less dominant position in comparison with rival factories in the towns.

The latter, on the other hand, being unable to compete in products of average quality because of the high cost of urban labour have concentrated on products of higher quality – mainly figured fabrics and fine expensive cloths. . . .

Coming now to the present state of technical progress in this important industry [of the printing of fabrics] we see that considerable advances have been made both from the chemical and mechanical point of view – with this difference that the chemical inventions have generally been of French origin and the mechanical of English origin.

The reason for this is that – in order to maintain their reputation and retain their customers – the French have been forced constantly to make innovations and to raise step by step the quality of their output to a position of undoubted superiority. Consequently the French have sought, in the secrets of chemistry, the means of re-awakening the interst of the jaded by new combinations of colours. The English, on the other hand, produce an enormous quantity of goods for the masses and since they aim not so much at high quality as at speedy production and low prices they seek to secure this by improvements in their machinery. . . .

Fast madder dyes are always the most important as far as cotton fabrics are concerned and all that is necessary is to try and produce pure colours in a simple manner. Thus in 1854 we took over from the Germans the use of silicate of soda as a fixing agent. And we learned from the English the use of madder dye [pink coffine] and quercitron.

Round about 1854 and 1855 there was a reaction. On the one hand we began to use plastics on a large scale – that is to say dyes of impalpable powder which were fixed by means of the whites of eggs, coal-ashes, as well as white zinc, madder lacquer, green Guiquet etc. The consumption of the whites of eggs became so considerable that it was necessary to seek for substitutes, and albumen of blood, gluten and similar substances were successfully used.

On the other hand, we have seen the appearance of those brilliant and transient colours that have led to a veritable revolution in taste and in modern varieties [of printing]. The year 1855 initiated a fruitful period of inventions and the appearance of a new colour – murex – which caused such a sensation that everyone felt that new paths were opening for inventors. And in fact inventors appeared one after another. No sooner had murex been successfully used with cotton than there appeared 'French purple' (a modified orchil) and a whole series of colours derived from coal tar – violet, red (magenta) and indigo blue. These splendid colours – unfortunately far from stable – took the place of madder-dyes for the light fabrics and enabled us to manufacture those extremely elegant and graceful fabrics which our machines turn out today in eight colours. The same result could not be secured with madder-dyes.

At the same time our manufacturers have realised the need to develop continuity of production, to use more mechanical devices in order to facilitate all operations, making them more regular, rapid and economical. Thus in bleaching manual labour has been greatly reduced and work has been speeded up. Recently it has again been possible to save time by using high-pressure apparatus.

Handprinting with metal plates has greatly benefited by the ever more widespread use of stereotyping and by the heating apparatus (which is a gas-heated stamp that burns the design in wood and so makes the original matrix).

With regard to the engraving of rollers for printing we should mention particularly the use of the pantograph and of galvanoblasty. Many improvements have also been made in roller printing. . . .

In 1862 the various industries of Alsace – excluding spinning mills, weaving sheds, fabric-printing works, and metal establishments – were using 135 steam engines of 1,581 h.p. In 1851 the same branches of manufacture used only 20 steam engines of 44 h.p.

Today in all the industries of Alsace there are 473 steam engines of 11,027 h.p. and 147 engines of 7,377 h.p. driven by water power. In 1851 Alsace had only 163 steam engines of 3,565 h.p. and 74 engines of 4,818 h.p. driven by water power.* . . .

11/7 Hosiery Industry in Saxony

Evidence of WILLIAM FELKIN and J. E. TENNENT, Minutes of Evidence taken before the Select Committee . . . (on) The Exportation of Machinery (Parl. Papers, 1841, VII), (**a**) Felkin, p. 149; (**b**) Tennent, pp. 92, 102–103.

a 2120. Do you know any thing of the progress of late years of the hosiery trade in any state of Europe? – The increase has chiefly taken place in Saxony.

2121. Are you aware whether, as regards the advance which has been made in Saxony, the article is produced by hand or produced by machinery? – It is all one class of production; inanimate power is not applied to the manufacture of stockings in any part of the world to any extent worth notice.

2122. But is it by hand or the stocking-frame? – The stocking-frame; the use of the stocking-frame has considerably increased in Saxony, and in other parts of Germany. . . .

2124. Do they meet us at present in neutral countries? – Decidedly; in some countries, where the workmanship is thrown in simply, and a very common or slight article, they are successful competitors with us in third markets.

2125. Are you aware why they have succeeded so well in rivalry with us? – From the circumstance of their having turned their attention to this as a staple production, whereas formerly it was so small as only to supply the local districts of the country in which it was, Saxony and the surrounding countries; the frames were spread over a large district, now they are more

* The statistics given for machines driven by water power apply to industry properly so-called and do not include water-driven corn mills or saw mills in the country districts. (footnote in original).

congregated together, and the means of supplying the raw material are more easy, so that they get the raw material at less cost. There is one particular reason, however, which may be properly stated in answer to the question, and that is the fact, that in Saxony most of the workmen have a small quantity of ground connected with their dwellings, and the manufacture of stockings is not as it is in this country the sole means of the support of the persons engaged in it; consequently they can go to market with their products, and they do not keep back those products generally merely on account of some comparatively slight difference in the price they might receive for them.

2126. Do you think that the circumstance of the artisans having plots of ground, which they must attend to, leads to a better division of labour, and that thereby they produce cheaper and in better qualities than employed as they are here? – I think the prime cost is frequently reduced of articles which are made by parties who are not entirely dependent upon the business in which they are engaged, but have other collateral means of support.

b Almost all the manufactures in Saxony are domestic manufactures; they are carried on in the houses of the parties themselves; this applies to the woollen, the hosiery, the lace, the linen, and the flax; machinery cannot be employed successfully under such a system of manufacture; the demand only exists where the manufacture is concentrated in large mills and factories; those do not exist in Saxony in any branch of trade, arising, in the first place, from the want of capital, and, secondly, from the abhorrence which the people have to be enclosed in factories; they would much rather work in their own houses, even at lower wages, than be shut up in mills. . . .

4519. The domestic manufactures to which you allude as being so prevalent in Saxony are the linen and some branches of the woollen? – Yes, and the hosiery and the lace; another reason of the limited demand for machinery in Saxony is, that the power-loom is little known there, weaving being by the hand-loom.

4520. Are there very large bleaching establishments in the valley round Chemnitz? – Yes, there are.

4607. Has machinery been applied to lace-making and bobbinet in Saxony, and if so, with what success? – It has been attempted; but it has been, in every instance, a most lamentable failure.

4608. To what do you ascribe that failure? – To the invention of machinery for the production of lace and bobbinet in England; previous to that, the manufacture of lace was altogether a manual operation; the raw material was of little or no value; the labour expended upon it constituted its entire and exclusive value; that labour was instantly superseded by the introduction of machinery, and a proportionate decrease took place in the prices of production.

4609. Was the manufacture in Saxony the same as we find it in the pillow-lace of Buckinghamshire and other parts? – Yes.

4610. The consequence of the improvements in England has been, that we have been enabled entirely to supersede the manufacture of that pillow-lace, even at the low wages of Saxony? – Not altogether; there is still some pillow-lace made in Saxony, for which the looms have not been set in this country; perhaps no manufacture in the entire range of European produce has exhibited so extraordinary reduction in point of price, by the application of machinery, as the article of lace . . . the invention, therefore, of this machine in England is one of the most striking illustrations of the interference of machinery with hand labour, inasmuch as it has almost annihilated that branch in Saxony.

4611. Are you aware of any attempt to introduce machinery on a large scale into Saxony for the purpose of manufacturing lace and bobbinet? – It was attempted; but so far as I understand the history of the bobbinet machine, the successive alterations which have been made in it have very rapidly succeeded one another. In the year 1830 a company was formed at Chemnitz by joint stock, with a view to manufacture bobbinet, and some frames were imported from England, and others made from them, they serving for models; for three or four years a small dividend was made upon the shares, but at length English competition and English improvements came on them so rapidly, that the prices were reduced so as actually to become less than the cost of the labour; the machines were disposed of to some Austrian speculator and the whole undertaking was abandoned in 1836, and no attempts have since been made to renew the effort. . . .

4612. Is there still a large manufacture of lace by hand in Saxony? – In the other branches of lace-making, to which machinery has not yet been applied, there is very considerable employment for the peasant in Saxony: I understand that between 30,000 and 40,000 peasants, throughout every district of Saxony, are employed in the manufacture of lace.

4614. They are not tied down to the production of a certain quantity in a certain time, but they carry it to market as they are able to produce it, with reference to their other occupations? – Yes; I was informed that a dexterous work-woman would produce in a week lace, the wages on which would not amount to more than a dollar,* or a dollar and a half. I should mention, in regard to this trade, that the government have endeavoured to give it every encouragement; schools for the purpose of teaching to make lace, and schools of design for the purpose of promoting improvements in its construction,

* See Glossary.

have been established in a number of the villages at the expense of the government.

4615. . . . A very large amount of employment has been given in consequence of the invention of the bobbinet machine; large quantities of bobbinet lace are now sent over to Hamburgh, and are, through agents, given out to the peasantry of Saxony, where they are embroidered by hand, and returned to Hamburgh and to England to be sold as Saxon lace.

4616. Then the cheap labour of Saxony would enable the British manufacturer to send out his bobbinet to be embroidered there in the same way as, I believe, has been the case formerly, if it does not exist still, in Scotland, where many articles were sent to be tamboured from Scotland to Belfast, and the north of Ireland? – Precisely so; I understand that upwards of 20,000 country women throughout Saxony receive entire or partial employment in the performance of that work.

4617. Is that confined to any particular part of Saxony, or does it spread itself over the whole breadth of the country? – Over the whole face of the country; but the population engaged in the bobbinet lace making and embroidery are, for the most part, in the mining district about Fribourg, the wives and daughters of the miners occupying themselves with this employment during the absence of their relations below ground. . . .

4621. The general tenor of your evidence leads the Committee to conclude, that the Saxons are far below the English in the use of machinery, even if they had the possession of it? – That is clearly my opinion – an opinion formed not from an observation on one branch of manufacture alone, but on all the branches which I visited in Saxony; I found that their production in cotton, even from the most superior machinery, was infinitely inferior to our own; and with regard to calico printing, in which England owes her present superiority to the existence of her machinery, and to her skilful use of it, I actually saw machines of English construction standing idle in the workshops of calico printers in Chemnitz, who stated to me that they were unable to employ them to advantage, and that they found it cheaper to continue the old system of hand labour.

II/8 Lyons Silk Industry, 1834

JOHN BOWRING, Second Report on the Relations between France and Great Britain (Parliamentary Papers, 1835, XXXVI), pp. 29–45.

. . . The silk manufacturer in France is subjected to many disadvantages. He pays a higher price for the raw and thrown material than either his Swiss or Italian competitor, and a higher price for labour. He bears a considerable burthen of local taxation, and is interfered with by many trade regulations which are very unfriendly to the developement of his capabilities. Many of the articles he employs in his manufacture, if of foreign origin, are either wholly prohibited, or so heavily loaded with duties as to be effectually denied to him. The cotton twist and woollen yarn of England are absolutely excluded. The long wool of England is visited with a duty of 33 per cent., and they are both materials of the greatest importance to him. He buys his iron at 150 to 200 per cent. advance on English prices; his fuel at an enormous advance; and he has to contend with all the difficulties of an anti-commercial system for his returns. There are few countries from whence he can import goods in payment for his exports; as the French commercial policy has loaded all articles, not the produce of her colonies, with intolerable imposts. If he want indigo from England he must pay two freights; so must he, if he desire to purchase East India or China silk in the British market. In fact, at every step there is some impediment in the way of his success, which has been created for the benefit of some partial interest or other. Notwithstanding this, the silk manufacture of France is the least protected of all the branches of French industry. It stands therefore on more safe and solid ground, its growth being natural and unforced.

. . . Weaving wages are, at Lyons, St. Etienne, and other places, divided between two individuals. Half goes to the owner of the looms, half to the labouring weaver. The loom owner is called a *maître ouvrier*, or *chef d'atelier*, the subordinate weaver, a *compagnon*. About three-sevenths of the looms are worked by *maître ouvriers*, one-seventh by children and apprentices, and three-sevenths by *compagnons*. For the lower-priced plain stuffs a great number of women are employed as weavers, and as the wages are exceedingly low, this quality of goods has been mostly abandoned by men. Formerly there was a difference of nearly half in the earnings of the weaver engaged in figured goods over the weaver of plain goods. The Jacquard mechanism, by simplifying the work, has nearly equalized the two.

The master weaver who has three looms is supposed to receive from the two which he does not himself work about 900 fr. per annum, £36. His rental will be about 150 fr.: cost of lodging his two compagnons, 80 fr.: remains, 670 fr. The weavers who are most prosperous are those who, with three or four looms, can employ their children to weave on them, and so receive the whole of the wages paid by the manufacturer. Three looms will clear to a family from 1,500 fr. to 1,600 fr. per annum, £60 to £64 per year.

The maître ouvriers represent that their net receipts from the looms, after the payment of the expense of mounting, winding, quills, &c., is not more than one-fifth of the sum paid by the manufacturer, i.e. if 10 fr. be the sum gained by the loom, 5 fr. will be received by the compagnon, 3 fr. will be spent in the different charges, &c., and 2 fr. will go to the proprietor of the loom.

At an estimate of 3 ells per day the compagnon's average earnings will be about 30 sous.* On new articles, however, his gains are from 2 to 3 francs, and those of the maître ouvrier will be increased in proportion. . . .

Most of the maître-ouvriers are married; the assistance of a woman is more valuable than the additional expense is burthensome. Of the maître-ouvriers the greater number can read and write, as they have accounts to settle with the manufacturer. Of the compagnons, a great proportion of whom come from the agricultural districts, less than half are able to read and write. Their readings are principally confined to newspapers and romances. . . . A very intelligent weaver describes the situation of his fellows in the following terms:

'The chef d'atelier occupies his own home. The furniture and utensils are his, with the exception of the remisses and reeds, which, in plain goods, almost always belong to the manufacturer. Some master weavers have remisses, but they are the least numerous, especially among the satin weavers. The compagnons and apprentices generally dwell with the master, who furnishes them whatever they require for food, light, &c. When the compagnon has his meals provided by the master weaver, he generally pays from 9 to 11 sous (equal from 4½*d.* to 5½*d.*) The consumption of the weaver is usually one-half litre of wine when his work is heavy, and one-quarter litre when it is light: his meal employs half an hour, and his day's work is from sixteen to eighteen hours. There is too much of confraternity between the master and the compagnon.' . . .

The average hours of labour at Lyons and its neighbourhood are sixteen; but when the demand is active, it is usual for the weavers to work eighteen or twenty. In answer to many inquiries on this head, I find fourteen, fifteen, and sixteen hours stated as the average term. In summer, they usually rise at 4 o'clock and go to bed at 10 o'clock. In winter they rise at 6 or 7 o'clock, and lie down at 11. They breakfast at 8 or 9 o'clock on bread and cheese; they dine at 1 o'clock on soup, animal food, and potatoes, and sup at night generally on cheese and bread. They eat salad with most of their meals in the vegetable season. . . .

There is an institution at Lyons, as well as in all the principal manufacturing towns of France, which is found of great value for the settling of questions between manufacturers, as to copyright and other disputes, between manufacturers and artisans, whether as regards wages, manner in which work has been done, or otherwise, or between masters and apprentices, &c. This is the *Conseil des Prudhommes*, who are chosen by annual

* See Glossary.

election, and consist of nine councillors nominated by the manufacturers, and eight by those weavers who possess four looms. They hold their sittings in the evening, after the labours of the day are over, and have the power of settling all questions to the amount of 100 fr.* without appeal; and for any greater sum, with the reservation of the right of appeal to the Tribunal of Commerce. But the appeals are rare. They are vested with the power of summons, of seizure, and with that of imprisonment to the extent of three days: they act in the first instance rather as a court of conciliation than of judicature, examine parties, suggest remedies for grievances, and prevent much vexation and expensive litigation. . . .

The Conseil des Prudhommes had its origin in a decree of Buonaparte, dated in 1806, and has undergone sundry modifications since its first establishment. . . .

The number of cases that are yearly decided are from 4,000 to 4,500; the number of appeals less than 100; and of the appeals very few have led to a reversal of the decree of the Council. . . .

A state of things very like that at Lyons exists in many respects at St. Etienne. When the labouring weaver, who is called at St. Etienne the *ouvrier*, uses the loom of a master weaver, who is called the *passementier*, he allows to the passementier half of his earnings. The ouvrier's gains are small; he takes three meals a-day, principally of soup. The passementier eats animal food twice a-day, and drinks usually a bottle of wine, of the value of 30*c*., or 3*d*. English.

The proprietors of the 18,000 single-hand looms are little farmers, inhabiting the mountainous district around St. Etienne, St. Chamond, and St. Didier: some of them dwelling at a distance of as much as 30 miles from the abode of the manufacturer. There are few cottages without one loom or more, and the occupation of weaving fills up the hours which are not employed in the business of the small farm. The looms are rude and cheap, averaging perhaps not more than 15fr. to 16fr. in value, and will continue to render less and less to the agricultural weaver as improvements are introduced into the looms of the towns, and as improved machinery alters and shifts the value of hand-labour. The greater dexterity too of the weaver, whose pursuit is uninterrupted, will interfere more and more with the mountain peasant, whose time and attention are drawn upon by different claims. The passementier is gradually becoming a little capitalist; he possesses, on an average, from 2 to 5 looms, and some have as many as 10 or 12: he is more prone to introduce improvements, more immediately acted on by the competition and conversation of his neighbours; he is far more advanced in civilization, his existence is more social, he reads more and thinks more, and

* See Glossary.

has many more objects of desire and of ambition. Pastoral manufacturing must, I think, be more and more interfered with: its cheapness will be more than compensated by the skill of the intelligent artisan. The farm, as more productive, will absorb the little earnings of the agricultural weaver, while the accumulations of the passementier will all go towards manufacturing improvement.

11/9 Lyons Silk Industry, 1842

SAMUEL LAING, *Notes of a Traveller on the Social and Political State of France, Prussia, Switzerland, Italy and other parts of Europe during the present century* (London, 1842), pp. 358–361. (G.P.J.)

Lyons . . . is the second city in France. . . . In 1831 it contained 165,459 inhabitants. . . .

In this chief seat of the silk manufacture in France . . . the manufacturing arrangements are apparently ill-adapted to the improvement, extension or even the future existence of its trade, against the competition of England, Prussia, and Switzerland. The old leaven of the corporation system sticks to Lyons; and the distress in which her operatives are so frequently plunged that their whole existence, it may be said, is distress, is very much the consequence of a faulty arrangement of business not suitable to the times. The master-manufacturer has no factory and workmen constantly in his employ. He merely buys the raw material, and gives it out to be sorted, spun, dyed and put in a state for the silk weaver. In these operations, which are not conducted in his own premises or factory, he has but very imperfect checks upon embezzlement, and none upon waste. . . . In Lyons, in the silk trade, the laying or preparing the pattern for the loom is the work of independent workmen; although the patterns are produced by a draughtsman, who is generally a partner with the master-manufacturer. The weavers again are independent workmen also, living and working each in his own shop, with two or three looms for the different kinds of fabric, and with journeymen to work them. He lodges and boards the journeymen, finds the loom and the work, and gets one half or one third of their earnings, according to the regulations or customs of the craft, as established for the different stuffs or fabrics. The master-weaver is paid for the work by the master-manufacturer so much per ell. . . .

It is evident that the eye and superintendence of the master-manufacturer cannot be given to quality and economy, where every operation essential to the manufacture is not under one roof, or one guidance, with partners and managers attending it, and with workmen responsible directly to one head, and whose hands are always kept employed in the same kinds of work. . . . In all that regards the preparation of the silk, and the texture and quality of the stuffs, the English excel the French manufacturers, and in economy so decidedly, that the ell of silk stuff which cannot be produced at Lyons under the cost for labour of 120 to 125 centimes costs in labour only 40 centimes in England. A certain number of privileged workmen are alone entitled to set up as masters in the weaving and other branches of the silk manufacture at Lyons, and are entitled to exclude others from the exercise of their trade. They must have served as apprentices and as journeymen for certain periods, and cannot set up for themselves without large fees of entry for the freedom of the craft, be the demand for looms ever so great. . . . The only argument in favour of this system of corporate privileges is, that it allows the small capitalist as well as the large to live. . . . The weaver with his two or three looms has an independent existence; . . . he is one of a body far more valuable in social relation than the two or three great capitalists who supersede this body of middle class manufacturers. But this is, unhappily, the natural and unavoidable progress of manufacturing industry.

11/10 Lyons Silk Industry, 1857

H. HOWARD, Lyons, Report dated 22 September 1857, in *Reports made by H.M. Secretaries of Embassies and Legations on the Manufactures and Commerce of the Countries in which they Reside* (Parliamentary Papers, 1857-8, LV. 2444), pp. 59-61.

The silks of Lyons are pre-eminently distinguished by the brilliancy of their dyes, by the superiority of their patterns, and by the exquisite taste of their designs. Whence, it may be asked, does this superiority arise? The factories of Manchester contain all that is excellent in mechanical contrivances; the English artisan is as industrious, and is, I would believe, in many respects superior to the race that swarm in the suburbs of La Guillotière, or La Croix Rousse. . . .

An answer to the inquiry is, I believe, to be found; as an Institution known under the name of 'L'École de la Martinière' exists, where, at the present moment, 900 boys of the working classes receive a gratuitous education. . . . Lyons is admitted to be indebted to it for her ablest workmen, for the skill of her draughtsmen, and for the taste of her designers.

The institution known under the name of the 'École de la Martinière,' in Lyons, was founded by a native of that town, General Martin, who was for many years in the English East India Company's service. Its object is to give instruction to the children of the working classes of the Department* of the Rhone. Instruction is principally directed to science and art as applied to industry.

The school accommodates on an average 500 day-boarders, and its expenses vary from 80,000 to 100,000 francs* annually. The peculiarity of the

* See Glossary.

establishment consists not so much in what is taught, as in the manner in which the instruction is conveyed. The teaching (if I may use the expression) is simultaneous, that is to say, the pupils are disciplined to respond collectively to a certain series of signals, which, while saving time, singularly simplifies the task of the professor. This mode of instruction, though very simple and easily understood by the pupil, must be witnessed to be thoroughly appreciated; it is difficult to explain in writing its precise nature; the result obtained, however, is continued attention during twelve hours on the part of the pupil, who is so placed as to be unable to take advantage of the greater ability or greater industry of his neighbour. The boy is made conscious that he must rely exclusively on himself, and that he must devote all his energies to the task.

I should observe that the instruction given at the 'Ecole de la Martinière' is gratuitous; admission to it is, therefore, confined to the children of the working classes of Lyons and of the Department. Another school, however, called the 'École Centrale Lyonnaise,' has, within the last year, been opened by M. Arlès Dufour, where, under the direction of the same professors, a similar system is adopted. Here, however, barring a small annual payment, there are no restrictions as to admission. . . .

Instruction is given in chemistry, drawing, writing, mathematics, morals, physics, the theory of silk manufacture, modelling, and moulding.

The drawing-class is peculiar, inasmuch as the pupils copy models and every species of machine without the aid of instruments. They are thus made acquainted with the forms of machines, the uses of which are subsequently explained to them by the professor.

The workshops ('ateliers de travail') form another interesting department: turning, joinery, and iron-filing, are the occupations of the workshop. Prizes are given in all three classes for the best work. The atelier, although the work is compulsory (sixty hours during the session), is considered by the pupil as a place of recreation.

The modelling and moulding class of this institution is another peculiar and prominent feature. The object of this class is to create a pure taste for ornamental forms, whereby the pupils may be enabled hereafter, as masons or plasterers, to understand and appreciate the ornamental works which they may be called upon to execute. In this class prizes are likewise given, and all the pupils model or mould the same thing in a given time. In the room devoted to this class, the collection of models (the work of former pupils who have excelled in the art) are disposed on the walls.

Many of the foremen of the factories of Lyons, and many good chemists (I am assured) have been pupils of the 'École de la Martinière.'

11/11 Progress of Continental Machinery

a J. C. SYMONS, *Art and Artisans at Home and Abroad* (Edinburgh, 1819), pp. 174–176.
b M. N. BRIAVOINNE, *De l'industrie en Belgique* (2 vols., Brussels, 1839), I, pp. 302–305. (Ed. Tr.)

a Belgium, from her mineral riches and other topographical facilities, naturally takes the lead in the progress of Continental machinery. I have already alluded to the leviathan establishment of Mr John Cockerill at Seraing, employing 3,000 workmen, with seven skilful English engineers superintending the chief departments, and combining English skill with the advantage of cheap labour. The motive power consists of steam-engines of 900 horse power; and Mr Cockerill not only supplies machinery to all parts of the Continent, but has branch establishments in three different countries. In addition to spinning machinery of every description, steam-engines, both stationary and locomotive, are supplied to France, Germany, and Russia.

It is difficult to name any large enterprise of manufacturing industry, whether in Belgium, Holland, Russia, or the immense territory of the Prussian league, with which Mr Cockerill is unconnected, either as a shareholder or as the engineer from whom the machinery emanates. He has spinning-mills of flax, or cotton, or wool, in almost all the chief districts for these manufactures in the Prussian and Belgian dominions. Mr Cockerill's name is on all the locomotive engines on the Belgian railroads, and I was told that he is the contractor for those now forming in Prussia.

Mr Cockerill's father, who established this gigantic concern, came over to Belgium a common blacksmith, and could neither write nor read, I believe, till the day of his death.

Mr Cockerill, extensive as are his enterprises, by no means monopolizes the making of machinery. Of those now commencing there are the Messrs Fairburn, who have issued prospectuses of an establishment, which was to be formed at the large factory already built at Malines, near the railroad station. Mr William Fairburn is to superintend the heavy department for engines, locomotives, &c. and Mr Peter Fairburn that for spinning-machinery, and especially for flax-spinning. There can be no question that this establishment will rival any in England. In addition to these is the company of the Phenix at Gand, on a very large scale, and in which English and Scotch engineers are already engaged. There is likewise another at Brussels, of the existence of which some mystery is made. I owe the knowledge of it to Sir Hamilton Seymour, who kindly accompanied me to see it, and owing to his good offices we obtained the unusual favour of being allowed to inspect the interior. It is of large dimensions, covering 2½ bonniers of about 6,500 square

* See Glossary.

feet each. This establishment belongs to one of the *Sociétés anonymes*,* of which the Banque Nationale is said to be at the head. 500 workmen, of nearly all nations except France, whose operatives are not in repute in Belgium, are employed. Some of Sharp and Roberts's machinery was there. The present motive power is not above 36 horse.

There are several old established machine-makers in different towns in Belgium, but few on the same scale as those I have named. The fact is, that this industry is yet in the first stage only of its development. Mr Cockerill told Sir Hamilton Seymour, that he had all the new inventions over at Seraing ten days after they came out in England.

b Machines for the spinning and weaving of cotton, with all the improvements which had been introduced in England, came into production at Seraing in 1825.

Most of the machines which have been manufactured there since then have been exported chiefly to Russia, Spain, Italy and Germany. Since 1827 power looms have been made at Seraing.

Since 1828 mechanical presses similar to those produced in England have been made there. All of these have been bought by the Germans; not a single one remains in Belgium.

In 1834 and 1835 a large quantity of machines for the grinding and polishing of glass, for the Saint-Gobin factory, were constructed in the works.

Immediately after the opening of the railway from Brussels to Malines, Mr. Cockerill was able to supply locomotives which can compete in all respects with those which had been obtained previously from England; in September, 1836, seven of these were in construction, including a giant-sized one for Russia. When new machines appear in England, Seraing obtains them to use as models, and supplies them afterwards not only to Belgium but to the entire continent.

The advantage of Seraing over the English establishments is especially noticeable in the price of engines for steam-powered boats, the construction of which requires a small amount of material and a great deal of labour. As regards every sort of steamboat, the Seraing establishment can rival England in every respect relating to quality and finish.

Everything in the mechanical arts which has been developed and produced in England to lessen the work-load is found at Seraing; among other things there are several machines for planing iron, cast iron and brass (it is possible to see one machine on which pieces 30 feet in length can be planed); a machine for making holes in iron; a machine for sawing beams and planks;

* See Glossary.

a machine for planing wood. . . . This establishment also possesses a great variety of lathes and boring machines.

Anyone visiting Seraing, whether he tries to take in the entire establishment or to examine specific sections, is soon astonished. This establishment, in its present state, is the result of eighteen years' work; the developments it has received have been progressive, and have resulted from an expansion of business; and yet one is so impressed by the admirable manner in which the various parts of this whole establishment seem to be interrelated, that it seems it could only have been planned and erected at a single attempt. Between the coal mines, the iron works and the workshops, a division exists which is sufficient to prevent any confusion and yet not sufficiently pronounced to destroy the unity of the works; the workers are in sufficient proximity to help each other and yet not sufficiently near to be a hindrance.

When you approach Seraing you are warned in advance of the importance of the establishment by the numerous steeples or smoking chimneys but when you are at the very gate of Seraing, the silence and order are such that you would never imagine you are only a few steps from 2,000 workers and machines. . . .

Also, to appreciate fully the contribution of the founders of Seraing, it is insufficient to insist on the utility of the works for the country, the numerous apprentices who have been trained there, and the incentive it has given to Belgian machine construction; it is necessary to emphasise again the perfection of the internal organization, the excellent lay-out of the establishment, the contented appearance of the workers; . . . but the greatest service without doubt which Seraing has rendered to Belgium – and everyone agrees on this – is that of having trained in a short space of time a large number of skilled mechanics.

The examining jury of the National Exhibition in 1835, having looked at the work of several industrialists, even though they had not exhibited any of their goods, referred to Mr. John Cockerill in the following terms:

We have reached the unanimous opinion that we should . . . award the Gold Medal to Mr. John Cockerill. It would be superfluous to enumerate here all the claims of this great industrialist to national recognition. We limit ourselves to recording that Mr. Cockerill was one of the first to introduce the coking process into Belgium, and the treating of cast iron with coal; that his spinning of cotton and carded wool at Liège, his cotton printing and his paper works at Andenne are organized on a very large scale, employ a considerable number of workers and produce goods which are as noteworthy for their cheapness as for their beauty; finally, his various machine factories have contributed most powerfully to the progress which so many branches of Belgian industry have made during the last fifteen years.

11/12 Engineering Industry in Belgium and France

Evidence of G. WITHERS to the Select Committee on the Exportation of Machinery [*see* Document **11/7**], pp. 43, 63-66.

561. Has machine-making made any considerable progress in Belgium? – Very great progress.

562. Where are the principal establishments located? – At Ghent, Malines, Brussels, Tirlement, Liege and Verviers.

563. Are those for the manufacture of cotton, woollen and flax machinery? – Yes: steam-engines, steam-boats, locomotives, and all descriptions of machinery.

564. How many hands are employed at the works which you have named; have you made that a subject of inquiry? – Yes; in round numbers I should say at least 8,000; but there are a great many machine-makers in a very small way, employing two, three, four, five and six workmen, in villages and small towns, which I have not named, especially for machinery for making cloth.

565. Are those latter parties machine-makers, or employed to keep machinery in repair? – They make machines.

566. Is the machinery made in those towns to which you have referred made for home use in Belgium, or is any portion of it destined for export? – The greater part of it is for exportation.

567. To other parts of the continent? – To other parts of the continent, and even to South and North America, Egypt and Turkey. . . .

571. *Chairman.*] Has not machine-making improved greatly in Belgium since the year 1838? – It has improved very much indeed. . . .

572. To what do you attribute the improvement you refer to? – To the extraordinary impulse given to manufacturing speculations by joint-stock companies, which are called Societés Anonymés. [sic]

573. Do you mean by Societés Anonymés manufacturing concerns for machinery? – Yes, machinery of all descriptions; in the first place, joint-stock companies were established for working coal-mines; when those joint-stock companies got into operation at the coal-mines, they necessarily wanted a great deal of machinery, such as engines, and not being able to obtain it, they turned their attention immediately to joint-stock companies for making those engines, so that the one society gave rise to the other. It was in the same way with machinery: there were joint-stock companies, flax-spinning joint-stock companies for the manufacture of stuffs, for paper making, for pianofortes; and, in short, joint-stock companies for almost every thing; their wanting a great quantity of machinery encouraged joint-

stock companies to make machinery, because they could not have it from England.

574. Are we to understand that the operations of joint-stock companies have extended to the production of cotton-twist, and of flax, and silk fabrics, as well as to the mere preparation and manufacture of machinery for those purposes? – Yes; there is a joint-stock company for silk, it is now making its machinery at Liege; Reynier Poncelet is making the Jacquard looms for weaving silk.

575. Mr. *Brotherton.*] What number of partners generally constitute a joint-stock company? – As many as choose to buy shares; it depends upon the amount of capital.

576. Are they under any Act of Parliament, or under any charter of incorporation? – In Belgium it merely requires the permission of the minister to form a joint-stock company.

577. *Chairman.*] The effect of the establishment of these joint-stock companies has been to bring together in a collected shape a capital which few individuals in that country were capable of furnishing individually? – That is the case.

883. Can you give the Committee any information as to the state of machine making in France, and particularly in reference to the progress which has been made since 1837; and will you be good enough to state the causes of that progress since that period? – Machine-making has been gradually improving, for a great number of years, in France; it did not take that rapid turn in France which it did in Belgium; the import duty being very high on the one hand, and the impossibility of getting it from England, made machine-making a very good speculation in France, and machine-makers have very much improved within the last 10 years.

888. What do you conceive to be the number of machine-makers in France, and who are the principal ones, and where are they principally located? – It would be impossible to say the number of machine-makers in France: you will find them all the way from Calais to Toulouse; they are spread over the whole face of the country; but for the cloth-manufactories, you find them at Arras, Rheims, Sedan, Elbeuf, Paris; for cotton-machinery, they are at Lisle, Lille, Roubaix, Douai, Cambray, Paris, and in Alsace, Rouen and various parts of the country; for lace-machinery, lace-making, Calais, Dunkirk, Lisle, St. Quentin, Lyons; but besides those places, I have before observed, there is a great deal of machine-making in France by small masters employing 8 or 10 workmen each.

889. Are the cotton, worsted, cloth and lace manufacturers of France all supplied, more or less, with machinery manufactured in the country? – All of them.

890. Wholly, or in part? – Wholly, I believe.

891. Mr. *Villiers.*] Have you any means of knowing whether cotton-machinery is increasing in amount? – According to their own report, manufacture is not increasing much, and machinery is not.

892. *Chairman.*] Can you give the Committee any particulars of the origin of machine-making in France? – Machinery has always been made in France, ever since the existence of manufactures; but it took a very particular turn during Napoleon. An Englishman, of the name of Douglas, went over there about 1798, and was very much encouraged by Napoleon, and he got over most of our inventions that were in existence at that time, and worked from them, as models, in France. . . .

896. You think our machinery is superior to theirs? – Yes, but only to a certain extent; 'cheaper and better,' 10 years ago, were different expressions from what they are to-day; their machinery was very inferior to ours 10 years ago, but now it is inferior to a small extent only. . . .

924. Was there not in Paris, in the year 1839, an exposition of all the recent improvements in machinery? – Yes, there was.

925. Were you present during that period? – I went to look at it.

926. Can you state what was the opinion at which you arrived, as regards the progress of machine-making in France, from the result of your observation on that occasion? – I saw the exposition in 1834, and, comparing the two together, I was struck with the very great improvement which they had made in engineering and machine-making generally; there were all descriptions of machines, from the locomotive to the simplest machine employed in our manufactures, and the difference was very much in favour of the advance. In point of general finish, I saw nothing inferior to our own machinery.

927. Would you say, then, that it was a superior class of machinery to that in Belgium? – In general appearance it was much superior; but I do not think in reality that it was. They have a different way of finishing in France; they put a higher finish, but it is merely French polish, not in the real fitting up of the machine.

928. Then the French can, in fact, supply themselves with machinery? – To any amount.

929. Have they any surplus? – They have a surplus, which they might export if they had a demand for it; but Belgium has cut them out of the trade of late years. They have a surplus number of hands, and tools, and means of making machinery; they have lately made a great deal of machinery for paper-making, to send out to Russia and Spain.

11/13 Backwardness of German Machinery Manufacture

Evidence of CHARLES NOYES to the Select Committee on the Exportation of Machinery [*see* Document **11/7**], pp. 85-88, 91.

4436. Did you visit any machine-making establishments at Hamburgh? – I did; and I think the condition of the manufactory which I visited at Hamburgh is a very fair practical illustration of what I have just been saying, of the anxiety which prevails throughout Germany to obtain English machinery. The manufactory to which I refer, is that of Messrs. Gleichman & Busse; this is a manufactory which has been constructed within the last two years, and I found them working with English iron, with English coals, with English models, all their tools English, their director an Englishman, and of the 150 hands who were in their employment, 90 were likewise English; and they informed me, that notwithstanding the expense to which they must be put in all those items of carriage from England, they still were enabled to make machinery so as to undersell the smuggled machinery which came over from England; and that from using their English materials, and applying their English skill, they found a favourable impression that their work was equal to English.

4442. You stated that the number of hands in this establishment at Hamburgh were 150, of which 90 were English; did that include the whole number? – No; it included the whole number that were then employed, but the works were calculated for 300 hands.

4443. What were the particular machines that they were employed in making? – They professed to make machinery of every description, both for power and for action; steam-engines, hydraulic presses, machinery for spinning, and likewise locomotives. At the time I was there, a large iron steam-boat was on the stocks, intended for the navigation of the Elbe; that, I should think, was an undertaking likely to be successful; for some iron steam-boats had been previously brought out from England for the purpose of navigating the Elbe above Hamburgh, but in consequence of the straining in the long sea voyage, and the shallow construction of the vessels, they were found to be so seriously injured, that no resource was left except to build them in Germany itself.

4444. Did you find that they were confining themselves, to any considerable extent, to the manufacture of that description of machinery which is considered to be prohibited by our rules in this country? – No, they seemed to be manufacturing, generally, every description of machinery.

4445. Do you recollect to have seen any machinery for the spinning of cotton? – Yes.

4446. They were making not only machinery for the spinning processes, but for the preparation? – Yes.

4447. They were constructing machinery for the first operations? – Yes; at the time of my visit they were very busily engaged, likewise, in the preparation of some flax machinery, which they told me was designed for Russia, and some they had been likewise exporting to Prussia.

4448. Did you inquire into the cost of the coals to them, which you said were imported from this country? – Their coals were all English; they were brought from Newcastle; and they told me that they could import it themselves at a cost of 15*s*. per ton, but that there were parties there who imported the English coals, and that they could not purchase from them under 17*s*. 6*d*. . . .

4453. From all the opportunities which you have had from visiting this establishment, and making inquiries respecting it, are you of opinion that it was one of a promising character, and which was then either remunerating, or had a prospect of eventually remunerating those engaged in it? – Such was their own report to me, and it was confirmed by several mercantile gentlemen with whom I afterwards conversed in Hamburgh.

4454. The means of communication into the heart of Germany is, I presume, by the Elbe itself? – By the Elbe itself, as far as Magdeburg, and from Magdeburg either by the Havel, or by the railroads, which are now extending in various directions towards Berlin: one is already open to Leipsic, and thence to Dresden. . . .

4457. From your own observation, as regards the finish of the machines which you examined, and the general style and character of the work which you saw; what is your impression with reference to its quality? – The finish of their spinning machinery seemed to me to be very fine indeed; but with regard to their castings they were particularly coarse, so much so as to lead to an observation on my part to the director.

4458. Did that appear to you to arise from want of skill on their part, or from the sand from which they cast it? – I can scarcely ascribe it to either, because they were English workmen, and they were working with English sand.

4459. Mr. *T. Parker.*] Do they make the tools with which the machinery is constructed? – They were all English tools that were used at Hamburgh.

4460–1. They do not attempt to make the tools with which the machinery is constructed? – Not at present; but they distinctly told me that it was within their power to do it, and that in all probability they would.

4462. Without the aid of English tools, they would not be able to make the machinery? – They express their ability to make tools for themselves; but I should doubt it very much, as I found elsewhere, especially in Belgium, that where parties were manufacturing their own tools, they were worse in execution and higher in price than if imported from England.

4463. *Chairman.*] Amongst other places, you visited Berlin? – I did.

4464. Did you examine any of the machine-making establishments there, and in what position did you find them? – I found at Berlin the most enterprising and systematic exertions made on the part of the Government to obtain a command of the manufacture of machinery; I found no expense spared for that purpose; and the exertions quite astonished me. There is one very important institution at Berlin, called the 'Gewerbe Institut,' which is a large establishment for practical education, combining design with almost every branch of manufactures into which science and mechanics enter. The pupils for this institution are selected from similar provincial schools throughout Prussia, and they are sent as a mark of honour to the head institution at Berlin, where they obtain their education, and are likewise even paid a salary during the period of their attendance: in going through the rooms of this institution with the professor, Mr. Wedding, I saw suites of apartments completely filled with models of English machines: the professor informed me that they had in it models of every machine in use in Great Britain for the manufacture of cotton, flax, silk and wool, and likewise a number from America and Germany; that by these means they were not only enabled to have our recent improvements, but, what was a matter of importance which we cannot command, that they were enabled frequently to combine in the same machine two distinct English patents. The system he told me was, that this machinery, as soon as produced in England, was immediately imported at the expense of the Government, and set up at the Gewerbe Institut; that it was proved; that a working model was immediately made from it, to be deposited in the institution, and that the original was presented as an honorary prize by the Government to some manufacturer in Prussia, who had distinguished himself in the peculiar branch to which it was applicable. In the Institut, likewise, the pupils were taught to make the machinery themselves; they were supplied with the tools, and they were permitted to carry away the machines which they themselves had constructed: I cannot but look upon the whole of this system as a most surprising effort made on the part of the Government to obtain a command of the manufacture of machinery, which is at the present moment so important a feature in English manufactures.

4465. Mr. *T. Parker*] Does this example on the part of the Government appear likely to produce any general effect upon the introduction of machinery? – I should say that it does; for those who were pupils in this institution have commenced the manufacture of machinery in all the districts of Prussia, from north-east to south-west. The Committee have already had evidence with reference to the state of the manufacture of machinery in the Rhenish Provinces of Prussia, and at Aix-la-Chapelle: the other great quarter in which it is located is in Silesia, at Breslau, to which unfortunately my time did not permit me to go; so that my observation was confined to central Prussia, Brandenburgh and Berlin, and there I found numerous establishments, in all of which were persons who had been educated at the Gewerbe Institut, and had become manufacturers under the immediate auspices of Government.

4466. *Chairman.*] What is the number of pupils who were maintained at this institution? – At the period of my visit there were but 80.

4467. Do you know what is the sum annually placed at the disposal of Government in order to keep up this institution? – I do not; the pupils, I was told, receive each 300 dollars* a year; but I think some information connected with that institution is given in the Report of Dr. Bowring upon the Prussian Commercial League, so that it is unnecessary for me to go further into it.

4502. *Chairman.*] Saxony is a great manufacturing country, is it not? – I presume, in proportion to its geographical extent and its population, Saxony is the most manufacturing country in Europe; there is scarcely a village in Saxony which has not some staple production, and scarcely a house that does not combine with agricultural pursuits some branch of mechanical industry.

4503. Is machinery extensively made in Saxony, as well as used? – The manufacture of machinery is more generally spread over Saxony than it is over Prussia, or any other manufacturing country of Europe; I think in Saxony I have a list of 18 manufactories of machinery, great and small.

4504. Mr. *Stansfield.*] Is there much capital employed? – No, not much; they are generally very small manufactories, and there is a very considerable division of labour among them; they are situated in those parts where the manufactures are situated, for the purpose of making or repairing the machinery incidental to those manufactories.

4505. *Chairman.*] In what part of Saxony did you find the greatest number of machine-making establishments? – The country about Chemnitz is the chief seat of manufacture.

4506. Which is itself the chief seat of the cotton manufactures? – Yes.

4507. Did you visit any particular machine-making establishments at Chemnitz? – I visited, at Chemnitz, the works of a joint-stock company for the manufacture of machinery, which are the largest in the kingdom; the firm is the 'Sachischen-Machinen-bau Compagnie.'

* See Glossary.

11/14 Russian Machinery Manufacture

Evidence of M. CURTIS to the Select Committee on the Exportation of Machinery [*see* Document **11/7**], pp. 115-118.

1575. Can you give the Committee any information as to the state of the imperial manufactory in Russia? – I know that it is carried on to a considerable extent from various conversations I have had with Lieutenant-general Alexander Wilson, the person who has the conducting and superintendence of the establishment, and who is a native of England.

1576. Is that the establishment of Alexandrofski? – Yes, I have seen lithographic drawings of the works, and they are on a very extensive scale; they are for the purposes of spinning, weaving, dying and bleaching of cotton goods, and the spinning and weaving of linen; they make beautiful damask table-cloths and a variety of other articles of that description; they have likewise a very extensive machine-making establishment there; they make wire cards there for the making of which they were furnished with machines from Mr. Dyer's establishment; in fact, they carry on very extensive works there; they are the only parties allowed to make the ordinary playing cards as distinguished from wire-cards; the Government monopolize exclusively the right of making those cards, and that business is carried on there. The works are, as I have said, on a large scale; boys are educated there; they introduce the Russian youths, who serve a period of apprenticeship; there are sleeping apartments, and general arrangements both for boarding and lodging the parties occupied in the works; schools, churches, and hospitals in case of sickness; besides which, there are at Colpeny much larger works where they manufacture steam-engines, mill-wright work and also iron steam-boats; there are foundries for the purpose of casting the ordnance both for the army and the navy; and they make there some of the most beautiful mathematical instruments that it is possible to make; in fact, I have never seen them equalled in this country; I believe some of the first makers of mathematical instruments in London have stated that they have never yet been able to equal them, and that it would be hardly worth their while to go to the expense of finishing them to such a degree, for they could not get the price for them; I have seen some specimens of the most beautiful workmanship I ever saw. . . .

1580. Is this a private or a royal establishment? – It is a royal establishment, or rather there are two establishments; they are supplied with the best tools; that I know, from the orders which General Wilson has given in this country to tool-makers; no expense whatever is spared in furnishing those establishments with the best possible tools.

1581. Mr. *T. Parker.*] Who is General Wilson? – The manager or director of those works, in fact the head person who gives directions and carries on the works as if he were sole proprietor; he has a certain sum allotted to him, and he has nothing to do but to apply for any money he wants, and he gets a grant for it. As far as I have understood from General Wilson, I believe the principal object of these establishments is to introduce particular manufactures and rather with a view of instructing the natives than as a matter of profit. . . .

1584. You do not know whether it is a royal monopoly? – It is carried on under the government, but the government would, I apprehend, allow other establishments to be formed in Russia. . . .

1586. Mr. *T. Parker.*] Are there any English operatives in either the works at Alexandrofski or Colpeny? – There are; the chief parties directing those works are either Englishmen or Scotchmen; the person who was manager and has been there for a length of time has now, in conjunction with some other parties in St. Petersburgh, established a very extensive cotton-spinning manufactory; parties going there are well paid and made as comfortable as they possibly can be; every encouragement is given to them, and I think few parties that go there return to this country. . . .

1599. *Chairman.*] To revert to Russia; do you suppose that if the present law preventing the exportation of machinery from this country were repealed, they would cease to be machine-makers at Alexandrofski and the imperial establishment at Colpeny, to which you have referred? – I do not believe they would, for I believe those works are carried on more with the view of giving encouragement or instruction to parties in machine-making than with a view of profit; I cannot say whether they make profit or not.

11/15 A Large-scale German Iron Undertaking, 1848

T. C. BANFIELD, *Industry of the Rhine: Series II – Manufactures* [*see* Document **11/4**], pp. 37-47. (G.P.J.)

A visit to the docks and workshops of Haniel, Huyssen and Jacobi must not be omitted by any who would inform themselves of the state of the machine-manufacture in Germany. The greater part of the steam-tugs now plying on the Rhine have been built by this house. . . . On going on board one, the Franz Haniel, we found. . . . She was altogether of iron . . . nearly every pound of iron used had been raised at their own mines, smelted, rolled and finished at some of their own works. . . . We drove first to Sterkerade, the seat of the blast-furnaces, and of the commencement of these works, which now rank amongst the largest in Europe. . . . The iron is like a great deal found in the coal strata of England, bog iron-ore, and when worked up alone produces iron of no better quality than Scotch or at most Welsh pig. To improve its quality Messrs. Haniel have acquired large mines of red hematite, although at a great distance, being situated on the Upper Lahn in the duchy of Nassau. They have water-carriage to Ruhrort, and bring the ore across the Rhine in the vehicles that take coals thither, at a low cost. . . . The furnaces at Sterkerade were charged when we saw them with the ores so mixed, and with a mixture of coals and charcoal. The blast was heated by gas taken from the top of the furnace, and although the works are so old yet the modern improvements had not been neglected . . . the chief business done at Sterkerade is casting (both from the blast and cupola furnaces) of the small wares called in German 'pottery'. This term includes, besides actual pots and pans, the small stoves that are used on the Lower Rhine in every house. . . . The furnaces at Sterkerade having ample employment in these and other large and small castings, the pig-iron chiefly worked up at the rolling-mill of Oberhausen is smelted at another establishment, a few miles distant, 'Antoni Hütte', where there are three blast-furnaces. But a great deal of foreign iron, Belgian or English, as the prices happen to range, is worked up; mixed, however, as far as is practicable, with the iron of the country, which is considered to improve its quality.

The casting-house at Sterkerade is on a large scale, as two blast-furnaces and two cupola-furnaces stand in it. . . . Sterkerade and Antonihütte employ together about 400 hands. Being old establishments, nearly all the workmen live with their families in the village, which is a little world of itself, or come to their work from places two or three miles distant. Nearly all are little landowners, with at least gardens to their cottages; for although the neighbourhood now has a cultivated appearance, yet it is not so long since all was heath, and land was to be had on very cheap terms. These works have given it a very different value. . . . Oberhausen . . . lies about three miles to the east of Sterkerade. . . . The works of Oberhausen, from a hasty view, may be estimated to stand upon about as much ground as those of Low Moor in Yorkshire. . . . The central part of the works is occupied by the rolling mill, round which 37 puddling and reheating furnaces are ranged, each with its hammer and rolls to correspond. . . . Nasmyth's steam-hammer, and the Scotch mill to supersede the puddling hammer, may be seen here. . . . The attention of Messrs. Haniel, Huyssen and Jacobi is wisely directed as much to the 'morale' as to the 'matériel' of their works. . . . As more than 1,000 hands are employed at Oberhausen. . . . With a view to lessen the inconvenience of distant lodging, a refectory is established on the premises, where the men get a bowl of soup, with meat in it, vegetables and sufficient bread, for about sixpence, served in a neat and comfortable manner; the room answering for a place to warm themselves in during the winter season. This last provision is especially requisite in iron-works in Germany, where the temperature often varies from 150° at the furnaces, and 90° at the rolls, to the freezing-point, or below it, without. Beer is sold on the premises for the workmen but no spirits, and they have opportunity enough of heating their little coffee-kettles, without one of which no man of the Lower Rhine goes to work.... Another good arrangement in these works is the obligatory deposit of a small portion of wages in the savings' bank ... it tends to raise the moral feeling of the men, and to excite self-respect, qualities to which this firm wisely trusts in all cases.

11/16 A Belgian Colliery, c.1840

MATHIAS DUNN, *View of the Coal Trade of the North of England* (London, 1844), pp. 190–192.

I had an opportunity of seeing the operations of the colliery of Grand Hornu, three miles to the westward of Jemappe, in the Hainault district, and said to be upon the most extensive and improved scale in the country. It is about 330 yards deep, and very similar in its arrangements to that of Produit.

The principal pumping engine has a 74 inch cylinder, upon the high pressure principle, with a 7 feet stroke in the cylinder, and 6 feet in the pit, the depth of which is nearly 190 fathoms, and the pumps, ranged in no less than 10 columns, are of 12 inches diameter. Three cylindrical boilers are attached to this huge engine, each 6 feet by 40 feet, with one fire and a single tube each, through which the flame passes. The pressure required for this enormous engine, is only 7 or 8 lbs, per square inch.

A very splendid erection of offices, workmen's houses, a foundry, and engine building establishment, are attached to this colliery, which used formerly to work 6 or 7 pits, and to raise 800 tons per day, employing 2,300 or 2,400 people, and making very large profits; but a couple of pits are now all that are required.

The colliery was founded about 40 years ago, by a Mons. Degorge, who had to struggle through great difficulties; but at length he lived to reap from it a large fortune. His widow resides upon the premises, which is one of the few extensive collieries in Belgium, carried on by a private family.

It is situated at the bottom of the basin, and has already worked more or less in 15 seams of the Flenu (the highest beds), which is a coal of fine quality, but soft. A good deal of this coal is conveyed to the Parisian market, by means of the spacious canals which intersect the country, and connect it with France. The distance from hence to Paris is about 180 miles and the cost of transit nearly as much as the value of the coals.

The seams lie at an inclination of about one in nine degrees, and for the most part rest upon a soft fire clay thill, which serves the hewer to curve in. According to the customary mode of conducting their workings, they prefer the thin to the thick seams, inasmuch, as the goaves or hollows are more readily stowed up, and the working of a five or six feet seam would be utterly impracticable under the present system.

I could not discover that they apply any ventilating furnaces at these collieries; but they have a pneumatic spiral ventilator, wrought by a steam engine. I had no opportunity of comparing its results; but I was far from being impressed with the feeling, that it was comparable to the ventilating furnace.

Ordinary working places are two or three yards wide; but owing to the working off the pillars, and the continual state of creep, every thing appeared to me in great confusion, and I particularly remarked the crushed state of the solid coal.

A vast number of persons, mostly women, and an exorbitant quantity of timber are required, to counteract this perpetual and injurious pressure, and the ventilation appeared to me very faint, ineffective, and inadequate to subdue the naturally high temperature; but most fortunately for every one concerned, the coal seems to produce no inflammable gas. . . .

The colliers use nothing but linen and cotton clothing, which must be attended with grievous consequences, in case of fire.

In fiery collieries, they frequently advert to the ventilating furnace; but on account of the accumulated inflammable air in the goaves, and the contiguity to the upcast pits, they dare not apply it in the ordinary way; they, therefore, provide a recess towards the upper part of the shaft, in which the furnace is placed, and which is fed with fresh air, brought from the surface, by means of a brattice or adjoining pit.

I had not an opportunity of seeing the district of Valenciennes, across the French frontier; but was told that some of their coal pits are 620 metres in depth, and that the workmen are not allowed any other means of ascending or descending, than by ladders.

The mode of managing the coals aboveground is very inferior to the method practiced in England. The cuffat tub, 7½ feet by 3 feet, and containing 30 cwt. of coals, is *upended* by a chain and winch upon a platform, where the coals are shovelled, and hacked, and cleaned, under a very heavy breakage. A few wide horizontal bars are fixed upon the said platform, over which they are raked by numerous females, into either waggons or oblong baskets placed across a sort of rolley, by which they convey them to the canal; these baskets contain 5 or 6 cwt. each. The small coal is then barrowed up into large heaps, until the time of sale arrives; and the large coals are selected by hand, into the two denominations of Gayettes and Gayletteries.

II/17 The Anzin Mining Company

A. GARCENOT, *Les bassins houillers du nord ouest de l'Europe: Les mines d'Anzin, Étude historique et technique* (Paris, 1884), pp. 13-16. (Ed. Tr.)

In 1830 the total output of the Anzin Company was 500,000 tons; the importation of Belgian coal into France principally from the areas to the west of Mons was 511,000 tons. Thus whilst the Anzin Company had only doubled its output between 1815 and 1830 the importation of Belgian coal had increased by 158%.

... However, for twenty years great improvements had been brought about in the management of the works; transport in the galleries by means of wheeled tubs had gradually replaced all the old methods; the rectangular shafts had become polygonous; the progress of mechanical knowledge had allowed the replacement of horses by machines, which, although very low powered were, nevertheless indicative of the advances which had been made both in methods and ideas.

The coal industry entered into an age of great prosperity; the establishment of the railways was to precipitate developments by rapidly increasing new outlets and stimulating the industries of Northern France.

Thus, in 1840, extraction of coal at Anzin had increased to 623,000 tons; the importation of Belgian coal had become even more rapid and at that time amounted to 749,000 tons; consumption needs grew more rapidly than Anzin production; the Company redoubled its efforts.

But in view of the ever-increasing consumption, several prospecting companies had, for some years, made numerous sinkings around the concessions granted to the Anzin Company, and had found coal, particularly at Vicoigne, where the thin coal seams of the Fresnes-Vieux-Condé range had been worked since 1838. The competition of the Vicoigne coal with the coal mined at Fresnes-Vieux-Condé forced the Anzin Company, after a fierce struggle, to lower the selling price of coal below the net cost, and with the object of ruining its young rival, to buy out the Hasnon Company and its interests in the Vicoigne Company; then in 1843 to come to an agreement with the Vicoigne Company for the sale of Anzin and Vicoigne thin coals; the Anzin Company was granted the sole right to sell the thin coals of the two companies for ninety-nine years; Vicoigne was to have only a third of the total profits on sales; Anzin was to receive two-thirds.

The rapid development of the workings of the Douchy Company (founded in 1822) also began to affect the Anzin Company, as a result of the competition it introduced with its high quality coals.

Prospecting continued ... between Douai and Leforest to discover in the west the extension of the Valenciennes coalfield, where M. Bracquemont, chief engineer of the Vicoigne mines, had confirmed the existence of coal in 1844; this guaranteed further problems for the Anzin Company.

Its struggle with the Vicoigne Company had been very costly; the Anzin Company feared a fierce competitive struggle, in spite of the considerable increase in coal consumption in the industrial regions of the north of France, and the vast market which was opened up for its business; thus it hastened to accept the proposals for an association which the Dourges Company made to it in 1852, conjointly with the Vicoigne Company, in the secret hope of a future agreement, similar basically to that which it had already contracted with the latter.

The tendency of the Anzin Company to extend its influence over the growing coal workings in the Pas-de-Calais coalfield is clearly shown in its circular to shareholders on the 20 June 1857, especially in the following passages:

> The discovery of the coal basin in the Pas-de-Calais was of vital interest to the future of our Company. The Management could not remain indifferent to an event of such importance. After having reflected deeply about its situation it thought that it could not do better than to become involved in new enterprises, in order, in the first place, to become clearly aware of what was happening; secondly, to contribute to developments, as a matter of common interest, by encouraging the principles of a soundly regulated industry; thirdly, and finally, to share in the prosperity and to indemnify itself against any adverse effects which might have arisen, if it so happened that the rapid development of the other coal companies affected Anzin; a situation which up to now has not occurred.

11/18 Fluctuations in French and Belgian Coal Mining

A. BURAT, *L'industrie houillère en 1868* (Paris, 1869), pp. 1-6. (Ed. Tr.)

For the first time for many years, we have to testify to a break in the increasing progress of coal production in France and Belgium.

Since the end of 1867 a persistent crisis has seriously affected a large number of industries which consume industrial coal; as a result serious difficulties have arisen in disposing of both fine and unpicked coal in the principal markets, selling prices have weakened and this has restricted output.

. . . Coal sales in 1867 had been quite favourable, and it was only in the last six months of that year that the symptoms of the crisis which affected the industry in 1868 began to manifest themselves. The demand for coal for a hard winter prevented the immediate appreciation of the gravity of these first symptoms, but . . . the 1867 output, already affected by the slackening demand for industrial coal, did not reach the level which had been previously forecast.

. . . During 1868, the coalfields of the Nord and the Pas-de-Calais, Mons and Charleroi have been affected by the fact that there are no markets for industrial coal.... Most of the Belgian pits are on a five-day week, a situation which created riots at Charleroi, which were especially regrettable, since they could result only in unemployment. In August 1868 the adjudication for the Belgian State Railways took place. The prices fixed in 1867 at 8 francs 50 to 9 francs 50 for small coal were made at 5 francs 45 to 6 francs 40; i.e. a reduction of more than 3 francs.

... Some people might have regarded this as a favourable state of affairs. But really, it is a symptom of the industrial recession which is gripping Belgium. In France the reductions have been less pronounced, and there is every reason to hope that in the course of 1869 the situation will revert to normal.

When the coal industry is studied over a period of time, the study assumes a special interest; it is possible to follow the general upward swing in production and it is noticeable that stationary coal production, or a recession, coincides with grave circumstances which have all-pervading social effects.

There is proof of this assertion in the table on page 339, which gives the figures for French coal production and consumption since 1830.

The industrial history of the country is related exactly by these figures.

Between 1815 and 1830 the first large-scale industrial establishments were founded in France. Each year brought some progress, which was based chiefly on the completion of canals and river improvements.

1830 was characterised by a break in production and consumption. It took three years for the 1829 levels to be regained, but ... the railways from St. Étienne to Lyons, and from Grand'Combe to Beaucaire and the establishment of mail steamers laid the foundations for new bursts of activity.

Railways were gradually extended and metallurgical establishments multiplied and increased in number. The vast establishments of Allier, Moselle, the Nord and the Franche Comté were developed in addition to the already existing centres in Saône-et-Loire, Aveyron and the Loire. Workshops for the production of railway materials, locomotives and machines of all kinds were founded everywhere. 1848 stopped this trend, and it took five years for industry to recover its equilibrium. In 1853 the economy was again buoyant; 1855-1866 was a period of vertiginous expansion characterised by an unprecedented development in business and enterprise.

Such progress was very difficult to sustain, and although the reasons are not yet clear, the break came at the end of 1867 and continues into 1868....

We regret that we do not have the figures for the production and consumption of coal in 1868, but for the Nord and Belgium these figures must be lower than those for 1867.

	Production		*Consumption*	
1830	1,862,665	tons	2,493,944	tons
1831	1,760,385	,,	2,301,726	,,
1832	1,962,855	,,	2,520,159	,,
1833	2,057,631	,,	2,736,662	,,
1834	2,489,840	,,	3,214,405	,,
1835	2,506,416	..	3,288,258	,,
1836	2,841,946	,,	3,814,905	,,
1837	2,980,735	,,	4,081,186	,,
1838	3,113,252	,,	4,304,887	,,
1839	2,994,861	,,	4,180,753	,,
1840	3,003,382	,,	4,256,711	,,
1841	3,410,199	,,	4,979,892	,,
1842	3,592,084	,,	5,203,415	,,
1843	3,692,539	,,	4,293,508	,,
1844	3,782,739	,,	5,576,850	,,
1845	4,202,091	,,	6,343,069	,,
1846	4,469,542	,,	6,608,884	,,
1847	5,153,200	,,	7,618,273	,,
1848	4,000,400	,,	6,222,305	,,
1849	4,049,100	,,	6,528,678	,,
1850	4,540,000	,,	7,130,284	,,
1851	4,780,000	,,	7,438,263	,,
1852	4,903,000	,,	7,958,500	,,
1853	5,938,000	,,	9,422,100	,,
1854	6,827,000	,,	12,856,800	,,
1855	7,453,100	,,	12,298,700	,,
1856	7,925,700	,,	12,896,200	,,
1857	7,901,800	,,	13,147,500	,,
1858	7,352,600	,,	12,893,000	,,
1859	7,482,600	,,	13,262,200	,,
1860	8,303,700	,,	14,270,300	,,
1861	9,423,300	,,	15,402,800	,,
1862	10,290,300	,,	16,274,600	,,
1863	10,709,700	,,	16,513,100	,,
1864	11,242,600	,,	17,491,500	,,
1865	11,300,000	,,	17,800,408	,,
1866	12,000,000	,,	20,217,380	,,

11/19 Coal Mining in Germany and Belgium, 1858

M. JODLBAUER, *Wirthschaftliche Wandernotizen* [*see* Document **11/5**], pp. 27–29. (Ed. Tr.)

There has been a great revolution in the economic conditions of the coal and iron industry. The two are so closely linked to each other that we shall not treat them separately here. In some regions coal is the first condition of production and it will remain so wherever there is no large fall of water to substitute water power. Its low price of 8 shillings a ton in Manchester has secured manufacturing industry for that town, as for similar reasons in Sheffield; it supports the Belgian iron industry in the Meuse valley between Namur and Liege, and in Germany it has conjured up huge works, as it were overnight, in Westphalia and the Rhine Province, notably in the Ruhr district. The price rise in the course of recent years called forth constant trial borings, and during the past year many sites were covered by boring apparatus. In Werden, and still more in Düsseldorf, mine shares were the sole topic of conversation; this is understandable, if we consider that the price rose by over 50% and that coal fetched 7–8 Sgr. per Schäffel.* As a rule, coal is won in deep mines, except in the Hanover area where some coal of poor quality is won by level mining. It is in deep mining that the advantages of the steam engine are most obvious; between the Ruhr and the Rhine, near Ruhrort, coal is found 910 feet deep, which could not otherwise be won, as it is impossible to drive an adit from the workings. A steam engine of 190 horse power, burning coal out of the mine itself, raises 13 cubic foot of water with each lift every 14 seconds; another steam engine raises the coal, a weight of 16 Schäffel to a height of 93 Lachter* in 57 seconds; as the work continues day and night, the output per day is over 2,200 Schäffel, at a minimum price of 4,842 Thaler*; despite this large output, no stocks have been accumulated.

In the nature of things coal cannot bear a high cost of transport, and the mine owners therefore attempt to persuade all projected railway companies to lay out their lines as closely as possible to their pits. Thus the Steele-Vohwinkel Railway, which branches off the Elberfeld-Düsseldorf line, was built solely for the transport of iron and coal. Actually, it is the Belgian coalmines which enjoy the most favourable geographical position, and this explains the great increase in Belgian coal mining and the low price of Belgian coal. The coal pits or levels are in the Meuse valley, close by the river and the railway; the gauge of the private tramroads leading from the pithead to the main railway is mostly the same as that of the main lines, so that their trucks can be brought right into the pits and are loaded directly by the miners. As these tramroads often form an inclined plane, i.e. the coal is

* See Glossary.

lifted right at the beginning to a height above that of the main line, transport is downhill and saves further cost and trouble. The local blast furnaces are sited hard by the iron mines and are so constructed as to allow the coal to be brought in on the railway without further unloading direct to the top of the furnaces and tipped into them. Several of the blast furnaces have canals close by them, connecting the works with the Meuse; saving on transport costs is a leading principle of the Belgian coal and iron industry, and this is in particularly sharp contrast to the iron industry of the Siegland.

11/20 Repeal of Prussian Mining Law, 1860

a Regulations for the Ruhr area of 16 June 1860, to carry out the Act of 21 May 1860.

b Protest of Miners of the Dortmund District to the Dortmund Mine Office (Bergamt), 11 September 1860.

Printed in GERHARD ADELMANN (ed.), *Quellensammlung zur Geschichte der sozalien Betriebsverfassung* . . . [see Document 5/4], pp. 127–130. (Ed. Tr.)

a *Regulations of enforcement, 16 June* 1860

(1) The mine owner operating under the supervision of the Mining Authority shall in future not be subject in the winning or use of his minerals to the control of the latter except as may be necessary to preserve the continuance of mining, the safety of the workings, the surface above ground in the interest of private and public traffic, and the life and health of the workmen.

The Mining Authority shall be competent to pass the working plans submitted by the mine owner or his agent.

(2) Contracts between the mine owner and the managers, the other officials and the miners, are left wholly to the free agreement of the contracting parties; the Mining Authority shall cease in future to take part in the employment or discharge of the above persons, as well as in the fixing and payment of shift wages and bonds.

(3) The Mining Authority confirms the works regulations promulgated by the mine owners for their works.

(4) Any contract between the mine owner and his miners may be cancelled, unless otherwise agreed, on fourteen days' notice open to either of the contracting parties. . . .

(7) The mine owner or his agent is obliged to provide a certificate to any miner leaving his employ, showing the type and duration of his employment, and, if required, also his conduct, which has to be attested by the police authority without charge. If he refuses to issue this certificate, the police authority shall provide it at his expense, and he shall be liable to a fine of from one to five Taler.*

* See Glossary.

(8) No mine owner or his agent may employ miners of whom they know that they have been employed in mining in the past, unless they are shown the leaving certificate issued by the last employer or the police authority respectively (7 above). Breaches of this regulation shall be punished by a fine of up to ten Taler and, in case of inability to pay, by imprisonment.

(16) Mine owners or their agents who seek to induce miners or the authorities to commit acts or to grant concessions, by conspiring with the owner of another mine to stop work, or to dismiss or refuse to employ miners unwilling to accept their demands, as well as all those attempting to persuade others to such acts, shall be punished by up to one year's imprisonment.

(17) Miners who seek to induce mine owners, their agents or the authorities to commit acts or to grant concessions, by conspiring to stop work or to prevent it in one or more mining company or attempting to persuade others to conspire in this manner, shall be punished by up to one year's imprisonment.

(18) Miners absenting themselves from their work without lawful cause and without permission or withdrawing from their work, or who are guilty of gross disobedience or persistent obstructiveness, shall be fined 20 Taler or given equivalent prison sentences.

b *Complaint of the Miners*

Honourable Royal Mining Office,

The Act of 21 May 1860 is already having a grievous effect. As early as 15 August we asked that the 8-hour shift be left in being, but already in the Margaretha pit – confirmed or not, we cannot tell – 9-hour shifts have been introduced. Including both winding times, the miner, the poor fellow who has the most dangerous, unhealthy and least well paid job, must therefore serve for 10 hours.

In consequence, the largest part of the men there have stopped work. No doubt other mines will follow their example. But the total result will be that thousands of miners will leave their trade and the pits will be greatly embarrassed.

The new constitution between the mining companies and the miners has only been desired by a few individuals, going about their design in devious ways. Thus a certain Otto has been collecting large numbers of signatures petitioning for a change in the regulations without allowing the signatories to see the contents of the document they were signing.

There may originally have been few or many arguments in favour of the Act: it has been proved a failure in practice and will never prove a success for any of those concerned. First, it so undermined the position of the miners that they regret having entered their trade. For the miner has to leave his hearth even if he is not guilty of any moral offence, if he merely caught his superior or employer in a bad mood.

Most miners are married and no longer young, but no one is asked about this when he is being discharged.

Secondly, the pits suffer considerably by frequent change of personnel, and if the companies think they are getting an advantage out of sacking the registered miners and employing day labourers instead, they will soon see how wrong they are. . . .

11/21 Rise of the French Iron and Steel Industry and its problems

a J. J. BAUDÉ, *De l'enquête sur les fers et des conditions du bon marahé permanent des fers en France* (Paris, 1829), pp. 46–49. (Ed. Tr.)

b F. MARSHALL, *Industry and Trade in France* [*see* Document **9/4**], pp. 179–186, 203–204.

a In France, most of the works in the Franche Comté, Champagne, Berry, Burgundy and Normandy carry out the two operations [of making iron] using charcoal, and it cannnot be denied that iron produced in this way has real superiority.

Other establishments, such as Gondrecourt (Meuse), Hayange (Moselle), Fourchambault (Nièvre), St. Julien, Lorette and Terrenoire (Loire), and Le Creusot (Saône-et-Loire), make only mineral fuel iron but 'treat'* charcoal iron and coke iron which is produced in the neighbourhood.

We have then, simultaneously, the different processes, which have succeeded one another in England. . . .

In the charcoal process four tons of charcoal are needed to produce one ton of iron. A ton of charcoal costs usually 75 francs†; thus on this hypothesis fuel accounts for 300 francs in the price of a ton, of which 150 francs is spent on the smelting of the ores and 150 francs on the conversion of cast iron into iron.

In the process using coke, 11 tons are needed to obtain one ton of bar iron; of these eleven tons, eight are employed in the smelting of the ores and three in the treatment of the pigs. If we use the prices prevailing at St. Étienne, the amount of fuel needed to produce one ton of iron costs 88 francs in those establishments which are near to the coal mines: 50 francs are spent in obtaining pig iron, and 38 on treating it.

From what has been said, it can be appreciated that the only works which use charcoal and can remain in business in coal-producing areas, are those which set quality production against the high price of their iron. Up to now,

* i.e. Puddle. We are indebted to Mr. W. K. V. Gale for his help at this point [Eds.]
† See Glossary.

it would seem almost impossible, even in England, to make really fine iron by using coke; iron produced in some forges will have little to fear from the competition of iron made by using coke processes because such iron cannot be used in the same way; indeed, it can be said that in certain respects the increasing use of these coarser forms of iron will create new uses for this fine iron.

The more consumers become aware of their real interests, the more they will acknowledge that at present the difference in the durability of good and bad iron is a more important factor than price, and they will look with increasing favour on the former.

These advantages relating to fuel can be neutralised to some extent by the inaccessibility of raw materials. That is what has happened at St. Étienne, of which we have just written; thus the cast iron obtained there is not much cheaper than that of the Franche Comté. The only advantage possessed by the large furnaces of the coal-producing area is that because coal is abundant, their productive limits are regulated purely by market demand whereas the charcoal based producers are restricted by the limited availability of supplies of wood.

In France, and particularly in Burgundy and in the Franche Comté, the pig iron being given, its conversion into one ton of iron costs:

Charcoal	—	150 francs
Workers	—	20 francs
Cost of Management, upkeep, rent of workshop, interest, etc.	—	40 francs
Total	—	210 francs

In England the same process costs today

Fuel	—	25 francs
Labour	—	28 francs
Interest	—	12 francs
Total	—	65 francs

The price of fuel at St. Étienne is the same as in England, and therefore the best method of production has been to treat the pig iron of the Saône area by the English processes. The iron of Burgundy and the Franche Comté flowed principally to Lyons, St. Étienne and towards the Rhône; it was thought that, excluding transportation costs, the St. Étienne iron would be 153 francs per ton cheaper but this expectation has not been realized and the anticipated profits have been diminished by the outlay which has been necessary to meet the obstacles which every new industry has to face.

b The development of the French iron trade during the last forty years is one of the striking features of the industrial history of the century.

11/21 *Rise of the French Iron and Steel*

With the single exception of the Creusot works, which were established in 1783 on a joint deposit of both iron and coal, and where coke has always been used as fuel, iron was, until 1821, exclusively smelted in France with wood charcoal. This system of manufacture was natural enough in a country which even now possesses twenty-one millions of acres of forest, offering an almost inexhaustible supply of charcoal, where until a very recent date the use of coal was virtually unknown, and where iron ores, though abundantly distributed over the surface, are rarely found in the neighbourhood of coal-fields. . . .

In 1821, which date may be taken as the point of departure of the present state of the trade, there existed in France 348 charcoal works, which produced in that year 183,700 tons of iron (pig and bar together), and 2 coke works producing 3000 tons. But in 1861 the proportions had become so radically changed, that while the make of charcoal iron, of both classes, had got up to 507,000 tons, that of coal and coke iron had risen from 3000 to 1,053,700 tons. The creation of this totally new industry is the work of the last forty years; its effect has been not only to multiply eightfold the total production of 1821, but to reduce the price by two-thirds, so enabling France to begin to compete with England in parts of the European market. It certainly may be classed among the most important results which French trade has attained since the Restoration.

This immense progress has not, however, been effected without damaging the old charcoal trade. . . . but by the introduction of new processes and better administration, considerable economies have been effected in the cost of production. . . .

The trade in all its branches is not carried on under favourable circumstances, as compared with England or Belgium. The laws which regulate it are onerous and restrictive. No iron-master is allowed to become possessor of mines for his own exclusive use; all he has is a preferential right to draw ore from the neighbourhood, and anybody else may put up works alongside him and use the same mineral. Furthermore, since the law of 1810, no iron-master can acquire coal mines. The object of this singular legislation is to prevent monopoly or coalition of interests, and to give the public the benefit of the competition which the obligatory division of mineral property was expected to produce. The result is, of course, identically the contrary. Although the average price of iron ore is lower in France than in England, especially in consideration of its generally superior quality, it and the coal to work it are bought by the French iron-masters at prices which include not only royalties to the state and the landowner, but also a profit to the seller. Ores and coal are regarded in France rather as merchandise than as raw material, and the price of manufactured iron includes everywhere, with the unimportant exception of a few of the older works which possessed mines of their own before 1810, the two first profits of the dealers in this merchandise plus that of the iron-master himself. Coal at the pit costs in France about twice as much as in England, not because it is worth that difference, but because, as was shown in the preceding chapter, the coal-owners are masters of the market and fix their own prices.

The transport of coal and ore is another heavy charge; indeed, many French iron-masters assert that their expenses for coal and carriage alone amount to 5*l.* 15*s.* per ton of iron produced, which is as much as the present sale price of Welsh bar. . . . This question of transports, so important for a trade which employs such heavy raw material, is aggravated by the circumstance that the iron-masters can do nothing to help themselves in the matter. The power of cheapening local carriage by the construction of private roads or railways may be said not to exist, for they can only be established on the same conditions as apply to ordinary public works. No one can make himself a branch line, even on his own land, without first obtaining a regular concession, with all its formalities and responsibilities; and when it is got, the railway must be constructed and worked under the direct supervision of the government engineers, who have the right to alter the plans. Even the use of water power is almost as costly as steam, from the endless restrictions and charges attached to its employment. Another burden occurs in the heavy direct taxation imposed on all manufacturers, not only on their buildings and establishments, but also on the very right to trade. No industry can be carried on in France without a patent or certificate of permission, the cost of which rises in proportion with the nature and importance of the business. Some of the large iron firms pay from 4000*l.* to 8000*l.* a year in taxes on their special position as manufacturers. It is true that the income tax presses almost equally heavily on many English firms, but that is a general charge which they support in common with every one else, while the French law levies payments on the particular occupation pursued. . . .

As a compensation for all these special disadvantages, the French coal iron trade has had one great advantage; it was established with the example of England to guide it from the beginning; it was able to start under the best known conditions of arrangement and direction; time and money were not wasted in trials; and the machinery put up at the very outset was of the best workmanship and great force. . . .

The production of steel has risen rapidly. In 1826 the total made amounted to 4915 tons; in 1859, the latest date to which official quantities are published, it reached 22,988 tons, of which 13,243 tons were forge steel, 5810 cemented, and 3915 cast.* M. Petin, of Rive de Gier, told the Tariff Committee that he

* *Statistique de l'Industrie Minérale*, pp. 487, 499. (F. Marshall.)

alone now makes 6000 tons of steel a year. The progress has been stimulated by the numerous new applications for which steel has been used in France during the last four or five years. Not only is it employed for tires, axles, cylinders, and other heavy parts of machinery, but M. Petin is now manufacturing railway wheels entirely of cast steel, and in one piece. . . .

11/22 French Industry at Mid-Century

Great Exhibition of the Works of Industry of all nations, 1851 (3 vols., London, 1851), III, pp. 1168-1169.

A VARIETY of circumstances contribute to render this collection, next to that of the United Kingdom, one of the most attractive and extensive in the Exhibition. The lengthened and successful experience enjoyed by France in exhibitions of national industry gave to the exhibitors an advantage not possessed by the majority of those contributing to the Exhibition, so far, that is to say, as concerned the arrangement and execution of the minor details inseparable from a display of this description. The results of these national expositions of French industry, and their effect upon the industrial progress of the people, and the development of art applied to the things of life, have been unquestionably great, and these are now presented to notice in a palpable form. The constant intercourse between this country and France, with the facility existing in both of the means of transport, seems to account, in some degree, for the large preponderance of French contributions on the Foreign side. But to this consideration must also be added others which have sensibly operated in giving an impetus to the contributors from France, but less strongly affecting those of other exhibiting States.

No class of the Exhibition, considered in its philosophical subdivision, has been left unrepresented by the French exhibitors. In Raw Materials, Machinery, Manufactures, and Fine Arts – the four grand Sections into which the thirty Classes resolve themselves – specimens of every variety are exhibited. The total number of exhibitors amount to about 1,750, and the area occupied by their contributed articles is very large, both on the north and south sides of the Main Eastern Avenue, and in the Galleries. It is to be regretted that some misconception originally existed with reference to this Catalogue, which was with difficulty removed, the result tending, in the first instance, to the production of a very condensed notice of the articles extending little beyond a mere enumeration of the objects. By much exertion, this obstacle to the production of a descriptive catalogue was eventually overcome, and although necessarily much condensed, and assuming, even in its present state, in many parts, the appearance of a summary notice of the objects, this Catalogue wears a very different aspect to that originally prepared. This cause has in some degree also delayed its appearance.

The principal features only of this large and valuable collection can be indicated in this notice. Among the Raw Materials, the beautiful specimens of raw and thrown silk must attract universal admiration. This is a department of industry which is constantly assuming greater importance. The samples of silk wound by modifications of the customary processes are of great beauty; and an interesting specimen of cocoons in the frames in which the silkworms are reared and permitted to spin the wonderful envelope of the pupa, gives a good idea of the manner in which the culture of these insects is carried on. The hemp, wool, and other textile materials exhibited are likewise interesting. The successful application of philosophy to manufacturing chemistry for a considerable time has produced good results in this department of industry. It is a universally admitted fact that, for some of the more delicate chemical preparations, such as vegetable alkaloids, the productions of the French manufacturer excel those of other nations. The grosser products are likewise exhibited: in these, however, the same success is not so manifest as in similar productions of British exhibitors, probably because the latter are generally manufactured on a very large and extensive scale. The cements and various specimens of paints exhibited have their special value and interest. Specimens of metals and of skill in metallic manipulation are also shown, – in particular, some large specimens of beaten copper and rolled brass, and specimens illustrative of the iron manufactures. Articles of prepared food are also largely exhibited.

A good collection of Machinery is likewise shown. It includes, among many objects of interest, a large prime mover in the form of a turbine water-wheel, a mechanical contrivance for the development of power from the descent of water, of recent introduction, and already of extensive application to the cotton and silk factories of France, and to other mills. The power developed by the fluid in motion is very great, and the arrangement of the machine extremely compact and effective. The mules for cotton-spinning, the carding engines for cotton and wool, and the endless paper-making machines, form objects of instructive comparison with the magnificent display of similar machines in the British collection. The kitchen apparatus, boilers, and numerous other machines are likewise of an instructive character. The philosophical instruments and musical instruments, inclusive of the organ in the Nave, form also an interesting group of objects. Optical instruments of different kinds are exhibited in great perfection.

Among the Manufactures, attention cannot fail to be claimed by the gorgeous productions of the silk-looms of Lyons, which are arranged in cases in the Gallery. The cotton manufactures, and those of wool and linen, are not less interesting. Wherever these admit of the introduction of a design, even in the commonest articles, there the peculiar and graceful indications of artistic feeling, which render the patterns produced popular, even among those who may not be able to recognise the cause of their harmony, are manifest. The skilful arrangement of many of these articles adds much to their attractiveness in the Exhibition. The splendid tapestries of the Gobelins, and of other national manufactories, as that at Beauvais, form, perhaps, one of the most interesting features of the whole collection. They are accompanied by specimens also of Sèvres porcelain, the articles in which, inclusive of vases, paintings, &c., are of great rarity and costliness. The furniture exhibited partakes of the usual character of the French productions of this class, and many indicate the employment of talent of a high order in their design and execution.

This collection is extremely rich in those articles which form so large and important a feature in Parisian industry – articles of bijouterie, vertû, &c., and jewellery. The multitude of objects exhibited in this class, and their variety, strongly suggest the idea of a great demand for such elegances, and of the existence of many skilful designers occupied in their production. The beautiful display of jewels exhibited by Her Majesty the Queen of Spain, and the jeweller of that Court, attract universal notice. The specimens of paper and printing exhibited include a number of objects of interest; and the coloured and other lithographs, and stereotypes by new processes, evidence much progress in this department. Photographs on paper and on silver (Talbotype and Daguerreotype) are exhibited, and form a very interesting collection. The French photographers have made great progress in the art of the Talbotype (an English discovery), and beautiful pictures taken by modifications of that process are shown. Those taken on glass plates, of which the positive pictures or proofs only are shown are, in some instances, taken by a process largely employed to obtain photographs for the Royal Commissioners in illustration of the Juries' Reports. Objects of sculpture and of the fine arts are likewise exhibited, and add to the interest of the collection.

The whole collection forms a fit illustration, and also an adequate one, of the present state of the industry of France; and it is interesting to regard it, also, as in some degree offering an exemplification of the effect of exhibitions of industrial products upon the nature and quality of the articles produced. The excellence and abundance of the objects of minute art would appear to indicate a high state of refinement; but their perfection forms, however, an observable contrast to the state of articles of a more ordinary character, and extensive demand. Although much has been done in the improvement of these articles, they do not admit of comparison with the perfect execution and manufacturing skill displayed in those of a more costly description. That improvement in the manufacture of these commoner articles of life, which is now rapidly extending in France, may be in part attributable to the powerful encouragement to the production of this class of objects constantly offered at the National Expositions at Paris.

11/23 Parisian Industry

a A. AUDIGANNE, *L'industrie contemporaine, ses caractères, et ses progrès chez les différents peuples du monde* (Paris, 1856), pp. 464-467. (Ed. Tr.)

b M. A. MOREAU DE JONNÈS, *Statistique de l'industrie de la France* (Paris, 1856), pp. 329-330. (Ed. Tr.)

a The various industrial applications of Parisian art had for a long time enjoyed an exceptional and unchallenged reputation; but the exhibition of 1855 will have greatly strengthened this reputation. It is quite remarkable to see Parisian manufacture remain unrivalled, in spite of the examples and instruction it provides, in all the arts where good taste is an essential condition of success. . . . The praise for this success has been rightly given to the various people who participate in the processes of production. Perhaps, however, insufficient attention has been paid to the more general factors which exert a powerful, if indirect, influence upon industrial production.

It is always public taste which determines tastes in manufacture. But from which source does the public derive its ideas concerning beauty? Certainly, refinement is related to the development of civilisation itself; it is one of the most undeniable manifestations of social progress. Perfection in the industrial arts derives, then, from the very principles which constitute the character of the people . . . the position occupied by the industrial arts in France in general, and more particularly in Paris, is, therefore, the consequence of efforts which have been made through the centuries to make these common bonds of ideas and sentiments a distinctive attribute of our society. All men who have contributed either by extending intellectual horizons or in consolidating the bases of our society, have contributed in a more or less direct way to the development of this public appreciation of beauty. Here is why we excel in works which demand taste, whilst we encounter competition in those processes which depend upon tenacity, the spirit of enterprise, and commercial savoir-faire.

Thus the superiority of Paris in the sphere of artistic industries is easily explained by its rôle in the general development of civilisation. The part assigned to these important influences cannot lessen that which belongs to the manufacturers, designers and workers engaged in industrial production. Although there is a degree of inequality in the demands made upon the workers, the work of each of them is accomplished under the stimulus of a common inspiration. The artistic industries are precisely those which demand the highest skills in workmanship. They demand from the worker not only physical strength, but also dexterity and accuracy; often they even demand a real feeling for art.

The characteristics attributable to Parisian work are found not only in the work which Paris itself produces. It exerts a considerable influence on a large number of industries which are practised far from its walls. Indeed when one studies the comparative situation of our manufacturing towns, it is soon evident that there are great differences according to whether their products go to the great market in the capital. All the manufacturers who produce for the Paris market are stimulated to a greater or lesser degree by this and they are kept constantly on their toes. Rapid growth, and a new vitality become noticeable in a place as soon as the demands of Paris seem to penetrate there. ... The manufactories which produce goods traditionally and exclusively for consumption in isolated parts of France or else only for the foreign market, remain engulfed in a general torpor. Routine, unvaried routine, dominates their activity.

How does this difference arise? ... One can easily account for it by reference to the general circumstances we have just related, and several secondary factors, we have yet to mention. An intimate although imperceptible relationship exists between consumers and manufacturers. The taste of the first reacts powerfully on the activity of the second. If the buyers are not very exacting, and are unchanging in their tastes, why should the manufacturer depart from his well-established ways? Why should he involve himself in new expenditure, in uncertain enterprises? Since he is not obliged to vary his work to dispose of his products, he does not create anything new. Moreover, Paris centralises consumer opinion; it gathers together, by a thousand channels, all the evidence relating to the satisfaction or discontent which prevails regarding commerce. It is wonderfully placed to inform the manufacturers about this, who thus receive a salutary impetus either to expand or modify their production.

b SURVEY OF MANUFACTURING PRODUCTION IN PARIS, 1848

Extracted from the Statistics of the Chamber of Commerce

	Establishments	Value of Production	Number of workers
Gunsmithery	126	3,277,000 f.	707
Fine Jewellery	88	41,599,000	4,392
Artificial Jewellery	342	61,525,000	2,182
Steel Jewellery	57	4,963,000	1,975
Hosiery, Knitted goods	262	4,754,000	2,650
Candles	38	7,804,000	307
Metal buttons	31	4,194,000	1,349
Toys, knick knacks	63	4,321,000	2,199
Bricks, Tiles	30	2,759,000	567
Bronze founders	38	5,050,000	2,711
– Works	188	18,493,000	2,711
Embroidery	552	6,007,000	3,964
Coachbuilding	199	19,307,000	3,758
Shawls	224	9,889,000	2,190
Bookbinding	361	5,375,000	3,772
Hats	628	16,762,000	4,090
Straw Hats	116	6,800,000	2,300
Braziery	205	5,963,000	1,208
Curriers	272	23,424,000	2,431
Cabinet Making	1,831	27,982,000	8,889
Cotton Spinning	35	7,230,000	2,103
Wool Spinning	16	5,966,000	1,066
Gas Lighting	3	2,080,000	403
Gas Appliance Manufacture	22	3,785,000	707
Metal Smelting	77	10,933,000	1,979
Clock Making	978	9,410,000	2,283
Lithographic Printing Houses	292	7,798,000	2,388
Typographical Printing Houses	84	15,247,000	4,530
Blinkers	35	19,288,000	538
Distilling	119	8,276,000	318
Machine Making	238	25,647,000	6,612
Goldsmithying	42	14,322,000	671
Papers	99	3,070,000	3,291
Wallpaper	139	10,227,000	849
Lacemaking	992	28,404,000	9,494
Morocco Leather	80	4,292,000	672
Leather Glovemaking	182	14,268,000	1,950
Furriery	86	4,336,000	638
Plated metal goods	54	6,332.000	791
Pianos, Harps	194	11,486,000	2,889
Wool combing	20	7,189,000	1,075
Pottery – baked earth	32	1,090,000	444
Chemical products	41	3,459,000	188
Pharmaceutical products	197	6,353,000	188
Saddlery	283	8,915,000	1,601
GENERAL TOTAL	10,168	514,282,000 f.	131,638

11/24 Gilds in Austria and Germany

a Reports made by H.M. secretaries of Embassies and Legations etc., Report from H. ELLIOTT; Vienna, 18 January 1858 (Parliamentary Papers 1857–58. V), pp. 110–111.

b THOMAS HODGSKIN, *Travels in the North of Germany* . . . [*see* Document **3/3**], II, pp. 176–185.

a But however great may have been the depressing effects upon commerce, resulting from [other] causes, they sink almost into insignificance, if compared with the evils arising out of the system of 'Guilds and Trades,' which so effectually stifles all development of industry and energy among the lower commercial and industrial classes.

Its depressing effect upon every branch of industry is readily understood when it is remembered what an effectual impediment it raises against all efforts of individual ingenuity and activity. Each workman, from the day of his apprenticeship, may be said to be bound to one narrow branch of trade, from which there is no escape. If, later in life, he finds his tastes or instincts draw him in another direction, he must not follow them, unless he is willing again to commence life over again, and to pass through the regular rotation. If he perceives that his business might be readily expanded in a manner to be alike advantageous to himself and to the public, he is probably obliged to abandon all thoughts of it, from finding that he would encroach upon the privilege of some other guild. If, as in other countries happens every day, a workman chance to show some peculiar mechanical genius, he has here no prospect of turning his talents to account, unless they chance to lead him in the identical direction in which he had first been started in life.

Nor is patient plodding industry allowed a fair chance. The workman must work for the 'meister', and for him alone; for although his master may not give him work sufficient to occupy the half of his time, if he venture to work upon his own account he at once falls under the lash of the law, and the half-employed tailor or shoemaker who, in his leisure hours, makes and sells a coat or a pair of shoes to support his family commits a punishable offence.

The shopkeepers are subjected to similar annoyances and restrictions. No one can open a shop without a license, obtained upon his giving proof of possessing a certain amount of capital, and the evidence which is required of this, although entirely inefficacious for the object intended, is in its form vexatious in the extreme, for not even the production of the full amount of the money is accounted sufficient proof for the purpose. The license also, when granted, only authorizes him to sell a certain class of articles arbitrarily determined upon, and no attempt must be made to deal in goods which have been placed in another category, however intimately connected they may be with his own trade. If an opportunity were to offer itself to him of making an advantageous purchase of goods which he is certain of being able to retail with profit, he must not avail himself of it unless they come within the narrow limits of his license; and above all if, in the town where he is established, general trade is declining, or his own branch of it overloaded, he has no power of moving and of setting up somewhere else where they [sic] may happen to be an opening for him.

These regulations make it difficult for a foreigner to set up establishments in Austria, and the consequence is, that inventions and improvements are often in operation in other countries long before they are adopted here.

The whole system is, in fact, that of a complicated monopoly, or rather of a complication of monopolies, all jealous of any encroachment on their own privileges, but of which each member is content to submit to vexatious regulations and restrictions in order to secure to himself immunity from that public competition which he rightly believes would lead to his ruin if it did not stimulate him to greater exertion and industry than he has been in the habit of bestowing on his business.

Monopolies thus pervade the whole empire, and the Government appear to have considered that the only method of encouraging commerce was to increase the number of them, and have seldom, therefore, shown a backwardness in granting what are here called 'exclusive privileges.'

b All these are set in motion, and kept in motion by a law common to the corporation of every trade. According to this law, every apprentice is obliged to travel, or, as it is called, *wandern*, for three years from the expiration of his apprenticeship, in search of knowledge, before he is allowed to settle in any city as a master in which guilds are yet in existence. This is one of the most important regulations of these guilds in which they differ from the corporations of our own country.

From the minute division of landed property which has been described, it might be expected that Germany would be, like Ireland, overrun with a famished and a degraded population. It is certainly far less so than our sister island; and possibly much of this evil may have been prevented by the wisdom of a regulation also common to all the trades. This is, that no journeyman shall marry. If he do, – if he even impregnate a woman, – he is banished from their society, he can obtain no employment in the trade, and he has no resource but common daily labour to save him from starving.

These two regulations, which seem very important, are not, however, invariably praise-worthy. It is not a rational objection to a man marrying, that he is a journeyman, though it be a very rational one, that he is not able to maintain a wife and family; and many men set up for masters before they otherwise would, in order to obtain the privilege of marrying.

There is possibly no method by which men who have a sufficient stock of previous knowledge, and who desire to increase it, may improve themselves more than by travelling. It appears to have been from this idea that the law was made which obliges every young man, after his term of apprenticeship is expired, to seek work abroad as a journeyman, for three years, before he can settle as a master. Many people of this description, however, must be perfectly unfit to travel, and it leads them into much dissipation.

It is degrading, and often destructive to the upright independence of young men, to wander about the country with a privilege to beg. I have had various opportunities, in fact, of witnessing the dissipation which the practice of wandering produces, to say nothing of the idleness necessarily occasioned by so frequently being out of employment. All the trades have different rules as to the manner of treating their wandering brethren when they arrive at any town in which guilds are established. Some make it a rule to give them only a lodging, others a lodging and a certain sum of money, and others, as the smiths, assemble at their house of call whenever any brethren arrive, and pass the night in jollity and mirth. All travelling journeymen have regular passports called wandering-books, and the regulations by which they are to be governed, such as not to stay longer than twenty-four hours in any one town, if they do not find employment, such as to beg in a regular manner, and apply to the magistrates for what is called the *Zehrpfennige*, subsistence-money, are printed in the first page. Such passports were formerly given by the magistrates of the towns, and were then called certificates. I have reason to believe, from some police reports that I have seen, that a great part of all the persons sent out of different towns as vagabonds are wandering journeymen.

The German mechanics, from seeing various cities, from mixing with a variety of men, possess in general a great deal of knowledge, and of freedom in opinion and action; but they are poor in spirit, averse to labour, and more given than the other classes of the society to joviality and dissipation. The advantages of travelling, when men themselves like it and choose it, and are fit to travel, are very great, but to compel the whole of so large a class of men as the journeymen mechanics to travel, by a law, is so absurd as to prescribe precisely the same regimen to the sick and to the healthy. When it was first made, also, there was little other communication between towns than what arose from people visiting them; there was no post, no press, and no periodical publications to give an account of improvements; and then, compelling the younger members of the guilds to travel in search of knowledge was much more rational than at present. One great advantage, apparently, of this law, is, that it keeps the journeymen on a level with the demand for their labour. The assistance afforded them by the corporations when they are compelled to wander, protects them from absolute distress, and, constantly circulated about the country, they are always conveyed to the spot where they are most wanted. Yet we know from experience, that this beneficial effect can be produced by the mere demand for labour, without a law to enforce and compel men to go where they are wanted.

The makers of guild laws have erred, as almost all law-makers err, from not distinguishing two things which are in themselves essentially distinct and different. These are, a *desired line of conduct*, and a *law* to compel that line of conduct.

The guilds are not at present universally established in Germany, though formerly there was not a single trade through the whole country, not even that of floating rafts down rivers, but what had its own guild laws. Guilds are abolished through the whole of the Prussian territories, and in Bavaria. The monarchs have laid a tax on every trade, by requiring every person to pay for permission to exercise it. They pay soldiers, but tradesmen must pay them. Guilds were abolished wherever the French power reached, but they are now again restored in various places, in Hannover for example, to all their former privileges. There are some towns free from them, but they are the offspring of towns, and are still generally found in all the large ones. They were originally combinations of men, so well for political as for other purposes, but they have long ceased to take any part either in the government of the towns, with the exception of the Hanse towns, or in the government of the country.

Two of the guild laws, whose influence is most important, have been mentioned. A third regulation is, that every person wishing to practise any art, whose members form a guild, must serve three or four years as an apprentice to learn that art; and there is no one, not even that practised by merchants, which has not a guild; so that every species, almost, of industry, is subject to this restriction. No journeyman can be employed who has not served a regular apprenticeship. Some trades, such as butchers, bakers, chimney-sweepers, are called close trades. Others are open. In the former only a limited number of masters is allowed in any one town, from a supposition that more could not obtain a living; in the latter the number is not limited. After serving an apprenticeship, and travelling as a journeyman, every person who wishes to establish himself as a master must first make some finished piece of work, called a *Meisterstück*, to prove his capability to work. If he is not the son of a citizen, he must buy the right of citizenship in the town where he wishes to settle. The price, of course, is various in different towns. It has long been a law that certain trades shall be only carried on within the walls of towns, and no journeyman dare do a piece of work on his own account. He must be employed by a master regularly established in a town. Formerly this privilege was confined to fewer towns than at present, and formerly those masters who settled in the country were obliged to enrol themselves in the guild of some town, and contribute to its expence. There were formerly still more hindrances to becoming a master. A man was obliged, for example, in some towns, to have a house of his own before he could be a tailor, and to prove himself not to belong to any family which had been ennobled.

These regulations were originally made by members of the trades themselves, and not by the governments. They have failed in their laudable efforts to ensure good workmen by sending them to travel, and by making them give proofs of their ability. I can safely assert, that all the common trades, such as tailors, shoemakers, bakers, smiths, have not attained so great a degree of perfection in Germany as in England. What may also possibly be deemed a proof of their uselessness is, that *milliners*, who have no guilds, are as clever in Germany as in other countries. It has been justly observed, that most of the great improvements which have of late years been made in the machinery and manufactories of England, have been made by persons not apprenticed to the arts they have improved, consequently, even the fewer restrictions as to apprenticeships which are found in England than in Germany, by hindering ingenious men from following the bent of their inclination, have been pernicious to improvements. The most manufacturing part of Germany is the country about the Rhine, and there, I believe, guild laws have been long abolished. The guild laws, therefore, of Germany, extending to every trade, may be considered as having in part caused the Germans not to make the same progress in manufactures as we have made. And as they regulate so many of the actions of men, they may also be regarded as aiding to produce that unenterprising character which is ascribed generally to the Germans.

The partial abolition of these regulations, and the works which have been written in Germany on the subject of guilds, prove that our neighbours are sensible of their injurious nature; however, it is impossible to avoid remarking, that the observations have been chiefly or wholly made by men whose profession was learning. I have talked to several tradesmen on the subject, and never met with but one individual, and he was a journeyman, whose years of wandering were expired, and who could not get settled, in which the tradesmen did not approve of the guild laws. The momentary abolition of them by the French gave a sort of licence to journeymen. Every one who could pay the tax on trades set up for a master, and a vast deal of poverty and misery were the consequence. This fact by no means proves the wisdom of the guild laws, though it throws some light on the effects of abolishing them by an arbitrary decree. It is, indeed, at present, an admitted fact in Germany so well as in Britain, that all such regulations as the guild laws prevent much good.

It ought not, however, to be the government which should abolish them. Its interference is above all things to be deprecated, and its only duty on this subject is to refuse its support to them, and leave them to be abolished by the rest of the society refusing to submit to them.

11/25 Foreign Contributions to German Industrialization

T. C. BANFIELD, *Manufactures*, etc. [*see* Document **11/4**], pp. 236-237, 242-243.

The quantity of zinc smelted in the Rhenish district is given for 1846 at 2616 tons. It has hitherto chiefly been confined in this province to an establishment belonging to M. Rheinhard, opposite Ruhrort, and the French Company at Stollberg. The mining-lists, however, name no less than forty-seven zinc-works in all Prussia. Another large joint-stock company, established under the firm of the Société Metallurgique, [sic] was not at work in 1846. A considerable quantity of zinc-ore (calamine) is gained on the Prussian territory, which is smelted in Belgium. A curious diplomatic dilemma gave occasion to this. By the treaty of Vienna a certain portion of the frontier of Prussia towards Belgium was to run due north and south at a given point. When the measurement was undertaken, the commissaries started a difficulty about the variation of the compass. They could not agree; and at length it was settled that the magnetic pole should decide the direction of the line one year, and the real pole for the year following. It so happens that a portion of the mines of the Vieille Montagne Company, whose furnaces are at Liège, are situated within this debateable limit, and, in consequence of the arrangement of the Prussian crown, draws the usual royalty from them in every alternate year. The whole of Prussia now yields about 10,000 tons of zinc, of which the greater part is smelted in Silesia. But the new companies establishing will, in all probability, very much increase the production, as they work with blende, or sulphate of zinc, in addition to the calamine or carbonate, which has hitherto almost exclusively been used. Zinc has greatly fluctuated in value, and is now low in price; but the first Rhenish smelters produced it at 15*l*. per ton, certainly with no great profit.

The new works at Stollberg, those of the Arnsau and Obernhof Companies, and the large works at Mühlheim, are all managed by young Frenchmen, élèves of the Ecole des Mines at Paris. Their knowledge appears to reflect great credit on that establishment; although, after some residence in the German mining-districts, they are disposed to show great respect to the information of the educated German miners. These French companies have commenced their operations with full confidence in the power of a good manufacturing organization, and, as they are well backed with capital, it is likely that they will realize their expectations.

Many interesting establishments lie within a short distance of Düren. Near Eschweiler, two stations distant in the direction of Aix-la-Chapelle, are iron-works that form creditable specimens of manufacturing industry in Germany. At the extensive mill of Messrs. Michaelis and Co., close to the railway between Eschweiler and Stollberg, rails are rolled in a style that quite equals the best efforts of English manufacturers. The material is a mixture of English and Belgian iron, which yields a durable and tough rail. The upper workmen are, as is common in large establishments in this part of Germany, Belgians or French. The labourers are mostly German. The large works of John Cockerill, near Liège, formed for many years a school that Germany did not possess, and hundreds of workmen acquired there the skill in working rolls and steam-hammers, that has since proved to them a source of unfailing profit. Puddlers and roll masters, instructed at Seraing, obtain wages nearly equal to those paid in England, if they are known to be steadily conducted. The work contains several sets of rail-rollers, with the corresponding puddling and reheating furnaces. Instead of a hammer the new compressor used in England may be seen there. The production is calculated at 20 tons of rails per week.

11/26 The Russian Iron Industry at Mid-Century

L. TĘGOBORSKI, *Commentaries on the Productive Forces of Russia* (2 vols., London, 1855), II, pp. 110–111, 116–121.

... We cannot be blind to the fact that most of our iron-masters, reposing on the cushion of protection, long neglected to follow the progress of this industry in foreign countries: any improvements introduced have been very recent and very exceptional; and as all experience has shown that improvement in the process of manufacture is invariably followed by increased production and diminished price, perhaps no better proof could be adduced of the unprogressiveness of ours than is afforded by the steadiness of our prices and the trifling increase of our production.... From the official returns of the department of mines ... we perceive in the course of one-and-twenty years an increase of 20 per cent. upon pig iron, and within the last twelve years an increase of 32 per cent. in the production of bar iron.... The quantity of pig iron produced, being the true index to the progress of production, we find that an increase of 20 per cent. in the course of one-

and-twenty years, or less than 1 per cent. per annum, is exceedingly trifling, especially in reference to a period during which the metallurgic industry of other countries has made such notable progress, and the demand for iron has increased in a measure totally beyond comparison with any preceding epoch. . . .

Formerly we exported iron to the extent of 2,300,000 poods*: this exportation has gradually decreased to a third of that quantity, – a natural enough circumstance, when it is remembered that whilst prices have been falling everywhere else, they have remained stationary with us. But the fact that we still continue to export from 700,000 to 800,000 poods, shows of itself that, notwithstanding the enormous reduction in the price of English irons, such is the superiority in quality of ours, that we could successfully compete in foreign markets if we only introduced those improvements which would have the effect of reducing the cost of production.

In regard to home prices, according to the preceding data, it cannot be alleged that they are much higher than in other countries (England excepted), if we consider only the prices at first hand at the place of production; but the aspect of matters is greatly altered when we consider the current market prices in different parts of the empire. . . .

Here we find the market prices rising almost to double in proportion as we remove farther from the place of production; and we know cases in which the Uralian iron, sold at Nijni-Nowgorod for 1 rouble or 1 rouble 10 kopecks per pood, fetched in the western provinces 3 roubles and upwards. Such differences of price for the same article are found in no other country: in France and Germany prices may vary from one province to another between 5 and 10 per cent., but seldom more, except for a different quality. The cause of this state of things in Russia is threefold: 1st. The geographical position of our chief iron mines. 2ndly. The bad state of our means of communication. 3rdly. The conditions of our home trade. The great seat of our iron manufacture is the Ural; that is, the eastern extremity of European Russia. . . .

Out of the fifty governments* of European Russia, there are but fourteen, or rather thirteen – for the product of Kostroma is quite insignificant – which produce iron. Of these thirteen, Perm alone furnishes more than three-fifths, and Perm and Orenburg together – two governments situated in the far east of the empire – nearly two-thirds of the total quantity produced. Of the eleven remaining governments there are but four of which the production exceeds the average wants of their population.

Thus we have upwards of 10 million poods of pig, or a corresponding quantity of bar iron, to be distributed from these six governments over the

* See Glossary.

whole remainder of European Russia, that is to say, over an area of more than 70,000 geographical square miles; moreover, of these six governments there are but two, namely, Kalouga and Nijni-Nowgorod (producing about 12½ per cent. of the total quantity), which are in the least degree centrical, whilst the other four – Perm, Orenburg, Wiatka, and Olonetz, which furnish about 82 per cent. of the total production – are situated at the eastern and northern extremities of European Russia.* A distribution so unequal of a metal of such prime necessity is not found in any other country . . .

The circumstances which we have just adverted to, joined to the difficulties of communication, of themselves explain the enormous differences in the prices of this metal; but to these must be added other circumstances connected with the iron trade of the interior. In consequence of the position of our principal iron works, the fair of Nijni has become not only their principal, but almost their sole market, so that the trade has got entirely into the hands of the Nijni merchants, and one or two houses of Moscow and Jaroslaw, who find themselves in a position to dictate the price both to the consumers and to those producers who have not capital enough to enable them to hold on – a category which unluckily comprehends not a few of our iron-masters. The iron which has arrived at Nijni during the navigation seldom reaches the distant governments before the end of several months, often not till the navigation of the following year is opened, when it comes charged with the heavy interest which the merchant requires for his outlay; and it generally has to pass through the hands of a succession of petty merchants and retail dealers before reaching the consumer in the distant provinces.

The high price of iron is a great evil, both for agriculture and for most branches of industry, – a truth so generally recognised, that it seems trivial to repeat it. Experience has also shown that there are few articles of which the consumption is so elastic, or so much regulated by price. Where cheap, as in England and the free ports of Germany, it often takes the place of wood and stone; where dear, wood usurps the place of it, even for those purposes for which the use of iron seems the most natural of any.

* We do not wish to attach undue importance to these approximative calculations, regarding them merely as the basis of a general sketch of the geographical position of our mines, and of the relations of the iron-producing districts with those which they supply with that metal. (Tęgoborski's note.)

11/27 Industry in Spain

S. T. WALLIS, *Glimpses of Spain*, or *Notes of an Unfinished Tour in 1847* (New York, 1849), pp. 86-89.

If there be any city, in the world, which sits under its own vine and fig-tree, it is Malaga. From time immemorial, as every body knows, it has lived by fig, wine, and grape. . . .

Of late years, much attention has been given in Malaga to manufactures, and they now begin to be a matter of important consideration. There is a large and prosperous iron foundry, upon the beach to the right of the harbor, and the tall chimney of the extensive establishment, upon the other side of the city, is one of the most conspicuous objects as you go in from sea. I had thought, at first, that the last mentioned works were devoted, exclusively, to the manufacture of iron, but having an opportunity of visiting them shortly after my arrival, I was surprised to see the extent and variety of the purposes, to which a very heavy capital was applied. Don Manuel Heredia, one of the principal proprietors, an intelligent and cultivated gentleman, did me the favor to accompany me through the establishment. A large and well appointed factory of coarse cottons and linens, though but a few months in operation, employed some six or seven hundred artisans. The iron foundry, occupying, at times, four or five hundred people, was complete in all the appliances needful for the smelting of the metal, and its manufacture into wire, tin blocking, and fine castings. Then there were chemical works, on an extensive scale, with all buildings and apparatus in the best style, and on the most approved modern principles. The machinery was mostly of British manufacture, and the chief engineer, and some of the superintendents of the different branches, were English. The operatives were all natives, and it was some time before I could be reconciled to seeing the jaunty jacket and *sombrero calañes*, so unromantically occupied among the looms and furnaces. Don Manuel informed me, that they found the people both willing to labor and apt to learn. The wages they received were so much higher than the ordinary rate of compensation among the working classes, that there was no difficulty in securing, always, as many hands as the establishment required. The iron ore comes from Marbella, where the Heredias have likewise an extensive foundry, and with these and their lead furnaces at Adra, they give employment to upward of two thousand people. Their establishments have, too, I learn, been largely increased since my visit. From the high price of fuel, and the difficulty of obtaining it, together with the necessarily heavy outlay in founding a new branch of industry, it is conceded that these establishments require, as certainly they deserve, the protection of the government against foreign competition. Captain Widdrington however mentions, that, on one occasion, the Heredias, being unable to complete a large contract, imported two thousand tons of iron from England, as a substitute, and suffered a serious loss, from the inferiority of the foreign article to their own. It would seem, from this, that the Spanish manufacture might readily be made to take care of itself, within a reasonable period. Indeed there could be no doubt of it, if active and judicious measures were adopted, for the proper working of the immense coal-beds of the Asturias, and the other mines of that necessary fuel, with which the Peninsula is so well provided. The iron mines of Marbella are inexhaustible, and produce from seventy to eighty per cent. of the very best metal. Catalonia and the northern provinces are equally fortunate, in the possession of mines of the very best quality, and it needs only some little of ordinary energy and wisdom, on the part of the government and the people, to make the production of iron a source of the largest wealth and prosperity. A few more such men as Heredia the elder, would work miracles. He was self-made, and yet died enormously wealthy, after a life of great mercantile enterprise and success. . . .

Malaga is indebted to Heredia, among other things, for a very pretty establishment, after the manner of the Passage Panorama, in Paris, called the *Pasage de Heredia*, and containing the finest shops in the city. It is there you find the best of the beautiful clay images, for which Malaga was first made famous by the celebrated sculptor Leon, whose descendants still carry on the manufacture. The rival establishment of José Cubero is not far off. These works are not only remarkable, as delineations of costume, and illustrations of life and manners in Spain, but sometimes reach a very high point of art, in their composition and the perfection and finish of their details.

Chapter 12 Commercial Policy

Introduction

One of the first measures passed after the fall of the *ancien régime* was the abolition of internal tolls in France, accompanied by protection against foreign imports as demanded by native industries (**6/2**). The protectionist sentiments evident then were immeasurably strengthened when Europe emerged after the Peace of 1815 open to the penetration by a British industry transformed, in isolation from the Continent, by its industrial revolution during the intervening war years. Everywhere unprotected textile and metallurgical industries clamoured for protection, justifying their demands either on the grounds of the traditional mercantilist doctrines, or on new, forward-looking claims as 'infant industries'.

In Germany the campaign was strengthened by the nationalist feeling aroused during the Napoleonic wars, which saw in the abolition of the internal tolls that still hampered traffic within the country (**3/3**), and in a simultaneous erection of common tariff barriers against outside countries, a means not only of preserving and fostering German industry, but also of creating a unified country in spite of the dynastic and separatist provisions of the Peace of Vienna. A good summary of these views is contained in List's petition to the Assembly at Frankfort in 1819 (**12/1**).

In the event, the petition proved to be abortive and the Assembly remained impotent, and it was the Zollverein which was to turn these proposals into reality, on the initiative not of the Liberal bourgeoisie, but of the Prussian bureaucracy. In the slow evolution from a Prussian internal tariff system to an almost pan-German Customs Union, the critical step was the Treaty of 1833, which united the most important states of the North, the South, and the Centre, including Prussia, Bavaria, Württemberg and Saxony (**12/2**, **12/3**). The extent to which the Zollverein performed for Germany what the revolution had achieved for France may be judged from the expansion of its interests beyond tariffs and taxation, to include rationalisation of the coinage, and ultimately the creation of the German Reich on Prussia's terms (**14/3**, **14/4**, **14/5**).

In France the power of the bourgeoisie ensured the maintenance of a high protective tariff wall (**3/11**, **3/13**, **12/4**). It required the power of Napoleon III, encouraged by his free-trade advisers and driven by his own political aims, to reverse this traditional policy by the commercial treaty with Britain in 1860 (**12/5**, **12/7**). For Britain it represented a major victory in her efforts to liberalise the world's trade at a time when she could hope to defeat most other makers of manufactured goods in fair competition; for France the shock administered to some of her more exposed industries, hitherto safe behind tariff walls, was great, and was cushioned by some (not very considerable) Government loans on easy terms (**12/8**), while the healthy cold blast of competition served to stimulate some French industries to greater exertions, and others kept their markets by the quality of their products (**12/9**, **12/10**). For both countries, however, the political motives were at least as strong as the economic (**12/5**, **12/6**).

Whatever the motives, the Treaty of 1860 ushered in a period of freer trade in Europe, extended by 'most-favoured nations' clauses which spread the reductions achieved by each contracting country to all the others. Prussia, a partner to several of these treaties, used them skilfully to extend her own hold over Germany at the expense of Austria, whose high tariffs obliged her perforce to remain outside the charmed circle (**12/11**). The Free Trade era was not destined to survive very long: its structure began to be dismantled less than twenty years after its inauguration. Nevertheless, it cannot be pronounced a total failure, for the experience of foreign example, foreign competition and foreign investment which it encouraged, helped to lay the foundations of the modern industry which was built up in the last quarter of the century in Western and Central Europe.

12/1 Petition for a Customs Union by German Merchants and Manufacturers, 1819

LUDWIG HÄUSSER, *Friedrich List's Gesammelte Schriften* (3 vols., Stuttgart & Tübingen, 1850-1), II, pp. 15-21. (Ed. Tr.)

A most humble Petition, of the German merchants and manufacturers assembled in Frankfort on Main at the Easter Fair, for the repeal of the tariffs and customs duties within Germany, and for the creation of a general German tariff system based on the principle of retaliation against neighbouring countries. Presented by Professor List from Tübingen as plenipotentiary of the petitioners. 20 *April* 1819.

The Honourable the Federal Diet.

We the undersigned German merchants and manufacturers assembled at the Frankfort Fair, bowed down by the sorry condition of German trade and industry, approach the highest authority within the German nation, in order to reveal the causes of our suffering and to beg for assistance.

In a country in which it is notorious that the majority of factories have ceased production or drag on a miserable existence, in which the fairs and markets are filled with the products of foreign nations, in which the majority of merchants have become almost totally inactive, does it still need further proof that the evil has reached its highest degree?

Either the cause of this horrifying decay of German industry and trade lies with the individual, or it lies with Society. But who can accuse the German*s* [*sic*] of lacking artistic sense or industry? Did not his praise [*sic*] become proverbial among the peoples of Europe? Who can deny him an enterprising Spirit? Did not those who allow themselves to be used as the salesmen of foreigners once lead the world's trade? It is solely in the order of Society in Germany that we find the cause of the evil.

Enlightened freedom is the precondition of the whole physical and spiritual development of man. Just as the human spirit is held down by any fetters on the exchange of ideas, so the welfare of nations is crippled by any chains put on the production and trade of physical goods. The nations of the earth can reach the highest level of material well-being only if they establish general, free and unlimited trading relations among themselves. But if they want to weaken each other, they should not only impede import and export and the transit of foreign goods, by prohibitions, surcharges, bans on shipping, etc., but abolish mutual communication altogether.

There is a view, which has become a dogma among politicians, though its erroneousness is beyond question among all educated merchants or manufacturers: and that is, that home industry can be brought into being by customs and tariff duties. Such imposts become, on the one hand, the coveted prizes of the black marketeer, who thereby imperils at the same time the alleged main objective of the State (the increase in home industry) and the alleged subsidiary objective (the collection of revenue). On the other hand, they react adversely on the existing home industries, for the country whose own goods are taxed will put the same fetters on the imports from the taxing country.

To be sure, if the neighbouring country does not pay back in the same coin, if it allows itself quietly to be impoverished and ruined by import prohibitions and protective tariffs, then the tariff system may be beneficial to one party. This is the case among Germany's neighbours. Surrounded by British, French, Dutch, etc., customs, Germany as a whole does nothing which might induce those other countries to extend general free trade, by which alone Europe could reach the highest stage of civilization.

To make up for this, the Germans restrict each other all the more. Thirty-eight customs frontiers cripple trade inside the country, and achieve approximately the same effect as if each limb of the human body were separately tied up so that the blood should on no account flow from one to the other. In order to trade from Hamburg to Austria, from Berlin to Switzerland, it is necessary to cross ten countries, to study ten tariff systems, and to pay ten sets of transit duties. But he who has the misfortune to live near a frontier where three or four States meet, spends all his life among hostile customs officers; he has no fatherland.

This is a bleak outlook for men who want to be active and productive; they look across the Rhine with envious eyes, where a great nation can trade from the Channel to the Mediterranean, from the Rhine to the Pyrenees, from the Dutch frontier to Italy on free rivers and open highways without ever meeting a customs officer.

Tolls and customs duties, like wars, can be justified only in defence. The smaller the county erecting customs barriers, the greater the evil, the more does it choke the people's activity, and the higher the costs of collection; for small countries have frontiers everywhere. Hence the thirty eight customs barriers are much more damaging to the German people than a similar barrier on the frontier of Germany, even if the latter were three times as high. And thus the strength of the same Germans who once, in the days of the Hanseatic league, traded with the whole world under the protection of their own warships, is wasting away owing to thirty eight tariff and customs systems.

We believe that we have enumerated sufficient grounds to persuade the Honourable the Federal Diet that only the abolition of the customs and tariffs inside Germany, and the creation of a common tariff frontier for the whole Confederation, can help the German trading and industrial classes, and thus the whole German economy, back on its feet again. The main reason which is usually put forward against this measure is the loss of revenue of the individual states. This objection, however, is easy to refute, for

(1) No Government has as yet openly avowed that it is levying tolls and duties solely for the sake of the revenue; on the contrary, it can be proved from most preambles to customs duties acts that the duties have been imposed to increase native industry. But if we can show that far from doing so, the duties are ruining native industry, the incidental effect that the budgets are partly covered by them cannot be sufficient reason to maintain them.

(2) The revenue from the duties levied by the Confederation as a whole will cover a large part of the shortfall. The rest could be raised by direct taxation with great advantage both to the States and the commercial and industrial classes. The Governments would thereby be able to relinquish one branch of the administration requiring much supervision and effort; and the citizens would gain the savings of the considerable administrative expenses.

(3) If we consider this at a level higher than that of mere finance, the gain to be achieved by the German states by abolishing their internal customs barriers appear immeasurably larger. It must at last be freely admitted that

customs offences are no longer considered wrong even by our most law-abiding citizens. The individual feels in a state of war against the customs system and fights it with the weapons of cunning. But nothing is a greater danger to the morals of nations than if Governments force citizens to break the law, especially if they belong to the educated classes. Nothing is more detrimental to the public esteem of the Government, than if a part of the civil service (the customs personnel) is in a state of open hostility to the people.

(4) Finally, the nature of the German Confederation itself imperatively demands the measures proposed by us. The unification of the powers and interests of all branches of the German people, for the advancement of defence abroad, and national welfare at home (in so far as this cannot be achieved by the individual Governments), is the object of the Confederation. But the interests of the German people are endangered not merely by the sword of other nations; their customs duties are a canker eating away German prosperity. It is thus that we explain the obligations of the Confederation, to defend us not only with armed might, but by a Federal customs union. A Confederation of States, like any other human society, will exist only in form and never in substance, unless it rests on the unification of interest of all individuals. Therefore we look upon the customs frontiers inside Germany which treat the people of other German States in the same way as they treat foreigners, as fetters which prevent the improvement of national welfare as well as of national feeling.

Following all this, may we be permitted to make mention of the immediate cause of this our humble petition, the new Prussian customs tariff? This tariff, we openly admit, seemed to be directed not so much against imports from France or England as against trade within Germany. The tariffs are fixed by weight. Since foreign nations send mostly fine quality goods to Prussia, while the neighbouring countries, whose high quality goods industry had already been crippled by British industry, market mostly coarse and bulky goods, the actual tariff paid by foreign goods amounts to only 6 per cent., while the German have to pay mostly 25-30, at times even 50 per cent., which is as good as a formal prohibition of imports.

The transit duties appear equally oppressive. Ordinary woollen goods, for example, are to pay transit duties of 6 Rthlr. 18 Gr. 8 hl. per cwt., which has a gross value of 150 Rthlr., i.e. about 4½ per cent. Thereby the whole of Germany would become tributary to Prussia in respect of all those goods which pass along the Rhine, the Weser and the Elbe on their way to the fairs at Leipzig, Naumburg and Frankfort.

However, we soon recover from our dismay if we reflect that the maintenance of this tariff law would soon totally ruin all German trade, and that it is therefore diametrically opposed to the spirit of the German Confederation. One is therefore inevitably led to the conviction that the Prussian Government, which is forced by the situation of its territories to desire above all others a state of total free trade, intends to use this tariff system to induce the other States of Germany to agree to general free trade. This assumption almost becomes a certainty if one takes into account the declaration of the Prussian Government that it is willing to conclude special commercial treaties with its neighbours.

The humble signatories recognise in this an important hint, drawing attention to what has to be done, and accordingly take the liberty to submit to the Honourable the Confederate Diet this petition:

(1) That all customs and tariffs inside Germany be abolished; but instead
(2) a customs system be set up against foreign nations, based on retaliation until they shall also recognise the principle of European free trade.

The humble signatories are well aware that the damage done by the internal customs and tariffs within Germany should be proved in greater detail, together with calculations how they affect individual States, cities and branches of commerce and industry.

But since they are at the moment unable to fill these gaps they promise, on return to their homes, to draft such comparative reports in collaboration with the whole of commerce and industry in their countries, and submit these humbly in due course.

And your Petitioners will ever pray. . . . [here follow the signatures of 70 German merchants and manufacturers from Saxony, Bavaria, Wurttemberg, Electoral Hesse, Baden, Hesse-Darmstadt and Nassau].

Frankfort, 14 April 1819.

A large number of signatures of other German merchants and manufacturers who are in agreement with this petition is still outstanding. In view of the urgency of the matter, however, it was judged best not to delay for their sake, and they will therefore be submitted later in due course.

Professor List

Plenipotentiary for the General German Association of Commerce and Industry, Frankfort on Main.

12/2 The Zollverein Treaty of 1833

Between Prussia, Bavaria, Wurttemberg, the Electorate of Hesse, and the Grand Duchy of Hesse; concluded 22 March 1833. Adhesion of Saxony, 30 March; adhesion of the Principalities of Anhalt and of the Duchy of Saxony, 11 May. Exchange of Ratifications, 11 November 1833 (Parl. Papers, 1840, VI), pp. 455-459.

The contracting powers, penetrated with a lively solicitude for whatever may contribute to the freedom and extension of commerce and industry in their respective states, and, consequently, of Germany in general, have opened negociations with a view to give fuller effect to the treaties already existing between them for such objects, and for this purpose they have . . . agreed to the following convention, subject to ratification:—

Article 1st. – The various associations of custom-houses, already existing in the said states, shall for the future form, by virtue of a common system of custom-houses and of commerce, a General Association, which shall include all countries comprised in such associations. . . .

4th. – Within the territories of the contracting powers there shall be similar laws relative to duties of import, export, and transit; but such modifications as, without injury to the common object, shall necessarily arise, whether from the spirit of general legislation of each of the contracting states, or from local interests, shall be made by each individual state.

For this reason, in establishing a custom-house tariff, there may be made, with regard to the import and export duty on certain articles of minor consideration, and with regard to the transit-duty, according as the channels of commerce may require, such exceptions to the principles of imposition generally adopted as may be particularly desirable to such and such states; provided, however, such exceptions are not prejudicial to the general interests of the Association.

The administration of the import, export, and transit duties, and the organization of the authorities who shall be constituted in all the states of the Associations, shall be placed upon the same footing, but without losing sight of the particular relations existing in these countries. The laws and regulations which shall be assimilated under this point of view by the contracting states are the Custom-house Law, the Custom-house Tariff, and Custom-house Regulations.

They shall be considered as integral parts of the present convention, and published along with it.

5th. – No change, addition, nor exception can be made in the Custom-house legislation, including the tariff and Custom-house regulations (Article 4), but by consent of the contracting parties, and in the same manner as provided for the adoption of laws. This clause extends to all arrangements for establishing rules tending to change generally the administration of the Custom-house.

6th. – After execution of the present convention, there shall be within the contracting states a freedom of commerce and intercourse, and a community of duties in all respects in conformity with the stipulations contained in the following articles.

7th. – Reckoning from this date, therefore, all import, export, and transit duties shall cease to be levied on the common frontiers of the associated Custom-houses, which have hitherto existed between Prussia and Hesse, and Bavaria and Wurtemberg. Consequently, all articles which have free circulation in one of the said territories may be introduced into the others freely, and without charge, with the single exception –

1st. Of objects which form a state monopoly, playing cards and salt, according to Articles 9 and 10.

2nd. Of indigenous productions, which, in the interior of the contracting states, are subject to unequal duties, or else which pay a duty in one of the states, and are exempt in those of another, which render them subject to an equalising duty, according to Article II.

Lastly. – Articles which cannot be imported or imitated without invading patents, or privileges granted by one of the contracting states which may have granted such privileges for the whole term of the present convention.

8th. – Without any prejudice to the freedom of commerce, or exemption from duties stipulated in Article 7th, the conveyance of articles of commerce, which according to the tariff of the common Custom-house, are subject to an import and export duty in passing the exterior frontiers, cannot take place from the kingdoms of Bavaria and Wurtemberg in the kingdom of Prussia, the territories of the Elector of Hesse and of the Grand Duchy of Hesse, and *vice versâ*, except by the ordinary routes and highways, and by the navigable rivers; for this purpose there shall be established at the internal frontiers offices for declaration, where the conductors of goods shall be obliged to present their manifest, or bill of conveyance, and shall point out the goods they are conveying from one country to another. This regulation is not applicable either to the trade in raw productions in small quantities, nor to the frontier retail trade, or of fairs, nor to passengers' baggage. Neither shall any verification of the goods take place, except where the security for the receipt of the duties of equalization requires it. . . .

13th. – The contracting states reciprocally renew the adoption of the principle that the highway-duties, or other duties which have been substituted for them – as, for example, the fixed augmentation of customs established on the entry of merchandize into the kingdom of Bavaria and Wurtemberg, in substitution of the highway-duties, the rates for paving, ditching, bridges, and carriage, as well as all other rates of this character, under whatever names they may have been established, and without distinction, if they are levied for account of the state or of a commune – cannot be maintained or established except in proportion to the ordinary cost of repair and maintenance. The highway-rates at present existing in Prussia, conformably to the tariff of 1828, shall be taken as the maximum, and henceforth cannot be exceeded by any of the contracting states.

In virtue of the principle abovementioned, the duties of tolls and highway-rates shall be abolished where highways exist; the paving-duties are included in the road-duties, but in such mode that the latter may be levied conformably to the general tariff.

14th. – The contracting governments engage to co-operate in the establishment in their respective countries of a uniform system of weights and measures; they will immediately open negociations for this purpose, and will, in the first instance, direct their efforts to the adoption of a common custom-house weight.

Should the arrangements to be made for this purpose not be matured when the execution of the present convention shall take effect, each of the contracting states, in order to facilitate the despatch of merchandize and of the operations of the custom-house officers, will adopt, if it has not already been done, the weights and measures pointed out by the tariffs of the custom-houses, and the weights and measures which the other contracting states have adopted in their tariffs. . .

15th. – Water-duties, and duties for conveyance by rivers, including duties which are charged on the tonnage of the vessel, shall continue to be reciprocally charged on the navigation of the rivers to which the stipulations of the Congress of Vienna or the separate conventions of the states are applicable, according to the said stipulations, if there are no others contrary to them. With respect to this latter regulation the contracting states propose immediately to open negotiations relative to the navigation of the river Rhine and its tributaries, in order to come to some arrangement, by virtue of which the navigation-duties upon these rivers, which burthen the importation, exportation, and transit of goods, of all the associated countries, shall be always, excepting the examination-duties, if not wholly abolished, at least considerably lightened.

All the facilities which one of the associated states may accord to its subjects, with regard to the navigation of the said rivers, shall be equally enjoyed by the navigation of the associated states.

Upon the other rivers, to which neither the act of the Congress of Vienna, nor other conventions entered into between the states, are applicable, the water-duties shall be levied in conformity with the ordonnances of the respective governments. However, upon these rivers also, the subjects of the contracting states, their goods and vessels, shall be treated with perfect equality.

16. – From the date when the present common regulation of custom-houses shall be carried into effect all warehouse and harbour dues then existing in the territories comprised within the Custom-house union shall cease to be levied, and no one shall be obliged to despatch or warehouse his merchandize, but in the cases prescribed by the said common regulation of custom-houses, or the maritime regulation legally in force.

17th. – No canal, sluice, bridge, road, weighing-crane, or warehouse dues, nor any hiring for profit of establishments intended to facilitate communications, may be demanded, except for the actual use of such establishments or objects; and each state shall charge to the subjects of the other contracting states in the same ratio and the same manner as charged to their own subjects.

Wherever there is a weighing-machine or crane intended for the exclusive use of the officers of customs, no weighing charge shall be allowed to be made by the custom-house officers for any goods that have been once weighed.

18th. – The contracting states shall continue to employ their efforts to facilitate, by means of the adoption of uniform principles, the progress of industry, and to give the greatest latitude to the right which all subjects of each possess to seek for work and means of subsistence in the other states of the association.

From the period of the present convention being carried into effect the subjects of one of the contracting states, who seek for work in the exercise of a trade or employment in the territory of another state, shall pay no greater duties than are paid by native subjects exercising the same trade.

The manufacturers or artisans who make purchases only for their trade, and travellers who carry with them samples only of goods and not the goods themselves, for the purpose of obtaining orders, shall pay no other tax on the business they may transact in any state, except in that in which they reside; these persons, however, shall enjoy this exemption only provided they have acquired in the state where they are domiciled permission to exercise their trade by paying the taxes thereon, or in the case of their being employed in the service of some trader or native workmen paying the tax.

Those subjects of the contracting states who visit the fairs and markets which are held in each of the said states for the purpose of following their trade, or selling the productions of their labour, shall be treated everywhere as natives of the country where they may be.

19th. – The sea-ports of Prussia shall be open to the commerce of the subjects of all the contracting states, subject to the same duties as are paid by Prussian subjects. The consuls of each of the associated states who may be in the sea-ports or other commercial places of foreign trade shall be charged with the protection in all respects, and without distinction, of the subjects of each of the contracting states.

20th. – To protect their system of general Custom-houses from contraband trade, and to guarantee their duties on internal consumption from fraud, the contracting states have concluded a common cartel, which shall be carried into effect as soon as possible; but, at the latest, at the same time as the present convention.

21st. – The community of receipts established between the contracting states by the present convention shall have for its object the produce of the import, export, and transit duties which shall be received in the Prussian states, the kingdoms of Bavaria and Wurtemberg, the Electorate and Grand Duchy of Hesse, including those other countries which have already acceded to the system of customs of the contracting states. The produce of the duties above mentioned shall be divided amongst the contracting states in proportion to their population. From this community shall be excluded and reserved for the individual benefit of the respective governments—

1st. Taxes which are levied in the interior of each state upon indigenous productions, including equalizing duties, of which mention has been made in Article 11.

2nd. Navigation-dues mentioned in Article 15.

3rd. Duties of highways, dykes, ports, roads, canals, sluices, as well as weighing and warehousing, and all other dues of that nature, whatever may be their denomination.

4th. Custom-house fines and confiscation, which, with reservation of the share of the informers, shall remain for the government, through the extent of its dominions. . . .

37th. – If, when the execution of the present convention takes effect, there should not exist on all essential points a conformity of import-duties in the territories of the contracting powers, the latter bind themselves to take the requisite steps to secure the revenues of customs of the association from injury by the importation or accumulation of goods free from duty, or which are subject to a lower duty than charged by the tariff of the association.

38th. – In the event of other German states manifesting a wish to be admitted to the association, the high contracting powers declare themselves ready to comply with such wish, as far as they can do so without compromising the particular interests of the members of the association: in such cases these new admissions shall be made by virtue of conventions which shall be concluded for that purpose.

39th. – The governments of the contracting powers shall employ all their efforts to procure for their subjects all possible facilities and advantages by means of treaties of commerce with other states. . . .

41st. – The duration of the present convention, which shall take effect from the 1st January, 1834, is provisionally fixed for the 1st January, 1842. If during this period, and two years before its expiration at the latest, the contracting powers do not express their wish to terminate this union, it shall be considered as prolonged for twelve years, and so on from time to time for a further period of twelve years.

The last stipulation, however, is made only in case during the interval all the governments of the Germanic Confederation shall not have entered into arrangements which shall entirely fulfil the purposes of the present association of custom-houses, a purpose which is in conformity with the intentions announced in the 19th Article of the Germanic Confederation. In the event of measures being taken in the whole of the states of the Germanic Confederation relative to the freedom in the trade of provisions, the duties appointed by the tariff of the association relative to this trade will be modified in consequence.

12/3 British View of the Zollverein, 1840

JOHN BOWRING, Report on the Prussian Commercial Union (Parl. Papers, 1840, VI), pp. 381-389, 419-421, 434-436.

No doubt this great Union which is known in Germany by the name of *Zoll Verein* or *Zoll Verbände* (Toll Association or Alliance), derived its first and strongest influence from a desire to get rid of those barriers to intercommunication which the separate fiscal legislation of the various states of Germany raised among a people whom natural and national feelings, as well as common interests, would otherwise have connected more intimately and permanently together.

The Zoll Verein represents, in Germany, the operation of the same opinions and tendencies which have already effected so many changes in the commercial legislation of other countries. In the United Kingdom the Custom-house laws which separated Scotland and Ireland from England have been superseded by a general system applicable to the whole. In France the local barriers and the local tariffs have given way to a general and uniform system of taxation. Even before the Commercial League associated so many states in a common union, several less extensive combinations had prepared the way for a more diffusive intercourse. Between the states which do not form part of the Prussian League – as, for example, between Hanover and Brunswick and Oldenburgh – the same tariffs have been adopted, and the payment of duties in one of the states is sufficient to secure free sale or transit in the other.

The Commercial League is, in fact, the substantial representative of a sentiment widely, if not universally, spread in Germany – that of national unity. It has done wonders in breaking down petty and local prejudices, and has become a foundation on which future legislation, representing the common interests of the German people, may undoubtedly be hereafter raised. If well directed in its future operation, the Zoll Verein will represent the fusion of German interests in one great alliance. The peril to its beneficial results will grow out of the efforts which will be made, and which are already made, to give by protections and prohibitions an undue weight to the smaller and sinister interests of the Verein. But if its tariffs be so moderate and so judicious as to allow full play to the interests of the consumers in the field of competition – if there should be no forcing of capital into regions of unproductiveness or of less productiveness – if the claims of manufacturers to sacrifices in their favour from the community at large be rejected – if the great agricultural interests of Germany recover that portion of attention from the *commercial* union to which they are justly entitled – if the importance of foreign trade and navigation be duly estimated – the Zoll Verein will have the happiest influence on the general prosperity. And that the League has been much strengthened by the experience of its benefits – that its popularity is extending – that its further spreading may be confidently anticipated – appears to be indubitable. In fact the Zoll Verein has brought the sentiment of German nationality out of the regions of hope and fancy into those of positive and material interests; and representing as it does the popular feeling of Germany, it may become, under enlightened guidance, an instrument not only for promoting the peace and prosperity of the states that compose it, but of extending their friendly relations through the world. . . .

The Zoll Verein was not, as it has been often asserted to be, a union formed in hostility to the commercial interests of other states – it was not intended prematurely to create a manufacturing population in rivalry with or opposition to the manufacturing aptitudes of Great Britain – it was by no means the purpose of its founders to misdirect capital to unprofitable employment, to sacrifice agriculture to trade, or to encourage less the field than the factory. The Zoll Verein was the substantial expression and effect of a general desire among a great nation, split into many small states, but still of common origin, similar manners, speaking the same language, educated in the same spirit, to communicate, to trade, to travel, without the annoyance and impediments which the separate fiscal regulations of every one of their governments threw in the way....

There can be no doubt that the hostile tariffs of other nations, and especially the corn and timber laws of Great Britain, served greatly to strengthen the arguments in favour of the Commercial Union. It was felt necessary to extend the home market while foreign markets were closed, or only partially and irregularly opened, to the leading articles of German production....

Thus, while on the one hand the Zoll Verein was advocated as a measure of self-defence against the hostile legislation of foreign nations, it should not be forgotten that, as respects the confederated states, it represented the principles of unrestricted intercommunication....

The objects proposed by the Zoll Verein were the removal of all restrictions to communication and transit, the abolition of all internal custom-houses, the establishment of a common tariff and system of collection, and the repartition of the receipts on all imports and exports according to the population among all the members of the League.... The intention of the tariff is to admit raw materials without any, or on merely a nominal duty....

The Zoll Verein, by directing capital to internal, in preference to external trade, has already had a great influence in improving the roads, the canals, the means of travelling, the transport of letters – in a word, in giving additional impulse to inland communications of every sort. The isolation of the several German states, with separate fiscal interests, and often hostile legislation, prevented those facilities from being given to intercourse which are alike the evidence and the means of civilisation. On every side beneficial changes are taking place. Railways are being constructed in many parts of the German territory – steam-boats are crowding the German ports and coasting along the German shores – everything is transported with greater cheapness and rapidity....

On the whole Saxony is the portion of Germany which has profited most by its connection with the Commercial League, for in Saxony manufacturing industry was most developed, and in the competition with other states of the League Saxony had the vantage ground. To her especially it has opened a market of 26,000,000 of consumers, and closed the gates to a great extent against foreign rivals. Saxony being far more advanced in manufacturing aptitude than most of the their states, was enabled at once to take up a predominant manufacturing position. A considerable rise in the cost of the necessaries of life followed the greater demand for labour, and of course pressed heavily on all that species of labour, for which the Zoll Verein created no demand. Much capital was suddenly disturbed and made less productive; much was misdirected to objects for which there was an artificial, but not a durable demand, or in which competition with other parts of the

Zoll Verein, or with foreign countries, could not be profitably maintained.

One of the consequences of the spread of manufacturing industry within the Zoll Verein, will be to diminish the importance of the great German fairs, which have been for so many ages the periodical gathering-place of buyers and sellers, from the remotest regions. For the German producer being now in more immediate contact with the buyer and consumer than his foreign rival, and adopting more and more the habit of sending his travelling agents over all Germany, and even to foreign countries, will more readily and more regularly supply the wants of the population than they would be supplied from those marts which are only available at distant epochs; and in this way, too, German manufacturers, being on the spot, will more easily accommodate themselves to German tastes and fashions, and even create those tastes and fashions, than can be effected by the manufacturers of countries far removed; added to which, the increased facilities of intercommunication, lead to a more frequent arrangement of the necessities of supply and demand than were provided for by the periodical fairs. . . .

The Commercial League has anticipated, from its very origin, the union of other German states, the following stipulation being part of the Treaty:

'In the case that other German states should convey a wish to form a part of the Zoll Verein, as created by the present treaty, the high contracting parties agree to give effect to that wish, in as far as it is consistent with the general interests of the league.'

The writers in favour of the league have been anxious to point out to the excluded states the benefits of the union, particularly to Hanover, whose geographical position makes her adhesion to the union greatly desirable; and, were the tariff of the Zoll Verein lowered to the standard of the tariff of Hanover, the financial and commercial objections to her joining would lose much of their weight, and her junction would bring Brunswick with it, as these countries are already associated in a custom-house union.

None of the maritime kingdoms and states of Germany, with the exception of Prussia, form, nor are they likely to form for the present, part of the Commercial Union. Their duties are lower than those of the league; they have no manufactures to protect; they have no interest to create, equal to that which they would sacrifice (the interest of almost free trade) by joining the union, unless, indeed, by a wise and liberal policy, the tariffs of the league were made lower than those of the neighbouring states. Such a result would create a popular interest in its favour, would predispose the resisting districts to desire a union, would dispose foreign powers to look on the extension of the union with a friendly and encouraging eye, and would, of necessity, increase the power and influence of the whole confederation.

In fact, the lowering of the tariff of the Zoll Verein to a very moderate

rate of duties could not fail to draw into the union, several of the states which have a present interest in remaining independent. . . .

I have pointed out, in more than one part of this Report, that the operation of the tariff of the Zoll Verein is really prohibitory on a great number of articles, and, among them, the most important articles of British manufacture. The avowal of the Prussian government, that it was their intention only to levy a moderate duty of from 10 to 15 per cent., is by no means carried into effect by the rate of duties levied. It will be seen by my correspondence with your Lordship (Appendix XXXIII.), that I did not fail to represent to the Prussian authorities that the *legislation* of the tariff was by no means accordant with the expressed purposes of the superordinate authorities. I have given (Appendix XXX.) returns furnished me from the first sources of information, which show the per centage duty, which is, in fact, levied on the principal manufactures of cotton and woollen. This state of things is a substantial grievance; as it will be seen that, on cotton goods, the duties vary from 30 to 120 per cent, and on woollens from 20 to 50 per cent. I have explained that those duties which press so heavily, or prohibitorily, on so many articles, have this effect in consequence of the fixation of a certain amount of duty on the *weight* of the articles, without any reference to quality or fluctuations of prices. And as the standard of value was taken at an inordinately high estimate, the *ad valorem* becomes enormous; and has, of course, considerably increased by the fall of manufactured goods: for the duty remains stationary, however low may be the cost of the article. . . .

Much of the trade which was formerly carried on in direct importation from Manchester has ceased. One example will serve instead of many. There was a district in Berlin frequently called Petty Manchester, in the Spandauer street and neighbourhood, in which were many large warehouses of British cotton goods. They have almost wholly disappeared. The owners have retired from a losing trade, either on their savings, or have engaged in other adventures – some even in manufactures competing with England – so that all their influence, which was once on the side of free trade, is now flung into the protecting and prohibitory scale. And the evils of this state of things are increasing, and must increase. Up to the present moment the importation of articles in the early stages of manufacture, to which more labour is to be applied, in Germany, is important and increasing, and serves, to a large extent, to fill up the vacuum arising from the diminished importation of wholly manufactured articles. The various materials, the produce of our superior machinery – such as cotton, woollen, linen, silk, and other thread – metals in the earlier progress of manipulation – in a word, articles which stand almost in the situation of *raw materials* to be worked in the later stages of manufacturing industry – form a very large portion of the imports of the Zoll

Verein. They have been hitherto and are still imported at low rates of duty; but the protective system will as infallibly reach these in the progress of time as it has reached the articles of more complete manufacture, unless the field of intercourse be considerably extended by mutual modifications of the tariffs of Great Britain and Prussia. There will be a growing demand for higher duties on half-manufactured articles – a stronger desire to depend for their supply less upon the foreign and more on the home producer.... Thus the goods on which the manufacturing process is complete have been the first to experience the effects of the Prussian tariff; for it cannot be too often repeated that many of the articles wholly manufactured, for which there was formerly a large demand, have ceased to find their way to the markets of the Commercial Union. No woven goods of low quality can any longer be sold, and the tendency of the tariffs is at the same time to intrude more and more upon the higher qualities which still are enabled to hold their place (but not very firmly) in the markets of Prussia.

12/4 Protectionist Views in France, 1832

Budget Committee of the Chamber of Deputies, 1832. Translated in G. VILLIERS AND J. BOWRING, *First Report on the Commercial Relations between France and Great Britain* (Parl. Papers, 1834, XIX), pp. 74-76. (W.O.H.)

... If we admitted the food and raiment, and metals, and colonial products, and other objects which strangers would bring to our ports, we might, probably, save some hundreds of millions: should we be the richer in consequence? We think not; for the riches of a State are in the elements of labour; and when labour fails to find employment, misery is reproduced. And it is not only a question of comfort, but one of existence; for if wheat were introduced without duty from the Baltic and the Black Sea, our maritime shores would remain uncultivated, and the effect of a ruinous competition would affect, more and more, nearly the whole of our agricultural industry. And it is only so long as foreign harvests are abundant that they will provide for our wants; if they were insufficient, importations would cease, and we, at the same time, should be feeling the want of those resources which we should have allowed to perish: so that instead of a scarcity we should have a famine. Therefore let us own, that there are objects which a State ought always to produce, and with respect to which the theory of free-trade is inapplicable.

But we are told, France has elements of riches which are peculiar, to which competition would give value, and of which the most extensive demand would compensate her for the loss of the manufactures which might not be capable of competing with a rivalry. Do these riches belong to us exclusively and immutably? – Quite the contrary. The fruits of the earth are transplanted from one hemisphere to the other; manufactures are still more transitory. Look to India: a century has not elapsed since she manufactured cottons for the four quarters of the world; now it is England which supplies them. The invention of a machine has sufficed to produce this revolution.

But, it is said, protecting duties perpetuate routine habits, destroy emulation, and maintain the high price of produce. The facts prove the contrary. At no period did French industry make such rapid progress as since it has been shielded by the present system. Manufactures have reached perfection; internal competition has lowered prices, and the nation is enriched by an immense mass of active industry. It is loudly asserted, it is maintained, that Government cannot benefit industry; that they merely embarrass when they interfere with it. Yet is it not an advantage to industry when roads are made, when canals are dug, and when the mercantile shipping is protected by the navy of the State? Is it not Government which supports the activity of industry, by securing to all the administration of justice, the rights to property, and personal safety? The laws, we are told, cannot create wealth: no, certainly, they do not create it; but let those who deny their influence on the prosperity of empires, tell us why Spain is so wretched, and England so prosperous. No, laws do not create wealth, but they pave the way to it; they excite its production. Nations, like individuals, are authors of their fate.

Further, let the system which we defend be judged by its results. Since the period when it began to be practised amongst us, we have been proven by adversity; disastrous wars, and two invasions, have increased our national debt by several milliards, and the Budget to the amount of some hundreds of millions. Now, if it be true that, in spite of those disasters, France is not the less rich at this moment, we may well be partial to a system under which so much evil has been repaired in such a short space of time.

Observe, also, that for thirty years past the prosperity of our manufactures has reposed on this protecting legislation, constantly confirmed since, and which, by its duration, has acquired, in some measure, the guarantee of public faith. To abandon it before it has produced its fruits, would be the overthrow of fortunes and of subsistences; it would be staking the real well-being of the country against the uncertain advantages of a theory which has never yet been subjected to the proof of decisive experience. England is quoted: it is asserted that she gained nothing in defending herself against external competition; – that she renounces protective laws, of which she acknowledges the injuries and the defects. Undoubtedly, it would be exaggeration to attribute the rapid fortune of our neighbours solely to their commercial legislation, but it is certain that it has powerfully contributed to it. In fact, is it not under the system of protecting duties, of prohibitions, and of bounties, that English industry has risen to its high superiority? Is it not under favour of the privilege which the Navigation Act reserved for the British flag, that the nautical power of England has been developed? If, at the present day, she tempers the repulsive system, it is because she carried it to excess in using it: if she extols the benefits of competition, it is because, having attained the point of no longer fearing any, she has now only to seek and conquer markets.

And is it true that England has altered her system? – By no means. She has generalised the warehousing of foreign merchandise, but still under the inflexible condition of re-exportation. She has reduced the duty on wines, in order to render it more productive, for the mere benefit of the Revenue. In short, she has lowered some import duties, but only on articles which are produced cheaper by her than in any other part of the world. That is to say, our neighbours open their doors to all that it is impossible to import; while in reality they do not concede anything to other nations. Thus, you see, far from renouncing her commercial system, England fortifies and consolidates it: whilst modifying its application according to her new necessities, she maintains the principle invariably. Let us act like her; let us continue to encourage industry, to aid all the germs of national prosperity; let us not lower our Tariffs until our manufactures shall have been developed and perfected; let us beware of sacrificing the interests of our country to the pretended welfare of the world; of effacing the features of national distinction, – of that noble sentiment which animates the grandeur and glory of human society.

12/5 French Views on Economic Development and the Treaty of Commerce, 1859-60

a Persigny to Napoleon III, 1 August 1859. BIBLIOTHEQUE NATIONALE, *Nouvelles Acquisitions Françaises*, 23056.

b Persigny to Napoleon III, 21 November 1859. Printed in G. WRIGHT, 'The Origins of Napoleon III's Free Trade', *Economic History Review*, IX (1938-9), pp. 64-67.

c Napoleon to Fould, 5 January 1860. Printed in *Discours, Messages et Proclamations de S. M. Napoleon III*, 1849-1861 (I Série, Paris, 1861), pp. 160-162. (All W.O.H.)

a When I had the honour of submitting to you the suggestion of a peace-programme designed to develop the wealth of France and also to convince all Europe of your pacific intentions, I did not fail to make it clear to Your Majesty that this plan was not addressed to the present Ministry. I was surprised to receive your request to submit my proposals to the Council. . . .

The scheme itself falls into four parts: (1) agriculture, (2) industry, (3) reafforestation of mountain regions, and (4) artificial reservoirs to prevent floods and to irrigate farm-land.

Only the second suggestion concerning industry is likely to meet with political opposition. The representatives of industry have for so long completely dominated the councils of state that any changes – however cautious and however mitigated by the compensations suggested by Your Majesty – will be impossible [to achieve] by legislative means. As M. Rouher has stated to the Council, the problem can be solved only by way of a commercial treaty with England. I saw M. Rouher before my departure and I found that he was convinced that it was necessary for such action to be taken and that the opportunity was at hand. He is quite ready to submit to Your Majesty a very suitable plan if Your Majesty is resolved to take such action.

For my part I have seen Lord John Russell. . . . I asked him confidentially what he would be disposed to do if – and this I did not yet know – my Government desired to take steps to enter into such an arrangement. He replied that, like Lord Palmerston, he could see no purpose and no advantage in concluding a treaty with France since that country was at present inferior to England (from the point of view of industrial development) and could not compete with England. On the other hand if there were a political advantage to be gained from concluding a commercial treaty between the two countries Russell was prepared to make substantial sacrifices to secure such an advantage. He had often examined the supposedly insurmountable difficulties caused by the dues levied by certain English ports on foreign ships and he was prepared to overcome these difficulties and was ready to enter into negotiations with us on this very important matter.

I need hardly say that a commercial treaty with England would aim at replacing our prohibitions by fixed import duties; at reducing our duties on coal and coke – taking perhaps as a basis for discussion the present dues levied on the Prussian frontier . . . and the reduction of our duties on worked-iron and on steel. In return England would have to reduce her duties on wines, spirits, silks and certain popular articles of consumption. . . .

b . . . But to avert so grave a disaster (as war) we must do more than see to it that our newspapers adopt restrained language and follow a sound policy. We must give the English people positive proof that it is mistaken in supposing that Your Majesty wants to make war upon them. Nothing would do this more effectively than a union of the commercial interests of the two peoples. Let France embark upon the great peaceful public works of which I have already spoken. Let us make a commercial treaty with England. Then the prosperity of the two countries will soon lead to the calming of [violent] passions and to the removal of all suspicions. The peace of the two countries will be assured to the everlasting honour of your name. Circumstances favour a commercial treaty. The English Government desires good relations between the two countries as much as Your Majesty and consequently it is prepared to make real sacrifices. It is ready to reduce substantially its import duties on wines and spirits which is an important factor in the well-being of half France. England will agree to admit free of duty such Paris luxury goods as bronzes and fashions and this [concession] would assure you of the gratitude of the capital. In return England does not expect too rapid a reduction in our tariff. The removal of prohibitions will be a considerable step forward as far as France is concerned. As for coal and iron a reduction in transport costs would give [our industrialists] some compensation for the lowering of our import duties. St. Étienne asks for no privileges. As for Lille and Rouen you can offer the manufacturers the loans that they will need to buy more modern machinery. These steps would reduce the only opposition to be expected to this great economic reform which both the circumstances of our day and the interests of the country demand.

c Despite the uncertainties which still surround some aspects of the international situation, one can confidently predict a peaceful outcome. The time has therefore come when we should consider by what means a great impulse can be imparted to the various branches of the national economy.

With this object I lay before you the bases of a programme many aspects of which should be approved by the Chambers – which you should discuss with your colleagues with a view to preparing the most appropriate measures to give a vigorous impetus to agriculture, industry and commerce.

For a long time the truth has been proclaimed that one should multiply the means of exchange to secure the expansion of commerce; that lack of competition causes industry to stagnate and prices to remain high which prevents any increase of consumption; that agriculture itself will remain in its infancy unless there are capital developments in a prosperous industry. Hence everything depends on the successive development of the [various] elements of national prosperity! But the all-important problem is to decide within what limits the State should promote these various interests and what order of priority should be accorded to each.

Hence, before developing our foreign trade by exchanging our products, we must improve our agriculture and free our industry from all the shackles – within the country – that place it in a position of inferiority. Today not only are our large-scale industries hampered by a host of restrictive regulations, but also the welfare of the workers is far from having reached the level attained in a neighbouring country [i.e. Britain]. So it is only by a policy that will bring about a sound national economy – by creating [new] riches for the country – that we can raise the standard of living of the working classes.

With regard to agriculture it is necessary to enable this branch of the national economy to participate in the benefits of credit institutes; to clear the forests situated in the lowlands; to secure the reafforestation of the mountainous districts; to set aside a large sum every year for public works of drainage, irrigation and clearing. These public works by transforming barren districts into cultivated areas will enrich the communes* without burdening the State, which will recover the money it has advanced by selling some of the lands that will have been made fit for farming.

To encourage industrial production it is necessary to abolish all duties on the raw materials essential to industry. In exceptional circumstances there should be loans to industry at low rates of interest as has already been done for agriculture in respect of drainage – to assist in the improvement of plant.

One of the greatest services that can be rendered to a country is to improve the transport of essential raw materials for agriculture and industry. To secure this the Minister of Public Works will promote as quickly as possible the construction of new means of transport – canals, highways and railways – with the main object of sending coal and fertilisers to the places where producers need them most. The Minister will endeavour – by securing fair competition between railways and canals – to bring about a reduction in the cost of carriage of goods.

The measures to which we have referred will naturally lead to the expansion of trade by the extension of the means of exchange. It will then be necessary first to reduce by stages the duties on goods which are consumed on a large scale and also to change the system of prohibitive duties – which reduces our foreign trade – into one of protective duties.

By these means the output of agriculture will be raised. Industry – freed from internal shackles, assisted by the Government, stimulated by competition – will compete on favourable terms with foreign goods. Our trade, instead of languishing, will receive a new stimulus.

Wishing above all to maintain order in our finances, we now show how these improvements can be secured without financial disturbances.

The conclusion of peace has saved us from exhausting the proceeds of the war loan. A considerable sum is available from this source and, added to other funds, amounts to about 160 million francs.* If we ask the Corps Legislatif to authorise the application of this sum – in three annual instalments of 50 million francs* – we shall add considerably to the amounts already voted every year in the budget [for public works].

This exceptional source of revenue will not only facilitate the prompt completion of railways, canals, inland waterways, roads and harbours but it

* See Glossary.

will enable us to proceed more quickly with the renovation of our cathedrals and churches and the worthy encouragement of science, letters and the arts.

To compensate the Treasury for the temporary loss of revenue owing to the reduction of duties on essential raw materials and goods which are consumed on a large scale we propose to suspend the redemption of the National Debt. When the revenue expands again with the extension of commerce it will be possible to resume the repayment of the National Debt.

To sum up we propose –

(i) The removal of import duties on woollens and cottons;
(ii) Reductions in stages of import duties on sugar and coffee;
(iii) Improvements vigorously pursued in the means of transport;
(iv) reduction of tolls on canals and consequently a general lowering of transport costs;
(v) loans to agriculture and industry;
(vi) substantial useful public works;
(vii) abolition of prohibitions;
(viii) commercial treaties with foreign countries.

These are the fundamental bases of the programme which I desire you to bring before your colleagues. They should, without delay, prepare draft laws destined to bring this programme into effect. The programme will, I am firmly convinced, secure the patriotic approval of the Senate and the Corps Legislatif which will be eager to inaugurate with me a new era of peace and to promote the welfare of France. . . .

Napoleon.

12/6 British Views on the Commercial Treaty with France, 1860

a Lord J. Russell to Earl Cowley and Mr. Cobden; London, 17 January 1860.
b Earl Cowley to Lord J. Russell; Paris, 23 January 1860.
Both printed in *Correspondence respecting the Negotiation of a Treaty of Commerce with France* (Parl. Papers, 1860, LXVIII), pp. 492–498.

a My Lord and Sir,

HAVING received from Earl Cowley an intimation that in an interview which he had had with Count Walewski on the 22nd ultimo, that Minister stated the bases on which, according to the views of the French Government, a Treaty of Commerce might be concluded with England, I have now to acquaint you that Her Majesty has been pleased to appoint you jointly the Plenipotentiaries to negotiate such a Treaty. I therefore proceed to explain to you the views with which Her Majesty has been so advised, and by which you will be governed in the use of the authority you have received.

Her Majesty's Government are of opinion, that although the activity of trade, and the constant demand for labour in this country, are such as to leave no pressing necessity for opportunities of extension, yet the enlargement of commercial relations, always in itself desirable, ought to be more peculiarly an object of desire in the case of two countries prepared for such intercourse, like France and Great Britain, by local proximity, combined with considerable diversities of climate, productions, and industry. But over and above these considerations they attach a high social and political value to the conclusion of a Commercial Treaty with France. Its general tendency would be to lay broad and deep foundations in common interest and in friendly intercourse for the confirmation of the amicable relations that so happily exist between the two countries; and while thus making a provision for the future, which would progressively become more and more solid and efficacious, its significance at the present moment, when the condition of some parts of the Continent is critical, would be at once understood, and would powerfully reassure the public mind in the various countries of Europe. . . .

Her Majesty's Government consider that in measuring together the change to be reciprocally made in the Tariffs of the two countries, it is equitable to take into view the relative as well as the absolute nature of those Tariffs.

The rule of the French Tariff is high duty, in general, with a large measure of absolute prohibition.

The rule of the British Tariff is low duty, in general, with a large number of articles absolutely free; and likewise, with a small number of most important exceptions, of articles upon which high duties are imposed for fiscal purposes.

Taking these as the respective points of departure on the two sides, Her Majesty's Government are prepared to admit, as appears also to be the opinion of the French Government, that the proper basis for the operation will be, on the side of France, a general transition, so far as British commodities are concerned, from prohibition, or high duty, to duties at a moderate rate: and on the side of England, the total abolition of Customs duty on French productions, where fiscal considerations will permit it, and reduction to the lowest practicable point, together with the entire abandonment of any protective impost on behalf of a British, and against a French, commodity, where fiscal considerations will not allow total abolition.

Having stated the basis which appears suited to the proceeding, I have now to mention certain reserves which Her Majesty's Government have to make on behalf of England, and which, they presume, the Government of His Majesty the Emperor of the French may also make on behalf of France.

The freedom of each Government to regulate trade in all matters lying beyond the stipulations of the Treaty will remain entire: but it may be well, for the purposes of avoiding misapprehension, to specify points which might otherwise remain open to doubt. The two Governments will be free, for example, to extend to all countries the concessions they engage to make to one another; and this extension will, on the part of England, probably, be effected by a simultaneous act. . . .

There are three commodities to which the Government of France must, without doubt, attach the first importance, namely, brandy, wine, and silk.

With respect to brandy, the present duty is 15*s.* per gallon. The lowest point to which, for any British purpose, Her Majesty's Government could propose to reduce the duty, would be 10*s.* per gallon. If, nevertheless, you should find that by making a concession, even beyond what I have named, you can obtain from the Government of the Emperor satisfactory arrangements for early reduction of duty upon some important commodities, you are authorized to engage for the reduction of the duty on brandy to the same rate as that on British spirits brought from the Colonies, namely, 8*s.* 2*d.* per gallon.

The rates to be specified in the Treaty would be in all cases maximum rates, and would not preclude either Government from making any reduction it might think fit to make below such rates.

On the article of wine, the Government of Her Majesty will propose to Parliament to lay no duties on wine of French growth from and after the adoption of the Resolution by Parliament, higher than 3*s.* per gallon; thus at once diminishing by nearly one-half the present charge of 5*s.* 6*d.*, together with 5 per cent. thereon.

They would also propose that, on and after the 1st of April, 1861, the duty should be further reduced as follows, in degrees varying according to the quantity of proof spirit which may be contained in the wine. . . .

With respect to the third great article now under consideration, namely, silk manufactures, the Queen's Government will propose to Parliament an immediate and total repeal of the duties.

They will proceed in a similar manner with respect to the whole of the extensive and diversified class known as manufactured goods, whether enumerated or unenumerated, subject to the single and slight reserve I have described above, of a power to make, if need be, a very small number of special exceptions for a short time.

Of the articles which it is intended thus to liberate, I send you herewith a list. You will find that, besides manufactured goods, that list contains some articles of produce which are specially imported from France into this country. . . .

b MR. COBDEN and I had the honour to receive, on the 18th instant, your Lordship's despatch of the 17th instant, informing us that, in consequence of certain confidential communications made to me by Count Walewski, and conveyed to your Lordship in a despatch which I addressed to you on the 23rd ultimo, the Queen had been graciously pleased to appoint us to be joint Plenipotentiaries to negotiate a Treaty of Commerce with Plenipotentiaries to be named by the Emperor of the French, and containing instructions for our guidance.

Since the receipt of that despatch, Mr. Cobden and I have been daily for several hours, engaged with Messrs. Baroche and Rouher, the French Plenipotentiaries, in the performance of the duties entrusted to us. The way had been so completely cleared by Mr. Cobden's previous active exertions, that the task which I have had to perform has been comparatively light.

Your Lordship will find in the Treaty signed this day, which is transmitted herewith, the result of our negotiations. It will, I trust, meet with the approval of Her Majesty's Government.

It only remains for me and my colleague to express the hope that the generous and philanthropic views which have mainly induced Her Majesty's Government to contract this Treaty may meet with their reward by drawing closer the ties of friendship so necessary to the two great nations in whose name and for whose interests it has been concluded.

12/7 The Anglo-French Commercial Treaty of 1860

Text of the Treaty, printed in *Treaty of Commerce between Her Majesty and the Emperor of the French* (Parl. Papers 1860, LXVIII), pp. 1-9.

ARTICLE I

His Majesty the Emperor of the French engages that on the following articles of British production and manufacture, imported from the United Kingdom into France, the duties shall in no case exceed thirty per cent. *ad valorem*, the two additional decimes included.

The articles are as follows:

Refined sugar;
Turmeric in powder;
Rock crystal worked;
Iron forged in lumps or prisms;
Brass wire (copper alloyed with zinc), polished or unpolished, of every description;
Chemical productions, enumerated or non-enumerated;
Extracts of dye-woods;

Garancine;

Common soap of every description, and perfumed soap;

Stone-ware and earthen-ware, fine and common;

China and porcelain-ware;

Glass, crystal, mirrors, and plate-glass;

Cotton yarn;

Worsted and woollen yarn of every description;

Yarns of flax and hemp;

Yarns of hair, enumerated or non-enumerated;

Cotton manufactures;

Horse-hair manufactures, enumerated or non-enumerated;

Worsted and woollen manufactures, enumerated or non-enumerated;

Cloth list;

Manufactures of hair;

Silk manufactures;

Manufactures of waste and floss-silk;

Manufactures of bark and all other vegetable fibres, enumerated or non-enumerated;

Manufactures of flax and hemp;

Mixed manufactures of every description;

Hosiery;

Haberdashery, and small wares;

Manufactures of caoutchouc and gutta percha, pure or mixed;

Articles of clothing, wholly or in part made up;

Prepared skins;

Articles of every sort manufactured from leather or skins, included or not under the denomination of small wares, fine or common;

Plated articles of every description;

Cutlery;

Metal wares, whether enumerated or not;

Pig and cast-iron of every description, without distinction of weight;

Bar and wrought-iron, with the exception of the kinds specified in Article XVII;

Steel;

Machinery, tools, and mechanical instruments of every description;

Carriages on springs, lined and painted;

Cabinet ware, carved work, and turnery of every description; worked ivory and wood;

Brandies and spirits, including those not distilled from wine, cherries, molasses, or rice;

Ships and boats;

With respect to refined sugar and chemical productions of which salt is the basis, the excise or inland duties shall be added to the amount of the above specified duties.

ARTICLE II.

His Imperial Majesty engages to reduce the import duties in France on British coal and coke, to the amount of fifteen centimes for the hundred kilogrammes, with the addition of the two decimes.

His Majesty the Emperor also engages, within four years from the date of the ratification of the present Treaty, to establish upon the importation of coal and coke by land and by sea, a uniform duty, which shall not exceed that which is fixed by the preceding paragraph.

ARTICLE III.

It is understood that the rates of duty mentioned in the preceeding Articles are independent of the differential duties in favour of French shipping, with which duties they shall not interfere. . . .

ARTICLE V.

Her Britannic Majesty engages to recommend to Parliament to enable her to abolish the duties of importation on the following articles:

Sulphuric acid, and other mineral acids;

Agates and cornelians, set;

Lucifers of every description;

Percussion caps;

Arms of every description;

Jewels, set;

Toys;

Corks;

Brocade of gold and silver;

Embroideries and needle-work of every description;

Brass and bronze manufactures, and bronzed metal;

Canes, walking canes or sticks, umbrella or parasol sticks, mounted, painted, or otherwise ornamented;

Hats, of whatever substance they may be made;

Gloves, stockings, socks, and other articles of cotton or linen, wholly or in part made up;

Leather manufactures;

Lace manufactured of cotton, wool, silk, or linen;

Manufactures of iron and steel;

Machinery and mechanical instruments; tools, and other instruments;

Cutlery, and other articles of steel, iron, or cast iron;
Fancy ornaments of steel and iron;
Articles covered with copper by galvanic process;
Millinery and artificial flowers;
Raw fruits;
Gloves, and other leather articles of clothing;
Manufactures of caoutchouc and gutta percha;
Oils;
Musical instruments;
Worsted and woollen shawls, plain, printed, or patterned;
Coverlids, woollen gloves, and other worsted and woollen manufactures not enumerated;
Handkerchiefs, and other manufactures not enumerated, of linen and hemp;
Perfumery; cabinet ware, carved work, and turnery of every description;
Clocks, watches, and opera glasses;
Manufactures of lead, enumerated or not enumerated;
Feathers, dressed or not;
Goats', and other hair manufactures;
China and porcelain ware;
Stone and earthenware;
Grapes;
Sulphate of quinine;
Salts of morphine;
Manufactures of silk, or of silk mixed with any other materials, of whatever description they may be;
Articles not enumerated in the Tariff, now paying an *ad valorem* duty of ten per cent.; subject, however, to such measures of precaution as the protection of the public revenue may require, against the introduction of materials liable to Custom or Excise duties, in the composition of articles admitted duty free in virtue of the present paragraph.

ARTICLE VI.

Her Britannic Majesty engages also to propose to Parliament that the duties on the importation of French wine be at once reduced to a rate not exceeding three shillings a gallon, and that from the 1st April, 1861, the duties on importation shall be regulated as follows:

1. On wine containing less than fifteen degrees of proof spirit verified by Sykes's hydrometer, the duty shall not exceed one shilling a gallon.

2. On wine containing from fifteen to twenty-six degrees, the duty shall not exceed one shilling and sixpence a gallon.

3. On wine containing from twenty-six to forty degrees, the duty shall not exceed two shillings a gallon.

4. On wine in bottles, the duty shall not exceed two shillings a gallon.

5. Wine shall not be imported at any other ports than those which shall be named for that purpose before the present Treaty shall come into force; Her Britannic Majesty reserving to herself the right of substituting other ports for those which shall have been originally named, or of increasing the number of them.

The duty fixed upon the importation of wine at ports other than those named, shall be two shillings a gallon.

6. Her Britannic Majesty reserves to herself the power, notwithstanding the provisions of this Article, to fix the maximum amount of proof spirit which may be contained in liquor declared as wine, without, however, the maximum being lower than thirty-seven degrees.

ARTICLE VII.

Her Britannic Majesty promises to recommend to Parliament to admit into the United Kingdom merchandize imported from France, at a rate of duty equal to the excise duty which is or shall be imposed upon articles of the same description in the United Kingdom. At the same time the duty chargeable upon the importation of such merchandize may be augmented by such a sum as shall be an equivalent for the expenses which the system of excise may entail upon the British producer.

ARTICLE VIII.

In accordance with the preceding Article, Her Britannic Majesty undertakes to recommend to Parliament the admission into the United Kingdom of brandies and spirits imported from France, at a duty exactly equal to the excise duty levied upon home-made spirits, with the addition of a surtax of two pence a gallon, which will make the actual duty payable on French brandies and spirits eight shillings and two pence the gallon.

Her Britannic Majesty also undertakes to recommend to Parliament the admission of rum and tafia imported from the French Colonies, at the same duty which is or shall be levied on these same articles imported from the British Colonies.

Her Britannic Majesty undertakes to recommend to Parliament the admission of paper-hangings imported from France, at a duty equal to the excise tax, that is to say, at fourteen shillings per hundredweight; and cardboard of the same origin, at a duty which shall not exceed fifteen shillings per hundredweight.

Her Britannic Majesty further undertakes to recommend to Parliament the admission of gold and silver plate imported from France, at a duty equal to the stamp or excise duty which is charged on British gold and silver plate.

ARTICLE IX.

It is understood between the two High Contracting Powers, that if one of them thinks it necessary to establish an excise tax or inland duty upon any article of home production or manufacture which is comprised among the preceding enumerated articles, the foreign imported article of the same description may be immediately liable to an equivalent duty on importation. . . .

ARTICLE X.

The two High Contracting Parties reserve to themselves the power of levying upon all articles mentioned in the present Treaty, or upon any other article, landing or shipping dues, in order to pay the expenses of all necessary establishments at the ports of importation and exportation.

But in all that relates to local treatment, the dues and charges in the ports, basins, docks, roadsteads, harbours, and rivers of the two countries, the privileges, favours, or advantages which are or shall be granted to national vessels generally, or to the goods imported or exported in them, shall be equally granted to the vessels of the other country, and to the goods imported or exported in them.

ARTICLE XI.

The two High Contracting Powers engage not to prohibit the exportation of coal, and to levy no duty upon such exportation. . . .

ARTICLE XV.

The engagements contracted by His Majesty the Emperor of the French shall be fulfilled, and the tariffs previously indicated as payable on British goods and manufactures shall be applied, within the following periods:

1. For coal and coke, from the 1st July, 1860.

2. For bar and pig iron, and for steel of the kinds which are not subject to prohibition, from the 1st October, 1860.

3. For worked metals, machines, tools, and mechanical instruments of all sorts, within a period which shall not exceed the 31st December, 1860.

4. For yarns and manufactures in flax and hemp, from the 1st June, 1861.

5. And for all other articles from the 1st October, 1861.

ARTICLE XVI.

His Majesty the Emperor of the French engages that the *ad valorem* duties payable on the importation into France of merchandise of British production and manufacture, shall not exceed a maximum of twenty-five per cent. from the 1st of October, 1864....

ARTICLE XIX.

Each of the two High Contracting Powers engages to confer on the other any favour, privilege, or reduction in the tariff of duties of importation on the articles mentioned in the present Treaty, which the said Power may concede to any third Power. They further engage not to enforce one against the other any prohibition of importation or exportation, which shall not at the same time be applicable to all other nations.

ARTICLE XX

The present Treaty shall not be valid unless Her Britannic Majesty shall be authorized by the assent of Her Parliament to execute the engagements contracted by Her in the Articles of the present Treaty.

ARTICLE XXI.

The present Treaty shall remain in force for the space of ten years, to date from the day of the exchange of ratifications; and in case neither of the High Contracting Powers shall have notified to the other, twelve months before the expiration of the said period of ten years, the intention to put an end to its operation, the Treaty shall continue in force for another year, and so on from year to year, until the expiration of a year, counting from the day on which one or other of the High Contracting Powers shall have announced its intention to put an end to it.

The High Contracting Powers reserve to themselves the right to introduce by common consent into this Treaty, any modification which is not opposed to its spirit and principles, and the utility of which shall have been shown by experience.

ARTICLE XXII.

The present Treaty shall be ratified, and the ratifications shall be exchanged at Paris within the period of fifteen days, or sooner if possible.

In faith whereof, the respective Plenipotentiaries have signed it, and affixed thereto the seal of their arms.

Done in duplicate at Paris, the twenty-third day of January, in the year of our Lord one thousand eight hundred and sixty.

(L.S.) COWLEY.
(L.S.) RICHARD COBDEN.
(L.S.) V. BAROCHE.
(L.S.) F. ROUHER.

12/8 French Government Loans to Industry, 1860-61

A. DUNHAM, *The Anglo-French Treaty of Commerce* (Michigan, 1930), pp. 152-153.

Of the eighteen loans granted to constructors of machinery, totalling 1,417,000 francs, that given Mercier of Louviers in Normandy is of unusual interest, as the reporter said. We know from the posthumous book of Charles Ballot on the introduction of machinery into France, and from other sources, that Mercier was one of the great leaders of the industrial revolution in France, a man of real vision and remarkable energy. Mercier had printed at the time of making his application, March 14, 1861, the following letter, which was evidently sent to all the members of the Commission on loans. After speaking of the services he could render French manufacturers in supplying them with better equipment, which was the main object of the law of August 1, 1860, he said:

In the last ten years I have sold machines worth 8,000,000 francs* with the defective equipment of my shops, although with high protection, far higher than that which machines will have under the Treaty. When my shops are reorganized to meet the new needs I shall be able to produce machines to the value of 2,400,000 francs a year which would otherwise be imported. Even then my shops will be inferior in organization and equipment to English workshops which are able to specialize as I cannot, and which have all the industrial centres of the world as markets. In view of this competition I must lower my prices 20 per cent compared with last year. To do this and still get a legitimate profit of 10 per cent my enlarged shops must have all the economical methods and machine tools used in England. I plan to spend 550,000 francs of the loan [he asked for 700,000 and received 600,000 francs] on this and to use the rest to meet the increase in the volume of trade and to increase my circulating capital. The latter is necessary as I have always had to give customers long credit. This the English will not do. They deliver for cash down and often ask payment in advance. Only through these credits have many manufacturers been able to complete their equipment.

In the last six years I have spent over 150,000 francs to make looms running up to seven shuttles, so as to make even the most varied novelties. I have also worked on the replacement of the mule-jenny by the water-frame, which makes finer yarn and takes less room; and finally, on machines for making felt recently invented by Vouillan, who received a medal at the Exposition of Rouen. My shops as now equipped could not properly develop these new discoveries, and would force me to maintain high prices on the machines I alone sell. As guarantee I offer my shops, which will be worth 1,000,000 francs when enlarged and producing on an increased basis, and in the presence of the new foreign competition, which will be further increased by the application of the new treaties planned with Belgium and Germany.

According to the first report submitted in April, 1861, the Commission granted eighty-eight loans to textile manufacturers for the sum of 15,060,000 francs. The greater part of this went to the cotton industry, which was the most deserving of help because of the colossal development of the rival industry in England.

* See Glossary.

12/9 The French Textile Industry in the Face of British Competition

L. REYBAUD, *Le Coton* [*see* Document **11/6**], pp. 261-264. (Ed. Tr.)

An interesting document summarises and describes the condition of the Normandy industries, just when the old régime was about to fall; it is a report attributed to the lawyer Thouret . . . The date of this extract is significant. It is 1787, two years before the great political revolution, one year after a small commercial revolution which originated in the treaty of commerce concluded with England. To read this report is like reading an echo of what surrounds us today; the analogies are striking, and several of the nuances of the language are almost the same; 'English goods,' it is said, 'are imported and sold in the greatest abundance; and England persists in scorning the products of our industry. Several of our manufacturers in succession are reducing the numbers of their workers; some keep open their workshops to finish goods which they have brought in from England in an unfinished state. After finishing them, they sell them with their name and mark as French goods'. Today, we have the equivalent of this in the finishing of unbleached goods, which are brought into France duty-free, and are then re-exported. Other documents state that in the course of twelve months after the 1786 Treaty, the importation of English goods more than doubled, from 8 million to 18 million. From our customs documents it would be easy to illustrate a similar trend in the period after the signing of the 1860 Treaty. . . . In a comparison between English and French industry it so happens that Thouret's report examines the factors which lead to superiority or inferiority and . . . the debate centred around the same arguments which are still heard today, with very little variation either in content or form: 'England', it is said, 'opposes the industry of Manchester to that of Rouen. Manchester factories manufacture large quantities of cotton goods of all kinds. The examples of Manchester goods which have come into our possession seem to indicate that in general the cotton goods produced there are finer, and yet cheaper, than ours. Passing from this fact to an examination of its causes, it is found that the English have two positive, permanent factors which guarantee their superiority in cotton production. One is the low price of fuel necessary for the preparation and dressing of the material; coal, which in Rouen costs from 47·50 per barrel, weighing 2 milliers*, at Manchester costs only 9s. or 11 livres 10 sols. The other is the great economy effected by the English in the cost of manual labour, by using ingenious inventions to accelerate and simultaneously perfect the spinning process. The areas around Manchester and Lancashire are full of these great machines which . . . can be used to card, spin, weave, dress and finish the goods, and in the villages jennies, . . .

* See Glossary.

replace the old spinning wheels. The means by which the manufactories of this Généralité* can maintain their share of the trade are, therefore,

1. to concentrate on the search for, and the exploitation of coal mines, the existence of which is indicated at several places in the province;

2. to reduce the costs of manual labour in cotton production by the introduction of those machines which endow England with an industrial ascendancy which is so ruinous for our manufactures. . . .

12/10 English Imports into France, 1860

C. B. DEROSNE, *Ten Years of Imperialism in France: Impressions of a Flaneur* (London and Edinburgh, 1862), pp. 145–150.

For the general public the 1st of October was as good as a great racing day. The two first industrial people face to face in this struggle. This was at least the view taken of it, and considerable was the interest excited, as could be seen by the numerous groups which collected wherever the large affiches indicated the presence of English articles. The expectation was greatly disappointed. The French walked over the course, as the saying is, in this industrial race, and the verdict was 'ce n'est que cela.' Nor was the verdict unjust; a quantity of 'tapis à sujet,' with hideous figures, and in more hideous colours, but wonderfully cheap, and side by side rolls of the commonest staircase carpets, wellnigh for nothing. Further on, a display of all that Manchester can produce of most tasteless tissues in silk, cotton, and wool, pure or mixed. Then again, ties which reminded one of Houndsditch, or caricatures of Chinese porcelain, here and there wretched imitations of Scotch woollens, and this not in the cheap shops high up on the Boulevard du Temple, or in the Faubourg Montmartre, but in the most prominent and frequented parts. Further east, the display showed canvass-like calico, Californian shirts, a collection of all the refuse of Sheffield cutlery, and a collection of old unsaleable woollens and cottons.

The whole seemed almost like a farce. Where were the woollens of Scotland and of the west of England, the linens of Ireland, the cottons of Lancashire, the tissues of Bradford, Leeds, the tasteful wares of Staffordshire, the unparalleled cutlery of Sheffield, the carpets of Kidderminster, and the unrivalled articles of so many other places? Not a trace was seen of them.

There have been complaints accusing the French shopkeepers of foul play and downright trickery, of buying or imitating the worst sort of English goods, and selling them at double the price, in order to discredit English goods. These cases may have occurred, but the display was too generally

* See Glossary.

wretched for one not to seek for a cause elsewhere. English importers seem to have acted in the first instance as if Timbuctoo, Australia, or California, and not France, had been opened to their manufactures. To make a masterfeat of cheapness, and, at the same time, to get rid of all the old stores seems to have been the leading idea which prevailed.

It showed a total ignorance of the market opened, or else must be ascribed to bad and interested advice from the other side of the Channel. Whatever enthusiasts on both sides may say, the industry of the two countries is about on a par. The cost of production differs little or nothing in most articles. Each of the two has specialties in which it is superior; and as both have a large export trade, both manufacture two sorts of goods, one for home consumption, and the other for exportation. There was plenty of time to study these conditions, but it seems to have been used but indifferently. The importations of France to England would have shown that the specific superiority of each people in certain manufactures must form the basis of their reciprocal intercourse; at the same time, intelligent agents sent over, would soon have found which of the articles in which England excels could be naturalised with advantage in France.

If this had been done, it would have been found that the best goods manufactured for home consumption were the most necessary in the beginning. France has the credit of being essentially the land of fashion, and the credit is deserved. The problem was, therefore, to make English goods fashionable; that is, have them taken up by the upper classes. This done once, the lower classes would soon have imitated the example of their betters. But it will be long, if ever, that those bad articles, made for cheapness and exportation, will be accepted in that country.

First, there is an innate unwillingness to buy bad things merely because they are cheap. The French ouvrier prefers to be without them, or wait till he can afford something better.

Then there is another not less weighty reason which opposes itself to the adoption of these articles. It is the difference in the life led by the lower classes in France – their different ideas of necessaries and luxuries. Most English articles are calculated for home life and home comfort; while the French lower classes have little or no idea of home life, and certainly no notion of comfort. They remain at home when they can go nowhere else. In their atelier, or out-of-doors, and engaged in work the whole day, they prefer, in the evening, idling about in the streets, or going to a café or 'éstaminet,' until the time comes for going to bed. The ouvrier sleeps at home, but that is all. What is the use of cheap carpets, crockery, &c., to him? Carpet is a luxury, crockery almost useless, as he takes his meals at the next wine-shop, and goes with his family on Sundays to some 'éstaminet' at the barrières. If not with the man, with the French housewife, in the lower classes, saving and mending old things is almost a mania, which would scarcely find a satisfaction in buying bad things; she prefers good old things second or third hand.

It seems to me, therefore, that British importers have begun to work the new treaty at the wrong end, and have therefore their share as well as others in the small result which has been obtained hitherto. It is the consolation of England, that it must have reverses in the beginning of every war, and that this is a necessity which serves to develop her resources. It is a poor consolation, but may be applied likewise in the present industrial struggle. Having allowed to pass the first favourable moment, time alone can help to remedy the original mistake. As it is, a marked improvement is already visible since the first days of October; the best class of goods begin to appear gradually. On the other hand, French trading interest, relieved from the first panic, shows likewise a disposition to abandon that narrow-minded policy which may succeed for a moment, but can never be carried out for any length of time. It is this gradual understanding and approach of the two sides towards each other, which will lead to the true equilibrium in the new commercial relations of the two countries.

12/11 Austrian Protest over the Franco-Prussian Commercial Treaty of 1862

Austrian Memorandum, 9 May 1862. Printed in L. K. AEGIDI and A. KLAUHOLD, *Die Krisis des Zollvereins urkundlich dargestellt* (Hamburg, 1862), pp. 216-225. (W.O.H. Tr.)

As long ago as September 1861 Count Chotek [the Imperial Austrian representative in Berlin] handed to the Prussian Government a memorandum on the commercial treaty, which was then the subject of negotiation between Prussia and France. The purpose of this communication was to induce the Prussian Government not to include anything in that treaty which would impair the close relations established between Austria and the Zollverein by the treaty of 19 February 1853. . . . The Austrian Government urged:

1) that France should not, in future, be treated unconditionally as a most favoured nation, but that, in accordance with the precedent observed by Austria since 1851, an exception should be made in favour of those concessions which Prussia might grant to a German Federal State in view of the relations between members of the Germanic Confederation.

2) that the treaty should not be concluded for a longer period than that covered by the existing Zollverein treaties, that is to say, beyond the year 1865, and

3) that the Zollverein import duties should not be reduced to such an extent that Austria would find it necessary to use her treaty right to raise her 'intermediate duties'

(*Zwischenzölle*) against the Zollverein to such an extent as to make it not worth while for traders to pay on French goods sent to Austria *via* the Zollverein both the Zollverein import duty and the Austrian intermediate duty.

The reasons for these various requests are obvious. If they are ignored, the hope of closer co-operation between Austria and the Zollverein vanishes, first, because every concession made to her by members of the Zollverein is immediately granted to France and therefore loses value so far as Austria is concerned; secondly, because Austria's position is rendered more difficult since she must give up all hope of entering a customs union which is already bound by the French treaty; and thirdly, because it would be a new bar to mutual trade and no propitious preparation for the further negotiations provided for in the February treaty if Austria were now to find it necessary to withdraw some tariff concessions already made to Zollverein commerce.

The Prussian Government itself admits that this memorandum was received at a time when the French treaty was far from ready for signature and when indeed the differences of opinion which had arisen during the negotiations made it doubtful whether the treaty would be concluded at all. Prussia thus had every opportunity of respecting Austria's wishes.

Nevertheless the Austrian Cabinet received no answer to this memorandum either at that time or in the course of the subsequently resumed and very protracted Franco-Prussian negotiations until it was informed of the agreements initialled on 29 March 1862, – *agreements that contain all those provisions to which the Austrian Government have objected in the interests of the maintenance and extension of close commercial relations between the Hapsburg Empire and the Zollverein.*

The tariff concessions which these treaties grant to France are of such a nature as to make it necessary for Austria to undertake a thorough revision of the intermediate tariff agreed upon in 1853 for Austro-Zollverein commerce. Further, since the tariff concessions to France are contrary to both the letter and the spirit of the treaty of February 1853 and since they ignore the fact that the Austrian Government has never concealed its readiness to co-operate in progressive commercial reforms, they are a barrier to any possibility of the expansion of the February treaty and of the future customs union between Austria and the Zollverein....

In a dispatch of Count von Bernstorff to Freiherr Von Werther of 7 April the Prussian Government has explained its point of view in relation to the Austrian case. The arguments contained in this dispatch make it incumbent on the Austrian Government to explain frankly its very different conception of the situation both to Prussia and to the other members of the Zollverein....

Count Bernstorff states that the chief motive which has caused the

Prussian Government to conclude the treaty with France is not the tariff concessions made by France but the necessity of reforming the Zollverein tariff apart from such concessions.

It is only too manifest that Prussia's motive for signing the French treaty could not have been the extent of the commercial gains secured. The tariff reductions in mutual commerce are made mainly in fine goods in which France unquestionably leads in the markets of the world. But the reductions on general articles of commerce are less considerable and in one or two cases where the Zollverein has very low specific import duties, France raises her duties, according to the fineness of the goods, to a very considerable height or else hits Zollverein products by levying not inconsiderable *ad valorem* duties.

But although the Austrian Government fully recognises this fact it is unable to see why a treaty with France was a necessary preliminary to the reform of the tariff to which, as Count Bernstorff admits, the other members of the Zollverein had already agreed in principle. Nor is the Austrian Government able to see why, in view of the general recognition of the necessity of reforming the tariff, Prussia has always firmly rejected the repeated offers and urgent requests of Austria that the two Powers should co-operate to revise their duties on non-German goods. It is, however, true that Austria would not have agreed to this reduction of the Zollverein duties on the finest goods – duties which were already much too low – to the rates fixed by the Franco-Prussian treaty since this would have undoubtedly led to the ruin of many branches of Austrian industry. . . .

Prussia's commercial policy rests upon too old a tradition and too wide experience for it to be supposed that either a narrow theoretical view of the necessity and advantage of free trade or an exaggerated estimate of the extent of the market to be gained in France has led Prussia to conclude the Berlin agreements. The Austrian Government is far from desirous of enquiring into Prussia's *intentions*. But, in such circumstances, the Austrian Government can think of no other explanation of Prussia's action than the one which has been loudly enough expressed in Prussia's own press – namely that Prussia intends (by the adoption of a commercial system which Austria cannot accept owing to the position of her industry and finances and by the conclusion of a treaty which renders for ever impossible any closer connection between Austria and the Zollverein) to make the economic severance of Austria from the rest of Germany an accomplished and enduring fact. . . .

According to the dispatch, to which reference has frequently been made, it appears to be the wish of the Prussian Government that – in the event of the French treaty being accepted by the Zollverein as a whole – Austria should reduce her import duties [on non-German goods] rather than make full use of her treaty right to raise her intermediate tariff on articles imported from the Zollverein.... But the great majority of the tariff rates fixed by Prussia in the French treaty, particularly those on fine goods, are so low that Austria could not follow Prussia's example – even to the extent of maintaining the intermediate tariff at the existing level – without bringing about the ruin of many branches of her industry. In the event of the Franco-Prussian commercial treaty being accepted by the other Zollverein States the Austrian Government will have no alternative but to request early information as to the date on which the treaty comes into force and then to inform members of the Zollverein of the extent to which it proposes to use its treaty right to revise the Austrian intermediate tariff on Austro-Zollverein commerce.

The Austrian Government cannot admit that the Franco-Prussian treaty is merely one of those circumstances which were provided for by Article 4 of the commercial treaty of 19 February 1853, and that the Zollverein has fulfilled all its treaty obligations to Austria if it informs her in time of the tariff changes made in agreement with France. It is true that the contracting parties of the treaty of 1853 retained the right to make individual tariff changes. Neither party made changes in individual tariff rates, which appeared to be necessary, dependent upon the consent of the other but, according to Article 4 of the treaty, the other party merely had the right of making an equivalent increase in its intermediate tariff. There is, however, obviously an important difference between making alterations in individual tariff rates – which might be necessitated by changes of trading conditions in this or that article of commerce and which were not forbidden by the February treaty – *and a comprehensive revision of the entire method of charging duties which is wholly opposed to the basis of this treaty*. Individual duties can be reduced without doing violence to the solemnly declared intention set out by the contracting parties in the preamble to the February treaty to prepare the way for a customs union, or even without contravening Article 25 of this treaty which states that it is the purpose of the contracting parties *to assimilate their tariffs as much as possible*. Such individual tariff changes were provided for in Article 4. But a complete reform of the tariff – a revision which, instead of reducing the differences of the two tariffs, systematically increases them; a revision by which one party changes from a protective system to a system of low revenue duties, without enquiring whether the other party can do the same; a revision, further, which is carried out not by internal legislation but by a binding treaty with a third Power – such a reform is incompatible not only with Article 4 of the treaty of 1853 but with the preamble of the treaty which pledges the contracting parties to aim at the conclusion of an Austro-German customs union. It is also incompatible with Article 25 which provides that, if the customs union has not been set up by 1860, the parties are pledged at least to attempt to secure as great a measure of uniformity as possible between the two tariffs. The Austrian Government therefore feels that it is its duty – in its own interests as well as in the true interests of Germany – to state that *the acceptance of the agreements initialled at Berlin on 29 March 1862, by Prussia and France would, in its judgment, be a breach, on the part of the Zollverein, of the legal obligations existing between Austria and Zollverein as a result of the treaty of February 19, 1853.*

One final point. By article 31 of the commercial treaty, Prussia promise France not to set up any export prohibition that is not, at the same time, made to apply to all other nations. This article affects not merely commercial interests but it affects the German national union and the standing of the Germanic Confederation as a unified Power and as a military unit. Hitherto the Confederation has had the unquestioned right, for reasons of Germany's external defence, to forbid the export from any part of the Confederation of horses, arms, munitions, military stores etc to certain foreign markets or to all of them. The Austrian Government cannot reconcile Prussia's obligations under this Federal law with the provision in question in her treaty with France.

Chapter 13 Transport

Introduction

The expansion of the railway network is the most significant feature of European transport development in the nineteenth century. It stimulated heavy industry by its demand for raw materials, provided employment for a considerable labour force, embraced activities as disparate as sophisticated engineering and navvying, and brought into existence completely new industries such as engine building and coach construction. Such developments resulted in a significant extension of the market, increased mobility and, for some, the railways brought a personal fortune. There were other effects; the decay of already established forms of transportation, for some the loss of land, and in urban centres the loss of homes.

Road transportation still claimed a good deal of attention and it is clear that, whilst certain areas in France such as the Aisne Department reflected a progressive attitude towards improvement (**13/1**), many countries were inadequately served by their road network. According to Casimir Delamarre, in 1868 Spain had 20 times less the amount of road per square kilometre than France (**13/3**). In Spain almost all developments depended upon the caprice of the authorities, and it was impossible to find any compensation for road deficiencies in the development of a railway network. This too was virtually non-existent, and commercial centres were generally isolated islands with limited markets. A similar situation prevailed until well into the nineteenth century in Italy, where there was a noticeable geographical division between satisfactory and unsatisfactory areas, with the north receiving far better consideration than the poorer areas in the south, which had hardly any recognizable roads (**13/4**). As far as Russia was concerned, even as late as 1870 the road network had changed little since the eighteenth century. Here transport was easier in winter, when snow and ice provided a solid surface (**13/5b**), but generally the system did not guarantee the efficient movement of men and materials.

In neither Spain nor Russia was there a co-ordinated transport system; in Spain the whim of the Minister of Public Works, and in Russia the requirements of the Tsar, were more powerful factors than any economic considerations.

What of river and canal transport? In 1815 the Congress of Vienna had allowed for freer navigation on the rivers of the signatory powers (**13/7**). In 1824 in his report on French transport Becquey argued forcibly about the need for transport improvements and the advantages resulting from the interdependence of river and canal transport (**13/7**) and Chevalier's notes written in 1838 indicated that the most industrialized areas of France possessed a satisfactory and impressive canal system (**13/8**). Gradually and inexorably, however, all modes of transport came to be overshadowed by the railways.

Several significant features emerge from the documents dealing with the railway development, which had its origins in industrial concerns (**11/19**). It is clear that the central or State authorities played a significant part in the financing, authorizing and development of the network. This applies not only to France (**13/11, 13/12, 13/14**), but also to Belgium, where the system was 'planned and executed by the Government at public cost' (**13/9**), Italy (**13/16**), Russia (**13/18**), and Germany, where development proceeded at a State rather than a national level. It would be incorrect to assume, however, that private capital and initiative were absent or unimportant. Indeed, private capital was extremely important, not only for local development, but on an international plane. For example, French finance was involved in the later developments of the Russian network (**13/18**); and Claxton, the American Consul in Moscow, noted the interest and activity of the Barings and Rothschilds and the Hopes in Russian developments (**13/19**). During this period of international railway finance, France assumed a pre-eminent role, performing a similar function in Europe to that which Britain had played in the development of the French economy. The *Crédit Mobilier* was heavily involved in financing railway development (**14/9**) and evidence indicates that French investment activity spread into most areas of Europe (**14/10**).

Whilst contemporary advocates of railways extolled their benefits (**13/10** and **13/17a**), there was an international movement of men to match the international flow of capital investment. The significant developments of the French network were a feature of the Second Empire, by which time Britain had laid the nucleus of her own track and trained a large number of contractors, navvies and mechanics for this kind of work. France was able to draw upon this pool of talent, and seized the opportunity. British contractors were able to price their French counterparts out of the market (**13/13a**), and once the contractors were established they tended to employ British labourers. Europe found itself invaded by the railway navvies. With their skill and experience they were capable of undertaking work which Frenchmen were either unable or unwilling to execute, and their liberal spending benefited many local economies (**13/13a**). It is interesting to note that the local labour which undertook navvying had a similar outlook on life and similar *mores* to the English navvy. As a Victorian observer put it,

'The line between an Italian navvy and a brigand is slight, not to say evanescent' (**13/15**).

By such means and with such help the railways were built. As far as can be ascertained, they were constructed more cheaply than in Britain (**13/9**, **13/11**) and the benefits anticipated by List (**13/17a**), were gradually realized. By 1870 the railways had already assumed the role of originating, co-ordinating and extending significant developments in the European economy.

13/1 Condition of Roads in the Aisne Department

J. B. BRAYER DE BEAUREGARD, *Statistique du département de l'Aisne* (Laon, 1824), pp. 554-555. (Ed. Tr.)

The Royal roads which cross the Aisne Department* take a large amount of traffic; they are part of the network which links Paris with Strasbourg, Germany, Flanders and the Kingdom of the Netherlands, or else they facilitate relations between the Eastern Departments of France and the Depart- of the Nord and Belgium.

For some years the state of the roads has been much improved; in general, they are now in good condition. This improvement is due to the paternal government under which we live, the sound administration of the Prefects,* and the enlightened zeal of the engineers. The sums provided by the Royal Treasury and the expenses for repair and maintenance since 1814 amount to 4,585,000 francs.* It is calculated that at present their annual maintenance must cost at least 45 centimes per metre for the paved parts of the highway, and 75 centimes for the metalled parts.

For its part, the Conseil Général of the Department concentrates all its attention on Departmental roads. Through the successive credits voted since 1815, which amount to 828,000 francs, it has managed to finish or restore roads 1, 2, and 7, and is about to finish 6, 9, 11 and 12, and to construct the most difficult and frequented parts of the five remaining roads. However, they still require a considerable outlay before they can be used throughout the year; the Conseil Général recognised how much advantage would result for the Department from such action, and in its 1826 session it voted an extraordinary tax of 2 centimes for five years, to be used, in addition to the customary road funds so that the road developments could proceed more quickly. The annual maintenance of the twelve roads in the Department, in their finished state is estimated at 100,000 francs, i.e., at the cheapest, 35 centimes per metre.

The materials which are to be found in the Aisne Department for the

* See Glossary.

construction and maintenance of roads vary according to localities. The surroundings of Soissons and Laon possess quite abundant resources of sandstone for paved roadways; at the extremities of the South and North there are silicious stones for the metalled roads; but the centre area, i.e. the country between Oulchy-le-Château, Berry-au-Bac, Laon, Coucy-le-Château, Vic-sur-Aisne and Villers-Cotterêts, offers only inferior quality limestone for the metalled roads which are planned for, or already built in the area.

The service of the roads, Royal as well as Departmental, is entrusted to a chief engineer and three ordinary engineers, who have under their command a number of foremen.

13/2 French Carter Merchants, 1824

JOHN M. COBBETT, *Letters from France, containing Observations made in that Country during a Journey . . . in 1824* (London, 1825), pp. 252–253. (G.P.J.)

To a nasty little inn . . . at Sedan . . . where I found . . . a disobliging . . . landlady. She put me down to supper with six voituriers, men who carry on the internal trade of the country. Carters to all appearance, with blue smock frocks and blue and red night-caps on; who however behaved with all that innate politeness which distinguishes the Frenchman. . . . These men go about with an immense cart and horses, carrying from one town to another the goods that such town wants to sell and to buy. And they buy besides goods which they dispatch by public conveyances to Paris, there to be sold for them on commission. They find something to buy wherever they go that is wanted elsewhere. Here they buy cloth, at Brussells lace, at Verdun comfitures, at Limoges *chesnuts*, and so on. One man that was in this group had come from Bayonne since the end of August. He was at Avignon in September and at Dijon on the same days that I was there; from this place he goes to Brussells, thence to Paris and Nantes, and this is his mode of life. These people one meets all over the country, sometimes with a long string of one-horse carts, or large carts drawn by very large mules, but the expenses of so much land carriage eat up their profits as merchants.

13/3 Spanish Roads and Economic Retardation

C. DELAMARRE, 'La situation économique de l'Espagne', *Journal des Économistes* (1869), pp. 60–64. (Ed. Tr.)

The real obstacle [to the export of raw materials], which nothing can overcome and which is the chief cause of the deplorable economic condition of Spain, is the absence of communications.

13/3 *Spanish Roads and Economic Retardation*

This absence is greater than anything imaginable: it is absolute. Official statistics cannot be used in defence of the system. They prove only one thing: that so many kilometres of first, second or third-class roads have been classified and officially constructed, but this does not mean that travel is easy. On many different occasions we recall having seen stage-coaches pass into the fields which border on the first-class roads. . . . We also recall that there are provinces indicated as having numerous kilometres of road, of which not even the smallest section is passable.

Finally, there are some roads which are very well constructed, but which cease to be maintained, with the result that they became quite useless.

Do not forget, moreover, that these *carreteras* correspond to our *routes impériales*, and apart from these roads absolutely nothing exists. Let us assume for a moment that the official figures are true, and compare them with the present situation in France, where improvement is still rightly demanded.

At the end of 1864, according to official figures, Spain possessed altogether 14,547 kilometres of *carreteras* and since then, absorbed by its political situation, it has managed to construct only insignificant additions.

By contrast, France possessed altogether 320,044 kilometres; taking into account the area of the two countries, the following figures emerge, which are in a ratio of 1 to 20.

For Spain, 28·71 metres of roads per sq. kilometre.

For France, 591·57 metres of roads per sq. kilometre.

. . . the economic consequences of this deplorable condition are aggravated even more by the fact that the raw materials which have to be transported, are precisely those which are very heavy and cumbersome, relative to their value, and even more than manufactured goods require an economic system of transportation.

But it will be said that there are railways. It is true that railways perform a valuable function; but, in a vast country, what is the use of several isolated lines, which join the main centres, but which, because of the absence of roads, cannot enter into contact with the very territory they cross?

In all parts of Spain we have seen with our own eyes the donkey . . . with a load placed on its shoulders at the production centres. Does the reader know how many donkeys are needed to effect the loading of a mere eight-ton truck? 88 of them are needed. 1700 donkeys would be needed for a 20-carriage train, without counting another army of drivers!

In such conditions raw materials, which are always heavy or bulky, cannot make use of the railways. As a method of transport for raw materials the railway is already too costly; but if the railway journey must be preceded by a long journey on a donkey's back, it becomes absolutely impossible to transport raw materials by these means.

Spanish railways really cross Spain without establishing contact with the interior of the country. Railways are of considerable importance for commerce and consumers in the large towns, [and] they develop an area of several kilometres around the stations; but their influence stops at that point. What Spain needs are roads which cross the country in all directions and which permit each product to gain access cheaply either to a railway station or, preferably, to a port.

This has not been grasped in Spain, where, on the contrary, the introduction of railways has been regarded by the Administration as an excellent opportunity to dispense with the provision of sums for the construction of roads. As for the old roads, since most of them were parallel to the railways, it became increasingly useless to maintain them.

New roads were constructed only by virtue of particular circumstances which were irrelevant to the economic interests of the country. A new Minister of Works took office, and provided his local area with a good road; then another Minister succeeded him who, in his turn, did something completely different. But there was no overall plan; the result was that certain areas like Andalusia, which, I am assured, have never produced a Minister of Public Works, have found themselves deprived absolutely of all forms of communication.

On another occasion it is the ex-Queen who thinks it is time to undertake a journey in the Southern provinces. It is suddenly noticed that the town of Murcia, with a population of 40,000, has waited four years since the opening of the railway from Madrid to Alicante, for a decent road to join it to Novelda, the nearest station. In a few weeks the road in question is improvised, after a fashion, and the Queen just manages to pass through.

Both the railway companies and the country suffer from this state of affairs.

Without roads which allow raw materials to converge on railway stations, and permit the transportation of manufactured goods into the interior, the railways have no trade, and cannot make profits. In our opinion, this is the real cause of the deplorable financial position of the railway companies.

13/4 Roads in Northern and Southern Italy

I. SACHS, *L'Italie, ses finances et son développement économique, 1859-1884* (Paris, 1885) pp. 216-217. (Ed. Tr.)

In 1860 the various parts of Italy were characterized by an unequal distribution of roads. In the Northern parts of Italy and the central areas as far as Tronto, apart from a network of great roads constructed and maintained by the finances of the different States, there were many good roads which were constructed and maintained by provinces and communes. Without being everywhere complete or perfect, the network was nevertheless adequate for the needs of the population. In the Southern provinces the situation was quite different.

The areas around Naples were provided with several beautiful roads, which were in perfect condition, but whilst these roads around the capital were maintained, roads into the interior of the country in the mountainous provinces of the Abruzzi and Calabria, with the exception of the great roads called Consolari, and several roads maintained by the provinces in the area of Bari and Otranto, simply did not exist. In the Island of Sicily conditions were even worse. There, not a single road was constructed or maintained by the Government, which had granted financial and administrative autonomy to the island.

We have statistics to illustrate the inequality in the distribution of communications in the different parts of Italy. In 1863 we counted altogether 22,167 kilometres of national and provincial roads, an average of 8,509 metres of road per square myriametre.* In Tuscany the average was 15,414 metres; in the Marches and Umbria 13,228; in Lombardy 12,799; in the Romagna, 11,727; in Piedmont, 9,688; in Sicily, 9,045; in Parma and Modena 8,789; in the Neapolitan areas 6,474; and finally 3,524 metres in the island of Sardinia. The total length of road in 1863 was 85,959 kilometres, of which, 13,498 were national roads, 8,995 provincial roads and 63,466 communal roads.

13/5 Road Maintenance in Russia

a MARQUIS DE CUSTINE, *Russia* (3 vols., London, 1844), II, pp. 229–230; III, pp. 104–105, 250–251.

b D. M. WALLACE, *Russia* etc. [*see* Document **11/1b**], pp. 13–14, 20.

a To travel post on the road from Petersburg to Moscow, is to treat one's self for whole days to the sensation experienced in descending the *montagnes Russes* at Paris. It would be well to bring an English carriage to Petersburg, if only for the pleasure of travelling, on really elastic springs, this famous road, the best chaussée in Europe, according to the Russians, and, I believe, according to strangers also. It must be owned that it is well kept, although hard, by reason of the nature of the materials, which broken as they are in tolerably small pieces, form, in encrusting over the surface, little immovable asperities, which shake the carriages to a degree that causes something to

* See Glossary.

come out of place at every stage. As much time is thus lost as is gained by the speed at which they drive; for we rush along, in a whirlwind of dust, with the rapidity of a hurricane chasing the clouds before it. An English carriage is very pleasant for the few first stages; but in the long run, the necessity of a Russian equipage to withstand the pace of the horses and the hardness of the road, is discovered. The rails of the bridges are formed of handsome iron balustrades, and the granite pillars which support them are carved with the Imperial arms. This road is broader than those of England; it is also as even, although less easy: the horses are small, but full of muscle. . . .

If we are to believe the Russians, all their roads are good during the summer season, even those that are not the great highways. I find them all bad. A road full of inequalities, sometimes as broad as a field, sometimes extremely narrow, passes through beds of sand in which the horses plunge above their knees, lose their wind, break their traces, and refuse to draw at every twenty yards; if these sands are passed, you soon plunge into pools of mud which conceal large stones and enormous stumps of trees, that are very destructive to the carriages. Such are the roads of this land, except during seasons when they become absolutely impassable, when the extreme of cold renders travelling dangerous, when storms of snow bury the country, or when floods, produced by the thaw, transform, for about three months in the year, the low plains into lakes; namely, for about six weeks after the summer, and for as many after the winter season; the rest of the year they continue marshes.

I had forgotten to mention a singular object which struck me at the commencement of the journey.

Between Petersburg and Novgorod, I remarked, for several successive stages, a second road that ran parallel to the principal highway, though at a considerable distance from it. It was furnished with bridges and every thing else that could render it safe and passable, although it was much less handsome, and less smooth, than the grand route. I asked the keeper of a post-house the meaning of this singularity, and was answered, through my feldjäger, that the smaller road was destined for waggons, cattle, and travellers, when the Emperor, or other members of the Imperial family, proceeded to Moscow. The dust and obstructions that might incommode or retard the august travellers, if the grand route remained open to the public, were thus avoided. I cannot tell whether the innkeeper was amusing himself at my expense, but he spoke in a very serious manner, and seemed to consider it very natural that the sovereign should engross the road in a land where the sovereign is every thing. The king who said, '*I am France*,' stopped to let a flock of sheep pass; and under his reign, the foot-passenger, the waggoner, and the clown who travelled the public road, repeated our old adage to the princes whom they met: 'the highway belongs to every body:' what really constitutes a law is, not its letter, but the manner in which it is applied.

b In Russia, roads are nearly all of the unmade, natural kind, and are so conservative in their nature that they have at the present day precisely the same appearance as they had many centuries ago. They have thus for imaginative minds something of what is called 'the charm of historical association'. The only perceptible change that takes place in them during a series of generations is that the ruts shift their position. When these become so deep that fore-wheels can no longer fathom them, it becomes necessary to begin making a new pair of ruts to the right or left of the old ones; and as the roads are commonly of gigantic breadth, there is no difficulty in finding a place for the operation. How the old ones get filled up I cannot explain; but as I have never seen in any part of the country a human being engaged in road-repairing, I assume that beneficent Nature somehow accomplishes the task without human assistance, either by means of alluvial deposits, or by some other cosmical action best known to physical geographers. . . .

In the winter months travelling is in some respects pleasanter than in summer, for snow and frost are great macadamizers. If the snow falls evenly, there is for some time the most delightful road that can be imagined. No jolts, no shaking, but a smooth, gliding motion, like that of a boat in calm water, and the horses gallop along as if totally unconscious of the sledge behind them. Unfortunately, this happy state of affairs does not last long. The road soon gets cut up, and deep transverse furrows are formed. How these furrows come into existence I have never been able clearly to comprehend, though I have often heard the phenomenon explained by men who imagined they understood it. Whatever the cause and mode of formation may be, certain it is that little hills and valleys do get formed, and the sledge, as it crosses over them, bobs up and down like a boat in a chopping sea, with this important difference, that the boat falls into a yielding liquid, whereas the sledge falls upon a solid substance, unyielding and unelastic. The shaking and jolting which result may readily be imagined.

13/6 Rules concerning the free navigation of rivers

Règlements concernant la libre navigation des rivières. Annexe No. 16 de l'acte final du Congrès de Vienne du 9 Juin 1815, extracted from N. W. POSTHUMUS, *Recueil de documents internationaux relatifs à l'histoire économique de 1814 à 1924* (Amsterdam, 1925), pp. 2-4. (Ed. Tr.)

1. Articles concerning the free navigation of rivers which in their navigable

course divide or cross the various States, which have signed the declaration of 24 March 1815.

COMMON ARRANGEMENTS

Article 1. The powers which are divided or crossed by a common navigable river pledge themselves to regulate its navigation by common agreement. To this effect they shall nominate commissioners who shall meet, at the latest, six months after the end of the Congress, and who shall take as the basis of their work, the following principles.

PRINCIPLES

FREEDOM OF NAVIGATION

Article 2. Navigation in the entire course of the rivers indicated in the preceding article, from the point at which each of them becomes navigable to its mouth, shall be entirely free and nobody who conforms to the common rules of administration may be prevented from using the rivers for trading purposes. . . .

UNIFORMITY OF SYSTEM

Article 3. As far as possible, the system established for the collection of tolls as well as for the maintainance of administration, shall be the same for the entire course of the river, and unless prevented by local circumstances it shall be extended also to those branches and confluents which, in their navigable stretches, divide or cross the various States.

TARIFF

Article 4. To obviate the detailed examination of cargoes otherwise than in cases of fraud and illegality, navigation duties shall be fixed, so that they are uniform and invariable, irrespective of the nature of the merchandise. . . .

The amount of these duties, which under no circumstances may exceed those in force at present, shall be settled locally, which hardly permits the establishment of a general rule. The basic idea behind the tariff is the encouragement of commerce and navigation, and the duty on the Rhine may serve as an approximative norm. Once the tariff is in force, it may be increased only by a common arrangement among the riverine States, and additional duties may not be introduced.

COLLECTION BUREAUX

Article 5. The number of collection bureaux shall be fixed by law and kept at a minimum and no alteration shall be possible, otherwise than by common agreement, unless one of the States wishes to reduce the number of its own bureaux.

TOW PATHS

Article 6. Each riverine state shall undertake the maintenance of tow paths within its territory and any work which is necessary to remove obstacles to navigation. . . .

RIGHT OF PUTTING INTO PORT

Article 7. Rights of purveyance, of berthing and of putting in under stress of circumstances shall not be established. Those which already exist shall be abolished unless they are necessary or useful for commerce in general.

CUSTOMS

Article 8. The customs duties of the riverine states shall be quite distinct from the navigation duties. Regulatory arrangements shall prevent the customs officers placing any hindrance in the way of navigation; but all attempts at smuggling, with the help or assistance of boatmen, shall be watched for by the river police.

RULES

Article 9. All the above provisions shall be decided by common agreement and shall annul all previous arrangements. Once accepted, the agreement may not be altered, except with the consent of all the riverine states, and they shall be charged with carrying out the act in a manner which is suitably adapted to circumstances and localities.

(*Signed*) Humboldt, Clancarty, Dalberg, Wessenberg.

13/7 Internal Transport in France, 1824

France, Ministère de Travaux Publics, Administration Générale des Ponts et Chaussées, *Statistique des Routes Royales* (par BECQUEY) (Paris, 1824), pp. 6-7, 11-12. (Ed. Tr.)

Almost the entire Kingdom can share in the benefits conferred by a sound system of navigation. A new impetus to manufacturing and agriculture, the multiplication of exchange outlets, and consequently the growth of public wealth, will be the inevitable result of improvements in transport; at a time when Europe is tending to divert exports to the internal market, we must attach great importance to the creation of new markets which allow us to recoup in internal trade what we may lose in exports. This is an opportune moment, therefore, to trace all the efforts directed towards the prosperity of this internal trade which, apart from the advantages of not being subjected to external political changes, will always be more profitable.

I should add that in the completion of our internal navigation France would find another advantage which should also be taken into consideration. The roads would cease to be troubled by heavy traffic; they would always remain in good condition and their upkeep would be cheap. I do not think it is going too far to say that a good system of navigation would save 6 million francs per year.

We are creating all kinds of new wealth; unceasing competition and increasing production oblige us to push ahead with transport improvements.

Indeed, no other country has as much interest in the development of communications as France, which, because of its territory, its geographical position and the outlook of its people, contains all that is needed for a vigorous internal trade.

But these advantages can be fully enjoyed only with a co-ordinated, extensive and economical transport system. It is by these means that profitable economic relations are established among the remote provinces; for then, their agricultural or industrial goods are transported easily to all parts of the Kingdom. The importance of natural navigation also invites the attention of the Government. There is a need for improvement in this respect in several parts of the Kingdom; and most of the canals, the construction of which is equally desirable, will be of limited value if river and stream communications do not receive the improvements which they need. These two types of communication are inextricably linked; they cannot be regarded in isolation; the canals would lose part of their usefulness if navigation on the rivers and streams with which they connect, cannot be attempted without risk, or if costs were such that trade was obliged to go overland.

In France we have a striking example of the beneficial influence resulting from quick and inexpensive communication. The Department* of the Nord, rightly renowned for its industrial and agricultural riches, is also an area which is crossed by the greatest number of canals, and possesses one-sixth of all the canals in the Kingdom.

It is regrettable that the other areas of France have been unable to follow a similar path, but local circumstances have not been everywhere favourable; and moreover, however disposed the Government was to such new developments, it has been frustrated too often by financial considerations. Sometimes local interests have co-operated with the State, and sometimes also, groups of proprietors and capitalists, excited by the advantage which would accrue to them from the opening of a canal, have undertaken all construction expenses, but the system of local associations, as yet, has allowed only very limited development.

Different methods can be used to foster canal development; they can be developed at the State's expense or can be contracted out to companies which

* See Glossary.

bear the cost of construction in return for toll concessions on the traffic using the canals, or, finally, the resources of the State and private companies can be combined when the tolls and profits are inadequate to indemnify advances.

13/8 French Canal Development

M. CHEVALIER, *Des intérêts matériels en France* (Paris, 1838), pp. 93–97. (Ed. Tr.)

Anyone who casts his eye over a map of the French inland navigation system must be struck by the enormous difference which exists between Eastern and Western France. In Eastern France there is a series of lines of navigation in both the Northern and Southern parts of the territory; first of all, from Paris to the sea, via Amiens and the Somme; then from Paris in the direction of Valenciennes, Mons and the entire valley of the Scheldt with the network of branches covering the Departments* of the Nord and the Pas-de-Calais, and the impressive offshoots from the Oise, one going to Charleroi and the valley of the Sambre, and the other to Namur, Liège, and the valley of the Meuse via the Aisne and the Ardennes canal . . . Any traveller from Paris to the Mediterranean via Lyons can also choose between four canals.
1. From the Seine to the Saône via the Yonne and the Burgundy Canal;
2. From the Seine to the Saône via the Loing Canal, the Briare Canal, the Canal latéral à la Loire, and the canal from Charollais or 'Le Centre'.†
3. There is a third choice which differs from the latter in so far as the traveller can choose to go via the Yonne and the Nivernais Canal rather than the Briare and Loing Canals.
4. Finally, the last route meets the second to the North of Digoin, but to the South of this town it follows the edge of the Loire as far as Roanne and there meets the St. Étienne railway system which extends as far as Lyons. On the edge of the Mediterranean are the canals which terminate in the Rhône Valley. In the same area of France is the canal from the Rhône to the Rhine which joins Lyons to Strasbourg, Mulhouse and Basle. During the last session, the Chambers granted a considerable sum to the Seine and the Saône and voted for the canalisation of the Marne from Paris to Vitry, i.e. more than one third of the Grand Canal from Paris to Strasbourg. It is not my intention to refer to the lesser undertakings of either the Government or the Companies.

In the West there is only the Brittany Canal, the canalisation of parts of

* See Glossary.

† Le Centre: 'the region is one of rolling topography, rising towards the South, to the Massif Central, and enclosed on the East and West by the great bend of the Loire'. N. S. G. Pounds and W. A. Parker, *Coal and Steel in Western Europe* (London, 1957), p. 157. (Ed.)

the Isle, the Dordogne and the Sèvre, the recently voted improvements affecting the Lot, the Tarn and the Adour, and the almost insignificant work on the Midouze and the Baise. The Canal of the Midi straddles the East and the West, and neither can regard it as its exclusive possession. The canals in the West are shorter than those in the East. Incomparably smaller sums have been spent on them. There is no integrated canal system uniting various Departments and conferring unlimited social benefits by allowing everyone to profit from everyone else's prosperity. As if this were not enough . . . until now the canals in the West have enjoyed only a secondary commercial importance. The Brittany Canal, which is the largest and most expensive work carried out in the West, was conceived as an advantage militarily . . . to guarantee the provisioning of the Brest Arsenal rather than to increase agricultural and industrial production in Brittany, which at that time, however, was perhaps the most neglected of all our provinces.

For centuries the West has possessed a few important ports and there are several more which are clearly destined to be of prime importance. In the proximity of these ports the West has fertile land and heavily populated centres which are, or aim to be, manufacturing areas which one day will send their output to the ports and draw from the latter agricultural products and national, foreign or colonial goods. Nothing has been done to link these ports and to provide them with access to the Paris market, and to make it easier for the towns and areas of the interior to gain access to the Paris market and the coastal areas. Deprived of economic and rapid means of transport, connecting them to internal markets, all our Western ports are in a situation similar to that which existed at the time of the blockade. . . .*

Such is the tragic plight of Cherbourg, where we have already spent large sums . . . and Caen. The same applies to Nantes, and Bordeaux, La Rochelle, Rochefort and Bayonne.

If, in contrast to the decadence which characterizes all the other ports which were so flourishing under the old régime, Marseilles and Le Havre (which, in any case, does not belong to Western France), are quite prosperous, it is because Le Havre benefits from the Parisian hinterland at its rear, and its proximity to the canals of the North-East; and Marseilles, once the worst sections of the Rhône are negotiated, can distribute its imports via the magnificent Eastern canal network.

The Eastern part of France, then, is quite magnificent; it offers a large number of navigable routes, all beautifully constructed, extending from one extremity of the country to the other, joining the various provinces and bringing the products of the North into the South and carrying Southern foodstuffs to the North, linking the frontier and the interior and the agricul-

* The Continental blockade during the Napoleonic Wars. (Ed.)

tural and manufacturing areas with the ports, all, finally, converging on Paris, which is the most active centre of capital and business, and the most important centre of consumption. In the East there is hardly a single important town, with the exception of Rheims and Troyes, which, within its locality, cannot boast of either a canal or a river which has been, or is being, improved at the expense of the Treasury.

This invaluable advantage disappears as one enters the West. Between the two halves of France, the division of public work seems to have been settled along the lines of the feudal lord, with the motto 'Everything on one side, and nothing on the other'. Normandy is quite as fertile as Flanders, and is not less of a manufacturing area; yet Normandy has no canals, whilst Flanders is strewn with them. To the North of the Loire and to the West of the Seine, with the exception of Brittany no province is endowed with a good system of navigation, in spite of the advantages which would accrue to the area from the provisioning of Paris. A similar situation prevails to the South of the Loire, in the Vendée, Poitou, Limousin, Marche and Auvergne. Between the Loire and the Garonne there is absolutely no significant line of communication. The vast basin of the Gironde is completely isolated from the rest of France. The Canal du Midi remains unfinished; even the Canal des Deux Mers does not deserve the title of a canal, since it starts at Toulouse, and from Toulouse to Bordeaux the navigation of the river is usually quite impossible. And yet the canal flanking the Garonne which was intended to contribute to the revival of Bordeaux did not receive the approval of the Chamber during the last session.

13/9 Belgian Railways

RAWSON W. RAWSON, 'On Railways in Belgium', *Journal of the Statistical Society* (vol. 2, 1839), pp. 47–55. (G.P.J.)

Belgium is the first state in Europe which has established a general system of railways, embracing the whole of the kingdom, and planned and executed by the Government at the public cost. The project was first put forth in the year 1833, and the object proposed was to unite the principal commercial towns on one side with the sea, and on the other with the frontiers of France and Prussia. . . .

The first step which the Government took . . . was to employ a number of competent engineers . . . On the 1st of May, 1834, a law was passed authorizing the Government to carry their project into execution. Mechlin* was taken as the centre of the system with four branches extending from that

* Malines. (Ed.)

town, in different directions to each frontier.... The total length of the lines projected by the first law was 239¼ English miles, of which 159½ miles, or exactly two-thirds, are already completed.... By a subsequent law, dated the 26th May, 1837, the Government was authorized to extend the system by the construction of a line from Ghent through Courtray to the French frontier....

... The people have had the advantage of a much earlier introduction of this important means of communication than if the undertaking had been left to private speculation, – without risk to individuals, – without the interference of private interests, – on lines, perhaps, which of themselves would have offered no temptation to private enterprise, but which as parts of an extensive system will repay, either directly or indirectly, the money expended upon them....

The Belgian Government, however, does not restrain private enterprise upon any other lines than those entering into the general system....

The cost of the ten sections already completed, comprising the expenses of locomotive power, stations and buildings, was about £1,360,000 or £8,526 a mile.... The cost, however, of the four sections since completed ... appears to have amounted to £10,432 a mile.... It is worthy of notice that the estimates of the engineers made in 1833 have been exceeded on the above four sections by only 8 per cent.

... The lowest sum yet incurred in the construction of a well-executed railway in England is stated to be £10,000 a mile. This was the amount on the Newcastle and Carlisle and on the Wigan lines.... Others ... have amounted to £40,000 a mile. The cost of the Manchester and Liverpool line was £38,553 per mile.... The short line from London to Greenwich, of only three miles, has cost more than £600,000 or £200,000 a mile.... In France, the estimated expenses of four different projected lines between Paris and Havre vary from £15,400 to £21,400 a mile. In comparison, therefore, with England or France, Belgium possesses great advantages in the cheap construction of railways; but it falls as far short, on the other hand, of the United States of America. There the cost is stated to fluctuate between £2,000 and £6,000 per mile....

The following will show how far the Belgian surpass the English railroads in cheapness of fares:

Liverpool and Manchester		Average of Belgian lines	
Mails	2½d. per mile	Berlins	1½d. per mile
Coaches	2⅛d. ,, ,,	Diligences	1¼d. ,, ,,
Wagons	1½d. ,, ,,	Chars-à-banc	¾d. ,, ,,
		Wagons	½d. ,, ,,

13/9 *Belgian Railways*

. . . On an average each inhabitant [of Liverpool, Manchester and Warrington] may be supposed to take one trip in a year . . . the average number of trips to each inhabitant [of Brussels, Mechlin and Antwerp] . . . five per annum.

13/10 Belgian Railways and their Economic Effects

E. TEISSERENC, *Les travaux publics en Belgique et les chemins de fer* (Paris, 1839), pp. 118-121. (Ed. Tr.)

It has been repeated often, and rightly, that one of the great benefits conferred by railways is that of increasing the speed of business transactions. People said, 'When the great commercial centres are separated simply by a few hours of travel, instead of plunging into correspondence which is often abortive, one will go to these centres and at the same time, business will improve and become speedier.'

From that it would seem that postal revenues would diminish considerably as a result of railway development, especially in a country where railway fares are extremely low; nothing of the kind has happened, and although the principal towns of Belgium have been provided with this sort of rapid communication, at the same time postal revenue has not stopped rising . . . far from slowing up, it has quadrupled in the space of three years. The fact is that the social intercourse established by this immense movement of men has been maintained by letters.

To conclude the enumeration of the results produced by the influence of the Belgian railways, we ought to indicate its prodigious effects on the machine industry and commerce in general [and] the rapid growth in the revenues of the towns which it connects; for example, we could take the customs receipts of Antwerp which amounted to only 4,338,800 francs* in 1829, a period which has always been given as the high peak of Belgian industry, and which rose in 1838 to 6,238,800 francs; but these figures are complicated by several factors, which are easily identifiable but the relative importance of which is unknown.

Several other facts should be noticed because they are certain to be repeated in all those countries which engage seriously in material improvements. We refer to the increase in the price of land at the side of the railway; the cost of labour, the price of iron and the wood which is needed for sleepers. . . .

The value of land crossed by the railways has risen by a third; labour has risen in the same proportion; the rails which cost only 37 fr. 93 c. for every

* See Glossary.

100 kilograms in 1834 had risen to 42 francs by the end of 1837; indeed, for a time, as a result of increased costs, it became necessary to suspend the laying of a second line between Brussels and Antwerp. After this period competition in the development of coke and iron production led to a reduction in price. At the last adjudication, which took place on 5 September 1838, the supply of rails for the section from Ghent to Deynze-Petegem was settled at 34 francs per 100 kilograms.

Such have been the general consequences of the establishment of railways in Belgium. Our experience is still incomplete, the track is not yet finished, the goods service is unorganized and the future will doubtless reveal new information among which the effects on the transit trade will not be the least interesting. Already in 1835 the export and import merchandise carried through Belgium had risen to nearly 23 millions. . . .

This is a significant factor and one which illustrates better than any *a priori* argument, the excellent geographical situation of this country, relative to transit commerce. The organisation of merchandising services on the railway, the extension of the network up to the Prussian and French frontiers and the opening of the railway which is to unite Frankfurt, Karlsruhe and Basle will increase the importance of such activity in a proportion which is difficult to calculate, but which cannot fail to be considerable.

13/11 The Financing of Railways in France

JOSEPH DEVEY, *The Life of Joseph Locke, Civil Engineer, M.P., F.R.S.* (London, 1862), pp. 216-219.

'*Whilst, however, the direct control of the State has protected French railway enterprise from the rivalries of party interests, and the wasteful expenses of competition, and whilst it has been aided by subventions, loans, and guarantees, the Government has not lost sight of the advantages to be drawn from it in return. It has secured to the State the mail service of France, free of charge; it has laid a 10 per cent. tax on passengers, and on first-class goods; and these two items, alone, are now estimated to yield more than 5 per cent. on the whole of the £36,000,000 given in the shape of subventions. On behalf of the State there has, further, been secured the participation in dividends, on many of the lines, after a certain per-centage is paid to the shareholders; the low tariffs fixed for soldiers, sailors, prisoners, paupers, &c.; and, finally, the possession, at the end of their concessions, of all the railways in France, which up to this period are estimated at £173,000,000 sterling. It would thus

* From Joseph Locke's address in taking the chair as President of the Institution of Civil Engineers, 12 January 1858. (Ed.)

appear that the system has, so far, reconciled the two important interests of the promoters and of the State, with considerable success; that while substantial benefits have been secured to the latter, the former have been enabled to derive a liberal return for their outlay; in short, that the railway interest in France has not, as in England, been made a victim of public exigencies and of private cupidity.'

Another cause beneficial to railway property in France is, that the service which is there considered sufficient for public convenience is more limited, both in frequency of departures and in speed, than is required on English lines. On referring to the ordinary time-tables of main lines in both countries, the difference on this head to the advantage of France will be found equal to about 20 or 25 per cent. But were the departures and speed, on those English railways which are under the strain of direct competition, introduced into the comparison, the per-centage in favour of France would be nearly doubled.

Another custom which tends to diminish the expense of working is the employment of females on French railways, 'especially in certain offices of the booking department, as well at the principal, as at minor stations. At the level crossings, too, females are employed: the head of the family being engaged on the line, whilst his wife or daughter opens and shuts the gates when required. They are found quite equal to the men in the performance of the duties assigned to them, while they are content with lower wages. The usages of the country, where this kind of substitution takes place in many other departments of business, find nothing strange in a practice which, however convenient and economical, would be thought in many respects questionable in ours.'

'An element of considerable importance in the finance of French lines is the proportion of share capital to the amount raised on obligations, or bonds. In the whole of the capital provided by companies, amounting, as we have seen, to £137,960,000, there is less than £50,000,000 in shares, or about 37 per cent. of the whole; whilst the remaining 63 per cent, has been raised on obligations. The Company "du Nord," for instance, had an original share capital of £8,000,000, on a concession of about 370 miles of railway. It subsequently reduced its shares from 500 francs to 400 francs, making the capital £6,400,000, and it remained so fixed at the end of 1856, although its engagements were then increased to £13,000,000. The Company "l'Est" had an original share capital of £5,000,000. It has subsequently doubled its capital; but its engagements by new concessions were more than quadrupled, being nearly £21,000,000. The Paris and Lyons Company, with an original share capital of £4,800,000, subsequently raised to £5,280,000, has engagements estimated at nearly £14,000,000. The Company from Lyons to the Mediterranean, in like manner, has a share capital of £1,800,000, whilst its estimated engagements are £6,800,000. The Orléans and the Western Companies are in a similar condition, each having a share capital of £6,000,000. The former having £13,000,000, and the latter £17,500,000 of engagements by new concessions.'

13/12 State Support of French Railways

C. B. DEROSNE, *Ten Years of Imperialism* . . . [*see* Document **12/10**], pp. 107–111.

The first object to which (the) new method of Government assistance was applied was the railway system. It was a legacy bequeathed to the Imperial Government by its predecessors. While in England and America the construction of railways was left altogether to private enterprise, and Parliament and Congress, following their old traditions, refused to give exceptional privileges and monopolies, continental governments took an opposite course. Everywhere it was laid down as the rule that to Government must belong all initiative in the matter. Nowhere was this principle carried so much to an extreme as in France. Not only did the Government itself trace out the network of railways which was to be constructed, but it adopted as a rule that all railways should be in the hands of the Government, which would thus derive not merely a considerable source of revenue, but likewise a large patronage, and the control over this rapid means of communication in times of political crisis. The only qestion was, whether the Government should construct them altogether at its own expense, or whether, in consideration of the delay which would result from the impossibility of the Government making the large initial outlay rapidly enough, it would not be advisable to call to its aid private capitalists, allowing them to contribute a portion of the expenditure, and giving them in return short concessions for the working of the lines. Both views had their ardent supporters in the Chambers; and the end was an unsatisfactory compromise, which not only retarded in many cases the construction, but became the source of much waste in the outlay. The compromise was, that no general rule should be laid down, but that each case should be judged on its own merits. Thus some lines, like that from Paris to Lille, or the Chemin de fer de la Bretagne, were constructed directly by the Government, while others, like the Chemin de fer de l'Est, were constructed half by the Government and half by a company. In almost every such concession both the conditions and the terms of the concession varied. The law of 1842 became, however, the model for such concessions. According to this the State paid for earthworks and for one-third of the ground, the departments and commonalties paid for another third of the ground, and only the rest of the outlay was at the charge of the companies, which were further assisted by loans from the Government. In spite of these facilities the railways did not prosper; most of the companies were only kept up with the greatest difficulty; and on one of the most important lines, that of Paris and Lyons, the Government had actually to take back the concession, and continue the works on its own account. It was a case of killing with kindness. Instead of being stimulated to exertion, the companies relied on the Government, and in most cases lost all power of expansion. Each company endeavoured to become the most favoured; little rivalries ensued to the great disadvantage of the common interest. Private capital was unwilling to aid in an enterprise where Government authorities had so much power to interfere, and where the term of concession was too short to allow sufficient time for the development of a large remunerative traffic. The result of all this was, that at the establishment of the Imperial régime, not more than 3541 kilometres, or 1270 miles of railway, dragged on a wretched existence.

Invested, in 1852, with full powers of opening extraordinary credits for the construction of the large railway network decreed in 1842, the Imperial Government gradually reversed the whole system which had been introduced by its predecessors. The practice of constructing and working railways at the expense of the Government was from the outset condemned, and measures taken at once to form companies to take off the hands of the Government those lines which were its property. Although the idea of an ultimate reversion of all the principal railways to Government was not given up in theory, the uniform grant of a ninety-nine years' lease to the companies, instead, as before, of half that time, or even less, was virtually giving them a right of proprietorship. All companies were reconstructed on this basis. Liberal terms were given both to the companies which took the Government lines, and to the old ones which were still under large obligations for outlays made by Government; but at the same time the condition was imposed that they should greatly extend their respective lines. In order to facilitate this, every effort was made to effect a fusion of all the smaller lines into a few large ones, which should divide the whole territory of France into so many regions. At present the number of these lines has been reduced to six, and they comprise all the railways, with the exception of about sixty miles, which are still in the hands of the smaller companies. Government subventions were not altogether stopped, but they were every year more reduced. From 30 and 40 per cent of the outlay – their former proportion – they gradually sank to 20 per cent and less; until in 1857, when a large construction of branch railways (4000 miles) was decreed, subventions were in most cases dropped, and a guarantee of 4·65 per cent as interest and sinking fund on a certain maximum of expense for fifty years, was adopted as the rule. If the revenues of the old lines exceeded a certain sum per mile, the surplus was to be applied as part of the guarantee stipulated by the Government for the new branch lines; if these latter should at any time yield more than the guarantee, the surplus was to be used to repay the sums expended by Government as guarantee; and, after 1872, all revenues of old and new lines beyond a fixed sum were to be shared with the Government. The system of direct subventions was only kept up in exceptional cases, where the Government was specially interested from military or other motives; but, taking all this together, it is calculated that the proportion of expense borne by the Government in these branch lines amounts to no more than from 20,000 to 25,000 francs – £800 to £1000 – per kilometre, or about 7 per cent of the outlay, against £4000 per kilometre, or 30 per cent, which had been the average in the old lines.

By these means a complete revolution has within the last ten years, been effected in the French railway system. They have changed their character as government concerns, and have become private enterprises. The effect of this emancipation is plainly visible in the progress which railways have made since that time. From 3541 kilometres in 1851, they had risen in the beginning of this year 10,096, or above 5000 miles, and this result has been achieved at about one-half of the expense entailed on the Government by the former system. The whole expense of the construction alone may be calculated at 4,008,042,000 of francs, or an average of 397,000 francs* per kilometre; out of this, about one-fourth was contributed by Government, but while it had spent above 600 millions for the original 3541 kilometres constructed till 1851, it had contributed about 350 millions only for the 6557 constructed since that time. On the other hand, in spite of the heavy expenditure since 1852 (about 2603 millions of francs, not counting the rolling stock), the companies have become proverbial for their prosperity, and excite the astonishment of railway shareholders all over the world. The dividends vary between 7 and 15 per cent, and in some instances, as in the case of the Orleans railway, have reached 20 per cent. It would be superfluous to speak of the reaction which this extension of very rapid and cheap means of transport had on commerce and industry; but it will scarcely be an exaggeration to assume that both in point of time and of cost a reduction of three-fourths has been effected.

* *i.e.* approximately £25,000 per mile. Also see glossary. (Eds.)

13/13 English Railway Builders in France

a JOSEPH DEVEY, *The Life of Joseph Locke* . . . [*see* Document **13/11**], pp. 164-168.
b THOMAS BRASSEY (1st EARL BRASSEY), *Work and Wages* (London, 1872), pp. 79-83.

a He [Mr. Locke] soon found that the French contractors, being necessarily new to their work, demanded prices nearly double those which were asked by Englishmen, and that the work when done could not be half so much relied upon even for safety or durability. He was driven, then, to the necessity, in order to bring the works within his own estimate, to employ English contractors, already experienced in works of this kind, and who, besides the skilled labour then at their disposal, brought into France large troops of English navvies to execute the rough part of the contract. Here was another invasion more formidable than anything of the sort before. An army of labourers, fortified with spades, pickaxes, and mattocks, dispersed themselves over the country and took up a permanent position upon French territory.

. . . 'Following* in the wake of their masters, when it was known that they had contracted for works in France, these men soon spread over Normandy; where they became objects of interest to the community, not only by the peculiarity of their dress, but by their uncouth size, habits, and manners; which formed so marked a contrast with those of the peasantry of that country. These men were generally employed in the most difficult and laborious work, and by that means earned larger wages than the rest of the men. Discarding the wooden shovels and basket-sized barrows of the Frenchmen, they used the tools which modern art had suggested, and which none but the most expert and robust could wield; and often have I heard the exclamation of French loungers around a gang of navvies – '*Mon Dieu, ces Anglais, comme ils travaillent!*'

'The abundance of five-franc pieces on the Saturday at all the shops and places of trade soon made the distributors of them popular; and it was a remarkable fact, well known at the time, that in tunnelling, or other dangerous work, the French labourer could not be induced to join, unless an Englishman was at the head of the operations. The lawless and daring habits of this class of our countrymen sometimes brought them under the special notice of gensdarmes, who, however, soon discovered that it was better to humour, for a time, rather than to attempt to control them, during the excitement which always followed the receipt of their monthly wages.

'There was one complaint, however, which I think it right to notice,

* [From] Mr. Locke's address on his election as President [of the Institute of Civil Engineers], p. 18. (Devey's note.) The Presidential Address, Railway Building in England and France, was given on 12 January 1858. (Ed.)

regarding the employment of Englishmen in France. It was soon observed and complained of, that the Englishmen earned larger wages than the French, forgetting that the latter, at that time, were physically unequal to much of the work which had to be performed in constructing railways. A piece of coarse bread and an apple or pear, which then formed the ordinary meal of a French labourer, could not be set up against the navvies' beef or bacon, and none knew the difference so well as the contractors themselves, who always obtained the greatest amount of labour from the highest-paid workmen. Three or four francs a day were then expended more profitably on an Englishman than two francs on a Frenchman; whilst now, it is fair to state, that, by force of imitation, both in the mode of living and in the implements used, there is little, if any, difference in the relative values of the labour obtained from each. The Frenchman has learnt the effect of nourishing food, and the consequently higher rate he can obtain for his labour; so that the result is that this class of work is now entirely supplied by the native population. Thus, it appears, that the introduction of English railway labour, so far from having been a grievance, has, in fact, as previously in the cases of the iron trade and the machinery manufacture, considerably improved the condition of the French working classes.'

The same superiority which Mr. Locke found in the English labourer he also found in the English mechanic. France had only one or two manufactories for the construction of steam-engines, and these had furnished only a few locomotives of a very inferior sort. The main supply was got from England. He therefore determined to establish English workshops at Rouen, like those he had assisted to supervise at Newcastle, and brought over a supply of English mechanics for the purpose of teaching France to construct and repair her own engines, and enabling the company to rely on services entirely under its own control. In this matter he engaged the services of Mr. Buddicom, who constructed, at fixed prices, all the engines, carriages, waggons, and other stock required by the company, and who subsequently agreed to keep them in repair at a fixed rate per kilometre. The success of this experiment has proved most lucrative, both to the company and to Mr. Buddicom, who still continues his labours, and in a much wider field, for he now supplies engines and carriages to most of the companies in France. But no company, owing to these efforts, even at the present day, possesses rolling stock better adapted to railway service than that which has emanated from the workshops at Rouen.

b I will now give an interesting example, derived from my father's early experience in France, in the construction of the Paris and Rouen Railway in 1842. The Paris and Rouen Railway was the first large railway work executed on the Continent. About 10,000 men were employed in its construction, of whom upwards of 4,000 were Englishmen. . . . A special effort was made to secure the services of English workmen on this particular contract; because it was a question whether native workmen could be obtained in sufficient numbers, and it was still more doubtful whether they would possess the necessary skill and experience for carrying out railway works, which at that period were a novelty, even to English engineers, and entirely unknown on the Continent. Under these exceptional circumstances, a large body of Englishmen were sent over to Normandy. . . .

It is scarcely necessary to observe that the employment of English manual labour abroad must always be costly, and a somewhat doubtful policy. But in this particular case it was not found to be disadvantageous in a pecuniary point of view.

The contract for the Paris and Rouen line included some difficult works. There were four bridges across the Seine, and four tunnels, one of them one mile and five-eighths in length, passing through hard limestone. The English were chiefly employed on the difficult work. The French labourers drew away the stuff, or wound it up the shafts; but the mining was done by Englishmen. In the tunnels the skilled work was all done by them. At one time there were five hundred Englishmen living in the village of Rollebois, most of whom were employed in the adjacent tunnel. Although these English navvies earned 5*s*. a day, while the Frenchmen employed received only 2*s*. 6*d*. a day, yet it was found, on comparing the cost of two adjacent cuttings in precisely similar circumstances, that the excavation was made at a lower cost per cubic yard by the English navvies than by the French labourers.

In the same quarry at Bonnières, in which Frenchmen, Irishmen, and Englishmen were employed, side by side, the Frenchmen received three francs, the Irishmen four, and the Englishmen six francs a day. At those different rates, the Englishman was found to be the most advantageous workman of the three.

On the completion of the Paris and Rouen line, and the extension to Havre, most of the English navvies returned to their own country; and the Dieppe line was executed principally by native labour, although Englishmen were still employed on the more difficult work. On the Dieppe Railway French labourers earned from two and a half to three francs a day; and, when working by piece work, their earnings advanced to three and a half francs a day. The wages of Englishmen, employed as plate-layers and tippers, were about five francs a day. A large number of Belgians were employed on this contract, and they always earned one franc a day more than the Frenchmen. It should, however, be explained that the construction of railways had been considerably developed in Belgium before railway works were commenced in France. Upon the Caen line, which was executed about ten years later than the Dieppe line, Englishmen were still employed for tipping and plate laying, and on difficult work in the deep rock cutting. The wages of the Englishmen were five francs a day as before; while the usual earnings of the French labourers ranged from 2·75 to 3 francs and 3·50 francs a day. It is to be noted that the English workmen were employed by sub-contractors, whose interest was directly involved in the closest possible reduction of expenditure. Yet those most experienced practical men were of opinion, that the English were worth the much higher rate of wages which they received, when employed on a work of exceptional difficulty.

13/14 Railway Building in France in the Second Empire

A. AUDIGANNE, *Les chemins de fer aujourd-hui et dans cent ans chez tous les peup es* (2 vols., Paris, 1858-1862), II, pp. 95-104. (Ed. Tr.)

At the end of 1851 the financial crises which affected railway developments were virtually over. Nevertheless, what was needed to recover all lost ground, to ensure the prompt finishing of the railway network, was the energetic completion of lines which had already been agreed upon, and the vigorous renewal of concessions for future railway development. The period beginning in 1852 is characterised by a vigorous and varied development.

The beginning of 1852 saw the granting of the contract for the railway from Lyons to Avignon, and the concession of the railway from Paris to Lyons. Then, to mention only the principal lines, came the concessions of railways from Dijon to Besançon, from Saint-Quentin to the Belgian frontier, from the centre of France to Clermont, Roanne, and Chateauroux, from Mézidon to Le Mans, from Nantes to Caen and Cherbourg and from Bordeaux to Cette. All told, the total number for this year was 1,945 kilometres.

In addition to this extremely important extension of the network was a significant development by way of amalgamations. At first the Orléans Company, then the Lyons-Avignon Company became the nucleus of powerful combinations. Up to then the rare amalgamations of this kind which had been brought about, had been local, fortuitous events. This was true even for the recent amalgamation of 19 February 1852, between the Company of the North and the Saint-Quentin and Boulogne Companies.

The number of concessions in 1853 was equivalent to that of the preceding year (1,946 kilometres). The Grand Central, . . . obtained 374 kilometres of the firm concessions granted in that year, without counting contingent concessions granted to the Company, and it increased this some months later by absorbing the former railways of the Loire under the name of the Railways of the Rhône and Loire. Among the most prominent concessions we must mention the Bayonne and Perpignan lines granted to the Company of the Midi; the Lyons to Geneva line to the Company of that name; the line from Rheims to Mézières and Sedan, to the Ardennes Railway Company; the Nantes to Saint-Nazaire line and the Tours to Le Mans line to the Orléans Railway Company; and finally, the direct line from Paris to Mulhouse, which, including several branch lines, amounted to 618 kilometres, which was granted to the Strasbourg Company.

A temporary check came in 1854. This is easily accounted for by reference to circumstances resulting from the commencement of the long and glorious campaign in the Crimea. Concessions amounted to only 353 kilometres; these were granted almost exclusively for the completion of railway lines which had been already started. . . .

Business picked up again in 1855. At the beginning of the year, important concessions were announced. This time the railways spread their tentacles into a new territory. Nearly all the new lines were in regions which had been completely deprived of the benefit of railways. Thus whilst the Rouen, Le Havre, Dieppe, Cherbourg and St. Germain Companies amalgamated to become the Company of the West, 806 kilometres were added to the track, which had to cross the most remote parts of Brittany in going to the Northern coast of this territory to reach Redon, Saint-Malo and Brest. At the same time, other lines belonging to the Orléans Company penetrated into the Southern tip of the Brittany peninsula, and leaving the Paris to St. Nazaire artery at Savenay went on to Lorient, Quimper, and Chateaulin and to the right joined a branch line of the Company of the West at Redon. In a quite neglected part of France the Grand Central Company obtained concessions which extended into the Loire, Lot, Cantal, Haute-Vienne, Dordogne, Lot-et-Garonne and Aveyron Departments.* Its network extended then more than 1,000 kilometres, without including several provisional concessions. The total number of concessions effected in 1855 amounted to 2,485 kilometres. At this point the concessions belonging to the second phase of railway building finished. There were no concessions in 1856.

It was in the nature of things that the increase in size of the companies corresponded with a sharp increase in the amount of work which was undertaken. A period of unprecedented activity followed everywhere. Company competition increased. The amount of work undertaken, which totalled 3,558 kilometres at the end of the first phase (December 1851), increased to approximately 6,500 kilometres at the end of the second phase, i.e. in the

* See Glossary.

first months of 1857. Another element of growth: on 31 December 1851 the total sum spent on railway construction by the State, the Companies and the localities, amounted to 1,463,719,960 francs,* of which 579,484,564, francs were spent by the State, and 883,520,396 by the Companies. It is interesting to notice the growth of this expenditure.... On the 1st January 1855, the total increased to 2,161,597,775 francs, including 3,500,123 francs for development research; but the State's contribution which amounted then to 630,078,815 francs, had grown only by 50 millions i.e., less than one-tenth, whilst expenditure by the Companies had almost doubled. At the beginning of 1857 we find that out of a total expenditure of 3,080,494,973 francs the contribution by the State was only 661,308,315, francs; expenditure by the Companies increased to 2,419,186,658. The total expenditure, on railways at the end of the second period was therefore 3,080,494,973 francs.

13/15 Railway Building in Italy

F. P. COBBE, *Italics Brief Notes on Politics, People and Places in Italy in 1864* (London, 1864), pp. 30–33.

The line between an Italian navvy and a brigand is slight, not to say evanescent. As I have learned from a French gentleman in charge of large works on the Roman territories, the robberies which were daily practised on this line were something marvellous. Casernes† had to be built to shelter soldiers to superintend the men; and these casernes were stripped of their tiles, and of every removable object as fast as it was supplied. Stabbing was a common occurrence; one fellow murdering another, on one occasion, because in his sleep he had rolled over into his companion's bed, on the floor of some den they were occupying together. A man once came to M. S——, and, professing great interest in his affairs, acquainted him that he was robbed in every direction. M. S—— replied that he knew it was the case; he had tried every means to stop the evil, but found that, under the Roman government, he had no redress. 'Is it possible?' said the benevolent informer. 'No redress at all?' 'Too true,' said the Frenchman. 'Oh! then,' said the other, 'I see I need not be under any apprehensions'; and from that day forth he was the worst robber of the party.

Such were the mechanical and human agencies at the disposal of the Italian Government in making railways; yet, in a great measure, it has triumphed over all difficulties. The growth of steam-traffic in Italy since the Annexation would be surprising had there not been half such obstacles to encounter. In Piedmont in 1859, there were already more lines of railway

* See Glossary. † Barracks. (Ed.)

open than in all the rest of Italy together; while in Naples, which had been the first to introduce them into Italy, there were only a few miles (almost exclusively of passenger service) in the whole kingdom. Between 1859 and 1864, the increase has been pretty equal over the peninsula. When the war broke out in 1859 there were only 1472 kilometres of railways in activity from north to south. Of these, 807 were in Piedmont, 200 in Lombardy, 33 in Emilia, 308 in Tuscany, and 124 in Naples. In the beginning of 1864, 3965 kilometres were at work, forming 41 different railways. This is surely a very considerable step towards the free circulation of men in Italy, and consequently of the ideas they carry along with them.

The cost of the 1693 kilometres of railway made between 1859 and 1864, is between five and six hundred millions of francs. The Italian Government has now commenced the sale of these railways to private companies, thereby, as it is hoped, contributing a little to make up the tremendous deficit of the revenue.

Besides all this development of railways, and partly in consequence of it, the common roads of the country have been vastly extended and improved, especially in Naples and Sicily. Soldiers have been very judiciously set to aid this latter work, and have just opened a new road near Gargano. When it is understood that throughout large districts of Calabria and the Abruzzi, there have been hitherto *no roads at all* – only rude tracks between one populous village and another, and that this state of things was especially patronised by the Bourbon Government – propositions for road making being always discountenanced – it may be judged what a task the new government has got before it. The poor Communes, accustomed only to be taxed and pillaged, do not yet understand what can be meant by affording them grants for schools and roads, and sending them able engineers to lay out public works. 'What *does* the King want?' they say. 'What good will it do him, our being better off?' Governments existing for the benefit of the governed, not of the governors, is a new idea in Naples.

13/16 Developments of Italian Railways

S. JACINI, *L'Amministrazione dei Lavori pubblici in Italia dal 1860 al 1867* (Florence, 1867), pp. 12–13, 86–88. (Ed. Tr.)

State of the railway system before 1860

The information contained in the collection of laws and decrees relating to the construction of Italian railways, published in 1862 by this Ministry, and that contained either in the report which I had the honour to present to H.R.H. *il Principe Luogotenente del Regno* on 26 December 1861, or in the other report submitted to Parliament regarding the laws for the re-organization of the railway network, mean that at this point it is unnecessary to enter into minute details regarding the state of Italian railways at the time of the fall of the last Government and all that is required is the following table which indicates the position in 1859, i.e. at the beginning of the war which resulted in the unification of Italy.

	Kilometres in use	*In construction*	*Total*	*Approved*
Subalpine Province	807	59	866	—
Lombardy Province	200	40	240	180
Emilia Province	33	147	180	276
Marche and Umbria Provinces	—	—	—	360
Tuscany Province	308	16	324	362
Naples Province	124	4	128	128
Sicily Province	—	—	—	—
Totals	1472	266	1738	1306

From these figures it can be deduced at a glance that the Subalpine and Tuscany Provinces were already in possession of a railway network sufficiently developed and adequate to the demands made upon it by their commerce; in Lombardy the principal lines were laid, to which branch lines were later added; Emilia, however, had only 33 kilometres in use as opposed to 423 kilometres either in construction or planned for construction: in Umbria and the Marches not a single kilometre was in use; in the Neapolitan Provinces, where so many attempts at railway development had been thwarted by the government, only a few kilometres had been actually constructed; in the vicinity of the capital, mainly for pleasure-trips, and also to connect Naples with the fortresses of Capaci and Gaeta, rather than for the benefit of the area.

Progressive development of the railway network from 1860 onwards

Have all these railway developments in Italy since 1860 been successful, and have the sacrifices borne by the community so hopefully been worth while? It is this which we must now answer. It seems to me that the question is immediately resolved by an examination of the following table, from which this conclusion is drawn, that whilst at the close of 1859 there were approximately 1,590 kilometres in use, there are now 4,390; so that in the course of only seven years our railway network has increased by approximately 2,800 kilometres, without taking account of the Venetian railway, the 30 kilometres trunk line, of which from Rovigo to Pontelagoscuro has been constructed in the last few months, nor the lines which are very near to completion, nor those in use on Roman territory, the completion of which is owed in great measure to the efforts of the Italian Government.

Amount of line in use in Italy
(*not including the Venetian and Roman Provinces*)

On 31 December 1859	—	1,591	kilometres
,, ,, ,, 1860	—	1,693	,,
,, ,, ,, 1861	—	2,054	,,
,, ,, ,, 1862	—	2,288	,,
,, ,, ,, 1863	—	2,902	,,
,, ,, ,, 1864	—	3,359	,,
,, ,, ,, 1865	—	3,693	,,
,, ,, ,, 1866	—	4,394	,,

Including the line from Rovigo – Pontelagoscuro.

From these figures, which have taken account of the deduction which has to be made for trunk routes which are used by several lines, it follows that the following amounts of line have been brought into use:

in 1860	—	102	kilometres
,, 1861	—	361	,,
,, 1862	—	233	,,
,, 1863	—	614	,,
,, 1864	—	448	,,
,, 1865	—	344	,,
,, 1866	—	701	,,
Total	—	2,803	kilometres
Average for each year	—	400	kilometres

If account is then taken of the Venetian lines in use at the time of the union with the Kingdom of Italy, which amounted to approximately 412 kilometres, as well as the 264 kilometres in the Roman Province and the line from Foggia to Bovino, which came into use at this time, the total amount of line in use in all the Italian territory on 21 January 1867 was 5,104 kilometres, an amount which, within a few weeks, with the addition of the lines from Voghera to Pavia and Naples to Avena-Caserta, increased to 5,161.

This figure seems to be the most eloquent reply to the accusations of inertia and slackness which some have levelled at the Government, even more so when it is considered that the advantage for the state must not be measured simply by the number of kilometres constructed, but rather in the value and importance of the lines in question, as a result of which Susa and Brindisi and Udine and Naples are joined together without any break in their network, which is true for all the principal cities of the Peninsula.

Perhaps it may be objected that some lines have been constructed after the stipulated concessionary period; but it is worth reflecting that in the majority of cases these limits were fixed, more according to the wishes of the Government than by a detailed examination of the technical difficulties presented by their construction and the time needed to complete the contract. It should also be noted that if some lines have been slightly delayed, others, particularly the more important lines, have been completed before the expiry of the agreed period. Finally, it should be noted that some lines, such as those from Bologna to Pistoia and from Florence to Fuligano, presented serious problems of a constructional and planning nature, which necessitated serious study before any work was undertaken.

When in a country like Italy, in which large scale industry was hardly developed, in which terrain placed so many difficulties in the way of railroad construction, 400 kilometres have nevertheless been brought into use in each of the last seven years, the undertakings which have carried out this work and the administration which has promoted or directed it cannot be criticised for lack of action.

13/17 Promotion of the Leipzig-Dresden Railway

a Memorandum to the Saxon Government by F. LIST, printed in ERWIN BECKERATH AND OTTO STÜHLER, *Friedrich List, Werke, III. Schriften zum Verkehrswesen* (Berlin, 1929), pp. 157-165. (Ed. Tr.)

b Act to establish the Leipzig-Dresden Railway Company, 6 May 1835. Printed in W. E. ROTHE and A. RITTHALER (eds.), *Vorgeschichte und Begründung des deutschen Zollvereins 1815-1834* (3 vols., Fr. List Society, 1934), III/2, pp. 747-750. (Ed. Tr.)

a . . . I could not watch the astonishing effects of railways in England and North America without wishing that my German fatherland would partake of the same benefits, and. . . .

. . . having settled in Saxony for some years, I determined to devote my leisure time to exploring the relevant local conditions, as far as this is possible for a stranger, and although my researches were but superficial, their results were so important as to induce me to submit them to you for further examination.

Above all, the level and firm surface stretching in all directions from Leipzig, which seems to invite its inhabitants to put down rails without further preparation, makes this area particularly suitable for the building of railways. If the occasional sharp corners of the main roads, and their progress through the middle of villages and towns, had not formed an obstacle to railway building, it might even have been advisable to lay the rails directly on that part of the main roads at present obstructed by heaps of road-building materials, in which case a very strong railway of oak rails lined with iron would have cost scarcely more than 15,000 Taler* per German mile. That nature herself has done the work here . . . [is shown by the fact that] our American company spent 40,000 dollars per German mile to level the ground in the way in which nature has provided it here, while the rest of the permanent way cost only 15,000 dollars† . . .

All in all, I believe that the normal costs of a railway like our American one, calculated to transport annually 2-4 million cwt. coal for 7-10 years, after which it would cost 4,000 dollars per German mile to keep in repair, would come in our local terrain and with local Saxon wages to 50,000 Taler per German mile at the most, including all normal tunnels, embankments, bridges and compensation for land, but excluding all major bridges across the larger rivers, and major tunnels.

A second important consideration for this locality is its position as the heart of the German inland traffic, the printing and publishing trade, and the German factory industry.

The numbers of travellers inward and outward and in transit, including the visitors to the fair, is greater than in any other German city and would by itself justify the building of four railways of 20 miles length each. The present estimate, including those in transit, is 50,000 visitors. This would at least double to 100,000 if it were possible to make the 40 miles return journey to Leipzig for 5 Taler without spending more than 10 hours on the road; the gross revenue in that case would be 500,000 Taler, and the net revenue, after deduction of one third for costs, would be above 8% on a capital of 4 million Taler.

* See Glossary.

† [As it is] North American costs are lower than those of Saxony for:

land	3,000 Taler per German mile
timber	2,000 „ „ „ „
	5,000 Taler

against this, wages cost more by 45,000 Taler, so that railway building in Saxony would be cheaper by 40,000 Taler per German mile.

The quantity of freight inward and outward and in transit . . . should amount, including salt and other mining products, to at least 1½ million cwt., which would yield, on 20 miles at 10 Groschen per mile (half the present freight charges), 625,000 Taler, or, after deducting one third for costs, over 10% on the capital.

Finally there is the consumption of the city itself. All food-stuffs and fuels are more expensive than on the coast, and of worse quality. Timber is twice as expensive as in towns four or five miles away. While at these high prices the mass of the population can afford very little fuel, the hills eight miles to the South are full of coal. Factories using water or steam power are out of the question; the existing water mills are hardly sufficient for grinding the necessary flour; the black bread for the poorer part of the population is brought in from the countryside. One can see everywhere how the lack of a cheap means of transport keeps down population and industry. How otherwise are we to explain that the centre of German trade has only 40,000 inhabitants? Even if we take only the existing levels of consumption, c. 60,000 klafter* of wood would have costs of transport of 150,000 Taler (at 2½ Taler a cord); other articles of consumption may be estimated at as much again.

Railways would carry wood, turf and coal at less than half the present costs. Coal from Zwickau would cost only 1½–2 Groschen a cwt. more than at the pithead and would raise the city to an important manufacturing centre. Bavaria, where flour, meat and other foodstuffs are 50–100% cheaper than in Leipzig, could export its surplus to the Erzgebirge, the Elbe and the Hansa cities. . . . Cheaper food and fuel would partly enhance the well-being of the working classes, and partly lower money wages, increase population and increase the extent of industry. Cheap building materials and low money wages would encourage building and lower the rents in the new and more distant parts of the city. On the other hand, increased population and industry would increase the rents, and thereby the value of the houses, in the centre of the city, well placed for trade and industry. In one word: population, the number of buildings, industry, trade, and the value of land and houses in Leipzig would be doubled in a short space of time, and I do not doubt for a minute that this increase in value in Leipzig alone would in a few years exceed the total capital costs of the new railways.

In an appendix I subjoin a plan for a Saxon railway system, as well as I could make it without an actual survey. According to it, the line from Leipzig to Dresden would have branches to Zwickau, Chemnitz and Freiberg, and the line from Weimar to Gotha, to Frankfort on the Main and Bamberg; by the line to Halle, the Kingdom of Saxony would be linked with the salt mines and with the river Saale; by the line to Dessau, Wittenberg or Torgau,

* See Glossary.

the Elbe would be reached at a point at which it is still easily navigable. This network, which would not exceed 50 miles altogether, would meet all the needs of the Kingdom of Saxony. . . .

b 1. General permission is granted for the proposal to build a railwa between Leipzig and Dresden.
4. As soon as the constitution of the Railway Company is approved in accordance with the Statutes, and the plan for the building of the Railway is sufficiently detailed to permit the building of at least a part of it, the Committee of the Company is hereby assured, that the publication of the expropriation law submitted to the last diet of the Assembly and accepted by its bill sub-committee on 29 October 1834 shall be authorized, and orders given necessary for its completion.
5. Within the framework of this law and of the subsequent Government declaration, the Government hereby grants to the society operating under the name of the 'Leipzig-Dresden Railway Company' the rights of a joint-stock company to the exclusion of all similar enterprises to establish direct connection between Leipzig and Dresden, to build a railway between these towns and to extend it to the frontier at its own discretion, and recognizes this company as the enterprise to which the regulations under paragraph (4) will apply, and to whom the railway to be built shall be assigned as sole and irrevocable property.
6. The determination of fares and freight rates for persons, animals and goods shall remain subject to the control of the future board of the Railway Company, yet nevertheless the Government expects that the latter will keep the rates as low as possible in the interest of public transport, and is meanwhile satisfied with the provisional declaration made by the Committee, that the fares for passengers in the first class shall never in any circumstances exceed the rates of the Royal Saxon Mail, and for second class passengers shall not exceed the rates of the ordinary Royal Saxon Stage Coaches; and that the freight rates for commodities in the fastest carriages shall not exceed the freight rates on the Royal Saxon Ordinary Mails, and in the second and slower class of goods traffic shall not exceed the freight rates of ordinary carters at the same time, for the same quality of commodities and the same distance in similar conditions.

(b) *Statutes of the Leipzig-Dresden Railway Company*, dated 20 March 1837
1. The purpose of the joint stock company is the building of a railway from Leipzig to Dresden, its operation and its future extension to the frontier.
2. The required capital shall consist of 15,000 shares, issued in the name of the owner, each of 100 tlr.,* at 21 fl.*. . . .

* See Glossary.

8. The shareholders jointly form the 'Leipzig-Dresden Railway Company'. This latter is the owner of the railway together with all the buildings, equipment or machines, stocks and other requisite properties. . . .
20. The affairs of the Company shall be managed by a Board. The Company, however, shall be represented in its relationship with the Board, in all matters not specifically assigned to the General Assembly, by a Select Committee of 30 shareholders. . . .
35. The Select Committee selects according to paragraph 31 [i.e. with an absolute majority] five Directors and five Vice-Directors from amongst the shareholders. The result of the election shall be published. . . .
51. In order to manage its day-to-day business and in order to carry out its decisions, the Board shall select one General Manager and make public its selection. . . .
60. In case the share capital according to paragraph (2) and the debenture capital according to paragraph (9) shall not be sufficient for the completion and working of the railway, the Board together with the Select Committee shall have power to make up the capital shortfall either by (i) loan or (ii) the issue of new shares, or both. The total sum of the loan may not exceed one-third of the real issued and paid-up-capital. The same regulations shall apply to any future extension of the line to the frontier. . . .

13/18 Development of Railways in Russia

A. AUDIGANNE, *Les chemins de fer* . . . [*see* Document **13/14**], II, pp. 233–236. (Ed. Tr.)

With the exception of most of the Scandinavian lines, the Russian railways are the immediate continuation of the Central European lines. Consequently, the Moscow network is endowed with considerable interest. The first Russian railway building occurred long ago; the small line from St. Petersburg to Tsarsko-Silo (28 kilometres) was opened in 1828. Then in 1851 the line from St. Petersburg to Moscow was constructed and used by the State at great expense to the Treasury. This, however, was only a purely national line. The railway from St. Petersburg to Moscow could only become a European line by the connection, which was completed at this time, of the town of Peter the Great and the German lines. The formation of the Russian Railway Company marks the moment when this distant group of lines endeavours to link up with the European system. Accordingly, the ukase of 26 January, (7 February 1857), with which this Company originated, will always remain a memorable act in Russian history. The undertaking assumed colossal proportions. On the one hand, there was a network of 4,162 kilometres and funds of 11,000,000,000 francs*; on the other hand there was an alliance, with one exception, of the most powerful European financial houses. The enterprise, which was of the greatest importance for the Russian Empire, affected all Europe: it was to have important repercussions for European civilization.

...The 4,162 kilometres which constituted the network could be divided into two sections. The first included:

1. The line from St. Petersburg to Warsaw, with a branch line between this line and the Prussian frontier towards Koenigsberg, 249 kilometres;
2. The line from Moscow to Nijni Novgorod on the Volga, 427 kilometres.

The second section included:

1. The line from Moscow to Theodosia in the Crimea, via Kursk and the region of the lower Dnieper, 1,259 kilometres;
2. The line which branches from the former towards Kursk or Orel, passing to Dünaburg, and terminating at the port of Libau on the Baltic in the Courland, 1,227 kilometres.

In view of this enormous task, the first question is whether the importance of such developments for Russia was exaggerated. Certainly not: it was correct to believe the internal progress of the Empire would be powerfully served by the completion of such a project. Up to that point, the deplorable condition, or rather the absence, of communications, had constituted the most insuperable obstacle to the growth of the productive forces of the country. Alerted to her internal weaknesses by the Crimean War, Russia really attempted to provide herself with the means of easily concentrating her strength and encouraging economic expansion. The policy which gave rise to the railways was both far-seeing and intelligent. From the beginning, France lent generous support to the accomplishment of this plan, which was given a contrary welcome in England; one recalls the most jealous and hostile reception accorded by the English. Most of the English Press indulged in narrow minded polemics inspired at one and the same time by national vanity and the theory that the least degree of progress in Russia was a threat to British India. This outburst rejected with a rare bluntness the principle that the solidarity of interests among peoples is an essential prerequisite for political and social progress. To facilitate the construction of Russian railways was not to furnish the barbarian with a means of overflowing into European society, but rather to procure for civilisation some means of substituting itself for vanquished barbarism. If, by favouring the undertaking the French government performed an act of generosity towards Russia, it concluded an act of *haute politique*, as regards the destiny of civilisation.

* See Glossary.

13/19 Investment in Russian Railways

American Consular Reports, 1858, F. S CLAXTON, Consul in Moscow, 1 October, 1858, pp. 168–169.

The privilege for constructing and operating during eighty years the five trunk lines of roads was awarded to the four banking houses of Steiglitz & Co., St. Petersburg, and to the Barings, Rothschilds, the house of Hope Brothers, each taking one-fourth of the estimated capital required, and the government guaranteeing 4½ per cent. interest on a sum equal to 72,000 roubles, multiplied by the number of versts of rail to be laid; if the roads cost more per verst it was a loss to the company; if less, they are still to receive the stipulated interest upon the 72,000 roubles per verst.* These favorable conditions soon caused the shares to be much sought for out of Russia, and they were at a premium in London and Paris before they were apportioned among the foreign subscribers; but such was the suspicion of their people to that class of investment, and so little were they familiar with such enterprises, that, when the first instalment of 25 per cent. was about being due, Baron Steiglitz found himself with the great bulk of his stock on hand.

Through the then minister of finance he obtained a decree reducing the rate of interest in the government bank from 4 to 3 per cent. on all deposits; his scheme was successful, and the shares soon became quoted on the St. Petersburg exchange at 3 per cent. above par.

The crisis declared itself, and all securities abroad went down; but the Russians, congratulating themselves of having an investment so safe from all revulsions, kept the railway stock at a premium. As a natural consequence, every mail brought thousands of shares to be offered for sale in St. Petersburg; in effect, here and there, they continued to command a premium, and the demand for bills or specie to pay for this stock increased the debt of the country. Nor is this the worst of the transaction: the government had calculated that foreign capital would build their lines; it now finds that not one-fifth of the stock is held abroad, and that not only the public lost the premium paid, but that the purchase of material, rails, and machinery will continue to keep the balance of the trade against this market, and that all such will cost some 7 or 10 per cent, more than it was estimated, for when the calculation was made exchange was in favor of this country.

* *c.* £17,700 per mile. (Ed.) Also see Glossary.

Chapter 14 Banking and Finance

Introduction

The economic confusion of the first years of the French revolutionary governments, aggravated by civil war, uncertainty, famine, expropriation and ultimately foreign wars, was mirrored by the confusion into which the monetary system necessarily fell. The difficulties of maintaining a paper credit in such unstable conditions are well illustrated by the history of the *assignats*, though it should be stressed that they were in part an outcome of the nationalization of forfeited land, especially of church land, and that the dangers of monetary inflation were well understood at the time (**14/1**, **14/2**). Ultimately, the demand of the French bourgeoisie for a firm and rational monetary framework was met by the creation of a national currency based on the metric system (**6/5**, **14/3**). The lesson was not lost on the Germans, who, in the slow process of building up a unified, capitalist German state also had to overcome the irrational hindrances of local currencies, weights and measures by a unified metric and decimal system (**14/4**, **14/5**).

Another consequence of the consolidation of bourgeois interests after the revolutionary years was the codification and expansion of joint-stock enterprise. The Act of 1807 created the legal conditions in which investors could without undue cost or risk form companies that had the privileges of incorporation and limited liability, to exist side by side with the older commandite type of concern (**14/7**). The ease of company formation, while it helped the process of capital investment, also led to abuses by promoters and speculators, particularly evident in some of the financial booms around the middle of the century (**14/16**, **14/19**).

The growth of French industry and commerce also demanded more efficient banking facilities. Napoleon's plans for the Bank of France stressed the need for low interest rates and easy credit facilities (**14/6**). The expansion of the economy in the mid-century led to further banks, based on land and on other assets (**8/9**, **14/8**, **14/9**), and almost inevitably some of these foundations were marred by speculation, fraud and ultimate collapse.

In the less developed countries, like Germany, the State had to take a more direct interest to ensure that sufficient funds were made available for economic development. The peculiar constitution of the Bank of Prussia of 1846 (**14/11**), with its private supply of capital but executive control by the bureaucracy and thus ultimately by the Monarch, became the model for the later central bank, the *Reichsbank*. By the 1860s, as a prelude to the vast expansion of German industry in the following decade, the German economy was sufficiently developed to permit the foundation of (local) banks by private means (**14/12, 14/13**), though the appetite of industry for capital was so great in relation to the total available that these banks had to engage in large-scale industrial investments, besides carrying out their functions of facilitating commerce. Another example of the problems of an under-developed economy, in which the only major concentration of resources is in the hands of the Government is furnished by the foundation of the Austrian *Credit Anstalt* in the 1850s (**14/14**).

European economic development, however, was something that transcended the powers of individual Governments, and the overflowing of capital across the borders to seek its maximum returns wherever it might be found was one of the most characteristic features of the mid-nineteenth century. Railways were among the most important targets of such investment (**13/9, 13/19**). While Britain was the main source of overseas finance, France also (**14/10**), and before long Belgium, Holland and Germany became important sources of international capital funds (**11/25**), though much of this development belongs to the period after 1870. The Latin Union (originally of France, Belgium, Italy and Switzerland), which linked its coinage to the French franc, was another sign of the growth of the international economy (**14/15**). Finally, the course of economic fluctuations became a symptom of this growing inter-dependence. While a few still bore strong local elements, and at times individual countries were hit by speculative promotion booms (**14/16, 14/18**), the crises of 1857 and 1866 and the depressions which followed them, were clearly international in scope (**14/17, 14/19, 14/20, 14/21**).

High finance was the appropriate method for supplying capital to large-scale undertakings, but these were by no means the only ones, or perhaps even the most representative, before 1870. Much domestic, and even handicraft, industry survived where there were no technical advantages of scale, and in some cases they were even fostered by the rising factory industry as suppliers of components, while benefiting by the greater spending power which the latter created. Agriculture also continued to be organized in relatively small units. Just as agricultural credit needs came to be solved, in part, by co-operative banking (**9/10**), so the corresponding credit institutions for small-scale industry, the Schulze-Delitsch mutual banks, were developed with some success in Germany (**14/22, 14/23**).

14/1 The Assignats, 1790

Decree on Assignats, 17 April 1790. Printed in STEWART, *A Documentary Survey . . .* [*see* Document **5/10**], pp. 159–161.

1. Dating from the present year the debts of the clergy will be considered as national debts; the public treasury shall be responsible for paying the interest and the principal thereof.

The nation declares that whosoever give proof of having legally contracted with the clergy, and hold contracts of revenues assigned thereto, are considered creditors of the State. Accordingly, the nation appropriates and mortgages to them all property and revenues at its disposal, as in the case of all its other debts.

2. Ecclesiastical property sold or alienated by virtue of the decrees of 19 December, 1789, and 17 March last* is absolved and freed from every mortgage of the legal debt of the clergy with which it was formerly burdened, and no opposition to the sale of such property may be permitted on the part of the said creditors.

3. The *assignats*† created by the decree of 19 and 21 December, 1789, and sanctioned by the King, shall be legal tender among all persons throughout the entire extent of the kingdom, and shall be received as coin of the realm in all public and private banks.

4. Instead of the annual five per cent interest assigned thereon, only three per cent shall be granted, dating from 15 April of the present year; and the reimbursements, instead of being deferred until the times stated in the said decrees, shall take place successively by lot as soon as a sum of 1,000,000 in money is realized on the bonds given by the municipalities for the property they have acquired, and in proportion to the returns from the patriotic contribution for the years 1791 and 1792. If the payments have been made in *assignats*, such *assignats* shall be publicly burned, as hereinafter prescribed, and only a register of their numbers shall be kept.

5. The *assignats* shall be from 200 *livres* to 1,000 *livres* in value. Interest shall be computed daily; the *assignat* of 1,000 *livres* shall be worth one *sou* eight *deniers* per day; that of 300 *livres*, six *deniers*; that of 200 *livres*, four *deniers*.†

6. Every day an *assignat* shall be worth its principal plus the accrued interest, and it shall be accepted for such sum. At the end of the year the last bearer shall receive the sum total of the interest, payable on a stated day by

* The first of these decrees provided for a Special Bank which was to administer the *assignats* issued against the Church lands; the second decree dealt with the alienation of property. (Stewart's note.)

† See Glossary.

the Special Bank in Paris as well as in the various towns of the kingdom.

9. Until the sale of the designated national domains is effected, their revenues shall be deposited without delay in the Special Bank, to be used, after making deduction for charges, in the payment of interest on the *assignats*. The bonds of municipalities for the property acquired shall be deposited there likewise, and, in proportion to the returns in cash from the sales which the said municipalities make of such property, said money shall be deposited therein without delay and without exception, and their proceeds and that of the loans they make, according to the obligations they have assumed with the National Assembly, may not be used under any pretext except for the payment of interest on the *assignats* and for their reimbursement.

11. The 400,000,000 of *assignats* shall be used primarily for the exchange of notes of the Discount Bank, up to the amount of the sums due it by the nation, for the amount of notes it has remitted to the public treasury by virtue of the decrees of the National Assembly.

The surplus shall be deposited successively in the public treasury, for liquidating anticipations at their maturity and for reducing by a half year the interest in arrears on the public debt.

12. All bearers of notes of the Discount Bank shall have such notes exchanged for *assignats* of the same amount at the Special Bank before 15 June next; and at whatever time they present themselves during said interval, the *assignats* they receive shall always bear interest to their profit, dating from 15 April; but if they appear after 15 June, their interest shall be deducted from 15 April to the day of presentation.

13. Dating from the said 15 April, the interest assigned to the Discount Bank on the totality of *assignats* to be delivered thereto shall cease . . .

14/2 On the Dangers of Issuing Assignats, 1790

DU PONT DE NEMOURS, *The Dangers of Inflation*, translated by E. E. Lincoln (Boston, Mass., 1950), pp. 28-29, 55-58.

A citizen associated with this Assembly, Monsieur La Voisier, Assistant Deputy from the Bailiwick of Blois, supported by the authority of Hume, by that of Smith, and still more by that of common sense, has demonstrated perfectly that:

If suddenly the quantity of money [i.e., specie] were reduced by one-half, the prices of commodities relative to silver would decline by half, and the other nations would come to provide themselves here in our country with the merchandise which they needed, until we had acquired a quantity of money which would restore our prices to approximately the level of those which were current in the other countries; that, if, on the contrary, the quantity of money were suddenly doubled, the prices of our commodities would double, until, our money having flowed out to foreign countries, the equilibrium which ought necessarily to obtain, with small local differences, between the nations, had reestablished itself.

He has shown that the quantity of money in circulation is naturally limited by the needs of this circulation; since, silver being a medium of exchange that must be purchased, no one wishes to use or lay by in money, beyond that which is necessary for the service for which the money is intended.

He also has shown that, as metallic money is the only kind to which people everywhere attribute an equal value, and which can in consequence circulate among all peoples, we could not establish in this country a superabundance of two kinds of money, one real and the other fictitious, without the more precious kind, the minted money, passing to the foreign country until the inflation of our prices had ceased.

The paper money remaining with us, because the foreigners would not want it, and the level being able to reestablish itself only by the flight of *metallic* money, we should risk finding ourselves at the end almost totally stripped of 'minted' money.

It might even happen that our *assignats*, before being burned in proportion as the sales [of land] took place, – the last step in the operation, – after having given us for some time a superabundance of money, which was ruinous for the people whose subsistence would be extremely dear, [and] ruinous for our manufacturers who would be able to sell nothing to the foreigner, [that] the final result would be to deprive us almost wholly of every kind of money.

Silver driven out by paper, the paper burned after the sales [of land], you might be reduced to primitive barter until the course of business had brought back to you some other money.

Thus the nation would pass quite promptly through the two opposite extremes, from the greatest inflation to the greatest deflation of prices. It would not be possible in France to make any forward commitments, either for wages or for any kind of work or commerce. The most frightful perils for a nation, and particularly for a nation which has just given itself a new constitution, would be in these alternative crises, from which may your wisdom preserve our native land!

I ask you, therefore, Gentlemen, to permit yourselves [to issue] assignats only for the most indispensable public service, and to issue *national bonds* for all other uses which they can satisfy, and for which assignats have been urged without reason.

The proposed procedure is so simple, useful, moderate, fair, and prudent, that I believe it should be substituted for the system of *assignats*. I hope that it will have your votes. I have tried to include the provisions for it in the proposed draft of a decree which I submit to your intelligence [for your intelligent consideration].

PROPOSED DRAFT OF DECREE

The National Assembly has decreed and decrees that which follows:

Article I

Assignats will be issued only gradually, and only for amounts which may be considered indispensable by the National Assembly, in order to provide for armaments and for the other public expenses, until taxes shall be fully and entirely collected.

Article II

They will be offered, 1st, for the debt now due, because of supplies furnished to the departments*; 2nd, for the debt in arrears; 3rd, for the suspended redemption of national bonds bearing three per cent interest, which will be, at the choice of the holder, but not in quantities less than 200 livres, accepted on equal basis with assignats and with silver, in payment for the purchase of national lands. . . .

Article V

All the creditors of the State [on the account of lapsed fees, services and finance companies] will be able to offer the said national bonds to all their creditors, money lenders, for the acquisition of businesses, or for the making of advances and surety bonds, whether the said funds have been furnished on notarial obligations or under private deed, or by simple renewable notes, prior to the 15th of August of the present year. . . .

Article VI

All the other creditors of the State, even those of the debts not yet due, will be able to have their finances liquidated, by reason of the income from their contracts, and by demanding the redemption in national bonds such as will be equally admissible in the purchase of the national domains.

Article VII

All the minted money which will result from the sale of the national domains will be used to retire and redeem assignats, and when there are no more assignats, to retire and redeem national bonds.

Article VIII

In case all national bonds should not have been retired by the complete sale of the national domains, the remainder will be redeemed annually and progressively, in the period which will be fixed and according to the rules

* See Glossary.

which will very soon be established for the general redemption of the national debts. . . .

Is there any one of you who is very certain that the issue of *assignats*, which has been proposed to you, does not contain any danger?

Is there any one of you who is very certain that the operation of the *national bonds*, such as I have just proposed, is open to any objection, which does not apply with even more force to the assignats?

Does it not appear to you that, in the present position of this Empire, there is a great opportunity to act in such a manner that the interests of our creditors and of our lands which ought to pay them, and all the extraordinary transactions which we have to rush through, may be separated from the usual transactions of our agriculture, of our manufactures, and of our commerce, of which the work and plans ought to be respected as much as possible, likewise as little diverted as possible from their natural course?

Is there any one of you who does not feel that rural pursuits and those of the factories are the arch of safety, and that we should shudder when one risks touching them with a rash hand?

As for you, Gentlemen, if you have the least doubt, the cause of the assignats is lost; for, in doubt, it is not permissible to risk the destiny of one's fellow-citizens; and legislators are scrupulously constrained to hold themselves to the safest course.

14/3 Metric Coinage in France, 1803

Law of 7 Germinal, Year XI (27 March 1803). Printed in LEONE LEVI, *The History of British Commerce . . . 1763–1878* (2nd ed., London, 1880), pp. 99–100. (Ed. Tr.)

In the name of the French people, Bonaparte, First Consul, proclaims the following Decree to be a Law of the Republic. . . .

Decree

General Statement. Five grammes of silver, of nine-tenths fineness, shall constitute the monetary unit, which shall retain the name of the franc.*

PART I: PRODUCTION OF THE COINAGE

Art. I The silver coinage shall consist of quarter-franc, half-franc, three-quarter franc, franc, two-franc and five-franc pieces.

Art. II The standard shall be nine-tenths fineness, and one tenth alloy.

* See Glossary.

Art. III The weight of the quarter franc shall be 1·25 grammes, of the half franc, 2·5 grammes . . . and of the five franc piece, 25 grammes.

Art. IV The tolerance of fineness shall be, in the silver coinage, three thousandths either way.

Art. V The tolerance of weight shall be, for the quarter franc, six thousandths either way . . . and for the five franc piece, three thousandths.

Art. VI There shall be manufactured gold coins of twenty and forty francs.

Art. VII Their fineness shall be nine-tenth, and one-tenth alloy.

Art. VIII The twenty-franc pieces shall be weighed at the rate of 155 to the kilogram, and the forty-franc pieces at the rate of 77½.

Art. IX The tolerance of fineness shall be two thousandths either way.

Art. X The tolerance of weight shall be two thousandths either way.

Art. XI Those who bring gold or silver to the mint, shall be charged only the costs of manufacture. These costs are fixed at nine francs a kilogram of gold, and three francs a kilogram of silver.

Art. XII If the metal shall be below the monetary fineness, they shall bear the costs of their refinement. The amount of these costs shall be calculated according to the proportion of the metal which has to be refined in order to bring it up to the monetary fineness.

Art. XIII There shall be manufactured copper coins of two, three and five hundredths of a franc.

Art. XIV The two-centième piece shall weigh four grammes, the three-centième piece six grammes, and the five-centième, ten grammes.

Art. XV The tolerance of weight shall be one-hundredth above the weight.

(*Signed*) Bonaparte (First Consul)
Hugues B. Maret (Secretary of State).

14/4 Variety of Currency, Weights and Measures in Germany, 1837

ALEXANDER LIPS, *Der deutsche Zoll-verein und das deutsche Masz, Gewicht und Münz-Chaos* (Nuremberg, 1837), pp. 7-12. (Ed. Tr.)

. . . All the other nations of Europe have abolished the former varieties of coinage, weights and measures, at least within their countries, and have reduced them to a single system, used to advantage and with ease in their internal trade.

Not so in Germany! . . . We do not have *one* coinage, *one* unit of account expressed in three or four levels, as pounds, shillings and pence in England, or francs, sous and centimes in France, but there are here three separate systems of coinage which circulate side by side, and create embarrassment and loss for the merchant in every large foreign transaction, since they each are divided up differently, and have different names and values. Some States use the heavy Leipzig 18-fl.* system (or did, until recently, like Hanover), others use the later 'conventional' 20-fl. system, like Austria, Saxony, Brunswick with its Specie-Thaler, heavy Thaler and heavy Gulden; still others, like Prussia, mint the same quantity of silver (the fine Cologne Mark) into 21 fl. or 14 Thaler, which are not quite worth a heavy Thaler; and there is finally also the so-called 'light' or 24-system of the Rhenish or Frankfurt currency, valid in Bavaria, Wurttemberg, Baden, Darmstadt, Nassau, etc. All these different systems form a chaos, in which only those maggots, the money-changers and money-brokers crawl around happily, playing havoc with those who need to change their currencies, and brandishing over the nation one of its most terrifying scourges, the agio†.

No less extensive and deterrent is the variety of the weights and measures in Germany. In the case of the 3 or 4 different currency systems, at least one or the other dominates a few countries together; but weights and measures not only differ as between each German state, but even within each state, especially in regard to measures of volume or grain. There are Rhenish, Bavarian, Saxon, Prussian, Hessian, Badish, Wurttemberg, etc., feet, ells, fathoms and rods, hides, furlongs and miles; large and small Simmern, Malter, Scheffel, Mötte, Striche, Mäsz and Metzen, Halbe, Viertel, Geisel and Diethäuflein, large and small Maas, Halbe, Schoppen, Quarte and Kännchen, Pinten, Anker, Eymer, Ohm, Stück, Fuder and Zuläste‡; as well as heavy and light pounds, Frankfurt, Bavarian, Wurttemberg, Prussian, etc., cwt., which all differ from each other§ and to match this variety, and prevent even

* See Glossary.

† These different systems are expressed not only in varying numerical relationships, but also in different names. In Northern Germany they speak of heavy Thaler, Groschen and Heller, also Specie-Thaler; in Southern Germany, there are only Gulden, Kreutzer and Pfennigs. The Gulden as well as the Thaler may be either heavy or light. The Heavy Thaler divides up into 24 good Groschen or 30 silver Groschen, the light Gulden into 60 Kr(eutzer) or 20 Mariengroschen (3 Kr.) and 10 Six-Kreutzer pieces. The Convention or Specie Thaler divides into whole Gulden, half-Gulden or 36 Kr. pieces, twenties, tens and fives; the heavy Thaler into 1/3, 1/6 or 1/12 or 2 Groschen pieces. Besides these there are Albus, Weiszpfennigs, Batzen, Schillings, Landmünzen, Stüber, and in the far North, there circulates the Mark. Finally, foreign gold and silver coins are also current in Germany: Carolines, Louis d'ors, Friedrich d'ors, Max d'ors, Souverains, Ducats, old and new French dollars, Brabant dollars, Polish dollars, as well as paper money, such as notes of the Prussian Treasury, the Salt Office, the Overseas Trading Company, the Austrian Loan, etc. What a free-for-all, what a selection of coins, names and units of account! (Lips' note.)

‡ Mostly measures of volume for wet and dry goods. (Ed.)

§ Thus the Baden lb. is 4 loth lighter than the Bavarian, and the Bavarian cwt. is 10 lb. heavier than that of Frankfurt. In Wurttemberg the cwt. has 104 light lb., in the easiest calculations, the convenience of each state dictated in addition, the invention of its own weights, heavy and light pounds, hundredweights of 100 and more pounds (e.g. 104, 108, 110 pounds), so that even the hundredweight is not true to its name and does not divide into exactly 100 lb. In several states, all of these, and local weights and measures besides, are current side by side and intermingle.*

What useless number and variety of means of exchange! What a multitude of names and symbols! What variety without reason or purpose, what cancerous growth in one field, thought up out of selfishness and laziness! What unnecessary obstacles to all business; what hurdles for all purchases and sales! What hold-ups in payments, what losses altogether in time and money in every kind of traffic! What masses of hands and resources in all offices, constantly reducing the terms of one scale to another in useless and boring calculations! . . .

14/5 Plans to Unify the German Coinage, 1867

American Consular Reports, 1867, pp. 447–449: W. W. MURPHY, Consul-General in Frankfort/Main, 7 February 1868.

That measure which appears to be nearest realization is the establishment of a unit weight and measure, while the introduction of one standard coin seems to meet with more and greater difficulties. One would think it a very easy task for the Prussian government to establish at least a joint system of coinage for the North German Confederation. That this, however, is not

Frankfurt 108. In Wurttemberg there is the light Cologne lb. so that 107 lb. of Wurttemberg equal 100 lb. of Baden. In Sigmaringen they have both, a heavy and a light lb.

German weights and measures are not only varied, but imperfect. In Wurttemberg and Bavaria . . . the foot is divided into 12 instead of 10 parts. The fruit Maasz in Bavaria is too large, the liquid Maasz unduly small. The Maasz of Rhineland, Frankfurt, Darmstadt Electoral Hesse is almost twice as large as the small Bavarian one; the Ohm more than double as large as the small Bavarian Eymer. In Darmstadt they have a large fathom, but a small rod! . . . (Lips' note.)

* It is deplorable that the separate states do not even remove the variety arising from the incorporation of new territories. Only a few of them, like Prussia and Bavaria, have granted their people the benefit of a unified system of weights and measures. Thus . . . the Grand Duchy of Baden had in 1820 no fewer than 8 different measures of length, 3 different ells, 91 different measures of land and surface, 63 measures of wood, 163 measures of grain, or 'sester' or 'simmer', 163 kinds of Ohm and Eimer, 80 kinds of pounds; 163 towns each had their own standards of which several had no currency outside the locality, not counting 20 foreign measures. Some places even had two kinds of ell, one for precious, one for ordinary commodities. Gold and silver was measured by a weight, the Mark, different from that of bread and meat, as if those noble metals might be degraded by being treated with an ordinary weight or measure. . . . (Lips' note.)

the case, appears from the peculiar fact that there are still in force and operation eight different systems of coinage, currency, and account in the states and provinces forming the confederation. These are, first, the 30-thaler standard in Prussia proper, with a subdivision of the thaler into 30 groshens of 12 pennies each; second, the 30-thaler standard in the kingdom of Saxony and the duchies of Saxe-Gotha, Saxe-Altenburg, and Brunswick, with a subdivision of the thaler into 30 groshens of 10 pennies each; third, the 30-thaler standard in the grand duchies of Mecklenburg-Schwerin and Mecklenburg-Strelitz, and the duchy of Lauenburg, with a subdivision of the thaler into 48 skillings of 12 pennies each; fourth, the 30-thaler standard in the free cities of Hamburg and Bremen, with a subdivision of the thaler into two and one-half mark current, or 40 shillings of 12 pennies each; fifth, the system of calculating after the mark banco in the free city of Hamburg, and the city of Altona and neighborhood; sixth, the thaler gold standard in the free city of Bremen, with the louis d'or or pistole, containing at least $\frac{1}{84}$ part of a pound of fine gold, and estimated at five thaler, the thaler subdivided into 72 groats; seventh, the species thaler standard in Schleswig-Holstein, according to which the nine and one-fourth species thalers are containing one Cologne mark of fine silver, the thaler subdivided into 60 shillings current; and eighth, the last but not the least important, the South German or florin standard in Frankfort-on-the-Main, Nassau, the principality of Hohenzollern the duchies of Saxe-Meiningen and Saxe-Coburg, the principality of Schwarzburg-Rudolstadt, and the South German states not belonging to the North German Confederation, viz: the kingdom of Bavaria and Wurtemberg, and the grand duchies of Baden and Hesse-Darmstadt.

The greatest deficiency, however, of the present system is, that the Prussian government has not been able even to extend it over its own special territory, but under the prevailing circumstances has been necessitated to ordain a special law for its newly annexed territories. The same was issued on the 24th of August, 1867, and reads in translation as follows:

We, William, by the grace of God King of Prussia, &c., do hereby ordain with regard to the territories incorporated into the Prussian monarchy by the laws of the 20th of September, and the 24th of December, 1866, with the exclusion of the late Bavarian county of Kaulsdorf, as follows:

ARTICLE 1. The regulations about coinage valid within the old Prussian provinces, and especially the mint and coinage law of the 4th of May, 1857, shall also be of legal force for the territories incorporated into the Prussian monarchy by the aforenamed acts of law, with the exception of the territory of the late free city of Frankfort, with the restriction, however, that the current coins and silver change coined in the late kingdom of Hanover and the electorate of Hesse-Cassel after the thaler standard, as well as the copper coins of the said late electorate of Hesse, shall be made equal to the Prussian coins; and that the traders and merchants of the city of Altona and neighbourhood shall be allowed to calculate after banco mark.

ART. 2. The calculation of amounts, payable, according to agreement, in coin of the territories mentioned in article 1, not made equal to Prussian coin, shall be after the following rates:

1st. Ten Hanoverian pennies are to be equal to 12 Prussian pennies.

2d. Seven florins of South German standard are to be equal to four Prussian thaler.

3d. Five marks current are to be equal to two Prussian thaler.

4th. Four Danish rix thaler are to be equal to three Prussian thaler; fractions, when amounting to less than half a Prussian penny, shall not be counted, and when amounting to more than half a penny shall be counted a full penny. For running payments to be made by instalments, the latter regulation shall be binding only for the amount payable within the calendar year.

ART. 3. The coins of Schleswig-Holstein, Nassau and Hesse-Homburg, with the exception of the 'vereinsthaler,' that is to say, the thalers coined in accordance with the third article of the mint-union of the 28th of January, 1857, as well as the copper coins of Hanover, are to be drawn in and exchanged against Prussian coin at the rates specified in article 2. . . . Upon the expiration of said term of exchange, these coins shall be withdrawn from circulation and be no longer valid as legal tender.

ART. 4. Up to the 31st of September, 1867, everybody within the territories specified in article 1 shall be bound to accept in payment, also, those coins which are not made equal to Prussian coin, as well as up to that term the calculation after the former coins of the incorporated territories shall be permitted. . . .

In witness our own hand and the great royal seal. Given at the Castle of Babelsberg on the 24th of August, 1867.

WILLIAM. . . .

The German Zollverein has acquired such an importance of late, for the commercial intercourse of the world, that of course some arrangement ought to be made for the facilitation of the exchange of its coins against those of other leading commercial countries. Therefore, as the greater part of the latter have adopted the gold standard, it is proposed that also the German states should change the silver standard into the gold standard. . . .

A further proposal is the introduction of the decimal system or decimal subdivision of the current gold coin with the 'Vereins-Thaler,' that is to say the thaler coined in accordance with the mint treaty of the 24th of January, 1857, as the principal piece of silver change. As however, the division of the thaler into 30 groshens does not directly adapt itself to the decimal system, the greater part of the German boards of trade and commerce have decided in favor of its subdivision into 'drittel-thaler pieces,' or third part of a thaler, under the name of 'Reichsmark,' (R.) to be subdivided into 10 groshens of 10 pennies each. The 'Reichsmark' then would adapt itself to the Austrian florin of 100 'Neukreutzers,' and the south German florin of 60 kreutzers, thus, 1 reichsmark equal to 100 pennies, or 50 Austrian neukreutzers, or half Austrian florin, or 35 south German kreutzers; 10 pennies equal to 1 groshen, or 5 Austrian neukreutzers, 3½ south German kreutzers.

To the French system the 'Reichsmark' would adopt itself as follows: 4 reichsmark equal to 5 francs; 4 groshens equal to 50 centimes, or half florin; 4 pennies equal to 5 centimes.

With the English silver coin the reichsmark would compare as follows:

1 reichsmark equal to 10 groshens, or equal to 1 English shilling, or 12 English pence.

Should England adopt the decimal subdivision of the shilling, as has been proposed some years ago, then the new small coin would perfectly coincide with the English one....

14/6 Central Banking Policy in France

Correspondance de Napoléon Ier, publiée par l'ordre de l'Empéreur Napoléon III (32 vols., Paris, 1858-1870), XVII, pp. 497-500. (Ed. Tr.)

A note on the Bank of France.

The idea of instituting a Bank is to achieve a reduction in the rate of interest and to keep the rate as low as possible. In general, the prosperity of manufacturing and commerce depends upon a moderate rate of interest. The bankers, and what are commonly called 'money merchants', indulge in devious operations, which often frustrate this end. Competent discounting by a public bank neutralises the effect of these activities, and should re-direct the operations of the bankers themselves in this direction.... Everything which leads to the reduction of the rate of interest is consonant with the aims of the Bank.

Once these principles are accepted, it is easy to show that today, by the way it operates, the bank does not give the money market all the help which had been anticipated, and in some respects it exacerbates its problems.

The new shares issued by the Bank created new floating funds. All floating funds encourage speculation; speculation of any kind makes it difficult to keep down the rate of interest.

(The note goes on to state that although the Bank cannot buy its own shares, since this is contrary to the interests of shareholders, it is possible for it to purchase Government stock, and since the returns on the latter and the returns on the Bank's shares, Caisse de Service notes and Caisse d'Amortissement bonds exert a reciprocal influence, the Bank can thus influence interest rates.)

The Bank, the Caisse de Service, and the Caisse d'Amortissement are three public establishments which are equally interested in seeing that the 5%'s* are never quoted at a rate which allows too great a disproportion to arise between their yield and the discount rate of the bank, the interest given by the Caisse de Service on the funds which are deposited with it, and the interest offered by the Caisse d'Amortissement for deposits (*cautionnements*), etc.

* Government stock, yielding 5% interest. (Ed.)

As a result of the similarity and reciprocity of activities and interests of these three establishments, there is a need for them to guarantee that the return on the 5%'s is such that it never exceeds 6% when the Bank discounts at 4%, the Caisse de Service borrows at 4-5%, and the Caisse d'Amortissement also gives the same rate of interest.

A degree of stability in the 5% rate is therefore an element of harmony which should be maintained between the Bank discount rate, the rate of borrowings of the Caisse de Service and the rate of interest given by the Caisse d'Amortissement. The heads of these establishments should always be concerned with the maintenance of this harmony; and it would be assured by the effective agreement made by the heads of the three establishments with the approval of the Emperor, the effects of which would be as follows:

A fund of 60 millions, of which the Bank would contribute 30 millions the Caisse d'Amortissement 16, the Caisse de Service the remainder, would be specially designed to remove from the market any 5%'s offered at a rate, which would guarantee more than 6%. Every time the quotation exceeded 83 francs*, the three establishments would see that a sufficient quantity of 5%'s were sold to bring the return within its limits. . . . The three chiefs would meet each month to summarise the results of their operations and to plan measures to be taken according to the state of the market.

The presence of this capital (60 million francs), and its immediate application, when the system requires it, would protect the operations of the Stock Exchange from fluctuations in the rate of interest, which is as ludicrous, as it is dangerous both for public and private interests.

14/7 Joint Stock Companies in France

a Regulations of 31 December 1807 on the formation of a *société anonyme*. Printed in L. WOLOWSKI, *Des sociétés par actions* (Paris, 1838), pp. 24-25. (Ed. Tr.)

b *Journal of the Royal Statistical Society*, Vol. I (1838-39), pp. 84-85.

a *Article* 1 Individuals who wish to form a *société anonyme*† shall be obliged to conform to the *Code de Commerce*; and, in order to obtain the authorisation of the Government, they shall address a signed petition to the Prefect of their Department,† and in Paris they shall send the same to the Councillor of State, the Prefect of Police.

Article 2 The petition shall indicate the business which the *société* wishes to undertake, the period of its proposed existence, the residence of the petitioners, the amount of capital which the *société* must raise, and whether it is

* The price at which *rentes*, i.e. Government stock, would yield 6%. (Ed.)

† See Glossary.

intended to raise the latter by subscription or shares, the period of time in which this capital must be raised, and the place which has been chosen as the administrative centre, the method of administration, and the agreements made between the interested parties.

Article 3 If those who sign the petition do not by themselves constitute the entire *société*, and declare their intention of completing their organisation only when they have received Government approval, they must, in this case, control at least one quarter of the capital of the company, and pay for their quota immediately after the authorisation has been granted.

Article 4 The Departmental Prefects and in Paris the Prefect of Police shall ascertain the qualifications and characters of either the authors of the plan or the petitioners; they shall give their opinion on the usefulness of the concern, and the probability of its success; they shall declare if the enterprise appears contrary to public morality, and commercial practice, and order in general; they shall undertake investigations to ascertain whether the petitioners are fully capable of realising the quota for which they claim an interest. The documents, and the opinion of the Prefect shall be sent to the Minister.

Article 5 After examining the proposition, the Minister shall submit it to His Majesty in his Council of State, who shall accept or reject the petition.

Article 6 Nothing can be changed as regards the bases and aim of the *société anonyme* after receipt of the approval, unless the *société* obtains a new authorisation from the government in the manner prescribed above, under penalty of the suspension of the *société*.

b JOINT STOCK COMPANIES IN FRANCE.

The French Code of Commerce recognizes three kinds of Commercial Societies for purposes of a permanent nature; – viz., 1st, Societies 'en nom Collectif,' or Common Partnerships; 2d, Societies 'en Commandite,' or Firms with Sleeping Partners; and 3d, Anonymous Societies, or Joint-Stock Companies.

The first consists of a certain number of persons associated in a firm, in which their several names are included. Each partner is responsible for the whole, and there is no limit to his liability.

Societies 'en commandite' consist of several individuals, one or more of whom are alone responsible for the acts of the firm, and are liable to the whole extent of their property. Others, who embark a fixed amount of capital in the enterprise, and are called 'commanditaires,' or sleeping partners, take no share in the business of the society: their names do not appear in the firm, and they are responsible only to the extent of their registered investment. The law allows this sum to be divided into transferable shares.

The third class, or Anonymous Societies, resemble Joint-Stock Companies in this country. The capital is divided into shares, and each holder is liable only to the amount of those which he possesses. The business is carried on by a few individuals elected by the shareholders, who are not personally responsible to the public.

In a recent Report of a Committee of the French Chambers the following statement is given of the number of Companies of the two latter classes established in France, and registered in the Tribunal of Commerce at Paris, from the year 1826 to the close of 1837:

		Capital.	
	Number.	Fr.	£.
Societies 'en Commandite'	1106	1,117,098,740 =	44,683,948
Joint-Stock Companies	157	393,396,125 =	15,735,844

The average nominal capital of the first class is 40,000*l*., and that of the latter 100,000*l*.

With respect, however, to the above figures, it must be borne in mind that a considerable number of the Companies never commenced operations from want of funds; that another large portion realised only a very small part of their calls; and that a deduction must be made for the double entry of some Companies, which were first created 'en commandite,' and afterwards formed into Joint-Stock Companies. . . .

During the present year the number of Societies, 'en Commandite,' has increased in a remarkable degree. In January and February there were registered 67 Societies, with a capital of 118,022,000 fr., or 4,720,880*l*., divided into 219,212 shares. In March alone the capital of the Societies registered amounted to more than double that sum, viz., 274,572,000 fr., or 10,982,880*l*., divided into 399,635 shares.

It will be seen from the following classification of the Companies formed since 1826, that enterprises connected with periodical and general literature form a large proportion of the total number. Of the 1106 Companies, 401 relate to Journals, Periodicals, and Books; 95 to Manufactures of various kinds; 93 to Coaches and modes of Conveyance; 60 to Forges, the manufacture of Metals, and the Coal-trade; 52 to internal and foreign Navigation; 40 were Banks; 27 Assurance Companies; 25 Companies for agricultural purposes, for draining Marshes, &c.; 24 Theatres; and 289 were of a miscellaneous nature.

14/8 The Foundation of the Crédit Foncier

Decree of 30 July 1852 approving the Statutes. Printed in J. M. JEANNENEY and M. PERROT, *Textes de droit . . .* [*see* Document **3/10b**], pp. 198–199. (Ed. Tr.)

Article 1 By these articles, those present, subject to Government approval, establish a *société anonyme*, composed of the holders of the shares hereafter created.

Article 2 The aims of the organisation are:

(i) The lending of sums, on mortgage, to landed proprietors situated in the seven Departments* of the Appeal Court of Paris (Seine, Seine-et-Oise, Seine-et-Marne, Eure-et-Loir, Aube, Marne and Yonne), which the borrowers shall repay by means of annual payments, including interest and amortisation as well as costs of administration;

(ii) The employment, with Government authorisation, of any other system, having for its aim the facilitation of loans on real estate and the repayments of the same;

(iii) The creation of bonds, equal in value to the mortgage liabilities endorsed by the bank, producing an annual interest, redeemable by the drawing of lots, with or without bonuses, and bearing the name of 'landed bonds';

(iv) The transaction of business in these bonds;

(v) The acceptance as deposits, without interest, of sums which are to be covered by the creation of landed bonds.

Article 3 The organisation shall assume the name of the Banque Foncière de Paris, Société de Crédit Foncier.

Article 50 The properly constituted General Meeting represents the shareholders as a whole. It is composed of the two hundred most important shareholders.

Article 57 Resolutions are decided on a majority vote of the members present. All members with forty shares at any one time possess equal voting rights, although nobody may have more than five votes in his own name, nor more than ten in his name and as a proxy.

Each member of the General Assembly has the right to speak even if he does not possess forty votes.

Article 60 The borrower contracts the obligation to pay off his debts to the *société* within a twenty- to fifty-year period.

Article 63 The bank lends only on first mortgages.

Article 66 The bank accepts as security only those properties with a certain guaranteed income.

Article 67 The amount of the loan may not exceed half of the value of mort-

* See Glossary.

gaged property. The loan shall not exceed one-third of the value of vineyards and wooded property.

In any case, the pledged annual payment may not be greater than the total income from the property.

Article 69 The rate of interest on the sum borrowed is fixed by the Conseil d'Administration. It may not exceed 5%.

Article 71 The annual payment includes:

(i) interest;

(ii) amortisation, calculated on the rate of the interest and the duration of the loan;

(iii) an annual amount which may not exceed 60 centimes* per cent for the cost of administration.

Article 74 Furthermore, default in payment for a period of six months renders demandable the whole of the debt, one month after public notice.

Article 75 The debtors have the right to anticipate the repayment of the debt either in whole or in part. Anticipated payments shall be made according to the choice of the borrower either in the bank's landed bonds, similar to those issued in representation of the contracted debt. [sic] These bonds are received at par and must be impressed immediately with a stamp of cancellation. The funds arising out of anticipated payments shall be used as necessary to amortize or to redeem landed bonds.

Article 87 Landed bonds may not exceed the amount of the mortgage obligations endorsed by landed proprietors in favour of the bank.

14/9 The Activities of the Crédit Mobilier

a A. COURTOIS, *Histoire de la Banque de France* . . . [*see* Document **9/9**], pp. 206–208. (Ed. Tr.)

b *Journal of the Royal Statistical Society*, Vol. XXIII (1860), pp. 243–245.

a The second financial creation in 1852 was the Société Générale de Crédit Mobilier, which under a new and well-chosen name undertook a financial role hitherto more respected abroad than in France. Thus from 1835 the Société Générale de Bruxelles and the Banque de Belgique undertook jointly in Belgium discount and issuing business and industrial joint stock operations. The founders of the Crédit Mobilier – and this is the most original feature of their enterprise – separated these two functions, and created a bank concerned with the second rather than the first of these activities, a Crédit Mobilier, as it has been called since 1852. The reader will understand how difficult it is to indicate the operations of an institution of this nature; in general it can be said that its object is to support undertakings which, after study, it regards in a favourable light, by helping in the formation of: 1. the administrative framework; 2. the social capital, either shares or bonds, then in issuing the latter to the public with its moral guarantee. This role . . . is of inestimable value to society; but like all institutions it needs to be enlivened by the spur of competition, without which even the ablest people cannot produce really profitable results either for share-holders or for society as a whole, as the present example clearly indicates.

The Crédit Mobilier Français was capitalised at 60 million francs,* divided into share units of 500 francs. It was authorised by the decree of 18 November 1852. 120,000 shares were issued in 40,000 blocks. Participation in the first issue allowed subscription to the second, in the proportion of one to one, and the third issue was granted to subscribers of the two first issues in the proportion of one share for every two held of either of the two other issues.

This Société could create bonds to an amount ten times greater than its capital (600 millions); the following restriction was imposed upon it; the accumulated amount of sums received in the current account, and bonds, valid for less than one year, cannot exceed twice the amount of the issued capital (120 millions).

This Société was administered by a council of fifteen members, nominated by the shareholders. A Committee of five selected from the members of the council was charged with carrying out its decisions. Because of an oversight, which we should like to attribute only to the haste surrounding the formation of this important Société, a Conseil de Censure, nominated by shareholders to superintend the Société in their interest, which was a feature of the Bank of France and the Crédit Foncier and so many other *Sociétés anonymes*, was not a feature of the organization. Moreover, by law, the General Meeting was presided over by one of the members of the Board of Management who was naturally the President or one of the Vice-Presidents. These two points were serious; they deprived the administration of a salutary counterbalance. The subsequent history of the Société has proved this only too well.

We shall not enter into detail regarding the operations of this Société. . . . It is sufficient to recall that the Crédit Mobilier has co-operated in the foundation and establishment of the capital . . . of numerous companies. . . . As far as French companies are concerned, it is involved in the Rhône to Loire Railway, the Grand Central, the Dôle to Salins Railway, the Ardennes line, the line from Saint-Rambart to Grenoble (Dauphiné), and the Companies of the East, West and South, the Crédit Foncier de France, the 'Confiance', later the 'Paternelle' (a Fire Assurance Company), the General Maritime

* See Glossary.

Company (later called the Trans-Atlantic), the four companies resulting from the division of the former Civil Company of the Mines of the Loire, the General Omnibus Company of Paris, the General Shops and Entrepots of Paris, the Parisian Gas, Heating and Lighting Company, the Real Estate Company of the Rue de Rivoli (later called the Real Estate Company of Paris), the Southern Salt Company, the Imperial Carriage Company of Paris, etc. As regards foreign companies, 1. in Belgium, the Vieille Montagne Zinc Mines and Foundries Company; 2. in Germany, the Commercial and Industrial Bank of Darmstadt, the Austrian State Railway Company, the Eastern Railway Company of the Emperor Franz Joseph; 3. in Russia, the Grand Russian Railway Company; 4. in Switzerland, the Western Swiss Railway Company and the Central Swiss Railway Company; 5. in Spain, the Spanish Crédit Mobilier, the Royal Company for the Canalisation of the Ebro, the Northern Railway Company of Spain and the Cordova to Seville Railway Company, as well as the Spanish Phoenix (an insurance company) and the Madrid Gas Lighting Company, in which it has an indirect stake through the General Spanish Crédit Mobilier Company; 6. in Holland, the General Company of Netherlands Industry and Commerce; 7. in Italy, the General Italian Crédit Mobilier Company; 8. in London, the International Financial Society; 9. finally in Turkey, the Imperial Ottoman Bank – without including the Société's important participation in the underwriting of large loans both in France and abroad.

b VI.—*Credit Mobilier Society at Paris. – Condition and Operations in* 1859.

The Paris Correspondent of the *Economist* newspaper of 5th May (1860), describes as follows the results of the Annual General Meeting of the Shareholders of the *Société Général de Credit Mobilier*, held at Paris on 30th April (1860). The French money is converted into sterling at 25f. = £.

The Credit Mobilier Shareholders held their annual meeting on the 30th April (1860), and, as usual, the report presented by the directors has excited great interest. The dividend declared was, as had been expected, only 12 f. 50 c. per share, in addition to the interest of 5 per cent. per share, making 25 f. paid at the beginning of the present year. The sum is certainly deplorably small, but in 1858 and 1857 there were no dividends at all. In 1856 the dividend (in addition to the 5 per cent. interest) was 90 f.; in 1855, 178 f. 70 c.; in 1854, 34 f.; and in 1853, 25 f. Thus, then, it will be seen the Credit Mobilier is subject to striking fluctuations of good and ill fortune.

The report, after some general observations, and after stating that the Company subscribed 50,000,000 f. in the last loan of 500,000,000 f. raised by the Government, enters into somewhat elaborate detail respecting the co-operation of the Company in certain Spanish enterprises – the North of Spain and the Cordova to Seville Railways, and the Spanish Credit Mobilier. These affairs, it appears, have not obtained the support which had been hoped for from the Spanish people; but nevertheless, the intervention of the Company in them is justified on the grounds that they are good in themselves, and that the Company but follows the example set by English capitalists in supporting the Rouen

Railway at a time at which the undertaking met with little favour in France. The Russian Railways, in which the Credit Mobilier is largely interested, are next noticed, and a favourable account is given of their situation and prospects; among other things, I see the Commercial Treaty between England and France is set down as likely to be advantageous to these lines by creating a larger demand for Russian raw materials. The Austrian, the Dauphiné (French), and the Southern (French) Railways; the Paris Omnibuses, the Paris Gas, and the Paris Real Property (Immobilière) Companies, in all which the Credit Mobilier is concerned, are successively referred to; nor is the Compagnie Maritime – one of its pet projects – which has hitherto been very unfortunate, forgotten; indeed, its situation is represented as quite *coleur* [*sic*] *de rose* . . .

With reference to the preceding report, the *Times* of the 4th May (1860), contains the following comment:

According to the accounts submitted at the annual meeting of the Credit Mobilier Company at Paris, the balance of 360,000*l.*, which stood to the credit of the concern at the end of 1858, has dwindled to 60,000*l.* This result has occasioned great remark, since it appears wholly inexplicable, the Company being supposed to have enjoyed during the past twelvemonth almost exclusive opportunities of connecting itself most profitably with all such projects as have received countenance from the Government. The understanding at the meeting, however, seemed to be that no questions were to be tolerated. Scarcely forty shareholders attended, and one or two who had the courage to solicit information, are reported to have been immediately put down. At any time the danger of resistance from intractable shareholders is small, since by the statutes of the Company those only can claim to be present who have held at least 200 shares for six months. As a means of silencing inquirers on the present occasion, the unworthy trick was resorted to of threatening that the Board of Directors would resign if any 'mistrust' were exhibited. After the payment of a dividend, the available balance of profit and loss will be reduced, it is stated, to 1,260*l.*

14/10 French Foreign Investment

F. BLANC, *Des Valeurs Étrangères en France* (Paris, 1860), pp. 6, 8, 9, 10–12. (Ed. Tr.)

We believed we could assume a role in the development of European railways similar to that played by England in the development of our own network. Very few railway lines exist today on the Continent which have not been established principally by French capital.

It is recalled that from 1852 to 1856 a great industrial fever seized France. The Government thought it was necessary to check this expansion, which occurred everywhere even beyond our frontiers. . . . The public was forewarned that the Government would not authorise henceforth any *société anonyme** except those whose public usefulness was quite evident. And as capital threatened to transfer its interests to *sociétés en commandite*,* it was thought necessary to substantiate the memorandum of 9 March (which had placed limits on joint-stock operations) by a law which placed definite limits on joint-stock companies and rendered their formation almost impossible.

* See Glossary.

The effect of these measures was to increase the flow of capital abroad and to favour its outward movement to the detriment of our own industries.

Foreign stock issued on the Paris market and at present 'dealt in' on the Bourse represents a realised capital of 1,420 million francs,* as shown in the table below:

Austrian	Shares	500 fr.	400,000	—	200 mil.
—	Bonds	275 ,,	603,636	—	166
South Austria	Shares	500 ,,	750,000	(250 p.)	187
—	Bonds	275 ,,	156,250	—	273
Victor Emmanuel	Shares	500 ,,	100,000	—	50
Roman	Shares	400 ,,	170,000	—	68
—	Bonds	250 ,,	80,000	—	20
Russian	Shares	500 ,,	600,000	(150 p.)	90
West Swiss	Shares	500 ,,	800,00	(450 p.)	36
Central Swiss	Shares	500 ,,	72,000	—	36
N.E. Swiss	Bonds	500 ,,	57,416	—	29
N. Spain	Shares	500 ,,	200,000	(200 p.)	40
Sargossa	Shares	500 ,,	240,000	(400 p.)	96
—	Bonds	250 ,,	100,000	—	25
Cordova to Seville	Shares	500 ,,	36,000	—	18
—	Bonds	260 ,,	24,576	—	6
Seville to Xeres	Shares	500 ,,	47,000	—	24
—	Bonds	250 ,,	32,000	—	8
Tarragona to Reus	Shares	500 ,,	7,933	—	4
Hainault – Flanders ...	Shares	500 ,,	52,000	(300 p.)	15
—	Bonds	250 ,,	47,586	—	14
William of Luxembourg	Shares	500 ,,	50,000	(300 p.)	15
					1,420 mil.

Foreign railway lines, which have had only a temporary quotation and in which our capital has been very little involved, are not included in this account.

Nor do we include credit institutions such as the Darmstadt Bank, the various Spanish and Viennese banking establishments and the credit banks in Geneva and Turin. Although these different banks have raised most of their capital in Paris, we shall not consider this capital as immobilised abroad, as bank capital is essentially floating capital, and consequently can always be

* See Glossary.

realised unless it is intended for joint stock enterprises, which is the case at present with the various Spanish credits.

France's contribution to foreign enterprise could certainly be placed at a total figure of 1,420 millions. . . . But so that no-one can accuse us of exaggeration, we estimate it at one milliard francs.

14/11 Statutes of the Bank of Prussia, 1846

Printed in NICOLAUS HOCKER, *Sammlung der Statuten aller Actien-Banken Deutschlands* (Cologne, 1858), pp. 500–509. (Ed. Tr.)

CHAPTER I. THE TRANSACTIONS AND RESOURCES OF THE BANK

Purpose of the Bank

1. The Bank shall exist in order to facilitate the monetary circulation of the country, to further the use of capital, to support trade and industry and to prevent an undue rise in the rate of interest.

Transactions of the Bank

2. For these purposes the Bank is permitted to discount bills and money orders, as well as Government securities and bearer securities of municipalities and other public authorities, and to trade in them on its own account or on the account of public bodies; to grant credits and loans against sufficient security; to issue bills and money orders, to accept them and collect them on the account of others; to accept sums of money on deposit and current account, and to buy and sell bullion and coin.

Other trading transactions, particularly the trade in commodities, are and shall remain prohibited.

3. The Bank is further permitted to accept for safe keeping gold and silver, coined or otherwise, valuables, State securities and documents of all kinds, as well as sealed packages without examination of their contents against deposit certificates and for appropriate payment.

Bill transactions

4. The Bank shall discount only such bills payable locally and such terminable securities as have less than three months' currency remaining, and bear, as a rule, three respectable signatures. It is authorised, further, to buy and sell good bills on other localities at home and abroad, whenever it shall find it necessary, particularly for the acquisition of bullion and coin. . . .

The rate of interest

6. The Bank shall publish the rate of discount at which it will discount bills or grant loans or pawns; but it shall be free to fix a lower rate of interest

in general for loans against the security of precious metals. In its pawn trade it must not exceed a rate of 6%. . . .

Bank money of account

8. The Bank shall pay and make up its accounts in Prussian silver money, as laid down in our Coinage Act for the Prussian States of 30 September 1821 (No. 673).

Capital of the Bank

9. The working capital of the bank shall consist:

(*a*) of the capital contributed by the State and private shareholders (paras. 10, 11, 17) as well as of the capital reserve (para. 18);

(*b*) of the funds contributed by law and under State guarantee by the courts and public trustee authorities, churches, schools, charitable foundations and other public institutions (paras. 21–26).

Subscribed capital: (a) of private persons

10. The capital to be subscribed by private persons shall amount to 10 million Thlr., to be divided into 10,000 shares of 1,000 Thlr.* each, to be paid into the Bank in cash in Prussian silver coinage, 14 Thlr. to the Mark fine. . . .

Subscribed capital: (b) of the State

17. The capital to be subscribed by the State shall consist of the surplus of assets over liabilities in existence at present, to which the annual dividends on this capital (para. 36/2) shall be added.

We reserve the right to augment this capital not only by the annual profits due to the State (para. 36/4), but also out of other State funds. . . .

Note issue

29. The Bank is authorised to issue, according to the needs of its trade, demand notes upon itself as its own currency under the title of 'bank notes'.

No bank note may be issued of a denomination lower than 25 Thaler Prussian silver coinage. The total note issue is limited to 15 million Thaler, so that the Bank is entitled to issue, in addition to the 10 million issued under the Order of 11 April 1846, another 5 million.

But whereas the Bank has received . . . 6 million Thalers in bills in 1836 and 1837 against National Debt papers . . . it shall be entitled, three years after the date of this Act, on surrender of the said bills, to issue a further 6 million Thaler in bank notes.

The Bank is strictly prohibited from exceeding this total sum of 21 million Thaler without express legal enactment. . . .

* See Glossary.

14/11 *Statutes of the Bank of Prussia, 1846*

CHAPTER 2. THE CONSTITUTION AND ADMINISTRATION OF THE BANK

Organisation of the Institution

39. The central office in Berlin, together with its existing and future branch offices and agencies in the Provinces shall form a single institution independent of the financial administrative offices of the State.

No provincial office may be dissolved or restricted in its functions without our permission. We reserve the right of decision over the opening of additional provincial offices in the light of the needs of trade.

40. We reserve the right to alter the location of the head offices and branch offices of the Bank.

Supervisory Council of the Bank

41. The Bank shall remain under the general supervision of the State, which shall continue to be exercised by the Bank Supervisory Council.

42. The Council shall consist henceforth of (*a*) the President of the State Council, (*b*) the Minister of Justice for the time being (*c*) the Minister of Finance for the time being (*d*) the President of the Board of Trade for the time being and (*e*) another member selected by us.

It shall meet every quarter. Its proceedings shall be minuted in writing.

General Constitution of the Bank

43. The whole corporation shall be presided over by a Governor and Royal Commissioner, assisted by a Central Board.

44. All business shall be transacted by the Central Board and by the offices and agencies in the Provinces, unless it is expressly reserved for the Governor.

45. All officers of the Bank shall continue to remain responsible solely to us for the faithful and orderly conduct of their affairs, and shall keep all the rights and duties of the regular Civil Service.

No officer of the Bank may own a Bank share.

46. The Bank alone shall continue to be responsible for all payments, emoluments, and pensions of the staff, as also for the support of their dependants after their death. The budget for staff salaries and payments shall continue to be laid down by us on the advice of the Governor.

47. The shareholders shall exercise their rights by the major shareholders' meetings and by their elected committees according to the present Bank Act.

The Governor

48. The Governor is appointed by us and reports to us direct. He shall control the whole of the Bank administration in conformity with the present Act, with unlimited powers and on his personal responsibility. He shall

attend the meetings of the Supervisory Council, shall report to it the state of the Bank's affairs and all matters relating thereto, and shall give a general account of all its operations and contracts. . . .

The Central Board

55. The Central Board is the administrative and executive authority, within the directives issued by the Governor.

56. The Central Board shall consist for the time being of one chairman and five members. . . .

The appointment of the chairman and members of the Central Board shall be undertaken by us on the advice of the Governor of the Bank. They shall hold their posts for life and receive a fixed salary. . . .

The meeting of major shareholders

61. The meeting of major shareholders represents all the shareholders and is formed by the holders of the 200 largest holdings as recorded in the books of the Bank (paras 10, 13) on the date of calling the meeting, who are resident in our dominions and are capable of conducting their own affairs. In case of equal holdings the length of possession shall decide, and in cases of equal length, it shall be decided by lot.

62. The major shareholders' meeting shall take place at least once a year, in January or February in the city of the Central Office, and extraordinary meetings may be called at any time. . . .

65. The meeting of major shareholders shall receive the annual report and balance sheet (para. 97), elect the shareholders' central committee (para 66) and determine their dismissal (80), as well as the dismissal of the Provincial committees (107), pronounce upon any proposed increase in the capital, as well about its need as about the manner of its augmentation, and the consequential alteration in the proportions of the profits going to the private holders and to the State (para. 11) and shall decide on the consequent amendment of the Act, which may only proceed with the consent of the shareholders (para. 16). . . .

Friedrich Wilhelm, by the Grace of God, King of Prussia etc.

14/12 Criticism of German Credit (Note-issuing) Banks in the 1860's

Report of the Magdeburg Chamber of Commerce, 1860. Printed in P. GEYER, *Theorie und Praxis des Zettelbankwesens* . . . (Munich, 1867), Appendix xii, pp. 345–347. (W.O.H. Tr.)

Although we strongly support [the principles of] the greatest possible freedom of commerce – which we regard as undoubtedly the most certain means of promoting the public welfare and the expansion of trade and industry – and although we object with equal emphasis to any kind of privilege [secured] through Government Departments, nevertheless we hold the view that the greatest precaution should be taken with regard to the issue of paper money. We consider that the issue of paper money should be regulated by law in such a way as to prevent all irregularities. In Germany it is only in the last few years that we have had a greater freedom with regard to the issue of banknotes and in this short time we have already gained enough experience to realise that we should take stringent precautions [in this matter]. What has happened to all those mighty banks [founded with] such great hopes and from which so much benefit for the industrial development of Germany was expected? [They are] in a bad way and more or less bankrupt and their shareholders can see salvation only in prompt liquidations. Of course we are accustomed to hearing the misfortunes of these banks ascribed to Prussia's ban on banknotes* in a manner which soon leads to bad relations between Federal States. We believe, however, that generally the banks have been ruined owing to their own blunders and to incompetence or dishonesty on the part of their founders and directors. We regard the [Prussian] ban as a wise and very necessary regulation.

[Banks were] established in places lacking all the opportunities which lead to successful business. They recklessly unloaded their notes onto the public. Their statutes allowed them to embark upon transactions which no note-issue bank ought to be allowed to undertake and, in doing so, they placed themselves on a level with the [Paris] Credit [sic] Mobilier. By [their] loans [to industry] and by their policy of discounting [bills] they wantonly encouraged over-speculation and the wildest business activities. They misled people into setting up factories and other establishments by persuading them that the credit they were offering would be of a permanent nature. But they soon had to withdraw their support when their own credit was shattered and when their own notes – by which the [newly-established] firms were forcibly fed – no longer sufficed to support the original over-optimistic credit. It is usually believed that here in Germany ruinous bank crashes – such as have occurred in Great Britain and in the United States – are not possible or at any rate are unlikely. People think that [in Germany] they are reasonably protected from folly and incompetence by the supervision which the State exercises over the banks and by the regular publication of bank returns. That the first precaution – Government supervision – is a protection of doubtful value, particularly in the smaller States, is proved by the

* In 1855 the Prussian Government forbade the circulation in Prussia of non-Prussian notes which were worth less than ten Thalers. Saxony issued a similar decree. (W.O.H.)

financial returns of various banks that lie before us. In these financial returns and in the enterprises promoted by German banks of issue we find plenty of evidence to support our assertion that a bank can be ruined as quickly and as suddenly with Government supervision as without it. When we see that a bank, with an acknowledged deficit equal to a quarter of its original capital, is nevertheless allowed to pay a dividend to its shareholders, and when dubious and half-lost sums are included in bank-balances and bank-statements as if they were assets, we doubt whether we are so very far off from the road that will lead us to a state of affairs similar to that of the United States.

14/13 Request for a Private Note-issuing Bank in Königsberg, 1865

Report of the Königsberg Chamber of Commerce, 1865. Printed in P. GEYER, *Theorie und Praxis des Zettelbankwesens* . . . [*see* Document **14/12**], Appendix XIV pp. 349–352. (W.O.H. Tr.)

Throughout the whole of this year's report – from the general introduction to the special reports on individual branches of industry – we hear ever louder complaints of the lack of capital in this province [East Prussia]. The banking system is therefore of greater importance to us than it is to other districts and at other times. We undoubtedly need much better banking facilities for all our business activities. While we fully appreciate the services of those responsible for the management of the local branch of the Bank of Prussia we cannot regard this bank as satisfying all the needs of the [local] money market. The Bank of Prussia, through its headquarters in Berlin and its local branch in Königsberg, has for several years always handled most of the commercial business [*Lombardgeschäft*] – though borrowing (on the security of merchandise) is largely confined to the corn merchants and to the produce merchants. But in times of crisis the local branch of the Bank of Prussia, acting on a general policy [laid down in Berlin], has to restrict its loans on the security both of merchandise and of shares. . . . Therefore the need for facilities for discounting bills is very great. Naturally the local branch of the Bank of Prussia limits the number of bills that it will discount for any individual firm and every merchant fears that he may overstep this limit – although the facilities offered [by the local branch of the Bank of Prussia] are quite inadequate. Unlike other business centres we have no joint stock companies here which deposit their surplus monies in the local banks. Similarly there are far fewer agents of outside banks and financial houses in Königsberg than in the commercial centres of Western Germany. So we have to rely on the Private Bank of Königsberg and we regret that we cannot report favourably upon this institution. The board of directors of the Private Bank of Königsberg – influenced by two firms holding a large number of the bank's shares – has not appreciated the important fundamental functions of a banking institution. In these circumstances we have applied for a concession to establish a second private bank of issue in Königsberg. This proposed new bank would have equal rights of note issue with the [existing] Private Bank of Königsberg. We realise that informed economic opinion just now is hostile to any extension of the right to issue bank notes. But the position in practice [here] is different. The banking laws in force today, the present monopoly of the Bank of Prussia, and the existence [in Germany] of a number of private note issuing banks – so long as that situation prevails a new private bank which has not got the privilege of issuing notes would, in the initial stages of its development, find itself in a difficult position even in one of the busiest and most favourably situated Prussian commercial centres. But, in the circumstances we have mentioned, such a new bank [without the right to issue bank notes] could not come into existence at all in so remote a town as Königsberg which is short of capital. No outside business man would risk his capital on an experiment as yet quite new in Prussia and in so unfavourably situated a town as Königsberg.

14/14 Austrian Central Bank Policy, 1856

American Consular Reports, 1856, pp. 109–111: Anonymous Report from Vienna, 31 March 1856.

The history of the fluctuations in the value of Austrian paper money, since the bank suspended its specie payments, is not without interest. The imperial decree, by which this suspension was authorized and the circulation of the bank notes made compulsory, bears date the 2d of June, 1848. In November of that year the *agio* on silver was 5 per cent. In June, 1849, it had risen to 23 per cent.; but in consequence of the capitulation of Georgey, at Velagos, and the prospect of a favorable termination of the Hungarian war, it fell again in September of the same year to 5 per cent. The improvement, however, was not permanent. The agio commenced soon after to rise again; and in November, 1850, during the difficulties with Prussia, it reached its highest point, specie commanding a premium of 52 per cent.

For some time after this the paper currency underwent constant and great fluctuations in value, until in 1852, in consequence partly of measures taken by the government to improve the finance, and partly of the general political repose of Europe, the agio sunk again to 9 and 10 per cent. For the first three quarters of 1853 it stood, with slight variations, at that point. Then began the oriental trouble, and in March of the next year it had risen again to 44 per cent. From this period, though it fell at times to 18 and 20 per cent. no abiding change for the better took place until the middle of 1855, when it began steadily to fall, and on the 16th of January of this year, the day before the receipt of the news of the acceptance by Russia of the propositions of the allies, it had already attained the comparatively low point of 13 per cent. On the 3d of the present month (March) the agio was noted in the official papers at 2½, its lowest point since 1848.

This rapid improvement in the paper currency is undoubtedly due in a great measure to the prospect of peace in Europe. But other causes have helped to bring it about. The government may fairly, on the ground of its recent financial policy and measures, lay claim to a good share of the credit. . . .

The task which the ministry of finance had before it was a threefold one: to reduce the national expenditure, to place the bank in the way of resuming its payments, and to stimulate the enterprise and industry of the country, so as ultimately to increase the revenue of the state.

The first object, the reduction of the expenditures, was of indispensable and most present necessity. . . .

The next object aimed at was the relief of the bank, and here the chief thing to be done was for the state to pay the debt it owed to this institution.

That debt in 1855 may be considered as divided into three portions: one of sixty millions of florins*, the remainder of an old debt contracted before 1848, and already provided for by annual appropriations from the revenue of three and five millions of florins alternately, which will liquidate it in fifteen years. The second portion, originally one hundred and forty-seven millions, grew up in the financial troubles of 1848–'49, and amounted at the close of last year to forty-two millions. This had also been provided for by a fixed per centage in the instalments as they are paid in of the so-called national loan of 1854, by which it will be discharged in three years. The third and larger portion of the debt amounted to one hundred and fifty-five millions of florins, contracted during the last two years, and for this no provision has been made. To liquidate it the government now resolved on a step often suggested, but never before taken up, the transference, that is, to the bank, of crown domains to the value of one hundred and fifty-five millions of florins, giving to the bank the right not only to cultivate and manage the estates for its own benefit, but to sell them, and replenish its coffers with the proceeds. The terms of the transfer were such that the debt was only then to be held as discharged when the bank, either through the profits of the management or through the sale of the estates, had actually received the sum of one hundred and fifty-five millions.

* See Glossary.

The government thus paid its debt in the way least burdensome to itself, because the estates, so long as it cultivated them through its servants, yielded, as a matter of course, but a very small interest on the capital represented; and it provided at the same time for the final transfer of the property to private hands, in whose management it would undoubtedly increase in value, and become, through taxation, a source of revenue to the state.

After thus disposing of the debt due the bank, the government proceeded to augment very largely the powers and efficiency of that institution. This was done by making it what is called here a '*hypotheken*,' or mortgage 'bank,' that is, giving it, authority to loan money on the security of real estate, lands and houses.

Heretofore the bank could only make loans on state bonds. Its capital was at the same time increased by the issue of new shares to the amount of thirty-five thousand silver florins, and it was empowered to advance in loans on real estate over and above this sum a further amount of two hundred millions of florins, not, however, in its usual bills for circulation, but in notes bearing interest, and to be discounted, or sold like other paper in the market.

The bank was then given to understand that it must do its part in the work, by gradually increasing its specie fund and diminishing its circulation, so that, as soon as practicable, a normal relation between the two might be restored, and its payments of specie be resumed without danger.

According to the official statement made at the beginning of this month, there were over fifty-one millions of silver in the vaults, and the notes in circulation amounted to three hundred and seventy-four millions – an improvement in both respects on the exhibit of the preceding month. . . .

The third and last object which, as above stated, the government had in view, was to facilitate enterprise and industry, and develope generally the material resources of the country. The creation of the 'hypotheken bank,' just described, is regarded as one step in this direction, since that institution will have for its aim the furtherance and help of one of the most important interests of the empire – the agricultural – an interest, too, which, in the eastern provinces, Hungary, Gallicia, &c., owing to the change in the relation of the peasants to the landlords, effected since the revolution, and to the want of capital for the introduction of improved modes of culture, is in a state of comparative depression.

By means of another institution, called the '*Credit Anstalt fur Handel and Gewerbe*,' which went into operation in January of this year, the government hopes to assist the commercial and manufacturing interests, and to give an impulse to industrial undertakings generally throughout the empire. The capital of this institution is one hundred millions of florins, represented in five hundred thousand shares, at two hundred florins each, of which, however, only three hundred thousand shares, answering to sixty millions of florins, are to be for the present issued. Thus far, three instalments, of ten per cent. each, on the shares have been paid in. The powers of the institution are very extensive.

It can establish manufactures, build railroads, work mines, discount paper, take government loans, speculate in stocks – in short, engage, either by itself or in company with others, in almost every kind of commercial and industrial enterprise. One great advantage which the government anticipates from it is, the opening to the smaller manufacturers and tradesmen a source of credit which has hitherto failed them. Another benefit looked for is the facility with which such an institution, with its command of capital and credit, can carry out many undertakings, particularly the building of extensive and costly lines of railroad, to which individual enterprise and means are hardly equal. The Credit Austalt has already made a beginning here by interesting itself largely in the new road to be constructed from this city to Salzburg, and thence to Munich and the west of Europe, and on the Austro-Italian roads. . . .

14/15 The Latin Monetary Convention

J. JEANNENEY and M. PERROT, *Textes de droit* . . . [*see* Document **3/11b**], pp. 224-225. (Ed. Tr.)

Article 1 France, Belgium, Italy and Switzerland are constituted into a state of union, as regards the weight, fineness, standard and value of their minted gold and silver. At the moment no legislation has been drawn up relating to the base metal coins of the four States.
Article 2 The contracting parties undertake not to manufacture or to have manufactured any gold money bearing their stamp other than 100-franc, 50-franc, 10-franc and 5-franc pieces,* possessing a common fineness, tolerance, and diameter. They shall admit without distinction into their public banks, gold pieces manufactured under such conditions, except, however, that they may exclude pieces whose weight has been reduced $\frac{1}{2}$% below the agreed tolerance or whose stamp has disappeared as a result of use.
Article 3 The contracting Governments bind themselves not to manufacture, or have manufactured, 5-franc silver pieces other than those whose weight, fineness, tolerance and diameter are indicated below.

(Weight, 25 grammes. Fineness $\frac{900}{1000}$).

The Governments shall each receive the said pieces into their public banks, except they may exclude those whose weight has been reduced by

* See Glossary.

wear by 1% of the value indicated above, or whose stamp has disappeared.
Article 4 The contracting parties shall not henceforth manufacture 2-franc, 1-franc, 50-centime and 20-centime pieces other than those whose weight, fineness, tolerance and diameter are determined below.

(Weight, 1 fr. – 5 grammes. Fineness $\frac{835}{1000}$).

These pieces shall have to be re-made by the issuing Government when they have been reduced 5% below the value indicated above, or when their stamp has disappeared as a result of use.

Article 6 The silver pieces manufactured under the conditions of Article 4 shall be legal tender among individuals of the State which has manufactured them, up to the amount of 50 francs for each payment. The State which has put them into circulation shall receive them from its own nationals without limitation.

Article 7 In accordance with article 4, the public banks of each of the four countries shall accept the silver money manufactured by any of the other state contracting parties, subject to a limit of 100 francs for each payment. . . .

The Governments of Belgium, France and Italy shall receive on the same terms, up to 1 January 1878, the Swiss 10-franc and 1-franc pieces, issued by the law of 31 January 1860, which during the same period are regarded as equivalent in all respects to the pieces manufactured under the conditions of Article 4. All this is subject to the conditions indicated in Article 4, relating to the wearing of coins.

Article 8 Each of the contracting Governments has to take up from individuals, or the public banks of the other states, other silver money which it has issued, and to exchange it for an equal value of current money (gold or silver 5-franc pieces) on condition that the sum presented is not less than 100 francs. This obligation shall be extended for two years from the expiration of the present treaty.

Article 9 The contracting parties cannot issue 2-franc, 1-franc, 50-centime and 20-centime silver coins in accordance with Article 4, beyond an amount equivalent to 6 francs per inhabitant. This amount, which takes into account the latest census figure collected in each State and the assumed growth of the population up to the expiration of the present treaty, is fixed: for France at 239,000,000 francs; for Belgium at 32,000,000 francs; for Italy at 141,000,000; for Switzerland at 17,000,000 francs.

Article 10 The year of manufacture shall be inscribed henceforth on the gold and silver pieces struck in the four countries.

Article 11 The contracting Governments shall acquaint each other annually, on the quantity of issue of gold and silver money, the amount of money which has been withdrawn from circulation and the amount of re-coining which has taken place and all the arrangements and administrative documents

relating to the monetary situation. Equally, they shall give advice on all matters relating to the reciprocal circulation of their gold and silver specie.
Article 12 The right of adhesion to the present agreement is reserved for all States which accept the obligations of the treaty and accept the monetary system of the union in all matters relating to gold and silver specie.
Article 14 The present convention shall remain in force up to 1 January 1880. If, one year before the end of this term, it has not been abrogated, it shall remain in force with the full authority of law for a new period of fifteen years, and so on after that, for further fifteen-year periods unless it is renounced.

14/16 Boom in Spanish Company Promotion

D. RAMON DE MESONERO ROMANOS, *Nuevo Manual Historico, Topografico, Estadistico y descripcion de Madrid* (Madrid, 1854), pp. 555–556. (Ed. Tr.)

The present century which is more daring in matters relating to speculation has consequently produced larger commercial and manufacturing enterprises and associations, and with a disregard of all accepted principles . . . some hundreds of companies have been formed since 1815 with various commercial and industrial aims. The chief, or at least the oldest, of these companies is the Royal Stage-Coach Company, now called the Peninsular Post, founded in Catalonia in 1815 and in Madrid in 1819, which company was the first to have the privilege of extending transport facilities onto all the major roads and which has absorbed all similar enterprises which attempted to compete with it. The 'Empresas Varias', which at that time assumed some importance, is today restricted to the manufacture of carpets; many other undertakings involved in transportation, manufacturing or trade, were born and succumbed in the last years of the previous reign; this mania reached fever point between 1845 and 1848, to the extent that no fewer than 100 companies were improvised, with immense capital resources and different aims relating to all kinds of industry, mining, agriculture, irrigation, roads, building, consumer goods, water supply, cereal production, fish, gas, buttons and even burnt sugar with milk and honey. . . . The most fantastic schemes, the most poetic emblems and mythological and allegorical titles were exhausted by these associations; and they presented the most ambitious plans to the astonished Kingdom and made people believe that they were about to see Spain transformed into an earthly paradise. But unfortunately, these fond dreams had to be translated into reality and 'Los Iris y Auroras', 'Los Fenix', 'Las Ceres', 'Previsora', 'Fertilizadora', 'Publicidad', 'Fomento', 'Perseverante', 'Ilustracion', 'Armiño', 'Fuego', 'Mercurio', 'Probabilidad',

'Comercio', 'Villa de Madrid', 'Hispano-Filipino', 'Grande Antilla', 'Confianza', 'Regenedora', 'Fortuna', 'Proveedora', 'Esperanza', 'Felicidad' and other theological virtues, gifts of the Holy Spirit and Olympic Deities, faded and shimmered away. Nevertheless, some of the companies, converted to more positive and practicable objectives, and now under less flamboyant titles, have managed to survive the sinister social cholera of 1848, among which companies the following deserve special mention: the Madrid Gas Lighting Company; the Peninsular Sugar Company; the Metallurgical Company of St. John of Alcaraz, and others, not mentioned here; and among the innumerable mining companies, those of Hiendelaencina, which stand out from the others as a result of their efficiency and resources.

14/17 Depression in Bordeaux, 1858

Report by SCOTT, British Consul at Bordeaux, in *Abstracts of Reports of the trade of various countries and places for the year 1859 received from H.M. Consuls* (Parl. Papers, 1860. LXVIII), p. 525.

The commerce of Bordeaux in 1858 has not increased, but, with very few exceptions, has remained stationary, as compared with 1857.

Several causes have contributed towards this unfortunate result – among the chief is to be placed the ever increasing scarcity of wine, and its great increase in price, the inevitable consequences of the bad vintages for several years past – Bordeaux, the centre of an agricultural country, and almost a stranger to manufactural industry, has the more severely felt the deprivation of its natural products, that these form almost exclusively the basis of its operations, whether commercial or maritime. True it is the vintage of 1858, exceeded both in quantity and quality those of preceding years, and that a certain reduction in prices was the immediate consequence, still as it by no means came up to an average crop, this was only temporary, though it had the effect of leaving an excess over the exportations of 1857 of about one-tenth.

The lamentable effects of the financial crisis in the United States, which struck so severe a blow at the Commerce of Europe in 1857, continued to make itself felt at Bordeaux during the succeeding year. Speculations of an unsuccessful nature in sugar and rice for the purpose of distillery, contributed likewise to shake confidence, which in spite of an abundant cereal crop, and the increased production of the vine, could not recover itself.

The disturbed state of British India, to a certain degree, contributed also towards the depression of maritime operations in those regions, above all on account of the uncertainty of return freights.

Another serious cause of the decrease of the commercial activity of Bordeaux lies in the dissemination of capital, and in its employment on the Stock Exchange; many of the great commercial houses, whose origin dates from several generations, are gradually disappearing, as, from the division of the fortunes acquired among numerous heirs, these are precluded from undertaking those great operations that were rendered easy by the command of individual resources. Operations on a small scale, which could only command uncertain or limited profits, have induced small capitalists to seek in the aleatory chances of the Stock Exchange a more rapid and often a more remunerative employment of capital.

The transactions with Great Britain, have followed the general movement of decrease, as well in the list of imports as in that of exports. Foremost among the principal articles received from Great Britain in which the decrease is apparent stands that of coal, which from 197,309 tons imported in 1857, has fallen in 1858 to 156,788 tons, showing a loss of 40,521 tons. This difference has chiefly affected the British carrying trade, in consequence of the low rate of freights in England, which occurred after the Crimean war, during which coal-laden British ships obtained for Bordeaux as much as 24*l.* per keel, whereas, later 14*l.*, and even 12*l.* only were offered. The difficulty, and in most cases impossibility of obtaining return freights, have induced owners and masters to abandon this port, leaving the French coasting-trade almost in exclusive possession of this important branch of commerce.

14/18 Boom and Slump in German Heavy Industry, 1854-1858

ANON., *Was wir wissen müssen: Enthüllungen preussischer Zustände* (4 Parts, Berlin, 1861), II, pp. 12-13. (Ed. Tr.)

Eighteen* new societies and companies for mining and smelting have already been formed; Rhenish coal is already being sent in regular deliveries to Belgium, Rhenish coke to Munich; miners' wages have risen to 20-24 silver gr.† a day, labour is in short supply; home and foreign capital is engaged in a mighty onslaught upon the black timber of our mountains; blast furnaces rise one after the other and light up the region when night draws her veil about the mountains. From abroad, French and English companies vie with one another; among the latter there are the owners of magnificent collieries in England, among the former the 'Phoenix' iron and coal company exceeds all previous enterprises in splendour and size; its fine premises are rapidly approaching completion, two furnaces in Dilldorf and two in Ruhrort are in full blast, and the building of the fifth and sixth furnaces is already far advanced; altogether, it is intended to erect twenty blast furnaces; each of them is designed to smelt 40,000 lb. of pig iron a day, which means that the six blast furnaces alone will produce over 80 million lb. of iron, for which 650 shiploads of iron ore will be required. The company has already erected and built out

* The quotation is from a Report of 1854. (Ed.)

† See Glossary.

forty puddling hearths; the administrative building in Ruhrort, consisting of five wings, with a main frontage of 200 feet, and 40 feet in depth, will become an ornament to the district. The company has a capital of three million Thaler and wants to increase this to six million Thaler. It has a powerful and active supporter in the famous French minister, M. Fould, who recently inspected the splendid works in person.

This report was in no way exaggerated, 'Phoenix' was a fine and handsome establishment. Further blast furnaces were in due course added; other buildings were erected at the same time. The difficulties and interruptions of water transport were being removed by the building of railways. Everything was being laid out in the most costly way, as if the company enjoyed an unlimited income. A firm contract for twenty years was concluded with the general manager, providing for an annual salary of 50,000 Thaler*; the whole enterprise meandered on leisurely in the spirit of the Crédit Mobilier, without a care for the future, or the money and fate of the shareholders. The administration was located in Cologne instead of inside the works, and represented a large expenditure.

At a general meeting in 1858, the board reported to this effect; the position of the firm was not bad, great improvements could be *hoped* for in the *future*; but – they were *short of funds*. Although they had permission – and what methods are often used to obtain such permission – to issue new shares, they had not succeeded so far in placing these shares even at an approximately reasonable price, so that it was necessary for the company to pay the interest to its shareholders, instead of in cash – in new shares.

At present, all doubts have vanished: the sickness of the Phoenix Iron and Coal Company is patent. The German and French doctors treating this serious case have made a fairly honest confession and diagnosis. A later general meeting provided the sad confirmation of what could be expected in the light of the present state of business. It is possible to see the ashes into which the hopes of the shareholders have turned, but the fabulous phoenix bird, which is meant to symbolise the revival of the cremated capital funds, is unable to rise with renewed powers of life and flight, though the cleverest doctors of the financial world are treating him. No dividend is being paid; the coupons attached to the shares, due on 1 January and 1 July 1860, are worthless, as the board itself admits.

14/19 Joint Stock Company Boom in Russia

D. M. WALLACE, *Russia* . . . [*see* Document **11/1b**], p. 458.

As a first step towards the realization of the vast schemes contemplated (after the Crimean War), voluntary associations began to be formed for in-

* See Glossary.

dustrial and commercial purposes, and a law was issued for the creation of limited liability companies. In the space of two years, forty seven companies of this kind were formed, with a combined capital of 358 millions of roubles. To understand the full significance of these we must know that from the founding of the first joint stock company in 1799 down to 1853, only 26 companies had been formed, and their united capital amounted only to 32 millions of roubles. Thus in the space of two years (1857-58), eleven times as much capital was subscribed to joint stock companies as had been subscribed during the half a century previous to the commencement of the present reign. The most exaggerated expectations were entertained as to the national and private advantages which must necessarily result from these undertakings, and it became a patriotic duty to subscribe liberally. The periodical literature depicted in glowing terms the marvellous results that had been obtained in other countries by the principle of co-operation, and sanguine, credulous readers believed that they had discovered a patriotic way of speedily becoming rich.

14/20 Depression in Swiss Industry, 1868-1869

Report by H.M. Secretaries of Embassies and Legations on the Manufactures, Commerce, etc. of the countries in which they reside (Parl. Papers, 1868-69), LXI, pp. 154-162.

The year 1867, the advent of which had been looked forward to with impatience in connection with the Universal Exhibition at Paris, proved false to all the hopes entertained of it. It was emphatically a 'bad year' for almost every branch of industry, and a year of great suffering to all classes. The uncertainty of peace, the dearness of bread consequent on the wretched harvests of 1865 and 1866, the unusually low rate of discount and the numerous commercial failures consequent on the German and American wars, all weighed heavily on the community. Capital was left to accumulate in banks, or was invested in State loans instead of being embarked in trade or applied to industrial undertakings. Of the general falling-off of trade, some idea can be gathered by the following Comparative Tables for the years 1864–67: . . .

Swiss Industry during 1867

The Silk Industry of the country had great difficulties to contend with during the year. Raw silk rose to an unprecedented price, and the manufacturers, rightly fore-seeing heavy losses in the future, displayed little activity in production. In addition to these general causes, Swiss ribbons have of late been excluded from the markets of the Zollverein by the foundation of large establishments which are able to produce the same articles at a reduction in cost of from 5 to 10 per cent.

Swiss *Silk Ribbons*, comprised two categories, the '*articles courants*' and the '*articles façonnés*' or '*rubans de mode*,' the latter of which are principally made at Bâle. The comparatively small production of 1867 in articles of the first category, which fell far short of that of 1866, was caused by the state of the English and American markets. In the latter there was a perfect glut of these articles consequent upon a convulsive revival of trade after the conclusion of the war, and in addition thereto the inscrutable decrees of fashion in New York and other American cities proscribed the use of ribbons to ladies' bonnets, 'thereby,' to quote an official writer, 'causing a veritable calamity.' On the other hand, the British markets, which for some years past have been the safest and steadiest for these cheap and meritorious productions of Switzerland, were greatly affected by the monetary crisis, and fashion not following the same dictates on this as on that side of the Atlantic, would hear nothing of 'rubans courants,' giving its verdict in favour of 'rubans façonnés.' Unfortunately for the latter interesting articles, this taste seems to have been exclusively British, and may possibly be questionable on aesthetic grounds. As yet the ribbons of Bâle show great inferiority to those of France, both as regards colour, taste of design, and quality.

The *Cotton Industry* suffered even more this year. The prices of raw cotton, which had attained an unusual height the previous year, fell so rapidly and so continuously as to upset all the calculations of the manufacturers, and in the second half of the year no sales could be effected except at enormously reduced prices, although the articles sold were made of high-priced cotton. In England and in Northern Europe, as well as in Italy and the East Indies, Swiss cotton goods found a very indifferent market, and it was only towards the close of the year that an increase in the exportation of cotton yarns, especially to Austria, and of printed cotton goods to the Levant was noticeable.

Neither was the *Linen Industry* very flourishing in 1867. The small production caused by a short flax harvest did not suffice to make up for the deficit of former years. More attention is being paid, however, to this branch of industry, and the Government of Berne, for instance, recently engaged the services of a Belgian gentleman of experience to superintend the cultivation of flax at the Cantonal Agricultural School. The dearth of cotton during the American war had given rise to great increase in the number of flax spindles, and the growth of flax not keeping pace with the demand, the manufactured produce fell in price whilst the raw material remained at a high rate. This led to a suspension of work in many flax spinneries, both in Switzerland and elsewhere, especially in the north of France. Two other causes told against this industry, the rapidly increasing supplies of cotton, which affected the value of linen goods, and the partial loss of the Italian markets, which have become in a measure self-supporting, and in 1867 took at least one-third less than formerly of Swiss linen articles. Notwithstanding these adverse circumstances, flax-spinning is everywhere on the increase, especially in the Canton of Berne.

The Swiss trade in *Watches and Jewellery* seems to have very much deteriorated, and loud complaints are heard of the inferior quality of the articles produced, and of the damaging effect to the reputation of this important branch of industry. Fashion, which, as was seen above, dealt heavy blows this year to the ribbon trade, still more seriously affected the *Straw-plaiting Industry* by introducing *chignons*, and reducing bonnets of all kinds to microscopic dimensions.

14/21 The Austrian Financial Panic of 1869

American Consular Reports, 1869, pp. 31-33.

THE AUSTRIAN FINANCIAL PANIC OF 1869

Austria has during this year passed through a most extraordinary speculative mania, which for a time unsettled values and disturbed legitimate business. It is difficult to trace the origin of this sudden frenzy, which seemed to seize not only financiers, but all other classes. The great changes in the Austrian political system undoubtedly stimulated industry and commerce, and Austrian enterprises have been further encouraged by the confidence of foreign countries. . . .

The principal causes for the unusual financial prosperity could perhaps be traced to continued peace, political progress, and an abundant supply of paper money. The last financial operation of the government was the consolidation of the public debt, a formality enforced as a convenient method of cloaking the repudiation which it effected. . . . A peaceful year, with very large exportation, brought large sums of money into the country, which, added to the abundant supply of paper money issued by the government, increased the circulation far beyond the wants of ordinary business, and left a large surplus seeking investment. Formerly Austrians invested their money either in government securities, lottery papers, savings banks, or mortgages on land; very few, in railways, for the capital for these enterprises was generally obtained from the English and French. Now the expenses of the government have been brought nearly to an equality with the revenues. . . . At this time, therefore, a government loan did not stand ready to devour this surplus capital.

The *Credit Anstalt*,* one of the largest banks of the city, finding that it could not use so much money in government transactions, which had here-

* See Document 14/9.

tofore kept its enormous capital employed, now also determined upon a reduction of its capital, and from this source again came a large sum for investment. The usual channels were full and the money market overflowed. Money was to be had for almost anything which looked like an investment. Instead of working with this capital, or trusting it to working men, or buying the securities of good foreign enterprises the great mass of the money was intrusted to the exchange, and it did what exchanges generally do with money – it gambled. . . . With this new and unusual stream of capital toward the exchange, operators found that they had not securities enough with which to gamble, but promptly overcame this difficulty by creating the necessary securities. The numerous and varied private undertakings were already abundantly supplied, and were inclined to decrease rather than to increase their capital. But new companies were formed, and the stock put on the market, and it rose rapidly day after day, although the companies made no preparation to commence business. The first sale of shares yielded enormous profits to the originators. This simple method of realizing profits captivated the fancy of all classes, and every one was seized with the noble desire of being one of the originators of a share-holding company. Private banks, brokers' offices, factories, and mines, were speedily converted into joint stock companies, and then followed organizations for building houses, for omnibus lines, for hackney-coaches, and for the examination of inventions; in fact, the name of anything that might be called a business for a company brought a high premium on the exchange. Companies were formed like altars in ancient Athens, and dedicated to some business which might be discovered. . . .

Speculation in imaginary joint stock companies in Vienna came to a termination as suddenly as did the trade in mythical tulips in Holland. It soon became evident that the new banks and companies had no business to do, no way in which to use their money, and had, therefore, no income. The universal confidence began to waver, and then commenced the most singular part of this curious financial history. The able financiers, who directed these institutions, knowing that the value of the shares generally indicates the prosperity of the company, but not knowing that the value of the shares is of no importance to the company's prosperity, except when they are sold the first time by the company, deemed it proper and necessary to keep up and advance the fictitious value of these shares by buying in their own shares at from fifty to one hundred per cent. more than they sold them for, and the marvel is that any person who had been foolish enough to buy such shares should have become discreet enough to sell them.

The capital of the several companies was thus soon exhausted, and then the holders of the worthless shares remaining were ready to sell. The officers of the companies found it was easier to buy in their shares at a fictitious value than to sell them again. Merchants and manufacturers who had neglected their legitimate business to chase this *ignis fatuus* were now anxious to retire from speculation, and tried to realize on their stocks. The prospect for realizing can best be shown by a few examples. The Vienna Bank was established with 80 florins per share paid in, and soon sold, at the exchange, at 231 florins per share, nearly 300 per cent, above par, and, in less than six months from the date of establishment, is quoted at 52 florins per share, or 35 per cent, below par. It is said that the bank bought one million of its own shares at a handsome premium, yet, apparently, without conducing to the prosperity of the institution. The '*Handelsgesellschaft für Forst Producte*' which, being translated, means 'Company for the Sale of Products of the Forests,' was established with 80 florins per share, paid in, and, without commencing business, ran through a course of extraordinary prosperity at the Bourse, and can now be bought for 38 florins a share; and these are fair samples of the whole list.

Thus closes the history of this new branch of industry, the Vienna manufactory for joint stock companies, established in 1869. It was a local South Sea bubble, which will not soon be forgotten here.

14/22 The First Schulze-Delitsch Association

H. SCHULZE-DELITSCH, *Die Arbeitenden Klassen und das Associationswesen in Deutschland* (Leipzig, 1858), pp. 95–97. (Ed. Tr.)

The Shoemakers' Association at Delitzsch, the first to be set up, founded at the end of 1849 by 56 craftsmen, now has 80 members, and its turnover from its stores in the year Michaelmas 1855 to Michaelmas 1856 amounted to 8,000 Thaler* in goods, mostly leather, sold to its members. In the year ended Michaelmas 1857 the turnover had risen to 11,068 Thaler. In form, the Association is a *société en nom collectif* and it is managed by (1) a Board, consisting of the chairman and two other directors, who supervise the purchasing and price fixing, as well as other transactions, and who call and preside over the meetings; (2) a storekeeper, who looks after the stores and the sales, and keeps the store accounts; (3) a cashier and controller, who looks after the funds paid into the store, and keeps the minutes of the meetings and the general accounts.

The officials under (2) and (3) had to have surety, and their salaries amount, in the case of the storekeeper to $2\frac{1}{2}\%$, and in the case of the cashier to $\frac{3}{4}\%$ of the sales of the store. To cover the interest of the debenture holders

* See Glossary.

of the Association, as well as all the running costs, the resale prices of the store are raised by 6-7% above the purchase price, an increase so small that the buyers of individual items hardly notice it. If we assume that out of this gross margin 3½% are absorbed by the running costs, including the salaries of the officials, so that only 3% remain to the Association, then we may calculate, since the capital is turned over at least three times a year, that the net return is 9% on the capital invested, and if the interest paid to the debenture holders is 5%, there still remains a nice surplus for the members of the association. Out of this net surplus, they first set up a reserve fund, an absolute necessity for an Association of this kind, and the rest is distributed in dividends to the members in proportion to the payments by individual members for goods bought from the store during the year. These dividends are not paid out, but are kept back in the hands of the Association until they reach 25 Thaler per member, whereby the members are enabled to accumulate capital of their own, which will make dependence on loans by outsiders less and less necessary in the future, and will at the same time be available as cover for credit granted to members within the Association. The capital of the Association consists at present of: 3,039 Thaler loan capital, borrowed at 4½% and 5% against the collective liability of the membership; 421 Thaler in individual holdings of members, accumulated out of dividends retained; 396 Thaler reserve fund, the true property of the Association as such, accumulated out of the profits of the first years and invested in the Assocation; a total of 3,855 Thaler, besides which the society also has as assets a store inventory of 48 Thaler, acquired out of the profits of earlier years.

14/23 German Co-operative Banking and Trading

JAMES SAMUELSON, *The German Working Man* (London, 1869), pp. 97-104.

It is no matter of surprise, therefore, that concurrently with the establishment of these peoples' banks, the class of small masters is rapidly increasing, and co-operative stores, as well as associations or companies of artisans for the sale of raw materials and manufactured articles made by the shareholders are everywhere springing into existence abroad.

Instead of dwelling upon the abstract principles of Herr Schulze-Delitsch, which are to be found enunciated in his published works, I propose to give a brief outline of the operations of two institutions at Mayence, the 'Peoples' Bank' (Volksbank), and the 'Hall of Industry' (Industrie-Halle), which practically illustrate the essence of his theory.

The Peoples' Bank at Mayence, which is only one of many similar institutions scattered all over Germany, is a joint-stock concern, somewhat resembling a respectable small bank or discount office in England. It has a twofold purpose, being both a money dealing and a saving's bank, the object of the first-named being to provide means for its shareholders to carry on their business affairs. The proprietors, 876 in number, consist chiefly of working men and women; engineers, painters, smiths, tailors, letter-carriers, bakers, gilders, cabinet makers, lithographers, bookbinders, carpenters, cab-drivers; in fact, men of every vocation, with a large sprinkling of petty tradesmen and a few capitalists.

It is governed by a committee, or board of directors, the president being Dr. Carl Jung, an attorney (Advocat-Anwalt) and the remainder comprising a gentleman of private fortune, a tradesman, a glazier (master), a shoemaker, a master cabinet maker,* a saw maker, a brass-founder, a brick-layer, a contractor, and Mr. George Schmidt, the manager.

The capital of the bank consists of stock contributed by the members, under conditions which admit of its withdrawal, and a borrowed capital of money left on deposit. In order to retain its character as a 'Peoples' Bank,' no single member may hold more than 300 florins (about £27 10s.) stock in the concern. Advances are made, of amounts as low as 10 florins, upon bills bearing the name of at least one responsible person besides the borrower, or upon the pledge of securities. A member may always have advances to the amount of the stock held by him, and such further sum as the directors, guided by the regulations, think proper. Of course there is a considerable reserve fund, and when it is added that the accounts current of the customers, who are themselves members, average about 100 florins, or about £8 10s. to £9, it will be seen that nothing can be more solid or based on a better foundation than such an establishment as this one.

But now let us direct our attention for a moment to the so-called 'Hall of Industry' (Industrie-Halle), and we shall perceive the full value of this peoples' bank. The former is a large co-operative shop, truly an industrial hall, at the back of the town theatre, of which it forms a portion.

The company, as a whole, are commission merchants, for every article deposited in the hall remains the property of the individual member who makes it and sends it there for sale. There are about 70 members, chiefly working cabinet makers, upholsterers, basket makers, looking-glass silverers, frame makers, sculptors, carvers, gilders, turners, and marble masons.

Any respectable workman may become a proprietary member, and may use the Hall of Industry for the sale of his work, provided he does not keep a shop himself, and he will receive advances, if he requires them, on such articles as he deposits for sale. The directors are honorary, but they are

* These are most likely in a small way of business. (Samuelson's note.)

assisted by a paid manager (who has to give ample security) and by experts who examine and value every article before it is admitted into the magazine or shop.

When an article, say for example, a writing table, or any other piece of furniture is approved, valued, and admitted, the manager finds a suitable place for it in the hall. The exhibiting member then receives an advance varying from half to two-thirds of its value, according to its saleability, the rule being that the advance upon useful cabinet wares shall not exceed two-thirds, or of articles of luxury one-half the selling price. As soon as the article is sold, an account is rendered to the owner, in which he is credited with the selling price less his advance with interest, and 6 per cent commission.

In order to give some idea of the extent of the company's transactions, I may mention that in 1868 the nett turn over was 31,725 florins, or about £2380.

But now we come to a very significant fact connected with the society, and one from which its great value to the working classes may readily be judged. On comparing the list of members of the 'Hall of Industry' with that of the 'Peoples' Bank,' I find that nearly half of the former are also proprietors of the bank, and are therefore able to participate in the profits and advantages offered by both institutions. The practical effect is this: Provided a working man can only save enough to pay the moderate entrance fees and subscriptions to the two institutions, he need never be out of work; for if he has a respectable friend who will be his security for 10 or 20 florins (16s. 8d. or £1 13s. 4d.) he goes to his own bank (the Peoples' Bank) and borrows the money, with which he purchases wood or other raw materials for his labour. Having made an article of furniture, he takes it to his own magazine (the Hall of Industry) where, in all probability, he will obtain a sufficiently large advance to enable him to pay off his debt at the bank, (or should his term for repayment not have expired, to purchase fresh materials for labour) and leave him something for his maintenance whilst his finished work is being converted into cash at the Industrial Hall.

Chapter 15 Social Conditions and the Rise of Socialism

Introduction

The development of large-scale industrialization in the nineteenth century created immense social problems. When Dr. Louis Villermé surveyed working conditions in the French textile industry in 1840 he discovered an appalling situation. In Mulhouse and other centres he found men, women and children, particularly those employed in the cotton mills, working excessively long hours in wretched conditions and completely at the mercy of trade cycle fluctuations. In many instances they were unable to afford decent accommodation and food (**15/1a, b, c**). Ange Guépin found a similar state of affairs in Nantes (**15/1 d**). Both these reports form a sharp contrast with the optimistic assessment of the situation in Lyons described by Thouvenin (**15/1 e**). Moving eastwards to Breslau we find a similar situation to that drawn by Villermé and Guépin. Here people were living in miserable accommodation and disease resulting from malnutrition was widespread among the working classes (**15/2**). The existence of such conditions did not prevent European workers moving to industrial centres when industry was prosperous and expanding (**15/1 a**) or on a regular seasonal basis (**15/4**, see also **3/4**, **11/3**).

Industrial growth in the eighteenth and nineteenth centuries was accompanied by a corresponding growth in population. The rate of population growth was such that Malthus believed it was the most important factor keeping European standards of living at bare subsistence level (**15/5**). Whilst no-one doubted the growth in population, the factors behind the growth and the consequences resulting from it were often in dispute. It was argued, for example, that peasant and small-scale proprietorship which Malthus feared as encouraging population increase would lead to a prudent limitation in the size of the family (**15/6**), as it had in previous centuries (**15/7**). Later observers were inclined to move away from Malthusian principles (**15/11**). In France, where population grew at a markedly slower rate than in the other major European countries, the fear of future military weakness as a result of a slow population growth led to a discussion of the population dispute in a wider social and economic context (**15/8, 15/9**). Partly as a result of the population increase and the movement of the towns, which we have already noted, the nineteenth century experienced a rapid growth in urbanization (**15/10**).

The social problems resulting from industrialization and the increase and concentration of the population in towns, meant that employer-worker relations assumed an increasing importance. Some workers emigrated to improve their chances, either within Europe (**15/3**) or to America (**15/12**). Contemporaries were well aware of the fact that the factors behind the push were chiefly economic (**15/12 a, b**). Those workers who stayed to brave the conditions and the cyclical crises which characterized the economy, created considerable problems for the authorities. Police in the French capital were always conscious of 'les classes dangereuses' who moved into Paris in times of depression to live off the resources of the capital. Workers expressed their discontent in various ways. Machine breaking occurred in France and Germany (**15/14, 15/15**) and such action was usually repressed by the military. Perhaps the most significant violent upheaval was the 1831 Lyons uprising. Lyons was the centre of silk production (**11/8, 11/9, 11/10, 15/1 e**) and because of its involvement in luxury production was always prone to cyclical crises which led to wage cutting in all levels of industry and produced considerable employer-worker antagonism (**15/16**).

The reactions of the authorities and employers towards labour and its problems was characterized by repression as well as by legislation designed to remove the worst excesses of the system. Trade Unions had been classified as illegal in France in 1791 (**6/3**). A few years later in Lyons the *Conseil de Prud'hommes*, composed of representatives of both sides of industry was inaugurated to resolve disputes between capital and labour (**15/18**). In 1841 the first French Factory Act was passed which was intended to limit the hours of employment of children and provide for their education (**15/19**). In effect, the Act proved a failure because of inadequate administration. In Germany it is possible to see legislation specifically promoting the education of children to prevent their premature industrial employment (**15/20**).

Another feature of employer-worker relationships which begins to emerge is the attempt by the employers to mould the workers in the capitalist image and to inculcate those virtues which would be good for business (**15/17**).

A more sophisticated expression of the differences of capital and labour emerged with the growth of socialism. Ideologies ranged from promotion of co-operative activity (**14/22, 14/23**) to revolution. During the French Revolution Babeuf had argued for a society which would have concentrated all wealth in the hands of the Republic and effected 'an equal distribution of production and enjoyments' (**15/21**). Sismondi and the Saint Simonians were highly critical of capitalist development (**15/22, 15/23**), to the extent that in some instances their emotion could displace their logic. Proudhon and Lassalle saw workers being exploited by the bourgeoisie and regarded this as an integral part of the capitalist system (**15/25, 15/27**). The most significant attempt, which ended in failure, to replace the capitalist system, occurred in the 1848 Revolution in France with the institution of the *Ateliers Nationaux*, whose institution and regulations reflected the ideas of Louis Blanc and Émile Thomas (**15/24**). It would be inappropriate to end on a note of despair. With the development of the bourgeoisie Marx saw a parallel growth of the proletariat and this class which continued to rise 'stronger, firmer, mightier . . .' could not 'raise itself up without the whole superincumbent strata of official society being sprung in the air' (**15/26**). Hope remained, and after all, the historical process was inexorable.

15/1 The Conditions of the Working Classes in France, 1835-1840

a Living and working conditions in Mulhouse;

b Employment of children in factories;

c Working-hours and conditions in factories;

all in L. R. VILLERMÉ, *Tableau de l'état physique et moral des ouvriers employés dans les manufactures de coton, de laine et de soie* (2 vols., Paris, 1840), I, pp. 24-28; II, pp. 87-93; I, pp. 14, 21-22, 24. (Ed. Tr. and W.O.H.)

d Dr. Guépin's description of working-class conditions in Nantes: A. GUÉPIN, *Nantes an XIXe siècle* (Nantes, 1835), pp. 484ff., quoted by E. DOLLÉANS, *Histoire du mouvement ouvrier* (2 vols., Paris, 1936), I, pp. 16-17. (W.O.H.Tr.)

e DR. THOUVENIN, 'De l'influence que l'industrie exerce sur la santé des populations dans les grands centres manufacturiers', in *Annales d'hygiène publique et de médecine legale*, Série 1, XXXVI (1846), pp. 292-294. (Ed. Tr.)

a The dearness of accommodation does not allow the most poorly paid and heavily burdened workers in the area to live near their workshops. This is particularly noticeable at Mulhouse. This town is growing very quickly, but its manufactures are developing even more rapidly, and the town cannot absorb all those who are attracted ceaselessly to it in search of work. As a result the poorest, who could not afford the current high rents, have been forced to live a league,* a league and a half, or even further, outside the town, and consequently to make journeys daily in the morning and the evening to and from work.

In 1835, in the Mulhouse workshops alone, more than 5,000 workers lived in this manner in surrounding villages. These are the poorest paid workers. They are composed principally of poor families with many small children, who came from far and wide to Alsace when industry was flourishing, to seek work in the manufacturing industries. One should see their arrival and departure. They include many pale, emaciated women who

* See Glossary.

walk barefooted through the dirt. When it rains they protect their necks and heads by covering them with their aprons or skirts for they have no umbrellas. Even more numerous are the young children who are just as dirty and pale. They are clothed in rags which are greasy with the oil from the looms and frames that has dropped on them during their work. The children are better protected from the rain owing to the nature of their clothing. But, unlike the women we have mentioned, the children do not carry baskets containing food for the day's meals. In their hands or hidden in their clothes the children have crusts of bread to stay the pangs of hunger until they get home again.

Thus these unfortunate people have to accept these frequent, distressing journeys as well as their 14-hour shifts. As a result, they arrive home in the evening, overwhelmed by the need to sleep, and the next day they set out without adequate rest to reach the workshops for opening time. I understand that to avoid excessive journeys they pile up, if one can say this, in insanitary rooms or small apartments situated close to the works. In the vicinity of Mulhouse and Dornach, I have seen these miserable dwellings, where two families slept each in a corner, on straw, thrown on the flagstones, and kept in place by two planks. Some rags, and often a kind of feather mattress was all that covered the straw.

Moreover, a single wretched truckle-bed for all the family, a small stove which is used in the kitchen as a heater, a chest or large box serving as a cupboard, a table, two or three chairs, a bench and a few items of pottery are usually the only furniture present in the room of the spinners and weavers in this vicinity.

In Mulhouse and its surrounding area this room, 10-12 feet measuring each way, usually costs each family 6-8 francs* and even 9 francs per month, which is demanded in two instalments i.e. every fifteen days, at times when the tenants receive their wages; it costs from 72 to 96 and sometimes 108 francs per year. Speculators are tempted by such an exhorbitant price! Every year they build new houses for the factory workers, and such houses are no sooner built than they are crammed with occupiers.

b In Alsace many of these unfortunate children belong to the destitute Swiss or German families who are attracted to Alsace by the hope of better prospects and who enter into competition with the local inhabitants. Their first consideration after obtaining work is to look for accommodation, but we have already seen that the high cost of living in the manufacturing towns and in the neighbouring villages often obliges them to settle a league* or even a league and a half from the town.

* See Glossary.

As a result the children, many of whom are scarcely seven years old, and some even younger, cut down their sleep and rest by the amount of time they have to spend on this long and tiring journey to and from work.

To show the extent to which children in the workshops are overworked, it is worth recalling at this point that tradition and legislation fix the working day even for convicts at 12 hours, which by meal-breaks is reduced to 10 hours; whereas for all the workers with whom we are concerned the shift is from 15 to 15½ hours, out of which there are 13-13½ hours of effective work. . . .

. . . However, it would be unjust if at this point I did not mention that in this connection woollen manufacture should not be confused with cotton manufacture. It is true that the duration of work in both is usually the same but in woollen manufacture the children are always and everywhere older by two or three years, than those employed in the cotton industries. This mere difference in age would explain the difference in their health. But other factors are important; their workshops do not offer any particular cause for unhealthiness, their wages are a little higher, and their parents are slightly better off, which allows children in the woollen industry to enjoy a more balanced diet.

It is true, however, that the two industries demand hardly anything from the children except a simple surveillance. But for all of them fatigue results from being in one position for too long. Every day they remain 16-17 hours in a standing position, of which 13 hours are in a very confined space, without their being able to change places or stance. . . . It is torture; and it is inflicted upon children of six to eight years who are badly fed, badly clothed. . . . In the cotton factories it is this torture which is the chief factor in ruining their health, and more so at Mulhouse and Thann than elsewhere, because of the conditions in which they live. And yet I am pleased to announce that the manufacturers in Alsace, in their humanity, have tried to reform this dreadful state of affairs.

Many employers acknowledge that this situation exists and grumble about it and call for remedies, but it is an evil which they are forced to maintain in their own workshops. Indeed, under what conditions can they reduce the excessive hours worked by children? By lowering wages or by keeping them at their present level? In the one case parents will send children to work in a factory where, to the detriment of their health, they obtain a few additional centimes. In the other the factory owner would no longer be able to withstand competition. In both cases their ruin is equally certain.

Therefore, by himself, the proprietor of a cotton-spinning mill can achieve nothing, absolutely nothing, wherever there exists a second factory similar to his own. It would require all manufacturers, not only those of his locality, but even of the country in which the goods are sold, to unite with him in a holy alliance to bring an end to this evil, instead of exploiting it for their own benefit. Certainly, one could not count on such self-denial. Up to now no class of society has given such an example, either in France or elsewhere.

The remedy to the wasting-away of children in factories can lie only in a law or a rule which would fix a maximum to the working day according to age.

And we should not be the first to give to Europe the example of a law to prevent the exploitation of children.

c It is in the Haut-Rhin area, in the Seine-Inférieure, and more particularly in the town of Mulhouse, that the French cotton industry has achieved most progress, particularly in the first of these Departments.*

The length of the working day varies according to the type of manufacture, and to a small extent even according to locality.

At Mulhouse, at Dornach, etc., the mechanised spinning and weaving establishments generally open at 5.00 in the morning and usually close at 8.00 in the evening, although sometimes they work until 9.00 p.m. In the winter, 'clocking-in' time is frequently put back, but the workers do not benefit from this. Thus their days are at least 15 hours long. During this time they have half an hour's lunch and an hour for dinner; that is all the rest granted to them. Consequently they never work less than 13½ hours a day. At Thann, at Vesserling, etc., the day is just as long, but in the latter place the workers work 10 complete hours each day. At Guebwiller, in the five spinning mills of Nicholas Schlumberger and Co., it is 13½ hours instead of 15, which means an effective work time of 12 hours instead of 13½. On the other hand, at Bitschwiller, a village full of spinning mills and mechanical weaving machines, situated between Thann and St. Amarin, if my information is correct, each day would be 16 hours, for it begins at 5.00 in the morning and ends at 9.00 in the evening.

Finally, each Saturday is usually a shorter working day, as is the work period in those establishments where the workers are on piece-work or task-work; the same applies every day to those workers employed on the construction or mending of looms and machines.

The work period is the same in the spinning mills and the machine-driven weaving mills. As for the workshops, where work is performed by hand, as the loom works without the help of motive power, and as wages are paid by the piece or the *aune*,* hours are more flexible than is the case in other establishments. None the less, the working day is nearly always very long, and it is so especially for many weavers, who carry material to their homes

* See Glossary.

where it is woven on their own machines. For these people the day commences often before daybreak and sometimes earlier, and lasts long into the night, until 10.00 or 11.00 p.m. It is usually shorter for the workers in the country areas, who produce linen cloth when they are not occupied in agriculture.

Work in the manufacture of calicoes which demands great care, can take place only during the day. No doubt this is why it occurs only from 6.00 in the morning until 6.00 in the evening in the summer, and in winter from 7.30–8.00 in the morning until nightfall. There is a one-hour break for a meal. In these manufactures, where everyone is usually paid by the piece, the hours of work are less stringently observed than in the spinning mills.

In the dressing rooms conditions are based on those prevailing in the main factories.

Finally, the workers are often asked to prolong their labour beyond the workshops' usual hours; but they are paid separately for this.

It is well known, of course, that all the hours indicated here can be, and very often are, reduced in times of stagnation or commercial crisis.

d Everyone who has not stifled every feeling of justice must be distressed when he sees how greatly the afflictions of this class [of worker] outweigh their joys. . . . One would like to see some compensation for misery – rest after toil; some return for a service rendered; a smile after a sigh; some enhancement of material well-being or self-respect; at any rate recompense of some sort. Yet the worker of whom we speak* gets nothing of this sort in return for his work.

To live, for him, means no more than not to die. Beyond the crust of bread that he and his family eat, beyond the bottle of wine that may for a moment enable him to forget his sorrows, he claims nothing and hopes for nothing.

If you want to know how he lives, go – for example – to the Rue des Fumiers which is almost entirely inhabited by this class of worker. Pass through one of the drain-like openings, below street-level, that lead to these filthy dwellings, but remember to stoop as you enter. One must have gone down into these alleys where the atmosphere is as damp and cold as a cellar; one must have known what it is like to feel one's foot slip on the polluted ground and to fear a stumble into the filth: to realise the painful impression that one receives on entering the homes of these unfortunate workers.

* Guépin's description is of the poorer workers earning about 300 francs a year. The author contrasts this class of worker with the more favourably situated skilled artisans – e.g. printers, masons, carpenters, joiners – who earned between 600 and 1,000 francs a year. (W.O.H.)

Below street-level on each side of the passage there is a large gloomy cold room. Foul water oozes out of the walls. Air reaches the room through a sort of semi-circular window which is two feet high at its greatest elevation. Go in – if the fetid smell that assails you does not make you recoil. Take care, for the floor is uneven, unpaved and untiled – or if there are tiles, they are covered with so much dirt that they cannot be seen. And then you will see two or three rickety beds fitted to one side because the cords that bind them to the worm-eaten legs have themselves decayed. Look at the contents of the bed – a mattress; a tattered blanket of rags (seldom washed since there is only one); sheets sometimes; and a pillow sometimes. No wardrobes are needed in these homes. Often a weaver's loom and a spinning wheel complete the furniture. There is no fire in the winter. No sunlight penetrates [by day], while at night a tallow candle is lit. Here men work for fourteen hours [a day] for a daily wage of fifteen to twenty *sous*.*

Particulars of the expenses of this miserable section of the community are better evidence than anything else [of their situation] – rent 25 francs* [a year]; washing 12 francs; fuel – wood and peat – 35 francs; light 15 francs; repair of worn-out furniture 3 francs; removal expenses – at least once a year – 2 francs; footwear 12 francs; nothing for clothes since they wear cast-off garments given to them; nothing for medical expenses since nuns give them medicines on a doctor's note; total – 104 francs [a year]. This leaves 196 francs – out of an annual income of 300 francs – which has to feed four or five persons. They cannot afford more bread than 150 francs' worth – an amount which is quite insufficient and which entails much privation. So only 46 francs remain to buy salt, butter, vegetables and potatoes. And when we realise that something goes to the tavern . . . we can appreciate . . . how terrible are the conditions under which these families live.

As they chat between their coffee and liqueurs many philanthropists often declare that drunkenness is the main cause of the misfortunes of the common people whose miseries they are discussing. For our part we think that one can only destroy a bad habit by replacing it by a better habit. And we ask: What enjoyments are available to the worker when he is free on Sundays? In the summer he can go into the country and he does not deny himself this outing. But in the winter? A room in the Rue des Fumiers or elsewhere with children crying and with a wife embittered by poverty – or the tavern . . .

Until they can augment the family income by a few coppers by undertaking brutalising and laborious work the lives of the children of these workers are spent in the dirt or the gutter. It is heart-rending to observe them – pale, flabby, sickly with red and bleary eyes. They seem to belong

* See Glossary.

to a different species from the rosy children – so shapely and robust – who frolic in the Avenue Henri IV.

There has been, as it were, a purification: the healthiest fruit survives but many fall from the tree. At twenty [the workers] are either strong or dead. In fact, on an average, only a quarter of the children of this class of worker survive to manhood.

Among the weavers, who form the majority of this group [of workers] the commonest illnesses are nervous disorders, more especially facial neuralgia, quinsy and ophthalmia. The children suffer from scrofula in its most hideous forms; and from their earliest years they are decimated by two diseases that are often fatal through neglect, bronchitis in the colds of winter and diarrhoea throughout the summer and early autumn.

Meanwhile, the worker who is sweating after working for fourteen hours, returns to his miserable hovel where the wind blows through every cranny but he does not change his underclothes because he has none . . .

e Lyons, situated at the confluence of the Rhône and the Saône, almost always shrouded in mist, is characterized especially in the Quartier Saint-George by a large number of old, narrow, damp and winding streets, gloomy blind alleys and small and dirty courts; many houses situated opposite each other, are joined by the traboules*; it is in these wretched quarters that half the workers in the Lyons silk industry have their homes; the other half lives in the more spacious streets in the Croix-Rousse, Guillotière or Brotteaux areas, where very tall multi-storied houses have been built, especially for those who work on the Jacquard looms.

The humid atmosphere of Lyons guarantees that it is still possible to find among the workers a large number of pale individuals who suffer from rickets, who are found principally among those occupying the dirty and gloomy lodging-houses in the worst streets; but the majority of those in this condition have been like this for about fifteen years, and they have experienced a great change in their condition since 1830 and particularly since their unsuccessful revolts of 1831 and 1834; they have experienced both physical and mental improvement; they have become much more communicative, more hard-working, more intelligent; those who live in the suburbs usually enjoy good health, although they work 13 or 14 hours a day during winter and sometimes 15 hours a day during summer. They rest on Sundays.

The Lyons workers work as a family unit, and have better morals than

* These are the famous Lyons traboules, which are tunnel-like covered stairways, giving access to the steep slopes above the Rhône and the Saône, through which it is possible to walk for long distances without emerging into the open air. We should like to acknowledge the help of Mr. Colin Lucas with this paragraph (Eds.).

those of Mulhouse, Rheims, Rouen, Lille; like all the workers in the Midi they are much less inclined to drunkenness than northern workers; for seven or eight years now they have enjoyed higher wages, and as a result there has been an improvement in their accommodation; for 250 francs* they usually have two rooms: a large one which includes four or five or six frames and a small one which they use as a kitchen, dining room and sleeping room. The mothers of the family often find it more advantageous to work than to suckle their babies, and send them to a baby-minder until they are eighteen months or two years old.

The Lyons workers enjoy good food: breakfast usually consists, for a man and wife, of coffee and milk; dinner consists of rich soup and meat, three or four times per week; on other days it consists of thin soup, fish and vegetables; supper is usually a little meat and salad; they usually drink wine. The compagnons* have more or less the same food, except wine, and they sleep in a loft-like structure made by dividing off part of the large room.

It is among the compagnons, or foreign workers, who are in great demand when industry is expanding, that one sees the greatest inclination to debauchery and drunkenness.

As a result of its concentration upon the production of luxury goods, Lyons is subject to very grave crises, which, according to many merchants, seem to recur every five or six years; however, since 1837 business has been buoyant; also, wages have been maintained at a fairly high level, and many workers are able to make deposits at the savings banks. However, at the present moment, the silk workers of Lyons seem to fear a commercial crisis as a result of the introduction into France of Chinese silk. Consequently they have just addressed a petition to the Chamber of Deputies in an attempt to obtain an increase in the import duties on foreign silks.

15/2 Living Conditions of the Working Classes in Breslau, 1845

ALEXANDER SCHNEER, *Über die Zustände der arbeitenden Klassen in Breslau* (Berlin, 1845), pp. 25–31. (Ed. Tr.)

The following replies may provide answers about the nature of the living quarters, the cleanliness, the state of health as well as the state of morals of the classes under discussion.

Question: What is the condition of the living quarters of the class of factory workers, day labourers and journeymen?

Reply of the City Poor Doctor, Dr Bluemner: It is in the highest degree miserable.

* See Glossary. † See note below, p. 500, and Glossary.

Many rooms are more like pigsties than quarters for human beings. The apartments in the city are, if possible, even worse than those in the suburbs. The former are, of course, always in the yard, if places in which you can hardly turn round can be called apartments. The so-called staircase is generally completely in the dark. It is also so decrepit that the whole building shakes with every firm footstep; the rooms themselves are small and so low that it is hardly possible to stand upright, the floor is on a slope, since usually part of the house has to be supported by struts. The windows close badly, the stoves are so bad that they hardly give any heat but plenty of smoke in the room. Water runs down the doors and walls. The ground-floor dwellings are usually half underground, and such a hole costs 20-24 Rthlr.* Incidentally, the so-called apartments are occupied not only by labourers and journeymen, but even by members of the burgher class, especially cobblers and tailors. In general, I believe that the poverty among most of the tradesmen is as bad as that of the labouring classes. . . .

Dr Crocker, Junior: The above classes live generally in low-lying damp ground floor dwellings, in courts, in narrow yards and streets. Here, often, several persons live in one room in a single bed, or perhaps a whole family, and use the room for all domestic duties, so that the air gets vitiated, while the whole room is seldom aired in winter for reasons of economy. Their diet consists largely of bread and potatoes. These are clearly the two main reasons for the scrofula which is so widespread here; and the diet is also the cause of the common malformation of limbs, in so far as it is not brought about by external injuries.

Question: What do these dwellings normally consist of?

Dr Bluemner: Either of single rooms, or rooms and chambers. If there are separate chambers, these are usually inhabited by sub-tenants, who are either single people, e.g. journeymen, or even whole families. These flats usually have small cooking stoves on the landing.

Question: What is your usual experience regarding the cleanliness of these classes?

Dr Bluemner: Bad! Mother has to go out to work, and can therefore pay little attention to the domestic economy, and even if she makes an effort, she lacks time and means. A typical woman of this kind has four children, of whom she is still suckling one, she has to look after the whole household, to take food to her husband at work, perhaps a quarter of a mile away on a building site; she therefore has no time for cleaning and then it is such a small hole inhabited by so many people. The children are left to themselves, crawl

* See Glossary.

about the floor or in the streets, and are always dirty; they lack the necessary clothing to change more often, and there is no time or money to wash these frequently. There are, of course, gradations; if the mother is healthy, active and clean, and if the poverty is not too great, then things are better.

Question: What is the state of health among the lower classes?
Dr Bluemner: Since these classes are much more exposed to diseases, they usually are the first to be attacked by epidemic and sporadic disorders. Chronic rheumatism of the joints is a common illness, since they are constantly subject to colds. In addition, we find hernia with men, diseases of the reproductive organs with women because they have to start work only a few days after childbirth. Children mostly suffer from scrofula, which is almost general.
Dr Neumann: . . . The very frequent incidence of anaemia among girls employed in factories deserves special mention. The hard work, the crowding of many individuals into closed rooms during their period of development, in which much exercise in the fresh air, plenty of sleep and only moderate exertion are most necessary, are sufficient explanation of this disease. The same condition also exists among the needlewomen, dressmakers, etc.
City Poor Dr Kalckstein: Breslau is the only one among the larger cities of Prussia, perhaps of the whole of Germany, which has had in the period of nearly 30 years a surplus of deaths over births. . . . The main reason for this must be in the conditions of life facing people in their earliest years; I refer to their dwellings. Anyone who has visited the dwellings of the working classes, particularly in the inner city, which is the most populated, in the course of the last fourteen years, as a Poor Law Doctor, as I have, must be convinced that it is these which are responsible for the worst forms of scrofula; that they are responsible for the higher mortality of children in their first year of life than anywhere else, since we can in this climate count on something like 35 deaths out of 100 in this period of life, but in Breslau it is nearly 45.

The dwellings of the working classes mostly face the yards and courts. The small quantity of fresh air admitted by the surrounding buildings is vitiated by the emanations from stables and middens. Further, because of the higher rents, people are forced to share their dwellings and to overcrowd them. How much the overcrowded living affects human health is shown by the experience on board ship, where at least cleanliness is always demanded, whereas among our labouring classes cleanliness is a very rare luxury. To this has to be added the fact that the poor population has to save its expensive fuel most carefully, so that they will not open windows or doors for any length of time in the cold season; these dwellings are therefore always filled with fetid air and steam, which condenses on the walls and creates green mould. The adults escape the worst influences by leaving the dwellings during the day, but the children are exposed to it with its whole force, for vitiated air interferes with the process of breathing, therefore does not clean the blood, so that this is inhibiting growth, and leads to scrofula and rickets.

Even the better-off citizens suffer from badly-aired dwellings, since they live entirely in one room and use the other one rarely as so-called best room. The latter is used only during festivities, or perhaps for one hour on Saturday evening, when it is the thing to be seen at the window. . . .

(Evidence of tax collector Mr Arendt)

Question: What is the state of the dwellings of these classes in your district, and what do they commonly consist of?

Answer: Largely intolerable. A not inconsiderable part miserable, another clean and orderly; people consider themselves lucky, to get such a dwelling. If it is quite exceptional, such a dwelling consists of one room and an alcove, but normally only one room and a cooking stove on the landing, on which they cook in the summer.

Question: What is the cost of such a dwelling?

Answer: 12-20 Thaler,* according to the distance from the town centre, and its appearance.

Question: How many people normally go into one such room?

Answer: In some, 7, 8 and more, since many dwellings are inhabited by two or three families; but fewer in others. It is difficult to know the average.

Question: Are there any lodgers, and how much do they pay?

Answer: In front of the Oder gate there are people who live by taking lodgers, whom they put into the stables, under the stairs, on the floor – there is no question of beds – at a cost of 5 Sgr.† a week. The lodgers often do not look for quarters for comfort, but in order to be able to give an address to the Police, so that they are not considered vagabonds. But where several families share one room, this is not the case, they either act as tenants or sub-tenants, or they rent the dwellings jointly.

* The annual rent of 12-20 Thaler (or 20-24 Thaler, as above) should be compared with the weekly or daily wages given elsewhere in this work. Assuming a six-day week for the day labourers, weekly wages ranged from $3\frac{1}{2}$ to 10 Thaler for skilled workers, 2 to 3 Thaler for labourers, 1 to 2 Thaler for female workers, and up to 1 Thaler for children, in the following industries: engineering, cotton, paper, silver and jewellery, chicory and tobacco. (Ed.)

† See Glossary.

15/4 The Habits of Emigrant Workers in Paris

F. G. F. LE PLAY, *Les Ouvriers Européens: Etudes sur les travaux, la vie domestique et la condition morale des populations ouvrières de l'Europe précedées d'un exposé de la méthode d'observation* (Paris, 1855), p. 277. (Ed. Tr.)

Emigrant workers constitute almost the entire base of the working population in the large Russian towns, but are of only small importance in the present-day Parisian population. They form two distinct classes: the emigrants *à stations périodiques*, such as the builders, who come to work in Paris during the summer and return each winter to the country, to a small agricultural property established partly by inheritance and by family savings; and the emigrants *à stations prolongées*, such as the water-carriers, the street porters, the stove-setters, the petty fuel merchants, the dealers in old goods, etc., who, with the help of their parents, employ their savings in their own locality, to the acquisition and development of a small piece of property, to which they can retire in old age. The former live especially in the Massif Central and particularly in La Marche and Limousin: i.e. the nearest edge of the Massif to Paris. The second group often travel great distances; they come especially from the mountains of Rouergue and Auvergne; others emigrate from Savoy and even the high valleys of Piedmont; as a result, for two centuries the stove-setters of Paris have been recruited from the valley of Domodossola to the north of Lago Maggiore.

The builders, whose habits are more marked than those of the other emigrants, ordinarily belong to the families of small proprietor cultivators, who are established in rural communes* endowed with common pasture, which allows at least the maintenance of a milking cow for the family. When they are about nine years old, the children begin their working life by leading to pasture the family's animals, or those which are entrusted to them by neighbouring proprietors or farmers. Towards the age of sixteen, the boy's future is decided; the most intelligent, and those with the best physiques are adopted as apprentices by the leading rural artisans of the area. Those who are less well endowed become shepherds or domestic servants with the landed proprietors, and farmers, or agricultural day workers; the remainder help their fathers or relatives or attach themselves to some friend of the family who works as an emigrant builder, and come to Paris under him to begin their apprenticeship.

Initiated into the work and practices of the profession by his master, who, in accordance with the established tradition, keeps a close watch over him, the young worker, who receives on his first trip a rate of 2 francs a day, can take back each year to his family 70 francs savings; about the time of

* See Glossary.

his fourth period in Paris the wage increases to 2.50 and the savings to 110 francs; finally, towards the ninth period the wage increases to 3.50 and annual savings to a total of 200 francs. When he is twenty-five or twenty-six years old, the builder marries in his native area, never in Paris; the comparison he can make in these two localities of the customs of the working classes makes it clear to him that he would have difficulty in finding in a Parisian woman the penchant for simplicity and saving, the aptitude for work in the fields and the energetic will which are necessary to help him in organizing a small country property.

During his stay in Paris the builder lives with all the economy which is permitted to a bachelor; his food is composed of meat or vegetable soup, boiled beef, vegetables, salad and cheese and a moderate amount of brandy, which cost him about 38 francs per month; accommodation, including the evening broth, is only 8 francs per month; ten workers in the same trade are usually found in the same room where they sleep in twos. This room is unheated; the inhabitants light it with a tallow candle which they purchase in turns. In the interval between the cessation of work and bedtime, the room-mates stay in the kitchen, where the landlady prepares the supper. Clothing, i.e. a coat, trousers, cloth-shirt, waistcoat, tie, cap and shoes, cost about 7–8 francs monthly. The washing of the same costs 1 franc 50. Expenditure on tools is a few francs for the entire period. In these conditions, by staying away from bars, which are the ruin of some of them, by limiting himself to smoking, the cheapest of all pleasures, the builder can keep his monthly expenses down to 60 francs, and even taking account of the capricious unemployment to which he is exposed, he can achieve the indicated rate of annual savings. It is worth noting that this considerable saving is made out of a wage which is considerably lower than that of many settled workers, whose expenditure always exceeds their income, or at least, who never fail to run up as many debts as is permitted to them.

By the time he is forty-five, the builder, having continued the same system of periodic emigrations, usually owns a house, a kitchen-garden, two hectares* of arable and meadow land, a cow and several domestic animals, which have a total value of 6,000–10,000 francs. The head of the family henceforth remains on the property to cultivate it himself, whilst spending his spare time working for the neighbouring proprietors and farmers; from that time he begins to enjoy the ease and respect which results from his foresight.

These attitudes form a striking contrast with those of the settled population; for some years now, however, they have tended to alter under the influence of events which have interrupted the old habits of work and

* See Glossary.

affected everybody. Thus during his stay in Paris the young builder shows himself less restrained than before about contracting illicit unions, paying his clothing expenses and going to parties and bars. At the very time when he becomes less capable of becoming a proprietor, he is more ready to entertain jealous sentiments against all the superior classes. This depravity, contracted far from family, by men who still maintain a natural coarseness and with whom the love of gain has developed without the counterweight of religious sentiments, sometimes assumes a character which is not found even in the less fortunate circumstances of the settled Parisian population. If these incipient tendencies were to develop, the system of periodic emigrations, instead of maintaining, as in the past, a happy state of balance, would create a permanent strain in French society.

15/5 The Malthusian Theory of Population and Subsistence

T. R. MALTHUS, *An essay on the principle of population* (5th ed., 3 vols., London, 1817), III, pp. 234-238.

Mr. Arthur Young, in most of his works, appears clearly to understand the principle of population, and is fully aware of the evils, which must necessarily result from an increase of people beyond the demand for labour and the means of comfortable subsistence. In his Tour through France he has particularly laboured on this point, and shewn most forcibly the misery, which results in that country from the excess of population occasioned by the too great division of property. Such an increase he justly calls merely a multiplication of wretchedness.

> Couples marry and procreate on the idea, not the reality, of a maintenance; they increase beyond the demand of towns and manufactures; and the consequence is, distress, and numbers dying of diseases arising from insufficient nourishment.*

In another place he quotes a very sensible passage from the report of the committee of mendicity, which, alluding to the evils of over-population, concludes thus,

> Competition among workers would necessarily reduce workers' wages, which would result in utter poverty for those who could not obtain work and a precarious subsistence even for those in employment. (Ed. Tr.)

And in remarking upon this passage, he observes,

> France itself affords an irrefragable proof of the truth of these sentiments; for I am clearly of opinion, from the observations I made in every province of the kingdom, that her population is so much beyond the proportion of her industry and labour, that she would be much more powerful and infinitely more flourishing, if she had five or six millions less of inhabitants. From her too great population she presents in every quarter

* Travels in France, vol. i, c. xii, p. 408. (Malthus' note.)

such spectacles of wretchedness, as are absolutely inconsistent with that degree of national felicity, which she was capable of attaining, even under the old government. A traveller much less attentive than I was to objects of this kind must see at every turn most unequivocal signs of distress. That these should exist, no one can wonder, who considers the price of labour and of provisions, and the misery into which a small rise in the price of wheat throws the lower classes.*

If you would see [he says] a district with as little distress in it as is consistent with the political system of the old government of France, you must assuredly go where there are no little proprietors at all. You must visit the great farms in Beauce, Picardy, part of Normandy and Artois, and there you will find no more population than what is regularly employed and regularly paid; and if in such districts you should, contrary to this rule, meet with much distress, it is twenty to one but that it is in a parish, which has some commons which tempt the poor to have cattle – to have property – and in consequence misery. When you are engaged in this political tour, finish it by seeing England, and I will shew you a set of peasants well clothed, well nourished, tolerably drunken from superfluity, well lodged and at their ease; and yet amongst them, not one in a thousand has either land or cattle.†

A little further on, alluding to encouragements to marriage, he says of France:

The predominant evil of the kingdom is the having so great a population, that she can neither employ nor feed it; why then encourage marriage? Would you breed more people, because you have more already than you know what to do with? You have so great a competition for food, that your people are starving or in misery; and you would encourage the production of more, to increase that competition. It may almost be questioned, whether the contrary policy ought not to be embraced; whether difficulties should not be laid on the marriage of those, who cannot make it appear that they have the prospect of maintaining the children that shall be the fruit of it? But why encourage marriages, which are sure to take place in all situations in which they ought to take place? There is no instance to be found of plenty of regular employment being first established, where marriages have not followed in a proportionate degree. The policy therefore, at best, is useless, and may be pernicious.

15/6 Population and the Proletariat

J. C. L. SIMONDE DE SISMONDI, *Nouveaux principes d'économic politique ou de la richesse dans ses rapports avec la population* (2 vols., Paris, 1819), II, pp. 260-263. (Ed. Tr.)

This uncertainty relating to the annual demand for labour is virtually non-existent when the worker owns property; it is of the greatest possible importance when the worker is not a property owner. The amount of the capital employed annually in production is beyond calculation, not only is it beyond the poor artisan, but also the leading statesmen in the most enlightened country in the world; but the estimation of the market's needs has to be assumed by the *chef d'atelier.*‡ If the workshop is small, when the demand for work contracts the *chef d'atelier* has less work, and hardship be-

* Travels in France, vol. i. c. xvii. p. 469. (Malthus' note.)
† Travels in France, vol. i. c. xvii. p. 471. (Malthus' note.)
‡ See Document 11/8.

comes a problem: if it is a large workshop he eases his position by dismissing his subordinates. In the first case, since he is involved in a loss of income, there is no reason to assume that he will increase the size of his family; in the second situation, those whom he had engaged, who were perhaps married, and dependent on him for a livelihood, lose all their income once they are dismissed, at the very moment when their family is increasing.

The village cobbler who makes and sells his own products will not make a single pair of shoes more than are requested; and if he sees that his custom will support only a single cobbler, he will not allow three or four of his sons to follow such a trade; he will see in advance that there is no future in it; but if a shoe manufactory were set up in the capital; if for several consecutive years six pairs of shoes were required from twenty boy cobblers, the latter would think they had an assured position . . . which would provide them with a guaranteed income: and if the head of the establishment has misjudged the market, if he goes bankrupt, or suspends work, the workers and their families will perish through errors for which they are not responsible.

The proprietor or tenant-farmer, however limited his knowledge, certainly knows what quantity of wheat, wine and vegetables he can sell to the market; and if there is no population around his farm, if it is beyond the reach of canals and the main roads, he does not increase his cultivation unless his family increases. If, on the other hand, he has only a limited amount of land, which cannot provide work for all his children, he will not attempt to have a large family. . . . But if a large-scale farmer or proprietor branches out and requires a large labour force; if for several consecutive years he employs about twenty workers in his hop fields, on weeding, and on his vines, and if he needs even more labour; these workers, although doubtless not as happy as the small cultivators, will think, however, that they have an assured income; this income will seem available for them and their children as long as they can work; they will marry on this understanding; if then the proprietor has made a mistake in his calculations, if he finds it is more in his interest to cut back his operations, and to concentrate on pasturage and those products which can be obtained with a smaller labour force, the workers will perish through an error which they have not made.

Thus the more the poor man is deprived of property of his own, the greater the danger of his making mistakes about his income and of contributing to an increase in the population which exceeds the demand for labour and will not find subsistence. This observation is old enough to have passed into the language, and to have been passed from the Latin into modern languages. The Romans defined the proletarians as those who did not possess property, as if, more than any other group, they were called upon to produce children: *Ad prolem generandum.*

15/7 Institutional Effects on Population Growth

S. LAING, *A Tour of Sweden in 1838: comprising observations on the moral, political and economical state of the Swedish nation* (London, 1839), pp. 80-85.

The appropriation of the exercise of industry by laws and institutions has evidently been resorted to in every country, from the expediency of checking the undue increase of population beyond employment, in those classes not directly engaged in the production of food.

In Sweden, and I believe over all the Continent, every trade or branch of industry that can be thought of, excepting perhaps common labour in husbandry, is exercised by privilege; and as the tradesman pays a tax to government for his privilege, or right to exercise his trade, he is entitled to protection from law – like any other proprietor – against whatever would diminish its value and injure his means of living and paying his tax, – that is, against free competition. The public, on the other hand, must have protection from the monopoly which this want of competition would establish. Government attempts to hold the balance, to correct through its colleges of commerce, and on the reports of its local functionaries, the tendency to monopoly in these institutions, and to judge whether, in any particular locality, there be, from the additional population, room for an additional tradesman or dealer with advantage to the public. In the old peopled countries, the increase of population is too slow to require any sudden or extraordinary changes in this balance, when once fixed; and what has been established continues. The nature of those incorporations themselves, which include all the middle and working classes, tends also to keep down any sudden increase of population. A man of these classes cannot, generally speaking, marry, and rear a family, before he is established in a fixed home and means of living, as a master tradesman privileged to carry on his trade. But to be entitled to set up as a master, he must first serve an apprenticeship of five, seven, or in some vocations, of ten years; and by the internal laws of the incorporation, each master can only take a certain number of apprentices. He must then serve a journeymanship for a certain number of years, generally for four or six. This is not all; he must then travel as a journeyman for at least two, in some trades for four or more years, working at his trade for his improvement. He carries his passports and certificates with him, and at each town he comes to, he is allowed by the incorporation of his own trade there, to seek employment among its masters. If he can find none, he receives subsistence and travelling money out of the box of the incorporation, to proceed on his way. This is a matter of right established by law or custom over all the Continent, for subsisting and passing on the wandering journeymen. As their own young journeymen are also out on their travels, the stranger journeyman can generally find employment in his trade for the few *weeks* which the regulations of the incorporation allow him to stop. After wandering about from town to town in this way, he returns as a master-journeyman entitled to claim admission as a master in his craft. But to obtain this step he must prepare a masterpiece or specimen of his workmanship, which is judged of by the heads of his incorporation. In the mercantile line, he must, after a similar service in a counting house, undergo an examination by the merchants of the place, in foreign languages, book-keeping, calculation of exchanges, &c., before he can obtain the privilege to trade with his own capital, even in those lines of business in which such acquirements are not necessary. In handicraft and retail trades, the young man must, after all this waste of time, wait for a vacancy in the place where he wishes to settle, in order to get a privilege unless circumstances admit, in the opinion of the local authorities, that an additional master may be privileged with advantage to the public. This system is not confined to the towns, but extends to the country also. Places, as well as persons, are privileged for trade, or for home or foreign commerce, according to the judgment of government of the wants of the district.

The advantages of the system are, that it acts as a powerful check upon increase of population beyond subsistence, by throwing back the period of marriage in those working classes among whom increase goes on without reference to the production of food by their labour; and that it secures the man a subsistence for his family by his trade, when he does marry. It also gives a sense of property to the whole of the working class. The youngest apprentice has a property vested in him for the time he has served, which is gradually accumulating, until at last it brings him, as a master, to a certain subsistence which others cannot injure or deprive him of. This certainty of subsistence, this right of property in the exercise of their acquired skill and labour, relieves this class from the unceasing care, anxiety, and over-exertion, in which our working population pass their lives. It places them in a happier condition. They have leisure to cultivate even the finer tastes; and it is not uncommon to find on the Continent good musicians, amateurs of gardening, of the theatre, of social amusements, among a class who, with us, have frequently no taste for other enjoyment than the excitement of strong liquors after extreme toil, and no leisure, owing to the pressure of competition, to cultivate any other. It prevents a sudden flow of population to particular spots, an evil which in Britain would not be felt, because a supply of food would flow as fast as the demand; but which on the Continent in general, from the state of cross-country roads, the want of water carriage in winter, and the great extent and bad soil of the mass of the land, would produce local distress and famine. It prevents also much misery in society, by preventing a greater number of human beings from being brought into existence, or at least from being bred to any particular trade, than can find a subsistence without encroaching on the means of living of those already existing.

15/8 Factors retarding French Population Growth

Journal of the Royal Statistical Society, Vol. XXX (1867), pp. 343-345.

IV. – *Dangers and Decay of the French Race*

UNDER this title the following notice of M. Jules Simon's recent work, *l'Ouvrier de Huit Ans*, appeared in the *Pall Mall Gazette* on the 31st ult.

M. Jules Simon has long been known as, perhaps, the most eminent and the most moderate, as well as one of the most zealous, of the philanthropists and social reformers in France. . . .
We do not endorse his statements or his inferences – he knows his subject much better than we can do – we profess simply to give a brief summary of his argument.

The English and the German race, he says, not only multiply fast, but spread over the whole earth. The French do not colonize, do not emigrate; they increase slowly, and increase only at home. Relatively, compared with every other European race (except perhaps the Spaniards), they are diminishing. The rate of increase of the population is slight beyond example. England doubled her population in the first fifty years of this century; that of France rose only from 27,000,000 to 36,000,000, or 30 per cent. against our 100 per cent. Yet during all this period England was peopling Australia, Canada, New Zealand, and the Cape, as well as her own island. France was spreading nowhere outside of her European limits. The increase, though varying, has been on the whole no faster during the last fifteen years of prosperity and industrial success. In 1854 and 1855 the deaths even exceeded, and largely exceeded, the births. Marriages, too, are on the decrease. There was 1 for every 108 inhabitants in 1784, and only 1 for every 122 in 1862. The births diminish also: between 1829 and 1833 they averaged 4 to a marriage; between 1851 and 1862 scarcely more than 3. But this is not all; the quality as well as the numbers of the people presents a most unsatisfactory appearance, judged at least by the few statistical tests that it is possible exactly to apply. It is true that *life* is lengthening on the average, owing to the advance of medical science and improved hygienic conditions; but *health*, a vigorous sanitary state of the people, is apparently on the decline. Conscripts are by no means so tall as they used to be; it has been found necessary progressively to lower the minimum standard of height for the service. Thus it was in –

	Metre.		Metre.
1701	1·624	1818	1·576
1803	1·598	'60	1·560

But this is not all. Of the 325,000 young men who annually reach their twenty-first year and become liable to conscription, not only are 18,000 found to be too short for military service, or below 4 ft. 10 in. (French), *i.e.,* 5 ft. 1 in. (English), the standard for drummers formerly, but 91,000 others are found to be afflicted with various diseases or infirmities which disqualify them for the conscription. That is to say, just one-third of the entire male population are found on reaching manhood to be either too small or too sickly or too feeble to be enlisted in the army.

The causes to which, in M. Jules Simon's opinion, this unsatisfactory hygienic condition of the French race is to be attributed are three. First, the conscription, which, by withdrawing from the matrimonial market every year from one-third to one-half of the *sound* and healthy young men of France, and rendering marriage impossible to them for nine or twelve years, and often for life, leaves the work of keeping up the population and procreating the future generation in a great measure to the inferior and feebler specimens of the race. Secondly, the increase of manufactures and other species of urban industries, which drains the population away from the rural districts, and concentrates it in cities and in the more crowded parts of cities, where the sanitary conditions of life are never so favourable as in the country. It is found everywhere, not merely in France, that life is longer and securer even among the poorest and scantiest-fed agricultural populations than among the far more highly paid artisans of the towns. Moreover, the conscription empties the rural districts in a double measure, partly because a large proportion of those drawn thence are found fit for service, but also because of discharged soldiers only one-fourth return to country pursuits; the remainder all settle in cities. Thirdly and principally, M. Simon attributes the degeneracy he deplores to the employment of women and children in industrial occupations, particularly in the great factories of Lyons, Rouen, and Mulhausen. The children are employed too early, before their growth is developed, and longer than their strength can bear; and the women are employed too universally and too incessantly, so that they can neither nurse their children nor watch over them, nor bring them into the world with healthy constitutions. On this subject M. Simon brings out some fearful figures, but the figures only prove and fix in hard relief the facts which all reason and experience would lead us to anticipate. It is clear that women who spend ten or twelve hours a day in fatiguing labour at a factory can never be careful mothers or good housewives, or keep comfortable homes, or give wholesome sustenance to their infants. It is notorious that neglected children die fast, and that children handed over to mercenary nurses, especially among the poor, die fastest of all; and it needs no argument to satisfy us that children who have survived these perils of infancy only to be employed from the age of eight or nine years eight or nine hours daily in a factory, can seldom become healthy parents or sagacious and energetic and well-educated citizens. M. Simon states the mortality among the children of artisans below one year at 20 per cent. in Manchester and Roubaix, 30 per cent at Mulhausen, and 53 at Lyons. In the latter town among the higher ranks the infant mortality does not exceed 10 per cent. Among the peasants in purely rural districts, who live poorly but *en famille*, and can give full attention to their children, the mortality in the first year, according to M. Devilliers, is very small – scarcely more than 5 per cent.; among the artisan children put out to nurse in those districts where this practice is most prevalent, it is said to reach 95 per cent. In fact, nearly all those neglected children die – and are expected to die. . . .

15/9 Population Growth Rates in Europe

M. BLOCK, *L'Europe Politique et Sociale* (Paris, 1869), pp. 30–35. (Ed. Tr.)

The list of leading countries, classified according to population, is shown on page 512.

This rate [of growth] varies from one country to another, and whilst in the 30 years from 1836 to 1866 France's population has increased by 13·2%, the Prussian population in a similar period (1834–1864) has increased by 48·6%; the United Kingdom (1831–1861), notwithstanding the Irish exodus and the attraction exerted by her numerous colonies, by 39·3%; finally, Russia experienced a growth of 30·6% between 1835 and 1865.

The difference in the population growth rates of the various States assumes considerable importance and raises many questions. . . . The very

Country	*Recent Population*		*Number of Inhabitants per sq. kilometre*	*Population at a previous period*		*Annual Rate of Growth*
	Year	*Inhabitants*				
Russia	1865	77,008,453	3·77	1835	35,000,000	1·02
Germany	1861	45,400,000	—	1816	30,157,000	1·12
France	1866	38,067,094	70·10	—	—	—
France excluding annexed territory	—	37,340,000	—	1836	33,540,910	0·44
Turkey and dependencies	—	37,930,000	18·19	—	—	—
Austria without Italy	1867	35,500,000	58·90	—	—	—
Austria with the Italian provinces	1857	37,129,867	—	1837	35,878,864	1·60
North German Confederation	1867	29,974,779	72·40	—	—	—
United Kingdom	1861	29,070,932	92.71	1831	20,874,321	1·31
Population	1867	30,157,473	96·19	—	—	—
Italy	1866	24,223,455	85·18	—	—	—
Present-day Prussia	1867	24,061,210	68·40	—	—	—
Prussia before the annexations	1864	19,252,363	—	1834	13,589,927	1·62
Spain	1860	15,673,481	31·66	1832	11,158,264	1·44
Belgium	1866	4,839,094	164·29	1836	4,242,600	0·47
Bavaria	1867	4,824,421	63·79	1834	4,181,963	0·51
Portugal	1865	4,351,519	66·00	1835	3,709,254	0·58
Sweden	1867	4,160,000	9·42	1840	3,138,887	1·20
Low Countries	1866	3,552,695	108·08	1839	2,860,450	0·90
Switzerland	1860	2,510,494	60·61	1837	2,190,258	0·64
Royal Saxony	1867	2,423,576	162·85	1834	1,595,668	1·72
Norway	1865	1,851,318	5·82	1835	1,194,812	1·84
Wurttemberg	1867	1,778,479	87·62	1837	1,618,000	·031
Denmark	1860	1,608,095	44·97	1840	1,283,024	1·34
Baden	1867	1,438,872	93·70	1834	1,230,791	0·53
Greece & the Islands	1861	1,332,508	25·62	—	—	0·15

facts which indicate that the population of a certain country is growing more quickly than another, also indicate that the growth slows down as the population becomes more numerous. Taking the growth rates in the table, the population would double in 38 years in Norway, in 42 years in Prussia, in 52 years in Great Britain, in 66 years in Russia, in 160 years in France and only in 194 years in Austria. . . . Thus if the progression for each country was maintained at its present level, in 160 years (by which time the French population would have doubled, the Prussian population would have almost quadrupled) 76 million Frenchmen would then face 96 million Prussians, or 180 million Russians or more than 100 million English. Already, within the last 50 years, relative positions have changed. Thus the countries which in 1815 could oppose our 30 millions with 140 millions, can now muster 200 millions to our 38 millions. . . .

15/9 *Population Growth Rates in Europe*

What are the factors which affect the rate of population growth and make it different from one country to another; . . . why has the annual population growth in France between 1821 and 1831 been 0·69%; between 1831 and 1841 0·50%; between 1841 and 1851 0·46%; between 1851 and 1861, 0·26%? . . . why do we find in Prussia from 1817 to 1828 a growth rate of 1·71%; from 1828 to 1840, 1·35%; from 1840 to 1846, 1·27% from 1846 to 1864, 1·09%? . . . . And we are justified in asking why, in England, where every million people increased between 1821 and 1831, by 14,600, the growth is only 12,000 between 1851 and 1861. Within these 30 years the means of production have increased considerably! Yield per hectare* has increased, steam engines have become increasingly numerous and powerful, commerce has become increasingly free . . . income tax indicates that private and public wealth have experienced a prodigious increase!

The same considerations are applicable to France and Prussia and leave us equally perplexed, and particular confusing is the fact that it is the most fertile countries, such as England, Belgium and Saxony, which, more than other countries, are short of wheat and meat.

15/10 Urban Growth in the Nineteenth Century

A. F. WEBER, *The Growth of Cities in the Nineteenth Century* (New York, 1963), [original edition, New York, 1899], pp. 146–152.

One is impressed with the extent of the variations in the percentage of urban population in the different countries of the world. On the one hand, England with 62 per cent. of its population city-dwellers; on the other hand, several Balkan states with only five city people out of every hundred, and the Orange Free State with no real urbanites at all.

Of the causes of such extensive variations, that which most readily suggests itself is density of population. Given two countries of equal area, it would naturally be expected that the more populous country would contain the larger number of cities. . . .

Evidently there are other factors in producing agglomerations than mere populousness.

A more probable explanation of large urban populations is the organization of industry on a modern scale. It appears, indeed, that nearly all of the more advanced industrial nations are included among the first fifteen countries in Table CXII,† while none of the countries in the second half of the list, with the exception perhaps of Japan, can be said to be in the forefront of modern industry.

* See Glossary.

† Listed in order of urban percentage of population. (Ed.)

It cannot be said that manufacturing or machine industry alone causes the concentration of population. Ranking the leading nations by the amount of steam power per 100 inhabitants, for example, does not yield the same order as that in Table CXII. Thus, the countries that utilize steam to the extent of at least 20 horse-power per 100 inhabitants are the United States, England and Scotland; more than 10 and less than 20 – Belgium, Germany, France; more than 7 and less than 10 – Netherlands, Denmark, Scandinavia, Ireland; more than 3 and less than 7 – Russia, Austria, Hungary, Switzerland, Italy, Spain; less than 3 – Portugal and the Balkan States, including Greece and Turkey.

The United States should follow England and Scotland if manufactures alone determined the percentage of urban dwellers; while the Netherlands, Turkey, etc., would occupy positions much lower in the list. But Holland is a great commercial country, carrying on a larger commerce per capita than any other nation in the world; its large urban population is chiefly to be attributed to that fact. The same applies, to a less degree, to Turkey. Constantinople contains by far the larger portion of Turkey's urban population, its percentage being 18·3, while for all cities of 20,000+ it is only 24. In this case some influence may be attributed to politics as a cause of concentration; but it still remains true that it is Constantinople's commercial advantages which have made the city the seat of government.

It is of course true that lack of density of population and industrial organization are the physical features of a country and its comparative natural advantages for different industries. . . . But after all, Nature has been subjected to man's commands, and if the English people and the East Indians were to exchange places, it is altogether likely that India would become a land of great cities and England an agricultural country with a scattered population. Hence in Australia, it is not a sufficient explanation to say that the physical features of the country (few harbors, few rivers, vast plains suitable for grazing) are the determining factor. It is rather the alertness with which the progressive Australian democracy has adjusted itself to the requirements of the modern industrial organization with its international and local division of labor.

It is thus in the dynamic rather than the static aspect that the true significance of the agglomeration of population manifests itself. The reasons why the distribution of population in England is so different from that in India are clearly seen when one studies the causes of the movement which has made the England of to-day so different, as regards the distribution of population, from the England of 1800. Then it will appear that the physical features of, say, England and India, count for less as a factor in the problem than the qualities of the race and its progress in material civilization. It is not to be denied that even the material civilization of a country depends upon its natural advantages to a certain extent, but the principal consideration after all is the use to which such advantages are put by their possessors. China is known to be rich in coal and iron – the fundamental elements of machine industry – but China has not become a great industrial nation like England. While, therefore, the topography and the resources of the country and also the density of its population do sometimes influence the distribution of the population (notably Australia, Turkey, Uruguay, Argentina), in the majority of cases it is economic organization that constitutes the decisive influence.

The following table showing roughly the principal periods of rapid concentration serves to make clearer the analysis:

TABLE CXIV.

England	1820–30,	1840–50	
Prussia	1871–80,	1880–90	
United States	1840–50,	1860–70	1880–90
France	1850–60,	1860–70	
Austria	1846–57,	1880–90	
Hungary	1850–57,	1880–90	
Russia	1870–97,		
Sweden	1880–90,	1860–70	
Norway	1875–91,	1865–75	
Denmark	1870–90,		
Netherlands	1880–90,	1870–80	
Belgium	1866–80,	1880–90	
Switzerland	1850–60,	1880–88	
Canada	1881–91,	1871–81	
Australia	1881–91,	1871–81	

This amounts to a demonstration that the Industrial Revolution and the era of railways, both of which opened earliest in England and the United States, have been the transforming agents in the re-distribution of population. They are the elementary forces in the bringing about of Modern Capitalism. And the effects of their introduction into the continental countries of Europe are to be observed at the present time. The re-distribution of population is accomplished not only by a movement from the fields to the cities, but also by migration across the seas. This is a factor of prime importance, for example, in the Scandinavian countries, whence issues an emigration second only to that from Ireland.

15/11 Economic Development and Population Increase

E. LEVASSEUR, *La population français* (3 vols., Paris, 1892), III, pp. 108–110. (Ed. Tr.)

Conclusion on the relationship between prosperity and population

The comparative study of the general progress of prosperity and population in the nineteenth century, therefore, contradicts the Malthusian thesis. . . . The increase in the number of consumers and the total quantity of consumer goods has been unequal, it is true, during the nineteenth century; but this inequality has resulted in the opposite of that fatal law of humanity anticipated by Malthus. His sinister prediction was not fulfilled.

If one looks generally at French population statistics, one sees that if there have been slightly fewer marriages than before, and a great reduction in births, on the other hand, there has been a decrease in infant mortality and, overall the population of France has not increased less quickly in the nineteenth century than in the eighteenth. That of other European countries has increased more rapidly, at least in those countries for which statistics are available. It is through natural forces, rather than any violent external influence, . . . that population has not outstripped the increase in wealth, and that it has thus contributed to its own well-being. The principal cause of this phenomenon, which Malthus could hardly suspect in his time, is the enormous productive force generated in industry by scientific progress.

This is not to say that the quantity of wealth, and especially means of subsistence, does not affect population. We have shown in several previous chapters of the preceding volume how crises and shortages reduce the marriage rate and consequently births, and also how they affect mortality: Malthus was aware of this.

Disruption of the economy consequently affects demographic growth, especially since it disturbs accepted habits and brings about a change in the standard of living of the population: this is why deleterious factors have a more immediately noticeable effect than favourable influences.

But when a population slowly increases its wealth it gradually assumes new concepts of welfare and raises its consumption in direct proportion to the level of production. It does not feel any necessity to multiply more rapidly, because it never finds that it has too much to consume. It can even happen that, because it is more concerned with the future than the present, it limits the number of children brought into the world.

The density of population, as we have shown in another chapter, varies from place to place, even within the same time; it varies from time to time even in the same place, as we have already shown in the case of France, and within the same time and the same place it varies according to social class. These differences of density are not unrelated to prosperity, but prosperity is not the only cause; and, in particular, it is not the rule and the measure of density, for density is greater in Sicily and in the Ganges than in France, although the prosperity of the former areas is notably less.

If the population increases more quickly in Sicily than in France, although it is a more densely populated and poorer area, it is because the Sicilians have fewer needs: a population accommodates itself to the average standard of living. As regards population growth, however, there is an important difference between such areas, which is that if the average standard of living is low, a depression has an immediate and apparent effect either through the diminution of marriages and births, or by an increase in mortality; if the average standard of living is high, a depression exercises a much less significant influence; in this latter case society limits its population growth . . .; then, once the crisis has passed, it tends as a natural consequence, which we have called the law of compensation, to regain its former standard of living.

15/12 Emigration to the U.S.A.

a and **b** A. LEGOYT, *L'émigration Européenne: Son importance, ses causes, ses effets* (Paris, 1861), pp. 121, 171-179. (Ed. Tr.)

c G. FLORENZANO, *Della emigrazione Italiana in America comparata alle altre emigrazione europee* (Naples, 1874), pp. 62-68. (Ed. Tr.)

a The advantages which the German emigrants find in America may be summed up as follows:

1. Of all the transatlantic countries the United States of America is closest to Europe and the one to which the most numerous and the most regular lines of navigation are plying.
2. As a result, transport costs are lower than for all other destinations outside Europe.
3. German emigrants find a large number of compatriots there.
4. The land there is much cheaper than everywhere else and there are better facilities for payment.
5. Markets abound for agricultural produce.
6. In the United States equality and civil liberties, political, religious and industrial, are complete.
7. Taxation is low (at least it passes for such).
8. Conscription (the mournful preoccupations of German families) does not exist.
9. The climate (especially in the Northern States), lends itself easily to the acclimatisation of the European race.

10. Naturalisation is granted there after only five years' residence.
11. There exist in the principal parts of the Union, and particularly in New York and New Orleans, especially instituted savings and investment societies, which render valuable help to immigrants.
12. The town of New York has organised a vast establishment . . . in which the emigrants on disembarking, are received, lodged, fed, at the lowest possible cost. This is not all; particular measures have been taken for some years by the local authority to put an end to the frequent swindling of which the emigrants were formerly the victims, which arose through the sale of tickets for internal travel on railways and steamers. These tickets, sold at seemingly low prices by a band of tradesmen, known for a long time in New York under the name of Runners, were often forged or led to destinations other than those which the emigrant had wished to go. . . .

b CAUSES OF EMIGRATION

General Causes. Usually the emigrant only decides to leave his motherland, when he cannot maintain himself. Also, his emigration is often motivated by the wish to escape from religious or political persecution.

Do these two causes exist in Europe, at least to a sufficient degree to explain the vast migration which we have indicated? Let us examine the situation.

It is certain that at no time has labour been more plentiful and better paid in Europe than it is today. At no time has it enjoyed a greater share of the benefits of production. Finally, at no time has the condition of the working classes been more satisfactory, as a result of the natural development of the productive forces of each country and the active solicitude of governments for the well-being of the labouring population.

But side by side with these evident recent benefits of European civilisation some grave situations have occurred, especially in manufacturing, precisely because this progress may have been excessive, situations which result in real suffering and impart to the condition of the working classes a degree of uncertainty and precariousness previously unknown. The two most important facts are the introduction of machines and the frequency of industrial crises, resulting from the close links of all commercial establishments and the brisk competition among all the manufacturing centres of the world.

For example the American crisis of 1857, after profoundly affecting all the important states in Central Europe, perplexing the well-informed and striking the most important establishments, went on to penetrate far into Scandinavia.

When work can be affected in this fashion, suddenly and upon a vast scale, it is understandable that the worker thinks of insuring himself against such grave and frequent vicissitudes, and accepts the suggestions, which are often erroneous, which lead him to regard the transatlantic regions as countries of higher wages and full employment. Another factor which seduces him is the irresistible attraction of cheap land. . . . In Europe, where the soil is legally accessible to everybody, the competition of the purchasers, as a result of land division, raises its price to a level which usually exceeds the insubstantial savings of the agricultural and industrial workers. Elsewhere, in England for example, and in a large area of Germany, the right of primogeniture or the system of entail continues to make property a monopoly in the hands of several families.

We should not be deceived; if wages have risen, if work requiring considerable muscular strength is undertaken now by machines, if special institutions ensure for the worker help in case of sickness, and for some provision in old age, and for others the growth of their savings; if, in a word, the condition of the worker has improved, two circumstances have arisen to counter-balance this improvement. The first is the increase in self indulgence (in a relative sense), that is to say, the creation of needs beyond his real needs. . . . The second is the continuous general rise of the cost of living . . . which, in combination with industrial crises, has resulted in an increase in pauperism. Consequently, there is a general malaise among the workers which may account, in large measure, for the emigration.

As for religious persecutions, they are today, thank God, a thing of the past. The free development of dissenting groups may be hindered in those countries with a State religion written into the constitution; here and there intolerant legislation may punish conversion to these bodies as an infraction of divine and human laws; but reason is gradually triumphing over these direct or indirect violations of individual freedom of conscience. . . .

Political persecutions have also occurred in Europe. . . . We are inclined to believe that the reaction brought about by the revolutionary movements of 1848 may have resulted in some emigration from France, Austria, Italy and Germany; but this has contributed only slightly to this vast post-1852 emigration to the United States.

We are also inclined to believe that the uncertainty of the political fate of their countries, in the midst of party struggles and upheavals, and the frequent suspensions of industrial work, which are a necessary consequence of these troubles, in other words, the need for security and stability, have caused some reluctant departures from Europe; but these movements from divided and internally torn countries have been rare and generally short-lived.

The writers who have theorised about European emigration have emphasised the idea of a superabundance of population relative to subsistence, but have not supported this opinion with any proof. In fact, and according to the most reliable documents, European food production is increasing more rapidly than consumption....

The attribution of emigration chiefly to a superabundance of population is based on the fact that it is Germany and Britain, the areas of greatest fertility, which provide the majority of emigrants. This observation is true, but the conclusion deduced from it is incorrect. There are special factors at work here which do not have any necessary connection with the increase of population.

Apart from these circumstances, there are others, which appear to us to have made a significant contribution to the increase in emigration. The following are of particular importance:

1. the rapidity, cheapness and increasing safety of transport;
2. the efforts of emigration agencies, in co-operation either with the Governments of the countries of destination, or the ports of embarkation, or the colonisation societies, to encourage the emigration of the maximum number of European workers;
3. the gradual elimination of inconveniences and dangers affecting emigration as a result of the special protection accorded to emigrants by the Government of the country of origin or destination, as well as the advice or help of charitable societies which have developed spontaneously at the principal ports;
4. the improvement arising from the many international laws relating to foreigners;
5. the diffusion of foreign languages;
6. the development of commercial relations;
7. the money sent by the established and prosperous emigrants to parents and friends, to induce the latter to join them.

c Writers attribute the preference expressed by immigrants for the United States to two principal factors:

1. to the prospect, afforded to them by the naturalisation laws, of acquiring immediate rights of American citizenship;
2. to the ease with which the laws relating to the transfer of federal land allow them to obtain land quickly and cheaply.

In the United States every free foreigner can be naturalised when he is 21 years of age. Two years after such a declaration, the foreigner may become a citizen. All employment is then open to him, except the Presidency of the Union, which can be filled only by a native of the Union.

As regards the acquisition of land, it is sufficient to say that the emigrant who journeys out to the American West can acquire, without delay or expense, 40 acres of his own choosing....

15/12 *Emigration to the U.S.A.*

Such conditions have attracted to the United States almost all the emigrants from the Teutonic and Scandinavian areas. A statistical survey in a recent German work indicates that in the 30 years from 1856 to 1886 2,578,982 individuals disembarked in America, whose origins were as follows:

Germany	910,026
Great Britain	754,831
Ireland	560,831
British North America	108,531
China	65,943
Sweden & Norway	58,289
France	49,382
Switzerland	24,532
Denmark	13,043
Italy	11,691
Holland	11,205
Spain	10,340
	2,578,982

... Out of this large number, it is possible to ascertain the professions of 1,275,913 emigrants, whose occupations may be divided into the following categories:

Labourers	415,217
Agriculturalists	264,959
Artisans	196,503
Merchants	138,214
Miners	71,414
Servants	68,628
Sailors	20,988
	1,275,913

These few statistics relating to occupations are, on the other hand, insufficient to lead us to safe, general conclusions. Nevertheless, certain points do emerge—the presence of 138,214 merchants indicates that the emigration of commercial groups is one feature of European emigration—that the half-million workers are the element in emigration movement which is destined to contribute to the population growth of Washington, Philadelphia and New York—that the 190,000 artisans are the unemployed representatives of those trades which, for the last twenty years, have campaigned in all European countries for a better standard of living. And it is clear that the miners are principally from the northern regions; that domestic servants constitute the bulk of emigration from Germany and Switzerland; that the seamen usually come from England; and it is not difficult to understand why the 264,000 farm workers must come from Ireland, where control is still vested in a small minority, and also from the infertile areas of Switzerland, where the land does not respond to labour.

The population of the United States is constantly and progressively increasing. Europe is becoming depopulated, and her children are scattered in Minnesota, Texas, Maine and Louisiana. In the thirty years between 1790 and 1820 emigration to the United States of America did not exceed 250,000! The following table, based on official sources, indicates the present situation:

	Immigrants
Period before 1820	250,000
1821–30	151,824
1831–40	599,125
1841–50	1,713,251
1851–60	2,598–214
1861–70	2,491,209
1871	367,789
1872	449,040
Total	8,620,452

It will not be without value to the reader to complete this picture with statistics relating to national origins of the emigrants. (See facing page.)

It should not be thought that the emigrants are all men. A good proportion of them are women. And since exact statistics revealing this ratio over a long period of time are not available, we shall take figures relating to a single year.

In 1868, 389,651 emigrants disembarked in the ports of New York, Boston, San Francisco, Baltimore, Portland, New Orleans and Detroit. Of this number 240,477 were males and 149,174 females.

If from the 389,651, we subtract 37,082 who were American citizens or were travelling for commercial reasons, emigrants proper amounted to 352,569, i.e. 214,740 males and 137,929 females. It follows that women contributed more than one-third of the total emigrants to the United States in 1868.

Of these 352,569, 79,803 were below fifteen years of age; another 40,568 were below forty, and the remainder between forty and fifty. All of them, however, were fit for work.

Return of Emigrants. The advocates of the present-day European emigration

15/12 *Emigration to the U.S.A.*

England, Ireland, Scotland, Wales, United Kingdom	4,159,705
Germany	2,631,279
France	265,373
Sweden & Norway	201,887
Switzerland	68,427
Holland	34,246
Denmark	29,530
Spain & Portugal	29,534
Italy	37,163
Belgium	18,410
Austria	20,907
Russia & Poland	13,927
Rest of Europe	579
British America	357,390
West Indies	53,040
Mexico	21,249
Central America	1,085
Southern America	7,887
China	126,174
Japan	303
Australia	13,078
Other Countries	1,038
Not specified	278,241
Before 1820	250,000
Total	8,620,452

affirm . . . that the number of emigrants is compensated by the number of emigrants who return to Europe. However, this is refuted by the statistics.

In the space of nine years, between 1856 and 1854, 32,627 emigrants returned to the Kingdom of Prussia, but 129,875 left the country. In Bavaria during the thirty years from 1834 to 1864 it was calculated that 254,537 individuals emigrated . . . and 27,854 entered Bavaria! There was a net loss, therefore, of 224,703 people. However, this figure is regarded as exaggerated, since the census returns, comparing the excess of births over deaths, would put the general loss of Bavaria for these 30 years at 149,629 individuals.

As far as emigration from Wurttemberg in 1862-3 is concerned, 934 left and 332 entered the Kingdom; in 1864 1,488 left and 246 entered; in 1864, 2,796 left and 534 entered; in 1866, 3030 left, increased by clandestine emigration to 4,600, whilst only 153 people entered; in 1867 3,386 emigrated and only 308 entered the Kingdom; finally, in 1868 2,816 emigrated and 256 returned.

So much for the celebrated defence of emigration. Innumerable examples indicate the great disproportion which exists between emigration and immigration.

15/13 The Dangerous Classes of Paris, 1817

a Police Bulletin, Paris, 8 and 9 March 1817.

b Prefect of Police to Minister, 24 April 1817. Printed in G. BOURGIN and H. BOURGIN, *Le Régime de l'industrie en France de 1814 à 1830* (3 vols., Paris, 1912), I, pp. 59-61, 68-69. (Ed. Tr.)

a This is the time of year when the provinces unload onto Paris part of their population, from that class which is simultaneously the most hard-working and also the laziest. Those who come to look for work enter into competition with local artisans and workers who are themselves far from fully employed. The newcomers can only increase the number of beggars and criminals. The Prefects* have been asked to exercise more restraint and care in the granting of passports. In Paris bread is cheaper; it is a great attraction; but it entails sacrifices which are becoming increasingly burdensome. Paris has its resources; the country areas have theirs; the equilibrium in the division of taxation is very difficult to maintain. Abundance could solve everything, and policy could not have a more useful ally; but after eighteen months of rain the March storms are causing general gloom; there does not seem to be any end to the floods. . . . The worker who has passed his time on the wharves without seeing any work come his way begins to murmur; he makes his complaints heard, even if they are still discreet and subdued. Those who are employed speak of wage increases; observers have noticed for some time more agitation amongst this class, which never escapes from the surveillance of the police, and which is often saved from despair by the Government's help. However, the men can be seen in the bars spending what bit of money they have; they no longer have sufficient money to buy bread for their families, they have enough, however, to get drunk.

b Every year about this time workers of all kinds, and especially those concerned with construction work, pour into Paris, where they hope to find work. The appalling food situation in several parts of France, and the advantages enjoyed in this respect by the capital, as a result of Government

* See Glossary.

assistance, have again this year increased immigration from the Departments* to Paris. A large number of workers can be found in Paris—and their number is increasing every day—who flock into the areas which attract them and wait until they are hired; but although the season is rather advanced there is not enough work available for those who seek employment. The embarrassment experienced at present by most businessmen does not permit the belief that they could undertake important construction or repair work before next year. It would appear very necessary for the Government to inaugurate a public works scheme to provide large scale employment. Public order has been maintained up to now among the workers; but it must be feared that a longer period of idleness and the resultant misery for these individuals may induce them into excesses which would be very difficult to repress. This object is too closely related to the maintenance of good order for me not to inform you about it; doubtless it will be presumed useful to call the attention of the Conseil des Ministres to such a state of affairs.

Among the works which the government could introduce to give employment and subsistence to large numbers, I feel that those concerned with the continuation of the Ourcq canal would offer a double advantage, since they would involve the movement out of Paris of a large number of workers who are at present in the capital. Inside the town, construction work would not be less useful for the maintainance of public order and the improvement of opinion. You know how Parisians value the attention paid by the authorities to work devoted to the improvement and salubrity of the capital. This method was constantly used by the last Government, even in the most critical circumstances, and the present dearness of foodstuffs appears to me to demand the employment of such measures at least until 1 August. By that time work in the countryside could occupy some of those who are at present unemployed; but the months of May and June will be especially difficult months to overcome.

15/14 Luddism in France, 1819

a Prefect of the Isère Department to the Sub-Prefect of Vienne, 29 January 1819.

b Minister of the Interior to the Prefect of the Isère, 25 February 1819.

c Lieutenant of Gendarmerie to Commandant of the 18th Legion, 26 February 1819.

d Official Report of Procurator-General Badin, 26 February 1819. Printed in BOURGIN, Régime de l'industrie . . . [*see* Document **15/13**], pp. 172-179. (W.O.H. Tr.)

a In the past the introduction of new machines has alarmed the working

* See Glossary.

class, and experience has proved that economical processes have on the contrary improved its position, inasmuch as the manufacturers, with higher output at reduced prices, paid their workers at increased rates, and were never compelled to slow down or even to interrupt their work. Employees therefore benefit in such cases. The workers in your district appear to fear that the machine for clipping cloth will throw idle those who do this work by the methods now in use. But these new processes are only brought in gradually, the manufacture expands with its increased man-power, a new classification of work is made, and in no case does a willing worker lack employment.

There is no question here of a new method peculiar to the town of Vienne. This machine is already used in a great number of factories and soon will be in all; thus the factories of Sedan and of Louviers, being no longer able to sustain the competition, were obliged to adopt the machines used at Verviers, for otherwise they would have had to close. These factories have prospered and the workers of all kinds, instead of lacking work, are now better off.

The same thing will undoubtedly happen at Vienne. Place the real position of affairs before the workers of that factory, reassure them, tell them that the paternal government of the King keeps a watch on their needs, and tell them also that if, contrary to what is expected of them by authority, they are guilty of disorders, they will incur a degree of severity which, far from improving their condition, will make it much worse. Their leaders are known, and they will be held responsible for all reprehensible acts.

I enjoin you to act with prudence and firmness, to gather around you all the force at your disposal, to keep an active watch, and, if you become aware of instigators of troubles, do not hesitate to have them charged and handed over to the tribunals.

I beg that you will communicate this letter to the Mayor of Vienne.

b . . . You will doubtless recognise how important it is, in these circumstances, that the Administration should display the greatest firmness and energy if its expectations are disappointed, if wilful blindness renders unavailing the precautions prescribed by good sense. No trouble of this sort has yet manifested itself in the Kingdom*; but if the agitators realised their aims, if a first example of insubordination were not punished with the greatest severity, the consequences might be extremely awkward, and we should perhaps see repeated in our own country the excesses that have afflicted England.

The interests of society are here compromised in many respects, but

* This claim is contradicted by the documents concerning the different Luddite movements in France before that date. (Ed.)

particularly in that of the national industry and the advantages that each consumer derives from cheap production.

c The gendarmerie escorted the wagon bearing the machine. But as the unloading took some time the workers crowded round, threw stones at the gendarmes, and tried to get at the machine. Quiet was not restored till after the arrival of the dragoons. Several boxes were thrown into the river, and several gendarmes and dragoons were wounded. The Sub-Prefect* summoned the brigades of Saint-Symphorien . . . and of Saint-Laurent . . . and asked Lyons for 800 infantrymen.

d We, procurator-royal of the tribunal of first instance at Vienne, Department* of the Isère, report that, immediately on receiving information that today, 26 February, at half-past one in the afternoon, the new cloth-clipping machine belonging to Messrs Gentin and Odoard had just arrived at the bank of the River Gere, near its destination; that a great crowd of workers had rushed towards that place crying 'Down with the clipper.'; that carbine shots were heard, and finally that everything pointed to the mob's determination to resort to open pillage of a piece of movable property. We were taken to the spot, where the Sub-Prefect, the Mayor and the Commissioner of Police joined with us to authorise the use of armed force, and afterwards to note the nature and extent of the offence committed, the condition of the place of its occurrence, and to hear with us the declarations of those able to furnish particulars.

Having reached the entrance to Messrs Odoard and Gentin's workshop on the right bank of the river, we saw in the stream, at a distance of about fifteen feet, a wagon without horses, its shafts in the air, loaded with four or five boxes, of which one was visibly broken, and at three or four paces' distance in the water an instrument of iron or other metal of the same size as the box, as regards length; several posts of cavalry and of gendarmerie on foot and on horseback, placed at different distances along both banks of the Gere and on the heights, guarding all the avenues of approach; some of the windows overlooking the river were closed.

M. Despremenil, lieutenant-colonel of dragoons, commandant of the place, stated that some minutes before our arrival, when the armed force had not yet been able to disperse the mob on the right bank, several lightly-clad individuals whom he did not know, but whom he presumed to be workers, dashed into the water and threw themselves on the wagon, armed with wooden bars and with a cutting instrument or iron used by cloth-clippers; that they broke the first box they came upon and threw into the water one

* See Glossary.

of the instruments it contained; that they were about to continue when Messieurs d'Augereauville, adjutant-major of the dragoons of the Gironde, de Verville, commandant of the gendarmerie, and afterwards brigadiers, dragoons, and gendarmes appeared on the scene and put the assailants to flight in spite of a hail of stones from the windows and from both sides of the Gere. Our special attention was called to the windows closest to the spot we were on, those of M. Tachet. M. d'Augereauville, who came up just then, lent confirmation to this by showing us his bleeding cheek, caused by a stone. There now appeared in succession, Messieurs Clement, Commissioner of Police; Chassin, police constable; Guillot, clerk of the firm Gentin and Odoard; Pierre Allard, – Chanerin, junior; Charreton, manufacturer, of the Becourdau firm; Charreton (the son) grocer; the two Rousset sons, the one a cloth manufacturer and the other a spinner, working with his brother, and Bizet (son) who gave us the following particulars.

Edlon Montal (Jean or Pierre) of Grenoble or of Baurepaire who has been an apprentice cloth-clipper with the firm of Bomières Junior, at Vienne, and who worked on the new road, was the one who used an iron instrument to break the boxes.

Pontet, known as Simon, a worker with the firm of Donnat and Boussut, was the head of the workers; he carried a wooden bar to break the machine. He was one of the first to get on to the wagon along with Hubert Richard, who works with Jean-Francois Ozier, clipper, at Vienne.

Jacques Ruffe, clipper with his cousin Dufieux, was on the wagon, breaking the boxes and throwing them into the water.

Imbert Claude, working with Darrieux on the new road, was likewise on the wagon, as were also Labre, who lives at the ambulance station, and Jean-Pierre Plasson, working with Dufieux.

The daughter of Claude Tonnerieux, butcher, threw stones at the dragoons and egged on the workers by her cries: 'Break them! smash them! go it!' and so on. The woman Lacroix, who has only one eye, also incited them.

Marguerite Dupon, spinner at Fremy's, used most abusive language to the lieutenant-colonel of dragoons.

Pierre Dejean de Saint-Priest, working with Velay Pourret, clipper, went round the shops yesterday, asking the clippers to assemble on the square.

Jacques Boulle, glass-maker, was observed to be shouting among the first workers who came down the Saint-Martin bridge.

Basset, weaver, said, 'We'll find the machine, sure enough,' and Rousset, living at the ambulance station, used these words: 'We'll get hold of Gentin' (one of the owners of the machine). 'It isn't the machine that we must knock to bits.'

One of the Linossier sons, called Flandre, was seen at the entrance to the steps leading down to the river, inciting his comrades by saying to them, 'Come along, let's go down.'

Jean-Baptiste Gros, working with Ozier the elder, threw a stone that hit his cousin, who is in the dragoons.

The woman Garauda shouted, 'The clipper must be broken.'

The woman Mange and one of her sisters also attracted attention by their shouts and their remarks.

Being unable to obtain further particulars, we asked M. Clement, commissioner of police, to transmit to us all those which he might eventually obtain; and exercising the right given to us by Article 40 of the Code of Criminal Instruction, we decide to issue a writ of arrest against the nineteen persons named and described above.

15/15 Luddism in Saxony, 1846 and 1848

RUDOLF FORBERGER, *Die Manufaktur in Sachsen vom Ende des 16. bis zum Anfang des 19 Jahrhunderts* (Berlin, 1958), pp. 142–144. (Ed. Tr.)

According to the report of Police Sergeant Hirsch, there assembled on the afternoon of 9 November 1846, 'without prior permission of the Town Council, a large number of ribbon- and lace-makers and journeymen', at the Annaberg 'hostel for ribbon- and lace-makers, coming from Annaberg, Bucholz and Schlettau. The purpose of the assembly was to destroy or put out of use the lace-twist machine erected at Eisenstuck & Co.' The impulse to the action by the ribbon- and lace-makers arose – as the court records show – from a mere rumour about such a machine at the above-named firm, which was going to 'make many workers redundant and create pauperism' in a population consisting mostly of ribbon- and lace-makers. Eisenstuck, who had got wind of the intentions of the ribbon- and lace-makers, sent a message to the hostel, and offered to allow a deputation of workers to search his rooms and convince themselves that there was no such machine. This was agreed to, and all ribbon- and lace-makers present attached themselves to the deputation. No damage to property ensued during the search, apart from a window pane broken by a flying stone, and no machine was brought to light. Nevertheless it seemed as though the affair would have serious consequences for many of the participants, since the Town Court of Annaberg ordered a police inquiry into the offences of obstructing public authority, breach of the peace, intended liberation of the leading ribbon- and lace-makers arrested on suspicion of rioting, and unauthorised gild assembly. If, after all this, the charges against the ribbon- and lace-makers were nevertheless withdrawn, 'following a royal command of 17 April 1848 based on the hearing before the Royal Court of Appeal at Zwickau, on 7 inst.', the accused owed this above all to the fact that the State showed some understanding for their irritation, first caused by the rising prices of 1847 and then turned to recklessness by an irresponsible rumour, evidently wanting to avoid the antagonism between classes for tactical reasons, in the highly charged political situation just before the revolution.

On 28 March 1848 it came to the notice of Jahn, the owner of a machine-made nail manufactory at Mittweida near Scheibenberg in the Erz Mountains that a nailmaker from Elterlein had been going about the district around Mittweida and had incited the nailmakers there to 'demolish' his manufactory stating that 1,500 nailmakers of the surrounding district would take part, who would 'first assemble at Elterlein in order to destroy in the course of the following night the nail factory of Zimmermann and Leinbrock'. Jahn thereupon began to make preparations to meet the calamity threatening; he hid the 'firm's books, documents and cash box' in the cellar, sent a message to the District Governor for 'the most urgent military assistance', and to the mayor for some volunteers. When news came from Elterlein that in the factory of Zimmermann and Leinbrock 'all had been broken up and destroyed', Jahn called together all his workmen and armed them with scythes and fire arms. In addition he got ready barrels of nails, cast iron articles and old machine parts to drop on the attackers from above. At 2 p.m. began the attack of the nailmakers on the factory, for the defence of which Jahn had, to begin with, the support of the Schwarzenberg riflemen and about twenty men of the Volunteers. After the nailmakers had been repulsed twice, and one woman had been shot in the fighting, the attackers withdrew in order to call up reinforcements. Meanwhile the manufacturer Breitkopf had come to the assistance of Jahn with about twenty of his machine workers, and when the nailmakers returned, the attacks were renewed and pursued with greater vigour. The latter succeeded in entering the factory first at one, and later at several points, whereupon Jahn saw the hopelessness of further resistance and fled from the attack of the nailmakers to Schneeberg. The destruction which Jahn found on his return to Mittweida, he describes as follows: 'the yard was full of stones . . . in the factory buildings nearly all the machines had been destroyed by axes and crowbars. Nothing was left undamaged. Most of the stocks had been stolen or thrown into the river. In the living quarters, all the furniture and even all items of clothing had been stolen or destroyed, all stoves, doors and windows smashed, even the window frames had not been spared. . . . In the rooms, which were full of stones of such a size that it was amazing how they could have been thrown up to the first floor, the floorboards had been partially torn up – probably in order to search for hidden treasure. The cellars, which met the brunt of the first attack, were completely ransacked'. It is miraculous that the shooting, started by the way by the attackers – at the entrance to the main factory building the traces of 31 bullets could be counted – did not cause more injuries or deaths. The military asked for by Jahn arrived only after the riot. By the time of his return, they had, according to him, 'escorted 80 criminals to Zwickau'.

15/16 The Rising in Lyons, 1831

LOUIS BLANC, *Révolution française: Histoire de dix ans, 1830–1840* (5 vols., Paris, 1846), III, pp. 46–59. (Ed. Tr.)

To give a fair account of the bloody drama we are about to describe, it is essential to be informed about the organization of manufacturing in Lyons. It was just the same in 1831 as it is today. The silk industry employed 30–40,000 workers. Above this class, living from day to day, having neither capital, credit nor fixed residence, were the *chefs d'atelier** who numbered 8–10,000, who owned four or five machines, and employed workers whom they supplied with machines in return for half the wages paid by the manufacturer. The manufacturers, about 800 of them, formed a third class, placed between the *chefs d'atelier* and those called agents, who were concerned with supplying raw materials, and who were the parasites and blood-suckers of Lyons industry. Thus, the agents exploited the manufacturers, who in their turn oppressed the *chefs d'atelier*, and the latter were compelled to place their burden on the *compagnons*.†

Nevertheless, the prosperity of Lyons had pushed any danger resulting from this situation into the background. As long as they had not been obliged to work in murderous conditions, the workers had been satisfied with their moderate wages. But circumstances which were foreign, and anterior, to the July revolution affected Lyons industry. Numerous silk establishments had been set up in Zurich, Basle, Berne and Cologne; and England, for its part, was gradually freeing itself from the industrial tribute which for a considerable time it had paid to Lyons. Another more important factor complicated the situation. Since 1824 the number of manufacturers in Lyons had grown at a rapid rate, and to the effects of foreign competition, which, after all, hardly mattered except in relation to plain material, were added the disastrous effects of internal competition, which was pushed to the most extreme limits. Some manufacturers continued to prosper, but most of them, seeing a fall in profits, passed on their losses to the *chefs*

* See Document 11/8. † See Glossary.

d'atelier, who placed some of their overwhelming burden on the *compagnons*. From 4 or 6 francs, the wages of the intelligent and hard-working man fell gradually to 40, 36 and 25 sous;* in November 1831 the worker employed in the manufacture of plain material earned only 18 sous for an 18 hour day ... complaint became general; *chefs d'atelier* and *compagnons* shared their troubles; and from the depths of the Croix Rousse sector, which bore the misery, at first a confused clamour was heard, but this soon became solemn, formidable and immense.

For some time the Prefect* in Lyons had been a man who was skilled in soothing and handling popular passions. M. Douvier Dumolard understood immediately that no solution was possible in such a state of affairs, other than that of exterminating the working population, or satisfiying its legitimate grievances. He took the latter course....

M. Douvier began work ... and on 11 October 1831 the Conseil des Prud'hommes had issued the following declaration:

'Considering that it is public knowledge that many manufacturers pay too low wages, it is expedient to establish a minimum wage.'

M. Douvier Dumolard resolved to deal with this resolution, which fell perfectly within his province; and on the 15th, under his Chairmanship, the Chamber of Commerce, the Mayor of Lyons and mayors of the three town suburbs met to discuss the situation. It became clear at this meeting that the bases of the wage structure would be discussed in a contradictory fashion by the twenty-two workers, twelve of whom had already been delegated by their comrades, and the twenty-two manufacturers whom the Chamber of Commerce designated as representatives.

M. Douvier Dumolard could have, and ought to have, fixed the tariff himself; he did not have the courage; he contented himself with putting the two parties together.

On 21 October a new meeting was convoked at the Prefecture. The 25th of October had been fixed as a date for the definitive discussion of the rates of pay.

Among the delegates of both parties discussion centred upon the crying abuses which had crept into the factories, but particularly on the reduction of wage rates; and such was the moderation of the workers that those whom twelve years before the manufacturers were pleased to pay 8 sous had their wages reduced by one eighth.... The agreement was signed ... and the Conseil des Prud'hommes was charged with supervising its execution, and one day per week was fixed to listen to the complaints which might arise through bad faith.

Among the manufacturers there were men who were honest and en-

* See Glossary.

lightened; they regarded the tariff as a necessary brake on the cupidity of several large speculators, and as a sure method of moderating disastrous market fluctuations resulting from competition. But this was the sentiment of a minority, and the news of the establishment of a tariff was no sooner known than the anger of most of the manufacturers spilled over into recriminations and menaces.

Infractions of the tariff were increasingly numerous; the Conseil des Prud'hommes, retracting its former decisions, refused to take action against those who violated the agreement; in this extreme situation the unfortunate weavers resolved to cease all work for a week; during this period they were to walk around the town calmly and without creating any disturbance, and they agreed that they would greet all those manufacturers who had kept the agreement. But this very moderation inflated the pride of their enemies. . . .

On Sunday, 20 November, a review of the National Guard was to take place on the Place Bellecour. This review brought out all the elements of the discord which existed deep within the Lyons population. . . .

Everything seemed then to announce a battle on the morrow. At the meeting held at the Prefecture . . . it was decided that the five gate-ways which led from Lyons to Croix-Rousse would be occupied from day-break; that a battalion of the National Guard of Croix-Rousse and 300 men of the line would meet at 7.00 in the morning to prevent the formation of any mobs; that four battalions of the National Guard of Lyons and one from La Guillotière would assemble at the same time in their respective positions.

On Monday, 21 November, at 7.00 or 8.00 in the morning, the workers in a body of about three or four thousand, gathered together at the Croix-Rousse.

At their head they had one of their leaders, and they were armed with sticks. Their aim was not in any sense to engage the manufacturers in battle. All they wanted was a cessation of work until the tariff was recognized, and some workers went through the workshops to bring out those of their mates who were still at work. In the meantime, fifty or sixty guards appeared, and the Commanding Officer having cried 'My friends, we must sweep away that *canaille*', they advanced with bayonets. The indignant workers dashed forward, surrounded the platoon, disarmed some of the guards, and caused some of the others to flee. Soon the groups became more numerous, but they were not hostile. They spoke only of recommencing the peaceful demonstration of 25 October. With this in mind, the weavers, joining arms and walking four abreast, descended the Grand'Côte. The Infantry of the First Legion, specially formed by the manufacturers, resolutely advanced to meet the columns. Their anger had reached its highest point and several drew their cartridges from their pouches. Towards the middle of the Grand'Côte the two groups met face to face; the Infantry fired and eight workers fell seriously wounded; immediately, the column of which they were members retreated in disorder, up the Grand'Cote and back into the Croix-Rousse. In an instant the cry went up, combatants emerged from every house, armed with picks, shovels, stones, forks; some had rifles. Some individuals ran from side to side crying 'To arms! Our brothers are being killed!' Barricades were erected by women and children in every street; the insurgents, in possession of two cannons belonging to the National Guard of the Croix-Rousse, began to march on Lyons, preceded by drums, and waving in the air a black banner, bearing the inscription. 'Live by working or die by fighting!' It was eleven o'clock. . . .

15/17 Factory Rules in Berlin, 1844

Works Rules for the men employed in the Foundry and Engineering Works of the Royal Overseas Trading Co., Moabit. Printed in SCHRÖTER and BECKER, *Die deutsche Maschinenbau-industrie* . . . [*see* Document **10/3**], pp. 112-116. (Ed. Tr.)

In every large works, and in the co-ordination of any large number of workmen, good order and harmony must be looked upon as the fundamentals of success, and therefore the following rules shall be strictly observed.

Every man employed in the concern named below shall receive a copy of these rules, so that no one can plead ignorance. Its acceptance shall be deemed to mean consent to submit to its regulations.

(1) The normal working day begins at all seasons at 6 a.m. precisely and ends, after the usual break of half an hour for breakfast, an hour for dinner and half an hour for tea, at 7 p.m., and it shall be strictly observed.

Five minutes before the beginning of the stated hours of work until their actual commencement, a bell shall ring and indicate that every worker employed in the concern has to proceed to his place of work, in order to start as soon as the bell stops.

The doorkeeper shall lock the door punctually at 6 a.m., 8.30 a.m., 1 p.m. and 4.30 p.m.

Workers arriving 2 minutes late shall lose half an hour's wages; whoever is more than 2 minutes late may not start work until after the next break, or at least shall lose his wages until then. Any disputes about the correct time shall be settled by the clock mounted above the gatekeeper's lodge.

These rules are valid both for time- and for piece-workers, and in cases of breaches of these rules, workmen shall be fined in proportion to their earnings. The deductions from the wage shall be entered in the wage-book of the gatekeeper whose duty they are; they shall be unconditionally accepted as it will not be possible to enter into any discussions about them.

(2) When the bell is rung to denote the end of the working day, every workman, both on piece- and on day-wage, shall leave his workshop and the yard, but is not allowed to make preparations for his departure before the bell rings. Every breach of this rule shall lead to a fine of five silver groschen* to the sick fund. Only those who have obtained special permission by the overseer may stay on in the workshop in order to work. – If a workman has worked beyond the closing bell, he must give his name to the gatekeeper on leaving, on pain of losing his payment for the overtime.

(3) No workman, whether employed by time or piece, may leave before the end of the working day, without having first received permission from the overseer and having given his name to the gatekeeper. Omission of these two actions shall lead to a fine of ten silver groschen payable to the sick fund.

(4) Repeated irregular arrival at work shall lead to dismissal. This shall also apply to those who are found idling by an official or overseer, and refuse to obey their order to resume work.

(5) Entry to the firm's property by any but the designated gateway, and exit by any prohibited route, e.g. by climbing fences or walls, or by crossing the Spree, shall be punished by a fine of fifteen silver groschen to the sick fund for the first offences, and dismissal for the second.

(6) No worker may leave his place of work otherwise than for reasons connected with his work.

(7) All conversation with fellow-workers is prohibited; if any worker requires information about his work, he must turn to the overseer, or to the particular fellow-worker designated for the purpose.

(8) Smoking in the workshops or in the yard is prohibited during working hours; anyone caught smoking shall be fined five silver groschen for the sick fund for every such offence.

(9) Every worker is responsible for cleaning up his space in the workshop, and if in doubt, he is to turn to his overseer. – All tools must always be kept in good condition, and must be cleaned after use. This applies particularly to the turner, regarding his lathe.

(10) Natural functions must be performed at the appropriate places, and whoever is found soiling walls, fences, squares, etc., and similarly, whoever is found washing his face and hands in the workshop and not in the places assigned for the purpose, shall be fined five silver groschen for the sick fund.

(11) On completion of his piece of work, every workman must hand it over at once to his foreman or superior, in order to receive a fresh piece of

* See Glossary.

work. Pattern makers must on no account hand over their patterns to the foundry without express order of their supervisors. No workman may take over work from his fellow-workman without instruction to that effect by the foreman.

(12) It goes without saying that all overseers and officials of the firm shall be obeyed without question, and shall be treated with due deference. Disobedience will be punished by dismissal.

(13) Immediate dismissal shall also be the fate of anyone found drunk in any of the workshops.

(14) Untrue allegations against superiors or officials of the concern shall lead to stern reprimand, and may lead to dismissal. The same punishment shall be meted out to those who knowingly allow errors to slip through when supervising or stocktaking.

(15) Every workman is obliged to report to his superiors any acts of dishonesty or embezzlement on the part of his fellow workmen. If he omits to do so, and it is shown after subsequent discovery of a misdemeanour that he knew about it at the time, he shall be liable to be taken to court as an accessory after the fact and the wage due to him shall be retained as punishment. Conversely, anyone denouncing a theft in such a way as to allow conviction of the thief shall receive a reward of two Thaler*, and, if necessary, his name shall be kept confidential. – Further, the gatekeeper and the watchman, as well as every official, are entitled to search the baskets, parcels, aprons etc. of the women and children who are taking the dinners into the works, on their departure, as well as search any worker suspected of stealing any article whatever. . . .

(18) Advances shall be granted only to the older workers, and even to them only in exceptional circumstances. As long as he is working by the piece, the workman is entitled merely to his fixed weekly wage as subsistence pay; the extra earnings shall be paid out only on completion of the whole piece contract. If a workman leaves before his piece contract is completed, either of his own free will, or on being dismissed as punishment, or because of illness, the partly completed work shall be valued by the general manager with the help of two overseers, and he will be paid accordingly. There is no appeal against the decision of these experts.

(19) A free copy of these rules is handed to every workman, but whoever loses it and requires a new one, or cannot produce it on leaving, shall be fined 2½ silver groschen, payable to the sick fund.

Moabit, August, 1844.

* See Glossary.

15/18 The Conseil de Prud'hommes in Lyons

Law of 18 March 1808. Printed in J. JEANNENEY and M. PERROT, *Textes de droit* . . . [*see* Document **3/10b**], pp. 109-110. (Ed. Tr.)

Article 1 A Conseil de Prud'hommes shall be established at Lyons, composed of nine members, of whom five shall be manufacturers and four shall be *chefs d'atelier**.
Article 3 Manufacturers shall be ineligible if they have fewer than six years' experience or if they have been bankrupt. *Chefs d'atelier* shall be ineligible if they can neither read nor write, if they have not held their position for six years, or if they are confidants of information given to them by the workers.
Article 6 The Conseil de Prud'hommes is instituted to settle by arbitration the petty disputes which arise daily either between manufacturers and workers or between *chefs d'atelier* and *compagnons* and apprentices. It is also authorised to judge informally, without costs or appeal, those disputes which have not been settled by arbitration, and which involve up to 60 francs.
Article 9 All disputes relating to a sum greater than 60 francs† which it has not been possible to settle by arbitration shall be brought before the commercial court or a competent authority.
Article 10 . . . The Conseil de Prud'hommes shall be specially required to pronounce on contraventions of new or recently enacted laws or regulations.
Article 11 The *procès verbaux* drawn up by the Prud'hommes to verify these contraventions shall be sent to the competent tribunals, together with any articles which may be useful as evidence.
Article 12 The Conseil de Prud'hommes shall also pronounce on the complaints brought to it which relate to the stealing of raw materials by workers from their employers, and on the dishonest activities of the dyers.
Article 13 In the latter case, and on the written or oral request of the parties concerned, at least two of the Prud'hommes, including one manufacturer and one *chef d'atelier*, assisted by a public officer, may visit the manufacturers, *chefs d'atelier*, workers and *compagnons*.* The reports of the findings on the thefts or illegalities shall be sent to the Bureau général des Prud'hommes and any evidence relating to the conviction shall be sent to the competent tribunals.
Article 14 The Conseil de Prud'hommes has the power to take measures to protect trade secrets.
Article 34 A Conseil de Prud'hommes shall be established by a public administrative rule, in all the manufacturing towns where the Government thinks it is necessary.
Article 35 Its composition may vary from place to place, but its powers shall be the same.

* See Document 11/8. † See Glossary.

15/19 French Factory Legislation, 1841

J. JEANNENEY and M. PERROT, *Textes de droit* . . . [*see* Document **3/10b**], pp. 161–163. (Ed. Tr.)

Article 1 Children may not be employed, except on the conditions laid down by the present law,

(i) in any sort of manufacturing establishment which is operated by mechanical power or which requires continuous firing processes, nor in other departments of the same establishments;

(ii) in any factory employing more than twenty workers.

Article 2 In order to be admitted, children shall have to be at least eight years old. From eight to twelve years they may not be made to work for a period longer than eight hours out of twenty-four, with provision for rest periods. From twelve to sixteen years of age they may not be employed in work for more than twelve hours, with provision for rest periods. This work shall take place only between 5.00 in the morning and 9.00 in the evening.

Ages shall be verified by a certificate issued . . . by the Registrar.

Article 3 All work between 9.00 in the evening and 5.00 in the morning is regarded as night work. All night work is forbidden for children below thirteen years of age. If as a result of the breakdown of motor power or urgent repairs, their employment is necessary, children below thirteen years may work at night, counting two hours as three, between 9.00 in the evening and 5.00 in the morning. Night work for children over thirteen years of age . . . shall be accepted, if it is regarded as absolutely necessary, in those establishments with continuous firing processes which cannot be suspended. . . .

Article 4 Children below sixteen years of age may not be employed on Sundays and recognized feast days.

Article 5 No child under twelve years of age may be admitted unless his parents or his teachers prove that he attends one of the public or private schools in the locality. All children who are admitted shall have to attend school until the age of twelve. Children over twelve years of age shall be exempt from attending school when a certificate, granted by the mayor of their place of residence, affirms that they have received elementary primary instruction.

Article 6 The mayor shall be obliged to deliver a *livret* inscribed with the child's age, name, Christian name, birthplace and place of residence and period of elementary education, to the father, mother, or teacher of the child.

The industrialist shall write

(i) on the *livret* of each infant, the date of entry into the establishment and the date of departure;

(ii) on a special register, all the details referred to in the present article.

Article 7 It shall be possible by legislation:

(i) to extend the application of the regulations of the present law to manufactures other than those mentioned in the present article;

(ii) to raise the minimum age and reduce the amount of work laid down in the second and third articles, if the work demands too much from the children and affects their health;

(iii) to determine the factories where, as a result of danger or unsatisfactory conditions, children below the age of sixteen years may not be employed;

(iv) to forbid children to undertake various types of dangerous or hard work even in the workshops where they are admitted;

(v) to regulate the employment of children which has to be accepted in the continuous firing processes on Sundays and feast days;

(vi) to regulate the night work provided for in Article 3.

Article 8 Regulations must:

(i) Provide the necessary measures for the execution of the present law;

(ii) Ensure the maintenance of public morals and decency in the workshops and factories;

(iii) Ensure the primary instruction and religious teaching of the children;

(iv) Prevent all bad treatment and excessive punishment of children;

(v) Guarantee the conditions of salubrity and safety necessary for the life and health of the children.

Article 9 The heads of factories must have the present law, together with the relevant regulations of public administration, posted in each workshop, together with the internal management regulations which they are obliged to maintain to ensure the observance of the law.

Article 10 The Government shall establish a system of inspection to superintend the arrangements and ensure the execution of the present law. In each establishment the inspectors may look at the registers containing details relating to the present law; the internal management regulations, the *livrets* of the children, and the children themselves; they may be accompanied by a doctor appointed by the Prefect* or the Sub-Prefect.

Article 11 In cases of irregularity, inspectors shall draw up *procès-verbaux*, which shall serve as proof until the contrary is established.

Article 12 In case of any contravention against the present law or its execution, the proprietors or the workers of the establishments shall be brought before the Justice of the Peace in the canton* and punished with a small fine not exceeding 15 francs.*

Contraventions arising either from the admission of children below the

* See Glossary.

required age or through the working of excessive hours shall result in fines for each child improperly admitted or employed, although the total fine may never amount to more than 200 francs.

In case of repetition of the offences, the proprietors or directors of the establishments shall be brought before the Court of Summary Jurisdiction and condemned to a fine of 16 to 100 francs. Infringement of Article 2 may never involve a fine greater than 500 francs.

Repetition shall be taken to mean that a judgement has been pronounced against an offender during the preceding twelve months.

15/20 Factory Legislation and Public Education in Prussia

J. KAY, *The Social Condition and the Education of the People* . . . [see Document **9/11**], II, pp. 48–51.

At the German revolutions of 1848, one of the great popular cries was for *gratuitous* education. The governments of Germany were obliged to yield to this cry, and to make it the law of nearly the whole of Germany, that all parents should be able to get their children educated at the primary schools without having to pay anything for this education.

There are now, therefore, no school fees in the greatest part of Germany. Education is perfectly gratuitous. The poorest man can send his child free of all expense to the best of the public schools of his district. And, besides this, the authorities of the parish or town, in which a parent lives, who is too poor to clothe his children decently enough for school attendance, are obliged to clothe them for him, and to provide them with books, pencils, pens, and every thing necessary for school attendance, so that a poor man, instead of being obliged to pay something out of his small earnings for the education of his children, is, on the contrary, actually paid for sending them to school. This latter is an old regulation, and is one which has aided very greatly to make the educational regulations very popular among the poor of Germany.

I made very careful inquiries about the education of children in the principal manufacturing district of Prussia. I remained several days in Elberfeld, their largest manufacturing town, on purpose to visit the factory schools. I put myself there, as elsewhere, in direct communication with the teachers, from whom I obtained a great deal of information; and I also had several interviews on the subject with the educational councillors at Berlin, who put into my hand the latest regulations on this subject issued by the government.

The laws relating to the factory children date only from 1839, so that no notice of them whatever will be found in M. Cousin's report. They are as follows:

No child may be employed in any manufactory, or in any mining or building operations, before it has attained the age of *nine* years.

No child, which has not received three years' regular instruction in a school, and has not obtained the certificate of a school-committee, that it can read its mother tongue fluently, and also write it tolerably well, may be employed in any of the above-mentioned ways, before it has completed its sixteenth year.

An exception to this latter rule is only allowed in those cases, where the manufacturers provide for the education of the factory children, by erecting and maintaining factory schools.

If a manufacturer will establish a school in connection with his manufactory, and engage a properly educated teacher, he is then allowed to employ any children of nine years of age, whether they have obtained a certificate or not, on condition, however, that these children attend the school four eveings in every week, as well as two hours every Sunday morning, until they have obtained a certificate of proficiency in their studies.

The 'schulrath,' or educational minister in the county court, decides whether the factory school is so satisfactorily managed, as to entitle the manufacturer to this privilege. This minister also regulates the hours which must be devoted weekly to the instruction of the factory children.

Young people, under sixteen years of age, may not be employed in manufacturing establishments more than ten hours a day.

The civil magistrates are, however, empowered, in some cases, to allow young people to work eleven hours a day, when an accident has happened, which obliges the manufacturer to make up for lost time, in order to accomplish a certain quantity of work before a given day. But these licenses cannot be granted for more, at the most, than four weeks at a time.

After the hours of labour have been regulated by the 'schulrath' and the manufacturer, the latter is obliged by law to take care that the factory children have, both in the mornings and in the afternoons, a quarter of an hour's exercise in the open air, and that at noon, they always have a good hour's relaxation from labour.

'*No young person, under sixteen years of age, may, in any case, or in any emergency, work more than eleven hours a day.*' The children of Christian parents, who have not been confirmed, may not work in the mills during the hours set apart by the religious minister, for the religious instruction, which he wishes to give them preparatory to their confirmation.

The manufacturers, who employ children in the mills, are obliged to lay before the magistrate a list, containing the names of all the children they employ, their respective ages, their places of abode, and the names of their parents. If any inspector or teacher reports to the civil magistrate, that any child under the legal age is being employed in the mills instead of being sent to school, or if the police report the infringement of any other of the above-mentioned regulations, the magistrate is empowered and obliged to punish the manufacturer by fines, which are increased in amount on every repetition of the offence.

I examined the actual state of things in Elberfeld, one of the most important of the manufacturing districts of Prussia, and I found these regulations most satisfactorily put in force.

15/21 Babeuf's Concept of Society

BUONARROTI'S *History of Babeuf's Conspiracy for Equality:* translated and illustrated by Bronterre, [i.e. J. Bronterre O'Brian] (London, 1836), pp. 369-370.

It was due to the French Revolution to put in practical execution the conceptions of philosophy, hitherto regarded as chimerical. We have commenced the great work; let us finish it. Were we to stop at the point where we now are, humanity and posterity would have little to thank us for.

In order to pass from our present vicious state to the one I advocate, it is necessary:

1. To place all the existing wealth of the country in the hands of the Republic.

2. To make all the valid citizens work, each according to his capacity and actual habits.

3. To utilize the objects of labour, by bringing together those which mutually aid one another, and by giving a new direction to such as are only the effect of the existing stagnant masses of riches.

4. To bring together (so as to have a continued supply) into the public depots all the productions of the land and of industry.

5. To effect an equal distribution of productions and enjoyments.

6. To dry up the source of all property, of all individual or private commerce, and to substitute for them a wise distribution confided to the public authority.

7. To establish common halls of education, in which each individual should be trained to the employment or work most suitable to his strength and inclinations.

Thus egoism would be no longer the spring of action or the stimulus to labour for individuals, who, whatever the variety and use of their productions, would receive the same retribution in food, clothing, &c. &c.

From this consequence our rich folk elicit the two following objections:

1. The necessity of procuring subsistence, and the hope of ameliorating our condition in life are the great sources of labour and reproduction; this

necessity and this hope once destroyed, labour ceases, the spring of reproduction is dried up, and society perishes.

2. If every species of labour were to receive the same recompence, there would no longer exist any motive for pursuing those scientific researches, which produce discoveries useful to society.

I answer, 1st, It is easy to make every one understand that a few hours' occupation per day would secure to every individual the means of living agreeably, and permanently relieve him from those anxieties by which we are now continually undermined; and surely the man who now slaves himself to exhaustion in order to have a little, would work a little in order to have much. Moreover, the objection rests entirely upon the disagreeable idea we are accustomed to form of labour, which, if wisely and universally distributed, would become in our system a mild and delightful occupation, of which no person would have either the inclination or interest to elude his share.

2d. It is, I think, a well ascertained fact that the progress of science depends more on the love of glory than on the avidity for riches; and in this case, our society, truly philosophic, embodying every possible means of effectually and impartially honouring its benefactors, would have therefore a right to expect more from science than our present corrupted associations, in which genius and virtue, despised and devoted to indigence, have the mortification to behold folly and crime almost invariably loaded with riches and honour.

I have said enough to satisfy my readers in good earnest, that the principle of avidity and selfishness, which forms the basis of all our present institutions, is detestable; and that to terminate for ever the agitations, misfortunes, and tyrannies which divide and oppress us, we must replace ourselves in a veritable state of society, where each individual, having equal stake and interest, may derive an equal profit; for all the reasonings of the political economists will never convince men of sense and honesty that it is supremely just that those who do nothing should possess every thing, and chain down, brutalize, and maltreat those who doing everything, possess almost nothing.

15/22 Sismondi on the Evils of Machinery

S. de Sismondi, 'Maux causés par l'introduction des machines', printed in M. LEROY, *Les précurseurs du socialisme de Condorcet à Proudhon* (Paris, 1948), pp. 137–141. (Ed. Tr.)

It is not only an unchecked growth of population which can cause national suffering, by breaking the equilibrium between the supply of, and demand for, work. The introduction of a process which economises on manual labour forces the journeymen to be content with wages which are so wretched that the men can hardly support themselves . . . one is sometimes ashamed for humanity to see the depths of degradation to which it can descend, and what it can do voluntarily in its attempts to earn a living, and in spite of the advantages which society has derived from the division of labour and the manufacturing inventions, one is sometimes tempted to regret their existence after seeing the effects they have on the lives of individuals who were created our equals. . . .

The progress of craft work, the development of industry and consequently even wealth and prosperity have resulted in more economical production methods and the employment of fewer workers. Animals replace men in almost all agricultural tasks, and machines replace men in almost all manufacturing operations. . . .

We must now decide the course of our future development. According to the latest census figures, agriculture employs 770,199 families in England; in proportion to the amount of land in use and the value of output, this number is infinitely smaller than in any other European country; ought one to offer a prize to the individual who discovers how to do the same amount of work with 70,000 families and to the individual who could manage with 7,000? In England, commerce and manufactures employ 959,632 families, and this number is sufficient to supply not only England but half of Europe and half of the civilized inhabitants of America with manufactured goods. England is a great manufacturing country which, to maintain itself, is obliged to sell to all the known world. Ought one to offer a prize to the person who discovers a means of accomplishing the same work with 90,000 families or 9,000? If England succeeded in maintaining her current production and profit levels and in carrying out all the work in the fields and factories by steam-powered machines with a population only as large as Geneva, should the country be considered richer and more prosperous?

Mr. Ricardo says quite definitely, 'yes'. Provided, he says, that its net and real income and its rents and profits are the same, what does it matter if the population is 10 or 12 million? Well then! Prosperity is everything and men are absolutely nothing! . . . Truly all that now remains is to want the King to be alone in his Kingdom, constantly turning a handle, having all the work in England accomplished by automatons. . . .

A third of the workshops are already closed, and another third will soon have to be closed and all the shops are overflowing with goods! Everywhere goods are offered for sale at reduced prices which do not cover half the costs of manufacture, and all the letters from South America announce that the large consignments of goods which had been sent there can only be sold at a price which hardly covers freight charges; in this universal distress, where the worker is everywhere rejected and the English nation has given his place in society to the machine . . . incentives are still offered to the inventors of new machines, which would make redundant those workers who still have a trade. Certainly it seems that in the midst of so much suffering we could dispense with encouraging those who, in the short term at least, can only accentuate the suffering. The suppression of privileges granted to the inventor of new processes would probably not seriously affect scientific progress . . . but it would rid the workers of the feeling that in this time of distress the Government is also aligned against them.

15/23 The St. Simonian Critique of Laissez-Faire

'Incohérence et désordre de l'industrie', printed in M. LEROY, *Les précurseurs français* . . . [*see* Document **15/22**], pp. 198-202. (Ed. Tr.)

In industry, as in science, emphasis is centred entirely on individualism; the sole sentiment which dominates all thinking is egotism. The industrialist is very little concerned about society's interests. His family, his capital and the personal fortune he strives to attain, constitute his humanity, his universe, his god. All those pursuing the same career are inevitably enemies . . . and it is by ruining them that he attains personal happiness and glory.

Problems which are no less serious exist regarding the organisation of work. Industry possesses a theory, which it might be believed holds the key to the harmonisation of production and consumption. Now this theory itself is the principal cause of disorder; the economists seem to pose the following problem:

'If it is accepted that leaders of society are more ignorant than those they govern; if it is supposed, moreover, that far from favouring the development of industry, these leaders wished to hinder its development, and their representatives were the born enemies of the producers, what kind of industrial organisation is suited to society?'

Laissez-faire, laissez-passer! Such has been the inevitable solution; such has been the single, general principle which they have proclaimed. The economists have thought by this to resolve with a stroke of the pen all questions relating to the production and distribution of wealth; they have entrusted the realisation of their schemes to *personal interest*, without realising that the individual, irrespective of his insight, is incapable of assessing total situations. . . . Well then! what is the picture we see before us? Each industry, deprived of direction, without any guidance other than personal observation, which is always imperfect . . . strives to become informed about consumer needs.

Rumour has it that a branch of production offers wonderful prospects; all endeavour and capital are directed towards it, everyone dashes blindly into it.... The economists immediately applaud the stampede because in it they recognise the principle of competition.... Alas! What results from this struggle to the death? Several fortunate individuals triumph ... the price is the complete ruin of innumerable victims. A necessary consequence of this over-production in certain sectors, this unco-ordinated activity, is that the equilibrium between production and consumption is always affected. Innumerable crises result, those commercial crises which terrify speculators and frustrate worthwhile projects. Honest and hard-working men are ruined and morale is injured by such events; such people come to believe that to succeed something more than honesty and hard work are needed. They become cunning, shrewd and sly; they even boast about these characteristics; once they have assumed this position, they are lost [to humanity].

Let us add now that the fundamental principle, *laissez-faire, laissez-passer*, assumes that personal and social interests always coincide, a supposition which is disproved by innumerable facts. To select only one example, is it not clear that if society sees its interest in the establishment of a steam engine, the worker who lives by his hands cannot share this sentiment? The reply to the workers' objection is well-known; for example, printing is cited, and it is true that today it occupies more men than there were transcribers before its invention, therefore it is concluded and stated that in the long run a new equilibrium is obtained. An admirable conclusion! And until then what will happen to the thousands of hungry men? Will our reasoning console them? Will they bear their misery patiently because statistical calculations prove that in future years they will have food to appease their hunger?

15/24 Social Factories and National Workshops

a Conclusion to Louis Blanc's *The Organization of Labour*, first published in book form in 1839. Printed in R. POSTGATE, *Revolution from 1789 to 1906* (London, 1920), pp. 186-187.

b Émile Thomas, *Regulations for the French National Workshops*, Printed in PIERRE-ÉMILE THOMAS, *Histoire des ateliers nationaux* (Paris, 1848), pp. 59-73, extracted and translated from *Royal Commission of Labour: Foreign Reports* Vol. VI, France (1893), pp. 140-143 (W.O.H.)

a The Government should be regarded as the supreme director of production, and invested with great strength to accomplish its task.

This task would consist in availing itself of competition itself, to destroy competition.

The Government should raise a loan which would be applied to the foundation of *social factories* in the most important branches of the national industry.

This foundation, requiring the investment of considerable funds, the number of original factories would be rigorously limited; but by virtue of their very organisation, as will be seen in the sequel, they would be gifted with an immense power of expansion.

The government, being considered as the only founder of the *social factories*, must also provide them with Statutes. These, having been discussed and voted by the representatives of the nation, would have the force and form of laws.

All workmen giving guarantees of good conduct to be admitted to work in the social factories, as far as the original capital would provide instruments of labour.

Although the false and anti-social education given to the present generation renders it difficult to find elsewhere than in an increase of remuneration a motive of emulation and encouragement, the wages would be equal – and an entirely new education should change old ideas and customs.

For the first year, following the establishment of social factories, the government would regulate the hierarchy of workers. After the first year it would be different. The workmen having had time to appreciate one another, and all being equally interested, as will be seen, in the success of the association, the hierarchy would be appointed on the elective principle.

Every year an account of the net profits would be made out and divided into three portions: One to be equally divided among members of the association. The second – 1, for the support of the old, the sick and the infirm; 2, for the alleviation of the crises weighing upon other branches of industry – all labour owing mutual support to its fellows. The third, lastly, to be devoted to the furnishing of instruments of labour to those desirous of joining the association, so that it might extend itself indefinitely.

Into each of these associations, formed for trades which can be exercised on a large scale, could be admitted those belonging to professions whose very nature compels those pursuing them to be scattered and localised. Thus each social factory might be composed of various trades grouped about one great centre, separate parts of the same whole, obeying the same laws and sharing in the same advantages.

Each member of the social factory should be at liberty to dispose of his wages to his own convenience; though the evident economy and incontestable excellence of living in community could not fail to bring from the association for labour the voluntary associations of wants and pleasures.

Capitalists should be admitted into the association, and receive interest for their capital, to be guaranteed by the budget; but not participate in the profits unless in the capacity of workmen.

b (A) Regulations for Enrolments in Brigades

I. Enrolment in brigades will take place for the different districts (arrondissements) in the order, and at the time indicated by an order of the day sent to the offices of the mayors.

II. No enrolment in brigades takes place on Sundays or national holidays.

III. In order to be enrolled a workman must:

(*a*) Certify at the office of the mayor of his district, that he is over 16 years of age, or else fatherless, or the eldest of a family of six children.

(*b*) He must appear in person, and only on the day and at the hour specified for his district, provided with a note bearing his name, calling, address, the stamp of the mayor of his district, and dated at least the day previous to the enrolment.

(*c*) If a workman is on guard on the day of admission for his district, he shall ask leave from the officer in charge of the guard in order to go to the central bureau.

(*d*) A workman who desires to be enrolled in a brigade which has already been formed, must appear in person on the day and at the time fixed for his district, with a message from the chief of that brigade stating his own number, that of the company and of the service.

(*e*) A workman who has lost his book shall call at the inquiry office with a certificate from the chief of his company, in order to obtain a fresh one; he shall then pay 50 centimes.

(*f*) The workmen shall be organized by brigades made up of 56 of the men who are present. Each brigade which presents itself incomplete shall be completed by the latest arrivals of the following brigade. No brigade shall start uncompleted from the bureau of enrolment, except the last.

(*g*) Brigadiers and chiefs of squads are elected beforehand by the workmen; but their brigade or squad may be taken to fill up incomplete lists belonging to the same district. Their nomination is not confirmed until after the enrolment in brigades.

(*h*) Every day a lieutenant sent by the head of the district shall come to announce the service numbers of the companies and brigades to which newly enrolled workmen belong, in order that these numbers may be entered on their books. These books, moreover, shall bear the names and addresses of the managers (chefs de service) of the heads of companies, of the lieutenants, brigadiers, and heads of squads.

The Commissary of the Republic,
Director of National Works,
Emile Thomas.

B. (General Regulations for Workmen engaged on the Works or awaiting Engagements)

The Commissary of the Republic, Director of the National Works, considering that different orders of the day have hitherto regulated the measures adopted for the administration of these works.

That it is important to combine in one regulation the different orders of the day enumerated above:

Enacts the following provisions which have been discussed in a council of heads of the districts, and laid before the assembly of workmen's delegates engaged in the national works, who have adopted them in their entirety.

The payment of brigadiers, heads of squads, and workmen are fixed as follows:

Days of work			
	fr.*	c.	
Brigadiers	3	0	per day
Heads of squads	2	50	per day
Workmen	2	0	per day
Non-working days			
Brigadiers	3	0	per day
Heads of squads	1	50	per day
Workmen	1	0	per day

On Sundays work is suspended; brigadiers, heads of squads, and workmen receive no pay.

No person enrolled in a brigade shall be entitled to two days' work until after the first Monday following his enrolment.

Heads of squads, and workmen selected for guard duty on any day except Sundays, or legal holidays, shall be considered as discharging a public duty, and shall be entitled to the payment accorded for days of active work, provided that within 24 hours they deliver to the chief of their company the document summoning them on guard, stamped with the seal of the staff officer of their legion, which document must bear the Christian name of the workman. After 24 hours the document will not be accepted.

The document, handed as aforesaid to the head of the company, shall be transmitted to the director through the manager (chef de service) stating the

* See Glossary.

district, the service, the company, and the brigade to which the workman belongs.

Tickets for Relief in Kind

Tickets for bread, meat, and soup are distributed at the relieving office, 4, Rue de Chartres, between 8.a.m. and 4.p.m. every day to the indigent fathers of families belonging to each brigade, in the following proportion, and on presentation of the list given by the delegate, verified and visa'd by the chief of the company.

Bread

No. of Children	*Kilograms*	*Weight (Avoir)* *lbs.*	*ozs.*
1	¼	0	9
2	½	1	1
3	¾	1	10
4	1	2	3
5	1¼	2	12
6	1½	3	5
7	1¾	3	13
8	2	4	6
9	2¼	4	15
10	2½	5	8

Bread and Meat

(1) Fathers of families who are ill and treated at the hospital are not paid. Their wives and children shall receive assistance in bread, meat and soup daily.

(2) Fathers of families who are ill, but are treated at their own homes, receive working pay – that is to say, two francs; medicines and medical attendance are rendered gratis. In this case they are only entitled to the allowance of bread, meat, and soup granted to all indigent fathers of families.

Workmen at the Works

The heads of companies, lieutenants, brigadiers, heads of squads, and workmen must be assembled at half-past six at the meeting place, whence they are to be set out for the works.

The head of the district shall determine the hour of arrival at the works according to the distance to be traversed by the men in order to reach them.

The meal times are fixed as follows:

Morning meal,	1 hour, 9 to 10.
Evening meal,	1 hour, 2 to 3.

Work shall cease at six o'clock in the evening.

Two roll-calls at least shall be undertaken every day by the heads of companies. Any inspector passing through the works may demand a supplementary roll-call from the head of a company, or, in the absence of the latter, from the lieutenants, or even from the brigadiers.

Any workman failing to answer incurs a fine of 25 centimes. Failure to respond at two calls entails the loss of a day's pay.

Any workman who fails during two days to appear at his yard shall be struck off the lists, except in one of the circumstances provided for by the above order of the day regulating payment.

Any workman leaving the works for a moment without the permission of the head or deputy head of the company shall be fined 50 centimes.

The delegates shall not make inquiries of the workman, nor receive their claims during working hours.

Only the central delegates shall be admitted to the relieving offices; they must present the lists which have been handed them by the three other delegates.

Any workman neglecting his work, on being reported by the chief of his company, by the lieutenant, or inspector, shall be fined 50 centimes.

All gaming is prohibited during working hours; infractions of this clause shall entail a fine of 50 centimes.

Any workman, or person in charge of a squad or brigade, refusing to obey his superiors, or found under the influence of drink on the works, shall forfeit his day's pay. If he repeat the offence he shall be struck off the lists.

Under certain circumstances of a grave nature, not provided for in the regulations, the head of the district is authorised to suspend any officer or workman from his duties pending the decision of the administration. A report on the step taken shall be immediately made to the directors.

No officer elected by the workman can be deprived of his office until the matter has been inquired into by the administration.

Every workman must carry his book about his person, and show it at the first request of one of his superiors.

The heads of squads are always at the disposal of the brigadier to aid them in their duties.

Any brigadier or head of a squad deprived of his rank on the report of one of his superiors, may make a written appeal to the director, but should his claims not be found valid, he shall return to the ranks as a simple workman, and shall not be eligible for re-election.

No measure, purchase, or payment is valid without the written authority of the director.

Tools

The depôt for all tools belonging to the national work, is situated in the rue Chartres, No. 4.

Divisional depôts shall be established in the yard; the tools must be deposited there every evening. Special keepers, selected and appointed by the sub-director of stores, shall be responsible for the tools during the time they are not in use.

Commissary of the Republic,
Director of National Works,
Émile Thomas.

15/25 Proudhon on Exploitation

B. R. TUCKER (trans.), *What is Property? An inquiry into the principle of right and of government* (London, 1898), pp. 126-129.

While they [the proletariat] have been clearing away for their neighbour, they have done no clearing for themselves. One year's seed time and harvest is already gone. They had calculated that in lending their labour they could not but gain since they would save their own provisions; and, while living better, would get still more money. False calculation! they have created for another the means wherewith to produce, and have created nothing for themselves. The difficulties of clearing remain the same; their clothing wears out, their provisions give out; soon their purse becomes empty for the profit of the individual for whom they have worked, and who alone can furnish the provisions which they need, since he alone is in a position to produce them. Then, when the poor grubber has exhausted his resources, the man with the provisions (like the wolf in the fable, who scents his victim from afar) again comes forward. One he offers to employ again by the day; from another he offers to buy at a favourable price a piece of his bad land, which is not and never can be of any use to him: that is, he uses the labour of one man to cultivate the field of another for his own benefit, so that at the end of twenty years, of thirty individuals originally equal in point of wealth, five or six have become proprietors of the whole district, while the rest have been philanthropically dispossessed!

In this century of *bourgeoise* morality, in which I have had the honour to be born, the moral sense is so debased that I should not be at all surprised if I were asked, by many a worthy proprietor, what I see in this that is unjust and illegitimate? Debased creature! galvanized corpse! how can I expect to convince you, if you cannot tell robbery when I show it to you? A man, by soft and insinuating words, discovers the secret of taxing others that he may establish himself; then, once enriched by their united efforts, he refuses, on the very conditions which he himself dictated, to advance the well-being of those who made his fortune for him: and you ask how such conduct is fraudulent! under the pretext that he has paid his labourers, that he owes nothing more, that he has nothing to gain by putting himself at the service of others, while his own occupations claim his attention, – he refuses, I say, to aid others in getting a foothold, as he was aided in getting his own; and when, in the impotence of their isolation, these poor labourers are compelled to sell their birthright, he – this ungrateful proprietor, this knavish upstart – stands ready to put the finishing touch to their deprivation and their ruin. And you think that just? Take care! I read in your startled countenance the reproach of a guilty conscience, much more clearly than the innocent astonishment of involuntary ignorance.

'The capitalist,' they say, 'has paid the labourers their *daily wages.*' To be accurate, it must be said that the capitalist has paid as many times one day's wage, as he has employed labourers each day – which is not at all the same thing. For he has paid nothing for that immense power which results from the union and harmony of labourers, and the convergence and simultaneousness of their efforts. Two hundred grenadiers stood the obelisk of Luxor upon its base in a few hours; do you suppose that one man could have accomplished the same task in two hundred days? Nevertheless, on the books of the capitalist, the amount of wages paid would have been the same. Well, a desert to prepare for cultivation, a house to build, a factory to run, – all these are obelisks to erect, mountains to move. The smallest fortune, the most insignificant establishment, the setting in motion of the lowest industry, demand, the concurrence of so many different kinds of labour and skill that one man could not possibly execute the whole of them. It is astonishing that the economists never have called attention to this fact. Strike a balance, then, between the capitalist's receipts and his payments.

The labourer needs a salary which will enable him to live while he works; for unless he consumes, he cannot produce. Whoever employs a man owes him maintenance and support, or wages enough to procure the same. That is the first thing to be done in all production. I admit for the moment, that in this respect the capitalist has discharged his duty.

It is necessary that the labourer should find in his production, in addition to his present support, a guarantee of his future support; otherwise the source of production would dry up, and his productive capacity would become exhausted: in other words the labour accomplished must give birth perpetually to new labour – such is the universal law of reproduction. In this way, the proprietor of a farm finds: 1. In his crops, means, not only of supporting himself and his family, but of maintaining and improving his capital, of feeding his live-stock – in a word, means of new labour and continual reproduction; 2. In his ownership of a productive agency, a permanent basis of cultivation and labour.

But he who lends his services – what is his basis of cultivation? The proprietor's presumed need of him, and the unwarranted supposition that he wishes to employ him. Just as the commoner once held his land by the munificence and condescension of the lord, so to-day the working-man holds his labour by the condescension and necessities of the master and proprietor; that is what is called possession by a precarious* title. But this precarious condition is an injustice, for it implies an inequality in the bargain. The labourer's wages exceed but little his running expenses, and do not assure him wages for to-morrow: while the capitalist finds in the instrument produced by the labourer a pledge of independence and security for the future.

Now, this reproductive leaven – this eternal germ of life, this preparation of the land and manufacture of implements for production – constitutes the debt of the capitalist to the producer, which he never pays; and it is this fraudulent denial which causes the poverty of the labourer the luxury of idleness, and the inequality of conditions. This it is, above all other things, which has been so fitly named the exploitation of man by man.

15/26 Economic Development and the Class Struggle: The Communist Manifesto

KARL MARX and FRIEDRICH ENGELS, *The Communist Manifesto* (1847–48).

In proportion as the bourgeoisie, i.e. capital, is developed, in the same proportion is the proletariat, the modern working class, developed – a class of labourers, who live only so long as they find work, and who find work only so long as their labour increases capital. These labourers, who must sell themselves piecemeal, are a commodity, like every other article of commerce, and are consequently exposed to all the vicissitudes of competition, to all the fluctuations of the market.

Owing to the extensive use of machinery and to division of labour, the work of the proletarians has lost all individual character, and, consequently, all charm for the workman. He becomes an appendage of the machine, and it is only the most simple, most monotonous, and most easily acquired knack, that is required of him. . . .

Modern industry has converted the little workshop of the patriarchal master into the great factory of the industrial capitalist. Masses of labourers, crowded into the factory, are organised like soldiers. As privates of the industrial army they are placed under the command of a perfect hierarchy of

* *Precarious*, from *precor*, 'I pray'; because the act of concession expressly signified that the lord, in answer to the prayers of his men or slaves, had granted them permission to labour. (Note in original.)

officers and sergeants. Not only are they slaves of the bourgeois class, and of the bourgeois state; they are daily and hourly enslaved by the machine, by the overlooker, and, above all, by the individual bourgeois manufacturer himself. The more openly this despotism proclaims gain to be its end and aim, the more petty, the more hateful and the more embittering it is. . . .

The lower strata of the middle class – the small trades-people, shopkeepers and retired tradesmen generally, the handicraftsmen and peasants – all these sink gradually into the proletariat, partly because their diminutive capital does not suffice for the scale on which modern industry is carried on and is swamped in the competition with the large capitalists, partly because their specialised skill is rendered worthless by new methods of production. Thus the proletariat is recruited from all classes of the population. . . .

But with the development of industry the proletariat not only increases in number; it becomes concentrated in greater masses, its strength grows, and it feels that strength more. The various interests and conditions of life within the ranks of the proletariat are more and more equalised, in proportion as machinery obliterates all distinctions of labour, and nearly everywhere reduces wages to the same low level. The growing competition among the bourgeois, and the resulting commercial crises, make the wages of the worker ever more fluctuating. The unceasing improvement of machinery, ever more rapidly developing, makes their livelihood more and more precarious, the collisions between individual workmen and individual bourgeois take more and more the character of collisions between two classes. Thereupon the workers begin to form combinations (trades unions) against the bourgeois, they club together in order to keep up the rate of wages, they found permanent associations in order to make provision before hand for these occasional revolts. Here and there the contest breaks out into riots.

Now and then the workers are victorious, but only for a time. The real fruit of their battles lies, not in the immediate result, but in the ever expanding union of the workers. This union is helped on by the improved means of communication that are created by modern industry, and that place the workers of different localities in contact with one another. It was just this contact that was needed to centralise the numerous local struggles, all of the same character, into one national struggle between classes. But every class struggle is a political struggle. And that union, to attain which the burghers of the Middle Ages, with their miserable highways, required centuries, the modern proletarians, thanks to railways, achieve in a few years.

This organisation of the proletarians into a class, and consequently into a political party, is continually being upset again by the competition between the workers themselves. But it ever rises up again, stronger, firmer, mightier. . . .

All the preceding classes that got the upper hand, sought to fortify their already acquired status by subjecting society at large to their conditions of appropriation. The proletarians cannot become masters of the productive forces of society, except by abolishing their own previous mode of expropriation, and thereby also every other previous mode of appropriation. They have nothing of their own to secure and to fortify; their mission is to destroy all previous securities for, and insurances of, individual property.

All previous historical movements were movements of minorities, or in the interest of minorities. The proletarian movement is the self-conscious, independent movement of the immense majority, in the interest of the immense majority. The proletariat, the lowest stratum of our present society, cannot stir, cannot raise itself up, without the whole superincumbent strata of official society being sprung into the air. . . .

The essential condition for the existence and for the sway of the bourgeois class is the formation and augmentation of capital; the condition for capital is wage-labour. Wage-labour rests exclusively on competition between the labourers. The advance of industry, whose involuntary promoter is the bourgeoisie, replaces the isolation of the labourers, due to competition, by their revolutionary combination, due to association. The development of modern industry, therefore, cuts from under its feet the very foundation on which the bourgeoisie produces and appropriates products. What the bourgeosie therefore produces, above all, are its own grave-diggers. Its fall and the victory of the proletariat are equally inevitable.

15/27 Lassalle on the Iron Law of Wages and on Workers' Associations

FERDINAND LASSALLE, 'Open Letter to the Central Committee on the Calling of a General German Workers' Congress in Leipzig'; Zurich, 1863. In *Reden und Schriften* (ed. Bernstein, 3 vols., Berlin, 1893), II, pp. 421-434. (Ed. Tr.)

The iron law of economics, which determines the wages of labour under the present conditions, under the dominance of supply and demand for labour, is this: That the average wage is always reduced to the minimum level necessary to maintain the habitual subsistence and propagation of a people. This is the point around which the real wage always fluctuates, without ever being able to rise far above, or fall far below it. It cannot remain for long above it – otherwise the easier, better conditions would lead to an increase in the marriages and births among the working classes, and these would lead to an increase in the supply of hands, which would reduce wages to and below their former levels.

Equally, wages cannot for long fall below the necessary subsistence level, for then we should have emigration, abstention from marriage and from procreation and finally diminished numbers caused by misery, which would reduce the supply of labour and thus raise wages to their former levels.

Real wages therefore fluctuate constantly around their point of gravity, at times above it (prosperity in some or all industries) at times a little below (periods of more or less general depression and crisis).

The limitation of the average wage to the minimum level necessary for subsistence and procreation habitual to a people – this is, I repeat, the iron and cruel law determining the wages of labour under present conditions.

This law cannot be disputed by anyone. I can bring you as many witnesses for it as there are great and famous names in economic science, from the liberal school of economics itself, for it was this school which discovered and found the proof for this law. . . .

There is, even in the Liberal school, not a single economist of stature who denies it. Adam Smith and Say, Ricardo and Malthus, Bastiat and John Stuart Mill acknowledge it unanimously. . . .

Let us look for a moment more closely on the effect and nature of this law. . . .

From the total produce of labour, that part is deducted and distributed among the workers which is necessary for their subsistence (the wages of labour). The whole surplus of the produce goes to the entrepreneur.

It is therefore a consequence of this iron and cruel law that you . . . are necessarily excluded from the increased productivity caused by the progress of civilisation, i.e. from the increased produce, from the increased efficiency of your own labour! For you forever the minimum subsistence, for the entrepreneur always everything beyond it.

But since, by the rapid progress in productivity [the efficiency of labour], many industrial products fall to very low prices at the same time, it may happen that . . . you gain for a time a certain indirect advantage from the increased productivity of labour. This advantage does not accrue to you as producer, it does not alter your quota of the total produce of labour, it merely affects you as consumer, equally with the entrepreneur and even those not taking part in the productive process at all, whose position as consumers is improved in even greater measure than your own.

And even this advantage, accruing to you as men, not as workers, will disappear again according to this iron and cruel law, which always depresses the wages of labour in the long run to the consumption level of minimum necessary subsistence.

If now, further, such an increase in productivity of labour and the resultant extreme cheapness of several products occur suddenly, and if they occur at the same time as a prolonged increase in the demand for labour – then these disproportionately cheapened products may be absorbed into the concept of the habitual necessary minimum of subsistence. . . .

Thus, if various periods are compared with each other, the condition of the working classes in the later century or in the later generation may have improved *vis-à-vis* the condition of the working classes of an earlier century or an earlier generation, in so far as the minimum of the habitual necessary subsistence has meanwhile been raised a little. . . .

Whether you are better off than the worker of 80 or 200 years ago (if that should be the case) because the minimum habitual subsistence has been raised in the meantime – what value has this question for you, and what satisfaction can you derive from it? As little as the equally undisputed fact that you are better off than Hottentots and cannibals.

All human satisfaction depends always on the relation of the available consumption goods to the subsistence needs habitually established in any age, or, what amounts to the same thing, on the surplus of the available consumption goods over the lowest margin of the minimum necessary subsistence at any given time. An increase in the necessary minimum creates misery and want unknown in earlier ages. What want has the Hottentot for soap, what want has the cannibal for a decent overcoat, what want had the worker for tobacco, before the discovery of America, what want had the worker for a useful book before the invention of printing?

All human suffering and want therefore depends solely on the relation of consumption goods to the needs and habits existing at any given time. All human suffering and want and all human satisfaction, in other words every human situation, must be measured against the condition in which other men are placed at the same time in relation to habitual needs. Every situation of a class must therefore be measured solely in relation to the condition of other classes at the same time.

Even if it could be proved that the level of necessary subsistence conditions had been raised in various periods, that satisfactions previously unknown have become habitual needs and by that very development wants and sufferings previously unknown have been caused – your human situation has remained the same throughout that period; it is always this: to fluctuate around the lowest margin of the currently valid minimum subsistence level, being at times just above, and at times just below it.

Your human condition has therefore remained the same, for the human condition cannot be measured in relation to the condition of animals in the jungle, or of negroes in Africa, or of serfs in the Middle Ages, or of workers 200 or 80 years ago, but must be measured in relation to the situation of your contemporaries, the condition of other classes at the same time. . . .

To make the working class into its own employer – this is the means by which, and by which alone – as you will see in a moment – the iron and cruel law can be removed which determines the wages of labour.

If the working class becomes its own employer, all distinctions between wages and profits disappear, and with them, wages as such also, and in their place we have the return to labour of the whole produce of labour.

The abolition of profit by the most peaceful and simple method, by the organisation of the working classes into its own employer through voluntary associations, which alone can abolish that law which under present conditions distributes only the minimum necessary for subsistence to the worker as wage, and leaves all the surplus to the employer, that is the only true, the only just, the only non-visionary improvement of the condition of the working classes.

But how? Cast a glance at the railways, the engineering works, the shipyards, the cotton spinning mills, the weaving sheds, etc., and at the millions required for them, and then look into your empty pockets, and ask yourselves where you could obtain the massive capital sums required for the former, and how you could ever be able to run large-scale industry on your own account?

And it is true that nothing is more certain than that you will never accomplish this, as long as you remain solely and exclusively reduced to your isolated efforts as individuals.

For this reason it is the task of the State to enable you to do it, to take in hand the great issue of the free individual association of the working classes in a positive and helpful manner, and to make it its sacred duty to provide you with the means and opportunity for your self-organisation and self-association.

And do not be misled by the shouts of those who will tell you that every such intervention by the State destroys social self-help.

It is not true that I prevent someone from climbing a tower if I hand him ladder and rope for it. It is not true that the State prevents our children from educating themselves if it provides teachers, schools and libraries. It is not true that I prevent someone from ploughing his field on his own if I provide him with a plough. It is not true that I prevent someone from defeating a hostile army by his own hand if I give him the weapons to do it with. . . .

The true improvement of the condition of labour and of the working class as such, which it demands with justice, can be achieved only with the assistance of the State.

And equally, do not be misled by the shouts of those who begin to speak of Socialism or Communism and try to oppose you with such cheap slogans. Be convinced that they only want to mislead you or do not know themselves what they are talking about. Nothing is further from this so-called Socialism or Communism than this demand, under which the workers will, as today, keep their individual freedom, individual style of life and individual wages and will stand in no other relationship to the State than that of having received from it the necessary capital or credit for their association. But this is precisely the great historical role of the State, to facilitate and set in train the major steps in the progress of civilised humanity. This is its function. This is its purpose; it always has been and had to be. I want to give you a single example, in the place of the hundreds of examples which I could give you – the canals, high roads, mail services, steam packet lines, telegraphs, mortgage banks, agricultural improvements, the introduction of new industries, etc. – a single example, but one that is worth hundreds of others, and is a particularly close parallel: when the railways had to be built, in all the German States – and likewise in most countries abroad – with the exception of a few very small and scattered lines, it was the State that had to intervene in one form or another, mostly by at least guaranteeing the interest on the shares, and in many countries by far more drastic action.

The interest guarantee represented, in addition, the following favourable contract of the entrepreneurs – the rich shareholders – with the State: 'If the new enterprises are unprofitable, the burden falls on the State, i.e. on all the taxpayers, which is particularly on you, the large class of the propertyless! But if, on the contrary, the new enterprises are profitable, then the advantage – the high dividends – shall belong to us, the rich shareholders'. This is not invalidated by the fact that in some countries, as e.g. in Prussia, the State bargained for certain, and at the time very doubtful, advantages for the very, very distant future, advantages which could be more than matched by those that would arise from the support of associations of workmen.

Without this State intervention of which, as noted, the interest-guarantee was the mildest expression, we might even today be without railways on the continent!

At any rate, it is certain that the State had to take this action, that even the interest-guarantee alone represented an extremely active form of State intervention, that this intervention favoured the rich and propertied classes, which in any case dispose of all capital and credit and which therefore could have much more easily done without State intervention than you, and that this intervention was demanded by the whole of the bourgeoisie.

Why was there no campaign then against the interest-guarantee as an 'inadmissible intervention by the State?' Why was it not said then that the interest-guarantee threatened the 'social self-help' of the wealthy entrepreneurs of those joint-stock companies? Why was the interest guarantee not libelled as 'Socialism and Communism'?

But of course, that form of State intervention was in favour of the rich and propertied classes of society, and in that case it was quite permissible, and always was so! It is only in the case of an intervention in favour of the needy, the vast majority – only then does it become 'Socialism and Communism'! . . .

Moreover, however great the progress of civilization caused by the railways, it is minute compared with the enormous step forward in human progress which would be caused by the association of the working classes. For what good are all hoarded treasures and all the fruits of civilization, if they are to be available only to the few, and the rest of limitless humanity as a whole remains forever like Tantalus, snatching in vain at these fruits? Worse than Tantalus, for he, at least, did not himself produce the fruit, for which his parched palate was doomed to yearn in vain.

If ever the helpful intervention of the State was justified, it was in the case of this, the largest step in the progress of civilization known to history. . .

Glossary

ABROC *See* OBROK.

AIDES Exise Duties.

ARBITRIO Tax (Spanish).

ARE French measure of surface. Equivalent to 6046 square yards.

ARPENT French measure of surface, of 100 square perches, measuring, according to the perch, between $\frac{5}{6}$ acre and $1\frac{1}{4}$ acres.

ARRONDISSEMENT French administrative sub-division.

ASSIGNATS Paper money issued during the French Revolution, based on church property confiscated by the State. Over-issue resulted in inflation.

ATELIER DE CHARITÉ An organization concerned with public works relief under the jurisdiction of an Intendant.

AUNE Old French measurement, usually relating to cloth lengths. Equivalent to the ell.

BARSCHINA Russian feudal obligation, paid in labour services.

BOOR A peasant; the term, used for the Russian servile peasant, derived from the German 'Bauer' and the Dutch 'boer'.

BOYAR A Russian noble.

CABILDO Cathedral chapter

CANTON French administrative sub-division with a resident juge de paix.

CAPITAINERIES Certain districts in pre-Revolutionary France in which all rights to game had been granted to privileged individuals by the Crown.

CAPITATION French poll tax.

CHAMPART A feudal obligation in kind in pre-Revolutionary France which closely resembled the tithe.

CIENTO A Spanish tax adding 4% to the Alcavala tax.

CINQUANTIER Town police.

COMMUNE The smallest French administrative territorial division.

COMPAGNON Journeyman.

CONTRÔLE A registration tax on legal documents.

CORPS DE MÉTIER Gild.

CORVEÉ French obligation to perform labour services to the Sovereign or feudal lord.

DAUPHINES Small, coloured, woollen articles.

DENIER *See* LIVRE.

DENISCHIKI Officers' servants or batmen.

DÉPARTEMENT Administrative sub-division of France. *See also* PREFECT.

DÎMES INFÉODÉES Tithes which had passed under the control of the laity.

DOLLAR *See* THALER.

DOMAIN ENGAGÉ Land temporarily transferred by the crown.

DROITS D'ABORD ET CONSOMMATION Special import duties on fish from foreign fisheries.

DROIT D'AUBAINE In France the right of reversion to the Crown of the estate of deceased, non-naturalized citizens.

DROIT DE GUÊT ET GARDE This was originally a seigneurial privilege in France which required vassals to look after the safety of the seigneurial chateau. In time this became commuted for a money payment or a payment in kind.

DROITS DE TRAITES Traites were duties levied on goods when they entered and left France and on their movement between certain areas within France.

DROSKY, DROSHKY Low four-wheeled open carriage.

ÉCU A French monetary unit. Equivalent to 6 livres (*see* LIVRE).

EN COMMANDITE Form of joint stock company in France and other Mediterranean countries joining two types of partners: *commanditaires*, or sleeping partners, supplying capital in conditions of limited liability, and *commandités*, active partners with full liability.

FERMIER GÉNÉRAL DES MESSAGERIES French official in charge of inland transportation.

FIVE GREAT FARMS Tariff area in northern France before the Revolution.

FLORIN *see* GULDEN.

FOREIGN PROVINCES Tariff area in pre-Revolutionary France. Abolished during the Revolution.

FRANC French monetary unit, which replaced the LIVRE. Equivalent to 1 LIVRE 3 DENIERS (*see* LIVRE).

GABELLE The name given to pre-Revolutionary taxes on salt in France.

GÉNÉRALITÉ The major sub-division of civil government in eighteenth-century France. (*See* INTENDANT).

GOVERNMENT / GOUVERNEMENT Russian administrative province.

GULDEN (FL., FLORIN) Austrian monetary unit, divided into 60 Kreutzer (Kr.) The C.M. (silver) Gulden was worth about 2s., the W.W. (paper) Gulden, about 10d.

HAIDUK Hungarian drover originally. Later applied to attendants and mercenaries.

HECTARE Metric measure of surface, equals 100 Are or 2·47 acres.

HUBE (HUFE) The original full share of village land belonging to a peasant household, including arable, common and waste. It varied between 30 and 60 Morgen in different parts of Germany. 1 Morgen measured *c.* 25–27 Are in Northern parts of Germany ($\frac{2}{3}$ acre) and *c.* 31–36 Are ($\frac{5}{6}$ acre) in the southern parts.

INSPECTEUR AUX BOISSONS One of the pre-Revolutionary excise duties on wines in France.

INTENDANT French official in charge of provincial administration.

JURÉ A juré was one of the most senior members within a gild organization. Collectively the jurés formed the JURANDE.

KREUTZER (KR., XR) *See* GULDEN.

KLAFTER A volume measure of timber usually 144 cu. feet. The Prussian Klafter measured 3·386 in. i.e. 119·6 cu. feet or 4·43 cu. yds. English.

LACHTER German fathom, varying in different parts of the country between 1·9 and 2·0 metres, *c.* 6½ feet.

LEAGUE A variable measure of length. The English (nautical) League measured 3.456 statute miles; the French league measured 2.764 miles.

LIVRE French pre-revolutionary monetary unit. Divided into 20 sou (s) of 12 denier (d) each. The livre was worth approximately 10½d.–11d. of English money.

LIVRE (weight) A measurement of weight containing a number of ounces which varied according to time and place.

LOUIS French monetary unit. Roughly equivalent to 22 shillings.

MARK DE FER (MARQUE DE FER) A light excise duty on a variety of iron products.

MÉTAYER One who farms on the métayage system under which the farmer (métayer) pays rent in kind and the owner furnishes stock and seed.

MÉTIER *See* CORPS DE MÉTIER.

MILLIER 1000 kilograms.

MILLONES Spanish internal customs duties.

MOOJIK Russian peasant.

MORGEN *See* HUBE.

MYRIAMETRE 10 kilometres.

OBROK Russian feudal obligation, paid in money or kind.

PAYS D'AIDES Those areas of France where AIDES (*see above*) were levied. Basically the areas under the jurisdiction of the Cours des Aides of Paris and Rouen.

PAYS D'ÉLECTION Areas of France where administrative power lay with representatives of the central authority.

PAYS D'ÉTATS Unlike the PAYS D'ÉLECTIONS (*see above*), these areas enjoyed a semi-contractual relationship with the French Crown. Matters relating to taxation, for example, were discussed between representatives of the estate and the central authority.

POOD Russia measure of weight, *c.* 36 lb.

PORTION CONGRUE A feudal obligation in pre-Revolutionary France which was paid to the clergy.

PREFECT Administrator of a DÉPARTEMENT (*see above*).

PRIVILÈGE DES QUATRE CHARRUES Noblemen could farm, free of any obligation to pay the TAILLE, a piece of land which it was calculated would take four ploughs to till (The number in Normandy was 3.) In the Paris GÉNÉRALITÉ this amount of land was calculated at 120 ARPENTS, which was also a variable measure.

PROCUREUR DU ROI A Law Officer of the French Crown.

PROCUREUR GÉNÉRAL SYNDIC A Departmental legal figure who acted in a liaison capacity between the DÉPARTEMENT (*see above*) and the central authorities. His function was to ensure the execution of the law.

PROVINCES REPUTED FOREIGN Tariff area in pre-Revolutionary France. Abolished during the Revolution.

QUINTAL Old hundredweight, of 100 lb., varying with the weight of the local lb. The French quintal weighed 48·95 kg.

REICHSTHALER (RIXDOLLAR, RIXTHALER, RTHLR) *See* THALER.

ROBOT Feudal labour services in Slavic, especially Austrian lands. Regulated by the patent of 1775 and abolished in 1848 and 1849.

ROUBLE Russian monetary unit. The silver rouble contained *c.* 20 grammes of fine silver and was worth *c.* 2s. 1d.

RTHLR *See* THALER.

SAZHEN Russian measure of length: 2·13 metres or 7 feet.

SCHÄFFEL, SCHEFFEL German measure of volume, for grain. A Prussian Scheffel equalled *c.* $1\frac{1}{2}$ English bushels.

SEPTIER A French measure of volume, which varied between localities. The Paris septier measured *c.* 156 litres.

SGR (SILBERGROSCHEN) *See* THALER.

SOCIÉTÉ ANONYME A joint stock company with limited liability for all shareholders.

SOL TOURNOIS Literally a sol (sou) minted at Tournois. Usually equivalent to 12 deniers.

SOU French monetary unit, $\frac{1}{20}$ part of a livre or of a franc.

STÈRE 1 cubic metre. 35·3174 cu. feet.

STÜBER $\frac{1}{20}$ part of a Thaler, i.e. *c.* 2d.

SYNDIC The French local official, found particularly among rural communities which did not have a mayor, who acted on behalf of the community and administered its affairs.

TABAC The royal tobacco monopoly in France, controlling the importation cultivation and selling of tobacco.

TAILLE A principal direct tax of the Ancien Régime, imposed on non-noble and non-privileged landowners by the Crown in the PAYS D'ÉLECTIONS and in the PAYS D'ÉTATS by the Estates, who paid the Crown a regular indemnity (Don gratuit) for the privilege.

THALER German monetary unit. In the second half of the eighteenth century the 'Conventional' Thaler was fixed at 23·4 grammes of silver, and the Prussian Thaler at $\frac{1}{14}$ of a Mark or silver, or *c.* 3s. In 1821 it was divided into 30 Silbergroschen. (*Also see* Document No. 14/5.)

TRAMPING ARTISAN German craftsmen spent some years as 'journeymen' or tramping artisans, wandering from town to town under the auspices of their trade and improving their skill under different masters before submitting to their mastership examination.

TYAGLO Russian feudal obligation, paid in labour services.

VERST Russian measure of distance, 3500 feet or *c.* $\frac{2}{3}$ mile.

VINGTIÈME A 5% tax on revenue from land and other property, public offices and industry.

XR Kreutzer, *see* GULDEN.

Index